The Financial and Other Sanctions of the European Union

European Monographs Series Set

VOLUME 119

Editor

Prof. Andrea Biondi is Professor of European Law and Director of the Centre of European Law at King's College London

Introduction & Contents/Subjects

As the process of European integration assumes an increasingly complex character, the EU legal system continues to undergo sweeping changes. The European Monographs series offers a voice to thoughtful, knowledgeable, cutting edge legal commentary on the now unlimited field of European law. Its emphasis on focal and topical issues makes the series an invaluable tool for scholars, practitioners, and policymakers specializing or simply interested in EU law.

Objective

The aim is to publish innovative work appealing to academics and practitioners alike. The result is an original and ongoing library of detailed analyses, theories, commentaries, practical guides, and proposals, each of which furthers the cause of meaningful European integration. Cumulatively, the series may be regarded as a 'work in progress' engaged in building a sharply defined representation of law in Europe.

Readership

Academics and practitioners dealing with EU law.

The titles published in this series are listed at the end of this volume.

The Financial and Other Sanctions of the European Union

Natalia Charalampidou

Wolters Kluwer

Published by:
Kluwer Law International B.V.
PO Box 316
2400 AH Alphen aan den Rijn
The Netherlands
E-mail: lrs-sales@wolterskluwer.com
Website: www.wolterskluwer.com/en/solutions/kluwerlawinternational

Sold and distributed by:
Wolters Kluwer Legal & Regulatory U.S.
920 Links Avenue
Landisville, PA 17538
United States of America
E-mail: customer.service@wolterskluwer.com

ISBN 978-94-035-4357-4

e-Book: ISBN 978-94-035-4367-3
web-PDF: ISBN 978-94-035-4377-2

Table of Contents

The Author

Natalia Charalampidou is teaching International Environmental and Energy Law at the Faculty of Law of the Democritus University of Thrace in Greece. She is also assisting the editors of *Transnational Dispute Management* and *Periballon & Dikaio.*

Prior to focusing on teaching and academic research, she had joined high-profile law firms representing parties in transboundary complex litigation including US-style discovery and common law injunctions, public listings as well as investment arbitration.

Her areas of expertise include the Energy Charter Treaty, contaminated site investigation and remediation, environmental liability, solid and hazardous waste, environmental due diligence, prospection, research and exploitation of hydrocarbons, renewable electricity, energy compliance and smart grids and cities. She has over ten years of experience in the Energy and Environmental Law of Cyprus.

List of Abbreviations

AG	Australia Group
Am.J.Comp.L.	American Journal of Comparative Law
AMISOM	African Union Mission to Somalia
AML Directive	Anti-Money Laundering Directive (Directive (EU) 2015/849)
AML Regulation	Anti-Money Laundering Regulation (Regulation (EU) 2015/847)
ARSIWA	Articles on Responsibility of States for Internationally Wrongful Acts
BYIL	The British Yearbook of International Law
CAR	Central African Republic
CFSP	Common Foreign and Security Policy
DFI	Development Fund for Iraq
DPRK	Democratic People's Republic of Korea
DRC	Democratic Republic of the Congo
Dual-Use Regulation	Regulation for the Control of Exports, Transfer, Brokering and Transit of Dual-Use Items (Regulation (EU) 2021/821)
Econ. Policy	Economic Policy
EJIL	European Journal of International Law
EU	European Union
Eur.-Asia Stud.	Europe-Asia Studies
FATF	Financial Action Task Force
IAMB	International Advisory and Monitoring Board
ICLQ	International & Comparative Law Quarterly
Int'l Aff. (UK)	International Affairs (UK)
Int. Stud. Rev.	International Studies Review

IRISL	Islamic Republic of Iran Shipping Lines
J.C.&S.L.	Journal of Conflict and Security Law
J.Glob.Secur.Stud.	Journal of Global Security Studies
J. Mod. Afr. Stud.	The Journal of Modern African Studies
J.Pol.Econ.	Journal of Political Economy
J.W.E.L. & B.	Journal of World Energy Law and Business
JCPOA	Joint Comprehensive Plan of Action of 14 July 2015 (also known as the *Iran Nuclear Deal*)
MINUSCA	United Nations Multidimensional Integrated Stabilization Mission in the Central African Republic
MTCR	Missile Technology Control Regime
MTCR Annex	Missile Technology Control Regime Equipment, Software and Technology Annex (as of 21 October 2022)
NSG	Nuclear Suppliers Group
OSCE	Organization for Security and Co-operation in Europe
Politique Eur.	Politique Européenne
UAV	Unmanned Aerial Vehicle
UN	United Nations
UNAMID	African Union/United Nations Hybrid Operation in Darfur
UNIOGBIS	United Nations Integrated Peacebuilding Office in Guinea-Bissau
UNROCA	United Nations Register of Conventional Arms
WA-List	List of Dual-Use Goods and Technologies and Munitions List of the Wassenaar Arrangement (as of December 2022)
WA-DU-List	List of Dual-Use Goods and Technologies and Munitions List of the Wassenaar Arrangement – List of Dual-Use Goods and Technologies (as of December 2022)
WA-M-List	List of Dual-Use Goods and Technologies and Munitions List of the Wassenaar Arrangement – Munitions List (as of December 2022)
YEL	Yearbook of European Law

Preface

Violence and aggression can manifest in many forms: invasion of a neighbouring state; civil war; foreign armed groups operating in parts of a state; illegal exploitation of natural resources; foreign security forces occupying part of a neighbouring state; nuclear programs; ballistic programs; coup d'états; undermining an electoral process; armed groups fighting; recruitment and use of children for fighting; terrorist activities and attacks; large-scale displacement of persons; gang violence; absence of progress towards democratization; obstructing the search for a political solution; disproportionate use of police force; violent crackdown on political demonstrators; corruption. Each one of these manifestations is present not only in the physical world, as damage, but also in the legal realm, as a violation of a right. However, the appearance of violence and aggression in these two plateaus takes place neither simultaneously nor in the same sequence. Launching ballistic missiles is an act threatening damage, which then constitutes a threat to international peace and security. Delaying elections or obstructing the electoral process is a violation of a right, which then leads to people suffering damage.

Either way, the European Union (EU) has chosen to react to violence and aggression in states outside the block, including perpetrating terrorist acts, cyberattacks taking place within the Union and use of chemical weapons also in the Union, through the imposition of restrictive measures, as per the legal term it chose to use throughout the relevant legislative acts. It has done so in thirty-seven instances and considers to continue to do so.

The present monograph elaborates on the notion of restrictive measures, along with the question of whether restrictive measures and sanctions share the same meaning. It also elucidates the factual background against which each legislation imposing such measures has been adopted, as well as whether the EU imposed restrictive measures independently of the United Nations (UN) or in – full or partial – alignment with such. It then proceeds to examine the prohibitions imposed by the restrictive measures, including the abstract legal definitions of their objective components and the detailed lists depicting the same components, where it has been decided to do so, as in the case of nuclear, dual-use items and weapons. It equally portrays exemptions, derogations and grace periods, along with the cases, where national authorities are given the authority to authorize deviation from the imposed restrictive measures, under conditions determined by the EU. Finally, it was decided to make note of the fact that certain persons and groups, which pretty certainly seem to check all the boxes for designation under the respective legislative instruments, have been left out and are thus 'absentees'. A notable example would be the Conspiracy of Cells of Fire that aside from blowing up things, including sending time bombs to Europol, and causing loss of life, has been designated as a terrorist organization in the United States. The EU does not think so, raising many questions. Asking such questions appears – and is – bold; still, in view of the admission that the EU uses articles and news from the press to conduct designations, the temptation to ask, on the basis of press articles, why certain persons and groups are absent was too great to resist.

Importantly, it has been decided to consider all EU legislation and jurisprudence up to 31 December 2023. Later amendments of existing legislation, introduction of new laws and further decisions of the Courts of the EU were not entertained.

The present monograph would have not been conceived without the intriguing remarks and intellectually challenging comments of Prof. Mark Kantor and Young-OGEMID. I am deeply grateful to each one of them. I am also very much obliged to Prof. Constantine Antonopoulos and Prof. Hara Aroni for their invaluable advice and unwavering support. Prof. Ute Mager has been a paradigm setting the standards of scientific research that must be religiously followed; so has Prof. Dr Burkhard Hess; I wholeheartedly thank both of them. Many heartfelt thanks are due to Prof. Kurt Deketelaere for his steadfast support and kind understanding that he has shown me throughout many years. The editor, Prof. Andrea Biondi, and the publisher, Kluwer Law International and especially Gwen de Vries, have been exceptionally kind, patient, understanding and supportive; to them, I am indebted – very very very much.

Bon lecture!
Istanbul, January 2024.

CHAPTER 1
Sanctions and Restrictive Measures

§1 THE MEANING OF SANCTIONS AND RESTRICTIVE MEASURES

1. The terms *sanctions* and *restrictive measures* are here deemed to denote the same notion, that of 'restrictive measures involving the withdrawal of trade or benefits from a sender to a target or/and interruption of normal relations to the target to obtain political goals';[1] their lack of any inherent differentiation apart from the Union using *restrictive measures* (*mesures restrictives* in French, *restriktive Maßnahmen* in German, *beperkende maatregelen* in Dutch) as its official term,[2] leads to their understanding as synonyms[3] and therefore, they are used interchangeably throughout this monograph. Sanctions presuppose the interaction over time of at least two parties, called the sender and the target, whereby the sender intends to affect the target's actions.[4] They are essentially a political tool and are used to force sanctions targets, both states and non-state actors, to align with the targeting state's political preferences.[5]

2. The author of the sanctions discussed here is the European Union ('EU' or 'Union'). On the international scene, the Union seeks to advance in the wider world the rule of

1. Clara Portela, *Where and Why Does the EU Impose Sanctions?* 17(3) Politique Eur. 83 at 84 (2005) https://doi.org/10.3917/poeu.017.0083.
2. Pierre-Emmanuel Dupont, *Countermeasures and Collective Security: The Case of the EU Sanctions Against Iran*, 17(3) J.C.&S.L. 301 at 302 (2012) https://doi.org/10.1093/jcsl/krs020.
3. *See also* Council of the European Union, *Guidelines on Implementation and Evaluation of Restrictive Measures (Sanctions) in the Framework of the EU Common Foreign and Security Policy*, 15579/03, Brussels 3 Dec. 2003, p. 4.
4. Jonathan Eaton & Maxim Engers, *Sanctions* 100(5) J.Pol.Econ. 899 at 900 (1992) https://doi.org/10.1086/261845.
5. Tom Ruys & Cedric Ryngaert, *Secondary Sanctions: A Weapon Out of Control? The International Legality of, and European Responses to, US Secondary Sanctions* (braa007) BYIL 1 at 6 & 7 (2020) https://doi.org/10.1093/bybil/braa007.

law, the universality and indivisibility of human rights and respect for international law.[6] It differs from most regional international organizations in that it imposes sanctions against states outside its territory.[7] As a regional international organization, it adopts sanctions both included in a United Nations (UN) Security Council resolution and not included in such a resolution, the latter occasionally denoted as *autonomous* as opposed to the first considered *UN-mandated*.[8] The UN Security Council does so as it has been entrusted with the primary responsibility of maintaining international peace and security. It thus was given the power to determine what constitutes a threat to international peace and security and to take the measures necessary to avert this threat.[9] At the same time, sanctions decided within the framework of the UN are called multilateral, due to them reflecting the collective will of the members of the UN, as opposed to sanctions adopted by states outside the framework of the UN that are named *unilateral* and do not reflect such will.[10] Regardless, sanctions made within the framework of the UN as well as sanctions made within the framework of the EU are authored by organs with autonomous powers enshrined in the international treaties that created them, the CJEU ruled.[11] The EU imposes restrictive measures, irrespective of them being unilateral or multilateral, autonomous or UN-mandated, within the frame of its Common Foreign and Security Policy ('CFSP') with the desired effect of exerting pressure on the targets.[12] Certain UN sanctions had been preceded by EU sanctions and heavily influenced by the same.[13] This does not alter their close interrelationship, interaction and cross-fertilization.

3. The restrictive measures analysed in the ensuing chapters are *smart* (or *targeted*). The qualities and significance of smart sanctions are better understood, when viewed from the perspective of the origins of sanctions, discussed immediately below. as opposed to Smart sanctions are preferred over embargoes, as they are designed to focus upon the 'deliquent rulers' while avoiding adverse consequences for the general population.[14]

6. *Ahmed Abdelaziz Ezz and Others v. Council*, T-288/15, Judgment of 27 Sep. 2018, digital ECR, para. 59.
7. Andrea Charron & Clara Portela, *The UN, Regional Sanctions and Africa* 91(6) International Affairs 1369 at 1377 (2015) https://doi.org/10.1111/1468-2346.12452.
8. Pierre-Emmanuel Dupont, *Countermeasures and Collective Security: The Case of the EU Sanctions Against Iran* 17(3) J.C.&S.L. 301 at 311 (2012) https://doi.org/10.1093/jcsl/krs020.
9. *European Commission v. Yassin Abdullah Kadi*, Joined C-584/10 P, C-593/10 P and C-595/10 P, Judgment of 18 Jul. 2013, digital ECR, para. 104 ('Kadi 2013').
10. Julia Schmidt, *The Legality of Unilateral Extra-territorial Sanctions under International Law* 27(1) J.C.&S.L. 53 at 58 (2022) https://doi.org/10.1093/jcsl/krac005.
11. *Bank Melli Iran v. Council of the European Union*, C-548/09 P, Judgment of 16 Nov. 2011, para. 102 ('Bank Melli 2011').
12. *République bolivarienne du Venezuela v. Council*, T-65/18 RENV, Judgment of 13 Sep. 2023, digital ECR, para. 42 ('Venezuela 2023').
13. Michael Brzoska, *International Sanctions Before and Beyond UN Sanctions* 91(6) Int'l Aff. (UK) 1339 at 1341 & 1342 (2015) https://doi.org/10.1111/1468-2346.12449.
14. Alain Pellet & Alina Miron, *Sanctions*, in: R. Wolfrum/A. Peters (eds), Max Planck Encyclopedias of International Law (OUP 2013) para. 34.

§2 THE ORIGINS OF SANCTIONS

4. At the outset, it is noted that the Union sees itself obliged to contribute to the strict observance and the development of international law. Thus, upon adoption of an act, the Union is bound to observe international law in its entirety, including customary international law that is binding upon the institutions of the Union, the CJEU ruled.[15] Still, the principles of customary international law may be invoked before the EU Courts solely in so far as, first, those principles are capable of calling into question the competence of the Union to adopt the act in question and, second, the act in question is liable to affect rights which the person derives from EU Law or to create obligations under EU Law in his or her regard.[16]

5. This note is of significance in view of the multilateral (UN-mandated) sanctions discussed here, as the Union, being an international organization, is not and may not be a member of the UN under Article 3 of the Treaty of the UN.[17] It follows that the Union is not required to accept and carry out the decisions of the UN Security Council.[18] The resolutions of the UN Security Council always address states, that have the corresponding obligation to implement those in their national legal orders.[19] The Union is neither a member of the UN, nor an addressee of the resolutions of the UN Security Council, nor the successor of rights and obligations of the Member States for the purposes of public international law.[20] However, the Union is deemed bound by the obligations under the Treaty of the UN in the same way as its Member States by virtue of the founding treaties, the CJEU ruled.[21]

6. The restrictive measures adopted by the Union and discussed in the ensuing chapters are *smart* sanctions. They were preceded by economic sanctions, in the sense of measures having the quality of classic general trade embargos aimed at a country,[22] which were put into use, particularly after the end of the Cold War. Economic sanctions in this sense are broad-based and comprehensive with crippling economic and humanitarian effects.[23] Indicative of such sanctions is the comprehensive trade embargo

15. *Venezuela 2023* (n. 12) para. 87, citing *Air Transport Association of America and Others*, C-366/10, Judgment of 21 Dec. 2011, digital ECR, para. 101 ('Air Transport Association of America 2011'); and *Kadi and Al Barakaat International Foundation v. Council and Commission*, C-402/05 P and C-415/05 P, Judgment of 3 Sep. 2008, digital ECR, para. 291 ('Kadi 2008').
16. *Venezuela 2023* (n. 12) para. 87, citing *Air Transport Association of America* (n. 15) para. 107.
17. Magdalena Ličková, *European Exceptionalism in International Law* 19(3) EJIL 463 at 482 (2008) https://doi.org/10.1093/ejil/chn028.
18. *Ahmed Ali Yusuf and Al Barakaat International Foundation v. Council and Commission*, T-306/01, Judgment of 21 Sep. 2005, digital ECR, para. 242 ('Yusuf 2005').
19. Alain Pellet & Alina Miron, *Sanctions*, in: R. Wolfrum/A. Peters (eds), Max Planck Encyclopedias of International Law (OUP 2013) para. 44.
20. *Yusuf 2005* (n. 18) para. 242.
21. *Ibid.*, para. 243; *Chafiq Ayadi v. Council*, T-253/02, Judgment of 12 Jul. 2006, digital ECR, para. 116 ('Ayadi 2006').
22. *Yusuf 2005* (n. 18) para. 113; *Yassin Abdullah Kadi v. Council and Commission*, T-315/01, Judgment of 21 Sep. 2005, digital ECR, para. 90 ('Kadi 2005').
23. Daniel W. Drezner, *Sanctions Sometimes Smart: Targeted Sanctions in Theory and Practice* 13 Int. Stud. Rev. 96 at 97 (2011) https://doi.org/10.1111/j.1468-2486.2010.01001.x.

imposed on Iraq in 1990 that had devastating humanitarian consequences.[24] Economic sanctions were criticized as blunt coercive instruments that inflict a broad array of harm upon innocent populations.[25] Thus, in the present analysis the term financial restrictive measures has been chosen to denote the measures that the EU imposes with regard to funds and economic resources of specifically designated persons, and thereby to differentiate from the broad-based economic sanctions previously imposed.

7. In response to the criticism against comprehensive economic sanctions, smart sanctions were introduced[26] that discriminate and minimize adverse consequences for those not responsible for policies and actions.[27] Smart sanctions have the qualities of targeted and selective measures, such as financial sanctions, prohibition of travel, and embargos on arms or specific goods, so as to reduce the suffering endured by the civilian population of the country concerned, while nonetheless genuinely sanctioning the targeted regime and those in charge of it.[28] The purpose of this legal concept is to limit the undesirable effects of international sanctions on persons who are already suffering or who are not responsible for the situation in the third country concerned. To this aim, they are adopted against persons with sufficient links with the regime in question in order to qualify as 'rulers' or 'persons associated' with rulers.[29] They target leaders of third countries and persons associated with them, who are deemed to be responsible for the policies or actions that have led to the imposition of the restrictive measures concerned, irrespective of whether they are personally involved in the implementation of those policies and actions.[30] Paraphrasing the exception to the cardinal rule of corporate law, they pierce the 'state veil' and hold the persons designing, perpetrating and profiting from the wrongs at issue, who take refuge behind the state apparatus, accountable.

§3 THE LEGAL BASIS FOR ADOPTING SANCTIONS

8. The Courts of the EU have adjudicated that choosing a legal basis for sanctions must be based on objective factors that are amendable to judicial review including, in particular, the aim and the content of the measure.[31] Taking this into account, it is noted that the legislation on restrictive measures consists of a decision, or previously a

24. Thomas J. Biersteker, Marcos Tourinho & Sue E. Eckert, *Thinking about United Nations Targeted Sanctions*, in: T.J. Biersteker, M. Tourinho & S.E. Eckert (eds), Targeted Sanctions (Cambridge University Press 2016) p. 11.
25. Bryan R. Early & Marcus Schulzke, *Still Unjust, Just in Different Ways: How Targeted Sanctions Fall Short of Just War Theory's Principles* 21 Int. Stud. Rev. 57 at 57 (2019) https://doi.org/10.1093/isr/viy012.
26. Marise Cremona, *EC Competence, 'Smart Sanctions' and the Kadi Case* 28(1) YEL 559 at 567 (2009) https://doi.org/10.1093/yel/28.1.559.
27. Council of the European Union, Sanctions Guidelines, 5664/18, Brussels 4 May 2018, p. 8.
28. *Yusuf 2005* (n. 18) para. 113; *Kadi 2005* (n. 22) para. 90.
29. *Pye Phyo Tay Za v. Council*, C-376/10 P, Opinion of Advocate General of 29 Nov. 2011, digital ECR, para. 35.
30. *Aguy Clement Georgias and Others v. Council and Commission*, T-168/12, Judgment of 18 Sep. 2014, digital ECR, para. 87.
31. *Bank Melli* 2011 (n. 11) para. 66, following the approach of *Kadi* 2008 (n. 15) para. 182.

common position, paired with a regulation. Decisions are adopted within the framework of the Treaty on European Union, under Article 29 TEU, and regulations are adopted within the framework of the Treaty on the Functioning of the European Union, according to Article 215 TFEU.[32] These provisions of the Treaties provide the Council with the power to adopt acts containing independent restrictive measures, distinct from the measures specifically recommended by the UN Security Council.[33] Furthermore, the conferral of implementing power on the Council has been justified by the consistency required between the designations adopted within the framework of the CFSP and those adopted on the basis of the TFEU.[34]

9. The Council has a broad discretion as to what to take into consideration for the purpose of adopting restrictive measures.[35] The objectives guiding the Council's hand are the ones of promoting, in the wider world, democracy, the rule of law, the universality and indivisibility of human rights and fundamental freedoms, respect for human dignity, and respect for the principles of the UN Charter and international law. They aim to ensure, *inter alia,* the following: (i) fulfilment of the *erga omnes partes* obligations to respect the principles derived from general international law and international instruments of a universal or quasi-universal nature, in particular, Article 1 of the UN Charter; (ii) respect for fundamental rights, in particular, the prohibition of torture; (iii) respect for democratic principles; and (iv) protection of the rights of the child, the CJEU ruled.[36] It is here underlined that for this description the CJEU adopted the approach of the ICJ discussing diplomatic protection and depicting the then-contemporary customary international law, at a time, when only states were subjects of international law, and for individuals and groups to have rights and obligations under international law seemed a pipe dream.

10. The wording of Article 215 TFEU does not preclude a regulation adopted on the basis of that provision from conferring implementing powers on the Commission or the Council under Article 291(2) TFEU, where uniform conditions for the implementation of certain restrictive measures provided for in that regulation are necessary.[37] Within this frame, implementation comprises both the drawing-up of implementing rules and the application of rules to specific cases by means of acts of individual application.[38]

32. *Bank Melli* 2011 (n. 11) paras 71 to 73; *Bank Refah Kargaran v. Council*, C-134/19 P, judgment of 6 Oct. 2020, digital ECR, paras 23, 37 & 38, citing *PJSC Rosneft Oil Company v. Her Majesty's Treasury and Others*, C-72/15, judgment of 28 Mar. 2017, digital ECR, para. 89 ('Rosneft 2017'); Council of the European Union, *Sanctions Guidelines*, 5664/18, Brussels 4 May 2018, p. 6.
33. *Council v. Manufacturing Support & Procurement Kala Naft*, C-348/12 P, Judgment of 28 Nov. 2013, digital ECR, para. 109 ('Kala Naft'); *Venezuela 2023* (n. 12) para. 95. *See also National Iranian Oil Company v. Council*, C-440/14 P, Judgment of 1 Mar. 2016, digital ECR, para. 52 ('National Iranian 2016').
34. *Ibid.*, para. 63.
35. *Venezuela* 2023 (n. 12) para. 63.
36. *Ibid.*, para. 113, citing *Barcelona Traction, Light and Power Company, Limited*, ICJ, Judgment of 5 Feb. 1970, digital ICJ Reports paras 33 & 34 and *Questions relating to the Obligation to Prosecute or Extradite*, ICJ, Judgment of 20 Jul. 2012, digital ICJ Reports paras 68 to 70.
37. *National Iranian* 2016 (n. 33) para. 34.
38. *Ibid.*, para. 36, citing *Commission v. Council*, 16/88, Judgment of 24 Oct. 1989, digital ECR, para. 11.

The difference between the procedure under Article 215 TFEU and the one under Article 291(2) TFEU reflects the intention of establishing a distinction, on the basis of objective criteria, between the basic act and an implementing act.[39]

§4 INTERPRETATION

11. Interpretation of the Union acts that set out the legal framework for sanctions, is performed by the Courts of the EU, unsurprisingly. At the same time, the Council has issued guidelines[40] ('EU Guidelines') that have since been updated,[41] and offer an invaluable insight into definitions and standard wording used in the legal instruments, among other issues such as the principles guiding restrictive measures, expiration or review of restrictive measures.

12. The Courts of the EU, when determining the meaning of a provision of EU law, take into account its wording, context and objectives.[42] They further consider the different language versions of a provision of EU law and in case of divergence between such versions, they interpret it by reference to the purpose and general scheme of the rules of which it forms a part.[43] Similarly, in case of doubt about the text of a provision the need for uniform interpretation of EU acts requires that the text of a provision is interpreted and applied in the light of the versions drawn up in other official languages.[44] Specifically with regard to the use of the present participle, the CJEU ruled that it attributes nothing more than a general meaning to the relevant provisions (*see* more in this regard paragraph 78 below).

13. When EU law is tightly interwoven with resolutions of the Security Council of the UN, as predominantly the case is in the field of restrictive measures, interpretation takes place in light of the relevant rules of international law following the firm belief that EU law must respect international law in the exercise of its powers.[45] In truth, it

39. *National Iranian* 2016 (n. 33) para. 45.
40. Council of the European Union, *Guidelines on Implementation and Evaluation of Restrictive Measures (Sanctions) in the Framework of the EU Common Foreign and Security Policy*, 15579/03, Brussels 3 Dec. 2003.
41. Council of the European Union, *Sanctions Guidelines*, 5664/18, Brussels 4 May 2018.
42. *Al-Aqsa v. Council*, T-348/07, Judgment of 9 Sep. 2010, digital ECR, para. 97 ('Al-Aqsa 2010') citing *Jyske Finans A/S v. Skatteministeriet*, C- 280/04, Judgment of 8 Dec. 2005, digital ECR, para. 34.
43. *M and Others*, C-340/08, Judgment of 29 Apr. 2010, digital ECR, para. 44 ('M and Others'); *Plato Plastik Robert Frank GmbH v. Caropack Handelsgesellschaft mbH*, C-341/01, Judgment of 29 Apr. 2004, digital ECR, para. 64.
44. *Adib Mayaleh v. Council*, Joined T-307/12 & T-408/13, Judgment of 5 Nov. 2014, digital ECR, para. 92 ('Mayaleh'), citing *Deo Antoine Homawoo v. GMF Assurances SA*, C–412/10, Judgment of 17 Nov. 2011, digital ECR, para. 28.
45. *Yusuf 2005* (n. 18) para. 249, citing *Anklagemyndigheden v. Peter Michael Poulsen and Diva Navigation Corp*, C-289/90, Judgment of 24 Nov. 1992, digital ECR, para. 9 ('Poulsen'); *A. Racke GmbH & Co. v. Hauptzollamt Mainz*, C-162/96, Judgment of 16 Jul. 1998, digital ECR, para. 45 ('Racke'); *Yvonne van Duyn v. Home Office*, 41/74, Judgment of 7 Dec. 1974, digital ECR, para. 22. *See also Gerda Möllendorf and Christiane Möllendorf-Niehaus*, C-117/06, Judgment of 11 Oct. 2007, digital ECR, para. 54 ('Möllendorf').

occurs under the specific light of the respective resolution(s) of the UN Security Council that are implemented, as the wording of such resolution is to be considered.[46] The historical context in which the provision(s) at hand was adopted, is equally to be weighed up.[47]

14. Furthermore, as it will be seen below, the Courts of the EU perform the task of interpretation on the basis of judgments, with issues of fact and points of law that bear little resemblance to the objects pursued by the legislation on sanctions, such as cases discussing state aid.[48] Moreover, they have drawn inspiration from the provisions of other pieces of EU legislation, also unfamiliar with these objects, for instance, the fight against terrorism, such as the Directive on the right of the citizens of the Union and their family members to move within the territory of the Member States,[49] including their jurisprudence.[50]

15. Finally, in the event of plurality of available interpretations, the Courts of the EU give preference to the interpretation which renders the provision consistent with the general principles of EU law and more specifically, with the principle of legal certainty.[51]

§5 SCOPE AND STRUCTURE OF THE ANALYSIS

16. The restrictive measures that have been adopted by the Union are portrayed and analysed in the ensuing chapters in the following manner. First the European legislation imposing sanctions in regard to a situation within a specific territory is offered starting with the UN-mandated sanctions under the heading 'International Peace and Security' as the UN Security Council has the authority to take action with the aim to maintain or restore international peace and security under Articles 39 et seq. of the UN

46. *Council v. Aisha Muammer Mohamed El-Qaddafi*, C-413/21 P, Judgment of 20 Apr. 2023, digital ECR, para. 57 ('El-Qaddafi 2023'), adopting *Bank Melli* 2011 (n. 11) para. 104. *See also Criminal proceedings against Mohsen Afrasiabi*, C-72/11, Judgment of 21 Dec. 2011, digital ECR, para. 43 ('Afrasiadi'); and *Islamic Republic of Iran Shipping Lines and Others v. Council*, C-225/17 P, Judgment of 31 Jan. 2019, digital ECR, para. 71 ('Iran Shipping 2019').
47. *National Iranian Oil* 2016 (n. 33) para. 78.
48. *See*, for example, *People's Mojahedin Organization of Iran v. Council, T-256/07, Judgment of 23 Oct. 2008, digital ECR* para. 138 ('PMOI I') applying by analogy *Spain v. Lenzing*, C–525/04 P, Judgment of 22 Nov. 2007, digital ECR ('Lenzing') a case relevant to state aid.
49. Directive 2004/38/EC of the European Parliament and of the Council of 29 Apr. 2004 on the right of citizens of the Union and their family members to move and reside freely within the territory of the Member States amending Regulation (EEC) No. 1612/68 and repealing Directives 64/221/EEC, 68/360/EEC, 72/194/EEC, 73/148/EEC, 75/34/EEC, 75/35/EEC, 90/364/EEC, 90/365/EEC and 93/96/EEC, OJ L 158, 30 Apr. 2004, p. 77.
50. *Organisation des Modjahedines du Peuple D'Iran v. Council*, T-228/02, Judgment of 12 Dec. 2006, digital ECR, para. 149 ('OMPI') citing *Roland Rutili v. Ministre de l'intérieur*, 36/75, Judgment of 28 Oct. 1975, digital ECR and *Regina v. Secretary of State for Home Affairs, ex parte Mario Santillo*, 131/79, Judgment of 22 May 1980, digital ECR.
51. *M and Others* (n. 43) para. 64, citing *Privat-Molkerei Borgmann GmbH & Co. KG v. Hauptzollamt Dortmund*, C-1/02, Judgment of 1 Apr. 2004, digital ECR, para. 30.

Charter[52] (sanctions targeting: Iraq, Sudan, Lebanon, the Democratic People's Republic of Korea ('DPRK'), Somalia, Iran, Guinea-Bissau, Libya, the Central African Republic ('CAR'), Yemen, South Sudan, Mali and Haiti). The UN-mandated sanctions are followed by the territory-related autonomous sanctions, that are divided under the headings 'Human Rights' (targeting: Zimbabwe, Iran and Myanmar/Burma), 'Democracy and Human Rights' (targeting: Burundi, Venezuela and Nicaragua), 'Violent Repression and Political Stalemate' (targeting: Guinea and Syria), 'Misappropriation of State Funds' (targeting: Tunisia and Ukraine) and 'Interests and Security of the Union' (targeting: Türkiye). These headings have been inspired by the values and violations stated in the preamble to the respective EU legislation. Within the frame of the present monograph, this categorization serves as a tool for organization; no sharp distinction between them is intended. Nonetheless, it is significant to note that all these sanctions regimes have been decided at the EU level, as adopting a decision at the UN level failed.

17. Chapter 3 presents the restrictive measures that are targeting all aforementioned states per sector, beginning with a few remarks on their scope of application and specifics on decisions adopting restrictive measures. Then the financial sanctions are described and are followed by the additional restrictions on funds and financial services, sanctions on gold and precious metals, sanctions on cultural property, energy-related sanctions, sanctions on dual-use items, sanctions on arms and weapons as well as sanctions with regard to movement of persons and goods.

18. The ensuing chapters shift the focus to three batches of EU acts, each bound together by a common denominator, or at least seem to be so, and appear to be somehow more specific than the ones described above. Chapter 4 delves into the restrictive measures against non-state actors, those being terrorists, Usama bin Laden, the Al-Qaida network, the Taliban and ISIL (Da'esh) and the persons responsible for the assassination of Rafiq Hariri. Here the common element is terrorism. Chapter 5 is dedicated to the sanctions responding to Russia's aggression, that was later escalated into a war of aggression, against Ukraine. Inevitably the additional sanctions against Iran for supplying Russia with unmanned aerial vehicles ('UAVs') and against Belarus as well as the ones in view of attempts for destabilizing Moldova are also discussed therein. These restrictive measures are autonomous and therefore could not be discussed alongside the UN-mandated measures portrayed under the title 'International Peace and Security'. In view of their common denominator – Russia's aggression that has escalated into a war of aggression – and their unique factual background that binds them together, it was decided to dedicate a specific chapter to those and not discuss them among the other autonomous sanctions explained in Chapter 2. After all, no other sanctions are currently in force due to the invasion of a neighbouring state and war. In the last chapter, Chapter 6, 'new generation' restrictive measures are elaborated, which are equally autonomous. They have been titled so, as they depart from the established modus operandi of targeting specific *states* or *non-state actors*, or more accurately the leaders and the elite of a regime, and instead they target activities and

52. Charter of the United Nations and Statute of the International Court of Justice (San Francisco 1945) XV UNCIO 335.

behaviour of *anyone*, dumping the requisite of a 'rogue' state policy that is forced into change or a 'corrupt' leadership that is coerced into adopting the promoted political preferences. These sanctions target serious violations of human rights, cyber-attacks and chemical weapons.

19. Outside the scope of this analysis fall restrictive measures that have been adopted but are no longer in force, i.e., the ones targeting former Yugoslavia[53] and Uzbekistan.[54]

20. The analysis is largely based on the texts of the approximately eighty-one relevant Union acts (for a more specific account *see* the table of legislation at pp 372 et seq.). The standard wording promoted by the Union enables a welder of these legislative tools, whereas at the same time departures from these standards illuminate their differences. Much effort has been put into locating their roots and origins with regard to both the multilateral sanctions and the unilateral ones. Obviously the first trace their origins into the floors and corridors of the UN Security Council. The latter do so into the floors and corridors of the US Senate and the White House, or at the very minimum, they correlate to pieces of US legislation. One further curiosity has been satisfied: that of identifying the sources of the lists depicting dual-use items. These were created by international informal groups, further weakening the view that only states or international organizations qualify as actors under international law. Findings of the Courts of the EU have been taken into consideration, along with the views of scholars.

21. Unforgivably and unavoidably, the *travaux préparatoires* of the EU legislation imposing restrictive measures have been left unattended, as they are not publicly available. This note is of importance because the legislative history of a provision of EU law, which lies in the apposite *travaux préparatoires*, may reveal elements that are relevant to interpretation, according to settled jurisprudence of the Courts of the EU.[55] Shrouding these documents in secrecy deprives not only scholars but more importantly also the Courts of the EU from the opportunity to apply a method of legal interpretation. Furthermore, maintaining secrecy over the origins and roots of imposed sanctions is the antithesis of the open and transparent approach adopted by the UN Security Council. For instance, the arms embargo in view of the situation in the Democratic

53. Imposed by 96/184/CFSP: Common Position of 26 Feb. 1996 defined by the Council on the basis of Art. J.2 of the Treaty on European Union concerning arms exports to the former Yugoslavia, OJ L 58, 7 Mar. 1996, p. 1; lifted by Council Common Position 2006/29/CFSP of 23 Jan. 2006 repealing Common Position 96/184/CFSP concerning arms exports to the former Yugoslavia, OJ L 19, 24 Jan. 2006, p. 34.

54. Imposed by Council Common Position 2005/792/CFSP of 14 Nov. 2005 concerning restrictive measures against Uzbekistan, OJ L 299, 16 Nov. 2005, p. 72 and Council Regulation (EC) No. 1859/2005 of 14 Nov. 2005 imposing certain restrictive measures in respect of Uzbekistan, OJ L 299, 16 Nov. 2005, p. 23.; lifted by Council Regulation (EU) No. 1227/2009 of 15 Dec. 2009 repealing Regulation (EC) No. 1859/2005 imposing certain restrictive measures in respect of Uzbekistan, OJ L 330, 16 Dec. 2009, p. 48.

55. *See European Union Intellectual Property Office v. John Mills Ltd*, C-809/2018 P, Judgment of 11 Nov. 2020, para. 55; *A and Others*, C-24/2019, Judgment of 25 Jun. 2020, para. 37 ('A and Others 2020'); *BGL BNP Paribas*, C-548/2018, Judgment of 9 Oct. 2019, para. 25; *Inuit Tapiriit Kanatami*, C-583/11 P, Judgment of 3 Oct. 2013, para. 50; and *Pringle*, C-370/12, Judgment of 27 Nov. 2012, para. 135.

Republic of the Congo ('DRC')[56] (*see* in this regard paragraph 280 below) was preceded by resolutions expressing concern over the conflict and the illicit flow of arms into the region[57] and reports[58] all of which are publicly available.

22. The present monograph does not inspire to replace the datasets available on the restrictive measures.[59] The moving parts involved and the frequency upon which they are altered obstruct such an attempt. It is equally not inspired to analyse the effectiveness of the imposed restrictive measures on the targeted economic activity. This is a task for financiers left to the masters of this trade.[60] Still, it is here briefly remarked that throughout the years sanctions have encouraged the creation of organized crime syndicates and the development of transnational smuggling networks, and continue to do so to this day.[61] The monograph you hold at hand, or view in your browser, attempts to provide an overview of all restrictive measures that the Union currently imposes, not just of financial sanctions and not just from the viewpoint of human rights, against which the decisions can be challenged before the Courts of the EU. Thus, there will be talk about money and other financial instruments, along with gold, guns, weapons, military and dual-use items, paintings, tourism, art and luxury items, as well as energy, mining and quarrying. In certain instances, also questions shall be asked about persons predominantly absent from the designation lists; persons, who according to the press – one of the main evidentiary means of the Union, alongside publicly available sources of information, intelligence reports and other similar sources of information[62] (*see* in this respect paragraphs 155, 374 and 455 below) – threaten the values and the principles promoted in the old continent.

56. *See* S/RES/1493 of 28 Jul. 2003 para. 20.
57. *See*, for example, S/RES/1279 of 30 Nov. 1999 & S/RES/1457 of 24 Jan. 2003.
58. *See* S/2002/1146 of 16 Oct. 2002; S/2003/566 of 27 May 2003 and S/2003/653 of 17 Jun. 2003.
59. *See*, for example, EU, *Consolidated List of Persons, Groups and Entities Subject to EU Financial Sanctions*, available: https://data.europa.eu/data/datasets/consolidated-list-of-persons-groups-and-entities-subject-to-eu-financial-sanctions?locale=en (last visited: 22 Dec. 2023); Deutsche Bundesbank, *Sankionsregimes*, available: https://www.bundesbank.de/de/service/finanzsanktionen/sanktionsregimes (last visited: 22 Dec. 2023); European Commission, *EU Sanctions Map*, available: https://www.sanctionsmap.eu/#/main (last visited: 22 Dec. 2023).
60. *See*, for example, Tibor Besedeš, Stefan Goldbach & Volker Nitsch, *Financial Sanctions* Econ. Policy 263 at 266 et seq. (2017).
61. *See* Daniel W. Drezner, *Sanctions Sometimes Smart: Targeted Sanctions in Theory and Practice* 13(1) Int. St. Rev. 96 at 98 (2011) https://doi.org/10.1111/j.1468-2486.2010.01001.x; *Hear* the podcast: Jean Lee & Geoff White (hosts/reporters), Estelle Doyle (producer), *The Lazarus Heist, S2.9 Big spenders*, 22 May 2023, BBC World Service, wherever you get your podcasts.
62. *See Kim and Others*, Joined T-533/25 & T-264/16, Judgment of 14 Mar. 2018, paras 107-109 ('Kim and Others').

CHAPTER 2

Restrictive Measures in View of the Situation Within a Territory

23. The legislation of the EU imposing restrictive measures is complex, obscure, draconian and at the same time remarkably simple and almost predictable, to a great extent due to the promoted standard wording.

24. As already mentioned, the legal instruments deployed for the imposition of restrictive measures have the form of a decision – previously a common position – and a regulation. The latter reproduces, in essence, the position of the Union expressed in the corresponding decision, and thus implements it at the EU level,[63] as regulations are of general application, a particularly useful feature when the approach of the Union to a matter relating to the CFSP needs to be precisely reflected.[64]

25. Notwithstanding the obscurity generated when looking into countries, places and situations, the restrictive measures and the legislation introducing them can become quite lucid, when observed from the viewpoint of the violations that these laws address and the principles, goods and values that they seek to protect. At the outset, the first group of principles that the EU restrictive measures seek to protect are international peace and security. This set of measures is effortlessly distinguished due to a specific formalistic feature: implementation of resolutions of the UN Security Council. Other, non-UN-mandated, restrictive measures are triggered by the urge to protect human rights, as a reaction to violent repressions, political stalemates or misappropriation of state funds, as well as by the need to guard the interests and the security of the Union. They share the common element of the EU taking the initiative for their enactment, and thus qualifying as autonomous sanctions. They equally offer a solid basis for the view that normative concerns trigger EU sanctions, as the Union most often imposes sanctions in the context of democratization or human rights violations, including coups

63. *Venezuela* 2023 (n. 12) para. 65.
64. *Ibid.*, para. 78.

d'état[65] and *unauthorized* prospect for hydrocarbons. To the contrary the first set of measures that follow immediately below have been issued following, both in spirit and in time, resolutions of the UN Security Council.

§1 INTERNATIONAL PEACE AND SECURITY

26. The EU has enacted thirteen sets of legislation relating to restrictive measures for the protection of international peace and security that were first decided and imposed by the Security Council of the UN. In chronological order, protecting international peace and security caused the imposition of sanctions targeting Iraq, Sudan, Lebanon, the DPRK, Somalia, Iran, Guinea-Bissau, Libya, the CAR, Yemen, South Sudan, Mali and Haiti. It is here noted that maintaining international peace and security constitutes an objective of general interest that can justify restrictions of fundamental rights, such as the protection of property and the freedom to pursue a trade or profession, the CJEU has ruled.[66] In the paragraphs below the measures are described in correlation to the resolution of the UN Security Council that they seek to implement, as its precise wording along with the historical context assist their interpretation and understanding.[67]

27. Regardless, EU law confers on the Council's autonomous power that can and is exercised independently from the specifics set out in the apposite resolution of the UN Security Council. In other words, the EU legislation does not aim to merely give effect to the resolutions of the UN Security Council; rather, by conferring on the Council 'autonomous power' it has the object to ensure that the ends pursued by such resolutions 'are attained by means of adopting autonomous restrictive measures', the CJEU ruled.[68] Thus, the content and objectives of such resolutions cannot be deemed as a yardstick against which the compatibility of contested decisions with the principle of proportionality must be assessed, the CJEU continued.[69] The Court nevertheless did not rule out assessing the compatibility of any contested decision against other principles that could derive, for example, from the draft articles on the responsibility of international organizations.[70]

28. The specific restrictions on economic and financial relations with Iraq were envisioned in a common position[71] ('Common Position on Iraq'), whereas it has been

65. Andreas Boogaerts, *Beyond Norms: A Configurational Analysis of the EU's Arab Spring Sanctions* 14 Foreign Policy Analysis 408 at 411 (2018) https://doi.org/10.1093/fpa/orw052.
66. *Bank Melli* 2011 (n. 11) paras 114 to 116.
67. *El-Qaddafi*. 2023 (n. 46) para. 57, adopting *Bank Melli* 2011 (n. 11) para. 104. *See* also *Afrasiabi* (n. 46) para. 43; and *Iran Shipping* 2019 (n. 46) para. 71.
68. *Bank Melli Iran v. Council*, T-390/08, judgment of 14 Oct. 2009, digital ECR, para. 64 ('Bank Melli 2009').
69. *Ibid.*, para. 65; affirmed on appeal *Bank Melli* 2011 (n. 11) paras 107 & 108.
70. *See* A/66/10.
71. Council Common Position 2003/495/CFSP of 7 Jul. 2003 on Iraq and repealing Common Positions 96/741/CFSP and 2002/599/CFSP, OJ L 169, 8 Jul. 2003, p. 72, as last amended by Council Decision (CFSP) 2023/338 of 14 Feb. 2023 amending certain Council decisions and

chosen to enact them in the form of a regulation[72] ('Regulation on Iraq') for the purpose of avoiding distortion of competition.[73] These have been issued, in order to implement a series of resolutions of the Security Council of the UN, mainly those that were decided upon the invasion of Kuwait having caused loss of human life and material destruction;[74] established the oil-for-food program,[75] recognized the occupying powers in 2003; set sanctions against the previous government; established the Development Fund for Iraq ('DFI') and its audit oversight body, the International Advisory and Monitoring Board ('IAMB'); and terminated the oil-for-food program.[76,77] In the ensuing years, the UN Security Council has issued a number of resolutions welcoming the establishment of the *broadly representative* Governing Council of Iraq, establishing[78] and maintaining the United Nations Assistance Mission for Iraq[79] ('UNAMI'), authorizing a multinational force ('MNF') for the security and stability in Iraq[80] and extending its mandate,[81] establishing a sanctions committee[82] (the '1518 Iraq Sanctions Committee'), condemning terrorist attacks and terrorist financing[83] and extending the mandate of the DFI and the IAMB.[84]

29. The EU, in view of the civil war and with the aim of promoting lasting peace and reconciliation, issued restrictive measures in view of the situation in Sudan that were discussed in a common position[85] ('Common Position on Sudan') and were given effect

---

common positions concerning restrictive measures in order to insert provisions on a humanitarian exemption, OJ L 47, 15 Feb. 2023, p. 50.

72. Council Regulation (EC) No. 1210/2003 of 7 Jul. 2003 concerning certain specific restrictions on economic and financial relations with Iraq and repealing Regulation (EC) No. 2465/96, OJ L 169, 8 Jul. 2003, p. 6, as last amended by Commission Implementing Regulation (EU) 2023/2185 of 11 Oct. 2023 amending Council Regulation (EC) No. 1210/2003 concerning certain specific restrictions on economic and financial relations with Iraq, digital OJ L, 12 Oct. 2023.
73. Recital No. 8 to the preamble of Regulation on Iraq.
74. S/RES/661 of 6 Aug. 1990.
75. S/RES/986 of 14 Apr. 1995.
76. S/RES/1483 of 22 May 2003. On the oil-for-food program *see also* S/RES/1958 of 15 Dec. 2010 and S/RES/2390 of 8 Dec. 2017.
77. *See* recital Nos 1 and 2 to the preamble of the Regulation on Iraq.
78. S/RES/1500 of 14 Aug. 2003. *See also* S/RES/1546 of 8 Jun. 2004 and S/RES/2107 of 27 Jun. 2013.
79. S/RES/1557 of 12 Aug. 2004, S/RES/1619 of 11 Aug. 2005, S/RES/1700 of 10 Aug. 2006, S/RES/1770 of 10 Aug. 2007, S/RES/1637 of 8 Nov. 2005, S/RES/1830 of 7 Aug. 2008, S/RES/1936 of 5 Aug. 2010, S/RES/2061 of 25 Jul. 2012, S/RES/2110 of 24 Jul. 2013, S/RES/2169 of 30 Jul. 2014, S/RES/2233 of 29 Jul. 2015, S/RES/2299 of 30 Dec. 2016, S/RES/2367 of 14 Jul. 2017, S/RES/2421 of 14 Jun. 2018, S/RES/2470 of 21 May 2019, S/RES/2522 of 29 May 2020, S/RES/2576 of 27 May 2021.
80. S/RES/1511 of 16 Oct. 2003. *See also* S/RES/1546 of 8 Jun. 2004.
81. S/RES/1723 of 28 Nov. 2006.
82. S/RES/1518 of 24 Nov. 2003.
83. S/RES/1618 of 4 Aug. 2005, S/RES/2170 of 15 Aug. 2014, S/RES/2178 of 24 Sep. 2014, S/RES/2199 of 12 Feb. 2015, S/RES/2249 of 20 Nov. 2015, S/RES/2379 of 21 Sep. 2017.
84. S/RES/1905 of 21 Dec. 2009, S/RES/1956 of 15 Dec. 2010.
85. Council Decision 2014/450/CFSP of 10 Jul. 2014 concerning restrictive measures in view of the situation in Sudan and repealing Decision 2011/423/CFSP, OJ L 203, 11 Jul. 2014, p. 106, as last amended by Council Decision (CFSP) 2023/726 of 31 Mar. 2023 amending certain Council Decisions concerning restrictive measures in order to insert provisions on a humanitarian exemption, OJ L 94, 3 Apr. 2023, p. 48.

in the form of a regulation[86] ('Regulation on Sudan'). Said instruments were preceded by the UN Security Council imposing an arms embargo[87] and restrictions on persons impeding the peace process, constituting a threat to stability, committing violations of international humanitarian or human rights law and other atrocities and violating the arms embargo.[88] Beyond those, the UN Security Council has issued resolutions establishing[89] and maintaining the United Nations Mission in Sudan[90] ('UNMIS') and subsequently withdrawing it,[91] establishing the International Commission of Inquiry for investigating reports of violations of international humanitarian law and human rights law in Darfur and enquiring allegations of genocide,[92] creating[93] and maintaining an African Union/United Nations hybrid peacekeeping mission in Darfur[94] ('UN-AMID') whose mandate expired,[95] and establishing[96] and maintaining the United Nations Integrated Transition Assistance Mission in Sudan[97] ('UNITAMS').

30. The EU enacted restrictive measures in view of the situation in the DRC via issuing a decision[98] ('Decision on DRC') and a regulation[99] ('Regulation on DRC') in response to resolutions of the UN Security Council[100] and in correlation to the measures

86. Council Regulation (EU) No. 747/2014 of 10 Jul. 2014 concerning restrictive measures in view of the situation in Sudan and repealing Regulations (EC) No. 131/2004 and (EC) No. 1184/2005, OJ L 203, 11 Jul. 2014, p. 1, as last amended by Council Regulation (EU) 2023/720 of 31 Mar. 2023 amending certain Council Regulations concerning restrictive measures in order to insert provisions on a humanitarian exemption, OJ L 94, 3 Apr. 2023, p. 1.
87. S/RES/1556 of 30 Jul. 2004.
88. S/RES/1591 of 29 Mar. 2005.
89. S/RES/1590 of 24 Mar. 2005. *See also* S/RES/1663 of 24 Mar. 2006 and S/RES/1706 of 31 Aug. 2006.
90. S/RES/1627 of 23 Sep. 2005, S/RES/1709 of 22 Sep. 2006, S/RES/1714 of 6 Oct. 2006, S/RES/1755 of 30 Apr. 2007, S/RES/1784 of 31 Oct. 2007, S/RES/1812 of 30 Apr. 2008, S/RES/1870 of 30 Apr. 2009, S/RES/1919 of 29 Apr. 2010 and S/RES/1978 of 27.Apr. 2011.
91. S/RES/1997 of 11 Jul. 2011.
92. S/RES/1564 of 18 Sep. 2004.
93. S/RES/1769 of 31 Jul. 2007. *See also* S/RES/2148 of 3 Apr. 2014.
94. S/RES/1828 of 31 Jul. 2008, S/RES/1881 of 30 Jul. 2009, S/RES/1935 of 30 Jul. 2010, S/RES/2003 of 29 Jul. 2011, S/RES/2063 of 31 Jul. 2012, S/RES/2113 of 30 Jul. 2013, S/RES/2173 of 27 Aug. 2014, S/RES/2228 of 29 Jun. 2015, S/RES/2296 of 29 Jun. 2016, S/RES/2400 of 8 Feb. 2018, S/RES/2429 of 13 Jul. 2018, S/RES/2479 of 27 Jun. 2019, S/RES/2495 of 31 Oct. 2019, S/RES/2525 of 3 Jun. 2020 and S/RES/2559 of 22 Dec. 2020.
95. S/RES/2559 of 22 Dec. 2020.
96. S/RES/2525 of 3 Jun. 2020 and S/RES/2524 of the same date.
97. S/RES/2579 of 3 Jun. 2021.
98. Council Decision 2010/788/CFSP of 20 Dec. 2010, concerning restrictive measures against the Democratic Republic of the Congo and repealing Common Position 2008/369/CFSP, OJ L 336 of 21 Dec. 2010, p. 30, as last amended by Council Decision (CFSP) 2023/2768 of 8 Dec. 2023 amending Decision 2010/788/CFSP concerning restrictive measures in view of the situation in the Democratic Republic of the Congo, digital OJ L, 11 Dec. 2023.
99. Council Regulation (EC) No. 1183/2005 of 18 Jul. 2005 imposing certain specific restrictive measures directed against persons acting in violation of the arms embargo with regard to the Democratic Republic of the Congo, OJ L 193, 23 Jul. 2005, p. 1, as last amended by Council Regulation (EU) 2023/1565 of 28 Jul. 2023 amending Regulation (EC) No. 1183/2005 concerning restrictive measures in view of the situation in the Democratic Republic of the Congo, OJ L 190I, 28 Jul. 2023, p. 9.
100. The Security Council of the UN imposed, strengthened, expanded, extended and renewed arms embargo, travel bans and assets freeze via the following resolutions: S/RES/1493 of 28 Jul. 2003, S/RES/1596 of 18 Apr. 2005, S/RES/1649 of 21 Dec. 2005, S/RES/1698 of 31 Jul. 2006,

introduced thereby. The initial objective pursued by these measures was to create a climate conducive to the holding of elections and to bring an end to all human rights violations.[101] The UN Security Council had expressed concerns over the continued illegal exploitation of natural resources and over the continuation of hostilities in the eastern part of DRC, particularly in Kivu and Ituri. It had strongly condemned the recruitment and use of children in the same part of DRC and imposed an arms embargo,[102] that was later expanded and accompanied by a travel ban and assets freeze.[103] At the same time, the UN Security Council established the UN Organization Mission in the Democratic Republic of the Congo[104] that later bore the title UN Organization Stabilization Mission in the Democratic Republic of Congo ('MONUSCO').[105] It addressed conflict prevention and peaceful dispute resolution in the Great Lakes region.[106] It further expressed its grave concern at the continued presence of the Forces démocratiques de libération du Rwanda, ex-Rwandan Armed Forces/Interahamwe, and other Rwandan armed groups in the eastern part of DRC, while underscoring that the Actes d'engagement (Goma 2008) and the Nairobi communiqué (Nairobi 2007) represent a major step towards the restoration of lasting peace and stability in the Great Lakes region.[107] It later reiterated its deep concern due to ongoing military activities of the 23 March Movement and the continuation of serious violations of international humanitarian law by said armed group and other ones.[108]

31. Certain restrictive measures in respect of Lebanon were considered in a common position[109] ('Common Position on Lebanon') and were put into force throughout the

S/RES/1768 of 31 Jul. 2007, S/RES/1771 of 10 Aug. 2007, S/RES/1799 of 15 Feb. 2008, S/RES/1807 of 31 Mar. 2008, S/RES/1857 of 22 Dec. 2008, S/RES/1896 of 30 Nov. 2009, S/RES/1952 of 28 May 2010, S/RES/2021 of 29 Nov. 2011, S/RES/2078 of 28 Nov. 2012, S/RES/2136 of 30 Jan. 2014, S/RES/2198 of 20 Jan. 2015, S/RES/2293 of 23 Jun. 2016, S/RES/2360 of 21 Jun. 2017, S/RES/2478 of 26 Jun. 2019, S/RES/2528 of 25 Jun. 2020, S/RES/2582 of 29 Jun. 2021, S/RES/2667 of 20 Dec. 2022 & S/RES/2688 of 27 Jun. 2023.

101. *Gabriel Amisi Kumba v. Council*, T-163/18, Judgment of 12 Feb. 2020, digital ECR, paras 61 & 7 ('Kumba').
102. *See* S/RES/1493 of 28 Jul. 2003 recitals and paras 13 & 20.
103. *See* S/RES/1596 of 18 Apr. 2005.
104. S/RES/1279 of 30 Nov. 1999. Its mission was renewed and expanded by S/RES/1445 of 4 Dec. 2002, S/RES/1565 of 1 Oct. 2004, S/RES/1592 of 30 Mar. 2005, S/RES/1592 of 30 Mar. 2005, S/RES/1621 of 6 Sep. 2005, S/RES/1635 of 28 Oct. 2005, S/RES/1669 of 10 Apr. 2006, S/RES/1693 of 30 Jun. 2006, S/RES/1711 of 29 Sep. 2006, S/RES/1736 of 22 Dec. 2006, S/RES/1742 of 15 Feb. 2007, S/RES/1751 of 13 Apr. 2007, S/RES/1756 of 15 May 2007, S/RES/1794 of 21 Dec. 2007, S/RES/1797 of 30 Jan. 2008, S/RES/1856 of 22 Dec. 2008 and S/RES/1906 of 23 Dec. 2009.
105. *See* S/RES/1925 of 28 May 2010.
106. *See* S/RES/1653 of 27 Jan. 2006.
107. *See* S/RES/1804 of 13 Mar. 2008.
108. *See* S/RES/2076 of 20 Nov. 2012.
109. Council Common Position 2006/625/CFSP of 15 Sep. 2006 concerning a prohibition on the sale or supply of arms and related materiel and on the provision of related services to entities or individuals in Lebanon in accordance with UNSC Resolution 1701 (2006), OJ L 253, 16 Sep. 2006, p. 36. It has not been amended since.

EU in a regulation[110] ('Regulation on Lebanon'). These were put in place in order to comply with the measures decided by the UN Security Council following the efforts of the government of Lebanon to extend its authority over its territory through its own legitimate armed forces and the withdrawal of the Israeli forces from southern Lebanon that called for prevention of selling and supplying arms and related material to entities and individuals in Lebanon.[111] Other resolutions of the UN Security Council called for a cessation of hostilities and established the United Nations Truce Supervision Organization[112] ('UNTSO'), urged Israel to withdraw from Lebanese territory,[113] established[114] and maintained the United Nations Interim Force in Lebanon[115] ('UNIFIL'), established[116] and maintained the United Nations International Independent Investigation Commission[117] ('UNIIIC') to assist the local authorities in the investigation of the assassination of former Lebanese Prime Minister Rafiq Hariri and others (*see* in this respect paragraphs 389 et seq. below) and established the Special Tribunal for Lebanon to prosecute persons responsible for said terrorist attack and other related attacks that occurred in Lebanon.[118]

32. Restrictive measures against the DPRK were portrayed in a common position[119] ('Common Position on DPRK') and enacted in a regulation[120] ('Regulation on DPRK). The UN Security Council assessed that the nuclear test that the DPRK conducted on 9

110. Council Regulation (EC) No. 1412/2006 of 25 Sep. 2006 concerning certain restrictive measures in respect of Lebanon, OJ L 267, 27 Sep. 2006, p. 2, as last amended by Commission Implementing Regulation (EU) 2022/595 of 11 Apr. 2022 amending certain Regulations concerning restrictive measures and setting out a single list for the Annexes to those Regulations containing the contact details of Member States' competent authorities and the address for notifications to the European Commission, OJ L 114, 12 Apr. 2022, p. 60.
111. S/RES/1701 of 11 Aug. 2006.
112. S/RES/50 of 29 May 1948.
113. S/RES/425 of 19 Mar. 1978 and S/RES/509 of 6 Jun. 1982, S/RES/520 of 17 Sep. 1982.
114. S/RES/425 of 19 Mar. 1978 and S/RES/426 of same date. *See also* S/RES/427 of 3 May 1978 and S/RES/1701 of 11 Aug. 2006.
115. S/RES/523 of 18 Oct. 1982, S/RES/1310 of 27 Jul. 2000, S/RES/1337 of 30 Jan. 2001, S/RES/1461 of 30 Jan. 2003, S/RES/1496 of 31 Jul. 2003, S/RES/1583 of 28 Jan. 2005, S/RES/1614 of 29 Jul. 2005, S/RES/1655 of 31 Jan. 2006, S/RES/1697 of 31 Jul. 2006, S/RES/1773 of 24 Aug. 2007, S/RES/1832 of 27 Aug. 2008, S/RES/1884 of 27 Aug. 2009, S/RES/1937 of 30 Aug. 2010, S/RES/2004 of 30 Aug. 2011, S/RES/2064 of 30 Aug. 2012, S/RES/2115 of 29 Aug. 2013, S/RES/2172 of 26 Aug. 2014, S/RES/2236 of 21 Aug. 2015, S/RES/2305 of 30 Aug. 2016, S/RES/2373 of 30 Aug. 2017, S/RES/2433 of 30 Aug. 2018, S/RES/2485 of 29 Aug. 2019, S/RES/2539 of 28 Aug. 2020, S/RES/2591 of 30 Aug. 2021.
116. S/RES/1595 of 7 Apr. 2005.
117. S/RES/1644 of 15 Dec. 2005, S/RES/1655 of 31 Jan. 2006, S/RES/1686 of 15 Jun. 2006, S/RES/1748 of 27 Mar. 2007, S/RES/1815 of 2 Jun. 2008 and S/RES/1852 of 17 Dec. 2008.
118. S/RES/1757 of 30 May 2007. *See also* S/RES/1664 of 29 Mar. 2006.
119. Council Decision (CFSP) 2016/849 of 27 May 2016 concerning restrictive measures against the Democratic People's Republic of Korea and repealing Decision 2013/183/CFSP, OJ L 141, 28 May 2016, p. 79, as last amended by Council Decision (CFSP) 2023/2540 of 13 Nov. 2023 amending Decision (CFSP) 2016/849 concerning restrictive measures against the Democratic People's Republic of Korea, digital OJ L, 14 Nov. 2023.
120. Council Regulation (EU) 2017/1509 of 30 Aug. 2017 concerning restrictive measures against the Democratic People's Republic of Korea and repealing Regulation (EC) No. 329/2007, OJ L 224, 31.8.2017, p. 1, as last amended by Council Regulation (EU) 2023/720 of 31 Mar. 2023 amending certain Council Regulations concerning restrictive measures in order to insert provisions on a humanitarian exemption, OJ L 94, 3 Apr. 2023, p. 1.

October 2006 constituted a threat to international peace and security and in response placed a series of sanctions.[121] These were transposed into Union law by said instruments. These did not deter Pyongyang. In truth, since 10 February 20005, when the DPRK announced that it possessed nuclear weapons, Pyongyang has conducted two underground nuclear tests[122] as well as four further nuclear tests;[123] it has also launched or attempted to launch ballistic missiles on countless occasions,[124] sometimes underwater from submarines,[125] along with a satellite.[126] In 2018, the DPRK refrained from nuclear testing and missile test-firing as an expression of 'sincere goodwill and tolerance to meet the universal desire of the international community for peace and stability'.[127] This approach however did not last. Pyongyang went on with launching ballistic missiles, including short-range, IRBM-class and ICBM-class ballistic missiles,[128] as well as submarine launches,[129] and successfully placed a spy satellite in orbit.[130] The UN strongly condemns these actions and repeatedly called Pyongyang to

121. S/RES/1718 of 14 Oct. 2006.
122. These nuclear tests were conducted on 9 Oct. 2006 and 25 May 2009 and both were condemned by the UN Security Council (*see* R/RES/1718 of 14 Oct. 2006 and R/RES/1874 of 12 Jun. 2009 respectively).
123. These nuclear tests were conducted on 12 Feb. 2013, 6 Jan. 2016, 9 Sep. 2016 and 2 Sep. 2017; each one of them was condemned by the UN Security Council (*see* R/RES/2094 of 7 Mar. 2013, R/RES/2270 of 2 Mar. 2016, R/RES/2321 of 30 Nov. 2016 and R/RES/2375 of 11 Sep. 2017 respectively).
124. Ballistic missiles were launched on 5 Jul. 2006, 4 Jul. 2009, 12 Dec. 2012, 26 Mar. 2014, 29 Jun. until 13 Jul. 2014, 27 & 28 Apr. & 31 May 2016, 21 Jun. 2015, 2 Aug. 2016, 5 Sep. 2016, 14 Oct. 2016, 20 Oct. 2016, 11 Feb. 2017, 5 Mar. 2017, 19 & 21 Mar. 2017, 4 Apr. 2017, 15 Apr. 2017, 28 Apr. & 13 May 2017, 21 May 2017, 3 & 28 Jul. 2017 and 14 Sep. 2017; they were condemned, usually in the strongest terms, by the UN Security Council (*see* R/RES/1695 of 15 Jul. 2006, R/RES/1874 of 12 Jun. 2009, R/RES/2087 of 22 Jan. 2013, SC/11502 of 30 Jul. 2014, SC/12385-DC/3536 of 1 Jun. 2016, SC/12418-DC/3640 of 23 Jun. 2016, SC/12494-DC/3649 of 26 Aug. 2016, SC/12509 of 6 Sep. 2016, SC/12557-DC/3665 of 17 Oct. 2016, SC/12716-DC/3684 of 13 Feb. 2017, SC/12741-DC/3687 of 7 Mar. 2017, SC/12763-DC/3690 of 23 Mar. 2017, SC/12780-DC/3696 of 6 Apr. 2017, SC/12801-DC/3698 of 20 Apr. 2017, SC/12821-DC/3704 of 15 May 2017, SC/12831-DC/3705 of 22 May 2017 & R/RES/2356 of 2 Jun. 2017, R/RES/2371 of 5 Aug. 2017, SG/SM/18656-DC/3732 of 29 Aug. 2017, SG/SM/18678-DC/3735 of 15 Sep. 2017 respectively).
125. Such launches took place on 9 May 2015 and 23 Aug. 2016; these were condemned by the UN Security Council (*see* R/RES/2270 of 2 Mar. 2016, SC/12494-DC/3649 of 26 Aug. 2016).
126. A satellite was launched on 7 Feb. 2016 that was condemned in a press statement, as it used ballistic missile technology that could be employed to deliver nuclear weapons systems in violation of relevant UN Security Council resolutions (*see* SC/12494-DC/3649 of 7 Feb. 2016).
127. *See* GA/12214 of 11 Nov. 2019.
128. In 2019, the DPRK made two launches in May and two in July, five launches in August 2019, one in September, two in October and one in November. Pyongyang then launched ballistic missiles on 2 Mar. 2020, 9 Mar. 2020, 21 Mar. 2020 and 29 Mar. 2020, and continued on 25 Mar. 2021, 15 Sep. 2021, 28 Sep. 2021 and 19 Oct. 2021. In 2022, the most intense year of missile activity, the DPRK made fifty-nine launches in total, whereas in 2023 thirty-six.
129. Such a launch took place on 2 Oct. 2019, 19 Oct. 2021 and 7 May 2022.
130. *See* SC/15540 of 19 Dec. 2023; Editors, *Fact Sheet: North Korea Missile Test Activity*, 14 Nov. 2023 (updated 5 Feb. 2024), Centre for Arms Control and Non-Proliferation, available: https://armscontrolcenter.org/fact-sheet-north-korea-missile-test-activity/ (last visited: 31 Dec. 2023); Editors, *Missile Launches by North Korea, Ministry of Foreign Affairs of Japan*, available: https://www.mofa.go.jp/files/100469370.pdf (last visited: 31 Dec. 2023); Editors, *Chronology of Events: DPRK (North Korea)*, Security Council Report, 2 Sep. 2020, available: https://www.securitycouncilreport.org/chronology/dprk-north-korea.php (last visited: 31

take steps towards complete, verifiable and irreversible denuclearization.[131] The DPRK takes a different view, as expressed in letters to the UN Security Council arguing that 'strengthening its nuclear forces is a righteous choice to defend itself from the extreme moves from the US to stifle it'[132] and that missile launches are a 'self-defensive measure'.[133] On a final note, despite popular belief, Pyongyang has advanced science and technology at its disposal that allows it to design, organize and perform such tests and, most importantly, learn from them.[134] At the same time, violations of human rights in the DPRK are being reported repeatedly, accumulating to 'long-standing and ongoing systematic, widespread and gross violations of human rights'; these are being steadily condemned in the strongest terms by the General Assembly of the UN.[135]

33. Specific restrictive measures in view of the situation in Somalia were described in a Council decision[136] ('Decision on Somalia') and implemented in a regulation[137] ('Regulation on Somalia'), which have been enacted in compliance with the UN Security Council reaffirming the general and complete arms embargo against Somalia.[138] These measures were first imposed[139] and later elaborated and amended[140] by other resolutions[141] in view of the heavy loss of human life and widespread material damage that resulted from the conflict in the country. Other resolutions of the UN Security Council established[142] the United Nations Operation in Somalia I ('UNOSOM I') to monitor the ceasefire in Mogadishu and protect humanitarian convoys and

Dec. 2023); Editors, *North Korea's Missile Activity in 2022*, IISS, December 2022, available: https://www.iiss.org/sv/publications/strategic-comments/2022/north-koreas-missile-activity-in-2022/ (last visited: 31 Dec. 2023).

131. *See*, for example, SC/12780-DC/3696 of 6 Apr. 2017, GA/12214 of 11 Nov. 2019, SG/SM/19924 of 1 Jan. 2020, SC/15540 of 19 Dec. 2023.
132. S/2016/988 of 22 Nov. 2016.
133. A/71/796-S/2017/139 of 17 Feb. 2017.
134. On the U-turn of DPRK in relation to science, technology and cyber *hear*: Jean Lee & Geoff White (hosts/reporters), Estelle Doyle (producer), *The Lazarus Heist, S1.5 Cyber Warriors*, 17 May 2021, BBC World Service, *Wherever You Get Your Podcasts*.
135. *See*, among others, A/RES/78/218 of 22 Dec. 2023, A/RES/77/226 of 9 Jan. 2023, A/RES/76/177 of 10 Jan. 2022, A/RES/75/190 of 28 Dec. 2020, A/RES/74/166 of 27 Jan. 2020, A/RES/73/180 of 23 Jan. 2019 and A/RES/72/188 of 19 Jan. 2018.
136. 2010/231/CFSP: Council Decision 2010/231/CFSP of 26 Apr. 2010 concerning restrictive measures against Somalia and repealing Common Position 2009/138/CFSP, OJ L 105, 27 Apr. 2010, p. 17, as last amended by Council Implementing Decision (CFSP) 2024/1729 of 17 Jun. 2024 implementing Decision 2010/231/CFSP concerning restrictive measures in view of the situation in Somalia, digital OJ L, 17 Jun. 2024.
137. Council Regulation (EU) No. 356/2010 of 26 Apr. 2010 imposing certain specific restrictive measures directed against certain natural or legal persons, entities or bodies, in view of the situation in Somalia, OJ L 105, 27 Apr. 2010, p. 1, as last amended by Council Implementing Regulation (EU) 2023/1147 of 12 Jun. 2023 implementing Article 12 of Regulation (EU) No. 356/2010 imposing certain specific restrictive measures directed against certain natural or legal persons, entities or bodies, in view of the situation in Somalia, OJ L 151I, 12 Jun. 2023, p. 1.
138. S/RES/1844 of 20 Nov. 2008.
139. S/RES/733 of 23 Jan. 1992.
140. S/RES/1356 of 19 Jun. 2001, S/RES/1425 of 22 Jul. 2002, S/RES/1725 of 6 Dec. 2006, S/RES/1744 of 20 Feb. 2007, S/RES/1772 of 20 Aug. 2007.
141. *See* preamble to S/RES/1844 of 20 Nov. 2008 and recital No. 1 to the preamble of the Regulation on Somalia.
142. S/RES/751 of 24 Apr. 1992. *See also* S/RES/775 of 28 Aug. 1992.

distribution centres, established[143] and later withdrew the United Nations Operation in Somalia II[144] ('UNOSOM II'), created the Unified Task Force[145] ('UNITAF') for ensuring the delivery of humanitarian assistance, authorized the Intergovernmental Authority on Development ('IGAD') and the Member States of the African Union to establish a protection and training mission in Somalia,[146] authorized the African Union Mission to Somalia[147] ('AMISOM') and authorized action against piracy and armed robbery at sea.[148]

34. Over the last years restrictive measures against Iran have been enacted by the EU[149] ('Common Position on Iran' and 'Regulation on Iran'), which are giving effect to resolutions of the UN Security Council related to suspending all enrichment-related and

143. S/RES/814 of 26 Mar. 1993. *See also* S/RES/897 of 4 Feb. 1994.
144. S/RES/954 of 4 Nov. 1994.
145. S/RES/794 of 3 Dec. 1992.
146. S/RES/1725 of 6 Dec. 2006.
147. S/RES/1744 of 20 Feb. 2007. *See also* S/RES/1772 of 20 Aug. 2007, S/RES/1801 of 20 Feb. 2008, S/RES/1831 of 19 Aug. 2008, S/RES/1863 of 16 Jan. 2009, S/RES/1872 of 26 May 2009, S/RES/1910 of 28 Jan. 2010, S/RES/1964 of 22 Dec. 2010, S/RES/2010 of 30 Sep. 2011, S/RES/2072 of 31 Oct. 2012, S/RES/2073 of 7 Nov. 2012, S/RES/2093 of 6 Mar. 2013, S/RES/2102 of 2 May 2013, S/RES/2124 of 12 Nov. 2013, S/RES/2158 of 29 May 2014, S/RES/2182 of 24 Oct. 2014, S/RES/2232 of 28 Jul. 2015, S/RES/2297 of 7 Jul. 2016, S/RES/2355 of 26 May 2017, S/RES/2372 of 30 Aug. 2017, S/RES/2408 of 27 Mar. 2018, S/RES/2415 of 15 May 2018, S/RES/2431 of 30 Jul. 2018, S/RES/2472 of 31 May 2019, S/RES/2520 of 29 May 2020, S/RES/2563 of 25 Feb. 2021, S/RES/2568 of 12 Mar. 2021, S/RES/2614 of 21 Dec. 2021 and S/RES/2628 of 31 Mar. 2022.
148. S/RES/1816 of 2 Jun. 2008, S/RES/1838 of 7 Oct. 2008, S/RES/1846 of 2 Dec. 2008, S/RES/1851 of 16 Dec. 2008, S/RES/1897 of 30 Nov. 2009, S/RES/1918 of 27 Apr. 2010, S/RES/1918 of 27 Apr. 2010, S/RES/1976 of 11 Apr. 2011, S/RES/2015 of 24 Oct. 2011, S/RES/2077 of 21 Nov. 2012, S/RES/2125 of 18 Nov. 2013, S/RES/2246 of 10 Nov. 2015, S/RES/2316 of 9 Nov. 2016, S/RES/2383 of 7 Nov. 2017, S/RES/2442 of 6 Nov. 2018 and S/RES/2608 of 3 Dec. 2021.
149. Council Common Position 2007/140/CFSP of 27 Feb. 2007 concerning restrictive measures against Iran, OJ L 61, 28 Feb. 2007, p. 49 that was put in force via Council Regulation (EC) No. 423/2007 of 19 Apr. 2007 concerning restrictive measures against Iran, OJ L 103, 20 Apr. 2007, p. 1. These were amended by Council Common Position 2007/246/CFSP of 23 Apr. 2007 amending Common Position 2007/140/CFSP concerning restrictive measures against Iran, OJ L 106, 24 Apr. 2007, p. 67, that was put into force via Council Regulation (EC) No. 618/2007 of 5 Jun. 2007 amending Regulation (EC) No. 423/2007 concerning restrictive measures against Iran, OJ L 143, 6 Jun. 2007, p. 1. In turn these were amended by Council Common Position 2008/652/CFSP of 7 Aug. 2008 amending Common Position 2007/140/CFSP concerning restrictive measures against Iran, OJ L 213, 8 Aug. 2008, p. 58, which was put into force by Council Regulation (EC) No. 1110/2008 of 10 Nov. 2008 amending Regulation (EC) No. 423/2007 concerning restrictive measures against Iran, OJ L 300, 11 Nov. 2008, p. 1. Finally, said acts were amended by 2010/413/CFSP: Council Decision of 26 Jul. 2010 concerning restrictive measures against Iran and repealing Common Position 2007/140/CFSP, OJ L 195, 27 Jul. 2010, p. 39, as last amended by Council Decision (CFSP) 2023/2195 of 16 Oct. 2023 amending Decision 2010/413/CFSP concerning restrictive measures against Iran, digital OJ L, 17 Oct. 2023, which was put into force via Council Regulation (EU) No. 961/2010 of 25 Oct. 2010 on restrictive measures against Iran and repealing Regulation (EC) No. 423/2007, OJ L 281, 27 Oct. 2010, p. 1, later repealed by Council Regulation (EU) No. 267/2012 of 23 Mar. 2012 concerning restrictive measures against Iran and repealing Regulation (EU) No. 961/2010, OJ L 88, 24 Mar. 2012, p. 1, last amended by Council Implementing Regulation (CFSP) 2023/2196 of 16 Oct. 2023 implementing Regulation (EU) No. 267/2012 concerning restrictive measures against Iran, digital OJ L, 17 Oct. 2023.

reprocessing activities.[150] The EU reaffirms said suspension and emphasizes the importance of guaranteeing that Iran's nuclear program is exclusively for peaceful purposes.[151] The measures equally cover concerns over the non-establishment of full and sustained suspension of enrichment and reprocessing activities[152] and concerns over the construction of an enrichment facility at Qom.[153] At the same time, the EU due to serious and deepening concerns over the nature of Iran's nuclear program decided to take additional measures against Iran described in a common position[154] and enacted via a regulation.[155] With regard to the progressive adoption of EU measures, the CJEU noted that it reflected the need to broaden the range of the restrictive measures intended to achieve the objective of the Iranian nuclear program serving exclusively peaceful purposes and constraining Iran's development of sensitive technologies in support of its nuclear and missile programs.[156] In other words, the – legitimate – objective of these legislative acts is to prevent nuclear proliferation and to bring pressure to bear on the Islamic Republic of Iran to end the activities concerned, the CJEU ruled. It also confirmed that their objective is linked to the maintenance of international peace and security.[157] The restrictive measures that are set by these acts are preventive in nature, as they seek to prevent a risk of proliferation-sensitive nuclear activities in Iran.[158] In the meantime, the UN Security Council has endorsed the Joint Comprehensive Plan of Action[159] ('JCPOA') that was agreed by China, France, Germany, Russia, the United Kingdom, the United States, the EU and Iran in order to reach a comprehensive, long-term and proper solution to the Iranian nuclear issue.[160] In order to implement the JCPOA, the EU proceeded with adopting a decision[161] and amending the framework of restrictive measures by, mainly, suspending the measures concerning Iranian crude oil.[162] On a final note, the EU has taken additional measures against Iran due to deep concerns about the deterioration of the human rights situation in said country. These are portrayed in the ensuing subchapter (*see* in this regard paragraphs 42 et seq. below).

150. S/RES/1737 of 23 Dec. 2006.
151. S/RES/1747 of 24 Mar. 2007.
152. S/RES/1803 of 3 Mar. 2008.
153. S/RES/1929 of 9 Jun. 2010.
154. Council Decision 2012/35/CFSP of 23 Jan. 2012 amending Decision 2010/413/CFSP concerning restrictive measures against Iran, OJ L 19, 24 Jan. 2012, p. 22.
155. Council Regulation (EU) No. 267/2012 of 23 Mar. 2012 concerning restrictive measures against Iran and repealing Regulation (EU) No. 961/2010, OJ L 88, 24 Mar. 2012, p. 1, as last amended by Council Implemending Regulation (CFSP) 2024/2074 of 26 Jul. 2024 amending Decision 2010/413/CFSP implementing Regulation (EU) No. 267/2012 concerning restrictive measures against Iran, digital OJ L, 30 Jul. 2024.
156. *Iran Shipping* 2019 (n. 46) paras 105 & 108.
157. *Ibid.*, para. 104, citing *National Iranian Tanker Company v. Council*, C-600/16 P, Judgment of 29 Nov. 2018, para. 77 ('National Iranian Tanker'). *See* also *Kala Naft* (n. 33) para. 124.
158. *Afrasiabi* (n. 46) para. 44.
159. Joint Comprehensive Plan of Action (Vienna 2015), available at: https://www.europarl.europa.eu/cmsdata/122460/full-text-of-the-iran-nuclear-deal.pdf (last visited 31 Dec. 2023).
160. S/RES/2231 of 20 Jul. 2015.
161. Council Decision 2014/21/CFSP of 20 Jan. 2014 amending Council Decision 2010/413/CFSP concerning restrictive measures against Iran, OJ L 15, 20 Jan. 2014, p. 22.
162. *National Iranian Tanker* (n. 157) paras 16 & 17.

35. The situation in Guinea-Bissau has prompted the implementation of restrictive measures portrayed in a decision[163] ('Decision on Guinea-Bissau') and a regulation[164] ('Regulation on Guinea-Bissau'). The EU adopted these instruments in order to give effect to a 2012 resolution of the UN Security Council,[165] which strongly condemned the military coup of 12 April 2012 and the undermining of the conclusion of the democratic electoral process. It further underlined the need to restore constitutional order and to address its political, security and development challenges, while expressing concern about cases of looting, human rights violations and abuses, ill-treatment during detention and repression of peaceful demonstrations.[166] In the same resolution, the UN Security Council demanded the restoration and respect of constitutional order, the reform of the security sector, the politics and economy, combatting drug trafficking and fighting impunity.[167] The EU explains as grounds for adopting restrictive measures the *mutiny* of 1 April 2010 and the coup d'état of 12 April 2012[168] without any further elaboration. Taking a look into the political history of Guinea-Bissau, recurring violence and structural fragility are not infrequently present.[169] Guinea-Bissau has witnessed both successful coups d'état and failed coup attempts whereas the intervention of the military in politics is not unusual.[170] On 1 April 2010, a *strange* and *half-failed* coup took place, in the sense that the coup leaders successfully deposed and detained the General Chief of Staff, but failed to remove the Prime Minister, who enjoyed – literally – massive protection from the people.[171] In this regard, the UN Security Council expressed concern over the prevailing security situation and threats to the constitutional order and called the government to release all those detained in the events of 1 April 2010 or prosecute them with full respect for due process.[172] Here the UN preferred to use the term *events* and not *mutiny*, as the EU did, whereas in a

163. Council Decision 2012/285/CFSP of 31 May 2012 concerning restrictive measures directed against certain persons, entities and bodies threatening the peace, security or stability of the Republic of Guinea-Bissau and repealing Decision 2012/237/CFSP, OJ L 142, 1 Jun. 2012, p. 36, as last amended by Council Decision (CFSP) 2023/1598 of 3 Aug. 2023 amending Decision 2012/285/CFSP concerning restrictive measures in view of the situation in Guinea-Bissau, OJ L 196, 4 Aug. 2023, p. 23.
164. Council Regulation (EU) No. 377/2012 of 3 May 2012 concerning restrictive measures directed against certain persons, entities and bodies threatening the peace, security or stability of the Republic of Guinea-Bissau, OJ L 119, 4 May 2012, p. 1, as last amended by Council Regulation (EU) 2023/1593 of 3 Aug. 2023 amending Regulation (EU) No. 377/2012 concerning restrictive measures in view of the situation in Guinea-Bissau, OJ L 196, 4 Aug. 2023, p. 1.
165. S/RES/2048 of 18 May 2012.
166. *Ibid.*
167. *Ibid.*
168. Recital No. 1 to the preamble of the Regulation on Guinea-Bissau.
169. Brigit Embaló, *Civil-Military Relations and Political Order in Guinea-Bissau* 50(2) J. Mod. Afr. Stud. 253 at 253 (2012) https://doi.org/10.1017/s0022278x12000079. Especially on political violence that took place in 2009 *see* Security Council, Security Council Press Statement on Guinea-Bissau, SC/9677-AFR/1859 of 9 Jun. 2009, available: https://www.un.org/press/en/2009/sc9677.doc.htm (last visited: 31 Dec 2023).
170. *Ibid.*, p. 254. *See also* Issaka K. Souaré, *The African Union as a Norm Entrepreneur on Military Coups D'état in Africa (1952-2012): An Empirical Assessment* 52(1) J. Mod. Afr. Stud. 69-94 (2014) https://doi.org/10.1017/s0022278x13000785.
171. *Brigit Embaló* (n. 169), pp. 254, 274 & 275.
172. UN Security Council, *Statement by the President of the Security Council*, 22 Jul. 2010, S/PRST/2010/15.

different document, the UN characterized the same event as an *anti-constitutional incident*.[173] Two years later, on 12 April 2012, the armed forces of Guinea-Bissau ceased power. The next day, the coup leaders announced the detention of the Interim President, the Prime Minister and the Armed Forces Chief of Staff; they alleged that they had been forced to act due to an alleged secret agreement with Angola for the deployment of Angolan forces, in order to defend themselves against the Government's attempts to annihilate the armed forces.[174] Independently from and prior to these events, the UN had established the UN Integrated Peacebuilding Office in Guinea-Bissau ('UNIOGBIS') in view of political violence, the need to have free, fair and transparent elections for a full return to the constitutional order and the importance of all actors remaining committed to the security sector reform, the promotion of the rule of law and the fight against impunity and illicit drug trafficking.[175]

36. Restrictive measures have been further implemented in view of the situation in Libya via a common position[176] ('Decision on Libya') and a regulation[177] ('Regulation on Libya'). This is a new regulation consolidating, for the sake of clarity,[178] the EU legal instruments implementing resolutions of the UN Security Council that had been set out in earlier instruments.[179] The UN Security Council decided to introduce restrictive measures in view of the widespread and systematic attacks taking place against the civilian population that could amount to crimes against humanity and the plight of refugees forced to flee the violence.[180] It adopted further measures when violence increased and ongoing fighting by armed groups was taking place and in view of the threat posed by unsecured arms and ammunition and their proliferation, including through transfer to terrorist and violent extremist groups.[181] Shortly thereafter, concerned at the growing trend of terrorist groups in Libya proclaiming allegiance to the Islamic State and the Levant (ISIL/Da'esh), the continued presence of Al-Qaeda-linked

173. UNIOGBIS, UNIOGBIS about 1 April 2010 events, 2 Apr. 2010, available: https://uniogbis.unmissions.org/en/uniogbis-about-1-april-2010-events (last visited: 31 Dec. 2023).
174. UN Security Council, *Special Report of the Secretary-General on the Situation in Guinea-Bissau*, 30 Apr. 2012, S/2012/280.
175. S/RES/1876 of 26 Jun. 2009. *See also* S/RES/1949 of 23 Nov. 2010, S/RES/2030 of 21 Dec. 2011, S/RES/2092 of 22 Feb. 2013, S/RES/2103 of 22 May 2013, S/RES/2157 of 29 May 2014, S/RES/2186 of 25 Nov. 2014, S/RES/2203 of 18 Feb. 2015, S/RES/2267 of 26 Feb. 2016, S/RES/2343 of 23 Feb. 2017, S/RES/2404 of 28 Feb. 2018, S/RES/2458 of 28 Feb. 2018 and S/RES/2512 of 28 Feb. 2020.
176. Council Decision (CFSP) 2015/1333 of 31 Jul. 2015 concerning restrictive measures in view of the situation in Libya, and repealing Decision 2011/137/CFSP, OJ L 206, 1 Aug. 2015, p. 34, as last amended by Council Decision (CFSP) 2023/1439 of 10 Jul. 2023 amending Decision (CFSP) 2015/1333 concerning restrictive measures in view of the situation in Libya, OJ L 176, 11 Jul. 2023, p. 26.
177. Council Regulation (EU) 2016/44 of 18 Jan. 2016 concerning restrictive measures in view of the situation in Libya and repealing Regulation (EU) No. 204/2011, OJ L 12, 19 Jan. 2016, p. 1, as last amended by Council Regulation (EU) 2023/1433 of 10 Jul. 2023 amending Regulation (EU) 2016/44 concerning restrictive measures in view of the situation in Libya, OJ L 176, 11 Jul. 2023, p. 1.
178. Recital No. 3 to the preamble of Regulation on Libya.
179. *See* in this regard Council Regulation (EU) No. 204/2011 of 2 Mar. 2011 concerning restrictive measures in view of the situation in Libya, OJ L 58, 3 Mar. 2011, p. 1, as amended.
180. S/RES/1970 of 26 Feb. 2011.
181. S/RES/2174 of 27 Aug. 2014.

terrorist groups and individuals operating there and the threat posed by unsecured arms and ammunition in this state and their proliferation, the UN Security Council imposed further restrictive measures.[182] Moreover, the UN Security Council adopted resolutions for the protection of civilians imposing an arms embargo and a no-fly zone,[183] deployed[184] and maintained the United Nations Support Mission in Libya[185] ('UNSMIL') that among others was entrusted with assisting and supporting the national efforts to restore public security, promote the rule of law and initiating economic recovery. It further took action against illicitly exported crude oil,[186] expressed grave concern over the threat posed by terrorist groups in Libya proclaiming allegiance to ISIL/Da'esh,[187] authorized the interdiction of vessels used for migrant smuggling or human trafficking,[188] welcomed the Libyan Political Agreement,[189] called for the destruction of stockpiles of chemical weapons and the prevention of proliferation of arms and related material[190] and endorsed the conclusions of the Berlin Conference on Libya.[191]

37. Restrictive measures have been further enacted in view of the situation in the 'CAR' that were discussed in a council decision[192] ('Decision on CAR') and specified in a regulation[193] ('Regulation on the CAR'). These measures were decided by the UN Security Council that was concerned over the continuing deterioration of the security situation in the CAR and the absence of the rule of law, the multiple and increasing violations of international humanitarian law and widespread human rights violations and abuses and condemned the devastation of natural heritage and trafficking of

182. S/RES/2213 of 27 Mar. 2015.
183. S/RES/1973 of 17 Mar. 2011.
184. S/RES/2009 of 16 Sep. 2011.
185. S/RES/2022 of 2 Dec. 2011, S/RES/2040 of 12 Mar. 2012, S/RES/2095 of 14 Mar. 2013, S/RES/2144 of 14 Mar. 2014, S/RES/2208 of 5 Mar. 2015, S/RES/2213 of 27 Mar. 2015, S/RES/2238 of 10 Sep. 2015, S/RES/2273 of 15 Mar. 2016, S/RES/2291 of 13 Jun. 2016, S/RES/2323 of 13 Dec. 2016, S/RES/2376 of 14 Sep. 2017, S/RES/2437 of 3 Oct. 2018, S/RES/2486 of 12 Sep. 2019, S/RES/2542 of 15 Sep. 2020, S/RES/2595 of 15 Sep. 2021, S/RES/2599 of 30 Sep. 2021, S/RES/2619 of 31 Jan. 2022, S/RES/2629 of 29 Apr. 2022.
186. S/RES/2146 of 19 Mar. 2014, S/RES/2208 of 5 Mar. 2015, S/RES/2362 of 29 Jun. 2017 and S/RES/2441 of 5 Nov. 2018 and S/RES/2509 of 11 Feb. 2020.
187. S/RES/2214 of 27 Mar. 2015.
188. S/RES/2240 of 9 Oct. 2015, S/RES/2312 of 6 Oct. 2016, S/RES/2420 of 11 Jun. 2018, S/RES/2437 of 3 Oct. 2018, S/RES/2491 of 3 Oct. 2019, S/RES/2546 of 2 Oct. 2020 and S/RES/2598 of 29 Sep. 2021.
189. S/RES/2259 of 23 Dec. 2015.
190. S/RES/2017 of 31 Oct. 2011, S/RES/2022 of 2 Dec. 2011, S/RES/2298 of 22 Jul. 2016.
191. S/RES/2510 of 12 Feb. 2020. *See also* Security Council, *Letter Dated 22 January from the Permanent Representative of Germany to the United Nations addressed to the President of the Security Council*, S/2020/63 of 22 Jan. 2020.
192. Council Decision 2013/798/CFSP of 23 Dec. 2013 concerning restrictive measures against the Central African Republic, OJ L 352, 24 Dec. 2013, p. 51, as last amended by Council Decision (CFSP) 2023/2487 of 9 Nov. 2023 amending Decision 2013/798/CFSP concerning restrictive measures in view of the situation in the Central African Republic, digital OJ L, 10 Nov. 2023.
193. Council Regulation (EU) No. 224/2014 of 10 Mar. 2014 concerning restrictive measures in view of the situation in the Central African Republic, OJ L 70, 11 Mar. 2014, p. 1, as last amended by Council Regulation (EU) 2023/2506 of 9 Nov. 2023 amending Regulation (EU) No. 224/2014 concerning restrictive measures in view of the situation in the Central African Republic, digital OJ L, 10 Nov. 2023.

wildlife.[194] Further measures were agreed as the UN Security Council was alarmed by the increasing cycle of violence and retaliation and degeneration into a countrywide religious and ethnic divide and expressed grave concern at the threat to peace and security in the CAR arising from the illicit transfer, destabilizing accumulation and misuse of small arms and light weapons.[195] The UN Security Council had adopted other resolutions both before and after the aforementioned ones. These welcomed the Bangui Agreements, a peace agreement between the rebels and then-CAR President Ange-Félix Patassé mediated by the Presidents of Gabon, Burkina Faso, Chad and Mali,[196] and the creation of the Inter-African Mission to Monitor the Implementation of the Bangui Agreements[197] ('MISAB'), established[198] and maintained the United Nations Mission in the Central African Republic[199] ('MINURCA'), established[200] and maintained[201] the United Nations Mission in the Central African Republic and Chad ('MINURCAT') that was subsequently subsumed by the United Nations Multidimensional Integrated Stabilization Mission in the Central African Republic[202] ('MINUSCA'). Finally, certain other resolutions were related to the imposed sanctions.[203]

38. The situation in Yemen has propelled the EU to impose restrictive measures that were set out in a council decision[204] ('Decision on Yemen') and a regulation[205] ('Regulation on Yemen'). These had been previously decided in a resolution of the UN Security Council that condemned all terrorist activities and attacks against civilians, infrastructure, legitimate authorities, military and security facilities, supported a peaceful, inclusive, orderly and Yemeni-led political transition process, and welcomed

194. S/RES/2127 of 5 Dec. 2013.
195. S/RES/2134 of 28 Jan. 2014.
196. *See* in this regard S/1997/561 of 22 Jul. 1997.
197. S/RES/1125 of 6 Aug. 1997. *See also* S/RES/1136 of 6 Nov. 1997 and S/RES/1155 of 16 Mar. 1998.
198. S/RES/1159 of 27 Mar. 1998. *See also* S/RES/1182 of 14 Jul. 1998.
199. S/RES/1201 of 15 Oct. 1998, S/RES/1230 of 26 Feb. 1999, S/RES/1271 of 22 Oct. 1999.
200. S/RES/1778 of 25 Sep. 2007, S/RES/1861 of 14 Jan. 2009, S/RES/1922 of 12 May 2010, S/RES/1923 of 25 May 2010, S/RES/2088 of 24 Jan. 2013, S/RES/2121 of 10 Oct. 2013, S/RES/2127 of 5 Dec. 2013, S/RES/2134 of 28 Jan. 2014.
201. S/RES/1834 of 24 Sep. 2008.
202. S/RES/2149 of 10 Apr. 2014. In regard to MINUSCA *see also* S/RES/2212 of 26 Mar. 2015, S/RES/2217 of 28 Apr. 2015, S/RES/2264 of 9 Feb. 2016, S/RES/2281 of 26 Apr. 2016, S/RES/2301 of 26 Jul. 2016, S/RES/2387 of 15 Nov. 2017, S/RES/2466 of 15 Nov. 2018, S/RES/2448 of 13 Dec. 2018, S/RES/2499 of 15 Nov. 2019, S/RES/2552 of 12 Nov. 2020, S/RES/2566 of 12 Mar. 2021 and S/RES/2605 of 12 Nov. 2021.
203. S/RES/2196 of 22 Jan. 2015, S/RES/2262 of 27 Jan. 2016, S/RES/2339 of 27 Jan. 2017, S/RES/2399 of 30 Jan. 2018, S/RES/2454 of 31 Jan. 2019, S/RES/2488 of 12 Sep. 2019, S/RES/2507 of 31 Jan. 2020, S/RES/2536 of 28 Jul. 2020 and S/RES/2588 of 29 Jul. 2021.
204. Council Decision 2014/932/CFSP of 18 Dec. 2014 concerning restrictive measures in view of the situation in Yemen, OJ L 365, 19 Dec. 2014, p. 147, as last amended by Council Decision (CFSP) 2023/338 of 14 Feb. 2023 amending certain Council decisions and common positions concerning restrictive measures in order to insert provisions on a humanitarian exemption, OJ L 47, 15 Feb. 2023, p. 50.
205. Council Regulation (EU) No. 1352/2014 of 18 Dec. 2014 concerning restrictive measures in view of the situation in Yemen, OJ L 365, 19 Dec. 2014, p. 60, as last amended by Council Regulation (EU) 2023/331 of 14 Feb. 2023 amending certain Council regulations concerning restrictive measures in order to insert provisions on a humanitarian exemption, OJ L 47, 15 Feb. 2023, p. 1.

Yemen's efforts to strengthen women's participation process in political and public life.[206] Other resolutions of the UN Security Council deplored actions taken by the Houthis to dissolve parliament, take over Yemen's government institutions and hold Yemeni government officials under house arrest,[207] demanded Houthis' withdrawal from all seized areas,[208] endorsed the Stockholm Agreement[209] that was reached between the Houthis and the Government of Yemen in 2018,[210] endorsed the agreement reached by the Government of Yemen and the Houthis on the city of Hodeidah and the ports of Hodeidah, Salif and Ras Issa ('the Hodeidah Agreement') and established the United Nations Mission to support the Hodeidah Agreement[211] ('UNMHA'). Other resolutions related to the Yemen sanctions regime[212] and a more recent one declared the Houthis a terrorist group.[213]

39. Restrictive measures have been taken in respect of the situation in South Sudan that were portrayed in a council decision[214] ('Decision on South Sudan') and foreseen in a regulation[215] ('Regulation on South Sudan'). These legal instruments implement a resolution of the UN Security Council that was adopted due to alarm and concern regarding the conflict between the Government of South Sudan and opposition forces and the resulting great human suffering, including loss of life, displacement of people and loss of property.[216] Other decisions of the UN Security Council created[217] and maintained the United Nations Mission in South Sudan[218] ('UNMISS'), that was entrusted with supporting peace consolidation, providing good offices, advice and support to the Government of South Sudan, promoting popular participation in

206. S/RES/2140 of 26 Feb. 2014.
207. S/RES/2201 of 15 Feb. 2015.
208. S/RES/2216 of 14 Apr. 2015.
209. In this regard *see* S/2018/1134.
210. S/RES/2451 of 21 Dec. 2018.
211. S/RES/2452 of 16 Jan. 2019. *See also* S/RES/2481 of 15 Jul. 2019, S/RES/2505 of 13 Jan. 2020, S/RES/2534 of 14 Jul. 2020 and S/RES/2586 of 14 Jul. 2021.
212. S/RES/2204 of 24 Feb. 2015, S/RES/2216 of 14 Apr. 2015, S/RES/2266 of 24 Feb. 2016, S/RES/2342 of 23 Feb. 2017, S/RES/2402 of 26 Feb. 2018, S/RES/2456 of 26 Feb. 2019, S/RES/2511 of 25 Feb. 2020, S/RES/2564 of 25 Feb. 2021 and S/RES/2624 of 28 Feb. 2022.
213. S/RES/2624 of 28 Feb. 2022.
214. Council Decision (CFSP) 2015/740 of 7 May 2015 concerning restrictive measures in view of the situation in South Sudan and repealing Decision 2014/449/CFSP, OJ L 117, 8 May 2015, p. 52, as last amended by Council Decision (CFSP) 2023/726 of 31 Mar. 2023 amending certain Council Decisions concerning restrictive measures in order to insert provisions on a humanitarian exemption, OJ L 94, 3 Apr. 2023, p. 48.
215. Council Regulation (EU) 2015/735 of 7 May 2015 concerning restrictive measures in respect of the situation in South Sudan, and repealing Regulation (EU) No. 748/2014, OJ L 117, 8 May 2015, p. 13, as last amended by Council Regulation (EU) 2023/720 of 31 Mar. 2023 amending certain Council Regulations concerning restrictive measures in order to insert provisions on a humanitarian exemption, OJ L 94, 3 Apr. 2023, p. 1.
216. S/RES/2206 of 3 Mar. 2015.
217. S/RES/1996 of 8 Jul. 2011. *See also* S/RES/2241 of 9 Oct. 2015, S/RES/2252 of 15 Dec. 2015.
218. S/RES/2057 of 5 Jul. 2012, S/RES/2109 of 11 Jul. 2013, S/RES/2132 of 24 Dec. 2013, S/RES/2187 of 25 Nov. 2014, S/RES/2223 of 28 May 2015, S/RES/2280 of 7 Apr. 2016, S/RES/2302 of 29 Jul. 2016, S/RES/2304 of 12 Aug. 2016, S/RES/2326 of 15 Dec. 2016, S/RES/2327 of 16 Dec. 2016, S/RES/2392 of 14 Dec. 2017, S/RES/2406 of 15 Mar. 2018, S/RES/2459 of 15 Mar. 2019, S/RES/2514 of 12 Mar. 2020, S/RES/2567 of 12 Mar. 2021 and S/RES/2625 of 15 Mar. 2022.

political processes, and supporting the Government of South Sudan in conflict prevention, mitigation and protection of civilians. Other resolutions related to the sanctions regime.[219]

40. Restrictive measures have been also set in view of the situation in Mali; they are described in a council decision[220] ('Decision on Mali') and prescribed in a regulation[221] ('Regulation on Mali'), that had been initially contemplated by the UN Security Council. In view of its assessment that the situation in Mali continued to constitute a threat to international peace and security, the UN Security Council introduced a travel ban and asset freeze, while setting the designation criteria.[222] Furthermore, it responded positively to a request from Mali regarding an intervention force to assist the national forces to reclaim the northern half of the country,[223] authorized the deployment of an African-led International Support Mission in Mali ('AFISMA') in order to support national authorities and to contribute to the rebuilding of the capacity of the national defence and security forces,[224] established[225] and maintained the United Nations Multidimensional Integrated Stabilization Mission in Mali[226] ('MINUSMA') that had the mandate of stabilizing key population centres and support for the reestablishment of state authority throughout the country, support for the implementation of the transitional road map and protection of civilians, human rights and humanitarian assistance. Certain resolutions were related to the sanctions regime.[227]

41. Most recently, the situation in Haiti that has been assessed as a threat to international peace and security, prompted the UN Security Council to decide on a travel ban, assets freeze and targeted arms embargo,[228] restrictive measures that were later transposed into EU law[229] ('Decision on Haiti' and 'Regulation on Haiti'). The

219. S/RES/2290 of 31 May 2016, S/RES/2353 of 24 May 2017, S/RES/2428 of 13 Jul. 2018, S/RES/2471 of 30 May 2019, S/RES/2521 of 29 May 2020, S/RES/2577 of 28 May 2021 and S/RES/2633 of 26 May 2022.
220. Council Decision (CFSP) 2017/1775 of 28 Sep. 2017 concerning restrictive measures in view of the situation in Mali, OJ L 251, 29 Sep. 2017, p. 23, as last amended by Council Decision (CFSP) 2023/2799 of 11 Dec. 2023 amending Decision (CFSP) 2017/1775 concerning restrictive measures in view of the situation in Mali, digital OJ L, 12 Dec. 2023.
221. Council Regulation (EU) 2017/1770 of 28 Sep. 2017 concerning restrictive measures in view of the situation in Mali, OJ L 251, 29 Sep. 2017, p. 1, as last amended by Council Regulation (EU) 2023/720 of 31 Mar. 2023 amending certain Council Regulations concerning restrictive measures in order to insert provisions on a humanitarian exemption, OJ L 94, 3 Apr. 2023, p. 1.
222. S/RES/2374 of 5 Sep. 2017.
223. S/RES/2071 of 12 Oct. 2012.
224. S/RES/2085 of 20 Dec. 2012.
225. S/RES/2100 of 25 Apr. 2013. *See also* S/RES/2164 of 25 Jun. 2014.
226. S/RES/2227 of 29 Jun. 2015, S/RES/2295 of 29 Jun. 2016, S/RES/2364 of 29 Jun. 2017, S/RES/2391 of 8 Dec. 2017, S/RES/2423 of 28 Jun. 2018, S/RES/2480 of 28 Jun. 2019, S/RES/2531 of 29 Jun. 2020 and S/RES/2584 of 29 Jun. 2021.
227. S/RES/2432 of 30 Aug. 2018, S/RES/2484 of 29 Aug. 2019, S/RES/2541 of 31 Aug. 2020 and S/RES/2590 of 30 Aug. 2021.
228. S/RES/2653 of 21 Oct. 2022, paras 3 to 5 & 15 to 18, 6 to 10 and 11 to 14 respectively.
229. Council Decision (CFSP) 2022/2319 of 25 Nov. 2022 concerning restrictive measures in view of the situation in Haiti, OJ L 307, 28 Nov. 2022, p. 135, as last amended by Council Decision (CFSP) 2023/2575 of 13 Nov. 2023 amending Decision (CFSP) 2022/2319 concerning restrictive measures in view of the situation in Haiti, digital OJ L, 14 Nov. 2023.

international community is concerned about the – still unsolved – assassination of the president of Haiti, Jovenel Moïse, in July 2021.[230] Since that same year, the UN Security Council has been expressing the urgent need to organize inclusive, peaceful, free, fair, and transparent legislative and presidential elections with the full, equal and meaningful participation of women.[231] It has also noted the extremely high levels of gang violence and other criminal activities[232] whereby gangs, and not the Haitian National Police, control vital ports and fuel terminals.[233] The UN Security Council further expressed concern over the illicit trafficking and diversion of arms and related materials of all types[234] as well as over illicit financial flows that enable armed gangs to operate.[235] In view of these, the UN Security Council reiterated its deep concern over the protracted and deteriorating political, institutional, economic, security, human rights, humanitarian and food security crises unfolding in Haiti.[236]

§2 HUMAN RIGHTS

42. Violation of human rights has propelled the EU into action in the sense of setting out restrictive measures, in view of the situation in Zimbabwe, Iran and Myanmar/ Burma.

43. Starting with Zimbabwe, restrictive measures are envisioned in a council decision[237] ('Decision on Zimbabwe') and set out in a regulation[238] ('Regulation on

Council Regulation (EU) 2022/2309 of 25 Nov. 2022 concerning restrictive measures in view of the situation in Haiti, OJ L 307, 28 Nov. 2022, p. 17, as last amended by Council Regulation (EU) 2023/1569 of 28 Jul. 2023 amending Council Regulation (EU) 2024/1803 of 24 Jun. 2024 amending Regulation (EU) 2022/2309 concerning restrictive measures in view of the situation in Haiti, digital OJ L, 25 Jun. 2024.

230. *See* Yamiche Alcindor & Ali Rogin, *Who Assassinated the Haitian President, and Why? Here's What We Know So Far*, PBS 7 Jul. 2021, available: https://www.pbs.org/newshour/show/who-assassinated-the-haitian-president-and-why-heres-what-we-know-so-far (last visited: 31 Dec. 2023); UN, *UN Condemns 'Abhorrent' Assassination of Haiti President Jovenel Moïse*, UN News 7 Jul. 2021, available: https://news.un.org/en/story/2021/07/1095422 (last visited: 31 Dec. 2023). *See also* Editors, *'Cup of blood': Haiti Official Decries Impunity in Moise killing*, Aljazeera 6 Jul. 2023, available: https://www.aljazeera.com/news/2023/7/6/cup-of-blood-haiti-official-decries-impunity-in-moise-killing (last visited: 31 Dec. 2023).
231. Paragraph 5 S/RES/2600 of 15 Oct. 2021; para. 3 R/RES/2645 of 15 Jul. 2022; preamble to R/RES/2653 of 21 Oct. 2022.
232. Preamble to S/RES/2600 of 15 Oct. 2021; preamble to R/RES/2645 of 15 Jul. 2022; preamble to R/RES/2653 of 21 Oct. 2022.
233. Preamble to R/RES/2653 of 21 Oct. 2022.
234. Preamble to R/RES/2645 of 15 Jul. 2022; preamble to R/RES/2653 of 21 Oct. 2022.
235. *Ibid.*
236. Preamble to S/RES/2600 of 15 Oct. 2021; para. 3 R/RES/2645 of 15 Jul. 2022; preamble to R/RES/2653 of 21 Oct. 2022.
237. Council Decision 2011/101/CFSP of 15 Feb. 2011 concerning restrictive measures against Zimbabwe, OJ L 42, 16 Feb. 2011, p. 6, as last amended by Council Decision (CFSP) 2023/2686 of 27 Nov. 2023 amending certain Council Decisions concerning restrictive measures in order to insert provisions on humanitarian exceptions, digital OJ, 28 Nov. 2023.
238. Council Regulation (EC) No. 314/2004 of 19 Feb. 2004 concerning certain restrictive measures in respect of Zimbabwe, OJ L 55, 24 Feb. 2004, p. 1, as last amended by Council Regulation

Zimbabwe') for the purpose of avoiding any distortion of competition.[239] The Council expressed serious concern about serious violations of human rights by the Government of Zimbabwe, including violations of the freedoms of opinion, of association and of peaceful assembly.[240] In 2008, the UN Security Council had prepared a draft resolution expressing concern over the irregularities of the presidential election, the violence and intimidation and the humanitarian situation that called for ceasing the attacks and introducing an arms embargo, transit restrictions and funds freezing.[241] Still, this remained a mere draft as it failed to find unanimous support. At that same time, the EU introduced such measures[242] noting that the violence organized and committed by the authorities of Zimbabwe had turned the presidential election into a denial of democracy.[243]

44. In parallel to the aforementioned restrictive measures in view of the situation in Iran, which were initially decided by the UN Security Council (*see* in this respect paragraph 34 above), more restrictive measures have been discussed in a council decision[244] ('EU Decision on Iran') and a regulation[245] ('EU Regulation on Iran'). The Council decided those, as it was concerned over the deterioration of the human rights situation in Iran and in particular over the dramatic increase in executions in recent months and the systematic repression of citizens who face arrests for exercising their legitimate rights to freedom of expression and peaceful assembly. It also condemned the use of torture and other cruel, inhuman and degrading treatment.[246] In this regard, it is here noted that in 2010 the Secretary-General of the UN submitted to the General Assembly of the UN a report on the situation of human rights.[247] The issues that concerned the EU are identified in said report, which in conclusion encouraged the Government of Iran to address the highlighted concerns and to continue to revise the national legislation.[248] Further reports on this subject have been tabled before the

(EU) 2023/2694 of 27 Nov. 2023 amending certain Council Regulations concerning restrictive measures in order to insert provisions on humanitarian exceptions, digital OJ L, 28 Nov. 2023.

239. Recital No. 5 to the preamble of Regulation on Zimbabwe.
240. Recital No. 1 to the preamble of Regulation on Zimbabwe.
241. S/2008/447 of 11 Jul. 2008.
242. Council Common Position 2008/632/CFSP of 31 Jul. 2008 amending Common Position 2004/161/CFSP renewing restrictive measures against Zimbabwe, OJ L 205, 1 Aug. 2008, p. 53.
243. Recital No. 2 to the preamble of Common Position on Zimbabwe.
244. Council Decision 2011/235/CFSP of 12 Apr. 2011 concerning restrictive measures directed against certain persons and entities in view of the situation in Iran, OJ L 100, 14 Apr. 2011, p. 51, as last amended by Council Implementing Decision (CFSP) 2023/1780 of 15 Sep. 2023 implementing Decision 2011/235/CFSP concerning restrictive measures directed against certain persons and entities in view of the situation in Iran, OJ L 228I, 15 Sep. 2023, p. 6.
245. Council Regulation (EU) No. 359/2011 of 12 Apr. 2011 concerning restrictive measures directed against certain persons, entities and bodies in view of the situation in Iran, OJ L 100, 14 Apr. 2011, p. 1, as last amended by Council Implementing Regulation (EU) 2023/1298 of 26 Jun. 2023 implementing Regulation (EU) No. 359/2011 concerning restrictive measures directed against certain persons, entities and bodies in view of the situation in Iran, OJ L 160I, 26 Jun. 2023, p. 1.
246. Recital No. 2 to the preamble of Council Decision 2011/235/CFSP.
247. General Assembly, The Situation of human rights in the Islamic Republic of Iran, Report of the Secretary-General, A/65/370 of 15 Sep. 2010.
248. *Ibid.*, p. 18, para. 55.

General Assembly of the UN,[249] which issued a resolution outlining the human rights situation in Iran that included the death penalty, the detention and treatment of persons deprived of their liberty, the situation of women, restrictions on freedom of expression and peaceful assembly and treatment of religious and ethnic minorities, discussed Iran's cooperation with international human rights mechanisms and made recommendations.[250]

45. The restrictive measures in respect of Myanmar/Burma were described in a council decision[251] ('Decision on Myanmar/Burma') and enacted in a regulation[252] ('Regulation on Myanmar/Burma'). These currently in force instruments are the last ones in a series of common positions and regulations imposing measures due to the absence of progress towards democratization and continuing violation of human rights.[253] The Security Council of the UN was neither unaware nor satisfied with the situation in Myanmar/Burma; much to the contrary a resolution[254] expressing deep concern at the slow pace of the process towards national reconciliation was vetoed by China and Russia, whereas the President of the Security Council in a statement[255] strongly deplored the use of violence against peaceful demonstrations and emphasized the importance of early release of all political prisoners and remaining detainees.

§3 DEMOCRACY AND HUMAN RIGHTS

46. Violation of human rights has been further viewed in conjunction with the deterioration of and undermining of democracy as a ground for enacting restrictive measures. The EU has done so in respect of the situation in Burundi, Venezuela and Nicaragua. Similarly, due to the threat to democracy and the rule of law, the EU has adopted additional restrictive measures with regard to Lebanon.

249. *See* General Assembly, Situation of human rights in the Islamic Republic of Iran, Note by the Secretary-General, A/68/503 of 4 Oct. 2013; General Assembly, Situation of human rights in the Islamic Republic of Iran, Report by the Secretary-General, A/69/306 of 12 Aug. 2014; General Assembly, Situation of human rights in the Islamic Republic of Iran, Note by the Secretary-General, A/69/356 of 27 Aug. 2014; General Assembly, Situation of human rights in the Islamic Republic of Iran, Note by the Secretary-General, A/70/411 of 6 Oct. 2015.

250. General Assembly, Resolution adopted by the General Assembly on 18 Dec. 2013, A/RES/68/184 of 4 Feb. 2014.

251. Council Decision 2013/184/CFSP of 22 Apr. 2013 concerning restrictive measures against Myanmar/Burma and repealing Decision 2010/232/CFSP, OJ L 111, 23 Apr. 2013, p. 75, as last amended by Council Decision (CFSP) 2023/2788 of 11 Dec. 2023 amending Decision 2013/184/CFSP concerning restrictive measures in view of the situation in Myanmar/Burma, digital OJ L, 11 Dec. 2023.

252. Council Regulation (EU) No. 401/2013 of 2 May 2013 concerning restrictive measures in respect of Myanmar/Burma and repealing Regulation (EC) No. 194/2008, OJ L 121, 3 May 2013, p. 1, as last amended by Council Implementing Regulation (EU) 2023/2789 of 11 Dec. 2023 implementing Regulation (EU) No. 401/2013 concerning restrictive measures in view of the situation in Myanmar/Burma, digital OJ L, 11 Dec. 2023.

253. Recital No. 2 to the preamble of 96/635/CFSP: Common Position of 28 Oct. 1996 defined by the Council on the basis of Art. J.2 of the Treaty on European Union, on Burma/Myanmar, OJ L 287, 8 Nov. 1996, p. 1.

254. S/2007/14 of 12 Jan. 2007.

255. S/PRST/2007/37 of 11 Oct. 2007.

47. Restrictive measures in respect of Burundi have been discussed in a Council decision[256] ('Decision on Burundi') and enacted in a regulation[257] (the 'Regulation on Burundi'). The EU remarked that cornerstones for resolving the crisis in Burundi were the Arusha Agreement for Peace and Reconciliation of 2000 and the Burundian Constitution that would lead to a consensus and a lasting political solution.[258] It then condemned the attempted coup along with any act of violence and abuse of the constitutional order, particularly the abuses attributed to the security forces.[259] These events equally concerned the UN Security Council that reiterated its conviction that only a genuine and inclusive dialogue based on the Constitution and the Arusha Agreement for Peace and Reconciliation of 2000, would enable a consensual solution to the crisis that Burundi faces.[260]

48. Restrictive measures in respect of Venezuela have been similarly discussed in a Council decision[261] ('Decision on Venezuela') and were set out in a regulation[262] (the 'Regulation on Venezuela'). The EU was deeply concerned at the continuing deterioration of democracy, the rule of law and human rights in Venezuela[263] and called for a solution to the crisis while fully respecting the rule of law and human rights, democratic institutions and the separation of powers.[264] It expressed concern specifically at the human rights violations and excessive use of force that took place on 26 July 2017. It further expressed regret at the decision of the national authorities to continue with the election of a Constituent Assembly on 2 August 2017.[265] The UN Security Council convened a meeting on the situation in Venezuela[266] and was later briefed thereon.[267] The United States proposed a resolution expressing deep concern that the

256. Council Decision (CFSP) 2015/1763 of 1 Oct. 2015 concerning restrictive measures in view of the situation in Burundi, OJ L 257, 2 Oct. 2015, p. 37, as last amended by Council Decision (CFSP) 2023/2686 of 27 Nov. 2023 amending certain Council Decisions concerning restrictive measures in order to insert provisions on humanitarian exceptions, digital OJ L, 28 Nov. 2023.
257. Council Regulation (EU) 2015/1755 of 1 Oct. 2015 concerning restrictive measures in view of the situation in Burundi, OJ L 257, 2 Oct. 2015, p. 1, as last amended by Council Regulation (EU) 2023/2694 of 27 Nov. 2023 amending certain Council Regulations concerning restrictive measures in order to insert provisions on humanitarian exceptions, digital OJ L, 28 Nov. 2023.
258. Recital No. 1 to the preamble of Council Decision (CFSP) 2015/1763. The *Arusha Peace and Reconciliation Agreement for Burundi* can be retrieved here: https://peacemaker.un.org/node/1207 (last visited: 31 Dec. 2023).
259. Recital Nos 2 and 3 to the preamble of Council Decision (CFSP) 2015/1763.
260. S/RES/2248 of 12 Nov. 2015. *See also* S/RES/2303 of 29 Jul. 2016.
261. Council Decision (CFSP) 2017/2074 of 13 Nov. 2017 concerning restrictive measures in view of the situation in Venezuela, OJ L 295, 14 Nov. 2017, p. 60, as last amended by Council Decision (CFSP) 2023/2686 of 27 Nov. 2023 amending certain Council Decisions concerning restrictive measures in order to insert provisions on humanitarian exceptions, digital OJ L, 28 Nov. 2023.
262. Council Regulation (EU) 2017/2063 of 13 Nov. 2017 concerning restrictive measures in view of the situation in Venezuela, OJ L 295, 14 Nov. 2017, p. 21, as last amended by Council Regulation (EU) 2023/2694 of 27 Nov. 2023 amending certain Council Regulations concerning restrictive measures in order to insert provisions on humanitarian exceptions, digital OJ L, 28 Nov. 2023.
263. Recital No. 1 to the preamble of Council Decision (CFSP) 2017/2074.
264. Recital No. 2 to the preamble of Council Decision (CFSP) 2017/2074.
265. Recital Nos 5 and 6 to the preamble of Council Decision (CFSP) 2017/2074.
266. S/PV.8452 of 26 Jan. 2019.
267. S/PV.8472 of 26 Feb. 2019.

presidential elections of 20 May 2018 were neither free nor fair and supporting the peaceful restoration of democracy and the rule of law in Venezuela.[268] This was vetoed by Russia,[269] which in view of the resolution having been drafted a year after the concerned event doubted the true intentions of the United States and argued that adoption of such a resolution would be equated with the UN Security Council removing one President of a sovereign country from office and installing another. Russia went as far as characterizing the same resolution as a legal theatre of the absurd.[270]

49. Undermining democracy and the rule of law, along with serious human rights violations and abuses and repression of civil society and democratic opposition have been the grounds for setting out restrictive measures in view of the situation in Nicaragua[271] (the 'Regulation on Nicaragua'). The accompanying council decision[272] ('Decision on Nicaragua') sheds a dim light on the events that triggered this response. These consisted of repression of the press and civil society, the use of anti-terrorist laws to repress dissenting opinions, the brutal repression of demonstrations by security forces that led to several hundred dead and injured and the arrest of citizens with irregularities and arbitrariness in detention and judicial procedures.[273] Still, the Report of the UN High Commissioner for Human Rights elucidates the facts. In April 2018 protests against the Government broke out throughout Nicaragua that turned into massive demonstrations and were violently dismantled by the police and pro-Government forces.[274] In the ensuing months human rights violations, including gross violations, such as disproportionate use of force by the police and ill-treatment and instances of torture in detention centres, were documented. At the same time, individuals were reported to have been injuring and killing police officers and members of the Sandinista political party, as well as destroying public infrastructure.[275] The authorities asserted that the repression of protests was a legitimate response to a failed *coup d'état* and denied, at the time, responsibility for human rights violations.[276] The European Parliament also reported, documented, assessed and condemned the restriction of the freedoms of expression, assembly and demonstration, breach of international standards in relation to judicial proceedings and endangering the right to information and academic freedom.[277] It further called for the immediate extradition of

268. S/2019/186 of 28 Feb. 2019.
269. S/PV.8476 of 28 Feb. 2019.
270. *Ibid.*, p. 2.
271. Council Regulation (EU) 2019/1716 of 14 Oct. 2019 concerning restrictive measures in view of the situation in Nicaragua, OJ L 262, 15 Oct. 2019, p. 1, as last amended by Council Regulation (EU) 2023/2694 of 27 Nov. 2023 amending certain Council Regulations concerning restrictive measures in order to insert provisions on humanitarian exceptions, digital OJ L, 28 Nov. 2023.
272. Council Decision (CFSP) 2019/1720 of 14 Oct. 2019 concerning restrictive measures in view of the situation in Nicaragua, OJ L 262, 15 Oct. 2019, p. 58, as last amended by Council Decision (CFSP) 2023/2686 of 27 Nov. 2023 amending certain Council Decisions concerning restrictive measures in order to insert provisions on humanitarian exceptions, digital OJ L, 28 Nov. 2023.
273. Recital No. 1 of Council Decision 2019/1720.
274. UN General Assembly, Human Rights Council, *Situation of Human Rights in Nicaragua*, A/HRC/42/18 of 17 Sep. 2019, p. 2, para. 5.
275. *Ibid.*, p. 3 para. 5.
276. *Ibid.*, p. 3 para. 6.
277. *See* European Parliament, Situation in Nicaragua P8_TA(2019)0219 of 14 Mar. 2019.

Alessio Casimirri, who lived at the time under the protection of the Nicaraguan Government, to Italy where he has been sentenced to life for the kidnapping and killing of Aldo Moro and the murder of his guards in 1978 in Rome.[278]

50. In addition to the legislative act already described (*see* in this regard paragraph 31 above), the EU has enacted further legislation in view of the situation in Lebanon[279] ('EU Decision on Lebanon' and 'EU Regulation on Lebanon'). In doing so, it expressed support for the Reform, Recovery and Reconstruction Framework ('3RF') to build back a better Lebanon.[280] The 3RF that was originally designed as a response to the needs created by the port of Beirut explosion is a collective and strategic partnership between the government of Lebanon, the civil society and the international community, whereas it evolved into facilitating an inclusive policy dialogue, long-term reconstructing critical assets, services and infrastructure and sustainable economic recovery across all Lebanon.[281] Furthermore, the EU expressed grave concern about the absence of a fully empowered government capable of meeting Lebanon's urgent needs and implementing critical reforms. It also noted that the economic, social and humanitarian situation in Lebanon continues to deteriorate, whereas the state's population pays an exceptionally high price for the inaction of their political leaders.[282] It therefore was ready to use all instruments at its disposal in order to contribute to a way out of the crisis and decided to adopt targeted restrictive measures against persons responsible for undermining democracy and the rule of law in Lebanon.[283]

§4 VIOLENT REPRESSION AND POLITICAL STALEMATE

51. Violent repression and political stalemate constitute another set of grounds that function as a base for issuing restrictive measures. The EU has invoked them when imposing sanctions on Guinea and Syria.

278. *Ibid.*, para. 8. *See also* European Parliament, Situation in Nicaragua P9_TA(2022)0238 of 9 Jun. 2022.
279. Council Decision (CFSP) 2021/1277 of 30 Jul. 2021 concerning restrictive measures in view of the situation in Lebanon, OJ L 277I, 2 Aug. 2021, p. 16, as last amended by Council Decision (CFSP) 2023/2686 of 27 Nov. 2023 amending certain Council Decisions concerning restrictive measures in order to insert provisions on humanitarian exceptions, digital OJ L, 28 Nov. 2023.
Council Regulation (EU) 2021/1275 of 30 Jul. 2021 concerning restrictive measures in view of the situation in Lebanon, OJ L 277I, 2 Aug. 2021, p. 1, as last amended by Council Regulation (EU) 2023/2694 of 27 Nov. 2023 amending certain Council Regulations concerning restrictive measures in order to insert provisions on humanitarian exceptions, digital OJ L, 28 Nov. 2023.
280. Recital No. 2 to the preamble of the EU Decision on Lebanon.
281. *See* UN Lebanon, *Lebanon Reform, Recovery and Reconstruction Framework: 3RF*, available: https://lebanon.un.org/en/111325-lebanon-reform-recovery-and-reconstruction-framework-3rf (last visited: 31 Dec. 2023); Reform, Recovery and Reconstruction Framework, *Lebanon Reform, Recovery and Reconstruction Framework* (3RF), available: https://www.lebanon3rf.org (last visited: 31 Dec. 2023); The World Bank, *Lebanon Reform, Recovery & Reconstruction Framework (3RF)*, 4 Dec. 2020, available: https://www.worldbank.org/en/country/lebanon/publication/lebanon-reform-recovery-reconstruction-framework-3rf (last visited: 31 Dec. 2023).
282. Recital Nos 5 to 7 to the preamble of the EU Decision on Lebanon.
283. Recital No. 8 to the preamble of the EU Decision on Lebanon.

52. Restrictive measures against Guinea had been discussed in a common position[284] and a Council decision[285] ('Decision on Guinea') and they were enacted in a resolution[286] (the 'Resolution on Guinea'). More specifically, the EU responded to the violent crackdown on political demonstrators in Conakry on 28 September 2009. It then called for the release of the arrested demonstrators and members of the opposition and urged all parties to take action to restore the rule of law and put the country back on the path towards constitutional rule and democracy.[287]

53. Similarly, brutal repression and political stalemate were the grounds for the imposition of restrictive measures against Syria[288] ('Regulation on Syria'), which were initially described in a decision[289] ('Decision on Syria'). The UN Security Council had drafted a resolution demanding that the Syrian authorities cease violations of human rights, allow the full exercise of human rights and fundamental freedoms, cease the use of force against civilians alleviating the humanitarian situation in crisis areas and ensure the safe and voluntary return of those who have fled the violence to their homes.[290] However, this remained merely a draft as it was vetoed by both Russia and China.[291] This was also the fate of another resolution, which demanded that the Syrian government cease all violence and protect its population, release all persons detained arbitrarily due to recent incidents, withdraw all Syrian military and armed forces from cities and towns, guarantee the freedom of peaceful demonstrations, allow access and movement for all League of Arab States' institutions and observer mission.[292] It remained merely a draft, as once again it was vetoed by Russia and China.[293]

284. Council Common Position 2009/788/CFSP of 27 Oct. 2009 concerning restrictive measures against the Republic of Guinea, OJ L 281, 28 Oct. 2009, p. 7, which was repealed on 24 Oct. 2010 by the ensuing Council decision.
285. Council Decision 2010/638/CFSP of 25 Oct. 2010 concerning restrictive measures against the Republic of Guinea, OJ L 280, 26 Oct. 2010, p. 10, as last amended by Council Decision (CFSP) 2023/2686 of 27 Nov. 2023 amending certain Council Decisions concerning restrictive measures in order to insert provisions on humanitarian exceptions, digital OJ L, 28 Nov. 2023.
286. Council Regulation (EU) No. 1284/2009 of 22 Dec. 2009 imposing certain specific restrictive measures in respect of the Republic of Guinea, OJ L 346, 23 Dec. 2009, p. 26, as last amended by Council Regulation (EU) 2023/2694 of 27 Nov. 2023 amending certain Council Regulations concerning restrictive measures in order to insert provisions on humanitarian exceptions, digital OJ L, 28 Nov. 2023.
287. Recital Nos 1 and 2 of the Council Common Position 2009/788/CFSP.
288. Council Regulation (EU) No. 36/2012 of 18 Jan. 2012 concerning restrictive measures in view of the situation in Syria and repealing Regulation (EU) No. 442/2011, OJ L 16, 19 Jan. 2012, p. 1, as last amended by Council Regulation (EU) 2023/2877 of 18 Dec. 2023 amending Regulation (EU) No. 36/2012 concerning restrictive measures in view of the situation in Syria, digital OJ L, 19 Dec. 2023.
289. Council Decision 2011/782/CFSP of 1 Dec. 2011 concerning restrictive measures against Syria and repealing Decision 2011/273/CFSP, OJ L 319, 2 Dec. 2011, p. 56. In the meantime, this has been repealed and currently in force is Council Decision 2013/255/CFSP of 31 May 2013 concerning restrictive measures against Syria, OJ L 147, 1 Jun. 2013, p. 14, as last amended by Council Decision (CFSP) 2023/2876 of 18 Dec. 2023 amending Decision 2013/255/CFSP concerning restrictive measures in view of the situation in Syria, digital OJ L, 18 Dec. 2023.
290. S/2011/612 of 4 Oct. 2011.
291. S/PV.6627 of 4 Oct. 2011.
292. S/2012/77 of 4 Feb. 2012.
293. S/PV.6711 of 4 Feb. 2012.

§5 MISAPPROPRIATION OF STATE FUNDS

54. Misappropriation of state funds, in one event in liaison with the violation of human rights, has been the ground for establishing restrictive measures in view of the situation in Tunisia and in Ukraine. The Courts of the EU found that the prosecution of economic crimes, such as misappropriation of public funds, is an important means of combating corruption, that itself constitutes, in the context of the external action of the Union, a principle falling within the scope of the rule of law.[294] Not every misappropriation of public funds in a third state justifies EU action with the objective of supporting the rule of law in that state, using the powers of the Union under the CFSP. It is necessary that the acts at hand are such as to undermine the legal and institutional foundations of the country concerned.[295] These foundations encompass principles of legality, the prohibition of arbitrary exercise of power by the executive, effective judicial review and equality before the law and respect for the rule of law in that state.[296]

55. In its usual modus operandum, the EU discussed the restrictive measures in view of the situation in Tunisia in a Council decision[297] ('Decision on Tunisia') and enacted a resolution (the 'Resolution on Tunisia').[298] In doing so, the Council reaffirmed its full solidarity and support with Tunisia and its people in their efforts to establish a stable democracy, the rule of law, democratic pluralism and full respect for human rights and fundamental freedoms. It then decided to adopt restrictive measures against persons responsible for the misappropriation of state funds and therefore deprived the people of the benefits of sustainable development of their economy and society and undermined the development of democracy in the country.[299]

56. Similarly, the EU has envisioned restrictive measures in view of the situation in Ukraine in a council decision[300] (the 'Funds Decision on Ukraine') and set them out in

294. *Edward Stavytskyi v. Council*, T-290/17, Judgment of 30 Jan. 2019, digital ECR. para. 69 ('Stavytsky'), citing *Yanukovych v. Council*, T-346/14, Judgment of 15 Sep. 2016, digital ECR, para. 141 ('Yanukovych').
295. *Stavytskyi (*n. 294) para. 70, citing *Yanukovych* (n. 294) para. 99.
296. *Stavytskyi* (n. 294) para. 72, citing *Yanukovych* (n. 294) para. 101.
297. Council Decision 2011/72/CFSP of 31 Jan. 2011 concerning restrictive measures directed against certain persons and entities in view of the situation in Tunisia, OJ L 28, 2 Feb. 2011, p. 62, as last amended by Council Decision (CFSP) 2023/2686 of 27 Nov. 2023 amending certain Council Decisions concerning restrictive measures in order to insert provisions on humanitarian exceptions, digital OJ, 28 Nov. 2023.
298. Council Regulation (EU) No. 101/2011 of 4 Feb. 2011 concerning restrictive measures directed against certain persons, entities and bodies in view of the situation in Tunisia, OJ L 31, 5 Feb. 2011, p. 1, as last amended by Council Implementing Regulation (EU) 2023/156 of 23 Jan. 2023 implementing Regulation (EU) No. 101/2011 concerning restrictive measures directed against certain persons, entities and bodies in view of the situation in Tunisia, OJ L 22, 24 Jan. 2023, p. 8.
299. Recital Nos 1 & 2 Council Decision 2011/72.
300. Council Decision 2014/119/CFSP of 5 Mar. 2014 concerning restrictive measures directed against certain persons, entities and bodies in view of the situation in Ukraine, OJ L 66, 6 Mar. 2014, p. 26, as last amended by Council Decision (CFSP) 2024/828 of 4 Mar. 2024 amending

a regulation[301] (the 'Funds Regulation on Ukraine'). Against the backdrop of unidentified armed men (Russian troops according to the delegation of Ukraine to the UN) blocking key sites such as airports, communications and public buildings in Crimea, as well as in the East and South of Ukraine,[302] the EU condemned all use of violence, called for an immediate end to it as well as full respect for human rights and fundamental freedoms. It decided to adopt restrictive measures against persons responsible for the misappropriation of state funds and persons responsible for human rights violations in Ukraine.[303] In the present set of measures, misappropriation of state funds was not correlated to the sustainable development of the economy; rather it shares the frontstage with human rights.

§6 INTERESTS AND SECURITY OF THE UNION

57. The EU deemed that its interests and security are threatened by the *illegal actions* of Türkiye in the Eastern Mediterranean that are *unauthorized*, and issued a decision[304] ('Decision on Drilling') and a regulation[305] ('Regulation on Drilling').

58. Hydrocarbon resources off the coast of Cyprus have been the cause of tensions for some time.[306] In February 2018, the EU noted that Türkiye blocked the drilling operations of ENI that was commissioned by Cyprus resulting in the abortion of the planned exploration activities. The EU, while emphasizing the sovereign rights to exploit their natural resources, stressed the need to respect the sovereignty of Member

---

Decision 2014/119/CFSP concerning restrictive measures directed against certain persons, entities and bodies in view of the situation in Ukraine, digital OJ L, 5 Mar. 2024.

301. Council Regulation (EU) No. 208/2014 of 5 Mar. 2014 concerning restrictive measures directed against certain persons, entities and bodies in view of the situation in Ukraine, OJ L 66, 6 Mar. 2014, p. 1, as last amended by Council Implementing Regulation (EU) 2023/449 of 2 Mar. 2023 implementing Regulation (EU) No. 208/2014 concerning restrictive measures directed against certain persons, entities and bodies in view of the situation in Ukraine, OJ L 67, 3 Mar. 2023, p. 1.
302. UN Security Council, 7124th meeting of Saturday, 1 Mar. 2012, 4:15 p.m. in New York, S/PV. 7124.
303. Recital Nos 1 & 2 of the Funds Resolution on Ukraine.
304. Council Decision (CFSP) 2019/1894 of 11 Nov. 2019 concerning restrictive measures in view of Turkey's unauthorised drilling activities in the Eastern Mediterranean, OJ L 291, 12 Nov. 2019, p. 47, as last amended by Council Decision (CFSP) 2023/2488 of 9 Nov. 2023 amending Decision (CFSP) 2019/1894 concerning restrictive measures in view of Turkey's unauthorised drilling activities in the Eastern Mediterranean, digital OJ L, 10 Nov. 2023.
305. Council Regulation (EU) 2019/1890 of 11 Nov. 2019 concerning restrictive measures in view of Turkey's unauthorised drilling activities in the Eastern Mediterranean, OJ L 291, 12 Nov. 2019, p. 3, as last amended by Council Regulation (EU) 2023/2507 of 9 Nov. 2023 amending Regulation (EU) 2019/1890 concerning restrictive measures in view of Turkey's unauthorised drilling activities in the Eastern Mediterranean, digital OJ L, 10 Nov. 2023.
306. Editors, *November 2019 Monthly Forecast, Europe, Cyprus*, Security Council Report, 31 Oct. 2019, available: https://www.securitycouncilreport.org/monthly-forecast/2019-11/cyprus-4.php.

States over their territorial sea and airspace.[307] One year later, the EU urged Türkiye to respect Cyprus' sovereignty over its territorial sea and its sovereign rights, whereas it expressed grave concern over Türkiye's statements over planned drilling activities, calling Türkiye to refrain from such *illegal actions*.[308] The call to refrain from *illegal actions* was reiterated.[309]

59. On Türkiye's part, the drilling activities performed by Turkish Petroleum were both notified to the UN and authorized by the government of Türkiye in the west of the island of Cyprus and by the 'Turkish Republic of Northern Cyprus' in the Karpas peninsula.[310] Türkiye further asserts that Greece and 'Greek Cypriot Administration' perform unilateral acts that ignore the rights and interests of Türkiye and 'Turkish Republic of Northern Cyprus', whereas at the same time, Türkiye has proposed to the EU to convene an inclusive conference on this matter.[311]

60. It seems that the EU does not attribute to two fundamental issues the apposite significance: the unresolved demarcation of maritime boundaries in the region, an issue also linked with the question of Palestine and the maritime boundaries that it is expected to have in case that the two-state solution prevails; and the unsettled Cyprus problem.[312] Instead of working towards resolving them via wielding its diplomatic power and encouraging the use of numerous dispute settlement mechanisms provided in the Convention on the Law of the Sea,[313] it chose to impose sanctions, the direst instrument at its disposal. History tells us that the last time that a state decided to

307. European Commission, *Commission Staff Working Document, Turkey 2018 Report*, SWD(2018) 153 final, Strasbourg, 17 Apr. 2018, p. 60, available: https://data.consilium.europa.eu/doc/document/ST-8080-2018-INIT/en/pdf.
308. Council of the European Union, *Association with Turkey – Establishment of the position of the European Union for the 54th meeting of the Association Council*, Brussels, 1 Mar. 2019, p. 7, available: https://data.consilium.europa.eu/doc/document/ST-6965-2019-INIT/en/pdf (last visited: 31 Dec. 2023).
309. European Commission, *Commission Staff Working Document, Turkey 2019 Report*, SWD(2019) 220 final, Brussels, 29 May 2019, p. 7, available: https://data.consilium.europa.eu/doc/document/ST-9816-2019-INIT/en/pdf (last visited: 31 Dec. 2023); European Council, *European Council meeting (20 June 2019) – Conclusions*, EUCO 9/19, Brussels, 20 Jun. 2019, available: https://data.consilium.europa.eu/doc/document/ST-9-2019-INIT/en/pdf (last visited: 31 Dec. 2023); Council of the European Union, *Turkish Drilling Activities in the Eastern Mediterranean – Council Conclusions*, 11257/19, Brussels, 15 Jul. 2019, p. 2, available: https://data.consilium.europa.eu/doc/document/ST-11257-2019-INIT/en/pdf (last visited: 31 Dec. 2023); Council of the European Union, *Council Conclusions on Turkey's Illegal Drilling Activities in the Eastern* Mediterranean, 13092/19, Brussels, 14 Oct. 2019, available: https://data.consilium.europa.eu/doc/document/ST-13092-2019-INIT/en/pdf (last visited: 31 Dec. 2023).
310. Republic of Türkiye, Ministry of Foreign Affairs, No.: 199, *Press Release Regarding the Activities of Our Drilling Ship Yavuz*, 10 Jul. 2019, available: https://www.mfa.gov.tr/no_199_-yavuz-sondaj-gemimizin-faaliyetleri-hk.en.mfa (last visited: 31 Dec. 2023).
311. Republic of Türkiye, Ministry of Foreign Affairs, No.: 321, *Press Release Regarding the Escalatory Activities of Greece and the Greek Cypriot Administration in the Eastern Mediterranean*, 2 Oct. 2021, available: https://www.mfa.gov.tr/no_-321_-yunanistan-ve-gkry-nin-dogu-akdeniz-de-gerginligi-arttiran-faaliyetleri-hk.en.mfa (last visited: 31 Dec. 2023).
312. *See also* Mehmet Bardakçı, *Turkey and the Major Powers in the Eastern Mediterranean Crisis from the 2010s to the 2020s* 70(3) Comparative Southeast European Studies 516 (2022) https://doi.org/10.1515/soeu-2021-0071.
313. United Nations Convention on the Law of the Sea (Montego Bay 1994) 1833 UNTS 3.

proceed with drilling in a disputed area, this was annexed by its neighbour (annexation of Kuwait by Iraq in 1991);[314] the subsequent imposition of financial sanctions[315] failed per se to ensure interests and security in the region leading to the Gulf Crisis and the deployment of military sanctions that expelled Iraq and re-established the previous government in Kuwait.[316] Naturally, the factual framework differs dramatically and so do the geopolitical dynamics. Nonetheless, it could be an indicator of how devout of meaning, or even counter-productive, restrictive measures can be in certain circumstances.

314. Ministry of Foreign Affairs, Japan, *Gaiko-Seisho (Diplomatic Bluebook) 1991*, in English, Chapter II, s. 1 subs. 1, available: https://www.mofa.go.jp/policy/other/bluebook/1991/1991-2-1.htm#Section%201.%20How%20the%20Gulf%20Crisis%20Began%20and%20Ended (last visited: 31 Dec. 2023).
315. R/RES/661 of 6 Aug. 1990.
316. Joseph O'Mahoney, *Denying the Spoils of War* (Edinburgh University Press 2018) p. 196.

CHAPTER 3

The Sanctions per Sector

61. In the ensuing paragraphs the specific sanctions are presented per sector, that being the financial sanctions (*see* in this regard paragraphs 72 et seq. below); further restrictions on funds and financial services (*see* in this regard paragraphs 171 et seq. below); sanctions on gold, precious metals and diamonds (*see* in this regard paragraphs 187 et seq. below); sanctions on cultural property (*see* in this regard paragraphs 196 et seq. below); energy-related sanctions (*see* in this regard paragraphs 199 et seq. below); sanctions on dual-use items (*see* in this regard paragraphs 241 et seq. below); sanctions on arms and weapons (*see* in this regard paragraphs 270 et seq. below) as well as sanctions with regard to the movement of persons and goods (*see* in this regard paragraphs 307 et seq. below). It has been decided to do so for practical and organizational reasons; nonetheless, it equally carries juridical significance, as the CJEU has been hesitant in freely transposing legal principles to sector-specific measures.[317]

62. It is with great regret that for their interpretation the reparatory documents shall not be used, as they are not publicly available. Thus, they can neither illuminate the adoption process nor facilitate the historical interpretation of terms and provisions.

63. Before describing the aforementioned restrictive measures, some brief notes on their scope of application (*see* in this regard paragraphs 64 et seq. below) and the decision to adopt them (*see* in this regard paragraphs 67 et seq. below) are made, as they are of a general nature and applicable to each one of the said measures.

§1 THE SCOPE OF APPLICATION OF THE SANCTIONS

64. In personam the EU provisions are applicable to any person inside or outside the territory of the Union who is a national of a Member State, to any legal person, entity

317. *Bank Mellat v. Council*, C-430/16 P, Judgment of 6 Sep. 2018, digital ECR, para. 50 ('Bank Mellat 2018').

or body incorporated or constituted under the law of a Member State as well as to any legal person, entity or body in respect of any business done in whole or in part within the Union.[318] Hence, all branches of EU banks must implement EU sanctions regardless of their location as the parent banks are legally liable for the activities of their branches.[319]

65. *In solum* the EU provisions are applicable within the *territory of the Union* (in regard to the definition *see* Annex I p. 311, at 333), including its airspace and on board of any aircraft or any vessel under the jurisdiction of a Member State.[320] The Union has not opted for extraterritorial restrictive measures, as the US has done.[321] Still, the Union acting as a contemporary evangelist strives to further the effect of some restrictive measures. To this end, it calls Member States to encourage third States to adopt similar ones both with regard to the restrictive measures that are independent of resolutions of the UN Security Council and with regard to measures related to such resolutions. The end goal is to maximize the impact of the adopted measures.[322]

66. *In temporis*, certain legislative acts, predominantly the common positions and the decisions prescribe their period of validity. More specifically, the Decision on Sudan and the Common Position on Lebanon provide that they shall be reviewed every twelve

318. Article 16(c), (d) & (e) Regulation on Iraq, Art. 19(c), (d) & (e) Regulation on Sudan, Art. 11(c), (d) & (e) Regulation on DRC, Art. 7(c), (d) & (e) Regulation on Lebanon, Art. 1(c), (d) & (e) Regulation on DPRK, Art. 17(c), (d) & (e) Regulation on Somalia, Art. 49(c), (d) & (e) Regulation on Iran, Art. 14(c), (d) & (e) Regulation on Guinea-Bissau, Art. 24(c), (d) & (e) Regulation on Libya, Art. 21(c), (d) & (e) Regulation on the CAR, Art. 18(c), (d) & (e) Regulation on Yemen, Art. 26(c), (d) & (e) Regulation on South Sudan, Art. 15 (c), (d) & (e) Regulation on Mali, Art. 13(c), (d) & (e) Regulation on Zimbabwe, Art. 15(c), (d) & (e) EU Regulation on Iran, Art. 10(c), (d) & (e) Regulation on Myanmar/Burma, Art. 17(c), (d) & (e) Regulation on Burundi, Art. 20(c), (d) & (e) Regulation on Venezuela, Art. 18(c), (d) & (e) Regulation on Nicaragua, Art. 18(c), (d) & (e) Regulation on Guinea, Art. 35(c), (d) & (e) Regulation on Syria, Art. 15(c), (d) & (e) Regulation on Tunisia and Art. 17(c), (d) & (e) Funds Regulation on Ukraine.
319. Matthias Efing, Stefan Goldbach & Volker Nitsch, *Freeze! Financial Sanctions and Bank Responses* 36(11) The Review of Financial Studies 4417 at 4423 (2023) https://doi.org/10.1093/rfs/hhad043.
320. Article 16(a) & (b) Regulation on Iraq, Art. 19(a) & (b) Regulation on Sudan, Art. 11(a) & (b) Regulation on DRC, Art. 7(a) & (b) Regulation on Lebanon, Art. 1(a) & (b) Regulation on DPRK, Art. 17(a) & (b) Regulation on Somalia, Art. 49(a) & (b) Regulation on Iran, Art. 14(a) & (b) Regulation on Guinea-Bissau, Art. 24(a) & (b) Regulation on Libya, Art. 21(a) & (b) Regulation on the CAR, Art. 18(a) & (b) Regulation on Yemen, Art. 26(a) & (b) Regulation on South Sudan, Art. 15(a) & (b) Regulation on Mali, Art. 13(a) & (b) Regulation on Zimbabwe, Art. 15(a) & (b) EU Regulation on Iran, Art. 10(c), (d) & (e) Regulation on Myanmar/Burma, Art. 17(a) & (b) Regulation on Burundi, Art. 20(a) & (b) Regulation on Venezuela, Art. 18(a) & (b) Regulation on Nicaragua, Art. 18(a) & (b) Regulation on Guinea, Art. 35(a) & (b) Regulation on Syria, Art. 15(a) & (b) Regulation on Tunisia and Art. 17 (a) & (b) Funds Regulation on Ukraine.
321. Joanne Scott, *Extraterritoriality and Territorial Extension in EU Law* 62(1) Am.J.Comp.L. 87 at 94 (2014) https://doi.org/10.5131/ajcl.2013.0009.
322. Article 4 Decision on Guinea-Bissau, Art. 16 Decision on Libya, Art. 11 Decision on South Sudan, Art. 8 Decision on Zimbabwe, Art. 5 EU Decision on Iran, Art. 11 Decision on Myanmar/Burma, Art. 5 Decision on Burundi, Art. 12 Decision on Venezuela, Art. 8 Decision on Nicaragua, Art. 6 Decision on Guinea, Art. 33 Decision on Syria, Art. 4 Decision on Tunisia & Art. 4 Funds Decision Ukraine.

months.[323] Other decisions set out that they shall be reviewed in accordance with relevant resolutions of the UN Security Council,[324] that they are vaguely under constant review,[325] or, while under constant review, they expire on a specific date[326] that usually is annually renewed. Not infrequently, legislative acts of the EU are repealed and the provisions of the new legislative acts correspond, essentially, to the repealed ones. The question arose whether the latter, new, provisions are to be interpreted as being applicable in a situation, whereby an agreement was made before they entered into force, but the final calculation of related costs takes place after the new provisions came into force. The CJEU noted that payments, which are part of a transaction characterized by an economic balance between the consideration given and the consideration received and constitute acts implementing an agreement concluded before the entry into force of the regulation at hand, do not, in itself, mean that they fall outside the scope of that regulation or of the prohibitions laid down therein.[327] It then acknowledged that the new legislative act is not applicable to the payments made under the already concluded agreement. Still, the final calculation of costs under the same agreement does fall under the provisions of the new legislative act, taking into account that the repealed and the now-in-force provisions were largely similar.[328]

§2 THE DECISIONS ADOPTING RESTRICTIVE MEASURES

67. Restrictive measures are disruptors. They are introduced in the ordinary course of business and discontinue the flow of goods and services. The degree and scope of disruption of the flow of goods and services lead to distinguishing between two categories of restrictive measures. On the one hand, restrictive measures can be of general application, the scope of which is determined by reference to objective criteria.[329] They interrupt or reduce, as the case may be, economic relations with a specific state as regards certain goods and services. They apply to objectively determined situations and a

323. Article 9 Decision on Sudan, Art. 4 Common Position on Lebanon.
324. Article 9(1) Decision on the DRC, Art. 36(1) Decision on DPRK, Art. 10 Decision on Somalia, Art. 26(1) Decision on Iran, Art. 5(1) Decision on Guinea-Bissau, Art. 17(1) Decision on Libya, Art. Decision on CAR, Art. 6 Decision on Yemen, Art. 6 Decision on Mali.
325. Article 12(1) Decision on South Sudan, Art. 10(3) Decision on Zimbabwe.
326. With regard to DRC, the relevant decision expires on 12 Dec. 2024 (Art. 9(2) Decision on DRC); with regard to Iran, it expires on 13 Apr. 2024 (Art. 6 EU Decision on Iran); with regard to Myanmar/Burma, it expires on 30 Apr. 2024 (Art. 12 Decision on Myanmar/Burma); with regard to Burundi, it expires on 31 Oct. 2024 (Art. 6 Decision on Burundi); with regard to Venezuela, it expires on 14 May 2024 (Art. 13 Decision on Venezuela); with regard to Nicaragua, it expires on 15 Oct. 2024 (Art. 9 Decision on Nicaragua); with regard to Guinea, it expires on 27 Oct. 2024 (Art. 8(2) Decision on Guinea); with regard to Syria, it expires on 1 Jun. 2024 (Art. Decision on Syria); with regard to Tunisia, it expires on 31 Jan. 2024 (Art. 5(1) Decision on Tunisia); with regard to funds misappropriation in Ukraine, it expires on 6 Mar. 2024 (Art. 5 Funds Decision on Ukraine); with regard to unauthorized drilling in the Mediterranean, it expires on 30 Nov. 2024 (Art. 8 Decision on Drilling).
327. *SH v. TG*, C-168/17, Judgment of 17 Jan. 2019, digital ECR, para. 58, citing *Möllendorf* (n. 45) paras 49 & 62 ('SH').
328. *SH* (n. 327) paras 94 to 99.
329. *Venezuela* 2023 (n. 12) para. 30, citing *Bank Mellat* 2018 (n. 317) paras 55 & 56.

category of persons viewed generally and in the abstract.[330] On the other hand, they target specifically designated natural and legal persons. These interrupt the flow of financial assets and economic benefits towards such persons, as per the particular designation in place.[331]

68. All restrictive measures have a preventive nature. Thus, the principle *non bis in idem* that relate to proceedings and penalties concerning an offence in respect of which a person has already been finally acquitted or convicted, finds no application.[332] It has been further found that they have a precautionary and, by definition, provisional nature. Thus, their validity always depends on whether the factual and legal circumstances which led to their adoption continue to apply and on the need to persist with them in order to achieve their objective, leading to the actual need for periodic renewal and amendment, as necessary.[333] The grounds for designating a person do not make the relevant restrictive measures criminal in nature.[334] Their implied, but clear, objective is to have an impact on the third state concerned.[335] Nonetheless, they are not intended as a reaction to an internationally wrongful act imputable to the state concerned through the temporary non-performance of the Union's international obligations. Consequently, they do not constitute countermeasures in the sense of International Law,[336] at least not according to the Courts of the EU.

69. The decisions adopting the measures described below are, most commonly, addressed to 'natural or legal persons, entities or bodies'[337] or 'persons, entities or bodies'.[338] In the paragraphs below the term *persons* shall be used to denote these phrases. Specifically with regard to the notion of legal persons, the CJEU specified that this concept refers, essentially, to entities having legal personality under the law of a Member State or a third State. It then went on to interpret Article 263 TFEU in the light of the principles of effective judicial review and the rule of law and concluded that a third State should have standing to bring proceedings, as a 'legal person', within the meaning of said article. Such a legal person governed by public international law is equally likely as any other person or entity to have its rights or interests adversely affected by an act of the EU and must therefore be able, in compliance with those

330. *Venezuela* 2023 (n. 12) para. 31.
331. *Ibid.*, paras 30 & 31, citing *Bank Mellat* 2018 (n. 317) paras 55 & 56.
332. *Iran Shipping* 2019 (n. 46) para. 59, citing *Afrasiabi* (n. 46) para. 44, and *Kadi*, 2013 (n. 9) para. 132.
333. *Kumba* (n. 101) para. 58, citing *Yusef v. Commission*, T-306/10, Judgment of 21 Mar. 2014, digital ECR, paras 62 and 63 ('Yusef'). *See also Alex Kande Mupompa v. Council*, T-170/18, Judgment of 12 Feb. 2020, para. 69 ('Mupompa') & *Antonio José Benavides Torres v. Council*, T-35/19, Judgment of 14 Jul. 2021, digital ECR, para. 50.
334. *Kumba* (n. 101) para. 85; *Mupompa* (n. 333) para. 97.
335. *Venezuela* 2023 (n. 12) para. 110.
336. *See* Art. 49 ARSIWA. *Venezuela* 2023 (n. 12) para. 92.
337. *See*, for example, Art. 2(1) & (2) Regulation on DRC, Art. 2(1) & (2) Regulation on Guinea-Bissau, Art. 5(1) & (2) Regulation on Libya, Art. 5(1) & (2) Regulation on the CAR, Art. 2(1) & (2) Regulation on Yemen, Art. 5(1), (2) & (3) Regulation on South Sudan, Art. 2(1) & (2) Regulation on Mali and Art. 3(1) & (2) Regulation on Haiti.
338. *See*, for example, Art. 4(2) Regulation on Iraq, Arts 5(3) & 15(1) Regulation on Sudan, Art. 34(4) Regulation on DPRK and Arts 23(1) & (2) and 23a(1) & (2) Regulation on Iran.

conditions, to seek the annulment of that act.[339] Furthermore, and still, within the notion of a *legal person* or *entity*, the CJEU specified that a person exercising functions conferring on him or her the power to manage an entity covered by restrictive measures may, as a general rule, himself or herself be considered to be involved in the activities that justified the adoption of the restrictive measures covering the entity in question.[340]

70. Exceptionally certain pieces of legislation entail some specific provisions. Such is the Regulation on Iran that specifies the term *Iranian person, entity or body* (in regard to the definition *see* Annex I p. 307). According to this statutory definition, said term stands for anyone related to Iran, whether it be the state or a natural or legal person of Iran, including entities owned or controlled by such persons.[341] Thus, the term *Iranian persons* in the paragraphs below shall have this meaning. In certain instances, mention is made to *government, public bodies, corporations of agencies or anyone acting on their behalf or at their discretion*. Jurisprudence ruled that these are general and abstract categories of persons and entities. The government at issue is not targeted by name through such provisions and therefore, the regulation at issue is of general application providing for restrictive measures of general application.[342] At the same time, the CJEU has affirmed that the respective states are affected by restrictive measures of general application;[343] nonetheless this in itself does not confer on them the right to be heard.[344]

71. The restrictive measures usually prohibit 'sale, supply, transfer or export' and 'import, purchase or transport'. It is highly probable and equally possible that selecting this line of words ensues the Union's willingness to implement with religious observance the resolutions of the UN Security Council as per the Member States' obligations under international law and the Charter of the United Nations. Such phrases, but for the word 'export', mirror the wording adopted in resolutions of the UN Security Council setting out restrictive measures.[345]

§3 FINANCIAL SANCTIONS

72. Restrictive measures related to funds, other financial assets and economic resources form the backbone of sanctions that Brussels has adopted. They entail, *ex*

339. *République bolivarienne du Venezuela v. Council*, C-872/19 P, Judgment of 22 Jun. 2021, digital ECR, paras 32 & 50.
340. *Mayaleh* (n. 44) para. 143, citing *Nabipour and Others v. Council*, T-58/12, Judgment of 12 Dec. 2013, digital ECR, para. 110.
341. Article 1(o) Regulation on Iran.
342. *Venezuela* 2023 (n. 12) paras 32 to 34.
343. *See*, i.e., Arts 2, 3, 6 and 7 Regulation on Venezuela.
344. *Venezuela* 2023 (n. 12) para. 43, citing *Atlanta v. European Community*, C-104/97 P, Judgment of 14 Oct. 1999, digital ECR, paras 34 and 35, and *Alpharma v. Council*, T-70/99, Judgment of 11 Sep. 2002, digital ECR, para. 388.
345. *See*, i.e., S/RES/2293 of 23 Jun. 2016 para. 2, S/RES/1718 of 14 Oct. 2006 para. 8(a), S/RES/2270 2 Mar. 2016 para. 8, S/RES/2551 of 12 Nov. 2020 para. 26, S/RES/1970 of 26 Feb. 2011 para. 8, S/RES/2174 27 Aug. of 2014 para. 8, S/RES/2648 of 29 Jul. 2022 para. 1, S/RES/2216 14 Apr. of 2015 para. 14, S/RES/2428 of 13 Jul. 2018 paras 4 & 5 and S/RES/2653 of 21 Oct. 2022 paras 11 & 13.

hypothesi, consequences which could cause harm to parties who are not responsible for the situation leading to their adoption.[346] By definition, such consequences affect, *inter alia*, the right to property and the freedom to pursue a trade or business of the persons affected.[347] The relevant legal materials follow a specific legislative pattern that involves the definition of the apposite terms, an outline of the restrictive measures that can be imposed and a description of the exceptions. This pattern is equally followed in the ensuing paragraphs.

73. Financial sanctions prescribe the freezing of all funds and economic resources belonging to or owned or held by certain persons.[348] At the same time, the prohibition mandates that no funds or economic resources shall be made available, directly or indirectly, to or for the benefit of certain persons.[349] The use of the words 'directly or indirectly' denotes that the restriction has been framed in particularly broad terms encompassing all acts necessary under the applicable national law if that person is in fact to obtain full power of disposal in relation to the funds or economic resources concerned.[350] The restriction encompasses any mode of making available an economic resource and therefore also any act which flows from the execution of a contract imposing mutual obligations and which has been agreed in exchange for payment of pecuniary consideration.[351] For funds to be regarded as being indirectly available to a designated person, it must be possible for those to be passed on to that person or for that person to have the ability to dispose of them via financial or legal links between the beneficiary of the funds and such a person.[352]

346. *Bank Mellat v. Council*, T-160/13, Judgment of 2 Jun. 2016, digital ECR, para. 204 ('Bank Mellat 2016'), citing *Melli Bank v. Council*, Joined T-246/08 and T-332/08, Judgment of 9 Jul. 2009, digital ECR, para. 111.
347. *Bank Mellat* 2018 (n. 317) para. 60, citing *Bosphorus*, C-84/95, Judgment of 30 Jul. 1996, digital ECR, para. 22 ('Bosphorus') and *Rosneft* 2017 (n. 32) para. 149.
348. Article 4(1) & (2) Regulation on Iraq, Art. 5(1) Regulation on Sudan, Art. 2(1) Regulation on DRC, Art. 34(1) Regulation on DPRK, Art. 2(1) Regulation on Somalia, Arts 23(1) & (2) and 23a(1) & (2) Regulation on Iran, Art. 2(1) Regulation on Guinea-Bissau, Art. 5(1) & (4) Regulation on Libya, Art. 5(1) Regulation on CAR, Art. 2(1) Regulation on Yemen, Art. 5(1) & (2) Regulation on South Sudan, Art. 2(1) Regulation on Mali, Art. 6(1) Regulation on Zimbabwe, Art. 2(1) EU Regulation on Iran, Art. 4a(1) Regulation on Myanmar/Burma, Art. 2(1) Regulation on Burundi, Art. 8(1) Regulation on Venezuela, Art. 2(1) Regulation on Nicaragua, Art. 6(1) Regulation on Guinea, Art. 14(1) Regulation on Syria, Art. 2(1) Regulation on Tunisia & Art. 2(1) Funds Regulation on Ukraine.
349. Article 4(3) Regulation on Iraq, Art. 5(2) Regulation on Sudan, Art. 2(2) Regulation on DRC, Art. 34(3) Regulation on DPRK, Art. 2(2) Regulation on Somalia, Art. 23(3) and 23a(3) Regulation on Iran, Art. 2(2) Regulation on Guinea-Bissau, Art. 5(2) Regulation on Libya, Art. 5(2) Regulation on CAR, Art. 2(2) Regulation on Yemen, Art. 5(3) Regulation on South Sudan, Art. 2(2) Regulation on Mali, Art. 6(2) Regulation on Zimbabwe, Art. 2(2) EU Regulation on Iran, Art. 4a(2) Regulation on Myanmar/Burma, Art. 2(2) Regulation on Burundi, Art. 8(2) Regulation on Venezuela, Art. 2(2) Regulation on Nicaragua, Art. 6(2) Regulation on Guinea, Art. 14(2) Regulation on Syria, Art. 2(2) Regulation on Tunisia & Art. 2(2) Funds Regulation on Ukraine.
350. *SH* (n. 327) para. 51, citing *Möllendorf* (n. 45) paras 50 & 51; *Criminal Proceedings Against E and F*, C-550/09, Judgment of 29 Jun. 2010, paras 66 & 74 ('E and F'); and *Afrasiabi* (n. 46) paras 39 & 40.
351. *SH* (n. 327) para. 51, citing *Möllendorf* (n. 45) para. 56.
352. *SH* (n. 327) para. 62.

74. Said dual restriction entails an objective element – the terms funds and economic resources as specified in the law – and a subjective element – the specific persons at the receiving end of the restrictions as designated by the competent sanctions committees and/or the Commission – along with the statutory duty to act and obligation to refuse directed to the financial sector. The CJEU refers to the subjective element as *general listing criterion*.[353]

I The Objective Element

75. The objective element is defined in the legislative documents in an almost uniform fashion. *Funds* (in regard to the definition *see* Annex I p. 307) means financial assets and economic benefits of every kind, that are then specified by a non-exhaustive list of such assets and benefits.[354] The definition of *funds* under the Regulation on Iraq is slightly different, as it adds one more item in the non-binding explanatory list, that being 'any other instrument of export-financing'.[355] It could safely be assumed that the EU drew its inspiration from the 1518 Iraq Sanctions Committee (*see* in this respect paragraph 80 below), which issued a relevant non-paper.[356] Although this paper does not unfold legally binding effects, apparently the EU decided to stay close to the suggested wording and adopted the definition to the letter.[357] Regulations imposing restrictive measures due to violations of human rights,[358] democracy and human rights,[359] violent repression,[360] misappropriation of state funds[361] and interests and security of the Union[362] have adopted the aforestated definition, with the exception of the Regulation on Zimbabwe[363] that follows the path of the Regulation on Iraq. On a final note, this separation might be merely of academic interest and debate in view of the generality embedded in the statutory definition of the phrase *including, but not limited to*.

76. The notion of *economic resources* (in regard to the definition *see* Annex I p. 307) complements the term *funds*, as it consists of assets of every kind that do not qualify as funds. The statutory definition is identical in all regulations implementing resolutions

353. *See*, for example, *National Iranian* 2016 (n. 33) paras 38 et seq.
354. Article 1(h) Regulation on Sudan; Art. 1(g) Regulation on DRC; Art. 2(12) Regulation on DPRK; Art. 1(a) Regulation on Somalia; Art. 1(l) Regulation on Iran; Art. 1(a) Regulation on Guinea-Bissau; Art. 1(a) Regulation on Libya; Art. 1(a) Regulation on Libya; Art. 1(h) Regulation on CAR; Art. 1(g) Regulation on Yemen; Art. 1(h) Regulation on South Sudan; Art. 1(g) Regulation on Mali; Art. 1(g) Regulation on Haiti.
355. Article 1(2)(h) Regulation on Iraq.
356. Security Council Committee established pursuant to resolution 1518 (2003), Non-Paper on the Implementation of paragraph 23 of Resolution 1483 (2003), unknown date, available: https://www.un.org/securitycouncil/sanctions/1518 (last visited: 31 Dec. 2023).
357. The last item on the 1518 Iraq Sanctions Committee, is included in the EU prohibition as it is listed in Annex II to the Regulation on Iraq (*see* in this respect para. 196 below).
358. Article 1(a) EU Regulation on Iran & Art. 1(g) Regulation on Myanmar/Burma.
359. Article 1(g) Regulation on Burundi, Art. 1(g) Regulation on Venezuela & Art. 1(g) Regulation on Nicaragua.
360. Article 1(d) Regulation on Guinea & Art. 1(j) Regulation on Syria.
361. Article 1(a) Regulation on Tunisia & Art. 1(g) Funds Regulation on Ukraine.
362. Article 1(g) Regulation on Drilling.
363. Article 1(b) Regulation on Zimbabwe.

of the UN Security Council,[364] the regulations enacted due to violation of human rights,[365] deterioration of democracy in conjunction with abuse of human rights,[366] violent repression,[367] misappropriation of state funds[368] and interests and security of the Union[369] with a single exception. The definition set out in the Regulation on DPRK differs, albeit in a minor way, as it adds the clarification 'including vessels, such as maritime vessels'.[370] In all probability, this clarification carries special weight in relation to that specific set of sanctions, as the 1718 DPRK Sanctions Committee (*see* in this respect paragraph 89 below) has the authority to designate vessels[371] engaging in prohibited activities.[372] Nonetheless, according to jurisprudence, the notion of 'funds and economic resources' is wide in scope, covering assets in kind, however acquired.[373] Within the frame of the sanctions against Iran, the CJEU took the view that an asset entails in itself a danger that it may be diverted in order to support proliferation-sensitive nuclear activities. Thus, it is not required that such an asset be immediately ready for use upon completion of the act at issue.[374]

II The Subjective Element

77. In contrast to the straightforwardness of the objective element that is almost uniform throughout the EU legislations, the subjective element is unique in each piece of legislation as it is interwoven with the circumstances that caused the introduction of the restrictive measures and form the purpose that may serve. Nonetheless, the subjective elements of the EU legislations can be separated into two groups, depending on whether the EU legislation in question transposes a resolution of the UN Security Council or not. In the former cases, a sanctions committee established under a

364. Article 1(3) Regulation on Iraq, Art. 1(e) Regulation on Sudan, Art. 1(d) Regulation on DRC, Art. 2(8) Regulation on DPRK, Art. 1(c) Regulation on Somalia, Art. 1(h) Regulation on Iran, Art. 1(c) Regulation on Guinea-Bissau, Art. 1(c) Regulation on Libya, Art. 1(e) Regulation on CAR, Art. 1(d) Regulation on Yemen, Art. 1(e) Regulation on South Sudan, Art. 1(d) Regulation on Mali and Art. 1(d) Regulation on Haiti.
365. Article 1(d) Regulation on Zimbabwe, Art. 1(c) EU Regulation on Iran & Art. 1(d) Regulation on Myanmar/Burma.
366. Article 1(g) Regulation on Burundi, Art. 1(d) Regulation on Venezuela, Art. 1(d) Regulation on Nicaragua & Art. 1(d) EU Regulation on Lebanon.
367. Article 1(f) Regulation on Guinea & Art. 1(f) Regulation on Syria.
368. Article 1(c) Regulation on Tunisia & Art. 1(d) Funds Regulation on Ukraine.
369. Article 1(d) Regulation on Drilling.
370. Article 2(8) Regulation on DPRK.
371. S/RES/2371 of 5 Aug. 2017. *See also* Security Council Committee established pursuant to resolution 1718 (2006), *Implementation Assistance Notice No. 1: Information to Assist UN Member States in Carrying out their Obligations under Security Council resolutions 1718 (2006), 1874 (2009), 2087 (2013), 2094 (2013), 2270 (2016), 2321 (2016), 2356 (2017), 2371 (2017) and 2375 (2017)*, 10 Aug. 2010 (updated 15 Nov. 2017) paras 9 et seq., available: https://www.un.org/securitycouncil/sanctions/1718/implementation-notices (last visited: 31 Dec. 2023).
372. *Ibid.* On the prohibited activities *see* S/RES/1718 of 14 Oct. 2006, S/RES/1874 of 12 Jun. 2009, S/RES/2087 of 22 Jan. 2013, S/RES/2094 of 7 Mar. 2013, S/RES/2270 of 2 Mar. 2016, S/RES/2321 of 30 Nov. 2016, S/RES/2356 of 2 Jun. 2017 and 2375 of 11 Sep. 2017.
373. *SH* (n. 327) para. 53, citing *E and F* (n. 350) para. 69.
374. *Afrasiabi* (n. 46) para. 47.

resolution of the UN Security Council undertakes the task of identifying and listing the designated persons and the institutions of the EU give effect to that designation in a dual-step procedure. In the latter cases, an EU institution, that being either the Council or the Commission, is entrusted with the task of designating persons that consists of a single-step procedure. As an exception, the legislative instruments setting out the restrictive measures in relation to the DRC, the DPRK, Iran, Libya, South Sudan and Mali blend the lines of said groups in the sense that the imposed restrictive measures are both UN-mandated and autonomous,[375] as it will be demonstrated below.

78. Before delving into the particular conducts and qualities that trigger designation either at the UN level or at the EU level, it is noted that all designation criteria use the present participle. This does not refer to a given period of time, in the sense of requiring that the conduct giving rise to the entry of a name on a designation list must be ongoing when the decision is taken to list or to maintain the listing. Rather, the present participle refers to the general meaning particular to legal definitions.[376]

A The Designations Performed by Sanctions Committees of the UN

79. Sanctions committees established by the UN designate persons with regard to Iraq, Sudan, DRC, DPRK, Somalia, Iran, Guinea-Bissau, Libya, the CAR, Yemen, South Sudan, Mali and Haiti. These committees designate persons applying criteria already decided by the UN Security Council. Not infrequently the criteria are designed for one specific party to a conflict, suggesting that the UN Security Council makes judgments about who are the peace spoilers.[377]

1 Iraq

80. Financial restrictive measures in relation to Iraq are directed against the previous Government of Iraq as well as public bodies and private companies controlled by that government, as long as on 22 May 2003 they are located outside Iraq and have been identified by the 1518 Iraq Sanctions Committee.[378,379] Furthermore, such measures are

---

375. *See also* Michael Brzoska, *International Sanctions Before and Beyond UN Sanctions* 91(6) Int'l Aff. (UK) 1339 at 1343 (2015) https://doi.org/10.1111/1468-2346.12449; Andrea Charron & Clara Portela, *The UN, Regional Sanctions and Africa* 91(6) International Affairs 1369 at 1379 (2015) https://doi.org/10.1111/1468-2346.12452.

376. *Kumba* (n. 101) para. 82 citing *PMOI I* (n. 47) para. 108. *See also Mupompa (n. 333)* para. 94.

377. Andrea Charron & Clara Portela, *The UN, Regional Sanctions and Africa* 91(6) International Affairs 1369 at 1381 (2015) https://doi.org/10.1111/1468-2346.12452.

378. According to Art. 1(1) Regulation on Iraq *sanctions committee* means 'the Committee of the Security Council of the United Nations which was established pursuant to paragraph 6 of Resolution 661 (1990)'. However, the mandate of that committee has lapsed and on 24 Nov. 2003 a new committee was established in order to continue identifying funds, financial assets and economic resources of the previous government of Iraq, Saddam Hussein and other senior officials of the former Iraqi regime. *See* S/RES/1518 of 24 Nov. 2003 and S/RES/1483 of 22 May 2003. Relevant materials, its works and mandate can be retrieved here: https://www.un.org/securitycouncil/sanctions/1518 (last visited:31 Dec. 2023).

directed against the former President Saddam Hussein, senior officials of his regime, immediate members of their families and legal persons, bodies and entities owned or controlled directly or indirectly by said persons or any person acting on their behalf or at their direction.[380]

81. This is the first instance, in many more that follow, where the notion 'owned or controlled' is used and lacks further specifications, with the exception of sanctions targeting Russia (*see* in this regard paragraph 436 below). The EU Guidelines provide though that *ownership* requires the possession of more than 50% of the proprietary rights of an entity or having a majority interest in it.[381] *Control* could be indicated by any of the following: (a) the right or power to appoint or remove members of the administrative, supervisory or management body of a legal person; (b) appointing solely as a result of exercising voting rights, a majority of the members of the administrative, management or supervisory bodies of a legal person, who have held office during the present and previous financial year; (c) controlling alone, pursuant to an agreement with other shareholders, a majority of shareholders' or members' voting rights in that legal person; (d) the right to exercise a dominant influence over a legal person, under an agreement entered into with that person, or to a provision in its Memorandum or Articles of Association, where the law governing that person permits its being subject to such agreement; (e) the power to exercise the right to aforementioned dominant influence without being the holder of that right; (f) the right to use all or part of the assets of a legal person; (g) managing the business of a legal person on a unified basis, while publishing consolidated accounts; and (h) sharing jointly and severally the financial liabilities of a legal person or guaranteeing them.[382]

82. Following the determination made by the 1518 Iraq Sanctions Committee, the Commission has the authority to amend the lists of designated persons set in the Regulation on Iraq[383] and therefore to allow for the legal effects of restrictive measures to unfold in relation to particular persons. The Regulation on Iraq is silent on the content of and the information to be provided in these annexes as well as on informing the addresses and offering them the opportunity to express their views and representations.

2 Sudan

83. Financial restrictive measures in relation to Sudan are targeting persons, who impede the peace process, constitute a threat to stability in Darfur and the region, violate international humanitarian or human rights law or commit other atrocities, violate the arms embargo and/or are responsible for offensive military overflights in

379. Article 4(1) Regulation on Iraq.
380. Article 4(2) Regulation on Iraq.
381. Council of the European Union, *Sanctions Guidelines*, 5664/18, Brussels 4 May 2018, p. 20.
382. *Ibid.*, pp. 20 & 21.
383. Article 11 and Annexes III & IV Regulation on Iraq.

and over the Darfur region, as designated by the sanctions committee[384] (the '1591 Sudan Sanctions Committee').[385]

84. At the EU level, the Council includes such a person in the list upon receiving the statement of reasons for that designation by the UN institution.[386] Thereafter, the Council communicates its decision to the addressee along with the statement of reasons providing it with the opportunity to present observations. In the event that the address of the addressee is unknown, such a notification takes place through the publication of a notice.[387] Should observations be submitted or substantial new evidence be presented, the Council is under the statutory obligation to review its decision and inform the addressee accordingly.[388] In such an event, the Council has the task to establish that the reasons on which it relied to take action against the person concerned are well founded. Further, the produced information or evidence has to support the reasons on which it based its action against the same person.[389] Within this frame, the element of time is significant, as the Council, as well as any other competent institution of the EU, is obliged to explain why the invoked reasons are still current when time has lapsed between the statements that served as the basis for designation and the actual adoption of the designation.[390] Retaining a person on the list of designated persons requires an up-to-date assessment of the situation and taking into account recent events and facts, when time has passed and the circumstances of the case changed.[391]

3 *The Democratic Republic of Congo*

85. Financial sanctions in view of the situation of the DRC are adopted at the level of the UN against persons engaging in or supporting acts undermining the peace, stability or security of the DRC. Indicatively, such acts include: actions violating the imposed arms embargo and related measures;[392] being political and military leaders of foreign

384. Under Art. 1(i) *sanctions committee* stands for 'the UN Security Council Committee established pursuant to paragraph 3 of UNSCR 1591 (2005)'. Relevant materials, its works and mandate can be retrieved here: https://www.un.org/securitycouncil/sanctions/1591 (last visited:31 Dec. 2023). *See also* Thomas Dörfler, *Why Rules Matter: Shaping Security Council Sanctions Policy in Counterterrorism and Beyond* 8(1) J.Glob.Secur.Stud. 1 at 15 & 16 (2023) https://doi.org/10.1093/jogss/ogac041.
385. Article 5(3) Regulation on Sudan. These listing criteria are identical to the ones set out in para. 3(c) of resolution 1591 (2005).
386. Article 15(1) & Annex I Regulation on Sudan.
387. *Ibid.*
388. Article 15(2) & Annex I Regulation on Sudan.
389. *El-Qaddafi* 2023 (n. 46) para. 68, adopting the approach of *Kadi* 2013 (n. 9) paras 121 & 122.
390. *El-Qaddafi* 2023 (n. 46) para. 69, adopting the approach of *Council v. LTTE*, C-599/14 P, Judgment of 26 Jul. 2017, para. 85 ('LTTE 2017').
391. *El-Qaddafi* 2023 (n. 46) para. 75, adopting the approach of *LTTE* 2017 (n. 390) para. 54 and *Council v. Kurdistan Workers' Party (PKK)*, C-46/19 P, Judgment of 22 Apr. 2021, paras 49 & 51 ('PKK 2021').
392. Articles 2a(1)(a) & 1a Regulation on DRC and Art. 1 Decision on DRC. *See* S/RES/1596 of 3 May 2005 paras 15 & 13; S/RES/1807 of 31 Mar. 2008 paras 11, 13(a) & 1; S/RES/1857 of 22 Dec.

armed groups operating in this state that hinder disarmament and voluntary repatriation or resettlement of combatants belonging to those groups;[393] being political and military leaders of Congolese militias, who obstruct the participation of their combatants in disarmament, demobilization and reintegration processes;[394] recruiting and using children in armed conflict;[395] acts constituting violations of human rights or international humanitarian law, including attacks on schools and hospitals;[396] obstructing access to humanitarian assistance or distribution thereof;[397] supporting groups involved in destabilizing the DRC through illicit exploitation and trade of natural resources;[398] participating in attacks against MONUSCO peacekeepers or personnel of the UN;[399] producing, manufacturing or using improvised explosive devices or otherwise assisting attacks with such devices;[400] providing financial, material or technological support to a designated person;[401] and performing acts on behalf of or at the direction of any designated person.[402] The designation is performed by the sanctions committee established under resolution 1533 of the UN Security Council[403] ('the 1533 Congo Sanctions Committee').[404] Upon the designation of a person by the 1533 Congo Sanctions Committee, the Council shall include such a

2008 paras 4(a) & 1; S/RES/2078 of 28 Nov. 2012 paras 4(a) & 1; S/RES/2136 of 30 Jan. 2014 paras 4(a) & 1; S/RES/2293 of 23 Jun. 2016 paras 7(a) & 1.

393. Article 2a(1)(b) Regulation on DRC. *See* S/RES/1649 of 21 Dec. 2005 para. 2(a); S/RES/1807 of 31 Mar. 2008 paras 11 & 13(b); S/RES/1857 of 22 Dec. 2008 para. 4(b); S/RES/2078 of 28 Nov. 2012 para. 4(b); S/RES/2136 of 30 Jan. 2014 para. 4(b); S/RES/2293 of 23 Jun. 2016 para. 7(b).
394. Article 2a(1)(c) Regulation on DRC. *See* S/RES/1649 of 21 Dec. 2005 para. 2(b); S/RES/1807 of 31 Mar. 2008 paras 11 & 13(c); S/RES/1857 of 22 Dec. 2008 para. 4(c); S/RES/2078 of 28 Nov. 2012 para. 4(c); S/RES/2136 of 30 Jan. 2014 para. 4(c); S/RES/2293 of 23 Jun. 2016 para. 7(c).
395. Article 2a(1)(d) Regulation on DRC. *See* S/RES/1698 of 31 Jul. 2006 para. 13; S/RES/1807 of 31 Mar. 2008 paras 11 & 13(d); S/RES/1857 of 22 Dec. 2008 para. 4(d); S/RES/2078 of 28 Nov. 2012 para. 4(d); S/RES/2136 of 30 Jan. 2014 para. 4(d); S/RES/2293 of 23 Jun. 2016 para. 7(d).
396. Article 2a(1)(e) Regulation on DRC. *See* S/RES/1698 of 31 Jul. 2006 para. 13; S/RES/1807 of 31 Mar. 2008 paras 11 & 13(e); S/RES/1857 of 22 Dec. 2008 para. 4(e); S/RES/2078 of 28 Nov. 2012 para. 4(e); S/RES/2293 of 23 Jun. 2016 para. 7(e).
397. Article 2a(1)(f) Regulation on DRC. *See* S/RES/1857 of 22 Dec. 2008 para. 4(f); S/RES/2078 of 28 Nov. 2012 para. 4(f); S/RES/2136 of 30 Jan. 2014 para. 4(f); S/RES/2293 of 23 Jun. 2016 para. 7(f).
398. Article 2a(1)(g) Regulation on DRC. *See* S/RES/1857 of 22 Dec. 2008 para. 4(g); S/RES/2078 of 28 Nov. 2012 para. 4(g); S/RES/2136 of 30 Jan. 2014 para. 4(g); S/RES/2293 of 23 Jun. 2016 para. 7(g).
399. Article 2a(1)(i) Regulation on DRC. *See* S/RES/2078 of 28 Nov. 2012 para. 4(i); S/RES/2136 of 30 Jan. 2014 para. 4(i); S/RES/2293 of 23 Jun. 2016 para. 7(i).
400. Article 2a(1)(k) Regulation on DRC. *See* S/RES/2641 of 30 Jun. 2022 para. 3.
401. Article 2a(1)(j) Regulation on DRC. *See* S/RES/2136 of 30 Jan. 2014 para. 4(j); S/RES/2293 of 23 Jun. 2016 para. 7(j).
402. Article 2a(1)(h) Regulation on DRC. *See* R/RES/1596 of 3 May 2005 para. 15; S/RES/2078 of 28 Nov. 2012 para. 4(h); S/RES/2136 of 30 Jan. 2014 para. 4(h); S/RES/2293 of 23 Jun. 2016 para. 7(h).
403. Article 1a(2) Regulation on DRC. *See* R/RES/1533 of 12 Mar. 2004 para. 8. Relevant material, its works and mandate can be retrieved here: https://www.un.org/securitycouncil/sanctions/1533/ (last visited: 31 Dec. 2023).
404. *See* in this regard Thomas Dörfler, *Why Rules Matter: Shaping Security Council Sanctions Policy in Counterterrorism and Beyond* 8(1) J.Glob.Secur.Stud. 1 at 15 (2023) https://doi.org/10.1093/jogss/ogac041.

person in the apposite annex[405] and thus, its designation shall come into effect throughout the EU.

86. At the same time, the Council, separately and independently from the aforementioned process, has been given the authority to impose financial sanctions on persons. The grounds that can support such a decision are very similar to the ones set by the UN Security Council. In detail, they include: obstructing a consensual and peaceful solution towards elections, including by undermining the rule of law;[406] planning, directing and committing acts that constitute serious human rights violations;[407] bearing responsibility for sustaining armed conflict, instability or insecurity, or supporting persons doing so;[408] inciting violence in connection with any of the aforementioned actions;[409] exploiting the armed conflict, instability and insecurity, including via illicit exploitation or trade of natural resources and wildlife;[410] and being associated with any person such as the ones described above.[411] To this end and once one of these grounds has been established, the Council performs the designation and amends the apposite annex accordingly.[412] Specifically with regard to the designation criterion of 'being associated with' a regime, the Courts of the EU compare the particular circumstances of each case before aligning with the approach of previously issued judgments; if they are not comparable to the case at hand, they refrain from adopting the conclusions reached.[413]

4 The Democratic People's Republic of Korea

87. Financial sanctions with regard to DPRK are directed at five groups of persons: (a) the persons designated by the sanctions committee;[414] (b) designated vessels;[415] (c) persons designated by the Council;[416] (d) persons associated with designated persons, in the sense of working on behalf of or at the direction of them and assisting them in the evasion of sanctions or violating the provisions of the Regulation on DPRK;[417] and (e) public entities and bodies of DPRK or of the Workers' Party of Korea, including persons acting on their behalf and bodies owned and controlled by them, as long as they are

405. Article 9(1) and Annex I Regulation on DRC.
406. Article 2b(1)(a) Regulation on DRC. On Art. 2b Regulation on DRC *see Évariste Boshab v. Council*, C-242/21 P, Judgment of 12 May 2022, digital ECR (available only in French) and *Évariste Boshab v. Council*, C-708/21 P, Judgment of 9 Feb. 2023, digital ECR (available only in French).
407. Article 2b(1)(b) Regulation on DRC.
408. Article 2b(1)(c) & (d) Regulation on DRC.
409. Article 2b(1)(e) Regulation on DRC.
410. Article 2b(1)(f) Regulation on DRC.
411. Article 2b(1)(g) Regulation on DRC.
412. Article 9(2) and Annex 1a Regulation on DRC.
413. *See*, i.e., *Johannes Tomana and Others v. Council and Commission*, T-190/12, Judgment of 22 Apr. 2015, digital ECR, paras 126-128 ('Tomana').
414. Article 34(4) and Annex XIII Regulation on DPRK.
415. Article 34(4) and Annex XIV Regulation on DPRK.
416. Article 34(4) and Annex XV Regulation on DPRK & Art. 27(1)(b) Decision on DPRK.
417. Annex 34(5) and Annex XVI Regulation on DPRK.

associated with activities prohibited by the UN Security Council, such as the nuclear and the ballistic missile programs, and do not fall in the aforestated categories.[418]

88. The Council in the exercise of its power to designate persons on its own initiative, that being the aforementioned third group, may proceed with listing when such a person is involved in DPRK's nuclear-related, ballistic missile-related or other weapons of mass destruction-related programs. Involvement has the form of having responsibility that includes support and promotion of such activities,[419] providing financial services or transfer of any financial or other assets or resources[420] and supplying items, materials, equipment, goods and technology.[421] Furthermore, the Council has the power to designate persons supplying arms and related materials of all types.[422] Persons eligible for designation do not have to directly perform these acts; they may equally perform them indirectly, in the sense of acting on behalf of or at the direction of the perpetrators or having ownership or control over the perpetrators.[423]

89. The Regulation on DPRK is silent on who or what the *sanctions committee* is. Nonetheless, there can only be little doubt that this is the committee established by the UN Security Council on 14 October 2006[424] (the '1718 DPRK Sanctions Committee') for two reasons. On the one hand, such a definition is stated explicitly in the accompanying Council decision;[425] on the other hand, the Regulation on DPRK transfers this resolution, alongside others subsequently adopted, into EU law.[426]

90. The process of listing a person, either following the designation of the 1718 DPRK Sanctions Committee[427] or due to a decision of the Council,[428] is similar to the one already explained (*see* in this respect paragraph 84 above) both as to communicating this fact to the interested person[429] and as to submitting observations and presenting substantial new evidence.[430]

5 Somalia

91. Restrictive measures due to the situation in Somalia are levelled at persons threatening the peace, security or stability of Somalia,[431] violating the arms embargo or

418. Annex 34(6) and Annex XVII Regulation on DPRK.
419. Article 34(4)(a) Regulation on DPRK & Art. 27(1)(b)(i) Decision on DPRK.
420. Article 34(4)(b) Regulation on DPRK & Art. 27(1)(b)(ii) Decision on DPRK.
421. Article 34(4)(c) Regulation on DPRK & Art. 27(1)(b)(iii) Decision on DPRK.
422. *Ibid.*
423. Article 34(4)(a), (b) & (c) Regulation on PRK & Art. 27(1)(b)(i), (ii) & (iii) Decision on DPRK.
424. S/RES/1718 of 14 Oct. 2006. Relevant material, its works and mandate can be retrieved here: https://www.un.org/securitycouncil/sanctions/1718 (last visited:31 Dec. 2023).
425. Article 1(1)(b) Decision on DPRK.
426. Recital Nos 1 & 2 to the preamble of Regulation on DPRK.
427. Articles 47(1) & 34(4) *ibid.*
428. Articles 47(2) & 34(4) *ibid.*
429. Article 47(4) *ibid.*
430. Article 47(4) *ibid.*
431. Article 2(3)(a) Regulation on Somalia, which corresponds to para. 8(a) of the UN Security Council resolution 1844 of 20 Nov. 2008, para. 1(a) of UN Security Council resolution 2002 of

the prohibited related assistance,[432] obstructing the delivery and distribution of or access to humanitarian assistance,[433] recruiting or using children in armed conflicts in Somalia, as long as they are political or military leaders,[434] and being responsible for violations of International Law involving the targeting of civilians in armed conflict.[435] These persons are designated by the sanctions committee[436] (the '751 Somalia Sanctions Committee').[437]

92. The process of listing a person following the designation of the 751 Somalia Sanctions Committee by the Council is similar to the one already explained (*see* in this respect paragraph 84 above) both as to communicating this fact to the interested person[438] and as to submitting observations and presenting substantial new evidence.[439]

6 *Iran*

93. Financial sanctions related to Iran are imposed by the sanctions committee established by the UN Security Council as well as by the Council of the EU. Within the frame of these restrictive measures, the CJEU has reached the conclusion that the restrictive measures adopted are progressive and justified by the lack of success of the measures adopted previously. Therefore, the designation criteria evolving over time have been extended.[440]

94. The UN Security Council or the *sanctions committee*[441] (the '1737 Iran Sanctions Committee') designates persons under resolutions 1737, 1803 and 1929.[442,443] In truth,

29 Jul. 2011, paras 1 and 3 of UN Security Council resolution 2060 of 25 Jul. 2012, para. 43 (a) of UN Security Council resolution 2093 of 6 Mar. 2013 and paras 42 and 43 of UN Security Council resolution 2385 of 14 Nov. 2017.

432. Article 2(3)(b) Regulation on Somalia, which corresponds to para. 8(b) of the UN Security Council resolution 1844 of 20 Nov. 2008, para. 1(b) of UN Security Council resolution 2002 of 29 Jul. 2011 and para. 43(b) of UN Security Council resolution 2093 of 6 Mar. 2013.
433. Article 2(3)(c) Regulation on Somalia, which corresponds to para. 8(c) of the UN Security Council resolution 1844 of 20 Nov. 2008 and para. 43(c) of UN Security Council resolution 2093 of 6 Mar. 2013.
434. Article 2(3)(d) Regulation on Somalia and para. 43(d) of UN Security Council resolution 2093 of 6 Mar. 2013.
435. Article 2(3)(e) Regulation on Somalia and para. 43(e) of UN Security Council resolution 2093 of 6 Mar. 2013.
436. According to Art. 1(e) Regulation on Somalia *sanctions committee* means 'the Committee of the Security Council established pursuant to UNSCR 751 (1992) concerning Somalia'. Relevant materials, its works and mandate can be retrieved here: https://www.un.org/securitycouncil/sanctions/751 (last visited: 31 Dec. 2023).
437. Article 2(3) Regulation on Somalia.
438. Article 12(1) Regulation on Somalia.
439. Article 12(2) Regulation on Somalia.
440. *Sharif University of Technology v. Council*, Case T-385/16 P, Order of 4 Apr. 2017, digital ECR, para. 56 ('Sharif 2017'), citing *Kala Naft* (n. 33) para. 126.
441. According to Art. 1(q) *sanctions committee* means 'the Committee of the United Nations Security Council which was established pursuant to paragraph 18 of United Nations Security Council Resolution ("UNSCR") 1737 (2006)'.
442. *See* S/RES/1737 of 23 Dec. 2006, S/RES/1803 of 3 Mar. 2008 and S/RES/1929 of 9 Jun. 2010.

this provision has fallen into utter desuetude as the UN Security Council decided to repeal the resolutions imposing sanctions, including providing for the establishment and maintenance of the 1737 Iran Sanctions Committee, on the implementation day of the JCPOA, that being 16 January 2016.[444]

95. At the same time, the Council has the power to impose financial sanctions on its own initiative on the grounds of certain persons' actions as well as on the grounds of certain persons' mere existence, as explained below. The persons eligible for listing due to their activities include three cases, as explained below. At the outset it should be noted that the adoption of restrictive measures against an entity does not presuppose that that entity has actually previously acted reprehensibly; the mere risk that the entity concerned may do so in the future is sufficient.[445] The first one includes engagement in Iran's proliferation-sensitive nuclear activities conducted contrary to the state's commitments in the JCPOA or the development of nuclear weapon delivery systems including the procurement of prohibited items, goods, equipment, materials and technology. Oddly this prohibition is enacted in two separate provisions[446] and merely the latter specifies the prohibited items, goods, equipment, materials and technology.[447] Nonetheless, the CJEU has specified that the expression 'nuclear proliferation' refers to activities infringing the Treaty on the Non-Proliferation of Nuclear Weapons[448] and thus to a category of military armaments.[449] Supporting the Government of Iran in respect of research and technology development in military or military-related fields satisfies the criterion discussed here where it relates to equipment or technology on the EU Common Military List, the procurement of which by the Islamic Republic of Iran is prohibited[450] (*see* in this regard paragraphs 272 et seq. below). Moreover, support of the government of Iran needs to possess certain quantitative or qualitative significance in order to satisfy the criterion at issue, as the judicature decided in response to arguments challenging the validity of this criterion on the ground that an Iranian taxpayer or official would be liable to be included on such a list in accordance with that criterion.[451]

96. The second case consists of assisting the evasion of and acting inconsistently with the Regulation on Iran and the Decision on Iran. Similar to the aforementioned and

443. Article 23(1) and Annex VIII Regulation on Iran.
444. Paragraph 7(a) S/RES/2231 of 20 Jul. 2015. *See also* U.S. Department of the Treasury, JCPOA Implementation, 16 Jan. 2016, available: https://home.treasury.gov/policy-issues/financial-sanctions/recent-actions/20160116 (last visited:31 Dec. 2023).
445. *Kala Naft* (n. 33) para. 84.
446. Article 23(2)(a) & Annex IX and Art. 23a(2)(a) & Annex XIII Regulation on Iran.
447. According to Art. 23a(a) specifies, in an unfortunate manner, these prohibited goods, as 'Annexes' to the Regulation on Iran, Decision 2010/413 and resolution 2231 of 20 Jul. 2015. It is unfortunate, as the Regulation on Iran has a number of annexes that deal with a number of issues and this in-clarity does not serve the prohibition.
448. Treaty on the Non-Proliferation of Nuclear Weapons (London, Moscow and Washington 1968) 729 UNTS 161.
449. *Sharif* 2017 (n. 440) para. 62.
450. *Sharif University of Technology v. Council*, T-52/15, Judgment of 28 Apr. 2016, digital ECR, para. 65 ('Sharif 2016'), confirmed by *Sharif* 2017 (n. 440) para. 63.
451. *Sharif* 2017 (n. 440) para. 64, citing *National Iranian 2016* (n. 33) paras 68 & 83.

equally strangely, this prohibition is enshrined in two separate provisions,[452] that nonetheless differentiate as they prohibit the violation of further legislative materials. Whereas, the latter mentions the JCPOA and the UN Security Council resolution 2231 as well as the Regulation on Iran and the Decision on Iran, the first one, unrealistically, prohibits the violation of resolutions 1737, 1747, 1803 and 1929 of the UN Security Council which have been repealed, as already explained above. Evidently, acting on behalf of designated persons, as well as being owned or controlled by designated persons is prohibited and results in the designation of anyone doing so.[453] The notion of 'owned or controlled' is not to be understood as under company law; rather the notion of 'control' is fairly broadly defined within the frame of restrictive measures ruled the Court of the EU.[454] Furthermore, the Court of the EU noted that acting under the control of a person and acting on behalf of a person should be equivalated.[455]

97. The third set of activities enclosures the provision of support, such as material,[456] logistical[457] and financial support,[458] to the Government of Iran, including entities controlled by that government and persons associated with the same.[459] The CJEU clarified that *support* implies a lesser degree of connection to the activities at hand than 'engagement' or 'direct association',[460] whereas *logistical support* is not limited to the activities of transporting goods or people but encompasses activities essentially relating to the methods and means of organization of an operation or process and to the making available of resources necessary for an activity or process to take place.[461] The criterion of *support to the government of Iran* has been added for the purpose of targeting a person's own activities that, even if they have no actual direct or indirect connection with nuclear proliferation, are nonetheless capable of encouraging it by providing this government with resources and facilities which allow it to pursue nuclear proliferation activities.[462] According to the CJEU and with regard to this particular designation ground, the Council carries out an assessment of the particulars of each specific case and determines which entities may be classified as entities 'owned or controlled'. This ground is independent of the one mentioned immediately above and does not have to

452. Articles 23(2)(b) and 23a(2)(b) Regulation on Iran.
453. Articles 23(2)(a) and 23a(2)(c) & (d) Regulation on Iran.
454. *Naser Bateni v. Council*, T-455/17, Judgment of 7 Jul. 2021, digital ECR, para. 123.
455. *Ibid.*, para. 94.
456. On material support *see, inter alia, Central Bank of Iran v. Council*, C-266/15 P, Judgment of 7 Apr. 2016, digital ECR, para. 45 ('Central Bank of Iran 2016').
457. On logistical support *see, inter alia, Iranian Offshore Engineering & Construction v. Council*, C-459/15 P, Judgment of 8 Sep. 2016, digital ECR, paras 53-56.
458. On financial support *see, inter alia, National Iranian Oil Company v. Council*, C-440/14 P, Judgment of 1 Mar. 2016, digital ECR, para. 85.
459. Article 23(2)(d) Regulation on Iran. *See Central Bank of Iran* 2016 (n. 456) para. 43, citing *National Iranian Oil Company v. Council*, T-578/12, Judgment of 16 Jul. 2014, para. 79 ('National Iranian 2014').
460. *Kala Naft* (n. 33) para. 80.
461. *National Iranian Tanker* (n. 157) para. 70.
462. *Central Bank of Iran 2016* (n. 456) para. 44, citing *National Iranian 2014* (n. 459) paras 80 & 81. *See also Sharif 2017* (n. 440) para. 59.

include the fact that the entity itself directly provides support to that government.[463] Specifically where the capital of an entity is entirely owned by an entity providing support to the government of Iran the designation criterion is satisfied.[464] However, where the capital of an entity is owned only by 60%, the same criterion is not satisfied per se.[465] On the issue of whether a parent company is able to exercise decisive influence over the conduct of a subsidiary, the CJEU has chosen to be guided by competition law-related jurisprudence.[466] Neither the existence of intermediary companies nor their number has any effect on the ability of a parent company to have a significant influence on the conduct of its subsidiary where the capital of the subsidiary and that of each of the intermediary companies is entirely owned by that parent company.[467]

98. The second group of persons is eligible for designation by the Council without conducting any specific activity; their existence suffices. Under this group, the persons eligible are: (a) members of the Islamic Revolutionary Guard Corps; and (b) a person owned or controlled by the Islamic Republic of Iran Shipping Lines ('IRISL'). As with the previous group, acting on behalf of those as well as being an entity owned or controlled by the same qualifies as a criterion for listing. Furthermore, persons providing insurance or other essential services to the same equally qualify for listing.[468]

99. The process of listing a person, either following the designation of the 1737 Iran Sanctions Committee,[469] a rather *mortuus* possibility as already explained, or due to a decision of the Council,[470] is similar to the one already explained (*see* in this respect paragraph 84 above) both as to communicating this fact to the interested person[471] and as to submitting observations and presenting substantial new evidence.[472]

7 Guinea-Bissau

100. Financial sanctions with regard to Guinea-Bissau are imposed on persons who have been identified as engaging in or supporting acts that threaten the peace, security

463. *Petropars Iran Co. et al v. Council*, T-433/12, Judgment of 5 May 2015, digital ECR, para. 63 ('Petropars Iran'), citing *Melli Bank v. Council*, C-380/09 P, Judgment of 13 Mar. 2012, digital ECR, paras 40 to 42 ('Melli Bank 2012').
464. *Petropars Iran* (n. 463) para. 64, citing *Melli Bank 2012* (n. 463) para. 79. *See also Melli Bank 2012* (n. 463) para. 56.
465. *Petropars Iran* (n. 463) para. 81, citing *Persia International Bank v. Council*, T-493/10, Judgment of 6 Sep. 2013, digital ECR, para. 106.
466. *Petropars Iran* (n. 463) para. 72, citing *Arkema v. Commission*, T-168/05, Judgment of 30 Sep. 2009, digital ECR, para. 71.
467. *Petropars Iran* (n. 463) para. 75.
468. Article 23(2)(c) & (e) Regulation on Iran.
469. Article 46(1) Regulation on Iran.
470. Articles 23(2) & (3), 46(2) & (3) and Annex IX and Arts 23a(2) & (3), 46(3) and Annex XIV Regulation on Iran.
471. Article 46(4) Regulation on Iran.
472. Article 46(5) Regulation on Iran.

or stability of the Republic of Guinea-Bissau or are associated with those.[473] They are the exception to the rule that UN sanctions in Africa are typically motivated by peace and security concerns. The Guinea-Bissau sanctions episode addresses exclusively an unconstitutional change in government.[474]

101. The designation takes place by the Council,[475] which alongside implementing the decisions of the sanctions committee[476] (the '2048 Guinea-Bissau Sanctions Committee')[477] proceeds with identifying such persons on its own initiative. The relevant process is similar to the one already explained (*see* in this respect paragraph 84 above) both as to communicating this fact to the interested person[478] and as to submitting observations and presenting substantial new evidence.[479]

8 Libya

102. Financial sanctions in relation to Libya are targeting persons predominantly in view of their actions and in some instances due to their possessions. The actions that can lead to listing are involvement in the former regime, violation of human rights, threatening peace, stability and security in Libya and owning or controlling misappropriated funds. More specifically, involvement with the former regime is understood as involvement in its repressive policies or otherwise associated with it and at the same time posing a continued risk to the peace, stability or security of Libya or to the successful completion of the Libyan political transition.[480] Committing serious abuse of human rights includes being involved or complicit in planning, commanding, ordering or conducting attacks, including aerial bombardments in violation of International Law on civilian populations or facilities.[481] Threatening the peace, stability or security in Libya and obstructing or undermining the successful completion of the Libyan political transition may include the following: (a) planning, directing, or committing acts in Libya that violate applicable international human rights law or international humanitarian law, or acts that constitute human rights abuses, in Libya;[482] (b) attacks against

473. Article 2(1) Regulation on Guinea-Bissau & Art. 2 Decision on Guinea-Bissau.
474. Andrea Charron & Clara Portela, *The UN, Regional Sanctions and Africa* 91(6) Int'l Aff. (UK) 1369 at 1372 (2015) https://doi.org/10.1111/1468-2346.12452.
475. Article 2(1) & Annex III Regulation on Guinea-Bissau.
476. The Regulation on Guinea-Bissau makes no mention of a sanctions committee. However, Decision 2012/285 both defines, at Art. 1(1)(a), and uses this term. Relevant materials, its works and mandate can be retrieved here: https://www.un.org/securitycouncil/sanctions/2048 (last visited:31 Dec. 2023).
477. *See* Annex III Decision 2012/285, where under 'identifying information' it states both the date of the UN designation and the relevant paragraph of the apposite resolution of the UN Security Council for some of the listed persons.
478. Article 11(2) Regulation on Guinea-Bissau.
479. Article 11(3) Regulation on Guinea-Bissau.
480. Article 6(2)(c) Regulation on Libya.
481. Article 6(2)(a) Regulation on Libya, which corresponds to para. 22(a) resolution 1970 of 26 Feb. 2011.
482. Article 6(2)(d)(i) Regulation on Libya, which corresponds to para. 4(a) resolution 2174 of 27 Aug. 2014 and para. 11(a) resolution 2213 of 27 Mar. 2015.

any air, land or sea port in Libya, or against a Libyan state institution or installation, or against any foreign mission in Libya;[483] (c) providing support for armed groups or criminal networks through the illicit exploitation of crude oil or any other natural resources in Libya;[484] (d) threatening or coercing Libyan State financial institutions and the Libyan National Oil Company, or engaging in any action that may lead to or result in the misappropriation of Libyan State funds;[485] (e) violating, or assisting in the evasion of, the provisions of the arms embargo in Libya;[486] (f) obstructing or undermining the elections planned for in the Libyan Political Dialogue Forum roadmap;[487,488] and (g) acting for or on behalf or at the direction of any of the above, or being entities or bodies owned or controlled by them or by listed persons.[489] Finally, owning or controlling Libyan State funds misappropriated during the former regime of Muammar Qadhafi in Libya which could be used to threaten the peace, stability or security of Libya or to obstruct or undermine the successful completion of its political transition leads to designation by the Council of the EU.[490] It is here noted that should a designated person have a stake in a non-designated person, the latter continues to conduct legitimate business, as long as it does not make available any funds and economic resources to the designated person.[491]

103. The designations take place either at the level of the UN Security Council by the sanctions committee[492] (the '1970 Libya Sanctions Committee') or at the level of the EU by the Council. Mainly, they apply the same criteria but the EU went further and extended them in order to include more persons and entities.[493]

483. Article 6(2)(d)(ii) Regulation on Libya, which corresponds to para. 4(b) resolution 2174 of 27 Aug. 2014 and para. 11(b) resolution 2213 of 27 Mar. 2015.
484. Article 6(2)(d)(iii) Regulation on Libya, which corresponds to para. 4(c) resolution 2174 of 27 Aug. 2014 and para. 11(c) resolution 2213 of 27 Mar. 2015.
485. Article 6(2)(d)(iv) Regulation on Libya, which corresponds to para. 11(d) resolution 2213 of 27 Mar. 2015.
486. Article 6(2)(d)(v) Regulation on Libya, which corresponds to para. 11(e) resolution 2213 of 27 Mar. 2015.
487. On the Libyan Political Dialogues Forum, which is based on the UN Security Council resolution 2510 of 11 Feb. 2020 visit: https://unsmil.unmissions.org/libyan-political-dialogue-forum (last visited: 31 Dec. 2023).
488. Article 6(2)(d)(vi) Regulation on Libya, which corresponds to para. 11 resolution 2571 of 16 Apr. 2021.
489. Article 6(2)(d)(vii) Regulation on Libya, which corresponds to para. 22(d) resolution 1970 of 26 Feb. 2011 and para. 11(f) resolution 2213 of 27 Mar. 2015.
490. Article 6(2)(e) Regulation on Libya. This does not constitute a designation criterion under the resolutions of the UN Security Council. However, the UN Security Council supports the efforts of the Libyan authorities to recover funds misappropriated by the Qadhafi regime and encourages the Libyan authorities and Member States that have frozen funds to consult each other regarding claims of misappropriated funds and related issues of ownership (para. 23 resolution 2213 of 27 Mar. 2015).
491. Article 7 Regulation on Libya.
492. According to Art. 1(f) Regulation on Libya. *sanctions committee* means 'the Committee of the United Nations Security Council which was established pursuant to paragraph 24 of UNSCR 1970 (2011)'. Relevant materials, its works and mandate can be retrieved here: https://www.un.org/securitycouncil/sanctions/1970 (last visited: 31 Dec. 2023).
493. Recital No. 9 to the preamble of Decision 2015/818.

104. The process of listing a person, either following the designation of the 1970 Libya Sanctions Committee[494] or due to a decision of the Council,[495] is similar to the one already explained, (*see* in this respect paragraph 84 above) both as to communicating this fact to the interested person[496] and as to submitting observations and presenting substantial new evidence.[497]

9 The Central African Republic

105. Financial restrictive measures in view of the situation in the CAR are aimed at persons identified by the sanctions committee[498] (the '2127 CAR Sanctions Committee') as persons threatening the peace, stability and security of CAR. Such are persons: (a) engaging in or providing support for acts that undermine the peace, stability or security of the CAR, including acts that threaten or impede the stabilization and reconciliation process or that fuel violence;[499] (b) acting in violation of the arms embargo[500] or having directly or indirectly supplied, sold, or transferred to armed groups or criminal networks in the CAR, or as having been the recipient of arms or any related materiel, or any technical advice, training, or assistance, including financing and financial assistance, related to violent activities of armed groups or criminal networks in the CAR;[501] (c) involved in planning, directing, or committing acts in the CAR that violate international human rights law or international humanitarian law, as applicable, or that constitute human rights abuses or violations, including those involving targeting of civilians, ethnic- or religious-based attacks, attacks on civilian objects, including administrative centres, courthouses, schools and hospitals, and abduction and forced displacement;[502] (d) being involved in planning, directing, or committing acts involving sexual and gender-based violence;[503] (e) recruiting or using children in armed conflict in the CAR, in violation of applicable international law;[504] (f)

494. Articles 6(1), 21(1) and Annex II Regulation on Libya.
495. Articles 6(2), 21(2) and Annex III Regulation on Libya.
496. Article 21(3) Regulation on Libya.
497. Article 21(4) Regulation on Libya.
498. According to Art. 1(i) Regulation on CAR *sanctions committee* means 'the Committee of the United Nations Security Council which was established pursuant to paragraph 57 of United Nations Security Council Resolution UNSCR 2127 (2013)'. Relevant materials, its works and mandate can be retrieved here: https://www.un.org/securitycouncil/sanctions/2127 (last visited: 31 Dec. 2023).
499. Article 5(3)(a) Regulation on CAR, which corresponds to para. 20 of resolution 2399 of 30 Jan. 2018.
500. This was established via para. 54 of resolution 2127 of 5 Dec. 2013.
501. Article 5(3)(b) Regulation on CAR, which corresponds to para. 21(a) of resolution 2399 of 30 Jan. 2018.
502. Article 5(3)(c) Regulation on CAR, which corresponds to para. 21(b) of resolution 2399 of 30 Jan. 2018.
503. Article 5(3)(d) Regulation on CAR, which corresponds to para. 21(c) of resolution 2399 of 30 Jan. 2018.
504. Article 5(3)(e) Regulation on CAR, which corresponds to para. 21(d) of resolution 2399 of 30 Jan. 2018.

providing support for armed groups or criminal networks through the illicit exploitation or trade of natural resources, including diamonds, gold and wildlife, as well as wildlife products, in or from the CAR;[505] (g) obstructing the delivery of humanitarian assistance to the CAR, or access to, or distribution of, humanitarian assistance in the CAR;[506] (h) involved in planning, directing, sponsoring, or conducting attacks against UN missions, international security presences and humanitarian personnel;[507] (i) are leaders of, or have provided support to, or acted for or on behalf of, or at the direction of, an entity that the Committee has designated;[508] (j) committing acts of incitement to violence, in particular on an ethnic or religious basis, that undermine the peace, stability or security of the CAR, and then engaging in or providing support for acts that undermine the peace, stability or security of the CAR;[509] and (k) involved in planning, directing, sponsoring or committing acts in the CAR that violate international humanitarian law, including attacks against medical personnel or humanitarian personnel.[510]

106. The process of listing a person following the designation of the 2127 CAR Sanctions Committee is performed by the Council and is similar to the one already explained, (*see* in this respect paragraph 84 above) both as to communicating this fact to the interested person[511] and as to submitting observations and presenting substantial new evidence.[512]

10 Yemen

107. Monetary restrictive measures in view of the situation in Yemen may be imposed on persons designated by the sanctions committee[513] (the '2140 Yemen Sanctions Committee') for being engaged in or providing support for acts that threaten the peace, security or stability of Yemen. More specifically these constitute of: undermining the successful completion of the political transition;[514] acting violently or attacking on essential infrastructure and therefore impeding the implementation of outcomes of the

505. Article 5(3)(f) Regulation on CAR, which corresponds to para. 21(e) of resolution 2399 of 30 Jan. 2018.
506. Article 5(3)(g) Regulation on CAR, which corresponds to para. 21(f) of resolution 2399 of 30 Jan. 2018.
507. Article 5(3)(h) Regulation on CAR, which corresponds to para. 21(g) of resolution 2399 of 30 Jan. 2018.
508. Article 5(3)(i) Regulation on CAR, which corresponds to para. 21(h) of resolution 2399 of 30 Jan. 2018.
509. Article 5(3)(i) Regulation on CAR, which corresponds to para. 22 of resolution 2399 of 30 Jan. 2018.
510. Article 5(3)(k) Regulation on CAR, which corresponds to para. 5 of resolution 2588 of 29 Jul. 2021.
511. Article 17(1) Regulation on CAR.
512. Article 17(2) Regulation on CAR.
513. According to Art. 1(h) Regulation on Yemen, *sanctions committee* stands for 'the Committee of the United Nations Security Council established pursuant to paragraph 19 of UNSCR 2140 (2014)'. Relevant materials, its works and mandate can be retrieved here: https://www.un.org/securitycouncil/sanctions/2140 (last visited: 31 Dec. 2023).
514. Article 3(1)(a) Regulation on Yemen, which corresponds to paras 17 & 18(a) of resolution 2140 of 26 Feb. 2014.

final report of the Comprehensive National Dialogue;[515] acting in violation of international human rights law or international humanitarian law or performing acts that constitute human rights abuses in Yemen, including sexual violence in armed conflict, or the recruitment or use of children in armed conflict in violation of International Law;[516] and acts violating the imposed arms embargo or obstructing the delivery of humanitarian assistance Yemen or access to and distribution of same within Yemen.[517]

108. The process of listing a person following the designation of the 2140 Yemen Sanctions Committee is performed by the Council and is similar to the one already explained, (*see* in this respect paragraph 84 above) both as to communicating this fact to the interested person[518] and as to submitting observations and presenting substantial new evidence.[519]

11 South Sudan

109. Financial sanctions with regard to South Sudan are addressed to persons responsible for or complicit in, or having engaged in, directly or indirectly, actions or policies that threaten the peace, security or stability of South Sudan. They shall be designated either initially by the sanctions committee[520] (the '2206 South Sudan Sanctions Committee')[521] or by the Council of the EU.[522] The latter may exercise its designation power while applying as listing criteria: (a) obstruction of the political process in South Sudan; (b) including by acts of violence or violations of ceasefire agreements; as well as (c) responsibility for serious violations of human rights in South Sudan; and (d) association with persons conducting such acts.[523] The listing criteria that the 2206 South Sudan Sanctions Committee is authorized to apply, are much more specific and, apart from threatening the peace, security and stability of South Sudan,[524] relate to the extending the conflict or obstructing reconciliation and peace talks,[525] threatening transition agreements and undermining the political process,[526] violating international human rights law or international humanitarian law or abusing human rights in South

515. Article 3(1)(b) Regulation on Yemen, which corresponds to para. 18(b) of resolution 2140 of 26 Feb. 2014.
516. Article 3(1)(c) Regulation on Yemen, which corresponds to para. 18(c) of resolution 2140 of 26 Feb. 2014 and para. 6 of resolution 2511 of 25 Feb. 2020.
517. Article 3(1)(d) Regulation on Yemen, which corresponds to para. 19 of resolution 2216 of 14 Apr. 2015.
518. Article 15(1) and Annex I Regulation on Yemen.
519. Article 15(2) Regulation on Yemen.
520. In Art. 5(1) Regulation on South Sudan, it is noted that *sanctions committee* denotes the committee established by para. 16 of the UN Security Council resolution 2206 of 3 Mar. 2015. Relevant materials, its works and mandate can be retrieved here: https://www.un.org/securitycouncil/sanctions/2206 (last visited: 31 Dec. 2023).
521. Article 5(1) and Annex I Regulation on South Sudan.
522. Article 5(2) and Annex II Regulation on South Sudan.
523. Article 5(2) Regulation on South Sudan and Art. 6(1)(b) Decision 2015/740.
524. Paragraph 14 of resolution 2521 of 29 May 2020.
525. Paragraph 15(a) of resolution 2521 of 29 May 2020.
526. Paragraph 15(b) of resolution 2521 of 29 May 2020.

Sudan,[527] targeting civilians,[528] planning, directing, or committing acts involving sexual and gender-based violence,[529] using or recruiting children by armed groups or armed forces in the context of the armed conflict,[530] obstructing the activities of international peacekeeping, diplomatic, or humanitarian missions,[531] attacking UN missions, international security presences and other peacekeeping operations and humanitarian personnel,[532] armed groups or criminal networks engaging in activities that destabilize South Sudan through illicit exploitation or trade of natural resources[533] and engaging in actions and policies having the purpose or effect of expanding or extending the conflict in South Sudan.[534]

110. The process of listing a person following the designation of the 2206 South Sudan Sanctions Committee is performed by the Council and is similar to the one already explained, (*see* in this respect paragraph 84 above) both as to communicating this fact to the interested person[535] and as to submitting observations and presenting substantial new evidence.[536] So is the listing on the initiative of the Council of the EU.[537]

12 Mali

111. Financial sanctions in relation to Mali target persons responsible for threatening the peace, security or stability in this country. The designation is performed by the sanctions committee[538] (the '2374 Mali Sanctions Committee')[539] as well as by the Council of the EU.[540] The 2374 Mali Sanctions Committee, according to EU law, has the power to designate persons engaging in hostilities in violation of the Agreement on Peace and Reconciliation in Mali,[541] obstructing and threatening the implementation of said agreement,[542] supporting and acting for and on behalf of said persons, including

527. Paragraph 15(c) of resolution 2521 of 29 May 2020.
528. Paragraph 15(d) of resolution 2521 of 29 May 2020.
529. Paragraph 15(e) of resolution 2521 of 29 May 2020.
530. Paragraph 15(f) of resolution 2521 of 29 May 2020.
531. Paragraph 15(g) of resolution 2521 of 29 May 2020.
532. Paragraph 15(h) of resolution 2521 of 29 May 2020.
533. Paragraph 15(j) of resolution 2521 of 29 May 2020.
534. Paragraph 16 of resolution 2521 of 29 May 2020 and para. 15 of resolution 2577 of 28 May 2021.
535. Articles 5(1) & 20(1) and Annex I Regulation on South Sudan.
536. Article 20(2) Regulation on South Sudan.
537. Articles 5(2) & 22(1) and Annex II and Art. 22(2) Regulation on South Sudan respectively.
538. According to Art. 1 Regulation on Mali the *sanctions committee* is 'the Committee of the Security Council established pursuant to paragraph 9 of United Nations Security Council Resolution UNSCR 2374 (2017)'. Still, its mandate expired on 31 Aug. 2023; *see* n. 549 below as well as https://main.un.org/securitycouncil/en/sanctions/terminated-sanctions (last visited: 31 Dec. 2023).
539. Article 2a and Annex I Regulation on Mali.
540. Article 2b and Annex Ia Regulation on Mali.
541. Article 2a(1)(a) Regulation on Mali, which corresponds to para. 8(a) resolution 2374 of 5 Sep. 2017.
542. Article 2a(1)(b) Regulation on Mali, which corresponds to para. 8(b) resolution 2374 of 5 Sep. 2017.

trafficking, smuggling and proceeds from organized crime,[543] are involved in attacks,[544] obstruct the delivery and distribution of humanitarian assistance,[545] violate international human rights law or international humanitarian law or abuse human rights,[546] are armed groups or armed forces using and recruiting children[547] and knowingly facilitate the travel of a listed person in violation of the travel restrictions.[548] The restrictive measures at the UN level failed to be renewed in summer 2023 due to Russia vetoing the adoption of the draft resolution.[549] The Council of the EU in its turn has the power to designate persons who are responsible for actions and policies threatening the peace, security and stability of Mali, obstruct and undermine the successful completion of the political transition and persons associated with them.[550]

112. The process of listing a person following the designation of the 2374 Mali Sanctions Committee is performed by the Council and is similar to the one already explained, (*see* in this respect paragraph 84 above) both as to communicating this fact to the interested person[551] and as to submitting observations and presenting substantial new evidence.[552] So is the listing on the initiative of the Council of the EU.[553]

13 Haiti

113. Financial sanctions in relation to Haiti target persons responsible for threatening the peace, security or stability in this country or having engaged in such actions.[554] Indicatively, such actions consist of: engaging in or supporting criminal activities and violence by armed groups and criminal networks;[555] supporting illicit trafficking and diversion of arms and related materiel including financial flows related thereto;[556]

543. Article 2a(1)(c) Regulation on Mali, which corresponds to para. 8(c) resolution 2374 of 5 Sep. 2017.
544. Article 2a(1)(d)(i), (ii) & (iii) Regulation on Mali, which corresponds to para. 8(d)(i), (ii) & (iii) resolution 2374 of 5 Sep. 2017.
545. Article 2a(1)(e) Regulation on Mali, which corresponds to para. 8(e) resolution 2374 of 5 Sep. 2017.
546. Article 2a(1)(f) Regulation on Mali, which corresponds to para. 8(f) resolution 2374 of 5 Sep. 2017.
547. Article 2a(1)(g) Regulation on Mali, which corresponds to para. 8(g) resolution 2374 of 5 Sep. 2017.
548. Article 2a(1)(h) Regulation on Mali. Resolution 2371 does provide for travel ban, but does not set out explicitly the facilitation of travel in violation of the travel ban as a listing criterium.
549. *See* Michelle Nichols, *UN Sanctions in Mali to End after Russia Blocks Renewal*, Reuters 30 Aug. 2023, available: https://www.reuters.com/world/russia-seeks-end-uns-mali-sanctions-monitoring-2023-08-30/ (last visited: 31 Dec. 2023). The draft resolution put forward by France and the United Arab Emirates: S/2023/638 of 30 Aug. 2023.
550. Article 2b(1)(a), (b) & (c) and Annex Ia Regulation on Mali.
551. Article 12(1) & (3) Regulation on Mali.
552. Article 12(4) Regulation on Mali.
553. Article 12(2), (3) & (4) Regulation on Mali.
554. Article 4(1) Regulation on Haiti.
555. Article 4(1)(a) Regulation on Haiti, which corresponds to para. 16(a) resolution 2653 of 21 Oct. 2022.
556. Article 4(1)(b) Regulation on Haiti, which corresponds to para. 16(b) resolution 2653 of 21 Oct. 2022.

supporting or financing a person performing any of the aforementioned actions;[557] acting in violation of the arms embargo or supplying, selling or transferring arms and related materiel to armed groups and criminal networks in Haiti;[558] planning, directing and committing acts in violation of International Human rights law or acts constituting human rights abuses;[559] planning, directing and committing acts involving sexual and gender-based violence in Haiti;[560] obstructing delivery of humanitarian assistance or access to and distribution of same;[561] and attacking personnel and premises of UN missions and operations.[562] The designation is performed by the sanctions committee[563] (the '2653 Haiti Sanctions Committee') as well as by the Council of the EU. The latter has the power to designate persons on the same grounds as the UN Security Council[564] and furthermore for undermining democracy or the rule of law through serious financial misconduct concerning public funds or the unauthorized export of capital.[565] The Council has also the authority to designate anyone associated with persons falling under the two categories explained above.[566]

114. The process of listing a person following the designation of the 2653 Haiti Sanctions Committee is performed by the Council and is similar to the one already explained, (*see* in this respect paragraph 84 above) both as to communicating this fact to the interested person and as to submitting observations and presenting substantial new evidence.[567] So is the listing on the initiative of the Council of the EU.[568]

B *The Designations Performed by Institutions of the EU*

115. The Council (exceptionally the Commission)[569,570] impose financial sanctions for a number of reasons, that share the common element of serious human rights

557. Article 4(1)(c) Regulation on Haiti, which corresponds to para. 16(c) resolution 2653 of 21 Oct. 2022.
558. Article 4(1)(d) Regulation on Haiti, which corresponds to para. 16(d) resolution 2653 of 21 Oct. 2022.
559. Article 4(1)(e) Regulation on Haiti, which corresponds to para. 16(e) resolution 2653 of 21 Oct. 2022.
560. Article 4(1)(f) Regulation on Haiti, which corresponds to para. 16(f) resolution 2653 of 21 Oct. 2022.
561. Article 4(1)(g) Regulation on Haiti, which corresponds to para. 16(g) resolution 2653 of 21 Oct. 2022.
562. Article 4(1)(h) Regulation on Haiti, which corresponds to para. 16(h) resolution 2653 of 21 Oct. 2022.
563. According to Art. 1(h) Regulation on Haiti the *sanctions committee* is 'the Committee of the Security Council established pursuant to paragraph 19 of UNSCR 2653 (2022)'. Relevant materials, its works and mandate can be retrieved here: https://www.un.org/securitycouncil/sanctions/2653 (last visited: 31 Dec. 2023).
564. Article 4a(1)(a)(i) to (viii) and Annex Ia Regulation on Haiti.
565. Article 4a(1)(b) and Annex Ia Regulation on Haiti.
566. Article 4a(1)(c) and Annex Ia Regulation on Haiti.
567. Article 16(1), (1b), (2) & (3) and Annex I Regulation on Haiti.
568. Article 16(1a), (2) & (3) and Annex Ia Regulation on Haiti.
569. Article 11(b) Regulation on Zimbabwe.
570. *See also* Tibor Besedeš, Stefan Goldbach & Volker Nitsch, *Financial Sanctions* Econ. Policy 263 at 270 (2017).

violations or lack of respect for human rights. More specifically, the Council of the EU designates persons responsible for serious human rights violations in Iran and persons associated with them.[571] Serious human rights violations along with undermining democracy or the rule of law are the listing criteria in view of the situation in Zimbabwe,[572] Myanmar/Burma and Burundi.[573] Within the legal framework of the measures targeting Myanmar/Burma, the Court of the EU underlined that the inclusion of family members of leading business figures prevents the circumvention of sanctions through the transfer of assets among family members.[574] It is noted that the Regulation on Myanmar/Burma lacks any designation criterion with regard to family members or leading business figures. It merely mentions the criterion of association with other persons eligible for listing.[575]

116. Specifically with regard to Zimbabwe, the Courts of the EU ruled that the reference to persons undermining democracy, respect for human rights and the rule of law relates to the conduct of the persons who perpetrated acts; thus the Council was led to assert that the leaders of Zimbabwe were responsible for an *escalation of violence, intimidation of political opponents and the harassment of the independent press, serious infringements of human rights and of the freedom of opinion, of association and of peaceful assembly* in the country or again a *systematic campaign of violence, obstruction and intimidation led by the Zimbabwean authorities*.[576]

117. Undermining democracy or the rule of law constitutes the listing criteria with regard to Lebanon.[577] Said criteria alongside repression of civil society and democratic opposition constitute the listing criteria with regard to Venezuela[578] and Nicaragua.[579] Freedom of expression cannot cloak media interventions, where public and targeted threats against political opposition, media and civil society were made, with a pretence of legitimacy.[580] Freedom of expression can be and is limited when this is provided for by law, with the intention to achieve an objective of general interest, as long as it is not excessive.[581]

118. In a similar vein, violent repression against the civilian population in Syria, benefiting from and supporting the regime are the listing criteria with regard to Syria.[582] Said criteria of *benefiting from the regime* and *supporting the regime*, brilliantly

571. Article 3(1) & Annex I Regulation on Iran.
572. Article 11(b) & Annex III Regulation on Zimbabwe and Art 5(1) Decision 2011/101.
573. Article 4a(3) & Annex IV Regulation on Myanmar/Burma and Art. 2(3) & Annex I Regulation on Burundi & Art. 2(1) Decision 2015/1763.
574. *Pye Phyo Tay Za v. Council*, T-181/08, Judgment of 19 May 2010, digital ECR, para. 72.
575. Article 4a(3)(f) Regulation on Myanmar/Burma.
576. *Tomana* (n. 413) paras 95, 96, 99 & 102.
577. Article 2(3)(a) & (b) and Annex I EU Regulation on Lebanon.
578. Article 8(3) and Annexes IV & V Regulation on Venezuela.
579. Article 2(3)(a), (b) & (c) & Annex I Regulation on Nicaragua and Arts 1(1) & 2(1) Decision 2019/1720.
580. *Diosdado Cabello Rondón v. Council*, T-248/18, Judgment of 14 Jun. 2021, digital ECR, paras 109-113 ('Rondón').
581. *Ibid.*, paras 120-123, citing *Kiselev v. Council*, T–262/15, Judgment of 15 Jun. 2017, digital ECR, paras 69, 72, 84 & 87 ('Kiselev').
582. Articles 1(a) & (b), 21 & Annexes II & IIa Regulation on Syria and Art. 19(1) Decision 2011/782.

underscore - at least in theory - the essence of smart sanctions that aim to hurt benefited target regime sympathizers and not politically weak groups, in contradiction to broad-based comprehensive sanctions.[583] The CJEU observed that as the previously adopted measures failed to put an end to the Syrian regime's repression against the civilian population, the Council decided to include said criteria in the apposite acts alongside the criterium of being responsible for the oppression.[584] The goal pursued through these measures is applying pressure to supporters of the Syrian regime persecuting civilian populations.[585] Being a natural person belonging to the family of the head of the state targeted by the restrictive measures fulfils the criterion of *benefiting from and supporting the regime*.[586] In addition to those, eligible for listing are leading businesspersons operating in Syria, members of the Assad or Makhlouf families, Syrian Government Ministers in power after May 2011, members of the Syrian Armed Forces of the rank of 'colonel' or the equivalent or higher in post after May 2011, members of the Syrian security and intelligence services in post after May 2011, members of the regime-affiliated militias and persons operating in the chemical weapons proliferation sector, as well as persons associated with them.[587] The criterion of *leading businesspersons* is an objective, autonomous and sufficient listing criterion rendering it unnecessary to demonstrate that there is any association between this category of persons and the Syrian regime.[588] The same applies to the other six criteria.[589] Nonetheless, the link with the Syrian regime is a rebuttable presumption. The specific person concerned may rebut this presumption by putting forward arguments or evidence capable of seriously calling into question the reliability of the evidence submitted by the Council or the Council's assessment.[590] It is explicitly stated in the respective acts that leading businesspersons shall not be included or retained on the list, if there is sufficient information that they are not associated with the Assad regime, do not exercise influence over it or do not pose a real risk of circumvention.[591] This rule must be understood as reflecting the different ways in which a person might favour the Syrian regime currently in place, without those ways being regarded as mutually exclusive, the Court decided.[592] Moreover, misappropriation of state funds, both by persons conducting such acts and by persons associated with them, is the listing criterium with regard to Tunisia[593] and Ukraine.[594] Further, in the case of Ukraine, persons eligible for listing include persons subject to investigation by the local authorities for the misappropriation of state funds and assets and for abuse of office as

583. Daniel W. Drezner, *Sanctions Sometimes Smart: Targeted Sanctions in Theory and Practice* 13(1) Int. St. Rev. 96 at 99 (2011) https://doi.org/10.1111/j.1468-2486.2010.01001.x.
584. *Mayaleh* (n. 44) para. 135.
585. *Bouchra Al Assad v. Council*, T-202/12, Judgment of 12 Mar. 2014, digital ECR, para. 117 ('Al Assad').
586. *Ibid.*, para. 97.
587. Articles 15(1a)(a), (b), (c), (d), (e), (f) & (g) & 21 Regulation on Syria.
588. *Abdelkader Sabra v. Council*, T-249/20, Judgment of 16 Mar. 2022, digital ECR, para. 130.
589. *George Haswani v. Council*, C-241/19 P, Judgment of 9 Jul. 2020, digital ECR, para. 66.
590. *Sabra* (n. 588) paras 131 & 133.
591. Article 15(1b) Regulation on Syria.
592. *Khaled Kaddour v. Council*, T-510/18, Judgment of 23 Sep. 2020, digital ECR, para. 151.
593. Article 2(1) & Annex I Regulation on Tunisia and Arts 1(1) & 2(1) & Annex Decision 2011/72.
594. Article 3(1) & Annex I Funds Regulation on Ukraine and Art. 1 Decision 2014/119.

a public office-holder in order to procure an unjustified advantage for him- or herself or for a third party and thereby causing a loss to public funds or assets.[595] Finally, restrictive measures with regard to Guinea rest on a unique listing criterium, that of the persons identified by the *International Commission of Inquiry*[596] as responsible for the 28 September 2009 events in Guinea, and persons associated with them.[597] Equally unique is the criterion set out in the Regulation on Drilling. It consists of responsibility for drilling activities in relation to hydrocarbon exploration and production and hydrocarbon extraction that take place within the territorial sea of Cyprus, in its exclusive economic zone or on its continental shelf that has not been authorized by the government of Cyprus.[598] This criterion is accompanied by the criterion of providing financial, technical and material support for such activities as well as by the one of being associated with these persons.[599]

119. In contrast to the variability and complexity of the listing criteria, the process of making the designating decision,[600] communicating it to the designated person,[601] providing the option to submit observations and present substantial new evidence[602] and the duty to review the list with the designated persons[603] is uniform with some exceptions. First, the legal text imposing restrictive measures in relation to Zimbabwe is silent on the matters of communicating the decision to the person concerned, the option to submit observations and furnish substantial new evidence and the duty to

595. Article 3(1a) Funds Regulation on Ukraine.

596. The Secretary-General of the UN decided to establish an international commission of inquiry to investigate the events of 28 Sep. 2009 in order to ascertain the facts, to identify the perpetrators with a view to ensuring that those responsible are held accountable. *See* Statement by the President of the Security Council, S/PRST/2009/27 of 28 Oct. 2009. The international commission prepared a report entitled 'Report of the International Commission of Inquiry mandated to establish the facts and circumstances of the events of 28 September 2009 in Guinea'. This is attached as Annex to the letter of the Secretary-General addressed to the President of the Security Council. S/2009/693 of 18 Dec. 2009.

597. Article 6(3) & Annex II Regulation on Guinea and Art. 4(1) Decision 2010/638.

598. Article 2(3)(a) and Annex I Regulation on Drilling and Arts 1(1) & 2(1) Decision on Drilling.

599. Article 2(3)(b) & (c) and Annex I Regulation on Drilling and Arts 1(1) & 2(1) Decision on Drilling.

600. Article 11(b) Regulation on Zimbabwe, Art. 12(1) EU Regulation on Iran, Art. 4i(1) Regulation on Myanmar/Burma, Art. 13(1) EU Regulation on Lebanon, Art. 13(1) Regulation on Burundi, Art. 17(1) Regulation on Venezuela, Art. 13(1) Regulation on Nicaragua, Art. 15a(1) Regulation on Guinea, Art. 32(1) Regulation on Syria, Art. 12(1) Regulation on Tunisia, Art. 14(1) Funds Regulation on Ukraine, Art. 12(1) Regulation on Drilling.

601. Article 12(2) EU Regulation on Iran, Art. 4i(2) Regulation on Myanmar/Burma, Art. 13(2) EU Regulation on Lebanon, Art. 13(2) Regulation on Burundi, Art. 17(2) Regulation on Venezuela, Art. 13(2) Regulation on Nicaragua, Art. 15a(2) Regulation on Guinea, Art. 32(2) Regulation on Syria, Art. 12(2) Regulation on Tunisia, Art. 14(2) Funds Regulation on Ukraine, Art. 12(2) Regulation on Drilling.

602. Article 12(3) EU Regulation on Iran, Art. 4i(3) Regulation on Myanmar/Burma, Art. 13(3) EU Regulation on Lebanon, Art. 13(3) Regulation on Burundi, Art. 17(3) Regulation on Venezuela, Art. 13(3) Regulation on Nicaragua, Art. 15a(3) Regulation on Guinea, Art. 32(3) Regulation on Syria, Art. 12(3) Regulation on Tunisia, Art. 14(3) Funds Regulation on Ukraine, Art. 12(3) Regulation on Drilling.

603. Article 12(4) EU Regulation on Iran, Art. 4i(4) Regulation on Myanmar/Burma, Art. 13(4) EU Regulation on Lebanon, Art. 13(4) Regulation on Burundi, Art. 17(4) Regulation on Venezuela, Art. 15a(4) Regulation on Guinea, Art. 32(4) Regulation on Syria, Art. 12(4) Regulation on Tunisia, Art. 14(4) Funds Regulation on Ukraine, Art. 12(4) Regulation on Drilling.

review. Second, the Regulation on Nicaragua does not provide for a review of the list of designated persons. Then, the persons eligible for listing with regard to Syria due to their family ties, occupation and public service (*see* in this regard paragraph 118 above) have the additional right to present evidence and observations as to why their resignation is not justified despite falling into these categories.[604] In other words, particularly in this case, the burden of proof is reversed with the listed persons having to prove that they are not a threat to peace, security and stability and do not violate human rights.

120. On a final note regarding the deciding authority at the EU level, the Regulation on Tunisia stands out and provides some detail as to the decision process within the Council. According to the apposite provision, the Council *acting upon a proposal by a Member State or the High Representative of the Union for Foreign Affairs and Security Policy shall establish and amend the list in the Annex.*[605] This stands in stark contrast to the other legal provisions that make mention solely of the Council deciding. Nonetheless, this is of little value in practice and it is highly unlikely that this is of general application. In any event, EU institutions in carrying out their task under certain legal instruments, may process personal data, including data related to criminal offences committed, criminal convictions and security measures concerning such measures. In such cases, the Council, the High Representative and the national competent authorities are 'controllers' in the sense of the Regulation on the processing of personal data by EU institutions.[606,607]

III The Statutory Obligations

121. The paragraphs that follow, discuss the obligations that the EU statutes impose on persons dealing with funds and economic resources controlled or owned by persons designated in the manner analysed above.

A The Duty to Act and the Obligation to Refuse

122. The duty to act consists of freezing all funds and economic resources, a prohibition that has considerable consequences for it may restrict the exercise of the targets' fundamental rights,[608] that is paired with not making any funds and economic

604. Article 32(2) 2nd sentence Regulation on Syria.
605. Article 2(1) Regulation on Tunisia.
606. Regulation (EU) 2018/1725 of the European Parliament and of the Council of 23 Oct. 2018 on the protection of natural persons with regard to the processing of personal data by the Union institutions, bodies, offices and agencies and on the free movement of such data, and repealing Regulation (EC) No. 45/2001 and Decision No. 1247/2002/EC, OJ L 295, 21 Nov. 2018, p. 39.
607. Article 51 Regulation on Iraq, Art. 19a Regulation on CAR, Art. 13a Regulation on Mali, Art. 15a Regulation on Burundi, Art. 18a Regulation on Venezuela, Art. 16 Regulation on Nicaragua and Art. 16a Regulation on Guinea. The Regulation on Iraq refers to Regulation (EC) No. 45/2001 that in the meantime has been repealed by Regulation 2018/1725 (n. 606).
608. *Bank Melli* 2011 (n. 11) para. 49.

resources available, the obligation to refuse. Both the terms *freezing of funds*[609] and *freezing of economic resources*[610] (in regard to the definition *see* Annex I p. 307) are statutory and defined in a manner uniform throughout the EU legislation. Once such freezing of funds and economic resources has been done, it has to be notified to the competent national authorities and the Commission, along with any other information that could facilitate compliance with the regulations, without prejudice to the laws on reporting, confidentiality and professional secrecy and, with regard to the sanctions on Iraq and Zimbabwe, without prejudice to Article 284 of the Treaty.[611] This information may only be used for the purposes for which it was provided or received.[612] However, in particular, in relation to Libya and the misappropriation of state funds in Ukraine, the same information may be shared with the relevant authorities of Libya, as well as of other Member States, where necessary, for the purpose of recovering misappropriated assets.[613]

123. The notion *made available* lacks a statutory definition. Nonetheless, the CJEU, noted that it has a wide meaning; instead of denoting a specific legal category of act, it

609. Article 1(4) Regulation on Iraq, Art. 1(g) Regulation on Sudan, Art. 1(f) Regulation on DRC, Art. 2(11) Regulation on DPRK, Art. 1(b) Regulation on Somalia, Art. 1(k) Regulation on Iran, Art. 1(b) Regulation on Guinea-Bissau, Art. 1(b) Regulation on Libya, Art. 1(g) Regulation on CAR, Art. 1(f) Regulation on Yemen, Art. 1(g) Regulation on South Sudan, Art. 1(f) Regulation on Mali, Art. 1(c) Regulation on Zimbabwe, Art. 1(b) EU Regulation on Iran, Art. 1(f) Regulation on Myanmar/Burma, Art. 1(f) EU Regulation on Lebanon, Art. 1(f) Regulation on Burundi, Art. 1(f) Regulation on Venezuela, Art. 1(f) Regulation on Nicaragua, Art. 1(e) Regulation on Guinea, Art. 1(i) Regulation on Syria, Art, 1(b) Regulation on Tunisia, Art. 1(f) Funds Regulation on Ukraine & Art. 1(f) Regulation on Drilling.
610. Article 1(5) Regulation on Iraq, Art. 1(f) Regulation on Sudan, Art. 1(e) Regulation on DRC, Art. 2(10) Regulation on DPRK, Art. 1(d) Regulation on Somalia, Art. 1(j) Regulation on Iran, Art. 1(d) Regulation on Guinea-Bissau, Art. 1(d) Regulation on Libya, Art. 1(f) Regulation on CAR, Art. 1(e) Regulation on Yemen, Art. 1(f) Regulation on South Sudan, Art. 1(e) Regulation on Mali, Art. 1(e) Regulation on Zimbabwe, Art. 1(d) EU Regulation on Iran, Art. 1(e) Regulation on Myanmar/Burma, Art. 1(e) EU Regulation on Lebanon, Art. 1(e) Regulation on Burundi, Art. 1(e) Regulation on Venezuela, Art. 1(e) Regulation on Nicaragua, Art. 1(g) Regulation on Guinea, Art. 1(h) Regulation on Syria, Art. 1(d) Regulation on Tunisia, Art. 1(e) Funds Regulation Ukraine & Art. 1(e) Regulation on Drilling.
611. Article 8(1) Regulation on Iraq, Art. 9(1) Regulation on Sudan, Art. 6(1) Regulation on DRC, Art. 50(1) Regulation on DPRK, Art. 9(1) Regulation on Somalia, Art. 40(1) Regulation on Iran, Art. 8(1) Regulation on Guinea-Bissau, Art. 18(1) Regulation on Libya, Art. 11(1) Regulation on CAR, Art. 9(1) Regulation on Yemen, Art. 14(1) Regulation on South Sudan, Art. 7(1) Regulation on Mali, Art. 8(1) Regulation on Zimbabwe, Art. 9(1) EU Regulation on Iran, Art. 4e(1) Regulation on Myanmar/Burma, Art. 8(1) EU Regulation on Lebanon, Art. 7(1) Regulation on Burundi, Art. 12(1) Regulation on Venezuela, Art. 8(1) Regulation on Nicaragua, Art. 12(1) Regulation on Guinea, Art. 29(1) Regulation on Syria, Art. 9(1) Regulation on Tunisia, Art. 8(1) Funds Regulation Ukraine & Art. 7(1) Regulation on Drilling.
612. Article 8(2) Regulation on Iraq, Art. 9(3) Regulation on Sudan, Art. 6(3) Regulation on DRC, Art. 50(3) Regulation on DPRK, Art. 9(2) Regulation on Somalia, Art. 40(3) Regulation on Iran, Art. 8(2) Regulation on Guinea-Bissau, Art. 18(2) Regulation on Libya, Art. 11(3) Regulation on CAR, Art. 9(3) Regulation on Yemen, Art. 14(3) Regulation on South Sudan, Art. 7(3) Regulation on Mali, Art. 8(3) Regulation on Zimbabwe, Art. 9(2) EU Regulation on Iran, Art. 4e(3) Regulation on Myanmar/Burma, Art. 8(3) EU Regulation on Lebanon, Art. 7(3) Regulation on Burundi, Art. 12(3) Regulation on Venezuela, Art. 8(3) Regulation on Nicaragua, Art. 12(3) Regulation on Guinea, Art. 29(2) Regulation on Syria, Art. 9(2) Regulation on Tunisia, Art. 8(3) Funds Regulation Ukraine & Art. 7(3) Regulation on Drilling.
613. Article 18(3) Regulation on Libya & Art. 8(4) Funds Regulation Ukraine.

encompasses all the acts necessary under the applicable national law if a person is effectively to obtain full power of disposal in relation to the asset concerned.[614]

B The Duty to Refrain from Circumvention

124. Equally important, participating knowingly and intentionally in activities aiming or effecting, directly or indirectly, the circumvention of the aforementioned duty and obligation is prohibited.[615] Such a prohibition is absent in a single legislation, which nonetheless prohibits the *promotion* of transactions related to the same duty and obligation.[616] According to jurisprudence, circumvention denotes activities which have the aim or result of enabling their author to avoid the application of that prohibition.[617] It therefore is to be understood as covering activities in respect of which it appears, on the basis of objective factors, that, under cover of a formal appearance which enables them to avoid the constituent elements of an infringement of said duty and obligation, nonetheless they have, as such or by reason of their possible link to other activities, the aim or result, direct or indirect, of frustrating said prohibition.[618]

125. Turning to the person performing, or attempting to perform the circumvention, the terms *knowingly and intentionally* imply an element of knowledge and an element of intent. These elements are met when a person deliberately seeks the object or the effect, direct or indirect, of circumvention connected therewith. They are equally met when the person in question is aware that his participation in such an activity can have that object or effect and accepts that possibility.[619] Furthermore, the perpetrator does not need to be a designated entity or person. In truth, transactions carried out with a view to circumvent the prohibitory measures by anyone are capable of infringing the duty to refrain from circumvention.[620] Thus, a non-designated entity that settles debts

---

614. *Afrasiabi* (n. 46) para. 40, citing *Möllendorf* (n. 45) para. 51.
615. Article 7(1) Regulation on Iraq, Art. 10 Sudan, Art. 7b Regulation on DRC, Art. 52 Regulation on DPRK, Art. 2(4) Regulation on Somalia, Art. 41 Regulation on Iran, Art. 3(3) Regulation on Guinea-Bissau, Art. 2(1)(b) Regulation on Libya, Art. 12 Regulation on the CAR, Art. 10 Regulation on Yemen, Art. 15 Regulation on South Sudan, Art. 8 Regulation on Mali, Art. 2(3) EU Regulation on Iran, Art. 4g Regulation on Myanmar-Burma, Art. 8 Regulation on Burundi, Art. 14 Regulation on Venezuela, Art. 9 Regulation on Nicaragua, Art. 6(4) Regulation on Guinea, Art. 14(3) Regulation on Syria, Art. 2(3) Regulation on Tunisia and Art. 9 Funds Regulation on Ukraine.
616. Article 6(3) Regulation on Zimbabwe.
617. *Afrasiabi* (n. 46) para. 60 citing *Johannes Henricus Maria van Binsbergen v. Bestuur van de Bedrijfsvereniging voor de Metaalnijverheid*, 33/74, Judgment of 3 Dec. 1974, digital ECR, para. 13, *Association des Centres distributeurs Édouard Leclerc and others v. SARL "Au blé vert" and others*, 229/83, Judgment of 10 Jan. 1985, digital ECR, para. 27 & *TV10 SA v. Commissariaat voor de Media*, C-23/93, Judgment of 5 Oct. 1994, digital ECR, para. 21.
618. *Afrasiabi* (n. 46) para. 62, citing *Emsland-Stärke*, C-110/99, Judgment of 14 Dec. 2000, digital ECR, para. 52 & *Halifax plc, Leeds Permanent Development Services Ltd and County Wide Property Investments Ltd v. Commissioners of Customs & Excise*, C-255/02, Judgment of 21 Feb. 2006, digital ECR, paras 74 & 75.
619. *Afrasiabi* (n. 46) para. 67.
620. *Europäisch-Iranische Handelsbank AG v. Council*, C-585/13 P, Judgment of 5 Mar. 2015, digital ECR, para. 78.

or makes payments on behalf of a designated entity has to satisfy itself as to the legality of the intended transaction; it is expected to do so by requesting authorization from the competent national authority, where applicable[621] (with regard to authorizations *see* paragraphs 132 et seq. below). The Court ruled that the danger of circumvention arises when a designated person delegates its activities to other entities, which although not owned by that person, act on its behalf or carry out certain activities in its name.[622]

126. Specifically in relation to the restrictive measures in view of the situation in Iraq, said the prohibition of circumvention is paired both with a prohibition to promote banned transactions and with the duty to inform the competent authorities at the national level as well as the Commission on circumventing the statutory provisions.[623]

127. In conjunction with the aforementioned statutory provisions, the aim to prevent circumvention has infiltrated the designation criteria. Within the frame of the Regulation on Iran, the CJEU took the view that, when an entity has been designated for providing support to the government of Iran,[624] or for being engaged in nuclear proliferation[625] (in relation to the designation criteria *see* paragraph 94 above), the possibility is created for that entity to exert pressure on the entities it owns or controls or that belong to it (in relation to this designation criterium *see* paragraph 95 above), in order to circumvent the effects of the imposed restrictive measures. Therefore, freezing the funds of such entities is both necessary and appropriate for the purpose of ensuring the effectiveness of the adopted measures as well as of making certain that those measures are not circumvented.[626] The Court adopted the same view within the frame of the Regulation on Syria[627] (in relation to the designation criteria *see* paragraph 115 above). Notably, providing assistance in circumventing restrictive measures has been actually set as an individual designation criterion with regard to Iran[628] (in relation to the designation criterion *see* paragraph 95 above).

128. A similar purpose serves the shareholding link criterion. Settled jurisprudence set within the frame of the sanctions targeting Syria, ruled that where a legal person is

621. *Ibid.*, para. 79.
622. *Islamic Republic of Iran Shipping Lines and Others v. Council*, T-14/14 and T-87/14, Judgment of 17 Feb. 2017, digital ECR, para. 76 ('Iran Shipping 2017').
623. Articles 7(1) & (2) and 4, 2 & 3 Regulation on Iraq.
624. Article 23(2)(d) Regulation on Iran. *See Petropars Iran* (n. 463) para. 62 & *Central Bank of Iran v. Council*, T-563/12, Judgment of 25 Mar. 2015, digital ECR, para. 64 ('Central Bank of Iran 2015').
625. Article 23(2)(a) & 23(2)(a) Regulation on Iran. *See Melli Bank 2013* (n. 464) para. 55 citing *Melli Bank* 2012 (n. 463) paras 39 & 58; *Islamic Republic of Iran Shipping Lines and Others v. Council*, T-489/10, Judgment of 16 Sep. 2013, digital ECR, para. 75.
626. *Petropars Iran* (n. 463) para. 62, citing *Melli Bank 2012* (n. 463) paras 39 and 58. *See also Iran Shipping 2019* (n. 46) para. 110.
627. *Syrian Lebanese Commercial Bank SAL v. Council*, Joined T-174/12 and T-80/13, Judgment of 4 Feb. 2014, digital ECR, para. 101 ('Syrian Lebanese'), citing *Melli Bank 2012* (n. 463) paras 39 & 58; *Amer Foz v. Council*, T-296/20, Judgment of 18 May 2022, digital ECR, para. 174, citing *Sharif v. Council*, T-540/19, Judgment of 28 Apr. 2021, digital ECR, para. 159 & by analogy *NIOC and Others v. Council*, T–577/12, Judgment of 4 Sep. 2015, digital ECR, para. 139 ('National Iranian 2015').
628. Article 23(2)(b) & 23a(2)(b) Regulation on Iran. *See Central Bank of Iran 2015* (n. 624) para. 64.

wholly owned by another person which undoubtedly must be covered by restrictive measures, that legal person must also be subject to those measures (in relation to this designation criterium *see* paragraph 115 above), by reason solely of that shareholding link, on condition that the measures by which the restrictive measures in question were adopted provide for their application to legal persons owned or controlled by persons already covered.[629] However, in a case discussing the Regulation on Syria that involved a shareholder holding the majority of the shares, albeit lacking the authority to nominate the majority of executive directors of the subsidiary as per the shareholder agreement in place, the Court found that the risk of exerting pressure for the purpose of achieving circumvention of the prohibitions did not exist.[630] Thus, holding the majority of the share capital does not automatically qualify the holder as owner or controlled for the purpose of the here-discussed restrictive measures.[631] It is noted that a holding of 48% or 49% is not sufficient by itself to justify the adoption of restrictive measures.[632] At the same time, the existence of intermediary companies does not affect the presumption that the parent company exercises decisive influence over the conduct of its subsidiary, the CJEU ruled.[633]

129. Finally, curbing the circumvention of restrictive measures is achieved also by listing family members of targeted natural persons, the Courts of the EU ruled (*see* in this regard paragraph 114 above). To this aim the competent organs of the EU may list family members of persons responsible for human rights violations, undermining democracy or the rule of law, or other violations, as the apposite legislative act may foresee, under the association criterion.[634]

130. Duties related to circumvention are also at play under other restrictive measures (*see* in this regard paragraphs 177, 206, 210, 279, 287, 299, 330, 350, 353, 382, 400, 439, 443, 455, 506 and 532 below).

IV The Exceptions

131. The statutory obligations explained above face a series of exceptions that can be divided into two groups. The first one consists of exceptions that are widely applied across all restrictive measures, whereas the second group consists of exceptions specifically targeted on certain set of measures, in all probability in view of their unique specifics. Both are discussed in the ensuing paragraphs.

629. *Syrian Lebanese* (n. 627) para. 102, citing *Melli Bank* 2012 (n. 463) para. 79 & *Melli Bank* 2013 (n. 464) para. 56.
630. *Syrian Lebanese* (n. 627) paras 105, 106 & 101, citing *Persia International* (n. 465) paras 103 to 113.
631. *Ibid.*, para. 119.
632. *Petropars Iran* (n. 463) para. 81. *See also Persia International* (n. 465) para. 106.
633. *Petropars Iran* (n. 463) para. 68.
634. *See Pye Phyo Tay Za* (n. 574) para. 72.

A Widely Applied Exceptions

132. The first group of widely applied exceptions includes cases related to the designated persons, financial institutions as well as third parties. Exceptions concerning the designated persons relate to their basic needs, that being payments for foodstuffs, rent or mortgage, medicines and medical treatment, taxes, insurance premiums and public utility charges, both of their own and of their dependent family members.[635] With regard to Mali this 'basic needs exception' may only be applied to natural persons.[636] Extraordinary expenses may also be grounds for derogation. However, in such events, the relevant competent authority after ascertaining the grounds that, in its view, justify an exceptionality, shall communicate those to the competent authorities of other Member States and to the Commission. This notification must take place at least two weeks prior to authorizing the release of frozen funds.[637] Still, when the designation is performed by a sanctions committee of the UN, said notification is addressed to the apposite sanctions committee[638] or the UN Security Council,[639] with the exception of the sanctions in relation to Iraq that provide for notification to the Commission.[640]

133. The second group of exceptions concerns directly the financial institutions that have frozen such funds and economic resources. In particular, it is set out that fees and service charges for routine holding and maintenance of frozen funds and economic resources may be paid. Where the designation was decided at the level of the UN Security Council, the relevant sanctions committee (or the UN Security Council in the case of Iran)[641] must have been informed at least five working days (or four days in the

635. Article 5(2)(a) Regulation on Iraq, Art. 6(1)(a)(i) Regulation on Sudan, Art. 3(1)(a) Regulation on DRC, Art. 35(1)(a) Regulation on DPRK, Art. 5(1)(a)(i) Regulation on Somalia, Art. 26(a)(i) Regulation on Iran, Art. 4(1)(a) Regulation on Guinea-Bissau, Art. 8(1)(a) Regulation on Libya, Art. 6(a)(i) Regulation on CAR, Art. 4(a)(i) Regulation on Yemen, Arts 6(a)(i) & 8(1)(a) Regulation on South Sudan, Art. 7(1)(a) Regulation on Zimbabwe, Art. 4(1)(a) EU Regulation on Iran, Art. 4b(1)(a) Regulation on Myanmar/Burma, Art. 3(1)(a) Regulation on Burundi, Art. 9(1)(a) Regulation on Venezuela, Art. 3(1)(a) Regulation on Nicaragua, Art. 8(1)(a) Regulation on Guinea, Art. 4(1)(a) Guinea-Bissau, Art. 16(a) Regulation on Syria, Art. 4(1)(a) Regulation on Tunisia & Art. 4(1)(a) Funds Regulation Ukraine.

636. Article 3(1)(a) Regulation on Mali.

637. Article 3(2)(a) & (3) Regulation on DRC, Art. 4(1)(d) Regulation on Guinea-Bissau, Art. 8(2)(a) Regulation on Libya, Art. 8(1)(d) Regulation on South Sudan, Art. 3(2)(b) Regulation on Mali, Art. 7(1)(d) Regulation on Zimbabwe, Art. 4(1)(d) EU Regulation on Iran, Art. 4b(1)(d) Regulation on Myanmar/Burma, Art. 3(1)(d) Regulation on Burundi, Art. 9(1)(d) Regulation on Venezuela, Art. 3(1)(d) Regulation on Nicaragua, Art. 8(1)(d) Regulation on Guinea, Art. 16(d) Regulation on Syria, Art. 4(1)(d) Regulation on Tunisia & Art. 4(1)(d) Funds Regulation Ukraine.

638. Article 6(2) Regulation on Sudan, Art. 3(2)(b) Regulation on DRC, Art. 35(2) Regulation on DPRK, Art. 5(2) Regulation on Somalia, Art. 8(2)(b) Regulation on Libya, Art. 7 Regulation on CAR, Art. 5 Regulation on Yemen, Art. 7 Regulation on South Sudan, Art. 3(2)(a) Regulation on Mali.

639. Article 28 Regulation on Iran.

640. Article 5(2)(d) Regulation on Iraq.

641. Article 26(a)(iii) & (b) Regulation on Iran.

case of Congo)[642] prior the date of the intended payment and within this time frame it has the power to object,[643] with the exception of the sanctions on Iraq and Guinea-Bissau that prescribe notification to the Commission and the other Member States.[644] Where the designation had been done at an EU level, the Commission and the other Member States are the authorities to be notified within an opaque time frame,[645] which in the case of Lebanon, Nicaragua, Tunisia and Türkiye is specified as two weeks[646] and four weeks in the case of Syria.[647] Further, with the exception of sanctions in relation to Iraq, interest or other earnings may be added to those accounts, as long as these are also frozen.[648]

134. The third group of exceptions relates to third parties in the sense of enforcement of contracts and judgments, payment of professional fees and crediting the accounts. More analytically, imposing sanctions does not bend the cardinal rule of *pacta sunt servanda,* in the sense that payments due under contracts, agreements or obligations are exempt as long as they were concluded or arose prior to the date on which the relevant person has been designated and these payments remain frozen in the accounts.[649] Specifically, payments made under a counter-guarantee agreement can be regarded as being used for the benefit of a listed person only if, on the basis of the bank

642. Article 3(1)(b) Regulation on DRC.
643. Article 6(1)(a)(iii) & (b) Regulation on Sudan, Art. 35(1)(a)(ii) & (b) Regulation on DPRK, Art. 5(1)(a)(iii) & (b) Regulation on Somalia, Art. 8(1)(c) Regulation on Libya, Art. 6(a)(iii) & (b) Regulation on CAR, Art. 4(a)(iii) & (b) Regulation on Yemen, Art. 6(a)(iii) & (b) Regulation on South Sudan, Art. 3(1)(c) Regulation on Mali, Art. 8(1)(c) & (2) Regulation on Guinea, Art. 4(1)(c) & (2) Regulation on Tunisia & Art. 4(1)(c) & (2) Funds Regulation Ukraine.
644. Article 5(2)(c) & (3) Regulation on Iraq, Art. 4(1)(c) & (2) Regulation on Guinea-Bissau.
645. Article 8(1)(c) & (2) Regulation on South Sudan, Art. 7(1)(c) Regulation on Zimbabwe, Art. 4(1)(c) EU Regulation on Iran, Art. 4b(1)(c) & (2) Regulation on Myanmar/Burma, Art. 3(1)(c) & (2) Regulation on Burundi, Art. 9(1)(c) & (2) Regulation on Venezuela, Art. 8(1)(c) & (2) Regulation on Guinea & Art. 4(1)(c) & (2) Funds Regulation Ukraine.
646. Article 3(1)(c) & (2) Regulation on Nicaragua, Art. 3(1)(c) & (2) EU Regulation on Lebanon, Art. 4(1)(c) & (2) Regulation on Tunisia & Art. 3(1)(c) & (2) Regulation on Drilling.
647. Article 16(c) & last sentence Regulation on Syria.
648. Article 8(2)(a) Regulation on Sudan, Art. 34(9) Regulation on DPRK, Art. 3(1)(a) Regulation on Somalia, Art. 29(2)(a) Regulation on Iran, Art. 6(1)(a) Regulation on Guinea-Bissau, Art. 12(1)(a) Regulation on Libya, Art. 10(2)(a) Regulation on CAR, Art. 8(2)(a) Regulation on Yemen, Art. 13(2)(a) Regulation on South Sudan, Art. 6(2)(a) Regulation on Mali, Art. 7(2)(a) Regulation on Zimbabwe, Art. 6(1)(a) EU Regulation on Iran, Art. 4d(4)(a) Regulation on Myanmar/Burma, Art. 6(2)(a) Regulation on Burundi, Art. 11(4)(a) Regulation on Venezuela, Art. 7(2)(a) Regulation on Nicaragua, Art. 7(2)(a) EU Regulation on Lebanon, Art. 10(2)(a) Regulation on Guinea, Art. 19(1)(a) Regulation on Syria, Art. 6(1)(a) Regulation on Tunisia, Art. 7(1)(a) Funds Regulation Ukraine & Art. 6(2)(a) Regulation on Drilling.
649. Article 8(2)(b) Regulation on Sudan, Art. 5(1)(b) Regulation on DRC, Art. 3(1)(b) Regulation on Somalia, Art. 29(2)(b) Regulation on Iran, Art. 6(1)(b) Regulation on Guinea-Bissau, Art. 12(1)(b) Regulation on Libya, Art. 10(2)(b) Regulation on CAR, Art. 8(2)(b) Regulation on Yemen, Art. 13(2)(b) Regulation on South Sudan, Art. 6(2)(b) Regulation on Mali, Art. 7(2)(b) Regulation on Zimbabwe, Art. 6(1)(b) EU Regulation on Iran, Art. 4d(4)(b) Regulation on Myanmar/Burma, Art. 6(2)(b) Regulation on Burundi, Art. 11(4)(b) Regulation on Venezuela, Art. 7(2)(b) Regulation on Nicaragua, Art. 7(2)(b) EU Regulation on Libanon, Art. 10(2)(b) Regulation on Guinea, Art. 19(1)(b) Regulation on Syria, Art. 6(1)(b) Regulation on Tunisia, Art. 7(1)(b) Funds Regulation Ukraine & Art. 6(2)(b) Regulation on Drilling.

guarantee agreement and the counter-guarantee agreements, those payments enable the beneficiary of the bank guarantee, who is also a designated person, directly or indirectly to secure enforcement of the bank guarantee.[650] The provisions on restrictive measures in view of the situation in DPRK require two more conditions to be satisfied, prior to paying amounts due. First, the contract may be not related to any item, operation, service or transaction for goods and technology that could contribute to nuclear programmes, programmes for weapons of mass destruction and ballistic missile programmes,[651] and for goods and technology included in the EU Common Military List (*see* in this regard paragraphs 273 et seq. below).[652] It can neither be related to the dual-use items (*see* in this regard paragraphs 239 et seq. below).[653] Cumulatively, the payment may not be received, directly or indirectly, by a designated person.[654] Thus, these two additional conditions neutralize the exception and strengthen the effects of the prohibition. Similarly, the restrictive measures in view of the situation in Iraq do not allow for payment of contracts under any circumstances as such a provision is absent.

135. Furthermore, certain set of restrictive measures provide for one more exception on the basis of contracts and obligations that have been concluded or have arisen, respectively, before the date of designation. The present exception relates to payment by a designated person as long as the obligation to refuse is not being breached. When these conditions are fulfilled, the competent authorities of the Member States have the authority to release frozen funds and economic resources and attach any conditions that they deem appropriate, following the exercise of their discretion. If the designation has been made by a sanctions committee, that needs to be informed within ten working days,[655] whereas when the designation is performed by the EU, the duty to inform relates to the other Member States and the Commission either prior[656] to or following the decision[657] or at an unspecified point in time.[658] In particular, the restrictive

650. *SH (n. 327)* para. 64.
651. Articles 36(2)(a) & 3(1)(a) & Annex II Parts II to IX Regulation on DPRK. Parts IV, V, VI, VII, VIII and IX to Annex II of said regulation bring into practice para. 25 to UN Security Council Resolution 2270 of 2 Mar. 2016, para. 4 to UN Security Council Resolution 2321 of 30 Nov. 2016, paras 4 & 5 UN Security Council Resolution 2371 of 5 Aug. 2017 and paras 4 & 5 UN Security Council Resolution 2375 of 11 Sep. 2017, respectively.
652. Articles 36(2)(a) & 7 Regulation on DPRK.
653. Articles 36(2)(a) & 3(1)(a) & Annex II Part I Regulation on DPRK and Annex I Dual Use Regulation.
654. Article 36(2)(b) and Annexes XIII, XV, XVI & XVII Regulation on DPRK.
655. Article 13 Regulation on Libya, Art. 9 Regulation on CAR, Art. 7 Regulation on Yemen, Art. 11 Regulation on South Sudan, Art. 5 Regulation on Mali & Art. 8 Regulation on Haiti.
656. In these cases the Member States and the Commission must be informed at least two weeks prior to granting the authorization. *See* Art. 7 EU Regulation on Iran & Art. 7 Regulation on Tunisia.
657. In these cases the Member States and the Commission must be informed within two weeks (Art. 5 Regulation on Mali, Art. 5 Regulation on Nicaragua, Art. 6(1) & (2) EU Regulation on Lebanon & Art. 5(1) & (2) Regulation on Drilling) or four weeks (Art. 4d(1) & (2) Regulation on Myanmar-Burma & Art. 11(1) & (2) Regulation on Venezuela).
658. Article 12 Regulation on South Sudan, Art. 5 Regulation on Burundi & Art. 6 Funds Regulation Ukraine.

measures in view of the situation in Iran set out the additional condition of not contributing to a prohibited activity, whereas the UN Security Council that must be notified, has the power to object.[659]

136. Finally, two set of restrictive measures, the ones in view of Libya and the ones in view of Syria, set out specific conditions that allow for derogation from the obligation to act and abbey. In relation to Libya and the frozen funds and economic resources located abroad on 16 September 2011, derogation is possible under a contract or an obligation that was concluded or arose prior to the designation when such a payment is not in breach of the obligation to abbey, it does not benefit the Libyan Investment Authority or the Libyan Africa Investment Portfolio and the 1970 Libya Sanctions Committee has been notified ten days in advance.[660] Turning to Syria, designated persons may perform payments under a contract or obligation done or undertaken before the date of designation, as long as such payment shall not be received directly or indirectly by the designated person. The competent authorities of the Member States that have the discretion to authorize such payments, may attach any conditions they deem appropriate.[661] Further, trade contracts in particular may allow for additional derogations. First, within two months of a designation, an entity may perform payments from frozen funds and economic resources that were received after the designation date, when such payment is due under a trade contract and it shall not be received by a designated person or entity both directly and indirectly.[662] In addition, trade contracts may allow for transfer by, through or to the Central Bank of Syria, under the conditions that the transfer relates to funds and economic resources, that the effected payment shall not be received by a designated person and that this action is not otherwise prohibited.[663] Specifically, transfers *by* the Central Bank of Syria must relate to funds and economic resources received and frozen after the designation date.[664] The sole purpose of those derogations is to avoid penalizing persons and entities not covered by the restrictive measures and trade not prohibited between the Member States and Syria. They do not serve the purpose of enabling the Central Bank of Syria to ordinarily operate.[665] In a similar pattern, transfers may be performed by, through or to the Commercial Bank of Syria with regard to funds and economic resources received from outside of the territory of the Union. Transfers *by* said bank must relate to funds and economic resources frozen after the designation date whereas the object of the trade contract permitting such derogation is restricted to medical supplies, food, shelter, sanitation and hygiene for civilian use.[666] Transfers *to the* same

659. Article 25 Regulation on Iran.
660. Articles 11(2) and 5(2) & Annex VI Regulation on Libya.
661. Article 20 & Annexes II and IIa Regulation on Syria.
662. Article 21 & Annexes II and IIa Regulation on Syria.
663. Article 21a(1)(b) Regulation on Syria.
664. Article 21a(1)(a) Regulation on Syria.
665. *Mayaleh* (n. 44) para. 152.
666. Article 21c(1)(a) Regulation on Syria.

bank may be allowed on the basis of trade contracts that meet essential civilian needs.[667]

137. Turning to enforcement of judgments, certain set of restrictive measures allow for payments due under judgments of ordinary courts, judgments of administrative tribunals and awards of arbitral tribunals, as long as they have been rendered prior to the designation date, they do not benefit the designated person and their recognition is not contrary to public policy *in the Member State concerned*.[668] At the same time, the funds and economic resources must be used to satisfy exclusively claims recognized therein,[669] whereas the apposite sanctions committee,[670] the UN Security Council[671] or the other Member States and the Commission,[672] as the case may be, have been notified. Under the same conditions, in certain sanctions regimes, a judicial, administrative and arbitral lien can be satisfied.[673] The restrictive measures in view of Iraq are slightly different, in the sense that neither any notification nor absence of benefit of

667. Article 21c(1)(b) Regulation on Syria.
668. Articles 7(a), (c) & (d) and 8(2)(c) Regulation on Sudan, Art. 7(a), (c) & (d) Regulation on DRC, Art. 36(1)(a), (c) & (d) Regulation on DPRK, Art. 6(a), (c) & (d) Regulation on Somalia, Art. 24(a), (c) & (d) Regulation on Iran, Art. 5(1)(a), (c) & (d) Regulation on Guinea-Bissau, Arts 9(1)(a), (c) & (d) and 12(1)(c) Regulation on Libya, Arts 8(a), (c) & (d) and 10(2)(c) Regulation on CAR, Art. 6(a), (c) & (d) and 8(2)(c) Regulation on Yemen, Art. 9(a), (c) & (d) Regulation on South Sudan, Art. 4(1)(a), (c) & (d) Regulation on Mali, Art. 7(1)(a), (c) & (d) Regulation on Haiti, Art. 5(1)(a), (c) & (d) EU Regulation on Iran, Art. 4c(1)(a), (c) & (d) Regulation on Myanmar/Burma, Art. 4(1)(a), (c) & (d) Regulation on Burundi, Art. 10(1)(a), (c) & (d) Regulation on Venezuela, Art. 5(1)(a), (c) & (d) EU Regulation on Lebanon, Art. 9(1)(a), (c) & (d) Regulation on Guinea, Art. 18(1)(a), (c) & (d) Regulation on Syria & Art. 4(1)(a), (c) & (d) Regulation on Drilling.
669. Article 7(b) Regulation on Sudan, Art. 7(b) Regulation on DRC, Art. 36(1)(b) Regulation on DPRK, Art. 6(b) Regulation on Somalia, Art. 24(b) Regulation on Iran, Art. 5(1)(b) Regulation on Guinea-Bissau, Art. 9(1)(b) Regulation on Libya, Art. 8(b) Regulation on CAR, Art. 6(b) Regulation on Yemen, Art. 9(b) Regulation on South Sudan, Art. 4(1)(b) Regulation on Mali, Art. 7(1)(b) Regulation on Haiti, Art. 5(1)(b) EU Regulation on Iran, Art. 4c(1)(b) Regulation on Myanmar/Burma, Art. 4(1)(b) Regulation on Burundi, Art. 10(1)(b) Regulation on Venezuela, Art. 5(1)(b) EU Regulation on Lebanon, Art. 9(1)(b) Regulation on Guinea, Art. 18(1)(b) Regulation on Syria & Art. 4(1)(b) Regulation on Drilling.
670. Article 7(e) Regulation on Sudan, Art. 7(e) Regulation on DRC, Art. 36(1)(e) Regulation on DPRK, Art. 6(e) Regulation on Somalia, Art. 9(1)(e) Regulation on Libya, Art. 8(e) Regulation on CAR, Art. 6(e) Regulation on Yemen, Art. 9(e) Regulation on South Sudan, Art. 4(1)(e) Regulation on Mali & Art. 7(1)(e) Regulation on Haiti.
671. Article 24(e) Regulation on Iran.
672. Article 5(2) Regulation on Guinea-Bissau, Art. 5(2) EU Regulation on Iran, Art. 4c(2) Regulation on Myanmar/Burma, Art. 4(2) Regulation on Burundi, Art. 10(2) Regulation on Venezuela, Art. 4(2) EU Regulation on Lebanon, Art. 9(2) Regulation on Guinea, Art. 18(2) Regulation on Syria & Art. 4(2) Regulation on Drilling.
673. Article 7(a) Regulation on Sudan, Art. 36(1)(a) Regulation on DPRK, Art. 6(a) Regulation on Somalia, Art. 24(a) Regulation on Iran, Art. 5(1)(a) Regulation on Guinea-Bissau, Art. 9(1)(a) Regulation on Libya, Art. 8(a) Regulation on CAR, Art. 6(a) Regulation on Yemen, Art. 9(a) Regulation on South Sudan, Art. 4(1)(a) Regulation on Mali, Art. 7(1)(a) Regulation on Haiti, Art. 5(1)(a) EU Regulation on Iran & Art. 9(1)(a) Regulation on Guinea.

     The Regulation on Venezuela, the Regulation on Myanmar/Burma, the Regulation on Burundi, the EU Regulation on Lebanon, the Regulation on Syria and the Regulation on Drilling do not foresee an exception for a lien.

designated persons is requested, whereas the regulation on prohibiting Iraqi claims[674] must not be breached.[675]

138. Legal costs are regulated in a separate provision, according to which payment of reasonable professional fees and reimbursement of incurred expenses with regard to legal services may be paid by frozen funds and economic resources. The competent authorities shall exercise their discretion, especially as the professional fees to be reimbursed must be reasonable, and shall dispatch the appropriate notifications to the appropriate sanctions committee that has the power to object within a certain period of time,[676] the UN Security Council with the same power[677] or, when the designation has taken place at EU level, to the Member States and the Commission either within a specific time frame[678] or at an unspecified time.[679] The Member States and the Commission may not object. The issue of whether fees are reasonable, and thus eligible for payment, is examined according to the principle of proportionality, one of the general principles of EU Law. Thereunder, the fees should be appropriate for attaining the legitimate objectives pursued by the legislation at issue and should not go beyond what is necessary to achieve them.[680] Should there be a choice between several appropriate ones, recourse must be had to the least onerous, whereas the disadvantages caused must not be disproportionate to the aims pursued.[681]

139. Finally, the aforementioned obligations do not prevent crediting frozen accounts by third parties, as long as the financial and credit institutions equally freeze such additions. The financial and credit institutions have to inform without delay the competent authorities about such transactions.[682] Exceptionally, the restrictive measures in view of the situation in Zimbabwe do not provide for such a derogation.

674. Council Regulation (EEC) No. 3541/92 of 7 Dec. 1992 prohibiting the satisfying of Iraqi claims with regard to contracts and transactions, the performance of which was affected by United Nations Security Council Resolution 661 (1990) and related resolutions, OJ L 361, 10 Dec. 1992, p. 1.
675. Article 6(1) Regulation on Iraq.
676. The appropriate sanctions committee may object within two (Art. 6(1)(a)(ii) & (b) Regulation on Sudan), three (Art. 5(1)(a)(ii) Regulation on Somalia), four (Art. 3(1)(b) Regulation on DRC) or five working days (Art. 35(1)(a)(i) & (b) Regulation on DPRK, Art. 8(1)(b) Regulation on Libya, Art. 6(a)(ii) & (b) Regulation on CAR, Art. 4(a)(ii) & (b) Regulation on Yemen, Art. 6(a)(ii) & (b) Regulation on South Sudan, Art. 3(1)(b) Regulation on Mali & Art. 6(1)(b) Regulation on Haiti).
677. Article 26(a)(ii) & (b) Regulation on Iran.
678. The notification must take place within two (Art. 3(1)(b) & (2) Regulation on Nicaragua, Art. 3(1)(b) & (2) EU Regulation on Lebanon & Art. 3(1)(b) & (2) Regulation on Drilling) or four weeks (Art. 4b(1)(b) & (2) Regulation on Myanmar/Burma, Art. 16(b) Regulation on Syria).
679. Article 5(2)(b) Regulation on Iraq, Art. 4(1)(b) & (2) Regulation on Myanmar/Burma, Art. 8(1)(b) & (2) Regulation on South Sudan, Art. 7(1)(b) Regulation on Zimbabwe, Art. 4(1)(b) EU Regulation on Iran, Art. 3(1)(b) & (2) Regulation on Burundi, Art. 9(1)(b) & (2) Regulation on Venezuela, Art. 3(1)(b) & (2) Regulation on Nicaragua, Art. 8(1)(b) & (2) Regulation on Guinea, Art. 4(1)(b) & (2) Regulation on Tunisia & Art. 4(1)(b) & (2) Funds Regulation Ukraine.
680. *Iran Shipping* 2019 (n. 46) para. 102, citing *Al-Aqsa v. Council and Netherlands v. Al-Aqsa*, Joined C-539/10 P and C-550/10 P, Judgment of 15 Nov. 2012, para. 122 ('Al-Aqsa 2012'); and *National Iranian Tanker* (n. 157) para. 76.
681. *Bank Mellat* 2016 (n. 346) para. 92, citing *Bank Melli* 2009 (n. 68) para. 66.
682. Article 5(1) Regulation on Iraq, Art. 8(1) Regulation on Sudan, Art. 5(2) Regulation on DRC, Art. 34(8) Regulation on DPRK, Art. 3(2) Regulation on Somalia, Art. 29(1) Regulation on Iran,

B Specific Exceptions

140. The regulations that freeze funds and economic resources, provide for some further exceptions that, unlike the preceding ones, are unique and exist within a specific regulatory frame in view of the situation in a specific state, or in some instances in more than one state.

141. The Regulation on Iraq sets out that frozen funds, economic resources and proceeds of economic resources shall be unfrozen in order to be transferred to the successor arrangements to the DFI[683] established by the Government of Iraq, as provided in the apposite provisions of resolutions of the UN Security Council.[684,685] This provision stands in accordance with the respective decision taken by the UN Security Council.[686]

142. The Regulation on DPRK provides an exception for funds and economic resources required to carry out the state's activities of its missions to the UN and its specialized agencies, related organizations and other diplomatic and consular missions.[687] The implemented resolution of the UN Security Council makes explicit mention of compliance with the Vienna Conventions on Diplomatic and Consular Relations.[688,689] A similar provision on authorizing the release of funds and economic resources for diplomatic missions, consular posts and international organizations enjoying immunities under International Law is foreseen in the restrictive measures in view of the situation in Iran,[690] Mali,[691] Myanmar-Burma,[692] Venezuela,[693] Nicaragua[694] and Syria.[695] The Regulation on Myanmar-Burma and the Regulation on Syria require

Art. 6(2) Regulation on Guinea-Bissau, Art. 12(2) Regulation on Libya, Art. 10(1) Regulation on CAR, Art. 8(1) Regulation on Yemen, Art. 13(1) Regulation on South Sudan, Art. 6(1) Regulation on Mali, Art. 6(2) EU Regulation on Iran, Art. 4d(3) Regulation on Myanmar/Burma, Art. 6(1) Regulation on Burundi, Art. 11(3) Regulation on Venezuela, Art. 7(1) Regulation on Nicaragua, Art. 10(1) Regulation on Guinea, Art. 7(1) EU Regulation on Lebanon, Art. 19(2) Regulation on Syria, Art. 6(2) Regulation on Tunisia, Art. 7(1) Funds Regulation Ukraine & Art. 6(1) Regulation on Drilling.

683. 'Development Fund for Iraq' stands for the Development Fund for Iraq held by the Central Bank of Iraq (Art. 1(6) Regulation on Iraq).
684. S/RES/1483 of 22 May 2003 and S/RES/1956 of 15 Dec. 2010.
685. Article 6(2) Regulation on Iraq.
686. That being para. 23 of resolution 1483(2003) of the UN Security Council. *See* recital No. 2 to the preamble of Council Regulation (EU) No. 85/2013 of 31 Jan. 2013 amending Regulation (EC) No. 1210/2003 concerning certain specific restrictions on economic and financial relations with Iraq, OJ L 32, 1 Feb. 2013, p. 1.
687. Article 34(7) of the Regulation on DPRK.
688. Vienna Convention on Diplomatic Relations (Vienna 1961) 500 UNTS 95; Vienna Convention on Consular Relations (Vienna 1963) 596 UNTS 261.
689. S/RES/2397 of 22 Dec. 2017 para. 22.
690. Article 27 Regulation on Iran.
691. Article 3b(1) and (2) Regulation on Mali.
692. Article 4b(1)(e) and (2) Regulation on Myanmar-Burma.
693. Article 9(1)(e) and (2) Regulation on Venezuela.
694. Article 3(1)(e) and (2) Regulation on Nicaragua.
695. Articles 16(e) & 16b Regulation on Syria.

notification of the Commission and the other Member States within four weeks,[696] the Regulation on Mali and the Regulation on Nicaragua within two weeks[697] and the Regulation on Venezuela within an unspecified period of time.[698] No notification requirement is set out in the Regulation on DPRK.

143. Funds, financial assets and economic resources required for the delivery of humanitarian assistance in DPRK may be unfrozen, as long as the competent authority of a Member State has obtained advance approval from the 1718 DPRK Sanctions Committee.[699] The implemented resolution of the UN Security Council makes explicit mention of its determination to avoid adverse humanitarian consequences for the civilian population of the DPRK and to facilitate the work of international and non-governmental organizations carrying out assistance and relief activities in the DPRK.[700] Furthermore, exempt from said prohibitions are funds and economic resources belonging to the Foreign Trade Bank or the Korean National Insurance Company (KNIC), under the condition that they are meant exclusively for humanitarian assistance undertaken by the UN, or alternatively for the official purposes of a diplomatic or consular mission in the DPRK.[701]

144. At the same time, humanitarian purposes may form the basis for authorizing the release of frozen funds and economic resources for humanitarian purposes, such as the delivery and facilitation of humanitarian aid, the delivery of materials and supplies necessary for essential civilian needs, medical products and the provision of electricity as well as for evacuations in relation to Libya,[702] Yemen,[703] Mali,[704] Myanmar-Burma,[705] Nicaragua[706] and Syria.[707] Should such be released, the authorities have the duty to inform other Member States and the Commission within two weeks,[708] with the exception of Myanmar-Burma, where the time frame for the notification is four weeks.[709] Specifically with regard to Libya, Mali, and Syria, such unfrozen funds and economic resources may be used for the evacuation of citizens of the Union and their family members.[710]

696. Article 4b(2) Regulation on Myanmar-Burma & Art. 16 Regulation on Syria.
697. Article 3b(2) Regulation on Mali & Art. 3(2) Regulation on Nicaragua.
698. Article 9(2) Regulation on Venezuela.
699. Article 34(7) of the Regulation on DPRK.
700. S/RES/2397 of 22 Dec. 2017 para. 25.
701. Article 37 Regulation on DPRK.
702. Articles 10 Regulation on Libya.
703. Article 3a Regulation on Yemen.
704. Article 3a(1) Regulation on Mali. It is silent on the information duty.
705. Article 4da(1) Regulation on Myanmar-Burma.
706. Article 6(1) Regulation on Nicaragua.
707. Article 16a(1), (2) & (3) Regulation on Syria.
708. Article 10 Regulation on Libya, Art. 3a(2) Regulation on Mali, Art. 6(2) Regulation on Nicaragua and Art. 16a(4) Regulation on Syria.
709. Article 4da(2) Regulation on Myanmar-Burma.
710. Article 10 Regulation on Libya, Art. 3a(1) Regulation on Mali, Art. 21b Regulation on Syria.

145. The 'humanitarian exemption'[711] introduced to the legislation of the Union following the relevant resolution of the UN Security Council,[712] permitted further authorization for unfreezing funds and economic resources with regard to DRC.[713] Both the wording chosen to introduce this exemption and the time limit for fulfilling the notification duty are identical to the exemption explained immediately above, including the provision of evacuation (*see* in this regard paragraph 144). More importantly, the 'humanitarian exemption' introduced to the UN-mandated sanctions[714] an exemption for funds and economic resources necessary for timely delivery of humanitarian assistance or other support of basic human needs, as long as the relevant activities are carried out by specific actors. These actors are the UN, other international organizations, humanitarian organizations having observer status with the UN General Assembly, non-governmental organizations funded by more than one state and participating UN appeals or humanitarian clusters coordinated by United Nations Office for the Coordination of Humanitarian Affairs ('UNOCHA'), their employees and implementing partners or appropriate other actors, as determined by the competent sanctions committee or the Council, as the case may be.[715] The 'humanitarian exemption' was later introduced to the unilateral sanctions[716] for the purpose of increasing consistency and coherence across the restrictive measures regimes in place in the Union.[717]

711. *See* recital No. 7 to Council Regulation (EU) 2023/720 of 31 Mar. 2023 amending certain Council Regulations concerning restrictive measures in order to insert provisions on a humanitarian exemption, OJ L 94, 3 Apr. 2023, p. 1.
712. R/RES/2664 of 9 Dec. 2022.
713. Article 4b Regulation on DRC.
714. The exemptions were introduced with three distinct pairs of legislative instruments: (a) Decision (CFSP) 2023/338 of 14 Feb. 2023 amending certain Council Regulations concerning restrictive measures in order to insert provisions on a humanitarian exemption, OJ L, 15 Feb. 2023, p. 50 & Council Regulation (EU) 2023/331 of 14 Feb. 2023 amending certain Council Regulations concerning restrictive measures in order to insert provisions on a humanitarian exemption, OJ L 47, 15 Feb. 2023, p. 1; (b) Council Decision (CFSP) 2023/726 amending certain Council Regulations concerning restrictive measures in order to insert provisions on a humanitarian exemption, OJ L 94, 3 Apr. 2023, p. 48 & Council Regulation (EU) 2023/720 of 31 Mar. 2023 amending certain Council Regulations concerning restrictive measures in order to insert provisions on a humanitarian exemption, OJ L 94, 3 Apr. 2023, p. 1; and (c) Council Decision (CFSP) 2023/1598 of 28 Jul. 2023 amending Decision 2012/285/CFSP concerning restrictive measures in view of the situation in Guinea-Bissau, OJ L 196, 4 Aug. 2023, p. 23 & Council Regulation (EU) 2023/1593 of 28 Jul. 2023 amending Regulation (EU) No. 377/2012 concerning restrictive measures in view of the situation in Guinea-Bissau, OJ L 196, 4 Aug. 2023, p. 1.
715. Article 4(4) Regulation on Iraq, Art. 5(4) Regulation on Sudan, Art. 2(2) Regulation on DRC, Art. 34(10) Regulation on DPRK, Art. 4 Regulation on Somalia, Arts 23(7) & 23a(7) Regulation on Iran, Art. 2(4) Regulation on Guinea-Bissau, Art. 5(5) Regulation on Libya, Art. 5(4) Regulation on CAR, Art. 2(3) Regulation on Yemen, Art. 5(4) Regulation on South Sudan, Art. 2(3) Regulation on Mali, Art. 5 Regulation on Haiti.
716. Article 7a Regulation on Zimbabwe, Art. 4da Regulation on Myanmar-Burma, Art. 4a Regulation on Burundi, Art. 9a Regulation on Venezuela, Art. 6 Regulation on Nicaragua, Art. 4 EU Regulation on Lebanon, Art. 8a Regulation on Guinea, Art. 4a Regulation on Tunisia. The EU Regulation on Iran, the Regulation on Syria, the Funds Regulation on Ukraine and the Regulation on Drilling lack such an exemption.
717. Recital No. 4 to the preamble of Council Regulation (EU) 2023/2693 of 27 Nov. 2023 amending certain Council Regulations concerning restrictive measures in order to insert provisions on humanitarian exceptions, digital OJ L, 28 Nov. 2023.

146. Similarly, funds and economic resources may be unfrozen for water for strictly civilian uses, as long as the Member State concerned consulted in advance with the Libyan authorities and notified the 1737 Iran Sanctions Committee. Both the Libyan authorities and the 1737 Iran Sanctions Committee have the authority to object within five working days of such notification. When none objects, the Member State may proceed with unfreezing funds and economic resources.[718] The same may take place for civilian public infrastructure[719] and resuming banking sector operations, including support or facilitating international trade with Libya.[720]

147. Iran, and its nationals, may acquire an interest in commercial activity involving uranium mining, production and use of nuclear materials and technology both within its territory and abroad, as long as the Security Council has approved in advance that specific activity.[721] The Security Council need not approve equipment for light water reactors, but the competent authorities of the EU Member States shall do so.[722] Further, funds and economic resources necessary for certain civil nuclear cooperation projects in Iran, as described in the JCPOA, may be unfrozen, under the terms and conditions set by the competent authorities of Member States.[723] That may also take place with regard to commercial activities involving uranium mining and the production or use of certain nuclear materials.[724]

148. Moreover, funds and economic resources may unfreeze for fuel and electricity for strictly civilian uses. The competent authority of the Member State concerned shall exercise its discretion and shall consult in advance with the Libyan authorities and notify the 1737 Iran Sanctions Committee. Both the Libyan authorities and the 1737 Iran Sanctions Committee have the authority to object within five working days of such notification. In the absence of such an objection, the competent authority may proceed with unfreezing funds and economic resources.[725] Under the same procedure, funds and economic resources for resuming production and sale of hydrocarbons in Libya may become unfrozen.[726] Similarly, essential energy needs of the civilian population in Syria may be satisfied by frozen funds and economic resources, as long as the competent authority that decides to do so, informs the competent authorities of the other Member States and the Commission at least four weeks prior to the authorization.[727]

---

718. Article 11(1)(a)(ii), (b), (d) & (e) Regulation on Libya.
719. Article 11(1)(a)(iv), (b), (d) & (e) Regulation on Libya.
720. Article 11(1)(a)(v), (b), (d) & (e) Regulation on Libya.
721. S/RES/2231 of 20 Jul. 2015, Annex B, para. 2(c). *See also* INFCIRC/254/Rev.12/Part 1 of 13 Nov. 2013 and INFCIRC/254/Rev. 9/Part 2 of 13 Nov. 2013.
722. Article 28a Regulation on Iran & S/RES/2231 of 20 Jul. 2015, Annex B, para. 2(c) subpara. 1.
723. Article 28b(a)(i) EU Regulation on Iran.
724. Articles 28b(a)(ii) and 2a(1)(d)(i) & (ii) Regulation on Iran. Regarding the nuclear material *see* the Nuclear Suppliers Group list specified in INFCIRC/254/Rev.9/Part 2 of 13 Nov. 2013.
725. Article 11(1)(a)(ii), (b), (d) & (e) Regulation on Libya.
726. Article 11(1)(a)(iii), (b), (d) & (e) Regulation on Libya.
727. Article 17 Regulation on Syria.

149. In Myanmar-Burma, frozen funds and economic resources may become available for the decommissioning of oil and gas wells, including waste disposal, site remediation activities required for safety and environmental restoration, related technical assistance, taxes, duties, salaries and social benefits to employees. However, funds and economic resources may be provided solely to the state-owned enterprise Myanmar Oil and Gas Enterprise, under conditions that the competent authority deems appropriate and only to the extent that they are necessary.[728]

150. Funds, financial assets and economic resources required for denuclearization in the DPRK may be unfrozen, as long as the competent authority of a Member State has obtained advance approval from the 1718 DPRK Sanctions Committee.[729] The implemented resolution of the UN Security Council reaffirmed its support for the Six Party Talks, called for their resumption and reiterated its support for the commitments set out in the Joint Statement of 19 September 2005, including the return of DPRK to the Non-Proliferation Treaty.[730,731]

V The Decisions Imposing Financial Sanctions

151. The designations that the Council performs resemble both measures of general application, in that they impose on a category of addressees determined in a general and abstract manner a prohibition on, *inter alia*, making funds and economic resources available to persons and entities named in the lists contained in their annexes, and a bundle of individual decisions affecting those persons and entities.[732] The fact that the persons and entities who are the subject of the restrictive measures imposed by the regulation at issue are expressly named, so that they appear to be directly and individually concerned by it, does not mean that that act is not of general application within the meaning of the second paragraph of Article 288 TFEU or that it is not to be classified as a regulation.[733]

152. In view of the desired surprise effect, that aims to ensure the effectiveness of the sanctions (*see* in this regard paragraph 364 below) no administrative procedure takes place prior to freezing funds.[734] More accurately, the measures are decided without prior communication to the target and with immediate effect.[735] Preventing the disclosure of information, including the statement of reasons, prior to the implementation of sanctions is based on compelling reasons touching on the security of the

728. Article 4db(a) and Annex IV.B. entry 10 Regulation on Myanmar-Burma.
729. Article 34(7) of the Regulation on DPRK.
730. *See* (n. 430) above.
731. S/RES/2397 of 22 Dec. 2017 para. 26.
732. *Council v. Bank Saderat*, C–200/13 P, Judgment of 21 Apr. 2016, digital ECR, para. 119 ('Saderat'), citing *Kadi 2008* (n. 15) paras 241 & 244, and *Gbagbo and Others v. Council*, Joined C-478/11 P to C-482/11 P, Judgment of 23 Apr. 2013, digital ECR, para. 56 ('Gbagbo').
733. *Saderat* (n. 732) para. 120, citing *Kadi* 2008 (n. 15) para. 241.
734. *Bank Melli* 2011 (n. 11) para. 90.
735. *Mayaleh* (n. 44) para. 110, citing *Kadi 2008* (n. 15) paras 333 to 340. *See* also *Syrian Lebanese* (n. 627) para. 139.

Union or of its Member States, including the conduct of their international relations.[736] Respect for the rights of the defence and, in particular, the right to be heard, does not require that the authorities, before first including a person or an entity on the list imposing restrictive measures, communicate the reasons for the listing to the person concerned prior to designating him, her or it.[737] In view of the described characteristics, there is no room for invoking the surprise effect as regards subsequent acts maintaining a person's name on the list.[738] However, the right of a person to be heard prior to adopting a subsequent decision must be respected, when the author of the imposed sanctions has new evidence; not, when the already communicated grounds are reiterated in the subsequent decision.[739]

153. Upon designating a person, the EU must comply with the set statutory requirements regarding the information to be provided in the relevant list, that being the grounds for the listing and, where available, information necessary for identifying the person concerned. With regard to natural persons, such information includes, indicatively, names, including aliases, date and place of birth, nationality, passport and identity card numbers, gender, address, if known, and function or profession. With regard to legal person, it includes names, place and date of registration, registration number and place of business.[740] In UN-mandated designations, the grounds and the information are listed, as provided by the UN Security Council or the relevant Sanctions Committee.[741] These requisites are set out in the legislative acts, in principle; occasionally the law is silent either on both the statement of reasons and the information for notification,[742] or solely on the statement of reasons.[743] When provisions of EU legislative acts require the Council to state individual and specific reasons for decisions

736. *Mayaleh* (n. 44) para. 86, citing *Bank Melli 2009* (n. 68) para. 81.
737. *Mayaleh* (n. 44) para. 110, citing *Kadi 2008* (n. 15) paras 338 & 339. *See also Syrian Lebanese* (n. 627) para. 137.
738. *Mayaleh* (n. 44) para. 114, citing *Makhlouf v. Council*, T-383/11, Judgment of 13 Sep. 2013, digital ECR, para. 42, and *Syrian Lebanese* (n. 627) para. 148.
739. *Tomana* (n. 413) para. 204, citing *Makhlouf* (n. 738) para. 43. *See also John Arnold Bredenkamp and Others v. Council and Commission*, T-66/14, Judgment of 21 Jul. 2016, digital ECR, para. 51 ('Bredenkamp'), citing *Al Assad* (n. 585) para. 71.
740. Article 11a(1) & (2) Regulation on Zimbabwe, Art. 3(2) & (3) EU Regulation on Iran, Art. 4a(4) & (5) Regulation on Myanmar-Burma, Art. 14(1) & (2) Regulation on Burundi, Art. 8(5) & (6) Regulation on Venezuela, Art. 14(1) & (2) Regulation on Nicaragua, Art. 14(1) & (2) EU Regulation on Lebanon, Art. 14 Regulation on Guinea, Art. 15(2) & (3) Regulation on Syria, Art. 3(1) & (2) Regulation on Tunisia, Art. 3(2) & (3) Funds Regulation on Ukraine and Art. 13(1) & (2) Regulation on Drilling.
741. Article 2a(2) & (3) Regulation on Congo, Art. 23(5) & (6) Regulation on Iran, Art. 6(3) & (4) Regulation on Libya, Art. 3(2) & (3) Regulation on Yemen and Art. 4(2) & (3) Regulation on Haiti. Specifically Art. 3(1) & (2) Regulation on Guinea-Bissau, Art. 47a(2) & (3) Regulation on DPRK, Art. 21 Regulation on South Sudan and Art. 2a(2) & (3) Regulation on Mali make no mention of information as provided by the UN.
742. No statutory requirements whatsoever as to the content of the lists are set in the Regulation on Iraq, the Regulation on Lebanon and the Regulation on Libya.
743. *See* Art. 16 Regulation on Sudan, Art. 14 Regulation on Somalia and Art. 18 Regulation on the CAR.

designating persons and make them known to such persons affected, it is sought to ensure observance of the principle of effective judicial protection.[744]

154. Regardless of the actual wording set out in the relevant EU legislative acts, the obligation of EU institutions to state reasons is laid down in Article 296 TFEU.[745] This requires that the statement of reasons must identify the actual and specific reasons why the Council considers, in the exercise of its discretion, that that specific restrictive measure must be adopted in respect of the person concerned. It further must be appropriate to the act in issue and the context in which it was adopted. The requirements that a statement of reasons is case-depended measured against the content of the measures, the nature of the reasons given and the interest which the targets, or other persons with direct and individual concern, may have in obtaining explanations. A statement of reasons need not specify all the relevant matters of fact and law, as the question of its adequacy is assessed with regard to its wording, its context and all legal rules governing that specific matter. Specifically, if a measure was adopted in circumstances known to the party concerned and these enable him or her to understand the scope of that same measure, the given reasons are deemed sufficient.[746]

155. It is noted that according to settled jurisprudence, the statement of reasons is an essential procedural requirement that is separate from that of the evidence of the alleged conduct; the latter concerns the substantive legality of the act in question and involves assessing the truth of the described facts and the classification of those facts as evidence, which satisfy the imposition of sanctions.[747]

156. The Courts of the EU have recognized the difficulty in obtaining specific evidence in a State beset by civil war or an authoritarian regime.[748] Nonetheless, evidence is expected to be sufficiently specific, precise and consistent to establish that there is a sufficient link between the person subject to a measure freezing his funds and the regime in question,[749] or to support any other reason for listing a certain applicant on the list in question.[750] Alongside publicly available sources of information, intelligence reports and other similar sources of information[751] the Council has used press articles to prove that a person was in a position to take significant decisions in relation to monetary policy,[752] that a person had links to a certain government or regime,[753] that

744. *Bank Melli* 2011 (n. 11) paras 47 & 48.
745. *El-Qaddafi* 2023 (n. 46) para. 65.
746. *Tomana* (n. 413) paras 142 & 143, citing *Council v. Bamba*, C-417/11 P, Judgment of 15 Nov. 2012, digital ECR, paras 52 to 54 ('Bamba').
747. *El-Qaddafi* 2023 (n. 46) para. 45, adopting the approach of *PKK* 2021 (n. 391) para. 55.
748. *Tarif Akhras v. Council*, C-193/15 P, Judgment of 7 Apr. 2016, digital ECR, para. 57.
749. *Tomana and Others v. Council*, C-330/15 P, Judgment of 28 Jul. 2016, para. 82; *Bashar Assi v. Council*, T-256/19, Judgment of 24 Nov 2021, digital ECR, para. 151; *Bureau d'achat de diamant Centrafrique (Badica) and Kardiam v. Council*, T-619/15, Judgment of 20 Jul. 2017, digital ECR, para. 61; and *Akhras* (n. 748) para. 61.
750. *Sabra* (n. 588) para. 53; *Khaldoun Al Zoubi v. Council*, T-257/19, Judgment of 24 Nov. 2021, digital ECR, para. 108; and *Bredenkamp* (n. 739) para. 57.
751. *See Kim and Others* (n. 62) paras 107-109.
752. *Mayaleh* (n. 44) para. 141.
753. *National Iranian Tanker Company v. Council*, T-565/12. Judgment of 3 Jul. 2014, digital ECR, para. 33; *Assaad v. Council*, T-426/21, Judgment of 8 Mar. 2023, digital ECR, paras 81 & 82;

a person supports a specific government and procures prohibited goods and technologies,[754] that a person has engaged with the government of a state in the military field,[755] and that a person has passed away.[756] The Council has further relied on the press to identify leading businesspersons providing material or financial support to the regime in question,[757] to establish political acts and statements[758] and even to conduct corporate due diligence.[759]

157. Turning to the requisite evidentiary standard, the Council applies the one suggested by the Financial Action Task Force ('FATF'),[760] namely, that freezing funds should be based 'on reasonable grounds, or a reasonable basis, to suspect or believe that such funds or other assets could be used to finance terrorist activity'.[761] The Court has approved this approach and confirmed that the reasons for inclusion can be based on 'suspicions of involvement in terrorist activities, without prejudice to the determination of whether those suspicions are justified'.[762]

158. Neither infrequently, not unusually the Council designates a person, the Courts of the EU then annul the apposite decisions insofar as they maintain the person's name on the lists due to various deficits and omissions, and consequently the Council proceeds with maintaining the same person's name on the lists.[763] It has been attempted to rely on res judicata against deciding to retain a person on the list, unsuccessfully though. The CJEU in rejecting the application of this principle noted that the relevant acts were adopted before the judgment in question was delivered. At the same time, the subject matter of, and cause of action in, the proceedings were not the same as those of the action that gave rise to that judgment. Furthermore, the principle of the force of res judicata extends only to the matters of fact and law actually or necessarily settled by a judicial decision.[764] It added that the reasons underpinning the retention of the

Mohamad Hamcho and Hamcho International v. Council, T-153/15, Judgment of 26 Oct. 2016, digital ECR, paras 80 & 81; *Samir Hassan v. Council*, T-572/11, Judgment of 16 Jul. 2014, digital ECR, para. 92.

754. *Bank Tejarat v. Council*, C-248/17 P, Judgment of 29 Nov. 2018, digital ECR, para. 40.
755. *Sharif 2016* (n. 450) paras 77 & 85.
756. *Tomana (n. 413)* paras 45 & 62.
757. *Sabra (n. 588)* para. 46; and *Khaled Kaddour v. Council*, T-461/16, Judgment of 31 May 2018, digital ECR, para. 101.
758. *Rondón* (n. 580) para. 112.
759. *Amer Foz v. Council*, C-524/22 P, Judgment of 11 Jan. 2024, digital ECR, paras 32, 47 & 48.
760. *See* Financial Action Task Force, *FATF Standards, FATF IX Special Recommendations*, 2008, p. 10, available: https://www.fatf-gafi.org/media/fatf/documents/reports/FATF%20Standards%20-%20IX%20Special%20Recommendations%20and%20IN%20rc.pdf (last visited: 24 Mar. 2022).
761. *Mohammed Al-Ghabra v. European Commission*, T-248/13, Judgment of 13 Dec. 2016, digital ECR para. 113 ('Al-Ghabra'); *Yassin Abdullah Kadi v. European Commission*, T-85/09, Judgment of 30 Sep. 2010, para. 60 ('Kadi 2010').
762. *Al-Ghabra* (n. 761) para. 116; *Kadi* 2013 (n. 9) para. 149.
763. *See*, i.e., *Aisha Muammer Mohamed El-Qaddafi v. Council*, T-322/19, Judgment of 21 Apr. 2021, digital ECR, paras 19 to 25 ('El-Qaddafi 2021').
764. *Ibid.*, para. 112, citing *National Iranian Tanker* (n. 157) para. 43.

applicant's name on the lists at issue did not constitute matters of fact and law actually or necessarily settled by the invoked final judgment.[765]

159. The statement of reasons must further be communicated to the targeted person. This obligation serves three purposes. It first enables the persons to whom restrictive measures are addressed to defend their rights in the best possible conditions. It equally enables them to decide with full knowledge of the relevant facts, whether there is any point in applying to the Courts of the EU. It lastly puts the same Courts fully in a position in which they may carry out the review of the lawfulness of the act in question in line with their duty under the TFEU.[766] Specifically with regard to the manner and timing of a notification, the following apply. The Council bears the obligation to communicate to the person concerned an act containing restrictive measures imposed on him or her, as provided for by the relevant legislation and it may not, in principle, discharge it.[767] Indirect communication of such acts through the publication of a notice in the Official Journal is permissible only if it is impossible for the Council to undertake individual communication. Were that not the case, the Council would readily be able to evade its obligation to undertake individual communication, the CJEU ruled.[768] In particular notification to an applicant's representative amounts to notification to the addressee only where such a form of notification is expressly provided for by legislation. It also does so, where there is an agreement to that effect between the parties as well as where the lawyer is duly authorized to accept such notification on behalf of his or her client.[769] Notification of the grounds on which the restrictive measures are based has to take place either when those measures are adopted or, at the very least, as swiftly as possible after their adoption, in order to enable those persons or entities to exercise their right to bring an action. This derives from the principle of effective judicial protection.[770]

160. The Courts of the EU have the authority to review the legality of a decision imposing financial sanctions. However, they shall not do so in light of WTO Agreements, such as the General Agreement on Tariffs and Trade.[771] When reviewing the

765. *El-Qaddafi* 2021 (n. 763) para. 112.
766. *Mayaleh* (n. 44) para. 105, citing *Heylens and Others*, 222/86, Judgment of 15 Nov. 2011, digital ECR, para. 28 and *Kadi* 2008 (n. 15) para. 337. *See also Bouchra Al Assad* (n. 585) para. 46 and *Tomana* (n. 413) para. 141, citing *Bamba* (n. 746) para. 49.
767. *See Aisha Muammer Mohamed El-Qaddafi v. Council*, T-681/14, Judgment of 28 Mar. 2017, digital ECR, para. 31 ('El-Qaddafi 2017'), citing *Mayaleh* (n. 44) para. 74.
768. *El-Qaddafi* 2021 (n. 763) para. 61, citing *Gbagbo (n. 732)* para. 61 & *Pshonka v. Council*, T-381/14, Judgment of 10 Jun. 2016, digital ECR, para. 41.
769. *El-Qaddafi* 2021 (n. 763) para. 64, citing *El-Qaddafi* 2017 (n. 767) paras 31 & 34. *See also Thoss v. Court of Auditors*, T-545/08, Order of 8 Jul. 2009, digital ECR, paras 41 & 42 and *BVGD v. Commission*, Joined T-104/07 and T-339/08, Judgment of 11 Jul. 2013, digital ECR, para. 146.
770. *Mayaleh* (n. 44) para. 54, citing *Bank Melli Iran v. Council*, Joined T-35/10 and T-7/11, Judgment of 6 Sep. 2013, digital ECR, para. 56.
771. Exceptionally they shall do so only where the Union intended to implement a particular obligation assumed in the context of the WTO, or where the act of the Union refers expressly to specific provisions of the WTO Agreements. *Venezuela* 2023 (n. 12) para. 107, citing *PSC Prominvestbank v. Council*, T-739/14, Judgment of 13 Sep. 2018, digital ECR, para. 133; *Fediol v. Commission*, 70/87, Judgment of 22 Jun. 1989, digital ECR, paras 19-22; *Nakajima v. Council*, C-69/89, Judgment of 7 May 1991, paras 29-32.

lawfulness of a decision, the Courts of the EU must satisfy themselves that that decision, which assumes individual scope for that person, has a sufficiently solid factual basis. That involves assessing the facts alleged in the statement of reasons on which the decision is based. Judicial review must concern whether these reasons, or, at the very least, one of those reasons, deemed sufficient in itself to support that decision, is substantiated.[772] With regard to time, the legality of an EU measure is assessed on the basis of the facts and the law as they stood at the time when the measure was adopted.[773] The competent EU authority bears the burden of establishing, in the event of a challenge, that the reasons relied on against the person concerned are well founded.[774] At the same time, the Courts of the EU carry out the assessment of the merits of a listing by examining the evidence not in isolation, but in the context in which it fits. Therefore, account may be taken of the context of the measures, of the fact that there was an urgent need to adopt such measures intended to put pressure on the respective regime in order for it to stop the violent repression against the population, or put an end to other condemned activities, and of the difficulty in obtaining more specific evidence in a state at civil war and having an authoritarian regime, where the case so is.[775]

VI The De-listing

161. Restrictive measures against a person may cease, as discussed briefly in the ensuing paragraphs. The relevant process depends on the authority that originally had designated such a person. When the designation has taken place at the level of the UN and the same authority decides to delist it, the Council shall amend the relevant list accordingly,[776] with the exception of the Regulation on Iraq where the Commission has been given the authority to do so.[777]

162. When the designation was decided at the level of the EU, a delisting can take place, as the relevant provisions set out the obligation of the Union to 'review [...] at regular intervals and at least every 12 months',[778] but for the acts targeting Nicaragua

772. *Mayaleh* (n. 44) para. 114, citing *Bank Melli 2009* (n. 68) para. 37.
773. *Sabra* (n. 588) para. 49, citing *Inuit Tapiriit Kanatami and Others v. Commission*, C-398/13 P, Judgment of 3 Sep. 2015, digital ECR, para. 22, and *National Iranian 2015* (n. 627) para. 112.
774. *Mayaleh* (n. 44) para. 138.
775. *Sabra* (n. 588) para. 42, citing *Anbouba v. Council*, C-605/13 P, Judgment of 21 Apr. 2015, digital ECR, para. 46.
776. Article 15(3) & Annex I Regulation on Sudan, Art. 9(5) & Annex I Regulation on DRC, Art. 47(5) & Annexes XIII and XIV Regulation on DPRK, Art. 13 & Annex I Regulation on Somalia, Art. 46(6) & Annexes VIII and XIII Regulation on Iran, Art. 21(5) & Annexes II and VI Regulation on Libya, Art. 17(3) & Annex I Regulation on CAR, Art. 15(3) & Annex I Regulation on Yemen, Art. 20(3) & Annex I Regulation on South Sudan, Art. 12(5) & Annex I Regulation on Mali.
777. Article 11(b) and Annexes III & IV Regulation on Iraq.
778. Article 47a(1) & Annexes XV, XVI and XVII Regulation on DPRK, Art. 46(7) & Annexes IX and XIV Regulation on Iran, Art. 11(4) & Annex I Regulation on Guinea-Bissau, Art. 21(6) & Annex III Regulation on Libya, Art. 12(6) & Annex Ia Regulation on Mali, Art. 12(4) & Annex I EU Regulation on Iran, Art. 4i(4) & Annex IV Regulation on Myanmar/Burma, Art. 13(4) & Annex

and Zimbabwe that do not do so. Nonetheless, the relevant provisions in the corresponding decisions foresee the obligation to keep these acts under constant review.[779] The view that delisting can take place is supported by the provisions of the corresponding decisions and common positions that establish the need for reviewing a listing when new evidence is presented,[780] along with the necessity for constant review and for renewal or amendment when the Council deems that its objectives have not been met.[781] The CJEU agrees.[782] Some legal instruments have adopted a different wording stating that the measures shall cease to apply when the Council determines that the conditions for their application are no longer met.[783] Within the frame of the Regulation on Libya, the CJEU held that the Council has the authority to maintain a person on the list concerned if it concludes that the reason for the initial listing is ongoing. To this end, it is required to verify whether, since the initial listing or since the last review, as the case may be, the factual situation has changed in such a way that it is no longer possible to draw the same conclusion. Furthermore, in view of the passage of time and in the light of changes in the circumstances of the case, the Council may be obliged to base the retention of that person on the list on an up-to-date assessment of the situation and to take into account more recent facts which demonstrate that that reason still obtains.[784]

163. The relevant process is initiated with a proposal by a Member State or the High Representative of the Union for Foreign Affairs and Security Policy towards the

I Regulation on Burundi, Art. 17(4) & Annexes IV and V Regulation on Venezuela, Art. 15a(4) & Annex II Regulation on Guinea, Art. 32(4) & Annexes II and IIa Regulation on Syria, Art. 12(4) & Annex I Regulation on Tunisia & Art. 14(4) & Annex I Funds Regulation Ukraine.

779. Article 10(3) Decision on Zimbabwe & Art. 11(b) Regulation on Zimbabwe and Art. 9 Decision on Nicaragua.
780. Article 15(2) Regulation on Sudan, Art. 9(4) Regulation on Congo, Art. 47(4) Regulation on DPRK, Art. 12(2) Regulation on Somalia, Art. 46(5) Regulation on Iran, Art. 11(3) Regulation on Guinea-Bissau, Art. 21(4) Regulation on Libya, Art. 17(2) Regulation on the CAR, Art. 15(2) Regulation on Yemen, Art. 20(2) Regulation on South Sudan, Art. 12(4) Regulation on Mali, Art. 16(2) Regulation on Haiti, Art. 12(3) EU Regulation on Iran, Art. 4i(3) Regulation on Myanmar-Burma, Art. 13(3) Regulation on Burundi, Art. 17(3) Regulation on Venezuela, Art. 13(3) Regulation on Nicaragua, Art. 13(3) EU Regulation on Lebanon, Art. 15a(3) Regulation on Guinea, Art. 32(3) Regulation on Syria, Art. 12(3) Regulation on Tunisia, Art. 14(3) Funds Regulation on Ukraine, Art. 12(3) Regulation on Drilling. No such provision is found in the Regulation on Iraq and in the Regulation on Zimbabwe.
781. Article 6(2) Decision on Mali, Art. 10(3) Decision on Zimbabwe, Art. 6(2) EU Decision on Iran, Art. 12 Decision on Myanmar/Burma, Art. 6 Decision on Burundi, Art. 13 Decision on Venezuela, Art. 9 Decision on Nicaragua, Art. 8(2) Common Position on Guinea, Art. 34 Decision on Syria, Art. 5(2) Decision on Tunisia & Art. 5 Funds Decision Ukraine.
782. *Torres* (n. 333) para. 49, citing *Kumba* (n. 101) para. 84.
783. Article 36(2) Common Position on DPRK, Art. 26(3) Common Position on Iran, Art. 17(2) Common Position on Libya.
784. *El-Qaddafi* 2023 (n. 46) para. 75, citing *LTTE* 2017 (n. 390) para. 54 and *PKK* 2021 (n. 391) paras 49 & 51.

Council, that reaches a decision,[785] sometimes unanimously[786] and less often as required by domestic political developments.[787]

164. Alongside the aforementioned procedures, the targeted persons are given the opportunity to present observations to the Council that it shall then review the decision and inform the person accordingly,[788] with the exceptions of persons designated under the Regulation on Iraq and the Regulation on Zimbabwe that are silent on this issue.

VII Limitation of Liability

165. The statutory provisions on restrictive measures limit the liability that could potentially arise from the imposition of such measures at a material level and at a procedural one.

166. Starting with the limitation at a material level, the aforementioned obligations and statutory duties are addressed to third parties other than the persons under the restrictive measures, those predominantly being private actors, such as banks, exporters and insurance companies. In truth such actors give effect to the legislation as they are the ones that proceed with freezing and abstain from making it available;[789] thus, it is quite likely that their actions will give rise to liability. The legislator has stepped in and defined the limits of their liability. More specifically, as long as freezing funds and economic resources and refusing to make such available is carried out in good faith and on the basis that such action is in accordance with the applicable regulation no liability of any kind shall arise unless these acts were the result of negligence.[790] Furthermore,

785. Article 12(2) Common Position on Libya, Art. 6(1) Decision on Zimbabwe, Art. 3(1) EU Decision on Iran, Art. 3(1) Decision on Burundi, Art. 5(1) Common Position on Guinea, Art. 30(1) Decision on Syria, Art. 2(1) Decision on Tunisia & Art. 2(1) Funds Decision Ukraine.
786. Article 33(2) Common Position on DPRK, Art. 23(2) Common Position on Iran, Art. 3(2) Decision on Mali, Art. 7(1) Decision on Myanmar/Burma, Art. 8(1) Decision on Venezuela, Art. 4(1) Decision on Nicaragua.
787. This has been stated with regard to Zimbabwe and Guinea. *See* Art. 6(1) Decision on Zimbabwe and Art. 5(1) Common Position on Guinea.
788. Article 15(1) & (2) Regulation on Sudan, Art. 9(3) & (4) Regulation on Congo, Art. 47(3) & (4) Regulation on DPRK, Art. 12(1) & (2) Regulation on Somalia, Art. 46(4) & (5) Regulation on Iran, Art. 11(2) & (3) Regulation on Guinea-Bissau, Art. 21(3) & (4) Regulation on Libya, Art. 17(1) & (2) Regulation on the CAR, Art. 15(1) & (2) Regulation on Yemen, Art. 20(1) & (2) Regulation on South Sudan, Art. 12(3) & (4) Regulation on Mali, Art. 16(1) & (2) Regulation on Haiti, Art. 12(2) & (3) EU Regulation on Iran, Art. 4i(2) & (3) Regulation on Myanmar-Burma, Art. 13(2) & (3) Regulation on Burundi, Art. 17(2) & (3) Regulation on Venezuela, Art. 13(2) & (3) Regulation on Nicaragua, Art. 13(2) & (3) EU Regulation on Lebanon, Art. 15a(2) & (3) Regulation on Guinea, Art. 32(2) & (3) Regulation on Syria, Art. 12(2) & (3) Regulation on Tunisia, Art. 14(2) & (3) Funds Regulation on Ukraine & Art. 12(2) & (3) Regulation on Drilling.
789. Julia Schmidt, *The Legality of Unilateral Extra-territorial Sanctions under International Law* 27(1) J.C.&S.L. 53 at 59 (2022) https://doi.org/10.1093/jcsl/krac005.
790. Article 9 Regulation on Iraq, Art. 11(1) Regulation on Sudan, Art. 7(1) Regulation on DRC, Art. 54(1) Regulation on DPRK, Art. 7 Regulation on Somalia, Art. 42(1) Regulation on Iran, Art. 7(1) Regulation on Guinea-Bissau, Art. 16(1) Regulation on Libya, Art. 13(1) Regulation on CAR, Art. 11(1) Regulation on Yemen, Art. 16(1) Regulation on South Sudan, Art. 9(1) Regulation on Mali, Art. 12(1) Regulation on Haiti, Art. 9 Regulation on Zimbabwe, Art. 8(1) EU Regulation on Iran, Art. 4f(1) Regulation on Myanmar/Burma, Art. 9(1) Regulation on

actions shall not give rise to any liability of any kind, if the acting person did not know and had no reasonable cause to suspect that their actions would infringe the measures set out in the regulation in question,[791] with the exception of the Regulation on Zimbabwe that is silent on this matter.

167. At the same time, the CJEU holds that it has jurisdiction to hear a claim for damages allegedly suffered by a person or entity, as a result of restrictive measures against it.[792] It may not of its own motion raise the issue of time limitation.[793] The applicant bears the burden of furnishing the evidence, in order to establish the fact and the extent of the allegedly suffered loss;[794] still, where it is difficult to express the damage in figures it is not absolutely necessary to particularize its exact extent in the application or to calculate the amount of the compensation claimed.[795] Turning to issues of substance, for non-contractual liability to incur the following conditions, that have to take place cumulatively,[796] must be satisfied: the institution's conduct must be unlawful, actual damage must have been suffered and there must be a causal link between the conduct complained of and the damage pleaded.[797] The unlawfulness of a legal act per se does not suffice for the first condition to be satisfied.[798] Moreover, a sufficiently serious breach of a rule of law that is intended to confer rights on individuals is necessary.[799] The damage suffered must be real and certain loss,[800] whereas it may be non-material, also classified as 'moral', in the sense of damage to the

---

Burundi, Art. 13(1) Regulation on Venezuela, Art. 13(1) Regulation on Nicaragua, Art. 10(1) EU Regulation on Lebanon, Art. 7 Regulation on Guinea, Art. 22 Regulation on Syria, Art. 8(1) Regulation on Tunisia, Art. 10(1) Funds Regulation Ukraine & Art. 9(1) Regulation on Drilling.

791. Article 4a Regulation on Iraq, Art. 11(2) Regulation on Sudan, Art. 7(2) Regulation on DRC, Art. 54(2) Regulation on DPRK, Art. 2(5) Regulation on Somalia, Art. 42(2) Regulation on Iran, Art. 7(2) Regulation on Guinea-Bissau, Art. 16(2) Regulation on Libya, Art. 13(2) Regulation on CAR, Art. 11(2) Regulation on Yemen, Art. 16(2) Regulation on South Sudan, Art. 9(2) Regulation on Mali, Art. 12(1) Regulation on Haiti, Art. 8(2) EU Regulation on Iran, Art. 4f(2) Regulation on Myanmar/Burma, Art. 9(2) Regulation on Burundi, Art. 13(2) Regulation on Venezuela, Art. 13(2) Regulation on Nicaragua, Art. 10(2) EU Regulation on Lebanon, Art. 11 Regulation on Guinea, Art. 28 Regulation on Syria, Art. 8(2) Regulation on Tunisia, Art. 10(2) Funds Regulation Ukraine & Art. 9(2) Regulation on Drilling.

792. *Post Bank Iran v. Council of the European Union*, T-559/15, Judgment of 13 Dec. 2018, digital ECR, paras 55 & 57 ('Post Bank Iran'), adopting the approach of *Safa Nicu Sepahan v. Council*, T-384/11, Judgment of 25 Nov. 2014, paras 45 to 149 ('Sepahan').

793. *Post Bank Iran* (n. 792) para. 64.

794. *Ibid.*, para. 70.

795. *Ibid.*, para. 71, following *Inalca and Cremonini v. Commission*, C-460/09 P, Judgment of 28 Feb. 2013, para. 104.

796. *Post Bank Iran* (n. 792) para. 85, following *Fahas v. Council*, T-49/07, Judgment of 7 Dec. 2010, paras 92 and 93 ('Fahas').

797. *Post Bank Iran* (n. 792) para. 83, following *FIAMM and Others v. Council and Commission*, C-120/06 P and C-121/06 P, Judgment of 9 Sep. 2008, para. 106; *Schneider Electric v. Commission*, T-351/03, Judgments of 11 Jul. 2007, para. 113; and *Sepahan* (n. 792) para. 47.

798. *Post Bank Iran* (n. 792) para. 93, following the approach of *Sepahan* (n. 792) para. 50; *see also Dole Fresh Fruit International v. Council and Commission*, T-56/00, Judgment of 6 Mar. 2003, paras 72 to 75.

799. *Post Bank Iran* (n. 792) para. 94, following, the approach of *Sepahan* (n. 792) para. 29.

800. *Post Bank Iran* (n. 792) para. 94, following *De Franceschi v. Council and Commission*, 51/81, Judgment of 27 Jan. 1982, para. 9; *Birra Wührerand Others v. Council and Commission*, Joined 256/80, 257/80, 265/80, 267/80, 5/81, 51/81 and 282/82, Judgment of 13 Nov. 1984, digital ECR, para. 9.

image or to the reputation of that person.[801] The claim for compensation for damage must give particulars of the nature of the damage alleged in connection with the conduct at issue and must quantify the whole of that damage, even if approximately.[802]

168. Furthermore, most regulations[803] provide a limitation of liability in relation to contracts and transactions that are affected by the imposed restrictive measures through the creation of procedural restrictions. More specifically, it is set out that claims in relation to such contracts and transactions, such as a claim for compensation or a claim under a guarantee, shall not be satisfied if they are made directly or indirectly by a designated person,[804] or with regard to the DPRK, Iran and Libya, by a designated person as well as by any such national and its government.[805]

169. Starting with the definitions, three key terms, those being 'claim', 'contracts and transactions' and, in some instances, 'affecting the performance of a contract or transaction', are statutory specified (in regard to the definitions *see* Annex I pp. 311 at 314, 314 and 311 respectively). *Claims* is in essence defined in a circular manner. It stands for any claim, as long as it has been made before the entry into force of the relevant regulation and it stands in connection with a contract or transaction.[806] *Contracts and transactions* is also defined in a circular manner. It includes any transaction of whatever form and whatever the applicable law, regardless of it comprising one or more contracts or similar obligations. Contract is then defined as any related provision arising in connection with the transaction.[807] Finally, a handful of set of restrictive measures specify the meaning of affecting the performance of a contract or transaction. According to those, the performance of a contract or transaction is

801. *Post Bank Iran* (n. 792) paras 108, 114 & 116, following the approach of *Sepahan* (n. 792) paras 80 & 83.
802. *Post Bank Iran* (n. 792) para. 113.
803. The Regulations on Iraq, Somalia, Guinea-Bissau, Zimbabwe, Guinea, Tunisia and the EU Regulation on Iran are silent on this matter.
804. Article 12(1) Regulation on Sudan, Art. 7a(1) Regulation on DRC, Art. 14(1) Regulation on CAR, Art. 12(1) Regulation on Yemen, Art. 17(1) Regulation on South Sudan, Art. 10(1) Regulation on Mali, Art. 13(1) Regulation on Haiti, Art. 4h(1) Regulation on Myanmar/Burma, Art. 10(1) Regulation on Burundi, Art. 15(1) Regulation on Venezuela, Art. 11(1) Regulation on Nicaragua, Art. 11(1) EU Regulation on Lebanon, Art. 27(1) Regulation on Syria, Art. 11(1) Funds Regulation Ukraine & Art. 10(1) Regulation on Drilling.
805. Article 53(1) Regulation on DPRK, Art. 38(1) Regulation on Iran, Art. 17(1) Regulation on Libya.
806. Article 1(b) Regulation on Sudan, Art. 1(a) Regulation on DRC, Art. 2(3) Regulation on DPRK, Art. 1(c) Regulation on Iran, Art. 1(b) Regulation on CAR, Art. 1(a) Regulation on Yemen, Art. 1(b) Regulation on South Sudan, Art. 1(a) Regulation on Mali, Art. 1(a) Regulation on Haiti, Art. 1(a) Regulation on Myanmar/Burma, Art. 1(a) Regulation on Burundi, Art. 1(a) Regulation on Venezuela, Art. 1(a) Regulation on Nicaragua, Art. 1(a) EU Regulation on Lebanon, Art. 1(a) Funds Regulation Ukraine & Art. 1(a) Regulation on Drilling. The Regulation on Libya and the Regulation on Syria do not set out a definition of *claims*.
807. Article 1(c) Regulation on Sudan, Art. 1(b) Regulation on DRC, Art. 2(5) Regulation on DPRK, Art. 1(d) Regulation on Iran, Art. 1(c) Regulation on CAR, Art. 1(d) Regulation on Yemen, Art. 1(c) Regulation on South Sudan, Art. 1(d) Regulation on Mali, Art. 1(b) Regulation on Haiti, Art. 1(b) Regulation on Myanmar/Burma, Art. 1(b) Regulation on Burundi, Art. 1(b) Regulation on Venezuela, Art. 1(b) Regulation on Nicaragua, Art. 1(b) EU Regulation on Lebanon, Art. 1(c) Regulation on Syria, Art. 1(b) Funds Regulation Ukraine & Art. 1(b) Regulation on Drilling. The Regulation on Libya does not set out a definition of *contract or transaction*.

regarded as having been affected by the measures imposed by the relevant regulation when the claim results from those measures, both directly and indirectly.[808] Under the jurisprudence of the Courts of the EU, the explained mechanism consists of three parts. First, the performance or execution of a contract or a transaction must have been affected by the adopted measures, thus requiring that the specific contract or transaction must have been the subject of such measures. Second, granting any claim connected to a contract or transaction is prohibited. Third, the claims under prohibition must have been made by the named entities or persons.[809] Within this frame and the specific case of counter-guarantee agreements, the CJEU ruled that the payment of the costs arising under counter-guarantee agreements by a first counter guarantor or by a second counter guarantor to the first counter guarantor cannot, in principle, be excluded from its scope.[810] When such agreements have been made between banks, the CJEU took the view that a bank may be regarded as an entity acting on behalf of the designated government and therefore causing a claim for payment to fall within the scope of the prohibition, whereby the relevant checks shall be made by the referring court.[811]

170. One further procedural limitation involves reversing the ordinary burden of proof, as set out in the national codes and legislation. Specifically during enforcement proceedings for a claim in the aforementioned sense, the person initiating such proceedings bears the onus of proving that the claim at hand is not prohibited.[812]

§4 FURTHER RESTRICTIONS ON FUNDS AND FINANCIAL SERVICES

171. The legal instruments imposing restrictive measures with regard to Syria and the DPRK impose additional restrictions on financial services. The Regulation on Iran contained similar provisions such as prohibiting the granting of financial loans and credits and establishing joint ventures for persons engaged in oil, gas and petrochemical industries and uranium mining,[813] as well as requiring authorization for the transfer of funds, prohibiting the opening of new bank accounts, establishing correspondent banking relationships, new representative offices and joint ventures, prohibiting

808. Article 53(2) Regulation on DPRK & Art. 38(2) Regulation on Iran.
809. *SH* (n. 327) paras 73 to 75.
810. *Ibid.*, para. 76.
811. *Ibid.*, paras 80 & 81.
812. Article 12(2) Regulation on Sudan, Art. 7(2) Regulation on DRC, Art. 53(3) Regulation on DPRK, Art. 38(3) Regulation on Iran, Art. 17(2) Regulation on Libya, Art. 14(2) Regulation on CAR, Art. 12(2) Regulation on Yemen, Art. 17(2) Regulation on South Sudan, Art. 10(2) Regulation on Mali, Art. 13(2) Regulation on Haiti, Art. 4h(2) Regulation on Myanmar/Burma, Art. 10(2) Regulation on Burundi, Art. 15(2) Regulation on Venezuela, Art. 11(2) Regulation on Nicaragua, Art. 11(2) EU Regulation on Lebanon, Art. 27(2) Regulation on Syria, Art. 11(2) Funds Regulation Ukraine & Art. 10(2) Regulation on Drilling.
813. Articles 17 to 22 (old version) Regulation on Iran.

selling and purchasing of public bonds, providing brokering services and insurance.[814] Nonetheless, said provisions have been repealed as a consequence of the JCPOA.[815,816]

172. The Regulation on Syria imposes further financial restrictions that come into place through the activities and vigilance of credit institutions,[817] their branches[818] and financial institutions,[819] as these have been statutorily defined (in regard to the definitions *see* Annex I pp. 311 at 315, 312, 319 respectively).

173. Syrian credit and financial institutions, those being institutions both domiciliated in Syria and controlled by persons in Syria,[820] may neither open a new bank account nor establish a new correspondent banking relationship with credit and financial institutions in the Union.[821] Moreover, they may not open a representative office or establish a branch or a subsidiary in the Union. This is ensured by prohibiting their authorization, the conclusion of relevant agreements and the acquisition and extension of a participation or acquisition of any ownership interest.[822] At the same time, credit and financial institutions in the Union are prohibited from opening a new representative office and establishing a new branch or subsidiary in Syria, as well as establishing a new joint venture with any Syrian credit and financial institution.[823]

174. Exceptionally, the competent authorities of the Member States may authorize the opening of a new bank account or representative office and the establishment of a new branch or subsidiary, when this is done for the purpose of assisting the civilian population in Syria. In this regard the ensuing three conditions must be fulfilled: the designated persons must not benefit therefrom; the Regulation on Syria must not be violated;[824] and the competent authority has to consult in advance the Syrian National Coalition for Opposition and Revolutionary Forces. If the latter has not expressed its views within thirty days, the relevant competent authority may proceed with its

814. Articles 30 to 35 (old version) Regulation on Iran.
815. The EU and its Member States undertook the commitment to terminate all provisions of the Regulation on Iran implementing nuclear-related sanctions as well as restrictive measures in the financial sector, the sector of oil, gas and petrochemical, the shipping, shipbuilding and transport sectors, the sector of gold and other precious metals, nuclear-proliferation, the sector of metals, software, arms, asset-freeze and visa bans, and certain other provisions, including definitions and general and final provisions. *See* Joint Comprehensive Plan of Action, S/RES/2231 of 20 Jul. 2015 Annex II points 1.1 to 1.10.1.2.
816. *See* Art. 1(11) & (15) Council Regulation (EU) 2015/1861 of 18 Oct. 2015 amending Regulation (EU) No. 267/2012 concerning restrictive measures against Iran, OJ L 274, 18 Oct. 2015, p. 1.
817. Article 1(d) Regulation on Syria and Art. 4(1)(1) Regulation (EU) No. 575/2013 of the European Parliament and of the Council of 26 Jun. 2013 on prudential requirements for credit institutions and amending Regulation (EU) No. 648/2012, OJ L 176 27 Jun. 2013, p. 1.
818. Article 1(a) Regulation on DPRK and Art. 4(1)(17) Regulation 575/2013.
819. Article 1(g) last sentence Regulation on Syria.
820. Article 1(n) Regulation on Syria.
821. Articles 25(1)(a) & (b) and 35 Regulation on Syria.
822. Article 25(2)(a), (b), (c) and (d) Regulation on Syria.
823. Articles 25(1)(c) & (d) and 35 Regulation on Syria.
824. Articles 25a(1)(b)(i), (ii) & (iii) and 14 Regulation on Syria.

decision.[825] It shall then inform within two weeks the other Member States and the Commission of the granted authorization.[826]

175. The ensuing restriction relates to Syrian public or public-guaranteed bonds issued after 19 January 2012, that being the date on which the Regulation on Syria came into force.[827] It is prohibited to sell and purchase such bonds, both directly and indirectly, to and from the State of Syria, including its public bodies, corporations and agencies, Syrian credit and financial institutions and their representatives as well as any person controlled by them.[828] It is also prohibited to provide brokering services with regard to such bonds to said persons and to assist said persons in order to issue such bonds by providing any service.[829] These prohibitions are absolute, as without any derogations or the possibility of an authorization.

176. In particular, the European Investment Bank is prohibited from making any disbursement or payment under any existing loan agreement with the State of Syria. Also, it is set out that it shall suspend all existing Technical Assistance Service Contracts relating to projects under the aforementioned agreements when they are intended for the benefit of the State of Syria.[830]

177. Furthermore, it is prohibited to provide insurance and re-insurance to the State of Syria and its public bodies, including their representatives and agents.[831] *Insurance* is defined as 'an undertaking or commitment whereby one or more natural or legal persons are obliged, in return for payment, to provide one or more other persons, in the event of materialization of a risk, with an indemnity or a benefit as determined by the undertaking or commitment'.[832] Further, *reinsurance* means 'the activity consisting in accepting risks ceded by an insurance undertaking or by another reinsurance undertaking or, in the case of the association of underwriters known as Lloyd's, the activity consisting in accepting risks, ceded by any member of Lloyd's, by an insurance or reinsurance undertaking other than the association of underwriters known as Lloyd's'.[833] It is equally prohibited to circumvent said prohibition.[834]

178. This insurance-related restriction is subject to a number of statutory exceptions. At the outset, providing compulsory or third-party insurance to Syrian persons based in the Union and insurance to Syrian diplomatic and consular missions in the Union are exempt.[835] Further, it is permitted to provide insurance, including health and travel insurance, to individuals acting in their private capacity and reinsurance relating thereto. It is also permitted to provide insurance and reinsurance to owners of vessels,

825. Article 25a(1)(c) & (2) Regulation on Syria.
826. Article 25a(3) Regulation on Syria.
827. Article 37 Regulation on Syria.
828. Article 24(a)(i), (ii), (iii) & (iv) Regulation on Syria.
829. Article 24(b) and (c) Regulation on Syria.
830. Article 23(a) and (b) Regulation on Syria.
831. Article 26(1)(a)(i) & (ii) Regulation on Syria.
832. Article 1(l) Regulation on Syria.
833. Article 1(m) Regulation on Syria.
834. Article 26(1)(b) Regulation on Syria.
835. Article 26(2) Regulation on Syria.

aircraft and vehicles that are not designated.[836] Lastly, insurance and re-insurance agreements concluded before 19 January 2012 fall outside the scope of the prohibition, as long as there is no prior contractual obligation on the part of the insurer or re-insurer to accept an extension or renewal of a policy.[837]

179. Finally, the Regulation on Syria prohibits the financing of certain enterprises.[838] As these enterprises are related to the oil and gas sector, they are portrayed under the restrictive measures in relation to energy (*see* in this regard paragraphs 200 et seq. below).

180. The Regulation on DPRK shares certain commonalities with the Regulation on Syria, starting with the identical definitions of *credit institution*, *branch* and *financial institution*[839] (in regard to the definitions *see* Annex I pp. 311 at 315, 312, 319 respectively). It also entails a number of identical prohibitions, those being selling and purchasing public and public-guaranteed bonds[840] issued after 19 February 2013,[841] as well as the prohibitions on opening an account, establishing a correspondent banking relationship, opening representative offices, establishing a joint venture and taking ownership interest,[842] which however may take place if the 1718 DPRK Sanctions Committee has authorized them.[843] Importantly, in the case of the DPRK, these measures have been decided beforehand by the UN Security Council, as a response to the nuclear test that the DPRK conducted on 12 February 2013,[844] with the exception of the bond-related restrictions that were introduced as autonomous measures of the Union alongside other sanctions adopted by the UN Security Council.[845]

181. The Regulation on DPRK sets out further restrictive measures, starting with a prohibition of the transfer of funds, including clearing of funds, to and from the DPRK.[846] *Transfer of funds* is specified as any transaction on behalf of a payer with a view to making funds available to a payee whereby the transaction could be carried out

836. Article 26(3) Regulation on Syria.
837. Article 26(4) Regulation on Syria.
838. Articles 13 & 14 Regulation on Syria.
839. *See* Art. 2(9), (1) and (6) Regulation on DPRK respectively.
840. Article 31(a), (b) & (c) Regulation on DPRK.
841. Article 5 Council Decision 2013/88/CFSP of 18 Feb. 2013 amending Decision 2010/800/CFSP concerning restrictive measures against the Democratic People's Republic of Korea, OJ L 46, 19 Feb. 2013, p. 28 and Art. 1(6) Council Regulation (EU) No. 296/2013 of 26 Mar. 2013 amending Regulation (EC) No. 329/2007 concerning restrictive measures against the Democratic People's Republic of Korea, OJ L 90, 28 Mar. 2013, p. 4.
842. Articles 24(a), (b), (c) & (d) and 30 Regulation on DPRK.
843. Article 25(1) Regulation on DPRK. If a Member State does proceed with such a derogation, it shall promptly notify the other Member States and the Commission (Art. 25(2) Regulation on DPRK).
844. These were the sanctions with regard to opening new branches, subsidiaries and representative offices of banks of DPRK abroad, *see* S/RES/2094 of 7 Mar. 2013, paras 12 & 13.
845. *See* Art. 1(2) Council Decision 2013/88, which implemented S/RES/2087 of 22 Jan. 2013 that makes no mention of measures related to bonds, and introduced Art. 2a to Council Decision 2010/800/CFSP of 22 Dec. 2010 concerning restrictive measures against the Democratic People's Republic of Korea and repealing Common Position 2006/795/CFSP, OJ L 341, 23 Dec. 2010, p. 32.
846. Article 21(1) Regulation on DPRK. *See* the relevant provision of the UN Security Council S/RES/2094 of 7 Mar. 2013 para. 11 & S/RES/2371 of 5 Aug. 2017 para. 13.

by electronic means or not, through a payment service provider or not. The payer and the payee being the same person does not affect the essence of this notion.[847] (in regard to the definition *see* Annex I p. 311 at 334).

182. Said prohibition is not immune to exemptions. First, it does not apply to any transfer of funds or transaction necessary for the official purposes of a diplomatic or consular mission of a Member State or an international organization enjoying immunities in the DPRK.[848] Further, it does not apply to two kinds of transactions that consist of two components: a quantitative element and the specific purpose served by the transaction. Transactions valued less than EUR 5,000 or equivalent that regard personal remittances are exempt from the said prohibition.[849] At the same time, transactions involving funds valued less than EUR 15,000 or equivalent may be exempted, when they serve the following purposes: (a) foodstuffs, healthcare including medical equipment, agricultural or humanitarian purposes;[850] (b) implementation of projects funded by the Union or its Member States for development purposes directly addressing the needs of the civilian population or the promotion of denuclearization;[851] (c) implementation of statutory exemptions or permitted trade contracts;[852] (d) transactions related to a diplomatic or consular mission or an international organization enjoying immunities under international law, under the condition that the intension behind such transactions is serving the official purposes of said missions or organizations.[853] Finally, regardless of the amount in question, said prohibition is inapplicable to any transfer of funds or transaction which is necessary for the official purposes of a diplomatic or consular mission of a Member State in the DPRK or an international organization enjoying immunities under international law.[854]

183. At the same time, it is prohibited for credit institutions, their branches and financial institutions that are located in the Union, regardless of the location of their head office,[855] to perform transactions with credit and financial institutions domiciled in the DPRK, as well as their branches, subsidiaries and any such institution controlled by persons domiciled in the DPRK.[856] The aforementioned exceptions (*see* in this regard paragraph 182 above) apply *mutatis mutandis.*[857]

184. By 31 May 2016, credit and financial institutions were obliged to implement a series of actions in accordance with resolution 2270 of the UN Security Council.[858] These actions included: closing any account with a credit or financial institution domiciliated in the DPRK; terminating any correspondent banking relationship with

847. Article 2(23)(a) & (b) Regulation on DPRK.
848. Article 21(3) Regulation on DPRK.
849. Article 21(5) Regulation on DPRK.
850. Article 21(4)(a) Regulation on DPRK.
851. Article 21(4)(d) Regulation on DPRK.
852. Article 21(4)(b) & (c) Regulation on DPRK.
853. Article 21(4)(e) Regulation on DPRK.
854. Article 21(3) Regulation on DPRK.
855. Article 2(6) Regulation on DPRK.
856. Article 21(2)(a), (b), (c), (d) and (e) Regulation on DPRK.
857. Article 21(4) and (5) Regulation on DPRK.
858. S/RES/2270 of 2 Mar. 2016.

such an institution; closing representative offices, branches and subsidiaries in the DPRK; terminating joint ventures with such an institution; and relinquishing any ownership interest in same institutions.[859] Exceptionally, certain representative offices, subsidiaries or accounts could remain operational, as long as the 1718 DPRK Sanctions Committee determined that this was required for humanitarian purposes, for the diplomatic and consular missions of the DPRK and for purposes consistent with the objectives of certain resolutions of the UN Security Council.[860,861]

185. When credit and financial institutions do engage in activities with credit and financial institutions domiciliated in the DPRK, they have to exercise enhanced vigilance by performing certain additional tasks and ensuring that precautionary measures are in place. More specifically, prior to establishing the business relationship or carrying out the transaction, they apply customer due diligence measures such as: identifying the customer and verifying the customer's identity on the basis of documents and information from independent sources; identifying the beneficial owner and taking reasonable measures to verify that person's identity; assessing and obtaining information on the nature of the business relationship; and conducting ongoing monitoring of the business relationship.[862] Interestingly, despite the acknowledged high risk of proliferation, the EU legislators place financing, credit and financial institutions under the statutory obligation to apply the ordinary customer due diligence measures and not the *enhanced* customer due diligence measures,[863] that would appear to be more apposite due to the evident geographical risk factor since the DPRK is subject to sanctions designated by the UN Security Council.[864] Further, in addition to said measures credit and financial institutions have to ensure compliance with anti-money-laundering and counter-terrorist-financing procedures as set out in EU legislation.[865] When transfer of funds takes place, they have to make sure that information on both payers and payees is provided as required under the AML-Regulation; should information be missing or be incomplete, they are under the obligation to refuse to process the transaction.[866] They also have to maintain records of the transactions, consisting of the original documents or copies admissible in judicial proceedings under the applicable national law for a period of five

859. Article 26(a), (b), (c), (d) and (e) Regulation on DPRK.
860. These are S/RES/1718 of 14 Oct. 2006, S/RES/1874 of 12 Jun. 2009, S/RES/2087 of 22 Jan. 2013, S/RES/2094 of 7 Mar. 2013, S/RES/2270 of 2 Mar. 2016, S/RES/2321 of 30 Nov. 2016, S/RES/2371 of 5 Aug. 2017.
861. Article 27(1) Regulation on DPRK.
862. Article 23(1)(a) Regulation on DPRK and Arts 13 & 14 Directive (EU) 2015/849 of the European Parliament and of the Council of 20 May 2015 on the prevention of the use of the financial system for the purposes of money laundering or terrorist financing, amending Regulation (EU) No. 648/2012 of the European Parliament and of the Council, and repealing Directive 2005/60/EC of the European Parliament and of the Council and Commission Directive 2006/70/EC, OJ L 141, 5 Jun. 2015, p. 73 (hereinafter 'AML Directive').
863. *See* in this regard Arts 18 et seq. AML Directive.
864. *See* Art. 18(3) and Annex III(3)(c) AML Directive.
865. Article 23(1)(b) Regulation on DPRK as well as AML Directive and Regulation (EU) 2015/847 of the European Parliament and of the Council of 20 May 2015 on information accompanying transfers of funds and repealing Regulation (EC) No. 1781/2006, OJ L 141, 5 Jun. 2015, p. 1 (hereinafter 'AML Regulation').
866. Article 23(1)(c) Regulation on DPRK.

years.[867] In addition, credit and financial institutions have a specific report duty in cases of suspicious transactions, including attempted transactions,[868] and suspicions of *proliferation financing*, in the sense of funds possibly contributing to the DPRK's programmes and activities related to nuclear, ballistic missiles, and other weapons of mass destruction.[869] It is here noted that the term *proliferation financing* is encountered as part of the phrase 'proliferation financing risk' in the Recommendations of the FATF[870] and more specifically in Recommendation 1. It is there set out that 'proliferation financing risk' refers 'strictly and only to the potential breach, non-implementation or evasion of the targeted financial sanctions obligations referred to in Recommendation 7', which foresees the obligation of states to implement targeted financial sanctions for the purpose of complying with resolutions of the UN Security Council with regard to the prevention, suppression and disruption of proliferation of weapons of mass destruction and its financing in the form of asset freezing and not making available funds and other assets to designated persons. Precisely this Recommendation 7 was welcomed by the UN Security Council[871] in its resolution that was implemented through the Regulation on DPRK.

186. Finally, it is prohibited to provide financing or financial assistance for trade with DPRK, including the granting of export credits, guarantees or insurance,[872] unless the 1718 DPRK Sanctions Committee has authorized it. Should such an authorization be granted, the Member State concerned shall inform the other Member States and the Commission within an unspecified frame of time.[873]

§5 SANCTIONS ON GOLD, PRECIOUS METALS, DIAMONDS AND LUXURY GOODS

187. The restrictive measures described here initiate the presentation of measures of general application reflecting a choice made by the Union in the field of international policy. Reference to government and public bodies, as will be seen in the ensuing paragraphs, does not alter this. No government per se is targeted by the measures explained below;[874] at least not in the sense of targeting a person and therefore attributing to these measures the nature of individual restrictive measures within the meaning of Article 275 TFEU.[875]

867. Article 23(1)(d) Regulation on DPRK and Art. 40(b) AML Directive.
868. Article 23(1)(f) Regulation on DPRK.
869. Article 23(1)(e) Regulation on DPRK.
870. Financial Action Task Force, *International Standards on Combating Money Laundering and the Financing of Terrorism and Proliferation: The FATF Recommendations*, Paris 2012-2022, available: https://www.fatf-gafi.org/content/dam/fatf-gafi/recommendations/FATF%20Recommendations%202012.pdf.coredownload.inline.pdf (last visited: 31 Dec. 2023).
871. S/RES/2270 of 2 Mar. 2016, preamble.
872. Article 32 Regulation on DPRK.
873. Article 33(1) & (2) Regulation on DPRK. For the corresponding provision of the relevant resolutions of the UN Security Council *see* S/RES/2094 of 7 Mar. 2013 para. 15 and S/RES/2270 of 2 Mar. 2016.
874. *Venezuela* 2023 (n. 12) paras 32 & 42.
875. *See Bank Mellat* 2016 (n. 346) para. 33.

188. Sanctions are imposed with regard to gold, precious metals and diamonds, which are not treated as unspecified legal terms; to the contrary, they are defined with reference to nomenclature codes taken from the *Combined Nomenclature*.[876] More specifically, the phrase 'gold, precious metals and diamonds' has been explained via correlation to CN Codes 7102, 7106, 7108 to 7111 and ex 7112.[877]

189. These goods may not be sold, supplied, transferred or exported both directly and indirectly to the government of the DPRK, its public bodies, the Central Bank of the DPRK, including anyone acting on their behalf and anyone owned or controlled by them.[878] Further, gold, precious metals and diamonds may not be imported, purchased or transported, directly and indirectly, when the relevant transaction involves the aforementioned bodies of the DPRK.[879] Moreover, technical assistance and brokering services, financing and financial assistance in relation to said goods may not be provided to any of said persons.[880] Said prohibitions with regard to gold, precious metals and diamonds have been set out, in all probability, as a response to the concerns expressed within the UN Security Council, whereby transfers of gold could be used in order to evade previously imposed restrictive measures.[881]

190. Identical restrictive measures on trade of gold, precious metals and diamonds have been imposed in view of the situation in Syria.[882]

191. As already explained, these restrictive measures are of general application. Therefore, the Council is not under any obligation to inform any person potentially affected by a new criterion of general application of the adoption of that criterion. The right to be heard in an administrative procedure concerning a specific person, which must be observed, even in the absence of any rules governing the procedure in question, cannot be transposed into the present measures in view of their general application.[883] The CJEU has accepted neither the application of Article 41(2)(a) of the Charter of Fundamental Rights, as it refers to *individual measures*, nor invoking jurisprudence of the ICJ,[884] as it relates to *countermeasures*.[885]

192. In a similar vein, sanctions have been imposed on *luxury goods*. For the purposes of providing context, it has been reported that luxury items, such as cognac, have been

876. *See* Art. 1(2) Council Regulation (EEC) No. 2658/87 of 23 Jul. 1987 on the tariff and statistical nomenclature and on the Common Customs Tariff, OJ L 256, 7 Sep. 1987, p. 1, as last amended by Council Regulation (EU) 2022/2465 of 12 Dec. 2022 amending Annex I to Regulation (EEC) No. 2658/87 on the tariff and statistical nomenclature and on the Common Customs Tariff, OJ L 322, 16 Dec. 2022, p. 81.
877. Annex IX Regulation on DPRK.
878. Article 11(a) Regulation on DPRK.
879. Article 11(b) Regulation on DPRK.
880. Article 11(c) Regulation on DPRK.
881. S/RES/2270 of 2 Mar. 2016 para. 37.
882. *See* Art. 11a and Annex VIII Regulation on Syria.
883. *Venezuela* 2023 (n. 12) para. 39, citing *Rosneft and Others v. Council*, T-715/14, Judgment of 13 Sep. 2018, digital ECT, para. 133; *Iran Shipping* 2017 (n. 622) para. 98.
884. *Gabčíkovo-Nagymaros Project (Hungary v. Slovakia)*, Judgment of 25 Sep. 1997, digital ICJ Reports, paras 83 & 84.
885. *Venezuela* 2023 (n. 12) paras 40 & 41.

shipped to the court and military of P'yŏngyang via a front company in Macau.[886] The term luxury goods has been defined with reference to nomenclature codes and it includes the following goods: horses,[887] caviar,[888] truffles,[889] wines, including sparkling wines,[890] cigars,[891] perfumes, toilet waters and cosmetics,[892] leather, saddlery and travel goods and handbags of a value exceeding EUR 50 each,[893] coats of a value exceeding EUR 75 each and other garments of a value exceeding EUR 20,[894] carpets,[895] pearls and jewellery,[896] coins and banknotes, which are not legal tender,[897] cutlery of precious metal,[898] tableware of porcelain and fine pottery,[899] items of lead crystal,[900]

886. *Hear* the podcast: Jean Lee & Geoff White (hosts/reporters), Estelle Doyle (producer), *The Lazarus Heist, S1.9 The Macau Connection*, 14 Jun. 2021, BBC World Service, wherever you get your podcasts.
887. CN Codes 0101 21 00 and ex 0101 29 90; point 1 of Annex VIII Regulation on DPRK.
888. CN Codes 1604 31 00 and 1604 32 00; point 2 of Annex VIII Regulation on DPRK.
889. CN Codes 0709 59 50, ex 0710 80 69, ex 0711 59 00, ex 0712 39 00, ex 2001 90 97, 2003 90 10, ex 2130 9090, ex 2104 10 00, ex 2104 20 00 and ex 2106 00 00; point 3 of Annex VIII Regulation on DPRK.
890. CN Codes 2203 00 00, 2204 10 11, 2204 10 91, 2204 10 93, 2204 10 94, 2204 10 96, 2204 10 98, 2204 21 00, 2204 29 00, 2205 00 00, 2206 00 00, 2207 10 00 and 2208 00 00; point 4 of Annex VIII Regulation on DPRK.
891. CN Codes 2402 10 00 and 2402 90 00; point 5 of Annex VIII Regulation on DPRK.
892. CN Codes 3303, 3304 00 00, 3305 00 00, 3307 00 00 and 6704 00 00; point 6 of Annex VIII Regulation on DPRK.
893. CN Codes ex 4201 00 00, ex 4202 00 00, ex 4205 00 50 and ex 9605 00 00; point 7 of Annex VIII Regulation on DPRK.
894. CN Codes ex 4203 00 00, ex 4303 00 00, ex 6101 00 00, ex 6102 00 00, ex 6103 00 00, ex 6104 00 00, ex 6105 00 00, ex 6106 00 00, ex 6107 00 00, ex 6108 00 00, ex 6109 00 00, ex 6110 00 00, ex 6111 00 00, ex 6112 00 00, ex 6112 11 00, ex 6112 12 00, ex 6112 19 00, 6112 20 00, 6112 31 00, 6112 39 00, 6112 41 00, 6112 49 00, ex 6113 00 10, ex 6113 00 90, ex 6114 00 00, ex 6115 00 00, ex 6116 00 00, ex 6117 00 00, ex 6201 00 00, ex 6202 00 00, ex 6203 00 00, ex 6204 00 00, ex 6205 00 00, ex 6206 00 00, ex 6207 00 00, ex 6208 00 00, ex 6209 00 00, ex 6210 10 00, ex 6210 20 00, ex 6210 30 00, ex 6210 40 00, ex 6210 50 00, 6211 11 00, 6211 12 00, 6211 20 00, ex 6211 32 00, ex 6211 33 00, ex 6211 39 00, ex 6211 42 00, ex 6211 43 00, ex 6211 49 00, ex 6212 00 00, ex 6213 00 00, ex 6214 00 00, ex 6215 00 00, ex 6216 00 00, ex 6217 00 00, ex 6401 00 00, ex 6402 20 00, ex 6402 91 00, ex 6402 99 00, ex 6403 19 00, ex 6403 20 00, ex 6403 40 00, ex 6403 51 00, ex 6403 59 00, ex 6403 91 00, ex 6403 99 00, ex 6404 19 10, ex 6404 20 00, ex 6405 00 00, ex 6504 00 00, ex 6505 00 10, ex 6505 00 30, ex 6505 00 90, ex 6506 99 00, ex 6601 91 00, ex 6601 99 00, ex 6602 00 00 and ex 9619 00 81; point 8 of Annex VIII Regulation on DPRK.
895. CN Codes 5701 00 00, 5702 10 00, 5702 20 00, 5702 31 80, 5702 32 00, 5702 39 00, 5702 41 90, 5702 42 00, 5702 50 00, 5702 91 00, 5702 92 00, 5702 99 00, 5703 00 00, 5704 00 00, 5705 00 00 and 5805 00 00; point 9 of Annex VIII Regulation on DPRK.
896. CN Codes 7101 00 00, 7102 00 00, 7103 00 00, 7104 20 00, 7104 90 00, 7105 00 00, 7106 00 00, 7107 00 00, 7108 00 00, 7109 00 00, 7110 11 00, 7110 19 00, 7110 21 00, 7110 29 00, 7110 31 00, 7110 39 00, 7110 41 00, 7110 49 00, 7111 00 00, 7113 00 00, 7114 00 00, 7115 00 00 and 7116 00 00; point 10 of Annex VIII Regulation on DPRK.
897. CN Codes ex 4907 00 30, 7118 10 00 and ex 7118 90 00; point 11 of Annex VIII Regulation on DPRK.
898. CN Codes 7114 00 00, 7115 00 00, ex 8214 00 00, ex 8215 00 00 and ex 9307 00 00; point 12 of Annex VIII Regulation on DPRK.
899. CN Codes 6911 00 00, 6912 00 23, 6912 00 25, 6912 00 83, 6912 00 85, 6914 10 00 and 6914 90 00; point 13 of Annex VIII Regulation on DPRK.
900. CN Codes ex 7009 91 00, ex 7009 92 00, ex 7010 00 00, 7013 22 00, 7013 33 00, 7013 41 00, 7013 91 00, ex 7018 10 00, ex 7018 90 00, ex 7020 00 80, ex 9405 10 50, ex 9405 20 50, ex 9405 50 00 and ex 9405 91 00; point 14 of Annex VIII Regulation on DPRK.

electronic items for domestic use of a value exceeding EUR 50 each,[901] electrical, electronic or optical apparatus for recording and reproducing sound and images of a value exceeding EUR 50 each,[902] transport vehicles of a value exceeding EUR 10,000 each,[903] clocks and watches,[904] musical instruments,[905] art works, collectors' pieces and antiques,[906] sports equipment,[907] as well as articles and equipment for billiard and casino games.[908]

193. It is prohibited to sell, supply, transfer, export, import, purchase and transfer, both directly and indirectly, such goods to and from the DPRK.[909] This prohibition is obviously intended to exert pressure on the regime's elite via obstructing access to treats enjoyed or withdrawing privileges in response to unwanted behaviour.[910] At the same time, it should not go unnoticed that luxury goods can be a component of money laundering. These goods can be used by money launderers to transform cash into

901. CN Codes ex 8414 51, ex 8414 59 00, ex 8414 60 00, ex 8415 10 00, ex 8418 10 00, ex 8418 21 00, ex 8418 29 00, ex 8418 30 00, ex 8418 40 00, ex 8418 81 00, ex 8422 11 00, ex 8423 10 00, ex 8443 12 00, ex 8443 31 00, ex 8443 32 00, ex 8443 39 00, ex 8450 12 00, ex 8450 19 00, ex 8451 21 00, ex 8452 10 00, ex 8470 10 00, ex 8470 21 00, ex 8470 29 00, ex 8470 30 00, ex 8471 00 00, ex 8472 90 40, ex 8472 90 90, ex 8479 60 00, ex 8508 11 00, ex 8508 19 00, ex 8508 19 00, ex 8508 60 00, ex 8508 80 00, ex 8509 80 00, ex 8516 31 00, ex 8516 50 00, ex 8516 60 10, ex 8516 71 00, ex 8516 72 00, ex 8516 79 00, ex 8517 11 00, ex 8517 12 00, ex 8517 18 00, ex 8517 61 00, ex 8517 62 00, ex 8517 69 00, ex 8526 91 00, ex 8529 10 31, ex 8529 10 39, ex 8529 10 65, ex 8529 10 69, ex 8531 10 00, ex 8543 70 10, ex 8543 70 30, ex 8543 70 50, ex 8543 70 90, ex 9504 50 00 and ex 9504 90 80; point 15 of Annex VIII Regulation on DPRK.
902. CN Codes ex 8519 00 00, ex 8521 00 00, ex 8525 80 30, ex 8525 80 30, ex 8525 80 30, ex 8525 80 91, ex 8525 80 99, ex 8527 00 00, ex 8528 71 00, ex 8528 72 00, ex 9006 00 00 and ex 9007 00 00; point 16 of Annex VIII Regulation on DPRK.
903. CN Codes ex 4011 10 00, ex 4011 20 00, ex 4011 30 00, ex 4011 40 00, ex 4011 90 00, ex 7009 10 00, ex 8407 00 00, ex 8408 00 00, ex 8409 00 00, ex 8411 00 00, 8428 60 00, ex 8431 39 00, ex 8483 00 00, ex 8511 00 00, ex 8512 20 00, ex 8512 30 10, ex 8512 30 90, ex 8512 40 00, ex 8544 30 00, ex 8603 00 00, ex 8605 00 00, ex 8607 00 00, ex 8702 00 00, ex 8703 00 00, ex 8706 00 00, ex 8707 00 00, ex 8708 00 00, ex 8711 00 00, ex 8712 00 00, ex 8714 00 00, ex 8716 10 00, ex 8716 40 00, ex 8716 90 00, ex 8801 00 00, ex 8802 11 00, ex 8802 12 00, 8802 20 00, ex 8802 30 00, ex 8802 40 00, ex 8803 10 00, ex 8803 20 00, ex 8803 30 00, ex 8803 90 10, ex 8803 90 90, ex 8805 10 00, ex 8901 10 00, ex 8901 90 00 and ex 8903 00 00; point 17 of Annex VIII Regulation on DPRK.
904. CN Codes 9101 00 00, 9102 00 00, 9103 00 00, 9104 00 00, 9105 00 00, 9108 00 00, 9109 00 00, 9110 00 00, 9111 00 00, 9112 00 00, 9113 00 00 and 9114 00 00; point 18 of Annex VIII Regulation on DPRK.
905. CN Codes 9201 00 00, 9202 00 00, 9205 00 00, 9206 00 and 9207 00 00; point 19 of Annex VIII Regulation on DPRK.
906. CN Code 9700; point 20 of Annex VIII Regulation on DPRK.
907. CN Codes ex 4015 19 00, ex 4015 90 00, ex 6210 40 00, ex 6210 50 00, 6211 11 00, 6211 12 00, 6211 20 00, ex 6216 00 00, 6402 12 00, ex 6402 19 00, 6403 12 00, 6403 19 00, 6404 11 00, 6404 19 90, ex 9004 90 00, ex 9020 00 00, 9506 11 00, 9506 12 00, 9506 19 00, 9506 21 00, 9506 29 00, 9506 31 00, 9506 32 00, 9506 39 00, 9506 40 00, 9506 51 00, 9506 59 00, 9506 61 00, 9506 69 10, 9506 69 90, 9506 70, 9506 91, 9506 99 10, 9506 99 90 and 9507 00 00; point 21 of Annex 21 to Annex VIII Regulation on DPRK.
908. CN Codes 9504 20 00, 9504 30 00, 9504 40 00, 9504 50 00 and 9504 90 80; point 22 of Annex VIII Regulation on DPRK.
909. Article 10(1)(a) and (b) Regulation on DPRK.
910. Julia Schmidt, *The Legality of Unilateral Extra-territorial Sanctions under International Law* 27(1) J.C.&S.L. 53 at 56 (2022) https://doi.org/10.1093/jcsl/krac005.

goods that can be resold or returned in exchange for cash.[911] Within the frame of the anti-money laundering policy of the Union the term 'high value assets' is used to denote such items.[912] Thus, the pursued aim in all probability is twofold: political pressure and slashing the flow of proceeds.

194. However, travellers' personal effects and goods of a non-commercial nature for travellers' personal use contained in their luggage are exempt.[913] In addition, goods necessary for the official purposes of diplomatic and consular missions in the DPRK and personal effects of their staff are also exempt.[914] Finally, transport vehicles may become exempt, if the specific transaction serves humanitarian purposes and the competent national authority has authorized it.[915] The prohibition of luxury items was first envisioned in resolutions of the UN Security Council,[916] that has been perhaps parsimonious in specifying the content of luxury items and qualified as such jewellery, transportation items,[917] luxury watches, items of lead crystal, recreational sports equipment,[918] rugs and tapestries valued greater than USD 500 as well as tableware of porcelain or bone china valued greater than USD 100.[919]

195. Trade in luxury goods is also prohibited with regard to Syria, whereby goods of a non-commercial nature contained in travellers' luggage are equally exempted.[920] The understanding of luxury goods under the Regulation on Syria[921] is quite similar, but not identical, to the one under the Regulation on DPRK.

§6 SANCTIONS ON CULTURAL PROPERTY

196. Trade in cultural property is also the target of restrictive measures both with regard to Iraq and Syria. The objective component of these measures consists of 'cultural property and other items of archaeological, historical, cultural, rare scientific or religious importance', an expression first encountered in resolution 1483 of the UN

911. Kristine Karsten, *Money Laundering: How It Works and Why You Should Be Concerned*, in: K. Karsten & A. Berkley (eds), Arbitration: Money Laundering, Corruption and Fraud (Paris: International Chamber of Commerce 2003) 15 at 21. On the significance of money laundering for DPRK's weapons programmes watch Financial Times, *North Korea and the Triads: Gangsters, Ghost Ships and Spies | FT Film*, 31 Mar. 2023, available: https://www.youtube.com/watch?v=o-6J5X9E-lE (last visited: 21 Dec. 2023).
912. *See*, for example, European Commission, *Commission Staff Working Document Accompanying the Document Report from the Commission to the European Parliament and the Council on the Assessment of the Risk of Money Laundering and Terrorist Financing Affecting the Internal Market and Relating to Cross-Border Activities*, SWD/2022/344 final, Brussels, 27 Oct. 2022, available: https://eur-lex.europa.eu (last visited: 21 Dec. 2023).
913. Article 10(2) Regulation on DPRK.
914. Article 10(3) Regulation on DPRK.
915. Article 10(4) Regulation on DPRK.
916. S/RES/1718 of 14 Oct. 2006 para. 8(a)(iii), S/RES/2094 of 7 Mar. 2013 para. 23.
917. S/RES/2094 of 7 Mar. 2013 Annex IV.
918. S/RES/2270 of 2 Mar. 2013 Annex IV.
919. S/RES/2321 of 30 Nov. 2016 Annex IV.
920. Article 11b(1) and (2) Regulation on Syria.
921. *See* Annex X Regulation on Syria.

Security Council[922] and reiterated in its later resolution 2199.[923] This expression is accompanied by an indicative list of these objects and elements with regard to Iraq, which are more than 50, 75, 100 or 200 years old, as the case may be, and are defined with reference to nomenclature codes,[924] includes archaeological objects, elements forming an internal part of artistic, historical and religious monuments, which have been dismembered,[925] pictures and paintings,[926] mosaics,[927] engravings, prints, serigraphs and lithographs,[928] sculptures,[929] photographs, films and negatives,[930] incunabula and manuscripts,[931] books,[932] printed maps,[933] archives,[934] collections,[935] means of transport[936] and other antique items.[937] Similar, but not identical, is the indicative list of objects and elements with regard to Syria.[938]

197. Trading as well as transferring such items into and from the territory of the Union is prohibited, if they have been illegally removed from locations in Iraq[939] and in Syria. With regard to the latter, it is further required that such act is in breach of Syrian law or international law, or that consent of their legitimate owner is absent. These conditions need no proof beyond reasonable doubt or on the balance of probabilities; reasonable grounds to suspect so suffices.[940] With regard to Iraq, these conditions are merely an indicative example of items the trade of which is forbidden.[941] The other indicative example of cultural items that may not be the object of trade, common in both Iraq and Syria, are items forming an integral part of either the public collections listed in the inventories of national museums, archives or libraries' conservation collection, or the inventories of religious institutions in these states.[942]

922. S/RES/1483 of 22 May 2003 para. 7.
923. S/RES/2199 of 12 Feb. 2015 para. 17.
924. Article 3 and Annex II Regulation on Iraq, Art. 11c and Annex XI Regulation on Syria.
925. Ex CN codes 9705 00 00 and 9706 00 00 points 1 and 2 of Annex II Regulation on Iraq.
926. Ex CN codes 9701 points 3 and 3A of Annex II Regulation on Iraq.
927. Ex CN codes 6914 and 9701, point 4 of Annex II Regulation on Iraq.
928. Ex CN codes Chapter 49, 9702 00 00 and 8442 50 99 point 5 of Annex II Regulation on Iraq.
929. Ex CN codes 9703 00 00 point 6 of Annex II Regulation on Iraq.
930. Ex CN codes 3704, 3705, 3706, 4911 91 80 point 7 of Annex II Regulation on Iraq.
931. Ex CN codes 9702 00 00, 9706 00 00, 4901 10 00, 4901 99 00, 4904 00 00, 4905 91 00, 4905 99 00 and 4906 00 00 point 8 of Annex II Regulation on Iraq.
932. Ex CN codes 9705 00 00 and 9706 00 00 point 9 of Annex II Regulation on Iraq.
933. Ex CN code 9706 00 00 point 10 of Annex II Regulation on Iraq.
934. Ex CN code 3704, 3705, 3706, 4901, 4906, 9705 00 00 and 9706 00 00 point 11 of Annex II Regulation on Iraq.
935. Ex CN code 9705 00 00 point 12 of Annex II Regulation on Iraq. *See also Collector Guns GmbH & Co. KG v. Hauptzollamt Koblenz,* Case 252/84, Judgment of 10 Oct. 1985, digital ECR.
936. Ex CN code 9705 00 00 and Chapters 86-89 point 13 of Annex II Regulation on Iraq.
937. Ex CN codes Chapter 95, 7013, 7114, Chapter 94, Chapter 90, Chapter 92, Chapter 91, Chapter 44, Chapter 69, 5805 00 00, Chapter 57, 4814, Chapter 93, 9706 00 00 point 14 of Annex II Regulation on Iraq.
938. It includes the aforementioned ex CN codes, with the exception of 8442 50 99 and 4911 91 80 that have been replaced by 8442 50 99 and 4911 91 80. *See* points 1-14 Annex XI Regulation on Syria.
939. Article 3(1)(a), (b) and (c) Regulation on Iraq.
940. Article 11c(1) Regulation on Syria.
941. Article 3(1)(c)(ii) Regulation on Iraq.
942. Article 3(1)(c)(i) Regulation on Iraq, Art. 11c(1) Regulation on Syria.

198. This prohibition does not apply on two occasions. The first once includes cultural items that have been exported from Iraq before 6 August 1990,[943] or from Syria before 15 March 2011.[944] These dates are not random. 6 August 1990 is the date on which the UN Security Council decided to take measures due to the invasion of Kuwait by Iraq.[945] 15 March 2011 is the date on which the UN Security Council prohibited the trade in Syrian cultural property and reaffirmed the ban on trade in Iraqi cultural property.[946] The prohibition on Syrian cultural property at the EU level ensued the restrictive measures of the UN Security Council for more than two years, as the ban became effective on 15 December 2013.[947] The second occasion where the prohibition of trade in cultural items is non-applicable is when the cultural items are being *returned* to the national institutions of Syria and Iraq.[948] *Import* of these items seems not to have any exceptions.

§7 ENERGY RELATED SANCTIONS

199. In addition to the aforementioned restrictions of financial nature (*see* paragraphs 136 to 138 above) the energy-related sanctions encompass prohibitive measures on coal, oil and gas, electricity production and nuclear energy.

I Sanctions with Regard to Coal

200. Sanctions on coal are imposed solely in view of the situation in the DPRK. Therein 'coal' has been defined as coal and solid fuels manufactured from coal,[949] lignite,[950] peat[951] and coke.[952] This item may not be imported, purchased and transferred from the DPRK.[953] Two exceptions are set out specifically with regard to coal import paired with

943. Article 3(2)(a) Regulation on Iraq.
944. Article 11c(2)(a) Regulation on Syria.
945. S/RES/1483 of 22 May 2003 para. 7, S/RES/661 of 6 Aug. 1990.
946. S/RES/2199 of 2015 para. 17. *See* recital No. 2 to the preamble of Council Regulation (EU) 2015/827 of 28 May 2015 amending Regulation (EU) No. 36/2012 concerning restrictive measures in view of the situation in Syria, OJ L 132, 29 May 2015, p. 1.
947. Recital No. 3 to the preamble of and Art. 1(4) Council Regulation (EU) No. 1332/2013 of 13 Dec. 2013 amending Regulation (EU) No. 36/2012 concerning restrictive measures in view of the situation in Syria, OJ L 335, 14 Dec. 2013, p. 3.
948. Article 3(2)(b) Regulation on Iraq and Art. 11c(2)(b) Regulation on Syria.
949. CN code 2701. Article 3(1)(e) and Annex V Regulation on DPRK.
950. CN code 2702. Article 3(1)(e) and Annex V Regulation on DPRK.
951. CN code 2703. Article 3(1)(e) and Annex V Regulation on DPRK.
952. CN code 2704. Article 3(1)(e) and Annex V Regulation on DPRK.
953. Article 3(1)(e) Regulation on DPRK. *See* S/RES/2270 of 2 Mar. 2016 para. 29 & S/RES/2321 of 30 Nov. 2016 para. 26 & S/RES/2371 of 5 Aug. 2017 para. 8. This prohibition stands next to the prohibition to import, purchase and transfer iron and iron ore in the sense of CN codes ex 26 01, 7201, 7202, 7203, 7204 10 00, ex 7204 30 00, ex 7204 41, ex 7204 49, ex 7204 50 00, ex 7204 50 00, ex 7205 29 00, ex 7205 29 00, ex 7206 90 00, ex 72 07, ex 72 08, ex 72 09, ex 72 10, ex 72 11, ex 72 12, ex 72 14, ex 72 15, ex 72 16 and ex 72 17. Article 3(1)(e) and Annex V Regulation on DPRK. *See* S/RES/2270 of 2 Mar. 2016 para. 29, S/RES/2321 of 30 Nov. 2016 para. 26 & S/RES/2371 of 5 Aug. 2017 para. 8.

one for coal export. Coal import may be approved by the competent authority of a Member State, as long as it has determined that the shipment originated outside the DPRK and was transferred through the DPRK solely for export from the port of Rajin (Rason).[954] This provision in all probability photographs the trans-shipment of Russia-origin coal through the Russia-DPRK Rajin-Khasan port, as decided by the UN Security Council.[955] Turning to the latter exception, for coal to be exported from the DPRK, the exporting state, that being Russia, has to notify in advance the 1718 DPRK Sanctions Committee about such an intended transaction. Unsurprisingly, the transaction in question may not relate to generating revenue for the nuclear or ballistic missile programs and other activities of the DPRK, prohibited by UN Security Council resolutions.[956,957] Member States having authorized such transactions in coal are obliged to notify the other Member States and the Commission.[958]

II Sanctions with Regard to Oil and Gas

201. The legislative instruments on Iraq, DPRK, Libya and Syria foresee specific restrictive measures with regard to oil and gas.

202. These instruments, with the exception of the Regulation on Libya, have taken the step to define the specific products of oil and gas that they regulate. The Regulation on Iraq specifies the terms 'petroleum, petroleum products and natural gas' as petroleum oils,[959] petroleum gases,[960] petroleum jelly,[961] paraffin wax,[962] 'slack wax' and 'scale wax',[963] residues of petroleum oils,[964] bitumen and asphalt,[965] bituminous mixtures,[966] acyclic hydrocarbons,[967] cyclohexane,[968] benzene,[969] toluene,[970] o-xylene,[971]

954. Article 4(2) Regulation on DPRK.
955. *See* S/RES/2397 of 22 Dec. 2017 para. 16, S/RES/2371 of 5 Aug. 2017 para. 8 and S/RES/2375 of 11 Sep. 2017 para. 18.
956. *See* S/RES/1718 of 14 Oct. 2006, S/RES/1874 of 12 Jun. 2009, S/RES/2087 of 22 Jan. 2013, S/RES/2094 of 7 Mar. 2013, S/RES/2270 of 2 Mar. 2016, S/RES/2321 of 30 Nov. 2016, S/RES/2356 of 2 Jun. 2017 and S/RES/2371 of 5 Aug. 2017.
957. Article 4(2) Regulation on DPRK. *See* S/RES/2397 of 22 Dec. 2017 para. 16, S/RES/2371 of 5 Aug. 2017 para. 8.
958. Articles 16g(2), 16e(2) & 4(3) Regulation on DPRK.
959. CN codes 2709 00 and 2710. Article 2 and Annex I Regulation on Iraq.
960. CN code 2711. Article 2 and Annex I Regulation on Iraq.
961. CN code 2712 10. Article 2 and Annex I Regulation on Iraq.
962. CN code 2712 20 00. Article 2 and Annex I Regulation on Iraq.
963. CN code ex 2712 90. Article 2 and Annex I Regulation on Iraq.
964. CN code 2713. Article 2 and Annex I Regulation on Iraq.
965. CN code 2714. Article 2 and Annex I Regulation on Iraq.
966. CN code 2715 00 00. Article 2 and Annex I Regulation on Iraq.
967. CN code 2901. Article 2 and Annex I Regulation on Iraq.
968. CN code 2902 11 00. Article 2 and Annex I Regulation on Iraq.
969. CN code 2902 20 00. Article 2 and Annex I Regulation on Iraq.
970. CN code 2902 30 00. Article 2 and Annex I Regulation on Iraq.
971. CN code 2902 41 00. Article 2 and Annex I Regulation on Iraq.

m-xylene,[972] p-xylene,[973] mixed xylene isomers,[974] styrene,[975] ethylbenzene,[976] cumene,[977] methanol,[978] lubricating preparations,[979] additives for lubricating oils[980] and petroleum sulphonates.[981] The Regulation on DPRK has defined the ensuing notions; 'refined petroleum products', 'crude oil' and 'aviation fuel'. The term 'refined petroleum products' stands for oils,[982] petroleum oils,[983] petroleum gases,[984] petroleum jelly,[985] paraffin wax,[986] wax,[987] residues of petroleum oils,[988] bitumen and asphalt,[989] bituminous mixtures,[990] lubricating preparations[991] and biodiesel.[992] 'Crude oil' means petroleum oils and oils obtained from bituminous minerals, crude, other than natural gas condensates.[993] The term 'aviation fuel' includes gasoline,[994] naptha-type jet fuel,[995] kerosene-type jet fuel[996] and kerosene-type rocket fuel.[997] Finally, the Regulation on Syria does set out definitions, not only of 'crude oil and petroleum products' but also of *activities* in the oil and gas sector. Accordingly, 'crude oil and petroleum products' means petroleum oils and oils obtained from bituminous minerals,[998] petroleum jelly,[999] petroleum coke,[1000] bitumen and asphalt[1001] and bituminous mixtures.[1002] Further 'exploration of crude oil' stands for the exploration for, prospecting for and management of crude oil reserves, as well as the provision of geological services in relation to such reserves.[1003] 'Refining of crude oil' means the processing, conditioning or preparation of oil for the ultimately final sale of fuels.[1004]

972. CN code 2902 42 00. Article 2 and Annex I Regulation on Iraq.
973. CN code 2902 43 00. Article 2 and Annex I Regulation on Iraq.
974. CN code 2902 44. Article 2 and Annex I Regulation on Iraq.
975. CN code 2902 50 00. Article 2 and Annex I Regulation on Iraq.
976. CN code 2902 60 00. Article 2 and Annex I Regulation on Iraq.
977. CN code 2902 70 00. Article 2 and Annex I Regulation on Iraq.
978. CN code 2905 11 00. Article 2 and Annex I Regulation on Iraq.
979. CN code 3403 19 10. Article 2 and Annex I Regulation on Iraq.
980. CN code 3811 21 00. Article 2 and Annex I Regulation on Iraq.
981. CN code 3824 90 10. Article 2 and Annex I Regulation on Iraq.
982. CN code 2707. Article 16d and Annex XId Regulation on DPRK.
983. CN code 2710. Article 16d and Annex XId Regulation on DPRK.
984. CN code 2711. Article 16d and Annex XId Regulation on DPRK.
985. CN code 2712 10. Article 16d and Annex XId Regulation on DPRK.
986. CN code 2712 20. Article 16d and Annex XId Regulation on DPRK.
987. CN code ex 2712 90. Article 16d and Annex XId Regulation on DPRK.
988. CN code 2713. Article 16d and Annex XId Regulation on DPRK.
989. CN code ex 2714. Article 16d and Annex XId Regulation on DPRK.
990. CN code ex 2715. Article 16d and Annex XId Regulation on DPRK.
991. CN codes 3403 11, 3403 19, ex 3403 91, ex 3403 99, ex 3824 99 92, ex 3824 99 93 and ex 3824 99 96. Regulation on DPRK.
992. CN codes 3826 00 10 and 3826 00 90. Regulation on DPRK.
993. CN code 2709 00 90. Article 16f and Annex XIe Regulation on DPRK.
994. CN codes 2710 12 31 to 2710 12 59. Article 3(1)(b) and Annex III Regulation on DPRK.
995. CN code 2710 12 70. Article 3(1)(b) and Annex III Regulation on DPRK.
996. CN code 2710 19 21. Article 3(1)(b) and Annex III Regulation on DPRK.
997. CN code 2710 19 25. Article 3(1)(b) and Annex III Regulation on DPRK.
998. HS codes 2709 00 and 2710. Article 1(e) and Annex IV Regulation on Syria.
999. HS code 2712. Regulation on Syria.
1000. HS code 2713. Regulation on Syria.
1001. HS code 2714. Regulation on Syria.
1002. HS code 2715 00 00. Regulation on Syria.
1003. Article 13(3)(a) Regulation on Syria.
1004. Article 13(3)(b) Regulation on Syria.

203. The restrictive measures with regard to oil and gas are diverse and heterogeneous; some relate to the enjoyment of proceeds, some to export and transfer, and others to financing such activities. More specifically, the Regulation on DPRK prohibits the sale, supply, transfer and export of crude oil,[1005] refined petroleum products[1006] and aviation fuel to the DPRK.[1007] Furthermore, aviation fuel may not be transported to the DPRK on board flag vessels or aircraft of Member States.[1008]

204. The transport of oil is at the front centre of the restrictive measures with regard to Libya. The relevant regulation sets out the prohibition to load, transport and discharge petroleum on *designated vessels* flying the flag of a Member State.[1009] *Designated vessels* are the ones designated by the 1970 Libya Sanctions Committee, not by an EU institution.[1010] It is further prohibited to accept or provide access to ports in the territory of the Union to designated vessels if the 1970 Libya Sanctions Committee has so specified.[1011] It is also prohibited to provide bunkering, ship supply services and any other servicing of vessels if the 1970 Libya Sanctions Committee has so decided.[1012] Finally, financial transactions aboard designated vessels are prohibited, provided that the 1970 Libya Sanctions Committee has so specified.[1013]

205. The legal instrument on Iraq does not prohibit per se the trade with petroleum, petroleum products and natural gas; rather, it imposes restrictions on the enjoyment of proceeds, as it provides that all proceeds from such sales shall be deposited into the DFI.[1014] Notably, the corresponding provision in the Common Position on Iraq allows for the application of these restrictions only until 30 June 2011,[1015] as does the apposite decision of the UN Security Council.[1016] Thus, it is arguable that these restrictions, although stated in a legal instrument currently in force, have expired.

206. The Regulation on Syria prohibits granting of any financial loan or credit to any Syrian person engaged in the exploration, production or refining of crude oil.[1017] In addition, it is prohibited to acquire or extend participation in such a person, as well as

1005. Article 16f Regulation on DPRK. *See* S/RES/2397 of 22 Dec. 2017 para. 4.
1006. Article 16d Regulation on DPRK. *See* S/RES/2397 of 22 Dec. 2017 para. 5.
1007. Article 3(1)(b) Regulation on DPRK. *See* S/RES/2270 of 2 Mar. 2016 para. 31. On alleged DPRK's illicit imports of oil *watch* Financial Times, *North Korea and the Triads: Gangsters, Ghost Ships and Spies | FT Film*, 31 Mar. 2023, available: https://www.youtube.com/watch?v=o-6J5X9E-lE (last visited: 21 Dec. 2023); The New York Times, *How a Mysterious Ship Helps North Korea Evade Oil Sanctions* | Visual Investigations, 22 Mar. 2021, available: https://www.youtube.com/watch?v=hDTCHdcPYTQ (last visited: 21 Dec. 2023).
1008. Article 3(1)(b) Regulation on DPRK. *See* S/RES/220 of 2 Mar. 2016 para. 31.
1009. Article 15(1) Regulation on Libya. *See* S/RES/2146 of 19 Mar. 2014 para. 12 & S/RES/2362 of 29 Jun. 2017 para. 2.
1010. *See* Art. 1(h) & Annex V Regulation on Libya and S/RES/2146 of 19 Mar. 2014 para. 11.
1011. Article 15(2) Regulation on Libya. *See* S/RES/2146 of 19 Mar. 2014 para. 10(b).
1012. Article 15(4) Regulation on Libya. *See* S/RES/2146 of 19 Mar. 2014 para. 10(c).
1013. Article 15(6) Regulation on Libya. *See* S/RES/2146 of 19 Mar. 2014 para. 10(c).
1014. Article 2 Regulation on Iraq. *See* S/RES/1483 of 22 May 2003 paras 20 and 21.
1015. *See* Arts 4, 5 & 7 Common Position on Iraq. With regard to the expiration *see* Council Decision 2011/100/CFSP of 14 Feb. 2011 amending Common Position 2003/495/CFSP on Iraq, OJ L 41, 15 Feb. 2011, p. 9.
1016. S/RES/1956 of 15 Dec. 2010.
1017. Article 13(1)(a) Regulation on Syria.

to create any joint venture with the same person.[1018] Finally, it is explicitly prohibited to circumvent these prohibitions.[1019]

207. Turning to the derogations to the prohibitions explained above, it is underlined that the prohibition set out in the Regulation on Iraq does not have any exceptions. The Regulation on DPRK does. Alongside the humanitarian exception that has already been explained (*see* in this regard paragraph 145 above), transactions in crude oil may be authorized by the competent authorities of the Member States, when the transaction is exclusively for humanitarian purposes and the 1718 DPRK Sanctions Committee has provided its prior approval.[1020] The same applies to aviation fuel.[1021] Similar - but not identical - is the exception with regard to transactions in refined petroleum products. These may be authorized by the competent authorities of Member States, provided that the transaction serves humanitarian purposes and a series of additional conditions, which have been inspired by the transposed resolution of the UN Security Council,[1022] are fulfilled. No persons associated with nuclear, ballistic missile programs and other prohibited activities under the relevant resolutions of the UN Security Council[1023] may participate.[1024] In addition, no revenue may be generated for said programs and activities prohibited under the same resolutions of the UN Security Council.[1025] Furthermore, the 1718 DPRK Sanctions Committee must have not notified the Member States that 90% of the aggregate annual limit has been reached.[1026] At this point, it is clarified that the resolution of the UN Security Council provides that sales, supply and transfer cease for the remainder of the respective year upon reaching 95% of said limit.[1027] The Member State concerned bears the obligation to notify the 1718 DPRK Sanctions Committee of the amount of the export along with information on all parties to the transaction every thirty days.[1028] Member States having authorized transactions in crude oil and refined petroleum products have to notify the other Member States and the Commission.[1029] Furthermore, an additional exception with regard to aviation fuel, aspired by common sense, is foreseen. Aviation fuel may be sold and supplied to civilian passenger aircraft exclusively for consumption during their flight to the DPRK and their return to their airport of origin.[1030]

1018. Article 13(1)(b) & (c) Regulation on Syria.
1019. Article 13(1)(d) Regulation on Syria.
1020. Article 16g(1)(a) & (b) Regulation on DPRK. *See also* S/RES/2397 of 22 Dec. 2017 para. 4.
1021. Article 4(1) Regulation on DPRK. *See* S/RES/2270 of 2 Mar. 2016 para. 31.
1022. *See* S/RES/2397 of 22 Dec. 2017 para. 5.
1023. *See* S/RES/1718 of 14 Oct. 2006, S/RES/1874 of 12 Jun. 2009, S/RES/2087 of 22 Jan. 2013, S/RES/2094 of 7 Mar. 2013, S/RES/2270 of 2 Mar. 2016, S/RES/2321 of 30 Nov. 2016, S/RES/2356 of 2 Jun. 2017, S/RES/2371 of 5 Aug. 2017, R/RES/2375 of 11 Sep. 2017 and S/RES/2397 of 22 Dec. 2017.
1024. Article 16e(1)(a) Regulation on DPRK. *See* S/RES/2397 of 22 Dec. 2017 para. 5.
1025. Article 16e(1)(b) Regulation on DPRK. *See* S/RES/2397 of 22 Dec. 2017 para. 5.
1026. Article 16e(1)(c) Regulation on DPRK.
1027. S/RES/2397 of 22 Dec. 2017 para. 5.
1028. Article 16e(1)(d) Regulation on DPRK.
1029. Articles 16g(2), 16e(2) & 4(3) Regulation on DPRK.
1030. Article 3(2) Regulation on DPRK. *See* S/RES/2270 of 2 Mar. 2016 para. 31.

208. With regard to Libya, designated vessels may have access to ports of the EU, where entry to such a port is necessary for an inspection, in case of an emergency or where the vessel is returning to Libya.[1031] Moreover, bunkering, ship supply services and any other servicing of vessels may be provided to designated vessels, where this is necessary for humanitarian or safety purposes and where the vessel is returning to Libya. The national competent authorities providing such authorization shall notify the 1970 Libya Sanctions Committee and the Commission.[1032] Financial transactions aboard designated vessels may take place, when they relate to accepting port fees upon entering an EU port for inspection, in the case of emergency and the designated vessel's return to Libya.[1033]

209. Lastly, the financial restrictions on Syrian persons engaged in the exploration, production or refining of crude oil are not applicable to the execution of obligations arising from agreements relating to the exploration, production and refining of crude oil made prior to 23 September 2011.[1034] Such agreements may also allow for extension of a participation in said Syrian persons relating to the exploration, production and refining of crude oil.[1035] These financial restrictions may further be lifted upon authorization of the competent authorities of the Member States. These authorities may allow, under terms and conditions that they deem appropriate, the above-described financial activities under the following conditions: (a) the intended activities aim to assist the Syrian civilian population, as long as they do not make available funds and economic resources to designated persons and the Regulation on Syria is not breached;[1036] and (b) the Member State concerned has consulted in advance the Syrian National Coalition for Opposition and Revolutionary Forces and this has given its views, or alternatively thirty days have passed since the request for consultation.[1037] When the competent authorities of the Member States provide such an authorization, they have to inform other Member States and the Commission within two weeks.[1038]

III Sanctions with Regard to Electricity Production

210. Sanctions against Syria have extended into electricity production. At the outset, it is prohibited to sell, supply, transfer and export certain equipment and technology when this shall be used in the construction and installation of new electricity power plants in Syria. Said equipment and technology includes certain steam[1039] and gas turbines,[1040] as

1031. Article 15(2) Regulation on Libya.
1032. Article 15(5) Regulation on Libya.
1033. Article 15(6) & (3) Regulation on Libya.
1034. Article 13(4)(a)(i) Regulation on Syria.
1035. Article 13(4)(b)(i) Regulation on Syria.
1036. Article 13a(1)(a)(i), (ii) & (iii) Regulation on Syria.
1037. Article 13a(1)(b) & (c) Regulation on Syria.
1038. Article 13a(3) Regulation on Syria.
1039. HS code 8406 81, Annex VII Regulation on Syria.
1040. HS code 8411 82, Annex VII Regulation on Syria.

well as electric motors and generators.[1041,1042] Also prohibited is providing technical and financial assistance, financing, as well as insurance and reinsurance.[1043] Further, Syrian persons engaged in the construction and installation of new electricity power plants face a series of financial restrictions. More specifically, they may not be granted any financial loan and credit.[1044] In the same vein, other persons may neither acquire nor extend participation in such persons nor create any joint venture with the same persons.[1045] Unsurprisingly, it is prohibited to participate in activities aiming to circumvent these prohibitions.[1046]

211. Exceptionally, steam and gas turbines, electric motors and generators may be sold, supplied, transferred and exported for new electricity power plants, when the relevant agreement was concluded before 19 January 2012, as long as the competent authority has been notified twenty-one calendar days in advance by the person intending to make use of this exception.[1047] Similarly, the financial restrictions are not applicable with regard to the execution of obligations arising from such agreements,[1048] whereas the same agreements may also allow for extension of a participation in Syrian persons engaged in the construction and installation of new electricity power plants.[1049]

IV Sanctions with Regard to Nuclear Energy and Nuclear Activities

212. In addition to the aforementioned restrictions to commercial activities involving nuclear materials and denuclearization and decommissioning of oil and gas wells (*see* in this regard paragraphs 147 et seq. above) sanctions with regard to nuclear energy are set out in view of the DPRK and Iran. They encompass an objective element and a subjective one.

A The Objective Element

213. The objective element consists of certain 'goods and technology' specified in detail in the relevant legal instruments.[1050] These goods and technology are targeted because they could contribute to the DPRK's nuclear-related programs and to Iran's activities, such as reprocessing- or enrichment-related or heavy water-related, that are inconsistent with the JCPOA.[1051]

1041. HS code ex 8501, Annex VII Regulation on Syria.
1042. Article 12(1)(a) and Annex VII Regulation on Syria.
1043. Article 12(1)(b) Regulation on Syria.
1044. Article 13(2)(b) & (1)(a) Regulation on Syria.
1045. Article 13(2)(b) & (1)(b) and (c) Regulation on Syria.
1046. Article 13(2)(b) & (1)(d) Regulation on Syria.
1047. Article 12(2) Regulation on Syria.
1048. Article 13(4)(a)(ii) Regulation on Syria.
1049. Article 13(4)(b)(ii) Regulation on Syria.
1050. Annex II Part II Regulation on DPRK and Annex II Regulation on Iran.
1051. Article 3(2) Regulation on DPRK & Art. 3a(2) Regulation on Iran.

214. Under the Regulation on DPRK the term 'goods and technology' includes a wide range of goods that at the same time qualify as dual-use items (*see* in this respect paragraphs 242 et seq. below). These are portrayed here, as although they are in truth related to nuclear energy, in the eyes of ordinary persons, they do not appear to do so. Within this frame 'goods and technology' include hollow cathode lamps, faraday isolators, optical gratings and fibres, nuclear reactor vessel components and testing equipment, nuclear detection systems, bellows-sealed valves, laser mirrors and lenses, pipes, vacuum pumps, shielded enclosures, natural uranium, depleted uranium, thorium and detonation chambers.[1052] It also includes special materials and related equipment such as bisphosphoric acid, fluorine gas, ring-shaped seals and gaskets, personal equipment for detecting radiation of nuclear origin, electrolytic cells, catalysts, aluminium and its alloys, magnetic metals, fibrous or filamentary materials, resin-impregnated or pitch-impregnated fibres, reinforced silicon carbide ceramic composites, tantalum, tantalum carbide, tungsten, tungsten carbide and alloys thereof, elemental powders of cobalt, neodymium or samarium or alloys or mixtures thereof, pure tributyl phosphate, maraging steel, metals, metal powders and material, soft magnetic alloys, graphite, steel alloys, carbon-carbon composite material, nickel alloys, titanium alloys, zirconium and zirconium alloys and explosive materials.[1053] In addition it encompasses materials processing such as vibration test systems, machine tools, components and numerical controls, balancing machines, remote manipulators, controlled atmosphere heat treatment furnaces or oxidation furnaces, pressure transducers, liquid-liquid contacting equipment, industrial equipment and components, multiple-seal, and seal-less pumps, centrifugal separators, sintered metal filters, spin-forming machines and flow-forming machines, equipment and reagents and open tanks or containers.[1054] Furthermore, said term covers electronics such as high voltage direct current power supplies, mass spectrometers, frequency chargers or generators, spectrometers and diffractometers, as well as sensors and lasers, such as yttrium aluminium garnet (YAG) rods, optical equipment and components, wave front corrector systems, argon ion lasers, semiconductor lasers, tunable semiconductor lasers and arrays, solid-state tunable lasers, neodymium-doped lasers, components of acousto-optics, radiation-hardened cameras and lenses, tunable pulsed dye laser amplifiers and oscillators, pulsed carbon dioxide lasers and other lasers.[1055] At the same time, it

1052. Points II.A0.001 to II.A0.014 of Part II to Annex II Regulation on DPRK that partially correlate to Nos 0A001, 0A001.j. & 1A004.c., 0B001.c.6. & 2A226 & 2B350, 0B001.g.5. & 6A005.e., 0B001.g.6. & 6A005.e.2., 2B350, 0B002.f.2. & 2B231, 0B006 and 0C001 of Annex I Part II Dual Use Regulation.

1053. Points II.A1.001 to II.A1.027 of Part II of Annex II Regulation on DPRK that partially correlate to Nos 1A001, 1A004.c., 1B225, 1A225 & 1B231, 1C002.b.4. & 1C202.a., 1C003.a., 1C010.a. & 1C010.b. & 1C210.a. & 1C210.b., 1C010 & 1C210, 1C107, 1C226, 1C116 & 1C216, 1C117 & 1C226, 1C003, 0C004 & 1C107.a., 1C116 & 1C216, 1A002.b.1., 1C002.c.1.a., 1C002.b.3., 1C002 & 1C202, 1C011 & 1C111 & 1C234, 1C239 of Annex I Part II Dual Use Regulation.

1054. Points II.A2.001 to II.A2.016 of Part II of Annex II Regulation on DPRK that partially correlate to Nos 2B116, 2B001 & 2B201, 2B119, 2B225, 2B226 & 2B227, 2B230, 2B350.e., 2B350.d., 2B350.i., 2B352.c., 2B352.d., 2B009 & 2B109 & 2B209, 2B350 & 2B352, 2B005 & 2B105 & 3B001.d., 2B350 of Annex I Part II Dual Use Regulation.

1055. Points II.A3.001 to II.A3.004 and Nos II.A6.001 to II.A6.013 of Part II of Annex II Regulation on DPRK that partially correlate to Nos 0B001.j.5. & 3A227, 0B002.g. & 3A233, 0B001.b.13. &

includes navigation and avionics, such as inertial navigation systems and specially designed components thereof, as well as aerospace and propulsion, such as explosive bolts, internal combustion engines and trucks.[1056] Finally, the term 'goods and technology' with regard to sanctions against the DPRK encompasses software and technology required for the development, production or use of the aforementioned items.[1057]

215. The same term with regard to Iran is quite similar, but not identical, as it includes in addition to the above glove boxes, toxic gas monitoring systems and helium leak detectors,[1058] maraging steels, fibrous or filamentary materials, propellants and constituent chemicals for propellants, lubricating materials and beryllium-copper,[1059] furnaces, electrical discharge machine tools, computer-controlled co-ordinate measuring machines, electron beam welding machines, laser welding and laser cutting machines, plasma cutting machines, vibration monitoring equipment, liquid ring vacuum pumps, rotary vane vacuum pumps, air filters,[1060] lasers, vacuum pressure gauges and microscopes[1061] and accelerometers.[1062]

216. On a final note and solely within the frame of DPRK, the described goods, software and technology are considered possibly contributing not only to nuclear-related programs but also to other programs related to weapons of mass destruction and to ballistic missiles.[1063]

B The Subjective Element

217. The subjective element consists of persons in the DPRK or the use of said goods and technology in the DPRK.[1064] Identical is the subjective element in the Regulation on

3A225 and 6A002 & 6A004.b., 6A004.a. & 6A005.e. & 6A005.f., 0B001.g.5. & 6A005.a.6. & 6A205.a., 0B001.g.5. & 0B001.h.6. & 6A005.b., 0B001.h.6. & 6A005.b., 0B001.g.5. & 0B001.h.6. & 6A005.c.1., 6A005.c.2.b., 6A203.b.4., 6A203.c., 0B001.g.5. & 6A005 & 6A205.c., 0B001.g.5. & 6A005 & 6A205.c., 6A005 & 6A205 of Annex I Part II Dual Use Regulation.

1056. Points II.A7.001 and II.A9.001 to II.A9.003 of Part II of Annex II Regulation on DPRK that partially correlate to Nos 7A001 & 7A003 & 7A101 & 7A103, 9A115 of Annex I Part II Dual Use Regulation.

1057. Points II.B.001 and II.C.001 of Annex II Regulation on DPRK.

1058. Points II.A0.015 to II.A0.017 Annex II Regulation on Iran that correlate to Nos 0B006, 0A001 & 0B001, 0A001 & 0B001.c. of Annex I Part II Dual Use Regulation.

1059. Points II.A1.012, II.A1.019, II.A1.024 to II.A1.026 Annex II Regulation on Iran that partially correlate to Nos 1C216, 1C111, 1C006 & 1C002.b. of Annex I Part II Dual Use Regulation.

1060. Points II.A2.006, II.A2.017 t0 II.A2.025 Annex II Regulation on Iran that correlate to Nos 2B226 & 2B227, 2B001.d., 2B006.a. & 2B206.a., 2B001.e.1.b., 2B001.e.1.c., 2B001.e.1., 2B116, 2B231 & 2B350.i., 2B231 & 2B235.i. & 0B002.f., 2B352.d. of Annex I Part II Dual Use Regulation.

1061. Points II.A6.013 to II.A6.016 Annex II Regulation on Iran that partially correlate to Nos 6A005.b, 0B001.b., 6B of Annex I Part II Dual Use Regulation.

1062. Point II.A7.002 Annex II Regulation on Iran that correlates to No. 7A001 of Annex I Part II Dual Use Regulation.

1063. Article 3(2) and Annex II Part II first sentence Regulation on DPRK.

1064. Article 3(1)(a) & (c) and Annex II Part II first sentence Regulation on DPRK.

Iran.[1065] This element differs from the subjective element explained in the financial sanctions, as in the legislation at hand focuses on the scope of the transaction, that is being used in the DPRK or Iran, as the case may be, and not on the person at the other end of the transaction, who can be anyone.

C *The Duty to Act and the Obligation to Refuse*

218. Cumulation of the subjective and the objective elements once again generates a duty to act and an obligation to refuse, albeit different ones with regard to Iran and the DPRK. They create an obligation to abstain from any trade involving such goods and persons.[1066]

219. The Regulation on Iran does not prohibit trade in the same goods and technology, but it does restrict it. Restriction takes the form of an authorization by the competent authorities of the Member States of the EU. More specifically, a prior authorization is required for their sale, supply, transfer or export to and purchase, import or transfer from Iran,[1067] for providing technical assistance[1068] and brokering services with regard to the same goods and technology[1069] and for providing financing and financial assistance.[1070] An authorization is also required before entering any arrangement with an Iranian person that would enable such a person to participate in commercial activities involving said goods and technology or increase his participation.[1071]

220. The competent authorities of the Member State, where the exporter is established, exchange information on requests for authorization via secure electronic means.[1072] In the process of evaluating the application, they consult the competent authorities of the Member State(s) that have the right to make known any objections within ten working days. In exceptional cases, any consulted state(s) may request for an extension of no more than thirty days. Should said states submit no objections within the explained time frame, it is deemed that they have no objection.[1073] Importantly, Member States have been given the option to request the denial of an authorization on the grounds of prejudice to their essential security interests. The

1065. Article 2a(1)(a) Regulation on Iran.
1066. Article 3(1)(a) & (c) and Annex II Part II Regulation on DPRK.
1067. Article 3a(1)(a) & (e) Regulation on Iran.
1068. On the statutory definition of 'technical assistance' *see* Annex I p. 311 at 331. Article 1(r) Regulation on Iran.
1069. Article 3a(1)(b) Regulation on Iran.
1070. Article 3a(1)(c) Regulation on Iran.
1071. Article 3a(1)(d) Regulation on Iran.
1072. Article 3a(5) Regulation on Iran and Art. 23(6) Regulation (EU) 2021/821 of the European Parliament and of the Council of 20 May 2021 setting up a Union regime for the control of exports, brokering, technical assistance, transit and transfer of dual-use items, OJ L 206, 11 Jun. 2021, p. 1, as last amended by Commission Delegated Regulation (EU) 2023/996 of 23 Feb. 2023 amending Regulation (EU) 2021/821 of the European Parliament and of the Council as regards the list of dual-use items, OJ L 138, 25 May 2023, p. 1 ('Dual Use Regulation').
1073. Article 3b(1) Regulation on Iran and Art. 14(1) Dual Use Regulation.

Member State receiving such a request is obliged to engage in consultations of a non-binding nature with the requesting Member State. The consultations between the two states are terminated within ten working days.[1074] The competent authorities are under a statutory obligation to refuse an authorization if they have reasonable grounds to determine that the relevant actions could contribute to activities related to reprocessing, enrichment, heavy water or other nuclear activities that are inconsistent with the JCPOA.[1075] Should the application for authorization concern a transaction that is essentially identical to a transaction denied under said ground, the concerned Member State shall consult the Member State that issued the denial.[1076] A further significant feature of the application, aside from the consultation, is the end-use statement in the specified form or an equivalent document that informs on the end-use and, as a basic principle, the end-use location of supplied items. Exporters applying for temporary exports are not requested to submit such a statement.[1077] All applicants stand under the statutory duty to provide all information required for their application to the competent authorities.[1078] Finally, the competent authorities have to notify the other Member States, the Commission and the High Representative of their intent to grant an authorization at least ten days before issuing the authorization.[1079]

221. If the competent authority decides not to grant the authorization due to concerns of reprocessing- or enrichment-related, heavy water-related or other nuclear-related activities inconsistent with the JCPOA, it shall notify the other Member States, the Commission and the High Representative. It shall also share the relevant information with them while complying with the confidentiality requirements.[1080]

222. The issued authorization is valid throughout the Union.[1081] If it has been issued in the absence of information on the end-use location, this may be requested at a later stage and the applicant shall provide it within a reasonable period of time.[1082] Further, if it has been issued despite a request for denial by another Member State on the grounds of prejudice to essential security interests, the issuing state shall notify accordingly the Commission and other Member States via secure electronic means.[1083] If it has been issued following consultations with Member States that refused to

1074. Article 3b(1) Regulation on Iran and Art. 14(2) Dual Use Regulation.
1075. Article 3a(4) Regulation on Iran.
1076. Article 3b(4) Regulation on Iran.
1077. Article 3a(6) and Annex IIa Regulation on Iran.
1078. Article 3a(3) Regulation on Iran.
1079. Article 3a(7) Regulation on Iran.
1080. Articles 3b(3) & 3a(4) Regulation on Iran. On confidentiality *see* Council Regulation (EC) No. 515/97 of 13 Mar. 1997 on mutual assistance between the administrative authorities of the Member States and cooperation between the latter and the Commission to ensure the correct application of the law on customs and agricultural matters, OJ L 082, 22 Mar. 1997, p. 1, as last amended by Regulation (EU) 2021/785 of the European Parliament and of the Council of 29 Apr. 2021 establishing the Union Anti-Fraud Programme and repealing Regulation (EU) No. 250/2014, OJ L 172, 17 May 2021, p. 110.
1081. Article 3b(1) Regulation on Iran.
1082. Article 3a(6s) Regulation on Iran.
1083. Article 3b(1) Regulation on Iran and Arts 14(2), 16(6) and 23(6) Dual Use Regulation.

authorize an essentially identical transaction, the issuing state has the duty to inform the other Member States, the Commission and the High Representative thereof as well as to provide all relevant information to explain the decision.[1084]

223. The authorization may be annulled, suspended, modified or revoked, where reasonable grounds exist for determining that the actions concerned would contribute to nuclear activities inconsistent with the JCPOA, such as activities related to reprocessing, enrichment and heavy water.[1085] Thereupon, the competent authorities notify the other Member States, the Commission and the High Representative and share all relevant information while communicating via secure electronic means and ensuring confidentiality.[1086]

D The Exceptions

224. The prohibition set out in the Regulation on DPRK has no exceptions, but for the humanitarian exception already explained (*see* in this regard paragraph 145 above). The obligation imposed via the Regulation on Iran does. The aforementioned procedure (*see* in this regard paragraphs 219 et seq. above) does not apply to goods and technology for light water reactors. Nonetheless, an end-use statement must accompany the submitted application for authorization, or alternatively, submission of the end-use location may be requested at a later stage.[1087] The issuing state shall inform the other Member States, the Commission and the High Representative of granted authorizations within four weeks.[1088]

225. Similarly, the aforementioned procedure (*see* in this regard paragraphs 219 et seq. above) does not apply to goods and technology related to necessary modifications of two cascades at the Fordow facility for stable isotope production, the export of Iran's enriched uranium in excess of 300 kilograms in return for natural uranium and the modernization of the Arak reactor based on the agreed conceptual design and, subsequently, on the agreed final design of such reactor.[1089] However, these do require authorization, whereby the competent authority ensures that all activities are undertaken in accordance with the JCPOA and an end-use statement has been submitted.[1090] The authority may request the submission of the end-use location at a later stage.[1091] Prior to issuing the authorization in question, the competent authorities notify other Member States and the Commission of their intention at least ten days in advance.[1092]

1084. Article 3b(4) Regulation on Iran.
1085. Articles 3b(2) & 3a(4) Regulation on Iran.
1086. Articles 3b(3) and 3a(4) & (5) Regulation on Iran and Regulation (EC) 515/97.
1087. Article 3c(1), (2) & (2a) Regulation on Iran.
1088. Article 3c(3) Regulation on Iran.
1089. Article 3d(1)(a), (b) & (c) Regulation on Iran.
1090. Article 3d(2)(a) & (b) Regulation on Iran.
1091. Article 3d(2a) Regulation on Iran.
1092. Article 3d(3) Regulation on Iran.

E Specifically the 'Trigger List'

226. The Regulation on Iran refers to certain goods and technology styled as 'goods and technology listed in Annex I'.[1093] In truth these goods and technology are the ones listed in the 'trigger list' of the Nuclear Suppliers Group (NSG) (*see* in this respect paragraph 246 below), as demonstrated in the ensuing paragraphs.[1094] In the same paragraphs, the goods and technology shall be described in a manner more succinct than their description in the EU act, albeit perhaps superfluous or unnecessarily detailed for the taste of jurists. It has been chosen to do so for the purpose of demonstrating that the 'goods and technology listed in Annex I' of the Regulation on Iran are the 'trigger list' of the NSG as well as a part of the Dual Use Regulation (*see* in this regard paragraphs 250 et seq. below). This also means that a specific item can fall under all three categories and thus, be subject to the respective prohibitions, restrictions or controls. It equally assists the correlation of EU legislation to the legislation of other states.

227. The 'goods and technology listed in Annex I' are listed under five separate categories. The first one is entitled 'Category 0: nuclear materials, facilities and equipment' and consists of: nuclear reactors and specially designed or prepared equipment and components therefor;[1095] plant for the separation of isotopes of 'natural uranium', 'depleted uranium' or 'special fissile materials', and specially designed or prepared equipment and components therefor;[1096] 'natural uranium' or 'depleted uranium' or

1093. Mark Bromley & Giovanna Maletta, *The Challenge of Software and Technology Transfers to Non-Proliferation Efforts*, Stockholm Peace Research Institute 2018, p. 18.

1094. The Regulation on Iran refers to the 'trigger list' as in INFCIRC/254/Rev.12/Part 1; this has been since revised twice and the currently valid version is INFCIRC/254/Rev.14/Part 1 of 18 Oct. 2019, available here: https://www.nuclearsuppliersgroup.org/index.php/en/guidelines/nsg-guidelines/guidelines-part-1 (last visited: 20 Dec. 2023).

1095. Point 0A001 of Annex I Regulation on Iran that correlates to No. TLBl.1 of the Nuclear Suppliers Group's control list. Subpoints 0A001.a, 0A001.b, 0A001.c, 0A001.d, 0A001.e, 0A001.f, 0A001.g, 0A001.h, 0A001.i, 0A001.j, 0A001.k correlate to Nos TLB1.1, TLB1.2, TLB1.3, TLB1.4, TLB1.5, TLB1.6, TLB1.7, TLB1.8, TLB1.9, TLB1.10, TLB1.11 respectively.

1096. Point 0B001 of Annex I Regulation on Iran that correlates to No. TLBl.5 of the Nuclear Suppliers Group's control list. Subpoint 0B001.b correlates to Nos TLB5.1.1, TLB5.1.1a to TLB5.1.1e, TLB5.1.2A.1, TLB5.1.2a2, TLB5.1.2b, TLB5.1.2c, TLB5.1.2d, TLB5.1.2e, TLB5.1.2f, TLB5.2.5 and TLB5.2.3. Subpoint 0B001.c correlates to Nos TLB5.3.1a, TLB5.3.2 to TLB5.3.5. Subpoint 0B001.d correlates to Nos TLB5.5.1, TLB5.5.2 to TLB5.5.6 and TLB5.5.10, TLB5.5.12. Subpoint 0B001.e correlates to Nos TLB5.6.1, TLB5.6.2, TLB5.6.3a, TLB5.6.3b, TLB5.6.4 and TLB5.6.5. Subpoint 0B001.f correlates to Nos TLB5.6.6, TLB5.6.7 and TLB5.6.8. Subpoint 0B001.g correlates to Nos TLB5.7.1 to TLB5.7.4 and TLB5.7.13. Subpoint 0B001.h correlates to TLB5.7.5 to TLB5.7.9, TLB5.7.12 and TLB5.7.13. Subpoint 0B001.i correlates to Nos TLB5.8.1 to TLB.5.8.6. Subpoint 0B001.j correlates to Nos TLB5.9.1a to TLB5.9.1d, TLB5.9.2 and TLB5.9.3. Subpoint 0B002 correlates to TLB5.2.1, TLB5.2.2, TLB5.2.4, TLB5.4.1, TLB5.4.2, TLB5.4.3, TLB5.4.5, TLB5.5.7, TLB5.5.9, TLB5.7.11 and TLB5.7.10. Subpoint 0B003 correlates to TLB7.1, TLB7.1.1 to TLB7 1.9. Subpoint 0B004 correlates to TLB6.1 to TLB6.9. Subpoint 0B005 correlates to TLB4. Subpoint 0B006 correlates to TLB3.1 to TLB3.5. Subpoints 0B007 correlates to TLB7.2.1 and TLB7.2.2.

thorium in the form of metal, alloy, chemical compound or concentrate;[1097] software specially designed or modified for the *development*,[1098] *production*[1099] or *use*[1100] of the goods described above;[1101] and *technology* for the development, production and use of the same goods.[1102] In reference to technology, it is clarified that technology directly associated with any such goods is controlled under the relevant provisions. This technology remains under control even when applicable to non-controlled goods. Still, it is not applicable to information *in the public domain*[1103] as well as to *basic scientific research*.[1104,1105]

228. The second category bears the title 'Category 1: special materials and related equipment'. It includes: systems, equipment and components, such as explosive detonators;[1106] test, inspection and production equipment;[1107] materials, such as aluminium and titanium alloys;[1108] software specially designed for certain goods;[1109] and technology for certain goods.[1110] With regard to technology it is noted that export

1097. Point 0C001 Annex I Regulation on Iran that correlates to No. TLA.1.1 of the Nuclear Suppliers Group's control list. Subpoints 0C002 correlate to TLA.1.2; 0C003 to TLB2.1; 0C004 to TLB2.2; and 0C005 to TLB5.3.1b.
1098. In regard to the statutory definition of *development see* Annex I, p. 311 at 318. Definitions of Terms Used in This Annex, Annex I Dual Use Regulation.
1099. In regard to the statutory definition of *production see* Annex I, p. 311 at 330. Definitions of Terms Used in This Annex, Annex I Dual Use Regulation.
1100. In regard to the statutory definition of *use see* Annex I, p. 311 at 335. Definitions of Terms Used in This Annex, Annex I Dual Use Regulation.
1101. Point 0D001 Annex I Regulation on Iran. Under the Nuclear Suppliers Group's control list *software* is specified as 'means a collection of one or more "programs" or "microprograms" fixed in any tangible medium of expression'.
1102. Point 0E001 Annex I Regulation on Iran. Under the Nuclear Supplier Group's control list *technology* means specific information required for the development, production, or use of any item contained in the List. This information may take the form of technical data, or technical assistance.
1103. In regard to the statutory definition of *in the public domain see* Annex I p. 311 at 325 Definitions of Terms Used in This Annex, Annex I Dual Use Regulation.
1104. In regard to the statutory definition of *basic scientific research see* Annex I p. 311 at 311. Definitions of Terms Used in This Annex, Annex I Dual Use Regulation.
1105. Nuclear Technology Note, Annex I Dual Use Regulation.
1106. Point 1A007 Annex I Regulation on Iran that correlates to Nos 6.A.1. and 6.A.2. of the Nuclear Suppliers Group's control list. Point 1A202 to No. 2.A.3., point 1A225 to No. 2.A.2., point 1A226 to No. 4.A.1. and point 1A227 to No. 1.A.1.
1107. Point 1B201 Annex I Regulation on Iran that correlates to No. 3.B.4. of the Nuclear Suppliers Group's control list. Point 1B225 to No. 3.B.1., point 1B226 to No. 3.B.5., point 1B228 to No. 4.B.2., 1B229 to No. 4.B.1., point 1B230 to No. 4.A.2., point 1B231 to No. 2.B.1., point 1B232 to No. 4.A.3., point 1B233 to No. 2.B.2. and point 1B234 to No. 5.B.7.
1108. Point IC202 Annex I Regulation on Iran that correlates to Nos 2.C.1 and 2.C.13. of the Nuclear Suppliers Group's control list. Point 1C210 to Nos 2.C.7.a, 2.C.7.b & 2.C.7.c, point 1C216 to No. 2.C.11, point 1C225 to No. 2.C.4., point 1C226 to No. 2.C.14., point 1C227 to No. 2.C.5., point 1C228 to No. 2.C.10., point 1C229 to No. 2.C.3., point 1C230 to No. 2.C.2., point 1C231 to No. 2.C.8., point 1C232 to No. 2.C.18., point 1C233 to No. 2.C.9., point 1C234 to No. 2.C.15., point 1C235 to No. 2.C.17., point 1C236 to No. 2.C.19., point 1C237 to No. 2.C.12., point 1C238 to No. 2.C.6., point 1C239 to No. 6.C.1.o, point 1C240 to No. 2.C.16. and point 1C241 to No. 2.C.20.
1109. Points 1D001 and 1B001 to 1B003 Annex I Regulation on Iran that correlates to No. 1.D.2. of the Nuclear Suppliers Group's control list. Points 1D201 and 1B201 to No. 1.D.3.
1110. Points 1E201 and 1A002, 1A007, 1A202, 1A225 to 1A227, 1B201, 1B225 to 1B234, 1C002.b.3. or .b.4., 1C010.b., 1C202, 1C210, 1C216, 1C225 to 1C241 or 1D201 that correlate to No. 1.E.1.

of technology required for the development, production or use of goods under control, underlies these provisions. Further, same technology remains under control even with regard to non-controlled goods. However, no controls apply to technology that is the minimum necessary for the installation, operation, maintenance (checking) and repair of those goods which are not controlled or whose export has been authorized. Controls are also not applicable to information on the public domain, to basic scientific research as well as to the minimum necessary information for patent applications.[1111]

229. The third category bears the title 'Category 2: materials processing'. The items listed are: crucibles;[1112] valves;[1113] machine tools;[1114] dimensional inspection or measuring systems;[1115] vibration test systems;[1116] isostatic presses in the sense of 'equipment capable of pressurizing a closed cavity through various media, such as gas, liquid and solid particles, to create equal pressure in all directions within the cavity upon a workpiece or material';[1117,1118] robots, in the sense of a 'manipulation mechanism, which may be of the continuous path or of the point-to-point variety, may use sensors, and has all the following characteristics: (a) is multifunctional; (b) is capable of positioning or orienting material, parts, tools or special devices through variable movements in three dimensional space; (c) incorporates three or more closed or open loop servo-devices which may include stepping motors; and (d) has 'user accessible programmability' by means of teach/playback method or by means of an electronic computer which may be a programmable logic controller, i.e., without mechanical intervention';[1119] end-effectors and control units;[1120] flow forming machines;[1121] centrifugal multiplane balancing machines;[1122] rotate manipulators;[1123] controlled atmosphere furnaces;[1124]

of the Nuclear Suppliers Group's control list. Points 1E202 and 1A007, 1A202 or 1A225 to 1A227 correlate to No. 1.E.1. Points 1E203 and 1A007, 1A202 or 1A225 to 1A227 correlate to No. 1.E.1.

1111. General Technology Note, Annex I Dual Use Regulation.
1112. Point 2A225 Annex I Regulation on Iran that correlates to No. 2.A.1. of the Nuclear Suppliers Group's control list.
1113. Point 2A226 Annex I Regulation on Iran that correlates to No. 2.A.3. of the Nuclear Suppliers Group's control list.
1114. Points 2B001 and 2B201 Annex I Regulation on Iran that correlate to No. 1.B.2. of the Nuclear Suppliers Group's control list.
1115. Points 2B006 and 2B206 Annex I Regulation on Iran that correlate to No. 1.B.3. of the Nuclear Suppliers Group's control list.
1116. Point 2B116 Annex I Regulation on Iran that correlates to No. 1.B.6. of the Nuclear Suppliers Group's control list.
1117. Definitions of Terms Used in This Annex, Annex I Dual Use Regulation.
1118. Point 2B204 Annex I Regulation on Iran that correlates to No. 1.B.5. of the Nuclear Suppliers Group's control list.
1119. Definitions of Terms Used in This Annex, Annex I Dual Use Regulation.
1120. Point 2B207 Annex I Regulation on Iran that correlates to No. 1.A.3. of the Nuclear Suppliers Group's control list.
1121. Point 2B209 Annex I Regulation on Iran that correlates to No. 1.B.1. of the Nuclear Suppliers Group's control list.
1122. Point 2B219 Annex I Regulation on Iran that correlates to No. 3.B.3. of the Nuclear Suppliers Group's control list.
1123. Point 2B225 Annex I Regulation on Iran that correlates to No. 1.A.4. of the Nuclear Suppliers Group's control list.
1124. Points 2B226 and 2B227 Annex I Regulation on Iran that correlate to Nos 1.B.4. and 1.B.7. of the Nuclear Suppliers Group's control list.

rotor fabrication or assembly equipment;[1125] pressure transducers, vacuum pumps and compressors;[1126] high-velocity gun systems;[1127] software specially designed for certain equipment,[1128] as well as software for electronic devices, even when residing in an electronic device or system, enabling such devices or systems to function as a 'numerical control' unit, capable of co-ordinating simultaneously more than four axes for contouring control;[1129] and technology in the aforementioned sense (*see* in this regard paragraph 218 above) for the development of the equipment and software already described.[1130]

230. The fourth category is entitled 'Category 3: electronics'. It encompasses the ensuing systems, equipment and components: certain electronic components;[1131] frequency changers or generators;[1132] high-power and high-voltage direct current power supplies;[1133] switching devices;[1134] certain generators and generator systems;[1135] multipoint initiation systems;[1136] mass spectrometers;[1137] striplines;[1138] software specially designed for said equipment;[1139] and relevant technology.[1140] Specifically with regard to technology, this is understood in the aforementioned sense (*see* in this regard paragraph 228 above) for the development, production[1141] and use[1142] of

1125. Point 2B228 Annex I Regulation on Iran that correlates to No. 3.B.2. of the Nuclear Suppliers Group's control list.
1126. Points 2B230, 2B231 and 2B233 Annex I Regulation on Iran that correlate to Nos 3.A.7., 3.A.8. and 3.A.9. of the Nuclear Suppliers Group's control list.
1127. Point 2B232 Annex I Regulation on Iran that correlates to No. 5.B.2. of the Nuclear Suppliers Group's control list.
1128. Points 2D001, 2D101, 2D201 and 2D202 Annex I Regulation on Iran that correlate to Nos 1.D.2. and 1.D.1 of the Nuclear Suppliers Group's control list.
1129. Point 2D002 Annex I Regulation on Iran that correlates to No. 1.D.3. of the Nuclear Suppliers Group's control list.
1130. Points 2E001, 2E002, 2E101 and 2E201 Annex I Regulation on Iran that correlate to No. 1.E.1. of the Nuclear Suppliers Group's control list.
1131. Point 1A201 Annex I Regulation on Iran that correlates to Nos 6.A.4., 3.A.4. and 5.B.1. of the Nuclear Suppliers Group's control list.
1132. Point 3A225 Annex I Regulation on Iran that correlates to No. 3.A.1. of the Nuclear Suppliers Group's control list.
1133. Point 3A226 and 3A227 Annex I Regulation on Iran that correlate to Nos 3.A.5. and 3.A.6. of the Nuclear Suppliers Group's control list.
1134. Point 3A228 Annex I Regulation on Iran that correlates to No. 6.A.3. of the Nuclear Suppliers Group's control list.
1135. Points 3A229, 3A230 and 3A231 Annex I Regulation on Iran that correlates to Nos 6.A.2., 5.B. and 6.A.5. of the Nuclear Suppliers Group's control list.
1136. Point 3A232 Annex I Regulation on Iran that correlates to No. 6.A.1. of the Nuclear Suppliers Group's control list.
1137. Point 3A233 Annex I Regulation on Iran that correlates to No. 3.B.6. of the Nuclear Suppliers Group's control list.
1138. Point 3A234 Annex I Regulation on Iran that correlates to No. 6.A.6. of the Nuclear Suppliers Group's control list.
1139. Points 3D002 and 3D225 Annex I Regulation on Iran that correlate to Nos 3.D.1 and 3.D.3 of the Nuclear Suppliers Group's control list.
1140. Points 3E001, 3E201 and 3E225 Annex I Regulation on Iran that correlate to No. 3.E.1 of the Nuclear Suppliers Group's control list.
1141. *Development* and *production* refer specifically to equipment and materials specified in 3A, 3B and 3C. Point 3E001 Annex I Regulation on Iran.
1142. Use refers solely to equipment described in 3A001.e.2., 3A001.e.3., 3A001.g., 3A201 and 3A225 to 3A234. Point 3E201 Annex I Regulation on Iran.

certain equipment as well as technology in the form of codes or keys to enhance or release the performance of the aforementioned frequency changers and generators.[1143]

231. The fifth and last category is 'Category 6: Sensors and Lasers' and includes the following: lasers;[1144] photomultiplier tubes;[1145] cameras and components;[1146] other lasers, laser amplifiers and oscillators;[1147] velocity interferometers;[1148] pressure sensors;[1149] specially designed software;[1150] and technology. This technology has the aforementioned meaning (*see* in this regard paragraph 228 above) and is used for certain equipment.[1151] It also means codes and keys for enhancing or releasing the performance of some cameras and imaging devices.[1152]

232. Trade in all these systems, equipment, components, software and technology (*see* in this regard paragraphs 217-221 above) is subject to prior authorization.[1153] The specific trade activities are described in detail and they are identical to the ones with regard to certain 'goods and technology' (*see* in this regard paragraph 219 above), with one exception. Participating in a partnership or joint venture refers to activities involving uranium mining, and production or use of nuclear materials listed in Part 1 of the NSG list, including making of loans or credit.[1154]

233. Pertinent to the authorization by the competent authority is the approval of the UN Security Council,[1155] with the exception of supply, sale and transfer of low enriched

1143. These frequency chargers and generators are the ones fulfilling the conditions stated in 3A225. Point 3E225 Annex I Regulation on Iran.
1144. Point 6A005 Annex I Regulation on Iran that correlates to No. 3.A.2. of the Nuclear Suppliers Group's control list.
1145. Point 6A202 Annex I Regulation on Iran that correlates to No. 5.A.1. of the Nuclear Suppliers Group's control list.
1146. Point 6A203 Annex I Regulation on Iran that correlates to Nos 5.B.3. and 1.A.2. of the Nuclear Suppliers Group's control list.
1147. Point 6A205 Annex I Regulation on Iran that correlates to No. 3.A.2. of the Nuclear Suppliers Group's control list.
1148. Point 6A225 Annex I Regulation on Iran that correlates to No. 5.B.5.a of the Nuclear Suppliers Group's control list.
1149. Point 6A226 Annex I Regulation on Iran that correlates to Nos 5.B.5.b and 5.B.5.c of the Nuclear Suppliers Group's control list.
1150. This software relates solely to cameras and imaging devices meeting the characteristics of 6A203.a. to 6A203.c. Point 6D203 Annex I Regulation on Iran that correlates to No. 5.D.2. of the Nuclear Suppliers Group's control list.
1151. This is the equipment described in 6A003, 6A005.a.2., 6A005.b.2., 6A005.b.3., 6A005.b.4., 6A005.b.6, 6A005.c.2., 6A005.d.3.c., 6A005.d.4.c., 6A202, 6A203, 6A205, 6A225 and 6A226. Point 6E201 Annex I Regulation on Iran that correlates to No. 5.D.1. of the Nuclear Suppliers Group's control list.
1152. This enhancement refers to cameras or imaging devices meeting the characteristics of 6A203a. to 6A203c. Point 6E203 Annex I Regulation on Iran that correlates to No. 5.D.1. of the Nuclear Suppliers Group's control list.
1153. Article 2a(1)(b) Regulation on Iran.
1154. Article 2a(1)(d)(i) & (ii) Regulation on Iran.
1155. Article 2a(3) Regulation on Iran.

uranium, certain equipment[1156] and items[1157] for light water reactors.[1158] The competent authorities, when evaluating the applications for authorization ensure that the requirements of the Guidelines of the NSG list have been met, to the appropriate extend, and that the rights to verify the end-use and end-use location of any applied item have been obtained from Iran and can be exercised effectively. They further have to provide a notification to the UN Security Council within ten days of the authorized activity as well as a notification to the IAEA.[1159] The exporters are under the obligation to supply the competent authorities with all relevant information required for their application.[1160]

234. Furthermore, the competent authorities have the discretion of requesting the approval of the UN Security Council with regard to activities related to any other goods and technology that, according to their assessment, could contribute to reprocessing- or enrichment-related or heavy water activities inconsistent with the JCPOA.[1161]

235. After an authorization is granted, the Member State concerned notifies thereof the Joint Commission,[1162] the other Member States, the Commission and the High Representative of the Union for Foreign Affairs and Security Policy within an unspecified time frame. It also informs them of any refusal of the UN Security Council to approve an authorization.[1163]

236. The aforementioned approval of the UN Security Council is also not needed for a specific set of cases. These are the supply, sale and transfer of items and technology, including providing financial assistance, investment and other services for the necessary modification of two cascades at the Fordow facility for stable isotope production, the export of Iran's enriched uranium in excess of 300 kilograms in return for natural uranium and the modernization of the Arak reactor based on the agreed conceptual design and, subsequently, on the agreed final design of such reactor.[1164] In these cases, the authorities have to ensure that all activities comply with the JCPOA, meet the requirements of the Guidelines of the NSG list and the rights to verify the end-use and

1156. This is the equipment covered by B.1 of INFCIRC/254/Rev.12/Part 1 specifically for light nuclear reactors. S/RES/2231 of 20 Jul. 2015, Annex B para. 2(c) subpara. 1.
1157. These are items, materials, equipment, goods and technology set out in INFCIRC/254/Rev. 9/Part 2 for exclusive use in light water reactors. S/RES/2231 of 20 Jul. 2015, Annex B para. 2(c) subpara. 1.
1158. Article 2b Regulation on Iran.
1159. Article 2c(1)(c) and (d) Regulation on Iran.
1160. Article 2c(3) Regulation on Iran and Arts 12(2) & 13(5) Dual Use Regulation.
1161. Article 2a(4) Regulation on Iran.
1162. 'Joint Commission' is a joint commission consisting of representatives of Iran and of China, France, Germany, the Russian Federation, the United Kingdom and the United States with the High Representative of the Union for Foreign Affairs and Security Policy, that is established to monitor the implementation of the JCPOA and will carry out the functions provided for in the JCPOA, in accordance with point ix of the JCPOA's 'Preamble and General Provisions' and Annex IV to the JCPOA. Article 1(u) Regulation on Iran. The reports of the Joint Commission are available here: https://www.un.org/securitycouncil/content/reports-joint-commission-established-jcpoa (last visited: 31 Dec. 2023).
1163. Article 2a(5) and (6) Regulation on Iran.
1164. Article 2d(1)(a), (b) and (c) Regulation on Iran.

end-use location of any supplied item have been obtained from Iran and can be exercised effectively.[1165] The competent authorities have to notify ten days in advance the UN Security Council and the Joint Commission, as well as within ten days following the activity the IAEA.[1166] They further have to inform within four weeks the other Member States, the Commission and the High Representative of the Union for Foreign Affairs and Security Policy.[1167]

F Specifically Graphite and Raw or Semi-Finished Metals

237. Graphite and raw or semi-finished metals, in the sense of raw or semi-fabricated graphite,[1168] corrosion-resistant high-grade steel,[1169] aluminium and alloys,[1170] titanium and alloys[1171] and nickel and alloys in the form of sheet, plate, tube or bar[1172] equally underlie restrictions. Their sale, supply, transfer and export to any Iranian person or for use in Iran must be previously authorized.[1173] Providing technical assistance and brokering services, as well as financing or financial assistance with regard to said metals must also be previously authorized.[1174]

238. An authorization shall not be granted if the competent authorities have reasonable grounds to determine that the described activity may be intended for use in connection with nuclear activities inconsistent with the JCPOA, Iran's military or ballistic missile programme or benefit the Iranian Revolutionary Guard Corps.[1175] An authorization is also not granted when the relevant contracts for delivery fail to include appropriate end-user guarantees.[1176] When a Member State decides to proceed with an authorization for a transaction essentially identical to a transaction that is still validly denied by another Member State, the aforementioned with regard to certain 'goods and technology' (*see* in this respect paragraph 219 above) apply *mutatis mutandis*.[1177]

239. The Member State concerned has the obligation to keep the other Member States and the Commission informed. When it decides to proceed with granting an authorization, it shall inform them at least ten days before granting it.[1178] When it refuses an

1165. Article 2d(2)(a), (b) and (c) Regulation on Iran.
1166. Article 2d(3)(a) and (b) Regulation on Iran.
1167. Article 2d(4) Regulation on Iran.
1168. HS Codes 2504 and 3801 point 1 of Annex VIIB Regulation on Iran.
1169. HS Codes ex 72 19 to ex 72 22, ex 72 25 to ex 72 28, ex 73 04 to ex 73 07 point 2 of Annex VIIB Regulation on Iran.
1170. HS Codes ex 7604, ex 7604 10 10, ex 7604 29 10, 7606, 7608 and 7609 point 3 of Annex VIIB Regulation on Iran.
1171. HS Codes ex 8108 90 point 4 of Annex VIIB Regulation on Iran.
1172. HS Codes ex 75 05, ex 7505 11, ex 7505 12, 7506, ex 75 07, 7507 11, 7507 12 and 7507 20 point 5 of Annex VIIB Regulation on Iran.
1173. Article 15a(1)(a) Regulation on Iran.
1174. Article 15a(1)(b) & (c) Regulation on Iran.
1175. Article 15a(2)(a)(i), (ii) & (iii) Regulation on Iran.
1176. Article 15a(2)(b) Regulation on Iran.
1177. Article 15a(5) Regulation on Iran.
1178. Article 15a(3) Regulation on Iran.

authorization, it shall inform them and the High Representative of the Union for Foreign Affairs and Security Policy within an unspecified time frame. This information duty also applies in cases of annulment, suspension, substantively modification or revocation of an authorization.[1179]

G *Specifically the Enterprise Resource Planning Software*

240. 'Enterprise Resource Planning software' is software used for financial accounting, management accounting, human resources, manufacturing, supply chain management, project management, customer relationship management, data services, or access control.[1180] Such software when designed specifically for use in nuclear and military industries is subject to all aforementioned restrictions and prohibitions (*see* in this regard paragraphs 237-239 above).[1181]

§8 SANCTIONS ON DUAL-USE ITEMS

241. Dual-use items are the subject of restrictive measures in view of the situation in the DPRK, Iran, Myanmar/Burma and Syria. They are statutory and defined within the regulatory frame of sanctions (*see* in this regard paragraphs 248 et seq. below). At the outset, it is noted that this notion refers to items capable of multiple uses, whereby the imposed restrictive measures aim to prevent these items from being used in an illegal way or serve a prohibited purpose. Thus, sanctions on dual-use items resemble the prohibition of money laundering *in reverse*. In money laundering the object is criminal proceeds; these are placed in the financial system, then layered or engaged in a series of movements to distance them from their source and finally integrated into a legitimate economy.[1182] In sanctions, items of the legitimate economy are layered or engaged in a series of movements to distance them from their source and finally, they emerge in the shadows of illegal use or serving banned purposes.[1183] And sometimes they grandstand in broad daylight. Tracks transferring ballistic missiles in military

1179. Article 15a(4) Regulation on Iran.
1180. Annex VIIA Regulation on Iran.
1181. Article 10d and Annex VIIA Regulation on Iran.
1182. Bernardo M. Crenades & David J.A. Cairns, *Transnational Public Policy in International Arbitral Decision-Making*, in: K. Karsten & A. Berkley (eds), Arbitration: Money Laundering, Corruption and Fraud (Paris: International Chamber of Commerce 2003) 65 at 70.
1183. For example, a medical imaging machine with a computer component also used in weapons manufacturing, made in Japan is sold to a Chinese company for use by a hospital in China. Should a sanctions inspector show up at that hospital, he or she is informed that the machine in question is actually used by a network of hospitals, causing a paper chase, while the machine has already made its way into the DPRK. *Hear* the podcast: Jean Lee & Geoff White (hosts/reporters), Estelle Doyle (producer), *The Lazarus Heist, S2.9 Big Spenders*, 22 May 2023, BBC World Service, wherever you get your podcasts.

parades of the DPRK's regime could be such an example; and so could be spray driers for baby food used for weaponized anthrax, a biological weapon.[1184]

242. Dual-use items are not merely entangled in the sanctions' legislation; they are specific items, depicted in specialized and highly detailed lists, which as a general rule are exported under a controlled regime (*see* in this regard paragraph 250 below). The specific list set out in the relevant EU legal instrument, that being the Regulation on Dual-Use Items[1185] (hereinafter 'Dual Use Regulation'), which implements the internationally agreed dual-use controls of the Chemical Weapons Convention,[1186] the Australia Group ('AG'), the Missile Technology Control Regime ('MTCR'), the NSG and the Wassenaar Arrangement.[1187]

243. The Chemical Weapons Convention, agreed in response to the Iraq-Kuwait conflict and Iraq's threats to use chemical weapons,[1188] banned categorically for the very first time an entire category of weapons of mass destruction. It supplemented, along with the Biological Weapons Convention,[1189] the Protocol for the Prohibition of the Use of War of Asphyxiating, Poisonous or Other Gases and of Bacteriological Methods of Warfare.[1190,1191] It prohibits chemical weapons from three distinct perspectives. First, it introduces an arms control obligation. Second, it entails a disarmament obligation, that being the obligation to destroy chemical weapons in the possession of a Member State, along with abandoned chemical weapons and chemical weapons production facilities. Finally, it prohibits the use of chemical weapons as a method of warfare.[1192]

244. Support of the regime established by the Chemical Weapons Convention, and the Biological Weapons Convention, and their aims is the objective of *the 'AG'*[1193] an

1184. *Hear* the podcast: Jean Lee & Geoff White (hosts/reporters), Estelle Doyle (producer), *The Lazarus Heist, S2.9 Big Spenders*, 22 May 2023, BBC World Service, wherever you get your podcasts.
1185. Regulation (EU) 2021/821 of the European Parliament and of the Council of 20 May 2021 setting up a Union regime for the control of exports, brokering, technical assistance, transit and transfer of dual-use items, OJ L 206, 11 Jun. 2021, p. 1.
1186. Convention on the Prohibition of the Development, Production, Stockpiling and Use of Chemical Weapons and on their Destruction (Geneva 1992) 1975 UNTS 45 (2000).
1187. Preamble to Annex I Dual Use Regulation.
1188. Dieter Fleck, *Developments of the Law of Arms Control as a Result of the Iraq-Kuwait Conflict* 13 EJIL 105 at 107-108 (2002) https://doi.org/10.1093/ejil/13.1.105.
1189. Convention on the Prohibition of the Development, Production and Stockpiling of Bacteriological (Biological) and Toxin Weapons and on Their Destruction, A/RES/2826(XXVI).
1190. Protocol for the prohibition of the use in war of asphyxiating, poisonous or other gases, and of bacteriological methods of warfare (Geneva 1925) 94 LNTS 65 (1929).
1191. Annamaria Viterbo, *Obligations Related to Transfers of CBRN Weapons and Dual-Use Items*, in: A. de Guttry et al. (eds), International Law and Chemical, Biological, Radio-Nuclear (CBRN) Events (Brill 2022), 439 et seq. (446).
1192. Michael Bothe, *Convention on the Prohibition of the Development, Production, Stockpiling and Use of Chemical Weapons and on their Destruction*, in: United Nations Audiovisual Library of International Law (Geneva: United Nations 2011) 2, available: https://legal.un.org/avl/ha/disarmament.html (last visited: 31 Dec.2023).
1193. Nineta Bărbulescu, *20 years of the Australia Group Coordination* (Romania: National Agency for Export Controls 2005), p. 7, available: https://www.dfat.gov.au/publications/minisite/theaustraliagroupnet/site/en/20years.pdf (last visited: 31 Dec. 2023).

informal forum of states' members to said conventions established in 1985, in response to Iraq's use of chemical weapons in the Iran-Iraq war.[1194] Annual meetings are held in Paris,[1195] The AG strikes the balance between allowing the export of dual-use items and prohibiting the proliferation of chemical and biological weapons,[1196] via establishing common control lists on chemicals, dual-use equipment, pathogens and toxins.[1197]

245. The *MTCR*, founded in 1987, is another informal political understanding among states. The states' partners to this voluntary association hold an annual plenary meeting chaired on a rotational basis seeking to coordinate their export licensing practices.[1198] Thus, they have drafted and since review, the *MTCR Guidelines*[1199] and the *Equipment, Software and Technology Annex,*[1200] which they agree to implement.[1201] In this manner, the MTCR adds one more layer of export control via screening transfers that 'could make a contribution to delivery systems, other than manned aircraft' for weapons of mass destruction.[1202] Any criticisms regarding its legitimacy became futile following resolution 1540 of the UN Security Council[1203,1204] which very recently has been reaffirmed.[1205]

246. The '*NSG*', established in 1974, is a group of nuclear supplier countries. Like MTCR, plenary meetings are held once a year, where the chair is being held on a rotational basis. The Permanent Mission of Japan to the International Organisations in Vienna acts as a point of contact.[1206] The NSG aims to contribute to the non-proliferation

1194. *Ibid.*, p. 2. *See also A. Viterbo* (n. 1191) p. 450.
1195. The Australia Group, The Origins of the Australia Group, available: https://www.dfat.gov.au/publications/minisite/theaustraliagroupnet/site/en/origins.html (last visited: 31 Dec. 2023).
1196. The Australia Group, *The Australia Group: an Introduction*, available: https://www.dfat.gov.au/publications/minisite/theaustraliagroupnet/site/en/introduction.html (last visited: 31 Dec. 2023).
1197. The Australia Group, *Australia Group Common Control Lists*, available: https://www.dfat.gov.au/publications/minisite/theaustraliagroupnet/site/en/controllists.html (last visited: 31 Dec. 2023).
1198. Timothy V. McCarthy, *The Missile Technology Control Regime*, in: Michael Barletta & Amy Sands (eds), Nonproliferation Regimes at Risk (James Martin Center for Nonproliferation Studies (CNS) 1999), p. 19.
1199. Missile Technology Control Regime, *Guidelines for Sensitive Missile-Relevant Transfers*, available: https://www.mtcr.info/de/mtcr-richtlinien/guidelines-for-transfer (last visited: 31 Dec. 2023).
1200. Missile Technology Control Regime, Equipment, Software and Technology Index, MTCR/TEM/2022/Annex of 21 Oct. 2022, available: https://www.mtcr.info/en/mtcr-annex (last visited: 31 Dec. 2023).
1201. Leonard S. Spector, *The Missile Technology Control Regime and Shifting Proliferation Challenges* 48(3) Arms Controls Today 14 at 14 (2018) https://doi.org/10.4324/9780203799826-13.
1202. Mark Bromley & Giovanna Maletta, *The Challenge of Software and Technology Transfers to Non-Proliferation Efforts*, Stockholm International Peace Research Institute 2018, p. 17.
1203. S/RES/1540 of 28 Apr. 2004 para. 3(d).
1204. Kolta Brockmann, Mark Bromley & Lauriane Hau, *The Missile Technology Control Regime at a Crossroads*, Stockholm International Peace Research Institute 2022, p. 19.
1205. *See* S/RES/2622 of 25 Feb. 2022.
1206. Nuclear Suppliers Group, Organization, available: https://www.nuclearsuppliersgroup.org/index.php/en/about/organisation (last visited: 31 Dec. 2023).

of nuclear weapons through the implementation of two sets of guidelines.[1207] The first relates to nuclear transfer. This is commonly referred to as the 'Trigger List', as the export of these items triggers the safeguards system set by the IAEA. The other set of guidelines relates to transfers of nuclear-related dual-use equipment, materials, software and technology.[1208]

247. The *Wassenaar Arrangement* ('WA'), also an informal group holding annual plenary meetings chaired by a participating state that is annually rotated,[1209] is the fourth and last multilateral export control regime.[1210] It has a Secretariat located in Vienna, Austria.[1211] The WA was established with the aim of contributing to regional and international security and stability through the promotion of transparency and greater responsibility in the transfers of conventional arms and dual-use goods and technologies.[1212] The participating states have compiled a list of dual-use goods and a munitions list,[1213] keep it under review and have agreed to implement it.

I Meaning of Dual-Use Items

248. 'Dual use items' are defined by an abstract legal definition and a much-detailed listing annexed to the Dual Use Regulation. According to the first one such are *items, including software and technology, which can be used for both civil and military purposes, and includes all goods which can be used for both non-explosive uses and assisting in any way in the manufacture of nuclear weapons or other nuclear explosive devices.*[1214]

249. The list of dual-use items consists of ten categories of items described below (*see* paragraphs 240 to 249 below). The description could seem superfluous or unnecessarily elaborate; still it has been deemed sensible in order to demonstrate the sources and roots of the listings and the correlation and connection among EU acts and the texts

1207. The Nuclear Suppliers Group: Its Guidelines, Origins, Structure, and Role, INFCIRC/539/Revision 8, para. 1, available: https://www.iaea.org/sites/default/files/publications/documents/infcircs/1997/infcirc539r8.pdf (last visited: 31 Dec. 2023).
1208. Sibylle Bauer, Kolja Brockmann, Mark Bromley & Giovanna Maletta, *Internal Compliance and Export Control Guidance Documents for the Nuclear Sector*, Stockholm International Peace Research Institute 2017, p. 1. The guidelines are available here: https://www.nuclearsuppliersgroup.org/index.php/en/guidelines/nsg-guidelines (last visited: 31 Dec. 2023).
1209. The Wassenaar Arrangement, *About Us*, available: https://www.wassenaar.org/about-us/ (last visited: 31 Dec. 2023).
1210. *Mark Bromley & Giovanna Maletta* (n. 1093) p. 4.
1211. The Wassenaar Arrangement, *Final Declaration*, The Hague, 19 Dec. 1995, para. 5, available: https://www.wassenaar.org/app/uploads/2021/12/Public-Docs-Vol-I-Founding-Documents.pdf (last visited: 31 Dec. 2023).
1212. The Wassenaar Arrangement, *Guidelines & Procedures, Including the Initial Elements*, December 2019, para. I.1., available: https://www.wassenaar.org/app/uploads/2021/12/Public-Docs-Vol-I-Founding-Documents.pdf (last visited: 31 Dec. 2023).
1213. The Wassenaar Arrangement, *Public Documents Vol. II, List of Dual-Use Goods and Technologies and Munitions List*, December 2022, available: https://www.wassenaar.org/control-lists/ (last visited: 31 Dec. 2023).
1214. Article 2(1) Dual Use Regulation.

compiled and agreed by said informal groups. It also supports the view that determining whether company's products are caught by product control lists is a complex and technical task.[1215] Sporadically, the definitions of certain terms as set out in these texts are portrayed.

250. The first category ('Category 0') is entitled 'nuclear materials, facilities and equipment'. It is identical to the category described above under nuclear energy and activities, and thus it is a part of the 'trigger list' of the NSG (*see* in this regard paragraphs 224 et seq. above), or, in other words, the Regulation on Iran adopted in its Annex I the first category of dual use items.

251. The second category ('Category 1') includes 'special materials and related equipment'. It lists the items, equipment and materials described above under nuclear energy and activities (*see* in this regard paragraphs 224 et seq. above) as well as the following systems, equipment and components: fluorinated compounds;[1216] composite structures and laminates;[1217] manufactures of non-'fusible' aromatic polyimides;[1218] protective and detection equipment and components not specially designed for military use;[1219] body armour and components thereof;[1220] equipment, specially designed or modified for the disposal of improvised explosive devices;[1221] charges, devices and components;[1222] resaturated pyrolized carbon-carbon components designed for space launch vehicles or sounding rockets;[1223] and equipment for the production or inspection of certain 'composite' structures or laminates.[1224] It also sets out the following test, inspection and production equipment: equipment designed to produce metal alloy powder or particulate materials with specific features;[1225] tools, dies, moulds or fixtures, for 'superplastic forming' or 'diffusion bonding' titanium, aluminium or their alloys with specific functions;[1226] equipment for the production of propellant and propellant constituents;[1227] specially designed nozzles;[1228] batch and continuous mixers;[1229] and

1215. Paul D. Burns et al., *Trade Sanctions and Export Controls: A Multijurisdictional Analysis for the Energy Sector* 3(2) J.W.E.L. & B. 214 at 224 (2010) https://doi.org/10.1093/jwelb/jwq003.
1216. Point 1A001 Annex I Dual Use Regulation.
1217. Point 1A002 Annex I Dual Use Regulation, which corresponds to No. 6.A.1. of the MTCR Annex.
1218. Point 1A003 Annex I Dual Use Regulation.
1219. Point 1A004 Annex I Dual Use Regulation.
1220. Point 1A005 Annex I Dual Use Regulation.
1221. Point 1A006 Annex I Dual Use Regulation.
1222. Point 1A008 Annex I Dual Use Regulation.
1223. Point 1A102 Annex I Dual Use Regulation, which corresponds to No. 6.A.2. of the MTCR Annex.
1224. Points 1B001, 1A002 & 1C010 and 1B101 Annex I Dual Use Regulation. Points 1B001, 1B101 and 1C010 correspond to Nos 6.B.1. and 6.C.1 of the MTCR Annex respectively.
1225. Points 1B002 and 1B102 Annex I Dual Use Regulation, which correspond to No. 4.B.3.d of the MTCR Annex.
1226. Point 1B003 Annex I Dual Use Regulation.
1227. Point 1B115 Annex I Dual Use Regulation, which corresponds to Nos 4.B.1. & 4.B.2. of the MTCR Annex.
1228. Point 1B116 Annex I Dual Use Regulation, which corresponds to No. 6.B.2. of the MTCR Annex.
1229. Points 1B117 and 1B118 Annex I Dual Use Regulation, which correspond to Nos 4.B.3.a & 4.B.3.b. of the MTCR Annex.

fluid energy mills.[1230] It further states the following materials: materials specially designed for absorbing electromagnetic radiation and materials for reduced observables usable in missiles or UAVs;[1231] metal alloys, metal alloy powder and alloyed materials;[1232] magnetic metals with specific characteristics;[1233] uranium titanium alloys;[1234] superconductive composite conductors;[1235] certain fluids and lubricating materials;[1236] ceramic powders, ceramic-matrix composite materials and precursor materials;[1237] non-fluorinated polymeric substances;[1238] unprocessed fluorinated compounds;[1239] fibrous or filamentary materials;[1240] certain metals and other materials typically used for nuclear heat sources;[1241] propellants and constituent chemicals for propellants;[1242] maraging steels, useable in missiles and materials for the fabrication of missiles components;[1243] titanium-stabilized duplex stainless steel;[1244] certain chemicals, which may be used as precursors for toxic chemical agents;[1245] human and animal pathogens and toxins with the exception of vaccines and immunotoxins;[1246] genetic elements and genetically-modified organisms;[1247] plant pathogens;[1248] and toxic chemicals and toxic chemical

1230. Point 1B119 Annex I Dual Use Regulation, which corresponds to No. 4.B.3.c. of the MTCR Annex.
1231. Points 1C001 and 1C101 Annex I Dual Use Regulation, which correspond to Nos 17.C.1. and 17.A.1. & 17.C.1. of the MTCR Annex, respectively.
1232. Points 1C002 and 1C102 Annex I Dual Use Regulation. Point 1C102 corresponds to No. 6.C.2. of the MTCR Annex.
1233. Point 1C003 Annex I Dual Use Regulation.
1234. Point 1C004 Annex I Dual Use Regulation.
1235. Point 1C005 Annex I Dual Use Regulation.
1236. Point 1C006 Annex I Dual Use Regulation.
1237. Points 1C007 and 1C107 Annex I Dual Use Regulation, which correspond to Nos 6.C.5. & 6.C.6 and 6.C.3, 6.C.4, 6.C.5 & 6.C.6 of the MTCR Annex respectively.
1238. Point 1C008 Annex I Dual Use Regulation.
1239. Point 1C009 Annex I Dual Use Regulation.
1240. Point 1C010 Annex I Dual Use Regulation, which corresponds to No. 6.C.1. of the MTCR Annex.
1241. Points 1C011 and 1C012 Annex I Dual Use Regulation. Point 1C011 corresponds to Nos 4.C.2.d. & 4.C.2.e. of the MTCR Annex.
1242. Point 1C111 Annex I Dual Use Regulation, which corresponds to Nos 4.C.2.a, 4.C.2.b., 4.C.2.c., 4.C.2.d., 4.C.2.e., 4.C.2.f., 4.C.2.g., 4.C.5., 4.C.6.c.1., 4.C.6.d.1., 4.C.6.e.1., 4.C.6.d.2., 4.C.6.d.4., 4.C.6.c.2. & 4.C.6.d.5 of the MTCR Annex.
1243. Points 1C116 and 1C117 Annex I Dual Use Regulation, which correspond to Nos 6.C.8. & 6.C. 7. of the MTCR Annex.
1244. Point 1C118 Annex I Dual Use Regulation, which corresponds to No. 6.C.9. of the MTCR Annex.
1245. Points 1C350 and 1C450 Annex I Dual Use Regulation, which corresponds to the precursor chemicals listed with the corresponding Chemical Abstract Service number in the Export Control List: Chemical Weapons of the AG as of 28 Feb. 2020.
1246. Point 1C351 Annex I Dual Use Regulation, which corresponds to 'Viruses', 'Bacteria', 'Toxins' and 'Fungi' of the List of Human and Animal Pathogens and Toxics for Export Control of the AG as of 28 Feb. 2020.
1247. Point 1C353 Annex I Dual Use Regulation, which corresponds to 'Genetic Elements and Genetically-modified Organisms' of the List of Human and Animal Pathogens and Toxics for Export Control of the AG as of 28 Feb. 2020.
1248. Point 1C354 Annex I Dual Use Regulation, which corresponds to the Core List (Bacteria, Fungi & Viruses) of the List of Plant Pathogens for Export Control of the AG as of 28 Feb. 2020.

precursors.[1249] Finally, it lists relevant software, such as software specially designed for analysis of reduced observables;[1250] and technology.[1251]

252. The third category ('Category 2') is entitled 'materials processing'. Aside the items mentioned above under nuclear energy and activities (*see* in this regard paragraphs 224 et seq. above), it includes anti-friction bearing and bearing systems;[1252] radial ball bearings;[1253] certain numerically controlled machine tools with specific characteristics;[1254] hot and other isostatic presses;[1255] equipment specially designed for the deposition, processing and in-process control of inorganic overlays, coatings and surface modifications and other equipment and process controls;[1256] computer controlled or numerical controlled coordinate measuring machines;[1257] rotary position feedback units and equipment for measuring surface roughness;[1258] robots with specific characteristics;[1259] compound rotary tables and tilting spindles;[1260] spin-forming machines and flow-forming machines;[1261] balancing machines and related equipment;[1262] motion simulators and rate tables with specific characteristics;[1263] centrifuges;[1264] chemical manufacturing facilities, equipment and components;[1265]

1249. Point 1C450 Annex I Dual Use Regulation.
1250. Points 1D002, 1D003, 1D101 and 1D103 Annex I Dual Use Regulation. Points 1D101 & 1D103 correspond to Nos 4.D.1. & 6.D.1. and 17.D.1. of the MTCR Annex, respectively.
1251. Points 1E001, 1E002, 1E101, 1E102, 1E103 and 1E104 Annex I Dual Use Regulation. Points 1E001, 1E101, 1E102, 1E103 & 1E104 correspond to Nos 6.E.1., 17.E.1., 6.E.2. & 6.E.1. of the MTCR Annex.
1252. Point 2A001 Annex I Dual Use Regulation, which corresponds to No. 3.A.7. of the MTCR Annex.
1253. Point 2A101 Annex I Dual Use Regulation, which corresponds to No. 3.A.7. of the MTCR Annex.
1254. Points 2B002 and 2B003 Annex I Dual Use Regulation.
1255. Points 2B004 and 2B104 Annex I Dual Use Regulation, which correspond to No. 6.B.3. of the MTCR Annex. Point 2B204 is related thereto and has been already mentioned under nuclear energy and activities.
1256. Points 2B005, 2B105 and 2B117 Annex I Dual Use Regulation. Points 2B105 & 2B117 Annex I Dual Use Regulation correspond to 6.B.4. & 6.B.5. of the MTCR Annex.
1257. Point 2B006.a Annex I Dual Use Regulation. Point 2B206.a is related and has been already mentioned under nuclear energy and activities.
1258. Points 2B006.c & 2B006.d Annex I Dual Use Regulation.
1259. Point 2B007 Annex I Dual Use Regulation.
1260. Point 2B008 Annex I Dual Use Regulation.
1261. Points 2B009 and 2B109 Annex I Dual Use Regulation. Point 2B109 corresponds to No. 3.B.3. of the MTCR Annex. Point 2B209 is related and has been already mentioned under nuclear energy and activities.
1262. Point 2B119 Annex I Dual Use Regulation, which corresponds to No. 9.B.2.a. & 9.B.2.b. of the MTCR Annex.
1263. Points 2B120 and 2B121 Annex I Dual Use Regulation, which corresponds to No. 9.B.2.c. & 9.B.2.d. of the MTCR Annex.
1264. Point 2B122 Annex I Dual Use Regulation, which corresponds to No. 9.B.2.e. of the MTCR Annex.
1265. Point 2B350 Annex I Dual Use Regulation, which corresponds to Nos I.1 to I.9 & I.10 of the Control List of Dual-Use Chemical Manufacturing Facilities and Equipment and Related Technology and Software of the AG as of 16 Aug. 2020.

toxic gas monitors and monitoring systems;[1266] biological manufacturing and handling equipment;[1267] relevant software;[1268] and technology.[1269]

253. The fourth category ('Category 3') relates to 'electronics'. In addition to the items mentioned above under nuclear energy and activities (*see* in this regard paragraphs 224 et seq. above), it includes: electronic items such as general purpose integrated circuits, microwave or millimetre wave items, acoustic wave devices, electronic devices and circuits containing components, manufactured from superconductive materials, high energy devices, rotary input type absolute position encoders, solid-state pulsed power switching thyristor devices, solid-state power semiconductor switches, and electro-optic modulators with certain characteristics;[1270] general purpose electronic assemblies, modules and equipment;[1271] spray cooling thermal management systems;[1272] and thermal batteries designed or modified for missiles, in the sense of rocket systems and UAV systems.[1273] It also includes the following test, inspection and production equipment: equipment for the manufacturing of semiconductor devices or materials;[1274] and test equipment specially designed for testing semiconductor devices.[1275] It further encompasses the following materials: hetero-epitaxial materials;[1276] resist materials;[1277] organo-inorganic compounds;[1278] hydrides of phosphorus, arsenic or antimony;[1279] and high resistivity materials.[1280] Finally, it includes relevant software and computational lithography software,[1281] and technology.[1282]

1266. Point 2B351 Annex I Dual Use Regulation, which corresponds to No. II. of the Control List of Dual-Use Chemical Manufacturing Facilities and Equipment and Related Technology and Software of the AG as of 16 Aug. 2020.
1267. Point 2B352 Annex I Dual Use Regulation, which corresponds to Nos I.1 to I.8 & I.10 of the Control List of Dual-Use Biological Equipment and Related Technology and Software of the AG as of 16 Aug. 2020.
1268. Points 2D003 and 2D351 Annex I Dual Use Regulation.
1269. Points 2E003 and 2E301 Annex I Dual Use Regulation. Specifically point 2E301 corresponds to No. III of the Control List of Dual-Use Biological Equipment and Related Technology and Software of the AG as of 16 Aug. 2020.
1270. Points 3A001.a to 3A001.i and 3A101 Annex I Dual Use Regulation, which correspond to Nos 18.A.1. & 18.A.2. and Nos 14.A.1., 14.A.1.b.1., 14.A.1.b.2., 15.B.5. of the MTCR Annex.
1271. Point 3A002 Annex I Dual Use Regulation.
1272. Point 3A003 Annex I Dual Use Regulation.
1273. Point 3A102 Annex I Dual Use Regulation, which corresponds to No. 12.A.6. of the MTCR Annex.
1274. Point 3B001 Annex I Dual Use Regulation.
1275. Point 3B002 Annex I Dual Use Regulation.
1276. Point 3C001 Annex I Dual Use Regulation.
1277. Point 3C002 Annex I Dual Use Regulation.
1278. Point 3C003 Annex I Dual Use Regulation.
1279. Point 3C004 Annex I Dual Use Regulation.
1280. Points 3C005 and 3C006 Annex I Dual Use Regulation.
1281. Points 3D001, 3D003, 3D004, 3D005 and 3D101 Annex I Dual Use Regulation. The latter corresponds to No. 15.D.1. of the MTCR Annex.
1282. Points 3E002, 3E003, 3E004, 3E101 and 3E102 Annex I Dual Use Regulation. The latter two correspond to No. 15.E.1. of the MTCR Annex.

254. The fifth category ('Category 4') has the heading 'computers'. It encompasses electronic computers specially designed to have specific specifications;[1283] digital computers and electronic assemblies;[1284] systolic array, neutral and optical computers;[1285] systems specially designed or modified for the generation, command and control or delivery of intrusion software;[1286] computers designed for use in specific space launch vehicles and sounding rockets;[1287] hybrid computers specially designed for modelling, simulation and design integration of space launch vehicles and sounding rockets;[1288] software;[1289] and technology.[1290]

255. The sixth category ('Category 5') bears the title 'telecommunications and information security' and contains the following items. Under *telecommunications* the following are listed: telecommunications systems, equipment, components and accessories with specific characteristics, functions and features;[1291] telemetry and telecontrol equipment designed or modified for missiles;[1292] telecommunications test, inspection and production equipment, components and accessories, specially designed for the development and production of specific equipment, functions and features;[1293] software;[1294] and technology.[1295] Under *information security,* which stands for 'all the means and functions ensuring the accessibility, confidentiality or integrity of information or communications, excluding the means and functions intended to safeguard against malfunctions. This includes *cryptography,*[1296] *cryptographic activation,*[1297] *cryptanalysis,*[1298] protection against compromising emanations and computer security', the items listed are: certain information security systems, equipment and

1283. Point 4A001 Annex I Dual Use Regulation, which corresponds to No. 13.A.1. of the MTCR Annex.
1284. Point 4A003 Annex I Dual Use Regulation, which partially corresponds to No. 14.A.1.b.2. of the MTCR Annex.
1285. Point 4A004 Annex I Dual Use Regulation.
1286. Point 4A005 Annex I Dual Use Regulation.
1287. Points 4A101, 9A004 and 9A104 Annex I Dual Use Regulation. Point 4A101 corresponds to 13.A.1.b. of the MTCR Annex.
1288. Points 4A102, 9A004 and 9A104 Annex I Dual Use Regulation. Point 4A102 corresponds to No. 16.A.1. of the MTCR Annex.
1289. Points 4D001 and 4D004 Annex I Dual Use Regulation.
1290. Point 4E001 Annex I Dual Use Regulation, which corresponds to the MTCR Annex.
1291. Point 5A001 Annex I Dual Use Regulation.
1292. Point 5A101 Annex I Dual Use Regulation, which corresponds to No. 12.A.4. of the MTCR Annex.
1293. Point 5B001 Annex I Dual Use Regulation.
1294. Points 5D001, 5A001, 5A002 and 5D101, 5A101 Annex I Dual Use Regulation. Point 5D101 corresponds to No. 12.D.3. of the MTCR Annex.
1295. Points 5E001 and 5E101 Annex I Dual Use Regulation. Point 5E101 corresponds to No. 12.E.1. of the MTCR Annex.
1296. In regard to the statutory definition of *cryptography see* Annex I p. 311 at 316 Definitions of Terms Used in This Annex, Annex I Dual Use Regulation, that corresponds to Definitions of Terms Used in These Lists of the WA-List p. 221.
1297. In regard to the statutory definition of *cryptographic activation see* Annex I p. 311 at 316. Definitions of Terms Used in This Annex, Annex I Dual Use Regulation, that corresponds to Definitions of Terms Used in These Lists of the WA-List p. 220.
1298. In regard to the statutory definition of *cryptoanalysis see* Annex I p. 311 at 316. Definitions of Terms Used in This Annex, Annex I Dual Use Regulation.

components;[1299] specific systems, equipment and components, for non-cryptographic information security;[1300] systems, equipment and components for defeating, weakening or bypassing information security;[1301] information security test, inspection and protection equipment;[1302] software;[1303] and technology.[1304]

256. The seventh category ('Category 6') is entitled 'sensors and lasers'. In addition to the items mentioned above under nuclear energy and activities (*see* in this regard paragraphs 224 et seq. above), it sets out the following: acoustic systems, equipment and components;[1305] optical sensors or equipment and components;[1306] cameras, systems and equipment specially designed and having specific characteristics;[1307] optical equipment and components;[1308] magnetometers, magnetic gradiometers, intrinsic magnetic gradiometers, underwater electric field sensors, compensation systems, and specially designed components therefor;[1309] gravity meters and gravity gradiometers;[1310] radar systems, equipment and assemblies with specific designs;[1311] radiation hardened detectors specially designed or modified for protecting against nuclear effects, such as electromagnetic pulse, and usable for missiles;[1312] masks and reticles, specially designed for optical sensors;[1313] optical equipment;[1314] pulse radar cross-section measurement systems, including such usable for rocket systems and UAV systems;[1315] optical sensor materials, optical materials[1316] and laser materials;[1317] software;[1318] and technology.[1319]

1299. Point 5A002 Dual Use Regulation.
1300. Point 5A003 *ibid.*
1301. Point 5A004 *ibid.*
1302. Points 5B002, 5A002, 5A003, 5A004 & 5B002 *ibid.*
1303. Point 5D002 *ibid.*
1304. Point 5E002 *ibid.*
1305. Point 6A001 *ibid.*
1306. Point 6A002 *ibid.*, which corresponds to Nos 18.A.2. & 11.A.2. of the MTCR Annex.
1307. Point 6A003 Annex I Dual Use Regulation.
1308. Point 6A004 Annex I Dual Use Regulation.
1309. Point 6A006 Annex I Dual Use Regulation, which corresponds to No. 9.A.8. of the MTCR Annex.
1310. Points 6A007 and 6A107 Annex I Dual Use Regulation, which correspond to No. 12.A.3. of the MTCR Annex.
1311. Points 6A008 & 6A108 Annex I Dual Use Regulation, which correspond to Nos 11.A.1. & 12.A.5. of the MTCR Annex.
1312. Point 6A102 Annex I Dual Use Regulation, which corresponds to No. 18.A.2. of the MTCR Annex.
1313. Point 6B002 Annex I Dual Use Regulation.
1314. Point 6B004 Annex I Dual Use Regulation.
1315. Points 6B008 & 6B108 Annex I Dual Use Regulation, which correspond to No. 17.B.1. of the MTCR Annex.
1316. Points 6C002 & 6C004 Annex I Dual Use Regulation.
1317. Points 6C005 Annex I Dual Use Regulation.
1318. Points 6D001, 6D002, 6D003, 6D102 & 6D103 Annex I Dual Use Regulation. Points 6D002, 6D102 & 6D103 correspond to Nos 11.D.1., 12.D.3. & 12.D.2. of the MTCR Annex.
1319. Points 6E001, 6E002, 6E003 & 6E101 Annex I Dual Use Regulation, which with the exception of point 6E003 correspond to the MTCR Annex.

257. The eighth category ('Category 7') relates to 'navigation and avionics' and includes: accelerometers, as well as such usable in missiles;[1320] gyros and angular rate sensors, as well as all types of gyros usable in missiles;[1321] inertial measurement equipment or systems designed for aircraft, land vehicles and vessels, including such usable in missiles;[1322] star trackers, also referred to as stellar attitude sensors or gyro-astro compasses;[1323] satellite navigation systems, that being a system consisting of ground stations, a constellation of satellites, and receivers, that enables receiver locations to be calculated on the basis of signals received from the satellites, and includes Global Navigation Satellite Systems and Regional Navigation Satellite Systems;[1324] airborne altimeters operating at certain frequencies and having specific qualities;[1325] underwater sonar navigation systems;[1326] passive sensors for determining bearing to specific electromagnetic source or terrain characteristics, designed or modified for use in space launch vehicles and sounding rockets;[1327] flight control systems and servo valves designed or modified for use in space launch vehicles and sounding rockets;[1328] guidance sets usable in certain missiles;[1329] test, calibration and alignment equipment designed for said equipment;[1330] equipment specially designed to characterize mirrors;[1331] equipment specially designed for the production of said equipment, including production facilities and equipment;[1332] software specially designed or modified for said equipment, including source code and other software;[1333]

1320. Points 7A001 & 7A101 Annex I Dual Use Regulation, which correspond to Nos 9.A.3. & 9.A.5. of the MTCR Annex.
1321. Points 7A002 & 7A102 Annex I Dual Use Regulation, which correspond to Nos 9.A.4. & 9.A.5. of the MTCR Annex.
1322. Points 7A003 & 7A103 Annex I Dual Use Regulation, which correspond to Nos 2.A.1.d., 9.A.6., 9.A.8., 9.A.1. & 9.A.7. of the MTCR Annex.
1323. Points 7A004 & 7A104 Annex I Dual Use Regulation, which correspond to No. 9.A.2. of the MTCR Annex.
1324. Points 7A005 & 7A105 and Definitions of Terms Used in This Annex, Annex I Dual Use Regulation. Said points correspond to No. 11.A.3. of the MTCR Annex.
1325. Points 7A006 & 7A106 Annex I Dual Use Regulation, which correspond to No. 11.A.1. of the MTCR Annex.
1326. Point 7A008 Annex I Dual Use Regulation.
1327. Points 7A115, 7A004 & 7A104 Annex I Dual Use Regulation. Point 7A115 corresponds to No. 11.A.2. of the MTCR Annex.
1328. Points 7A116, 7A004 & 7A104 Annex I Dual Use Regulation. Point 7A116 corresponds to Nos 10.A.1., 10.A.2. & 10.A.3. of the MTCR Annex.
1329. Point 7A117 Annex I Dual Use Regulation, which corresponds to No. 2.A.1.d. of the MTCR Annex.
1330. Point 7B001 Annex I Dual Use Regulation, which corresponds to Nos 2.B.2., 9.B.1. & 10.B.1. of the MTCR Annex.
1331. Points 7B002 & 7B102 Annex I Dual Use Regulation, which corresponds to No. 9.B.1. of the MTCR Annex.
1332. Points 7B003 & 7B103 Annex I Dual Use Regulation, which correspond to Nos 2.B.2., 9.B.1. & 2.B.1. of the MTCR Annex.
1333. Points 7D001 to 7D005 & 7D101 to 7D104 Annex I Dual Use Regulation. Points 7D002 & 7D101 correspond to Nos 2.D.3. & 9.D.1. and 2.D., 9.D.1, 10.D.1., 11.D.1. & 11.D.2. of the MTCR Annex. Point 7D102 corresponds to Nos 9.D.2., 9.D.3. & 9.D.4. Point 7D103 corresponds to No. 16.D.1.

and technology under the General Technology Note (*see* paragraph 217 above) and other technology for development and use of said equipment.[1334]

258. The ninth category ('Category 8') refers to 'marine'. It lists the following: submersible items and surface vehicles, both manned and unmanned, with specific qualities;[1335] specifically designed marine systems, equipment and components for submersible vehicles, for underwater use and for use with submersible vehicles and underwater swimming and diving equipment;[1336] special designed water tunnels;[1337] syntactic foam;[1338] software specially designed for said items;[1339] and technology under the General Technology Note (*see* paragraph 217 above) and other technology for development and use of said equipment.[1340]

259. The tenth category ('Category 9') relates to 'aerospace and propulsion'. It lists the following systems, equipment and components: aero gas turbine engines incorporating specific technologies or designed to power aircrafts to cruise at Mach 1 or higher;[1341] marine gas turbine engines designed to use liquid fuel and having specific qualities;[1342] specially designed assemblies and components incorporating certain technologies;[1343] space launch vehicles, spacecraft, spacecraft buses, spacecraft payloads, spacecraft on-board systems or equipment, terrestrial equipment, air-launch platforms and sub-orbital craft;[1344] liquid rocket propulsion systems containing certain systems or components;[1345] systems and components, specially designed for liquid rocket propulsion systems;[1346] solid rocket propulsion systems having specific capacity and components;[1347] components specially designed for solid rocket propulsion systems;[1348] hybrid rocket propulsion systems;[1349] specially designed components, systems and

1334. Points 7E001 to 7E004 & 7E101, 7E102, 7E104 Annex I Dual Use Regulation, which correspond to Nos 2.E.1., 9.E.1, 11.E.1. & 10.E.2. of the MTCR Annex.
1335. Point 8A001 Annex I Dual Use Regulation.
1336. Point 8A002 Annex I Dual Use Regulation.
1337. Point 8B001 Annex I Dual Use Regulation.
1338. Point 8C001 Annex I Dual Use Regulation.
1339. Points 8D001 & 8D002 Annex I Dual Use Regulation.
1340. Points 8E001 & 8E002 Annex I Dual Use Regulation.
1341. Point 9A001 Annex I Dual Use Regulation, which corresponds to No. 9.A.1. of the WA-DU-List and No. 3.A.1. of the MTCR Annex. According to the WA-DU-List aero gas turbine engines designed to power aircrafts to cruise at Mach 1 or higher is not used since 2022.
1342. Point 9A002 Annex I Dual Use Regulation, which corresponds to No. 9.A.2. of the WA-DU-List.
1343. Point 9A003 Annex I Dual Use Regulation, which corresponds to No. 9.A.3. of the WA-DU-List.
1344. Point 9A004 Annex I Dual Use Regulation, which corresponds to No. 9.A.4. of the WA-DU-List and to Nos 1.A.1. & 19.A.1. of the MTCR Annex.
1345. Point 9A005 Annex I Dual Use Regulation, which corresponds to No. 9.A.5. of the WA-DU-List and to Nos 2.A.1.a., 2.A.1.c. & 20.A.1. of the MTCR Annex.
1346. Point 9A006 Annex I Dual Use Regulation, which corresponds to No. 9.A.6. of the WA-DU-List and to Nos 3.A.8., 3.A.5. & 3.a.10. of the MTCR Annex.
1347. Point 9A007 Annex I Dual Use Regulation, which corresponds to No. 9.A.7. of the WA-DU-List and to No. 2.A.1. of the MTCR Annex.
1348. Point 9A008 Annex I Dual Use Regulation, which corresponds to No. 9.A.8. of the WA-DU-List and to Nos 3.A.3., 3.C.1., 3.C.2. of the MTCR Annex.
1349. Point 9A009 Annex I Dual Use Regulation, which corresponds to No. 9.A.9. of the WA-DU-List and to Nos 2.A.1.c.1. & 20.A.1.b. of the MTCR Annex.

structures for launch vehicles, launch vehicle propulsion systems and spacecraft;[1350] ramjet, scramjet and combined cycle engines;[1351] UAVs, unmanned airships, related equipment and components;[1352] further turbojet and turbofan engines;[1353] turboprop engine systems specially designed for UAVs;[1354] sounding rockets capable of a range of at least 300 km;[1355] liquid propellant rocket engines and gel propellant rocket motors;[1356] systems and components specially designed for liquid rocket propulsion and gel propellant rocket systems;[1357] solid propellant rocket motors, usable in complete rocket systems or UAVs;[1358] components specially designed for solid and hybrid rocket propulsion systems;[1359] hybrid rocket motors and specially designed components;[1360] composite structures, laminates and manufactures thereof specially designed for use in missiles;[1361] pulse jet and detonation engines usable in missiles and UAVs;[1362] further UAVs;[1363] launch support equipment;[1364] reentry vehicles usable in missiles;[1365] staging mechanisms, separation mechanisms and interstages usable in missiles;[1366] devices to regulate combustion usable in engines which are usable in missiles and UAVs;[1367]

1350. Point 9A010 Annex I Dual Use Regulation, which corresponds to No. 9.A.10. of the WA-DU-List and to Nos 6.A.1. & 3.A.2. of the MTCR Annex.
1351. Point 9A011 Annex I Dual Use Regulation, which corresponds to No. 9.A.11. of the WA-DU-List and to No. 3.A.2. of the MTCR Annex.
1352. Point 9A012 Annex I Dual Use Regulation, which corresponds to No. 9.A.12. of the WA-DU-List and to Nos 1.A.2., 19.A. & 9.A.6. of the MTCR Annex.
1353. Point 9A101 Annex I Dual Use Regulation, which corresponds to No. 3.A.1. of the MTCR Annex and to No. 3.A.1. of the MTCR Annex.
1354. Point 9A102 Annex I Dual Use Regulation, which corresponds to No. 3.A.9. of the MTCR Annex and to No. 3.A.9. of the MTCR Annex.
1355. Point 9A104 Annex I Dual Use Regulation, which corresponds to No. 1.A.1. of the MTCR Annex. However, the latter includes ballistic missiles and space launch vehicles as well and requires the capability of delivering at least a 500 kg payload. Point 9A104 also corresponds to Nos 1.A.1. & 19.A.1. of the MTCR Annex.
1356. Point 9A105 Annex I Dual Use Regulation, which corresponds to Nos 2.A.1.c.2. & 20.A.1.b.2. of the MTCR Annex.
1357. Point 9A106 Annex I Dual Use Regulation, which corresponds to Nos 3.A.3., 2.A.1.e., 3.A.5. & 3.A.10. of the MTCR Annex.
1358. Point 9A107 Annex I Dual Use Regulation, which corresponds to No. 20.A.1.b.1. of the MTCR Annex.
1359. Point 9A108 Annex I Dual Use Regulation, which corresponds to Nos 3.A.3. & 2.A.1.e. of the MTCR Annex.
1360. Point 9A109 Annex I Dual Use Regulation, which corresponds to Nos 3.A.6., 20.A.1.b. & 2.A.1.c. of the MTCR Annex.
1361. Point 9A110 Annex I Dual Use Regulation, which corresponds to No. 6.A.1. of the MTCR Annex.
1362. Point 9A111 Annex I Dual Use Regulation, which corresponds to No. 3.A.2. of the MTCR Annex.
1363. Point 9A112 Annex I Dual Use Regulation, which corresponds to Nos 19.A.2. & 19.A.3. of the MTCR Annex.
1364. Point 9A115 Annex I Dual Use Regulation, which corresponds to Nos 12.A.1. & 12.A.2. of the MTCR Annex.
1365. Point 9A116 Annex I Dual Use Regulation, which corresponds to No. 2.A.1.b. of the MTCR Annex.
1366. Point 9A117 Annex I Dual Use Regulation, which corresponds to No. 3.A.4. of the MTCR Annex.
1367. Point 9A118 Annex I Dual Use Regulation, which corresponds to No. 3.A.2. of the MTCR Annex.

individual rocket stages usable in complete rocket systems or UAVs;[1368] liquid or gel propellant tanks;[1369] umbilical and interstage electrical connectors specially designed for missiles, space launch vehicles or sounding rockets;[1370] and spraying or fogging systems, specially designed or modified for fitting to aircraft, lighter-than-air vehicles[1371] or UAVs.[1372] It further includes the following test, inspection and production equipment: certain manufacturing equipment, tooling and fixtures;[1373] on-line (real time) control systems, instrumentation (including sensors) or automated data acquisition and processing equipment;[1374] equipment specially designed for the production or test of gas turbine brush seals designed to operate at specific tip speeds and temperatures;[1375] tools, dies and fixtures for joining of metals for gas turbines;[1376] acoustic vibration test equipment;[1377] equipment specially designed for inspecting the integrity of rocket motors and using non-destructive test techniques;[1378] direct measurement wall skin friction transducers;[1379] tooling specially designed for producing gas turbine engine powder metallurgy rotor components;[1380] equipment specially designed for the production of certain items;[1381] wind tunnels for certain speeds usable for missiles;[1382] environmental chambers and anechoic chambers;[1383] specially designed production equipment and

1368. Point 9A119 Annex I Dual Use Regulation, which corresponds to Nos 2.A.1.a. & 20.A.1.a. of the MTCR Annex.
1369. Point 9A120 Annex I Dual Use Regulation, which corresponds to No. 3.A.8. of the MTCR Annex.
1370. Point 9A121 Annex I Dual Use Regulation, which corresponds to No. 11.A.5. of the MTCR Annex.
1371. In regard to the statutory definition of *lighter-than-air vehicles see* Annex I p. 311 at 329. Definitions of Terms Used in This Annex Annex I Dual Use Regulation that corresponds to Definitions of Terms Used in These Lists of the WA-List p. 226, Definition of Terms of the Control List of Dual-Use Biological Equipment and Related Technology and Software of the AG as of 16 Aug. 2020.
1372. Point 9A350 Annex I Dual Use Regulation, which corresponds to No. I.9 of the Control List of Dual-Use Biological Equipment and Related Technology and Software of the AG as of 16 Aug. 2020.
1373. Point 9B001 Annex I Dual Use Regulation, which corresponds to No. 9.B.1 of the WA-DU-List.
1374. Point 9B002 Annex I Dual Use Regulation, which corresponds to No. 9.B.2 of the WA-DU-List; Point 9B005 Annex I Dual Use Regulation, which corresponds to No. 9.B.5 of the WA-DU-List and No. 15.B.2. of the MTCR Annex.
1375. Point 9B003 Annex I Dual Use Regulation, which corresponds to No. 9.B.3 of the WA-DU-List.
1376. Point 9B004 Annex I Dual Use Regulation, which corresponds to No. 9.B.4 of the WA-DU-List.
1377. Point 9B006 Annex I Dual Use Regulation, which corresponds to No. 9.B.6 of the WA-DU-List and to No. 15.B.4.b. of the MTCR Annex.
1378. Point 9B007 Annex I Dual Use Regulation, which corresponds to No. 9.B.7 of the WA-DU-List.
1379. Point 9B008 Annex I Dual Use Regulation, which corresponds to No. 9.B.8 of the WA-DU-List.
1380. Point 9B009 Annex I Dual Use Regulation, which corresponds to No. 9.B.9 of the WA-DU-List.
1381. Point 9B010 Annex I Dual Use Regulation, which corresponds to No. 9.B.10 of the WA-DU-List.
1382. Point 9B105 Annex I Dual Use Regulation, which corresponds to No. 15.B.2. of the MTCR Annex. The MTCR provision makes mention of 'aerodynamic test facilities' which under the provided technical note includes not just wind tunnels, but also shock tunnels for the study of airflow over objects.
1383. Point 9B106 Annex I Dual Use Regulation, which partially corresponds to No. 15.B.4. of the MTCR Annex. However, MTCR provision makes mention just of 'environmental chambers' and none of 'anechoic chambers'.

production facilities;[1384] test benches and test stands for solid or liquid propellant rockets and rocket motors with specific characteristics;[1385] *insulation*[1386] material and *interior lining*[1387] usable in missiles;[1388] resin impregnated prepregs and metal coated fibre preforms;[1389] software, software specially designed or modified for the use of Full Authority Digital Electronic Engine Controls for propulsion systems and other software;[1390] and technology.[1391]

II Controls and Restrictions

260. Before elaborating on the particular restrictive measures that are imposed on dual-use items, it is here briefly noted that in general trade in dual-use items is subject to controls. The Dual Use Regulation establishes 'individual export authorisations',[1392] 'global export authorizations',[1393] 'national general authorizations'[1394] and 'Union general export authorizations'[1395] for dual-use items. Moreover, an authorization may be required for dual-use items that fit the relevant statutory definition but are not

1384. Points 9B115 & 9B116 Annex I Dual Use Regulation. The first point corresponds to Nos 2.B.2., 3.B.2. & 20.B.2. of the MTCR Annex and the latter to Nos 1.B.1., 2.B.1., 3.B.1., 19.B.1. & 20.B.1. of the MTCR Annex.
1385. Point 9B117 Annex I Dual Use Regulation, which corresponds to No. 15.B.3 of the MTCR Annex.
1386. 'Insulation' is applied to the components of a rocket motor and includes cured or semi-cured compounded rubber sheet stock containing an insulating or refractory material. It may also be incorporated as stress relief boots or flaps. Definitions of Terms Used in this Annex, Annex I Dual Use Regulation, which corresponds to the technical note of No. 3.A.3 of the MTCR Annex.
1387. 'Interior lining' suited for the bond interface between the solid propellant and the case or insulating liner is usually a liquid polymer based dispersion of refractory or insulating materials, e.g., carbon filled hydroxyl terminated polybutadiene (HTPB) or other polymer with added curing agents sprayed or screeded over a case interior. Definitions of Terms Used in this Annex, Annex I Dual Use Regulation, which corresponds to the technical note of No. 3.C.1 of the MTCR Annex.
1388. Point 9C108 Annex I Dual Use Regulation, which corresponds to Nos 3.C.1 & 3.C.2 of the MTCR Annex.
1389. Point 9C110 Annex I Dual Use Regulation, which corresponds to No. 6.C.1 of the MTCR Annex.
1390. Points 9D001, 9D002, 9D003 & 9D004 Annex I Dual Use Regulation, which correspond to Nos 9.D.1, 9.D.2, 9.D.3 & 9.D.4 of the WA-DU-List and Nos 3.D.3., 2.D.2 & 19.D.1 of the MTCR Annex. In regard to the statutory definition of *Full Authority Digital Electronic Engine Controls* *see* Annex I p. 311 at 324. Definitions of Terms Used in this Annex, Annex I Dual Use Regulation. It is noted that this is not identical to the definition of *Full Authority Digital Engine Control Systems* set out in the Wassenaar Arrangement (in regard to this *see* Annex I p. 311 at 324). Definitions of Terms Used in These Lists of the WA-List p. 223.
    Points 9D101, 9D103, 9D104 & 9D105 Annex I Dual Use Regulation, which correspond to Nos 1.D.1, 2.D.1, 3.D.1, 12.D.1, 15.D.1 & 20.D.1 and 16.D.1 and 2.D.2, 2.D.4, 3.D.2, 2.D.5 & 20.D.2 and 1.D.2 & 19.D.1 of the MTCR Annex, respectively.
1391. Points 9E001, 9E002 & 9E003 Annex I Dual Use Regulation, which correspond to Nos 9.E.1, 9.E.2, 9.E.3.a to g of the WA-DU-List pp. 164-168. Points 9E001 & 9E002 also correspond to the MTCR Annex. Points 9E101 & 9E102 that also correspond to the MTCR Annex.
1392. Articles 3(1), 12(1)(a) & 2(12) Dual Use Regulation.
1393. Articles 3(1), 12(1)(b) & 2(13) Dual Use Regulation.
1394. Articles 3(1), 12(1)(c) & 2(16) Dual Use Regulation.
1395. Articles 3(1), 12(1)(d) & 2(15) Dual Use Regulation.

listed[1396] in the categories explained above (*see* in this respect paragraph 249 above). For instance, such may be the case, when the competent national authorities inform the exporter that the item in question may be used for chemical, biological or nuclear weapons or other nuclear explosive devices or for missiles capable of delivering such weapons; or that the purchasing state or state of destination is subject to arms embargo.[1397] Especially with regard to exports to Syria, Member States are given the authority to prohibit or impose an authorization requirement on export to Syria for not listed dual-use items.[1398] On a final note, a request for authorization under this regulation is not granted, when there are reasonable grounds to believe that the end user might be a military end-user, the Border Guard Police or that the goods might have a military end-use.[1399]

261. Trade in, that being transport, import and export of, dual-use items is prohibited when it involves persons in the DPRK, Myanmar/Burma and Syria, or when the same goods and technology shall be used in the DPRK, Myanmar/Burma and Syria.[1400] In the two latter cases that share the common denominator of further prohibiting technical assistance, brokering services, financing and financial services related to dual-use items,[1401] an additional condition is set out. With regard to Myanmar/Burma that consists of the items in question being or might be intended for military use, military end-user or the Boarder Guard Police. Especially, where the end-user is the military of Myanmar/Burma, any dual-use item is deemed to be for military use.[1402] In relation to Syria, the additional requirement is the possible use of the items in question for internal repression, or for manufacturing or maintaining products for that purpose.[1403]

262. With regard to dual-use items and Iran, said activities are not prohibited per se; rather, they are controlled through necessitating a prior authorization.[1404] An authorization is also required for providing *technical assistance*, *brokering services*, *financing* and *financial services* as well as for making any arrangement for participation in a *partnership*.[1405] The use of such items in Iran that triggers the need for an authorization is not merely the subjective element of an Iranian person or their use in Iran; it is also required that these items could contribute to activities inconsistent with the JCPOA, such as reprocessing- or enrichment-related or heavy water-related activities.[1406]

263. The applicant for an authorization is expected to submit an end-use statement with information on the end-use as well as the end-use location of the items intended for supply. Still, information on end-use location may be provided at a later point in

1396. Article 3(2) Dual Use Regulation.
1397. Article 4(1)(a) & (b) Dual Use Regulation.
1398. Article 2d Regulation on Syria.
1399. Article 3a(2) Regulation on Myanmar/Burma.
1400. Article 3(1)(a) & (c) and Annex II Part I Regulation on the DPRK, Art. 3a(1) Regulation on Myanmar/Burma & Annex I Dual Use Regulation, Art. 2a(1)(a) Regulation on Syria.
1401. Article 3a(4)(a) & (b) Regulation on Myanmar/Burma, Art 3(1)(a) & (b) Regulation on Syria.
1402. Article 3a(1) Regulation on Myanmar/Burma.
1403. Article 2a(1)(a) Regulation on Syria.
1404. Article 3a(1)(a) & (e) and Annex II Regulation on Iran.
1405. Article 3(1)(b), (c) & (d) Regulation on Iran.
1406. Article 3a(2) Regulation on Iran.

time, should the competent authority opt for issuing an authorization despite the absence thereof.[1407]

264. The competent authority has a double information duty towards other Member States and the Commission. It first informs them of requests for authorization that it received via the mechanism established by the Dual Use Regulation (*see* in this respect paragraph 219 above).[1408] It shall also inform them, along with the High Representative of the Union for Foreign Affairs and Security Policy, of its intention to grand an authorization at least ten days prior to making the decision.[1409] Further, it may not issue an authorization, when it has reasonable grounds to determine that the actions concerned would contribute to the use of such items that trigger the need for an authorization, that being activities inconsistent with the JCPOA.[1410]

III Exceptions to Controls and Restrictions

265. Trade in dual-use items involving persons in the DPRK or their use in the same state may be authorized by competent authorities of Member States by way of derogation. Such an authorization, which shall include the terms and conditions deemed appropriate by said authorities, may be based on humanitarian purposes, such as food, agricultural and medical grounds.[1411] The pertinent condition for granting such an authorization is the approval of the 1718 DPRK Sanctions Committee.[1412]

266. In relation to Myanmar/Burma, the sale, supply, transfer and export of dual-use items may be authorized by the competent authorities of the Member States, when it is intended for specific purposes. These are humanitarian or protective use, use in de-mining operations, use for institution-building programmes of the UN and the EU, as well as for EU and UN crisis-management operations. Related financing, financial assistance and technical assistance may also be authorized.[1413]

267. The provisions in the Regulation on Syria bear more resemblance to the ones in regard to DPRK, as the transaction in question must relate to humanitarian purposes, such as food, agricultural and medicinal purposes. Moreover, use for the benefit of UN personnel, personnel of the EU or its Member States may also serve as a basis for an authorization.[1414] Further, specifically sale, supply, transfer or export of dual-use items is to be undertaken in accordance with the 'elimination of the Syrian Arab Republic's

1407. Article 3a(6) & (6a) Regulation on Iran.
1408. Article 3a(5) Regulation on Iran. and Art. 19(4) Dual Use Regulation.
1409. Article 3a(7) Regulation on Iran.
1410. Article 3a(4) Regulation on Iran.
1411. Article 8(1) Regulation on DPRK.
1412. *See* Art. 8(2) Regulation on DPRK. *See also* S/RES/2321 of 30 Nov. 2016 para. 46, S/RES/2371 of 5 Aug. 2017 para. 26 & S/RES/2397 of 23 Dec. 2017 para. 25.
1413. Article 4(1)(a), (b) & (c) Regulation on Myanmar/Burma.
1414. Articles 2a(2) & 3(3) Regulation on Syria.

chemical weapons program' and in consistency with the objective of the Chemical Weapons Convention.[1415]

268. As seen already under the Regulation on Iran (*see* in this respect paragraph 264 above) the competent authority of a Member State examining a request for authorization has information duties towards other Member States and the Commission. With regard to the DPRK, it must inform them of the request for approval that it submitted to the 1718 DPRK Sanctions Committee.[1416]

269. Should a competent authority of a Member State proceed with granting an authorization, it shall inform accordingly the other Member States and the Commission within four weeks,[1417] in some instances. In the case of Syria, this statutory duty refers solely to authorization of technical assistance, brokering services, financing and financial services;[1418] no such duty is set for providing authorization of export, transfer, supply and sale. The relevant provisions on dual-use items with regard to Myanmar/Burma are silent on this matter.

§9 SANCTIONS ON ARMS AND WEAPONS

270. Certain legislative acts impose restrictive measures on arms and weapons, that consist of military items, that being items in the EU Common Military List and arms and related materiel, equipment for internal repression, and finally missiles and other systems of delivery. Such restrictive measures are also denoted as additional nonfinancial sanctions.[1419] These are portrayed below.

I Sanctions with Regard to Military Items

271. Military items are placed under restrictive measures with regard to the situation in Sudan, the DRC, Lebanon, Yemen, South Sudan, Myanmar/Burma, Zimbabwe, the DPRK, Somalia, Iran, Libya, the CAR, Venezuela and Syria. On the whole, no technical assistance, no financing and financial assistance, and no brokering services may be provided for military activities, whereas arms and related materials may neither be provided, nor manufactured, maintained or used. The particular restrictive measures set out in the respective legislative acts and the exceptions, but for Somalia and Iran that provide for no derogation, are described below.

1415. Article 2a(3) Regulation on Syria and S/RES/2118 of 27 Sep. 2013 para. 10.
1416. Article 8(3) Regulation on DPRK.
1417. Article 8(4) Regulation on DPRK, Art. 3(3) Regulation on Syria.
1418. Article 3(3) Regulation on DPRK.
1419. With regard to export restrictions on military equipment between 2002 and 2015 *see* Matthias Efing, Stefan Goldbach & Volker Nitsch, *Freeze! Financial Sanctions and Bank Responses* 36(11) The Review of Financial Studies 4417 at 4431 (2023) https://doi.org/10.2139/ssrn.3338778.

A *The Range of Military Items*

272. Two groups of military items are the target of restrictive measures in view of certain states; a specific and an abstract one. The first group consists of the items listed in the *EU Common Military List* and the latter *arms and related materiel of all types*.

1 *The EU Common Military List*

273. The EU Common Military List is the equipment covered by the EU Code of Conduct on Arms Exports. It was first adopted in 2000 under the title 'Common List of Military Equipment by the EU Code of Conduct on Arms Exports'[1420] and has been since regularly reviewed taking into account similar national and international lists.[1421] It has been suggested that these lists are the small arms categories of the UN, the Organization for Security and Co-operation in Europe ('OSCE') and the WA;[1422] in truth, as shall be demonstrated below, the EU Common Military List is an exact replica of the Munitions List of the WA. Finally, at first glance, it would seem that the EU Common Military List and the list of dual-use items of the EU overlap. They do not. Military standards and specifications are the parameters separating equipment that could otherwise fall under both the list of dual-use items and the EU Common Military List.[1423]

274. The current valid version of the EU Common Military List was issued in 2022.[1424] It includes: 'smooth-bore weapons with a calibre of less than 20 mm, other arms and automatic weapons with a calibre of 12,7 mm (calibre 0,50 inches) or less and accessories';[1425] 'Smooth-bore weapons with a calibre of 20 mm or more, other weapons or armament with a calibre greater than 12,7 mm (calibre 0,50 inches), projectors specially designed or modified for military use and accessories';[1426] 'ammunition and fuze setting

1420. Council Declaration of 13 Jun. 2000, issued on the occasion of the adoption of the common list of military equipment covered by the European Union code of conduct on arms export (2000/C 191/01) OJ C 191, 8 Jul. 2000, p. 1.
1421. Recital No. to the preamble of Council Common Position 2008/944/CFSP of 8 Dec. 2008 defining common rules governing control of exports of military technology and equipment, OJ L 335, 13 Dec. 2008, p. 99.
1422. P. Holtom, *Transparency in Transfers of Small Arms and Light Weapons*, Stockholm International Peace Research Institute 2008, p. 50.
1423. *See*, for example, point 1A005 Dual Use Regulation and point ML13.d.2. EU Common Military List; point 1A006 Dual Use Regulation and point ML4.b.2.b. EU Common Military List; point 1A007 Dual Use Regulation and point ML8 EU Common Military List; point 1B102 Dual Use Regulation and point ML8.c.8. EU Common Military List.
1424. Council, Common Military List of the EU adopted by the Council on 17 Feb. 2022, OJ C 100, 1 Mar. 2022, p. 3 ('CML 2022').
1425. ML1 of the CML 2022, which corresponds to No. ML1 of the WA-M-List. Subpoints a, b, c & d of the CML 2022 correspond to Nos a, b, c & d of the WA-M-List.
1426. ML2 of the CML 2022, which corresponds to No. ML2 of the WA-M-List. Subpoints a, b, c & d of the CML 2022 correspond to Nos a, b, c & d of the WA-M-List.

devices';[1427] 'bombs, torpedoes, rockets, missiles, other explosive devices and charges'[1428] including aircraft missile protection systems; 'fire control, surveillance and warning equipment' and 'test and alignment and countermeasure equipment';[1429] 'ground vehicles and components'[1430] including tanks and other military armed vehicles; 'chemical agents, biological agents, riot control agents, radioactive materials';[1431] 'energetic materials and related substances' which encompass explosives, propellants and pyrotechnics among others;[1432] vessels of war, both surface and underwater, and special naval equipment;[1433] aircraft, lighter-than-air vehicles, UAVs, aero-engines and aircraft equipment as well as related equipment, and components;[1434] electronic equipment, spacecraft and components not specified elsewhere in the EU Common Military List;[1435] 'high velocity kinetic energy weapon systems and related equipment';[1436] 'armoured or protective equipment, constructions, components, and accessories';[1437] 'specialised equipment for military training or for simulating military scenarios';[1438] 'imaging or countermeasure equipment';[1439] 'forgings, castings and other unfinished products';[1440] 'miscellaneous equipment, materials and libraries';[1441]

1427. ML3 of the CML 2022, which corresponds to No. ML3 of the WA-M-List. Subpoints a & b of the CML 2022 correspond to Nos a, b, c & d of the WA-M-List.
1428. ML4 of the CML 2022, which corresponds to No. ML4 of the WA-M-List. Subpoints a, b & c of the CML 2022 correspond to Nos a, b & c of the WA-M-List. With regard to ML4 (b) of the CML 2022 *see* point 1A006 Annex I Dual Use Regulation.
1429. ML5 of the CML 2022, which corresponds to No. ML5 of the WA-M-List. Subpoints a, b, c & d of the CML 2022 correspond to Nos a, b, c & d of the WA-M-List.
1430. ML6 of the CML 2022, which corresponds to No. ML6 of the WA-M-List. Subpoints a & b of the CML 2022 correspond to Nos a & b of the WA-M-List.
1431. ML7 of the CML 2022, which corresponds to No. ML7 of the WA-M-List. Subpoints a, b, c, d, e, f, g, h & i of the CML 2022 correspond to Nos a, b, c, d, e, f, g, h & i of the WA-M-List.
1432. ML8 of the CML 2022, which corresponds to No. ML8 of the WA-M-List. Subpoints a, b, c, d, e, f, g & h of the CML 2022 correspond to Nos a, b, c, d, e, f, g & h of the WA-M-List. With reference to ML8 (c) (5) of the CML 2022 *see* points 1C011 & 1C230 Annex I Dual Use Regulation. With regard to ML8 (d) of the CML 2022 *see* point 1C111 Annex I Dual Use Regulation.
1433. ML9 of the CML 2022, which corresponds to No. ML9 of the WA-M-List. Subpoints a, b, c, d, e, f, g & h of the CML 2022 correspond to Nos a, b, c, d, e, f, g & h of the WA-M-List.
1434. ML10 of the CML 2022, which corresponds to No. ML10 of the WA-M-List. Subpoints a, b, c, d, e, f, g, h & i of the CML 2022 correspond to Nos a, b, c, d, e, f, g, h & i of the WA-M-List.
1435. ML11 of the CML 2022, which corresponds to No. ML11 of the WA-M-List. Subpoints a, b & c of the CML 2022 correspond to Nos a, b & c the WA-M-List.
1436. ML12 of the CML 2022, which corresponds to No. ML12 of the WA-M-List. Subpoints a & b of the CML 2022 correspond to Nos a & b of the WA-M-List.
1437. ML13 of the CML 2022, which corresponds to No. ML13 of the WA-M-List. Subpoints a, b, c & d of the CML 2022 correspond to Nos a, b, c & d of the WA-M-List. With regard to ML13 (d) of the CML 2022 *see* point 1A005 Annex I Dual Use Regulation.
1438. ML14 of the CML 2022, which corresponds to No. ML14 of the WA-M-List.
1439. ML15 of the CML 2022, which corresponds to No. ML15 of the WA-M-List.
1440. ML16 of the CML 2022, which corresponds to No. ML16 of the WA-M-List.
1441. ML17 of the CML 2022, which corresponds to No. ML17 of the WA-M-List. Subpoints a, b, c, d, e, f, g, h, i, j, k, l, m, n, o & p of the CML 2022 correspond to Nos a, b, c, d, e, f, g, h, I, j, k, l, m, n, o & p of the WA-M-List.

'production equipment, environmental test facilities and components';[1442] 'directed energy weapon systems, related or countermeasure equipment and test models';[1443] 'cryogenic and superconductive equipment';[1444] software and technology.[1445]

2 *Arms and Related Materiel*

275. 'Arms and related materiel of all types' is an abstract legal notion, as the legal instruments that make mention of it, do not specify it. They merely add a general description that reads 'including weapons and ammunition, military vehicles and equipment, paramilitary equipment, and spare parts for the aforementioned'.[1446] Interestingly, this particular wording was initially conceived at the level of the UN Security Council.[1447] Therefore, it could be suggested to take a look – and perhaps apply – the definition adopted by the UN, which reads 'small arms are those weapons designed for personal use'. It includes revolvers and self-loading pistols, rifles and carbines, sub-machine-guns, assault rifles and light machine-guns. *Small arms* is a notion accompanied by the notion of *light weapons* that stands for 'those designed for use by several persons serving as a crew' and include heavy machine guns, hand-held under-barrel and mounted grenade launchers, portable anti-aircraft guns, portable anti-tank guns, recoilless rifles, portable launchers of anti-tank missile and rocket systems, portable launchers of anti-aircraft missile systems, and mortars of calibres of less than 100 mm.[1448] At the same time, noteworthy is the notion of *major conventional arms* that forms the pillar of the United Nations Register of Conventional Arms[1449] (hereinafter 'UNROCA'). It consists of the following seven categories of arms: (i) battle tanks;[1450] (ii) armoured combat vehicles;[1451] (iii) large-calibre artillery

1442. ML18 of the CML 2022, which corresponds to No. ML18 of the WA-M-List. Subpoints a & b of the CML 2022 correspond to Nos a & b of the WA-M-List. On *production equipment see also* points 1B102, 1B115 Annex I Dual Use Regulation. With regard to ML18(h) *see* point 1B119 Annex I Dual Use Regulation.
1443. ML19 of the CML 2022, which corresponds to No. ML19 of the WA-M-List. Subpoints a, b, c, d, e & f of the CML 2022 correspond to Nos a, b, c, d, e & f of the WA-M-List.
1444. ML20 of the CML 2022, which corresponds to No. ML20 of the WA-M-List. Subpoints a & b of the CML 2022 correspond to Nos a & b of the WA-M-List.
1445. ML21 & ML22 of the CML 2022, which corresponds to Nos ML21 & ML 22 of the WA-M-List.
1446. Article 2(a) Regulation on Sudan, Art. 2(a) Regulation on Lebanon, Art. 1a(a) Regulation on Yemen, Art. 2(1) Regulation on South Sudan, Art. 3(1)(a) Regulation on Myanmar/Burma and Art. 2(a) Regulation on Zimbabwe.
1447. *See* with regard to Sudan: S/RES/1556 of 30 Jul. 2004 para. 7, S/RES/1591 of 29 Mar. 2005 para. 7, and S/RES/1945 of 14 Oct. 2010 para. 7; with regard to Lebanon: S/RES/1701 of 11 Aug. 2006 para. 15(a), last reaffirmed by S/RES/2650 of 31 Aug. 2022; with regard to Yemen: S/RES/2216 of 14 Apr. 2015 para. 14, last reaffirmed by S/RES/2624 of 28 Feb. 2022 para. 4; and with regard to South Sudan: S/RES/2428 of 2018 para. 4 last reaffirmed by S/RES/2633 of 26 May 2022 para. 1.
1448. A/52/298 of 25 Aug. 1997 paras 25 & 26.
1449. The UNROCA has been established by UN General Assembly Resolution on 'General and complete disarmament' of 6 Dec. 1991, A/RES/46/36.
1450. In regard to the statutory definition of *battle tanks see* Annex I p. 311 at 312. A/RES/46/36 p. 75.
1451. In regard to the statutory definition of *armoured combat vehicles see* Annex I p. 311 at 311. A/71/259 Annex I, Category II.

systems;[1452] (iv) combat aircraft and unmanned combat aerial vehicles ('UCAV');[1453] (v) attack helicopters;[1454] (vi) warships;[1455] and (vii) missiles and missile launchers.[1456]

276. The legal notion of 'arms and related materiel of all types' co-exists in the EU legislative acts with the equally unspecified term 'military activities' in the respective restrictive measures.[1457] Exceptionally, the Regulation on DPRK has adopted an even wider approach to the objects under restriction, as the relevant provision refers to 'items', excluding food and medicine, that are possibly destined for the armed forces of the DPRK or another state.[1458]

B Restrictions and Embargo

277. In the paragraphs below, the embargo on arms and on items on the EU Common Military List are described along with the terms that may lead to derogation therefrom.

1 Restrictions and Embargo on Arms and Related Materiel

278. The restrictive measures with regard to arms, also depicted as arms embargo, are multi-faceted. At the outset, they consist of the prohibition to provide technical assistance related to military activities to any person in Sudan, Lebanon, South Sudan, Myanmar/Burma and Zimbabwe or for use in the same states. In view of Yemen, the prohibition is addressed solely to designated persons.[1459] *Technical assistance* stands for 'any technical support related to repairs, development, manufacture, assembly, testing, maintenance, or any other technical service, and may take forms such as instruction, advice, training, transmission of working knowledge or skills or consulting services, including verbal forms of assistance'.[1460] Further, it is prohibited to provide financing and financial assistance related to military activities, such as grants, loans

1452. In regard to the statutory definition of *large-calibre artillery systems see* Annex I p. 311 at 328 A/58/274 para. 112.
1453. In regard to the statutory definition of *combat aircraft and unmanned combat aerial vehicles see* Annex I p. 311 at 313. A/71/259 para. 81.
1454. In regard to the statutory definition of *attack helicopters see* Annex I p. 311 at 311. A/71/259 Annex I, Category V.
1455. In regard to the statutory definition of *warship see* Annex I p. 311 at 335. A/61/261 para. 124.
1456. In regard to the statutory definition of *missiles and missile launchers see* Annex I p. 311 at 328. A/58/274 para. 112.
1457. Article 2(a) Regulation on Sudan, Art. 1a(2) Regulation on DRC, Art. 2(a) Regulation on Lebanon, Art. 1a(a) Regulation on Yemen, Art. 2(1) Regulation on South Sudan, Art. 3(1)(a) Regulation on Myanmar/Burma and Art. 2(a) Regulation on Zimbabwe.
1458. Article 5(1)(a) & (b) Regulation on DPRK.
1459. Article 2(a) Regulation on Sudan, Art. 1a(2) Regulation on DRC, Art. 2(a) Regulation on Lebanon, Art. 1a(a) Regulation on Yemen, Art. 2(1) Regulation on South Sudan, Art. 3(1)(a) Regulation on Myanmar/Burma and Art. 2(a) Regulation on Zimbabwe.
1460. Article 1(j) Regulation on Sudan, Art. 1(h) Regulation on DRC, Art. 1(1) Regulation on Lebanon, Art. 1(j) Regulation on Yemen, Art. 1(i) Regulation on South Sudan, Art. 1(h) Regulation on Myanmar/Burma and Art. 1(a) Regulation on Zimbabwe.

and export credit insurance,[1461] and in some sets of legislation, explicit reference to insurance and reinsurance is made as examples of financing and financial assistance.[1462] Furthermore, specifically the regulations on Sudan, the DRC and South Sudan prohibit the provision of brokering services with regard to military activities, whereas the latter also prohibits the provision of other services in relation to the same activities.[1463] *Brokering services* is defined as '(i) the negotiation or arrangement of transactions for the purchase, sale or supply of goods and technology, or of financial and technical services, from a third country to any other third country; or (ii) the selling or buying of goods and technology or of financial and technical services, that are located in third countries for their transfer to another third country'.[1464] Moreover, it is prohibited to provide, manufacture, maintain and use arms and related materiel of all types to any person in Sudan, Lebanon, South Sudan, Myanmar/Burma and Zimbabwe or for use in Sudan, Lebanon, South Sudan, Myanmar/Burma and Zimbabwe or to designated persons with regard to Yemen.[1465] Finally, it is prohibited to provide financing or financial assistance with regard to the sale, supply, transfer and export of arms and related materiel to any person in Sudan, Lebanon, South Sudan, Myanmar/Burma and Zimbabwe or for use in Sudan, Lebanon, South Sudan, Myanmar/Burma and Zimbabwe or to designated persons with regard to Yemen.[1466]

279. Parallel to the aforementioned prohibitions that are common throughout the regulations in view of Sudan, Lebanon, South Sudan, Myanmar/Burma and Zimbabwe, certain regulations provide for individual ones. The Regulation on Lebanon explicitly prohibits activities aiming to circumvent the prohibitions set.[1467] In a similar spirit, the Regulation on Zimbabwe prohibits activities promoting the prohibited transactions.[1468] Lastly, the Regulation on South Sudan prohibits the provision of technical assistance, financing, financial assistance or brokering services with regard to mercenary personnel in South Sudan or for use in South Sudan.[1469] The absence of the here-explained prohibitions in the other regulations could hardly be perceived as a free pass to perform such activities; doing so could qualify as acting in bad faith. In all

1461. Article 2(b) Regulation on Sudan, Art. 1a(2) Regulation on DRC, Art. 2(b) Regulation on Lebanon, Art. 1a(b) Regulation on Yemen, Art. 2(2) Regulation on South Sudan, Art. 3(1)(b) Regulation on Myanmar/Burma and Art. 2(b) Regulation on Zimbabwe. The Regulation on DRC does not make mention of any examples.
1462. Article 2(b) Regulation on Sudan, Art. 1a(b) Regulation on Yemen and Art. 2(2) Regulation on South Sudan.
1463. Article 2(a) Regulation on Sudan, Art. 1a(2) Regulation on DRC and Art. 2(1) Regulation on South Sudan.
1464. Article 1(a) Regulation on Sudan, Art. 1(i) Regulation on DRC and Art. 1(a) Regulation on South Sudan.
1465. Article 2(a) Regulation on Sudan, Art. 2(a) Regulation on Lebanon, Art. 1a(a) Regulation on Yemen, Art. 2(1) Regulation on South Sudan, Art. 3(1)(a) Regulation on Myanmar/Burma and Art. 2(a) Regulation on Zimbabwe.
1466. Article 2(b) Regulation on Sudan, Art. 2(b) Regulation on Lebanon, Art. 1a(b) Regulation on Yemen, Art. 2(2) Regulation on South Sudan, Art. 3(1)(b) Regulation on Myanmar/Burma and Art. 2(b) Regulation on Zimbabwe.
1467. Article 2(c) Regulation on Lebanon.
1468. Article 2(c) Regulation on Zimbabwe.
1469. Article 2(3) Regulation on South Sudan.

probability, the EU felt the need to adopt such provisions, that at first glance seem odd, for two reasons. First, they in order to follow closely the respective provisions of the resolutions of the UN Security Council.[1470]

280. The arms embargo on DPRK differs from the above. Sale, supply, transfer and export of any item, but for food and medicine, to the DPRK is prohibited when the exporter is aware or has reasonable grounds to believe that the items in question are destined for the armed forces of the DPRK. Said prohibition applies also to items that could support or enhance the operational capabilities of the armed forces of a state other than the DPRK.[1471] This deviation in the form of a 'catch-all' clause complies with the wording selected by the UN Security Council in the 2016 resolution[1472] that the EU legislation implemented.

2 *Restrictions and Embargo on Items on the EU Common Military List*

281. The restrictive measures with regard to items on the EU Common Military List and the situation in the DRC, the DPRK, Somalia, Iran, Libya, the CAR, Venezuela and Syria bear a striking resemblance to the ones related to arms and related materiel, explained above (*see* in this respect paragraphs 276 et seq. above), and more specifically to providing technical assistance[1473] and financing or financial assistance.[1474] At the same time, a few remarks deserve mention. The Regulation on Somalia does not bar technical assistance for said items to *any* person in that specific state, following the rule shaped by the other regulations. Rather, it sets such prohibition for all persons listed therein, reflecting the approach of the UN Security Council on 'targeted ban on arms transfers'.[1475] Further, the Regulation on DPRK prohibits not only providing but also obtaining such assistance.[1476] It is also noteworthy that, with regard to Syria, providing technical assistance related to goods and technology listed in the EU Common Military List is not prohibited. Finally, specifically with regard to the prohibition of financing and financial assistance for the sale, supply, transfer, maintenance and use of items of the EU Common Military List, for use in Somalia, it is set out that persons not acting in compliance therewith may not be held liable on one occasion. This may take place when such persons had not known and had no reasonable cause to suspect, that their actions would infringe this prohibition.[1477]

1470. *See* with regard to South Sudan S/RES/2428 of 13 Jul. 2018 para. 4.
1471. Article 5(1)(a) & (b) Regulation on DPRK.
1472. S/RES/2270 of 2 Mar. 2016 para. 8.
1473. Article 1a(1)(a) Regulation on DRC, Art. 7(a) Regulation on DPRK, Art. 8(1)(a) Regulation on Somalia, Art. 5(a) Regulation on Iran, Art. 3(1)(a) Regulation on Libya, Art. 2(a) Regulation on CAR and Art. 2(1)(a) Regulation on Venezuela.
1474. Article 1a(1)(b) Regulation on DRC, Art. 7(b) Regulation on DPRK, Art. 8(1)(b) Regulation on Somalia, Art. 5(b) Regulation on Iran, Art. 3(1)(c) Regulation on Libya, Art. 2(b) Regulation on CAR, Art. 2(1)(b) Regulation on Venezuela and Art. 3a(a) Regulation on Syria.
1475. *See* S/RES/1844 of 20 Nov. 2008 para. 7.
1476. Article 7(c) Regulation on DPRK.
1477. Article 8(3) Regulation on Somalia.

282. In addition, it is prohibited to provide technical assistance, financing and financial assistance with regard to armed mercenary personnel in Libya or for use in Libya.[1478] This prohibition also applies to mercenaries in the CAR or for use in the CAR, albeit in an extended form as it also includes transport and brokering services.[1479]

283. The prohibition on brokering services with regard to goods and technology listed under the EU Common Military List is prescribed only sparsely, as seen under arms and related materiel (*see* in this respect paragraph 287 above). It applies in the DRC, the DPRK, Iran, the CAR and Venezuela.[1480]

284. It is further prohibited to provide to the designated persons under the Regulation on Somalia *investment services* related to military activities or to supplying, transferring, manufacturing, maintaining and using goods and technology listed in the EU Common Military List.[1481] *Investment services* (in regard to the statutory definition *see* Annex I p. 311 at 327) include services such as orders with regard to financial instruments, portfolio management, investment advice and operation of multilateral trading facilities.[1482]

285. This specific prohibition reflects the 'targeted ban on arms transfers' as decided and imposed by the UN Security Council.[1483]

286. Moreover, it is prohibited to acquire or extend participation in any Iranian person engaged in manufacturing items of the EU Common Military List, as well as to create any joint venture with such a person.[1484] This prohibition echoes the one imposed with regard to crude oil in Syria (*see* in this regard paragraph 206 above).

287. Unsurprisingly, activities aiming to circumvent said prohibitions are not permitted. What is surprising though, is that such an explicit provision has been set out merely with regard to Somalia, Libya and Syria.[1485]

C Exceptions

288. But for the DRC, Somalia and Iran, the restrictive measures on items of the EU Common Military List do not apply in certain cases, as explained below. The existence of these derogations substantiates both the appropriateness of the adopted restrictive measures and that the same measures do not go beyond what is necessary to achieve

1478. Article 3(1)(d) Regulation on Libya.
1479. Article 2(c) Regulation on the CAR.
1480. Article 1a(1)(a) Regulation on DRC, Art. 7(a) Regulation on DPRK, Art. 5(a) Regulation on Iran, Art. 2(a) Regulation on CAR and Art. 2(1)(a) Regulation on Venezuela.
1481. Article 8(1)(c) Regulation on Somalia.
1482. Article 1(g) Regulation on Somalia.
1483. *See* S/RES/1844 of 20 Nov. 2008 para. 7.
1484. Article 5(c) Regulation on Syria.
1485. Article 8(2) Regulation on Somalia, Art. 3(1)(e) Regulation on Libya and Art. 3a(b) Regulation on Syria.

the objective pursued, therefore satisfying the principle of proportionality, the CJEU ruled.[1486]

289. Derogations are permitted, in some - not all - regulations, on the grounds of humanitarian purposes. In Libya,[1487] the CAR[1488] and Venezuela[1489] non-lethal military equipment intended solely for humanitarian or protective use is a ground for deviation from the cardinal rule of prohibiting the provision of technical assistance, financing and financial assistance. Similarly, prohibited items, assistance and brokering services may be allowed in the DPRK for humanitarian purposes, such as food, agriculture and medicine, as already seen under dual-use items (*see* in this regard paragraph 267 above).[1490] The EU provision refers to food, agriculture and medicine as examples that stipulate humanitarian purposes. It would seem that this choice of words is an unfortunate transplant from the resolutions of the UN Security Council, where it does make sense, as the exceptions refer to conventional arms, lists of certain items and technology[1491] as well as luxury items, unlike the EU derogation that refers solely to conventional arms.

290. Protective items form another group of derogations. Non-combat vehicles with ballistic protection for the use of personnel of the EU and its Member States in the DPRK are exempt from said prohibitions.[1492] This also applies to protective clothing for use by the same personnel in Libya, the CAR and Venezuela, although in Libya and Venezuela, use is explicitly extended to UN personnel, representatives of the media, humanitarian and development workers and associated personnel.[1493]

291. One more group of derogations involve assistance to governments and state institutions, actual or in-process. Technical and financial assistance and financing may be provided for non-lethal military equipment intended for institution-building programmes of the UN, the EU, the Member States of the EU as well as regional and sub-regional organizations in Venezuela,[1494] and for security and disarmament assistance to the government in Libya.[1495] In the latter case, the UN Security Council has decided to allow the provision of arms and related materials upon approval by the 1970 Libya Sanctions Committee, and has not restricted the derogation solely to 'non-lethal

1486. *Venezuela* 2023 (n. 12) paras 102 & 103.
1487. Article 3(2)(a) Regulation on Libya; *see* S/RES/1970 of 26 Feb. 2011 para. 9(a).
1488. Article 3(d) Regulation on the CAR; *see* S/RES/2648 of 29 Jul. 2022 para. 1(d).
1489. Article 4(1)(a)(i) Regulation on Venezuela.
1490. Article 8(1) Regulation on DPRK; *see* S/RES/2270 of 2 Mar. 2016 paras 8(a) & (b). The UN provisions refer to battle tanks, armoured combat vehicles, large calibre artillery systems, combat aircraft, attack helicopters, warships, missiles or missile systems as defined for the purpose of the United Nations Register on Conventional Arms as well as related materiel including spare parts.
1491. These are related to nuclear programmes (*see* S/2006/814) and ballistic missile programmes (*see* S/2006/815).
1492. Article 7(2) Regulation on DPRK.
1493. Article 3(2)(b) Regulation on Libya, Art. 3(b) Regulation on the CAR and Art. 5 Regulation on Venezuela. Use in the CAR requires notification to the 2127 CAR Sanctions Committee at least twenty days in advance.
1494. Article 4(1)(a)(i) Regulation on Venezuela.
1495. Article 3(2)(c) Regulation on Libya.

military equipment'.[1496] Technical assistance, financing, financial assistance and brokering services may also, exceptionally, be provided for supplying non-lethal equipment, including training, to the CAR security forces intended for the process of the Security Sector Reform in coordination with MINUSCA, when the 2127 CAR Sanctions Committee has been notified in advance.[1497] Similarly, said assistance, financing and brokering services may be allowed in the CAR for use by MINUSCA, missions of the EU, forces of France deployed therein and forces of states members of the UN that provide training and assistance.[1498] Parallel, weapons and ammunition, military vehicles and equipment may be supplied to the CAR for the state security forces in order to support the process of the Security Sector Reform, provided that the 2127 CAR Sanctions Committee has been notified in advance.[1499] According to the relevant resolution of the UN Security Council, the 2127 CAR Sanctions Committee has the power to approve the sale and supply of arms and other materiel as well as providing assistance and personnel in the CAR.[1500] No such provision exists under the Regulation on the CAR. Furthermore, material intended for crisis-management operations of the UN and the EU, as well as of regional and sub-regional organizations may be allowed in Venezuela.[1501]

292. Further, otherwise prohibited transactions related to items of the EU Common Military List and the DPRK may be authorized by competent authorities of the Member States of the EU, as long as the 1718 DPRK Sanctions Committee has approved a prior request,[1502] as already seen under dual-use items (*see* in this regard paragraph 264 above). Similarly, export of items of the EU Common Military List from Syria may take place, when they are undertaken in accordance with resolution 2118 of the UN Security Council[1503] and decisions of the executive council of the Organisation for the Prohibition of Chemical Weapons that are consistent with the objective of the Chemical Weapons Convention.[1504] In a similar way, technical assistance, financing, financial assistance and brokering services with regard to military activities in the DRC may be provided for the purpose of assisting MONUSCO or the African Union Task Force, under the condition that the 1533 Congo Sanctions Committee has been notified in advance and has been informed of all relevant information, such as the end-user, the proposed date of delivery and the itinerary of shipments, as the case may be. In the same manner, such assistance and services in the DRC may be provided for non-lethal military equipment intended solely for humanitarian or protective use.[1505] Parallel

1496. *See* S/RES/2009 of 16 Sep. 2011 para. 13(a); S/RES/2095 of 14 Mar. 2013 para. 10; and S/RES/2174 of 27 Aug. 2014 para. 8.
1497. Article 3(c) Regulation on the CAR.
1498. Article 3(a) Regulation on the CAR; *see* S/RES/2399 of 30 Jan. 2018 para. 1(a).
1499. Article 3(e) Regulation on the CAR; *see* S/RES/2648 of 29 Jul. 2022 para. 1(g).
1500. S/RES/2648 of 29 Jul. 2022 para. 1(h).
1501. Article 4(1)(a)(ii) Regulation on Venezuela.
1502. Article 8(2) Regulation on DPRK; *see* S/RES/2270 of 2 Mar. 2016 paras 8(a) & (b).
1503. S/RES/2118 of 2013 para. 10.
1504. Article 3b Regulation on Syria.
1505. Article 1a(2) Regulation on DRC; *see* S/RES/1807 of 31 Mar. 2008 paras 3(a), (b) & (c) and 5. The notification requirement has been repealed in December 2022; *see* S/RES/2667 of 20 Dec. 2022 para. 2.

thereto, the same assistance and services with regard to non-lethal military equipment in the DRC may be authorized by the competent authorities of Member States, when it is intended solely for humanitarian or protective use, as long as the activity in question has not already taken place.[1506]

293. The Regulation on DRC prescribes an interesting exception. It gives the competent authorities of the Member States the authority to authorize the provision of technical assistance, financing, financial assistance and brokering services for arms and related material, as long as they are intended for the support of or use by MONUSCO or the African Union Regional Task Force.[1507] It also does so, when such assistance and services have been approved in advance by the 1533 Congo Sanctions Committee.[1508] This exception is interesting, despite perhaps seeming ordinary at first glance, as *arms and related material* are not sanctioned; *items under the EU Common Military List* and *military activities* are.

294. Finally, two unique derogations are prescribed with regard to Venezuela. First, supply, sale, transfer and export of demining equipment and material used in demining operations may be authorized by the competent authorities of the Member States.[1509] The other exception, which does not require prior authorization is related to the execution of contracts concluded before 13 November 2017 and ancillary contracts, that are necessary for the execution of said contracts. Nonetheless, these contracts must comply with the provisions of Common Position 2008/944[1510] and they must have been notified to the competent authorities of the Member States within five working days of the Regulation on Venezuela entering into force.[1511]

295. On a final note, as has already been noted above, the restrictive measures regarding the EU Common Military List in Somalia are absolute. Nonetheless, the apposite resolutions of the UN Security Council do set out derogations. More specifically, the arms embargo does not apply to weapons and military equipment for use by UN personnel, including the United Nations Assistance Mission in Somalia ('UNSOM'), AMISOM, AMISOM's strategic partners and the European Union Training Mission.[1512] It also does not apply to such items destined for the sole use of states and international organizations against acts of piracy and armed robbery at sea, upon the request of the Federal Government of Somalia.[1513] Moreover, supplying protective clothing exported

1506. Article 1b(1)(b) & (2) Regulation on DRC.
1507. Article 1b(1)(a) & (c) Regulation on DRC.
1508. Article 1b(1)(d) Regulation on DRC.
1509. Article 4(1)(c) Regulation on Venezuela.
1510. Council Common Position 2008/944/CFSP of 8 Dec. 2008 defining common rules governing control of exports of military technology and equipment, OJ L 335, 13 Dec. 2008, p. 99, as last amended by Council Decision (CFSP) 2019/1560 of 16 Sep. 2019 amending Common Position 2008/944/CFSP defining common rules governing control of exports of military technology and equipment, OJ L 239, 17 Sep. 2019, p. 16.
1511. Article 2(2) Regulation on Venezuela.
1512. S/RES/2111 of 24 Jul. 2013 para. 10(a), (b), (c) and (d).
1513. *Ibid.*, para. 10(e).

to Somalia by UN personnel, representatives of the media and humanitarian and development workers as well as associated personnel for their personal use is permitted. Similarly, supplying non-lethal military equipment intended solely for humanitarian and protective use is permitted, as long as the 751 Somalia Sanctions Committee has been notified five days in advance.[1514] In parallel, the Federal Government of Somalia may be supplied with certain arms and weapons[1515] as long as a request for exemption has been submitted to the 751 Somalia Sanctions Committee and approved.[1516]

II Sanctions with Regard to Equipment for Internal Repression

A Meaning of 'Equipment for Internal Repression'

296. Equipment which might be used for internal repression in Libya, Myanmar/Burma, Zimbabwe, Iran and Venezuela, has been identified as a range of items that are not controlled by the EU Common Military List. These are: firearms, ammunition and related accessories;[1517] bombs and grenades;[1518] vehicles;[1519] explosive substances and

1514. *Ibid.*, para. 10(f) & (g).
1515. Arms and weapons that may be supplied to the Federal Government of Somalia are the following: (1) Surface to air missiles, including Man-Portable Air-Defence Systems (MANPADS); (2) Guns, howitzers, and cannons with a calibre greater than 12.7 mm, and ammunition and components specially designed for these. (This does not include shoulder fired anti-tank rocket launchers such as RPGs or LAWs, rifle grenades, or grenade launchers.); (3) Mortars with a calibre greater than 82 mm; (4) Anti-tank guided weapons, including Anti-tank Guided Missiles (ATGMs) and ammunition and components specially designed for these items; (5) Charges and devices intended for military use containing energetic materials; mines and related material; (6) Weapon sights with a night vision capability. *Ibid.* Annex.
1516. *Ibid.*, para. 7. *See also* S/RES/2444 of 14 Nov. 2018, S/RES/2142 of 5 Mar. 2014, S/RES/2385 of 14 Nov. 2017.
1517. These are: 1.1 firearms not controlled by ML 1 and ML 2 of the EU Common Military List; 1.2 ammunition specially designed for the firearms listed in item 1.1 and specially designed components therefor; and 1.3 weapon-sights not controlled by the EU Common Military List. Point 1 Annex I Regulation on Libya; point 1 Annex I Regulation on Myanmar/Burma; point 1 Annex I Regulation on Zimbabwe; point 1 Annex III Regulation on Iran; and point 1 Annex I Regulation on Venezuela.
1518. Point 2 Annex I Regulation on Libya; point 2 Annex I Regulation on Myanmar/Burma; point 2 Annex I Regulation on Zimbabwe; point 2 Annex III Regulation on Iran; and point 2 Annex I Regulation on Venezuela.
1519. These vehicles include: (3.1) vehicles equipped with a water cannon, specially designed or modified for the purpose of riot control; (3.2) vehicles specially designed or modified to be electrified to repel borders; (3.3) vehicles specially designed or modified to remove barricades, including construction equipment with ballistic protection; (3.4) vehicles specially designed for the transport or transfer of prisoners and/or detainees; (3.5) vehicles, including trailers, specially designed to deploy mobile barriers; (3.6) components for the vehicles specified in items 3.1 to 3.5 specially designed for the purposes of riot control, with the exception of vehicles specially designed for the purposes of fire-fighting. Point 3 Annex I Regulation on Libya; point 3 Annex I Regulation on Myanmar/Burma; point 3 Annex I Regulation on Zimbabwe; point 3 Annex III Regulation on Iran; and point 3 Annex I Regulation on Venezuela.

related equipment;[1520] protective equipment;[1521] simulators for training in the use of firearms;[1522] night vision, thermal imaging equipment and image intensifier tubes;[1523] razor barbed wire;[1524] knives;[1525] production equipment specially designed for said items; and specific technology for same items.[1526]

297. Equipment for internal repression is understood differently with regard to Syria. Initially, it was thought to adopt the aforementioned definition and include some dual-use items and other chemicals.[1527] However, the agreed text[1528] has stripped off

1520. These substances and equipment are: (4.1) equipment and devices specially designed to initiate explosions by electrical or non-electrical means, including firing sets, detonators, igniters, boosters and detonating cord, and specially designed components therefor; except those specially designed for a specific commercial use consisting of the actuation or operation by explosive means of other equipment or devices the function of which is not the creation of explosions (e.g., car air-bag inflators, electric-surge arresters of fire sprinkler actuators); (4.2) linear cutting explosive charges not controlled by the Common Military List; (4.3) other explosives not controlled by the Common Military List and related substances as follows: (a) amatol; (b) nitrocellulose (containing more than 12.5% nitrogen); (c) nitroglycol; (d) pentaerythritol tetranitrate (PETN); (e) picryl chloride; (f) 2,4,6-trinitrotoluene (TNT). Point 4 Annex I Regulation on Libya; point 4 Annex I Regulation on Myanmar/Burma; point 4 Annex I Regulation on Zimbabwe; point 4 Annex III Regulation on Iran; and point 4 Annex I Regulation on Venezuela.

1521. The here relevant protective equipment is not controlled by ML 13 of the EU Common Military List involves: (5.1) body armour providing ballistic and/or stabbing protection; and (5.2) helmets providing ballistic and/or fragmentation protection, anti-riot helmets, antiriot shields and ballistic shields, with the exception of equipment specially designed for sports activities and equipment specially designed for safety of work requirements. Point 5 Annex I Regulation on Libya; point 5 Annex I Regulation on Myanmar/Burma; point 5 Annex I Regulation on Zimbabwe; point 5 Annex III Regulation on Iran; and point 5 Annex I Regulation on Venezuela.

1522. These simulators are not controlled by ML 14 of the EU Common Military List. Point 6 Annex I Regulation on Libya; point 6 Annex I Regulation on Myanmar/Burma; point 6 Annex I Regulation on Zimbabwe; point 6 Annex III Regulation on Iran; and point 6 Annex I Regulation on Venezuela.

1523. These are not controlled by the EU Common Military List. Point 7 Annex I Regulation on Libya; point 7 Annex I Regulation on Myanmar/Burma; point 7 Annex I Regulation on Zimbabwe; point 7 Annex III Regulation on Iran; and point 7 Annex I Regulation on Venezuela.

1524. Point 8 Annex I Regulation on Libya; point 8 Annex I Regulation on Myanmar/Burma; point 8 Annex I Regulation on Zimbabwe; point 8 Annex III Regulation on Iran; and point 8 Annex I Regulation on Venezuela.

1525. These are military knives, combat knives and bayonets with blade lengths in excess of 10 cm. Point 9 Annex I Regulation on Libya; point 9 Annex I Regulation on Myanmar/Burma; point 9 Annex I Regulation on Zimbabwe; point 9 Annex III Regulation on Iran; and point 9 Annex I Regulation on Venezuela.

1526. Points 10 & 11 Annex I Regulation on Libya; points 10 & 11 Annex I Regulation on Myanmar/Burma; points 10 & 11 Annex I Regulation on Zimbabwe; points 10 & 11 Annex III Regulation on Iran; and points 10 & 11 Annex I Regulation on Venezuela.

1527. *See* European Commission & High Representative of the European Union for Foreign Affairs and Security Policy, Joint Proposal for a Council Regulation, amending Regulation (EU) No. 36/2012 concerning restrictive measures in view of the situation in Syria, JOIN(2012) 16 final of 1 Jun. 2012, pp. 7 et seq., available: https://eur-lex.europa.eu.

1528. Council Regulation (EU) No. 509/2012 of 15 Jun. 2012 amending Regulation (EU) No. 36/2012 concerning restrictive measures in view of the situation in Syria, OJ L 156, 16 Jun. 2012, p. 10.

the aforementioned definition and has maintained the dual-use items and other chemicals without any apparent reason for this deviation. Thus, the term *equipment that could be used for internal repression* with regard to Syria entails the items listed in Annex IA[1529] and the items of Annex IX.[1530]

B *Restrictions and Controls*

298. It is prohibited to sell, supply, transfer and export equipment that could be used for internal repression to any person in Libya, Myanmar/Burma, Zimbabwe, Iran, Venezuela and Syria or for use in the same states.[1531] It is also prohibited to import such equipment from Libya.[1532] Technical assistance for the same equipment is not allowed,[1533] just as financial assistance,[1534] with the exception of Libya as such a provision is absent, and brokering,[1535] but for Libya, Myanmar/Burma and Zimbabwe that are silent on this issue.

299. Further, the Regulation on Syria explicitly prohibits activities that aim to circumvent these restrictions.[1536] Specifically with regard to the items listed under Annex IX of the Regulation on Syria, exporting, providing technical assistance, brokering services, financing and financial assistance a prior authorization by the competent authorities of the Member States is required.[1537] This authorization to export such items shall be in

1529. This equipment includes: protective and detection equipment and components, UAVs, chemical manufacturing facilities, equipment and components, toxic gas monitoring systems and their dedicated detecting components, equipment capable of use in handling biological materials, chemicals, which may be used as precursors for toxic chemical agents, human pathogens, zoonoses and toxins, animal pathogens, genetic elements and genetically modified organisms, plant pathogens, toxic chemicals, software and technology (Annex IA Part 1 Regulation on Syria). It also includes certain chemicals at 95% concentration or greater and related technology (Annex IB Part 2 Regulation on Syria).

1530. These goods and materials processing are: certain chemicals at 95% concentration or greater, certain chemically defined compounds at 90% concentration or greater, floor-mounted fume hoods, full face-mask air-purifying and air-supplying respirators, class II biological safety cabinets or isolators, batch centrifuges, fermeters, conventional or turbulent air-flow clean-air rooms and self-contained filter units, chemical manufacturing facilities, equipment and related technology (Annex IX Regulation on Syria).

1531. Article 2(1)(a) Regulation on Libya, Art. 2(1) Regulation on Myanmar/Burma, Art. 3(a) Regulation on Zimbabwe, Art. 1a(1)(a) Regulation on Iran, Art. 3(a) Regulation on Venezuela and Art. 2a(1)(a) Regulation on Syria.

1532. Article 2(2) Regulation on Libya.

1533. Article 3(1)(b) Regulation on Libya, Art. 3(2)(a) Regulation on Myanmar/Burma, Art. 3(b) Regulation on Zimbabwe, Art. 1a(1)(b) Regulation on Iran, Art. 3(b) Regulation on Venezuela and Art. 3(1)(a) Regulation on Syria.

1534. Article 3(2)(b) Regulation on Myanmar/Burma, Art. 3(c) Regulation on Zimbabwe, Art. 1a(1)(c) Regulation on Iran and Art. 3(c) Regulation on Venezuela and Art. 3(1)(b) Regulation on Syria.

1535. Article 1a(1)(b) Regulation on Iran, Art. 3(b) Regulation on Venezuela and Art. 3(1)(a) Regulation on Syria.

1536. Article 3(1)(c) Regulation on Syria.

1537. Articles 2b(1) and 3(4)(a) & (b) Regulation on Syria.

accordance with the rules set out in the Dual-Use Regulation.[1538] No such requirement is set out with regard to technical assistance, brokering services, financing and financial services. Lastly, an authorization shall not be granted if said authorities have reasonable grounds to believe that the items in question might be used for internal repression or for manufacturing and maintaining products that could be used for the same scope.[1539]

C *Exceptions*

300. Sale, supply, transfer and export of equipment for internal repression in Myanmar/Burma may be authorized by the competent authorities of the Member States on the same grounds that trade of dual-use items may be authorized[1540] (*see* in this regard paragraph 265 above). Protective clothing is also exempt from the restrictions when it is exported temporarily to Myanmar/Burma by personnel of the UN, the EU, the Member States of the EU, representatives of the media, humanitarian and development workers and associated personnel and is intended solely for their personal use.[1541] The same exceptions are effective with regard to Venezuela[1542] and Zimbabwe[1543] but for crisis-management operations. The Regulation on Zimbabwe differs in one more point, as it allows the export of explosive substances and related equipment, including financial and technical assistance, as long as such items shall be used for civilian use in mining and infrastructure projects.[1544] A Member State considering to authorize the export of explosives shall have to inform the other Member States and the Commission at least two weeks in advance.[1545] The Regulation on Libya sets out exceptions merely for protective clothing and humanitarian or protective use.[1546] Lastly, with regard to Iran equipment that might be used for internal repression may be exported, when it is intended solely for the protective use of the personnel of the EU and of its Member States in Iran.[1547]

301. With regard to Syria, the exemptions on the EU Common Military List apply *mutatis mutandis* on items listed under Annex IA.[1548] Two additional exemptions are set out on the basis of the purposes that the items in question shall serve: humanitarian purposes; and for the benefit of personnel of the EU, its Member States and the UN.[1549]

1538. Articles 2b(3) Regulation on Syria and Art. 14 Dual-Use Regulation.
1539. Articles 2b(2) and 3(4) last sentence Regulation on Syria
1540. Article 4(1)(a), (b) & (c) Regulation on Myanmar/Burma.
1541. Article 2(2) Regulation on Myanmar/Burma.
1542. Articles 5 and 4(1)(b) Regulation on Venezuela.
1543. Articles 5 and 4(1)(a)(i), 4(1)(b), 4(1)(a)(ii) Regulation on Zimbabwe.
1544. Article 4a(1) & (2) Regulation on Zimbabwe and Art. 14 Dual-Use Regulation.
1545. Article 4a(4) Regulation on Zimbabwe.
1546. Article 2(3) & (4) Regulation on Libya.
1547. Article 1a(2) Regulation on Iran.
1548. Articles 2a(2) and 3(5) Regulation on Syria.
1549. Articles 2a(2) and 3(3) Regulation on Syria.

III Sanctions with Regard to Missiles and Other Systems of Delivery

A *Meaning of 'Missiles'*

302. Under the Dual Use Regulation, the term *missiles* is defined by the capacity load and the delivery range of the systems, that is half a ton and 300 km (in regard to the statutory definition *see* Annex I p. 311 at 328).[1550] On the basis of technical notes on the term *payload* according to the MTCR,[1551] it is understood that said term entails *ballistic missiles, space launch vehicles,*[1552] *sounding rockets,*[1553] *cruise missiles* and other *UAVs.*[1554]

303. Nonetheless, the specification of missiles under restrictive measures both differs from the aforementioned and lacks uniformity. The Regulation on DPRK targets two sets of items: items which could contribute to programmes of ballistic missiles of the DPRK;[1555] and key components for the ballistic missile sector.[1556] The first set of items has been already described, as they also qualify as items that could contribute to the state's nuclear-related programmes (*see* in this regard paragraphs 213 et seq. above). It is here noted that the same set of items further qualifies as items that could contribute to other weapons of mass destruction-related programmes. The second set of items involves nine goods related to aluminium, which at the same time qualify as dual-use items.[1557]

304. The Regulation on Iran sets under restrictive measures goods and technology listed in the MTCR list.[1558] Nonetheless, the listed goods and technology also qualify as dual use items[1559] and they have been already described (*see* in this regard paragraphs

1550. Definitions of Terms Used in This Annex, Annex I, Dual Use Regulation.
1551. 2. Definitions, MTCR Annex.
1552. In this regard *see* point 9A004 Annex I, Part I Dual Use Regulation.
1553. In this regard *see* point 9A104 Annex I, Part I Dual Use Regulation.
1554. In regard to the definition of UAV *see* Annex I p. 311 at 335. Definitions of terms used in this Annex, Annex I, Part I Dual Use Regulation.
1555. Annex II Part II Regulation on DPRK.
1556. Annex II Part III Regulation on DPRK.
1557. These are: unwrought aluminium (No. III.A1.001 Regulation on DPRK that corresponds to No. 1C002 Annex I Dual Use Regulation), aluminium waste and scrap (No. III.A1.002 Regulation on DPRK that corresponds to No. 1C002 Annex I Dual Use Regulation), aluminium powders and flakes (No. III.A1.003 Regulation on DPRK that corresponds to No. 1C111 Annex I Dual Use Regulation), aluminium bars, rods and profiles (No. III.A1.004 Regulation on DPRK that corresponds to No. 1C005 Annex I Dual Use Regulation), aluminium wire (No. III.A1.005 Regulation on DPRK that corresponds to No. 1C002 Annex I Dual Use Regulation), aluminium plates, sheets and strip, of a thickness exceeding 0.2 mm (No. III.A1.006 Regulation on DPRK that corresponds to No. 1C002 Annex I Dual Use Regulation), aluminium tubes and pipes (No. III.A1.007 Regulation on DPRK that corresponds to No. 1C002 Annex I Dual Use Regulation), aluminium tube or pipe fittings (No. III.A1.008 Regulation on DPRK that corresponds to No. 1C002 Annex I Dual Use Regulation) and stranded wire, cables, plaited bands and the like, of aluminium, not electrically insulated (No. III.A1.009 Regulation on DPRK that corresponds to No. 1C002 Annex I Dual Use Regulation).
1558. Article 4a(2) Regulation on Iran.
1559. These are the following points of Annex I Dual Use Regulation: 1A002, 1A102, 1B001, 1B002, 1B101, 1B102, 1B115, 1B116, 1B117, 1B118, 1B119, 1C001, 1C007, 1C010, 1C011, 1C101,

226 et seq. and 250 above), but for the following few items: chlorine trifluoride;[1560] certain software;[1561] vibration test systems;[1562] certain other software and technology;[1563] and certain other technology.[1564]

B Restrictions and Controls

305. Restrictions on missiles are set out in the Regulation on DPRK and in the Regulation on Iran. The restrictive measures with regard to the first state[1565] are identical to the ones imposed on dual-use items (*see* in this regard paragraphs 261 et seq. above). The restrictive measures with regard to Iran are also identical to those.[1566] In addition, they set out the prohibition of technical assistance, brokering services,[1567] financing, and financial assistance.[1568] They lastly prohibit any arrangement for participating, both independently, as well as via a joint venture or other partnership, in any Iranian person engaged in commercial activities involving missile technologies.[1569]

C Exceptions

306. The aforementioned restrictions on missiles within the scope of the Regulation on DPRK may be lifted for humanitarian reasons as well as upon authorization of the 1718 DPRK Sanctions Committee,[1570] as already seen under dual-use items (*see* in this regard paragraph 266 above). No exceptions are foreseen in Iran.

1C102, 1C107, 1C111, 1C116, 1C117, 1C118, 1D101, 1D103, 1E001, 1E101, 1E103, 1E104, 2A001, 2A101, 2B004, 2B009, 2B104, 2B105, 2B109, 2B117, 2B119, 2B120, 2B121, 2B122, 3A001, 3A101, 3A102, 3D101, 3E101, 3E102, 4A001, 4A003, 4A101, 4A102, 4E001, 5A101, 5D101, 5E101, 6A002, 6A006, 6A007, 6A008, 6A102, 6A107, 6A108, 6B008, 6B108, 6D002, 6D102, 6D103, 6E001, 6E002, 6E101, 7A001, 7A002, 7A003, 7A004, 7A005, 7A006, 7A101, 7A102, 7A103, 7A104, 7A105, 7A106, 7A115, 7A116, 7A117, 7B001, 7B002, 7B003, 7B102, 7B103, 7D002, 7D101, 7D102, 7D103, 7E001, 7E002, 7E003, 7E004, 7E101, 7E102, 7E104, 9A001, 9A004, 9A005, 9A006, 9A007, 9A008, 9A009, 9A010, 9A011, 9A012, 9A101, 9A102, 9A104, 9A105, 9A106, 9A107, 9A108, 9A109, 9A110, 9A111, 9A112, 9A115, 9A116, 9A117, 9A118, 9A119, 9A120, 9A121, 9B006, 9B105, 9B106, 9B115, 9B116, 9B117, 9C108, 9C110, 9D001, 9D002, 9D004, 9D101, 9D103, 9D104, 9D105, 9E001, 9E002, 9E101 and 9E102.

1560. Point 1C238 Annex III Regulation on Iran, which corresponds to No. 4.C.4.a.6 of the MTCR Annex.
1561. Point 1D001 Annex III Regulation on Iran, which corresponds to No. 6.D.1 of the MTCR Annex.
1562. Point 2B116 Annex III Regulation on Iran, which corresponds to No. 15.B.1 of the MTCR Annex.
1563. Points 2D001, 2D101, 2E001, 2E002 & 2E101 Annex III Regulation on Iran, which corresponds to Nos 3.D, 3.D.1, 6.D.2 & 15.D.1 of the MTCR Annex.
1564. Point 3E001 Annex I Regulation on Iran, which corresponds to the MTCR Annex.
1565. Article 3(1)(a) & (c) Regulation on DPRK.
1566. Article 4a & 4c Regulation on Iran.
1567. Article 4b(a) Regulation on Iran.
1568. Article 4b(b) Regulation on Iran.
1569. Article 4b(c) Regulation on Iran.
1570. Article 8(1) & (2) Regulation on DPRK.

§10 SANCTIONS AND MOVEMENT OF PERSONS AND TRANSFER OF GOODS

I Sanctions on Movement of Persons

307. With the exception of the set of measures targeting Iraq, Lebanon, Haiti, Tunisia and Ukraine, Union acts imposing restrictive measures foresee sanctions on movement of certain persons, styled as 'restrictions on admission'.

A The Restrictive Measures

308. The restrictive measures on movement of persons consist of the prohibition of an action, the objective element that is uniform throughout the legislative measures, by a certain person, and the subjective element that is tailored to the aims and scope of each legislative measure.

1 The Objective Element

309. The objective element is formed of preventing the entry into or transit through the territories of the Member States.[1571] This however does not oblige Member States to refuse their own nationals entry into their territory.[1572]

2 The Subjective Element

310. The subjective element, that being the persons eligible for non-admission to the Union, is, in principle, identical to the one explained under the financial sanctions (*see* in this respect paragraphs 79 to 120 above).[1573]

1571. Article 4(1) Decision on Sudan, Art. 4(1) Decision on DRC, Art. 23(1) Decision on DPRK, Art. 5(1) Decision on Somalia, Art. 19(1) Decision on Iran, Art. 1(1) EU Decision on Iran, Art. 8(1) & (2) Decision on Libya, Art. 2a(1) Decision on the CAR, Art. 2a(1) Decision on Yemen, Art. 3(1) Decision on South Sudan, Arts 1(1) & 1a(1) Decision on Mali, Art. 4(1) Decision on Zimbabwe, Art. 5(1) Decision on Myanmar/Burma, Art. 1(1) Decision on Burundi, Art. 6(1) Decision on Venezuela, Art. 1(1) Decision on Nicaragua, Art. 1(1) EU Decision on Lebanon, Art. 3(1) Decision on Guinea, Art. 1(1) Decision on Guinea-Bissau, Art. 27(1) & (2) Decision on Syria and Art. 1(1) Decision on Drilling.

1572. Article 4(2) Decision on Sudan, Art. 4(2) Decision on DRC, Art. 23(3) Decision on DPRK, Art. 5(2) Decision on Somalia, Art. 19(3) Decision on Iran, Art. 1(2) EU Decision on Iran, Art. 8(3) Decision on Libya, Art. 2a(2) Decision on the CAR, Art. 2a(2) Decision on Yemen, Art. 3(2) Decision on South Sudan, Arts 1(2) & 1a(2) Decision on Mali, Art. 4(2) Decision on Zimbabwe, Art. 5(2) Decision on Myanmar/Burma, Art. 1(2) Decision on Burundi, Art. 6(2) Decision on Venezuela, Art. 1(2) Decision on Nicaragua, Art. 1(2) EU Decision on Lebanon, Art. 3(2) Decision on Guinea, Art. 1(2) Decision on Guinea-Bissau, Art. 27(5) Decision on Syria and Art. 1(2) Decision on Drilling.

1573. Articles 4(1) & 3 Decision on Sudan, Arts 4(1) & 3 Decision on DRC, Art. 23(1) Decision on DPRK, Art. 2(1) Decision on Somalia, Art. 19(1) Decision on Iran, Art. 1(1) EU Decision on

311. Exceptionally, the restrictive measures on Iran set out additional groups eligible for restrictions on admission. These are persons designated by the UN Security Council for engaging in Iran's proliferation-sensitive nuclear activities contrary to JCPOA, or in developing nuclear weapon delivery systems, including via procuring prohibited items listed in Annex B to resolution 2231 of the UN Security Council.[1574] Other persons may enter the relevant list due to assisting already designated persons in evading the JCPOA or resolution 2231 of the UN Security Council or acting inconsistently thereto, as well as for having acted on behalf of or at the direction of such persons.[1575] Other persons who have engaged in said activities may also come under restrictions on admission, despite the lack of designation by the UN Security Council.[1576]

B The Exceptions

312. The restrictive measures on movement of persons do not apply, when the competent sanctions committee or the institutions of the Union, as the case may be, determine that travel is justified on grounds of humanitarian need, including religious obligations. They equally do not apply, when such deviation would further the objectives of the apposite resolution of the UN Security Council for the creation of peace, national reconciliation and stability in the respective state and region.[1577] Any authorization on these grounds is limited to the purpose for which it is given and to the persons concerned thereby.[1578]

313. Member States may authorize derogation from the aforementioned measures for persons designated by institutions of the EU on the grounds of: (a) urgent humanitarian need; and (b) attending intergovernmental meetings promoted or hosted by the EU or a Member State, as long as political dialogue directly promoting the policy objectives of the restrictive measures, including democracy, human rights and the rule of law, is

Iran, Art. 8(1) & (2) Decision on Libya, Art. 2a(1) Decision on the CAR, Art. 2a(1) Decision on Yemen, Art. 3(1)(a) & (b) Decision on South Sudan, Art. 1(1) Decision on Mali, 4(1) Decision on Zimbabwe, Art. 5(1) Decision on Myanmar/Burma, Art. 1(1) Decision on Burundi, Art. 6(1) Decision on Venezuela, Art. 1(1) Decision on Nicaragua, Art. 1(1) EU Decision on Lebanon, Art. 3(1) Decision on Guinea, Art. 1(1)(b) Decision on Guinea-Bissau and Art. 27(1) & (2) Decision on Syria and Art. 1(1) Decision on Drilling.

1574. S/RES/2231 of 20 Jul. 2015.

1575. Article 19(1)(d) & Annex III Decision on Iran.

1576. Article 19(1)(e) & Annex IV Decision on Iran.

1577. Article 4(3) Decision on Sudan, Art. 4(3) Decision on DRC, Art. 23(2) Decision on DPRK, Art. 5(3) Decision on Somalia, Art. 8(4) Decision on Libya, Art. 2a(4) Decision on the CAR, Art. 2a(5) Decision on Yemen, Art. 4(2) Decision on South Sudan, Arts 1(4) & 1a(9) Decision on Mali, Art. 4(5) Decision on Zimbabwe, Art. 1(3) Decision on Guinea-Bissau, The Decision on Iran does not contain such a provision.

1578. Article 4(4) Decision on Sudan, Art. 4(9) Decision on DRC, Art. 23(10) Decision on DPRK, Art. 5(4) Decision on Somalia, Art. 19(9) Decision on Iran, Art. 1(9) EU Decision on Iran, Art. 8(11) Decision on Libya, Art. 2a(5) Decision on the CAR, Art. 2a(6) Decision on Yemen, Art. 5(7) Decision on South Sudan, Art. 1(5) Decision on Mali, Art. 4(7) Decision on Zimbabwe, Art. 5(8) Decision on Myanmar/Burma, Art. 1(8) Decision on Burundi, Art. 6(8) Decision on Venezuela, Art. 1(8) Decision on Nicaragua, Art. 3(8) Decision on Guinea, Art. 1(10) Decision on Guinea-Bissau and Art. 27(11) Decision on Syria.

held.[1579] The Member State intending to grant such an exception must notify the Council, whose members may raise an objection within two working days. Despite any raised objections, the Council has the power to allow the proposed exemption via a qualified majority.[1580] Two notes must be made with regard to Iran. First, any intended derogation needs the previous approval of the UN Security Council. Second, an exemption may also be granted with the aim of furthering the objectives of resolution 2231 of the UN Security Council,[1581] including Article XV of the IAEA Statute.[1582] The notification requirement for authorizations referring to Yemen differs, as it only requires informing the 2140 Yemen Sanctions Committee within forty-eight hours.[1583]

314. The legal framework of Libya provides the Member States with the possibility to derogate from the imposed travel bank on two occasions. The first is the one explained in the preceding paragraph that requires notification to the Council and against which objection is possible.[1584] At the same time, the law assigns to Member States the power to determine on a case-by-case basis that entry or transit is required for the purpose of advancing peace and stability in Libya. On such an occasion, the Member State having decided so, has to notify the 1970 Libya Sanctions Committee within forty-eight hours.[1585]

315. Furthermore, the restrictions on admission automatically do not apply, when this is necessary for the fulfilment of a judicial process. No notification is required,[1586] with one exception where the Council must be informed.[1587] In certain cases, fulfilment of the judicial process is a ground for authorizing derogation from the travel ban, requiring notification to the Council and allowing for objections from members, as seen above (*see* in this regard paragraph 313 above).[1588] Other legislative acts are silent on this issue.[1589]

1579. Article 4(7) Decision on DRC, Art. 23(7) Decision on DPRK, Art. 19(7)(i) & (iii) Decision on Iran, Art. 1(8) Decision on Guinea-Bissau, Art. 5(5) Decision on South Sudan, Art. 1a(6) Decision on Mali, Art. 4(5) Decision on Zimbabwe, Art. 1(6) EU Decision on Iran, Art. 5(6) Decision on Myanmar/Burma, Art. 1(6) Decision on Burundi, Art. 6(6) Decision on Venezuela, Art. 1(6) Decision on Nicaragua, Art. 1 (3) EU Decision on Lebanon, Art. 3(6) Decision on Guinea, Art. 27(9) Decision on Syria and Art. 1(6) Decision on Drilling.
1580. Article 4(8) Decision on DRC, Art. 23(8) Decision on DPRK, Art. 19(8) Decision on Iran, Art. 1(9) Decision on Guinea-Bissau, Art. 5(6) Decision on South Sudan, Art. 1a(8) Decision on Mali, Art. 4(6) Decision on Zimbabwe, Art. 1(7) EU Decision on Iran, Art. 5(7) Decision on Myanmar/Burma, Art. 1(7) Decision on Burundi, Art. 6(7) Decision on Venezuela, Art. 1(7) Decision on Nicaragua, Art. 1 (8) EU Decision on Lebanon, Art. 3(7) Decision on Guinea, Art. 27(10) Decision on Syria and Art. 1(8) Decision on Drilling.
1581. S/RES/2231 of 20 Jul. 2015.
1582. Article 19 (10) and (7)(ii) Decision on Iran respectively.
1583. Article 2a(4) Decision on Yemen.
1584. Article 8(9) & (10) Decision on Libya.
1585. Article 8(5)(a) Decision on Libya.
1586. Article 1(4) Decision on Guinea-Bissau, Art. 8(5)(a) Decision on Libya and Art. 2a(3) Decision on Yemen.
1587. Article 4(3)(d) & (6) Decision on DRC.
1588. Article 1a(7) Decision on Mali, Art. 1(7) & (8) EU Decision on Lebanon, Art. 1(7) & (8) Decision on Drilling.
1589. These are the Decision on DPRK, the Decision on Somalia, the Decision on Iran, the Decision on Guinea-Bissau, the Decision on Libya, the Decision on South Sudan, the Decision on

316. Imposing said restrictive measures is without prejudice to obligations under international law, namely where a Member State is a host country of an international intergovernmental organization, such as the OSCE, or an international conference convened by the UN or under its auspices, as well as under a multilateral agreement conferring privileges and immunities or under 1929 Treaty of Conciliation between the Holy See and Italy,[1590] as explicitly stated in some EU legislative acts.[1591]

II Sanctions on Transfer of Goods

317. The restrictive measures on the transfer of goods are broken down into restrictions on cargo, vessels and aircraft.

A Sanctions with Regard to Cargo

318. Generally, cargoes related to the DPRK are inspected, whereas certain cargoes related to Iran may not be loaded or unloaded in ports of EU Member States. Cargo that originates from the DPRK, is destined for the DPRK, has been brokered or facilitated by the DPRK, including its nationals, individuals and entities and persons designated under resolutions 1718 and 2094 of the UN Security Council, or transported on a DPRK-flagged vessel, an aircraft registered in the DPRK or a stateless vessel or aircraft, is liable for inspection.[1592] Such cargo entails personal luggage and checked baggage within or transiting through the Union including airports, seaports and free zones. The inspection aims to ensure that cargo does not contain any items prohibited by certain resolutions of the UN Security Council[1593] and the Regulation on DPRK.[1594]

319. In the cases where cargo is transiting through the EU or is situated within the EU, but falls outside the scope of the aforementioned measure, it is still liable for

Zimbabwe, the EU Decision on Iran, the Decision on Myanmar/Burma, the Decision on Burundi, the Decision on Venezuela, the Decision on Nicaragua, the Decision on Guinea and the Decision on Syria.

1590. Inter Sanctam Sedem et Italiae Regnum Conventiones, Trattato fra la Santa Sede e l' Italia XXI Acta Apostolicae Sedis 209 et seq. (1929).

1591. Article 4(4) Decision on DRC, Art. 23 (4) & (5) Decision on DPRK, Art. 19(4) & (5) Decision on Iran, Art. 1(3) & (4) EU Decision on Iran, Art. 8(6) & (7) Decision on Libya, Art. 5(2) & (3) Decision on South Sudan, Art. 1a(3) & (4) Decision on Mali, Art. 5(3) & (4) Decision on Myanmar/Burma, Art. 1(3) & (4) Decision on Burundi, Art. 6(3) & (4) Decision on Venezuela, Art. 1(3) & (4) Decision on Nicaragua, Art. 1(3) EU Decision on Lebanon, Art. 3(3) & (4) Decision on Guinea, Art. 1(5) & (6) Decision on Guinea-Bissau, Art. 27(6) & (7) Decision on Syria and 1(3) Decision on Drilling.

1592. Articles 38(1)(a), (b), (c) & (d) and 34(4) and Annex XIII Regulation on DPRK.

1593. These are S/RES/1718 of 14 Oct. 2006, S/RES/1874 of 12 Jun. 2009, S/RES/2087 of 22 Jan. 2013, S/RES/2094 of 7 Mar. 2013, S/RES/2270 of 2 Mar. 2016, S/RES/2321 of 30 Nov. 2016, S/RES/2371 of 5 Aug. 2017.

1594. Article 38(1) Regulation on DPRK.

inspection, when there are reasonable grounds to believe that it may contain items prohibited by the Regulation on DPRK.[1595]

320. None of the aforementioned measures intrudes into the inviolability and protection of diplomatic and consular bags under the 1961 and 1963 Vienna conventions.[1596,1597]

321. Turning to the restrictions that certain Iran-related cargoes face, it is specified that the cargoes under restriction are cargoes of vessels owned or controlled by the IRISL and cargoes of vessels owned or controlled by designated entities owned or controlled by IRISL or acting on its behalf. These may not be loaded or unloaded in ports of EU Member States. They are neither to be impounded nor to be detained.[1598]

B Sanctions with Regard to Vessels

322. The imposed restrictive measures with regard to vessels include denial of servicing, access to ports and some other services, as well as seizure. Such measures are set in view of the situation in the DPRK and Iran. The term vessels lacks definition; albeit the term *a vessel crewed by the DPRK* stands for a vessel whose manning is controlled by a person of the DPRK or a vessel actually manned by nationals of the same state.[1599]

323. Servicing vessels of the DPRK, such as bunkering and ship-supply services, is prohibited, when the vessels in question carry prohibited items. Knowledge of such cargo may be based on information that provides reasonable grounds to believe so. This prohibition does not apply when the provision of said services is necessary for humanitarian purposes.[1600] Similar is the relevant provision in the Regulation on Iran, which prohibits servicing of vessels controlled by Iranians that carry either prohibited items or items listed in the EU Common Military List. Exceptionally servicing may take place for humanitarian purposes, like with regard to the DPRK, or safety purposes,[1601] unlike with regard to the DPRK. Said prohibitions apply for as long as cargo in such vessels is being inspected and seized or disposed of, as the case may be. Any seizure or disposal is performed, in accordance with the national legislation, at the expense of the importer or is recovered from anyone else responsible for the illicit supply, sale, transfer or import.[1602]

1595. Article 38(2) Regulation on DPRK.
1596. Vienna Convention on Diplomatic Relations (Vienna 1961) 500 UNTS 95 (1964) and Vienna Convention on Consular Relations (Vienna 1963) 596 UNTS 261 (1967).
1597. Article 38(4) Regulation on DPRK.
1598. Article 23(2) Regulation on Iran.
1599. Article 2(24) Regulation on DPRK.
1600. Article 38(4) Regulation on DPRK.
1601. Article 37(1) Regulation on Iran.
1602. Article 37(3) Regulation on Iran.

324. Furthermore, vessels related to the DPRK are denied access to ports in the territory of the Union. Vessels are related to the DPRK, when they are owned, operated or crewed by said state as well as when they are flagged to same state.[1603] Ownership needs neither be direct nor certain, when the alleged owner is a designated person or entity; reasonable grounds to believe so suffice. This level of certainty equally applies to control of such a vessel by a designated person and to the belief that it contains items prohibited under the Regulation on DPRK.[1604] Moreover, specifically designated vessels by the UN that are listed in the Regulation on DPRK are prohibited entry into ports of the Union.[1605] Lastly, no access to ports of the Union is provided to vessels refusing to be inspected, when such an inspection has been authorized by the flag state of the vessel or the state of registration. No such authorization is necessary, when the vessel in question is without nationality.[1606]

325. At the same time, it is prohibited to lease or charter vessels to the DPRK, designated persons and entities, other DPRK entities, other persons and entities that have assisted in violating resolutions of the UN Security Council,[1607] including persons and entities acting on their behalf or at the direction of them.[1608] It is also prohibited to procure vessel crew services from the DPRK.[1609] The same applies to owning, leasing and chartering any vessel flagged to the DPRK, including providing vessel classification services and associated services.[1610] It is similarly prohibited to apply for or to assist in the registration or maintenance on the register of any vessel controlled or owned by the DPRK or DPRK nationals, as well as any designated vessel,[1611] or any deregistered vessel under resolutions of the UN Security Council.[1612] Providing insurance or reinsurance services to DPRK vessels and to designated vessels is also not allowed.[1613]

326. Finally, DPRK vessels are seized, when the 1718 DPRK Sanctions Committee has so specified and the designated vessels are listed in the Regulation on DPRK.[1614] Currently, two vessels, three cargo vessels, three merchant vessels, three tankers, three oil tankers and one crude oil tanker have been designated as vessels subject to seizure since 30 March 2018.[1615]

1603. Article 39(1)(a) & (b) Regulation on DPRK.
1604. Article 39(1)(c) & (d) Regulation on DPRK.
1605. Article 39(1)(g) and Annex XIV Part B Regulation on DPRK.
1606. Article 39(1)(e) & (f) Regulation on DPRK.
1607. These are the following: S/RES/1718 of 14 Oct. 2006, S/RES/1874 of 12 Jun. 2009, S/RES/2087 of 22 Jan. 2013, S/RES/2094 of 7 Mar. 2013, S/RES/2270 of 2 Mar. 2016, S/RES/2321 of 30 Nov. 2016 and S/RES/2371 of 5 Aug. 2017.
1608. Article 43(1)(a) and Annexes XIII, XV, XVI and XVII Regulation on DPRK.
1609. Article 43(1)(b) Regulation on DPRK.
1610. Article 43(1)(c) and (d) & Annex XVIII Regulation on DPRK.
1611. Article 43(1)(e) & Annex XVIII *ibid.*
1612. Deregistration is set out in: para. 24 of S/RES/2321 of 30 Nov. 2016, para. 8 of S/RES/2375 of 11 Sep. 2017, para. 12 of S/RES/2397 of 22 Dec. 2017.
1613. Article 43(1)(e) & (f) and Annex XVIII Regulation on DPRK.
1614. Article 34(2) and Annex XIV Part A Regulation on DPRK.
1615. Annex XIV Part A Nos 1 to 15 Regulation on DPRK.

C Sanctions with Regard to Aircraft

327. The DPRK, Iran and Syria aircraft are subject to restrictions. Any aircraft operated by DPRK carriers or originating from the DPRK may not operate in the Union, in the sense of taking off, landing and overflying.[1616] Nonetheless, operations may take place for humanitarian purposes and other purposes consistent with the Regulation on DPRK, including landing for inspection and emergency landing.[1617]

328. At the same time, similarly to the sanctions with regard to vessels already explained (*see* in this regard paragraph 323 above), it is prohibited to lease or charter aircrafts to the DPRK, designated persons and entities, other DPRK entities, other persons and entities that have assisted in violating resolutions of the UN Security Council,[1618] including persons and entities acting on their behalf or at the direction of them.[1619] It is also prohibited to procure aircraft crew services from the DPRK.[1620]

329. Restrictions with regard to aircrafts of Iran, relate solely to cargo aircrafts and require reasonable grounds, but no absolute certainty, to determine that they carry items listed in the EU Common Military List or prohibited under the Regulation on Iran. Cargo aircrafts subject to these measures are such aircrafts that are owned or controlled, directly or indirectly, by an Iranian person, entity or body. When these conditions are met neither engineering services nor maintenance services may be provided, unless these are necessary for humanitarian purposes or safety.[1621] These prohibitions apply for as long as cargo in such vessels is being inspected and seized or disposed of, as the case may be. Any such seizure or disposal is done under the applicable national law, while the expenses are borne by the importer or are recovered from anyone else responsible for the illicit supply, sale, transfer or import.[1622] The formulation of this prohibition is almost identical to the prohibition of bunkering and ship supply services to Iranian vessels (*see* in this regard paragraph 323 above) and to DPRK vessels (*see* in this regard paragraph 323 above).

330. Lastly, cargo flights operated by Syrian carriers and all flights operated by Syrian Arab Airlines do not have access to airports in the Union. Circumventing this prohibition, including attempt to do so, is also prohibited.[1623] Nonetheless two exceptions apply. Aircrafts engaged in non-scheduled international air services do have

1616. Article 41(1) Regulation on DPRK.
1617. Articles 42 and 41(2)(a) & (b) Regulation on DPRK.
1618. These are the following: S/RES/1718 of 14 Oct. 2006, S/RES/1874 of 12 Jun. 2009, S/RES/2087 of 22 Jan. 2013, S/RES/2094 of 7 Mar. 2013, S/RES/2270 of 2 Mar. 2016, S/RES/2321 of 30 Nov. 2016 and S/RES/2371 of 5 Aug. 2017.
1619. Article 43(1)(a) and Annexes XIII, XV, XVI and XVII Regulation on DPRK.
1620. Article 43(1)(b) Regulation on DPRK.
1621. Article 37(2) Regulation on Iran.
1622. Article 37(3) Regulation on Iran.
1623. Article 26a(1) & (3) Regulation on Syria.

access to such airports, where landing is for non-traffic or non-commercial traffic purposes. The same applies to aircrafts engaged in scheduled international air services, as long as landing is for non-traffic purposes.[1624] Said restrictions do not apply to flights with the sole aim of evacuating citizens of the Union and their family members from Syria.[1625]

III Sanctions and Transfer of Goods

331. Generally, importing, exporting and transiting ordinary goods to, from and through the Union requires the disclosure of certain information assisting in risk analysis for these goods, as provided in the Union Customs Code.[1626] The 'pre-departure declaration' can have the form of a *customs declaration*,[1627] either standard or simplified,[1628] where the goods leaving the territory of the Union are placed under a customs procedure requiring such declaration, a *re-export declaration*[1629] or an *exit summary declaration*.[1630,1631] The customs office receiving a pre-departure declaration ensures that on the basis of the submitted declaration, a risk analysis takes place, primarily for security and safety purposes.[1632] Goods brought into the Union most times need to be covered by an *entry summary declaration*[1633,1634] which contains all particulars necessary for risk analysis, and also for security and safety purposes.[1635]

1624. Article 26a(1)(a) & (b) Regulation on Syria. *See also* Convention on International Civil Aviation (Chicago 1944) 15 UNTS 295 and International Air Services Transit Agreement (Chicago 1944) 84 UNTS 389.
1625. Article 26a(2) Regulation on Syria.
1626. Regulation (EU) No. 952/2013 of the European Parliament and of the Council of 9 Oct. 2013 laying down the Union Customs Code, OJ L 269 10 Oct. 2013, p. 1, as last amended by Regulation (EU) 2022/2399 of the European Parliament and of the Council of 23 Nov. 2022 establishing the European Union Single Window Environment for Customs and amending Regulation (EU) No. 952/2013, OJ L 317 9 Dec. 2022, p. 1.
1627. In regard to the definition of *customs declaration see* Annex I p. 311 at 316 Art. 5(12) Regulation (EU) 952/2013.
1628. *See* Arts 162 and 166 Regulation (EU) 952/2013 respectively.
1629. In regard to the definition of *re-export declaration see* Annex I p. 311 at 330 Art. 5(13) Regulation (EU) 952/2013 On this declaration *see* Arts 270 & 158-195 *ibid*.
1630. In regard to the definition of *exit summary declaration see* Annex I p. 311 at 319. Art. 5(10) Regulation (EU) 952/2013 On this declaration *see* Art. 271 Regulation (EU) 952/2013.
1631. Article 263(3) Regulation (EU) 952/2013.
1632. Article 264 Regulation (EU) 952/2013. *Risk analysis* is also mentioned in the old, and now repealed, Modernized Customs Code (Art. 176(1)(e) Regulation (EC) No. 450/2008 of the European Parliament and of the Council of 23 Apr. 2008 laying down the Community Customs Code, OJ L 145, 4 Jun. 2008, p.1) but not in the previous Community Customs Code (Council Regulation (EEC) No. 2913/92 of 12 Oct. 1992 establishing the Community Customs Code, OJ L 302, 19 Oct. 1992, p. 1).
1633. In regard to the definition of *entry summary declaration see* Annex I p. 311 at 319 Art. 5(9) Regulation (EU) 952/2013.
1634. Article 127(1) & (8) Regulation (EU) 952/2013. On the exceptions *see* Art. 127(2) Regulation (EU) 952/2013.
1635. Articles 127(5) and 128 Regulation (EU) 952/2013.

332. Certain, but not all, legislative acts on restrictive measures refer to said obligations, usually with the term pre-arrival and pre-departure information.[1636] In addition to these, the person having the duty to produce the customs declaration has to declare whether the goods are covered by the EU Common Military List or by the respective regulation. If the goods are subject to authorization, the same person is further obliged[1637] to specify 'the particulars of the export license granted'[1638] or 'the goods and technology covered by the export license granted'.[1639] In a different case, said person has to declare whether the respective goods are covered by the EU Common Military List *and* specify the particulars of the export license granted;[1640] thus requiring neither a declaration nor a specification with regard to other goods and technology, perhaps due to the fact that no other goods and technology are sanctioned in the relevant legislation. These additional elements are to be submitted either in written form or using a customs declaration, as appropriate.[1641] Finally, with regard to Iran any authorizations required under the apposite legislation need to be *presented* alongside the customs declarations.[1642]

333. From the provisions already explained three notes are to be taken. At the outset, unlike the general spirit and structure of the EU legislation on sanctions, the provisions requiring additional declarations alongside the ordinary customs declaration are neither identical nor duplicate; they merely bear a similarity, whereas the Regulation on Iran is clearly different. Second, many other pieces of EU legislation on sanctions provide for restrictions on dual use items, items on the EU Common Military List and equipment used for internal repression. Still, these are silent on any documentation to be submitted alongside the ordinary customs declaration.

1636. Article 4 Regulation on Libya, Art. 3a(1) Regulation on Somalia and Art. 9(1) Regulation on DPRK. The Regulation on Iran makes mention of 'advance information' determined in the summary declarations and customs declarations of the Community Customs Code (Art. 36 Regulation on Iran).
1637. Article 4 Regulation on Libya and Art. 9(1) Regulation on DPRK.
1638. Article 4 Regulation on Libya.
1639. Article 9(1) Regulation on DPRK.
1640. Article 3a(3) Regulation on Somalia.
1641. Article 4 Regulation on Libya, Art. 9(2) Regulation on DPRK and Art. 3a(5) Regulation on Somalia. The Regulation on DPRK allows for submission, aside in written form, in any other electronic form, deviating from the other two ones.
1642. Article 36 Regulation on Iran.

CHAPTER 4

Restrictive Measures Against Non-state Actors

334. Joining the fight against terrorism, the Union has imposed restrictive measures targeting terrorists in general as well as specific terrorists, those being Al-Qaida, ISIL (Da'esh) and the Taliban. Another set of legislative acts imposes sanctions due to a specific terrorist act, that being the assassination of Rafiq Hariri. Unlike the predecessors, the targets of this cluster of measures are non-state actors. This is a superordinate concept that encompasses all actors in international relations that are not states, such as individuals and companies, international organizations, terrorists and transnational criminal organizations.[1643] It arose in contingent circumstances, as pragmatism mandates to treat attacks by terrorist groups on an equal footing with attacks carried out by states.[1644] The common thread unifying all these diverse actors is the fact that they all wield power, albeit in different forms and extend; some contribute positively to security and stability, whereas others actively undermine it.[1645] Terrorists do the latter. Specifically within the frame of non-proliferation of weapons of mass destruction, *non-state actors* have been defined as 'individual[s] or entit[ies], not acting under the lawful authority of any State in conducting activities [...]'.[1646] More generally, it has been established that non-state actors have a legal personality, although different from the one that states have.[1647] They do bear obligations set out on a host of international

1643. Markus Wagner, *Non-state Actors* MPEIL (2013) para. 1; Andrea Teftedaria, Edwin Bakker et al., *Non-state Actors and Individuals*, in: Jan Rood & Rosa Dinnissen (eds), An Uncertain World: Clingendael Strategic Monitor (2013) 88.
1644. *Markus Wagner* (n. 1643) para. 26.
1645. Peter Wijninga et al., *State and Non-state Actors: Beyond the Dichotomy*, in: J. van Esch et al (eds), Strategic Monitor 2014: Four Strategic Challenges (Hague Centre for Strategic Studies 2014) 141.
1646. UN Security Council resolution 1540 (2004) of 28 Apr. 2004; *Markus Wagner* (n. 1643) para. 2.
1647. Daragh Murray, *How International Humanitarian Law Treaties Bind Non-state Armed Groups* 20 (1) J.C.&S.L. 101 at 120 & 121 (2015) https://doi.org/10.1093/jcsl/kru010.

instruments, most notably resolutions of the UN Security Council,[1648] and are bound by customary international law.[1649]

335. The majority of the sanctions discussed in the ensuing paragraphs are multilateral, or UN-mandated, as they have been decided by the UN Security Council. In one case, the EU decided took the initiative to devise and design additional measures. On the EU level, the restrictive measures take effect, usually, by the Council, and other times by the Commission, at a two-level procedure, most of the times. This two-level procedure preconditions a decision of the competent authority of a Member State at a national level or a decision of the Security Council or a sanctions committee at the UN level. Following such a decision, EU institutions take up the torch and proceed with issuing a common position and a regulation. The similarity of both the measures and the exceptions thereto bring the EU legal instruments closer, whereas their differences make them drift apart.

§1 RESTRICTIVE MEASURES WITH REGARD TO TERRORIST ACTS IN GENERAL

336. The extraordinary events of September 11, attacks of a shadowy transnational terrorist network, re-shaped the world in many ways, including blurring, if not annihilating, the line distinguishing freedom fighters from terrorists. Russia's President Vladimir Putin, who used the analogy of Chechnya to interpret September 11, personally offered his condolences over the 'series of barbaric terrorist acts targeted against innocent people' to President George Bush.[1650] The UN Security Council responded by adopting resolution 1373[1651] Therein it reaffirmed the need to combat by all means threats to international peace and security caused by terrorist acts and recognized the need to prevent and suppress the financing and preparation of any acts of terrorism. It equally reaffirmed the principle that every state has the duty to refrain from organizing, instigating, assisting or participating in terrorist acts in another state or acquiescing in organized activities within its territory directed towards the commission of such acts.[1652] The Union implemented it by adopting a common position[1653]

1648. Vladyslav Lanovoy, *The Use of Force by Non-state Actors and the Limits of Attribution of Conduct* 28 (2) EJIL 563 at 564 (2017) https://doi.org/10.1093/ejil/chx029.
1649. *Daragh Murray* (n. 1647) 108.
1650. John O'Loughlin, Gearóid Ó Tuathail & Vladimir Kollov, *A 'Risky Westward Turn'? Putin's 9-11 Script and Ordinary Russians* 56(1) Eur.-Asia Stud. 3 at 3, 7 & 9 (2004) https://doi.org/10.1080/0966813032000161428.
1651. R/RES/1373 of 28 Sep. 2001.
1652. *Ibid.*, preamble.
1653. Council Common Position of 27 Dec. 2001 on the application of specific measures to combat terrorism (2001/931/CFSP), OJ L 344, 28 Dec. 2001, p. 93, as last amended by Council Decision (CFSP) 2023/1514 of 20 Jul. 2023 updating the list of persons, groups and entities subject to Arts 2, 3 and 4 of Common Position 2001/931/CFSP on the application of specific measures to combat terrorism, and repealing Decision (CFSP) 2023/422, OJ L 184, 21 Jul. 2023, p. 33.

('Common Position on Terrorism') and a regulation[1654] ('Regulation on Terrorism'). It declared that terrorism is a real challenge to the world and to Europe and made clear that the fight against terrorism will be a priority objective of the Union.[1655] Combating the threats to international peace and security, which is the purpose of the measures set out by said legislative acts, is an objective of fundamental public interest for the international community, the Courts of the EU confirmed.[1656] The Union also clarified that combating the funding of terrorism is a decisive aspect of the fight against terrorism.[1657] Against this backdrop, the concrete measures and specific content of the EU acts are analysed below.

I Scope of Application

337. With regard to the scope of application the aforementioned (*see* in this respect paragraphs 64 et seq. above) apply *mutatis mutandis*.[1658] However, one additional aspect is pivotal thereto; the notion of *terrorist acts*. At the level of the Union, an act may constitute a terrorist act, as long as it is performed intentionally, has the potential to seriously damage a country or an international organization and is committed with the aim to seriously intimidate a population, or compel a government or an international organization to do or not do anything, or to seriously destabilize or destroy the structures of a country or an international organization[1659] (in regard to the definition *see* Annex I p. 311).

338. The measures described below are intended to prevent the perpetration of terrorist acts in this sense or the repetition of such acts; they do not seek to accompany or support national criminal procedures.[1660] Hence, they are based more on the appraisal of a present or future threat than on the evaluation of past conduct.[1661] It is precisely on this temporal point that said measures differentiate from the offences and

1654. Council Regulation (EC) No. 2580/2001 of 27 Dec. 2001 on specific restrictive measures directed against certain persons and entities with a view to combating terrorism, OJ L 344, 28 Dec. 2001, p. 70, as last amended by Commission Implementing Regulation (EU) 2022/595 of 11 Apr. 2022 amending certain Regulations concerning restrictive measures and setting out a single list for the Annexes to those Regulations containing the contact details of Member States' competent authorities and the address for notifications to the European Commission, OJ L 114, 12 Apr. 2022, p. 60.
1655. Recital No. 1 to the preamble of Regulation on Terrorism.
1656. *Yusuf* 2005 (n. 18) para. 298.
1657. Recital No. 2 to the preamble of Regulation on Terrorism.
1658. Articles 10(1) to (5) & 11 Regulation on Terrorism.
1659. Council Common Position of 27 Dec. 2001 on the application of specific measures to combat terrorism (2001/931/CFSP) OJ L 344, 28 Dec. 2001, p. 93, as last amended by Council Decision (CFSP) 2023/1514 of 20 Jul. 2023 updating the list of persons, groups and entities subject to Arts 2, 3 and 4 of Common Position 2001/931/CFSP on the application of specific measures to combat terrorism, and repealing Decision (CFSP) 2023/422, OJ L 184, 21 Jul. 2023, p. 33.
1660. *Al-Aqsa* 2012 (n. 680) para. 67 ('Al-Aqsa 2012').
1661. *PMOI I* (n. 48) para. 110; *Al-Aqsa* 2010 (n. 42) para. 142.

sanctions described under the directive on combating terrorism,[1662] which prescribes penalties for past conduct.[1663]

339. The definition of terrorism, as set out above, has been neither disputed nor challenged before the Courts of the EU to date. Still, they have noted the absence of a universally-accepted definition of the concepts of *terrorism* and *terrorist act*.[1664] The aforementioned definition is broad and is not confined within a specific territory. Arguing that no terrorist acts were perpetrated within the EU is irrelevant and has been rejected by the Courts of the EU.[1665] Still, a mere act of murder or attempted murder may not be regarded as an act of terrorism.[1666]

340. The objections that have been raised and discussed relate to the context of such acts. The most predominant one consisted of the argument that the persons in question were freedom fighters conducting armed conflict under international humanitarian law.[1667] This line of reasoning failed to convince the Courts of the EU, which maintained the view that existence of armed conflict, if any, does not preclude the application of the EU law relating to terrorism, should a terrorist act take place in the context of that conflict. In truth, such an act could also trigger the provisions of international humanitarian law on breaches of law of war.[1668] Another objection related to the function of the group in question that was in fact participating in a government and thus exercised sovereign authority, suggesting that the principle of non-intervention should be applied.[1669] The Courts of the EU could not agree with this suggestion deciding that the applicant was not a state within the meaning of international law and that the legitimate-government status may not be extended to groups to which some of its members are delegated.[1670] This line of reasoning per se seems to defy credulity, as a government is a representative of the State by which it has been appointed.[1671] The creation of an organ that functions as a government and its competence are domestic issues reserved to the national law of each individual

1662. Directive (EU) 2017/541 of the European Parliament and of the Council of 15 Mar. 2017 on combating terrorism and replacing Council Framework Decision 2002/475/JHA and amending Council Decision 2005/671/JHA, OJ L 88, 31 Mar. 2017, p. 6. *See* in particular Arts 11 and 18.
1663. *A and Others* 2020 (n. 55) para. 82.
1664. *OMPI* (n. 50) para. 104.
1665. *PMOI I* (n. 48) para. 148.
1666. *Jose Maria Sison v. Council*, T-341/07 Judgment of 30 Sep. 2009, digital ECR, para. 134 ('Sison 2009').
1667. *See Liberation Tigers of Tamil Eelam v. Council of the European Union*, Joined T-208/11 and T-508/11, Judgment of 16 Oct. 2014, digital ECR, para. 54 ('LTTE 2014'); *A and Others v. Minister van Buitenlandse Zaken*, C-158/14, Judgment of 14 Mar. 2017, digital ECR, para. 45 ('A and Others 2017').
1668. *LTTE* 2014 (n. 1667) para. 63; *A and Others 2017* (n. 1667) paras 88 and 97; *Hamas v. Council of the European Union*, T-400/10 RENV, Judgment of 14 Dec. 2018, digital ECR, para. 351 ('Hamas 2018').
1669. *Hamas* 2018 (n. 1668) paras 154, 366 & 367.
1670. *Hamas* 2018 (n. 1668) paras 156 & 157.
1671. *Certain Questions Relating to Settlers of German Origin in the Territory Ceded by Germany to Poland*, PCIJ Advisory Opinion No. 6 of 10 Sep. 1923, digital PCIJ Rep p. 22.

State.[1672] Thus, it would be more helpful, if the Courts of the EU had been willing to discuss and consider the other fundamental elements of a state under customary international law, those being a defined territory, a permanent population, the *effectiveness* of its government and the capacity to enter into relations with other States,[1673] should such a finding had been incumbent to reach a decision.

II The Restrictive Measures

341. The aim pursued by the measures described below is to combat terrorism and eliminate the threat to international peace and security caused by terrorist acts.[1674] It is aspired to achieve this by preventing the financing of acts of terrorism.[1675]

342. The restrictive measures mandated by the Regulation on Terrorism are twofold and share the common denominator of proscribing the use of assets. They consist of freezing funds and prohibiting financial services.

A Financial Sanctions

343. The Regulation on Terrorism provides for financial sanctions in the sense of freezing all funds, other financial assets and economic resources and preventing anyone from making available funds, other financial assets and economic resources.[1676]

344. The objective element of these measures differs from the pattern identified and described above, as it consists of the notion of *funds, other financial assets and economic resources*. It has been defined as 'assets of every kind, whether tangible or intangible, movable or immovable, however acquired, and legal documents or instruments in any form, including electronic or digital, evidencing title to, or interest in, such assets, including, but not limited to, bank credits, travelers' cheques, bank cheques, money orders, shares, securities, bonds, drafts and letters of credit'.[1677] This notion emulates the one of *economic resources* that was treated as a separate one in the aforementioned legislative acts as well as in the ones described below.

345. The targets of these measures are persons: committing, or attempting to commit, participating in or facilitating the commission of any act of terrorism; legal persons owned or controlled by such; and persons acting on their behalf or at their direction.[1678]

1672. Siegfried Magiera, *Governments* MPEPIL 2007 para. 5.
1673. Sean D. Murphy, *Democratic Legitimacy and the Recognition of States and Governments* 48(3) ICLQ 545 at 546 (1999) https://doi.org/10.1017/s0020589300063430.
1674. *PMOI I* (n. 48) para. 129.
1675. *A and Others2017* (n. 1667) para. 96.
1676. Article 2(1)(a) & (b) Regulation on Terrorism.
1677. Article 1(1) Regulation on Terrorism.
1678. Article 2(3) Regulation on Terrorism. The description of the actions rendering a person eligible for listing is remarkable close to the one in R/RES/1373 of 28 Sep. 2001 para. 1(c).

These form the subjective element of the prohibition. In this regard the following three issues must be highlighted: the notion of 'persons, groups and entities involved in terrorist acts'; the notion of ownership; and the notion of control.

346. The Courts of the EU within the frame of the regulation discussed here, adjudicated that the term *person* means someone or something with legal personality, and therefore both a natural and a legal person.[1679] At the same time *groups* and *entities* may be other types of social organizations, which although they do not have legal personality none the less, they exist in a more or less structured form.[1680] At the same time, it has been statutory set that the notion of *persons, groups and entities involved in terrorist acts* is broad and includes both persons committing terrorist acts and persons facilitating such acts, as well as entities owned by such persons and persons acting on their behalf (in regard to the definition *see* Annex I p. 311 at 330).[1681]

347. The criterion of *ownership of a legal person, group or entity* (in regard to the definition *see* Annex I p. 311 at 329) is satisfied, when such a person, group or entity is possessed by at least 50%; nonetheless a majority interest also suffices.[1682] Ownership within the framework of terrorism that is discussed here, is identical to the one set out in the EU Guidelines, albeit it predates them. Thus, it would be more appropriate to suggest that the Regulation on Terrorism influenced the EU Guidelines.

348. The criterion of *controlling a legal person, group or entity*[1683] (in regard to the definition *see* Annex I p. 311 at 314) is fulfilled, when the exercise of control is demonstrated by holding any of the following rights. That can be having appointed or having a right to appoint or remove the majority of a management body of such a person, controlling the majority of shareholders' voting rights, having the right both directly and indirectly to exercise a dominant influence over such a person, having the right to use assets of such a person, managing the business of such a person, sharing jointly and severally the financial liabilities of such a person, or guaranteeing same liabilities. As seen already with regard to ownership (*see* in this regard paragraph 347 above), this definition is identical to the one portrayed in the EU Guidelines, but the latter were issued after the Regulation on Terrorism.

349. When the objective and the subjective element have been satisfied, funds, other financial assets and economic resources are frozen,[1684] in the sense of preventing any move, transfer, alteration, use of or dealing with funds in any way that would result in any change in their volume, amount, location, ownership, possession, character, destination or other change that would enable the funds to be used, including portfolio management.[1685] There is no need for establishing that the transferred funds, were

1679. *Al-Aqsa* 2010 (n. 42) para. 57.
1680. *Ibid.*, para. 58.
1681. Article 1(2) Common Position on Terrorism.
1682. Article 1(5) Regulation on Terrorism.
1683. Article 1(6) Regulation on Terrorism.
1684. Article 2(1)(a) Regulation on Terrorism.
1685. Article 1(2) Regulation on Terrorism.

actually used to finance terrorist activities.[1686] At the same time, no funds, other financial assets and economic resources shall be made available.[1687] As this has a wide meaning encompassing all the acts necessary if a person or entity on the list is effectively to obtain full power of disposal in respect of the funds, other financial assets and economic resources concerned.[1688]

350. As a final remark, activities aimed to circumvent the explained prohibitions are prohibited.[1689]

B Prohibition of Financial Services

351. The other restrictive measure foreseen in the Regulation on Terrorism relates to financial services, which builds the objective element of this prohibition. The term *financial services* includes any service of a financial nature such as insurance, insurance-related and banking as well as asset management, credit reference, investment research and advice, and advice on acquisitions and corporate restructuring[1690] (in regard to the statutory definition *see* Annex I p. 311 at 323).

352. The subjective element of the restrictive measure is identical to the one explained above (*see* in this regard paragraphs 344 et seq. above). Thus, the aforementioned apply *mutatis mutandis*.

353. The restrictive measure consists of prohibiting the provision of financial services to designated persons or for their benefit.[1691] Participating in activities the object or effect of which is to circumvent this prohibition, is also prohibited.[1692]

354. On a final note, the principle of proportionality is absent from both the legislative text and the jurisprudence under the present regulation, but for a single succinct reference.[1693] Rather, it is preferred to discuss the *appropriateness* of the measures.[1694] In any event, the wording of the provision does not leave any room for considerations or manoeuvres.

III The Exceptions to the Restrictive Measures

355. The explained restrictive measures are subject to exceptions that can be granted by the competent authorities of the Member States under any conditions that they

1686. *E and F* (n. 350) para. 76.
1687. Article 2(1)(b) Regulation on Terrorism.
1688. *E and F* (n. 350) para. 67.
1689. Article 3(1) Regulation on Terrorism.
1690. Article 1(3) Regulation on Terrorism.
1691. Article 2(2) Regulation on Terrorism.
1692. Article 3(1) Regulation on Terrorism.
1693. *Al-Aqsa* 2012 (n. 680) paras 122 and 130.
1694. *See*, for example, *Al-Aqsa* 2012 (n. 680) para. 123; *LTTE* 2014 (n. 1667) para. 163.

deem proper. These statutory exceptions consist of exceptions for basic needs[1695] (*see* in this regard paragraph 132 above) and charges for maintenance of the accounts[1696] (*see* in this regard paragraph 133 above). Payments to a designated person may also be performed, as long as they are due under contracts made before the Regulation on Terrorism came into force and they are made into a frozen account within the Union[1697] (*see* in this regard paragraph 134 above). The Regulation on Terrorism lacks exceptions for extraordinary expenses (*see* in this regard paragraph 132 above), payments due to a contract by a designated person (*see* in this regard paragraph 135 above), enforcement of judgments and awards (*see* in this regard paragraph 137 above), crediting of accounts (*see* in this regard paragraph 139 above) and professional fees and incurred expenses (*see* in this regard paragraph 138 above). The latter has not hindered the CJEU from ordering costs both in favour of beneficiaries of frozen accounts and against them. Although the logic behind such a decision is reasonable, in the sense that the taxpayer cannot be expected to finance the legal struggles of persons involved in terrorists' acts, the departure from the letter of a statutory provision in an environment predominantly influenced by legal positivism, could be strange, especially when the author of a legal provision enjoys benefits from a provision that it did not dictate. This is even more so when other regulations on restrictive measures explicitly provide for payment of professional fees associated with legal services.

356. Finally, the Regulation on Terrorism allows for an exception to the described prohibitions with a view to the protection of the interests of the Community, which include the interests of its citizens and residents. This ground is not further elaborated. It is prescribed though, that the competent authorities of a Member State may grand an authorization after consultation with the competent authorities of the other Member States, the Council and the Commission. To this end, they are obliged to communicate to them the grounds on which they intend to grant an authorization or reject a request along with the conditions that they deem necessary for preventing the financing of acts of terrorism. Any comments made within two weeks are to be taken into account when they intend to grant an authorization.[1698]

IV The Decisions Imposing Restrictive Measures

357. At the outset, mention deserves the observation made by the CJEU with regard to the difference between the Regulation on Terrorism and the Regulation on Al-Qaida, which is analysed below (*see* in this regard paragraphs 386 et seq. below). The Court underlined that resolution 1373 of the UN Security Council mandating the freezing of assets and the prohibition of financial services that is implemented by the regulation discussed here, does not specify individually the persons targeted. It neither establishes a procedure for freezing their assets nor provides any safeguards for the designated

1695. Article 5(2)(1) & (2)(2)(a) Regulation on Terrorism.
1696. Article 5(2)(2)(b) Regulation on Terrorism.
1697. Article 5(2)(3) Regulation on Terrorism.
1698. Article 6(2) Regulation on Terrorism.

persons to be afforded the opportunity to challenge the measures imposed. Such *essentialia* are to be specified by states at the national level or, in the case of the Union, at the EU level.[1699] This observation equally signifies the differentiation of the regulation discussed here from the ones analysed in the chapter above.

358. Under the Regulation on Terrorism the procedure, which may culminate in freezing funds and assets takes place at two levels; at a national one and at the level of the Union.[1700] In this regard significant is the reciprocal duty among the Member States and the institutions of the Union to cooperate in good faith, enshrined in Article 4(3) of the TEU, that is especially binding in the area of Justice and Home Affairs.[1701] *In concreto* the Common Position on Terrorism[1702] introduces a specific form of cooperation between the Council and the Member States, as the Council defers the assessment to be conducted as far as possible to authorities of the Member States. This extends to recognizing potential restrictions on access to evidence or clues, legally justified under national law on grounds of overriding public policy, public security or the maintenance of international relations.[1703] Nonetheless, under exceptional circumstances, where the person concerned disputes on the basis of concrete evidence that the authorities of the Member States observed fundamental rights, the Court must ascertain whether those rights were observed.[1704] To date, the CJEU has not done so.

A The Procedure at the National Level

359. In the first phase, a competent national authority, in principle judicial, must take a decision within the meaning of Article 1(4) of the Common Position on Terrorism.[1705] The administrative and non-judicial nature of such a decision is not decisive for the application of this provision.[1706] More specifically, it is not required that this decision is taken in the context of criminal proceedings *stricto sensu*; it is sufficient that the national proceedings aim to combat terrorism.[1707] The scope of this requirement is to ensure that persons are included on the basis of a sufficiently solid factual basis.[1708]

360. From the wording of this provision[1709] the Courts of the EU concluded that administrative authorities are not excluded from the notion of *competent authority*, as

1699. *OMPI* (n. 50) paras 101 and 102.
1700. *Al-Aqsa* 2010 (n. 42) para. 78; *Sison* 2009 (n. 1666) para. 93.
1701. *LTTE* 2014 (n. 1667) para. 133; *Sison* 2009 (n. 1666) para. 94; *OMPI* (n. 50) para. 123; *Al-Aqsa* 2010 (n. 42) paras 79 and 80.
1702. Article 1(4) Common Position on Terrorism.
1703. *OMPI* (n. 50) para. 124, citing *Postbank v. Commission*, T-353/94, Judgment of 18 Sep. 1996, digital ECR para. 69.
1704. *Gamaa Islamya Êgypte v. Council*, T-643/16, Judgment of 10 Apr. 2019, digital ECJ para. 132 ('Gamaa Islamya Êgypte'), referring by analogy to *Minister for Justice and Equality (Deficiencies in the System of Justice)*, C-216/18, Judgment of 25 Jul. 2018, digital ECJ para. 36.
1705. *OMPI* (n. 50) para. 117.
1706. *Gamaa Islamya Êgypte* (n. 1704) para. 110.
1707. *Al-Aqsa 2010* (n. 42) para. 98; *Gamaa Islamya Êgypte* (n. 1704) para. 119; *LTTE* 2014 (n. 1667) para. 113.
1708. *LTTE* 2017 (n. 390) para. 26 ('LTTE 2017').
1709. *Al-Aqsa* 2010 (n. 42) para. 88.

long as: (a) those authorities are actually vested, in national law, with the power to adopt restrictive decisions against groups involved in terrorism; and (b) those authorities, although only administrative, may be regarded as 'equivalent' to judicial authorities.[1710] The latter takes place, when their decisions are open to judicial review.[1711] The concept of *competent authority* is not confined to the authorities of Member States; moreover, it may extend to authorities of third states,[1712] as it was done a number of times.[1713] However, in such a case, the Council must verify, whether that decision was adopted in accordance with the rights of the defence and the right to effective legal protection.[1714]

361. The decision of a competent authority may have two forms. It can be a decision to 'instigat[e] … investigations or prosecut[e]' in the sense of forming part of national proceedings seeking, directly and chiefly, the imposition on the person concerned of measures of a preventive or punitive nature, in connection with the combating of terrorism and by reason of that person's involvement in terrorism.[1715] A decision of a national judicial authority that rules only incidentally and indirectly on the possible involvement of the person concerned in a terrorist activity in a dispute concerning civil rights and duties does not satisfy this requirement.[1716] The requirement of 'precise information' and 'serious and credible evidence or clues' aims to establish that the involvement of the person concerned in terrorist activities is based on clues assessed as credible by the national authorities and has led them, at the very least to adopt measures of enquiry, without requiring the national decision to have been taken in a specific legal form or to have been published or notified.[1717]

362. The persons concerned do enjoy the protection of fundamental rights at this level. However, the authority to assess whether these are observed belongs to the national courts and not the Council.[1718]

B The Procedure at the EU Level: The Initial Decision

363. In the second phase, the Council, acting by unanimity – and not by qualified majority as it was originally suggested[1719] – must decide whether to include the party

1710. *LTTE* 2014 (n. 1667) para. 107; *Gamaa Islamya Êgypte* (n. 1704) para. 111.
1711. *PMOI I* (n. 48) para. 145; *Gamaa Islamya Êgypte* (n. 1704) para. 112.
1712. *LTTE* 2017 (n. 390) para. 22; *PKK v. Council*, T-316/14, Judgment of 15 Nov. 2018, digital ECR para. 64 ('PKK 2018').
1713. *See*, for example, *Gamaa Islamya Êgypte* (n. 1704) paras 75 & 81.
1714. *LTTE* 2017 (n. 390) para. 31; *Gamaa Islamya Êgypte* (n. 1704) para. 85; *PKK* 2018 (n. 1712) para. 65.
1715. *Sison* 2009 (n. 1666) para. 111; *Al-Aqsa* 2010 (n. 42) para. 101.
1716. *Al-Aqsa* 2010 (n. 42) para. 101.
1717. *Ibid.*, para. 69.
1718. *Gamaa Islamya Êgypte* (n. 1704) para. 132.
1719. Council of the European Union, *Amended Proposal for a Council Regulation on Specific Restrictive Measures Directed Against Certain Persons and Entities with a View to Combating Terrorism: 15201/01*, Interinstitutional File 2001/0228(CNS), Brussels, 11 Dec. 2001, digital database Consilium.

concerned in the list, on the basis of precise information or material in the relevant file, which indicates that a decision at a national level had been made. Verification of the existence of a decision of a national authority is an essential condition for the adoption of this initial decision.[1720] Specifically, the obligation to verify that decisions are 'based on serious and credible evidence or clues' concerns only decisions to instigate investigations or prosecution; it does not concern condemnation decisions, as dictated by the principle of sincere cooperation.[1721] However, the Council is under no obligation to include in the list any person in respect of whom a decision has been taken by a competent authority,[1722] and it does enjoy broad discretion in its assessment of the matters to be taken into consideration for the purposes of adopting restrictive measures.[1723]

364. The list of designated persons[1724] was initially incorporated in a council decision,[1725] and since June 2009 in regulations, later implementing regulations.[1726] Their nature is not an exclusively legislative one. At the same time, it is an act which imposes an individual economic and financial sanction.[1727] Regarding their content, it is set out that they must include sufficient particulars appended to permit effective identification of specific human beings, legal persons, entities or bodies.[1728] With regard to their form, the CJEU held that establishing a list does not necessarily mean that the authority did not carry out an individual appraisal in respect of each of those persons or entities prior to their inclusion in the lists, or that the appraisal must necessarily be arbitrary or unfounded.[1729]

365. In this context of imposing financial sanctions, safeguarding the right to a fair hearing is imperative.[1730] The following two aspects of this fundamental right are

1720. *OMPI* (n. 50) para. 117.
1721. *Gamaa Islamya Êgypte* (n. 1704) paras 141 & 142.
1722. *OMPI* (n. 50) para. 145.
1723. *PMOI I* (n. 48) para. 137; *OMPI* (n. 50) para. 159; *Sison* 2009 (n. 1666) para. 97; *People's Mojahedin Organization of Iran v. Council*, T-284/08, Judgment of 4 Dec. 2008, digital ECR para. 55 ('PMOI II').
1724. *See* Art. 2(3) Regulation on Terrorism.
1725. *See*, for example, the first issued decision: 2001/927/EC: Council Decision of 27 Dec. 2001 establishing the list provided for in Art. 2(3) of Council Regulation (EC) No. 2580/2001 on specific restrictive measures directed against certain persons and entities with a view to combating terrorism, OJ L 344, 28 Dec. 2001, p. 83.
1726. *See* the first issued regulation: Council Regulation (EC) No. 501/2009 of 15 Jun. 2009 implementing Art. 2(3) of Regulation (EC) No. 2580/2001 on specific restrictive measures directed against certain persons and entities with a view to combating terrorism and repealing Decision 2009/62/EC, OJ L 151, 16 Jun. 2009, p. 14. The regulation in power at the present time is Council Implementing Regulation (EU) 2021/1188 of 19 Jul. 2021 implementing Art. 2(3) of Regulation (EC) No. 2580/2001 on specific restrictive measures directed against certain persons and entities with a view to combating terrorism, and repealing Implementing Regulation (EU) 2021/138, OJ L 258, 20 Jul. 2021, p. 14.
1727. *OMPI* (n. 50) para. 98.
1728. Article 1(5) Common Position 2001/931.
1729. *LTTE 2014* (n. 1667) para. 115; *Gamaa Islamya Êgypte* (n. 1704) para. 122; *Hamas* 2018 (n. 1668) para. 274; *Hamas v. Council*, T-289/15, Judgment of 6 Mar. 2019, digital ECR para. 85 ('Hamas 2019 A').
1730. *OMPI* (n. 50) para. 108.

applicable, subject to expressions. First, the party concerned must be informed of the evidence adduced against it to justify the proposed sanction. Second, he or she must be afforded the opportunity effectively to make known her view on that evidence.[1731] Still, under circumstances involving freezing assets of persons identified as being involved in terrorist acts, the right to a fair hearing may be restricted.[1732] The Court has repeatedly held that if the aforementioned safeguards apply in such circumstances before the adoption of the initial decision to freeze funds, it could lead to jeopardizing the effectiveness of the sanctions. As a consequence, it continues, the manifestation of this right would be incompatible with the public interest objective pursed by Regulation on Terrorism.[1733] This line of argument generated the 'surprise effect' that financial sanctions are expected to have. Nonetheless, the persons concerned must have the opportunity to request an immediate re-examination of the initial measure. Such an opportunity is granted in the form of eligibility for filing an action before the Court of First Instance; thus both the fundamental rights of the persons concerned and the need for prevention of terrorism are ensured.[1734] Similarly, overriding considerations concerning the security of the Union and its Member States or the conduct of their international relations may preclude the communication to the parties concerned of certain evidence adduced against them and, in consequence, the hearing of those parties with regard to such evidence during the administrative procedure.[1735] Still, the general principle of observance of the right to a fair hearing requires, unless precluded by overriding considerations concerning the security of the Union and its Member States, or the conduct of their international relations that the evidence adduced against the party concerned, should be notified to it, in so far as possible, either concomitantly with or as soon as possible after the adoption of an initial decision to freeze funds.[1736] However, observance of this right does not require that the evidence adduced against the person concerned be notified to him or her before the adoption of an initial measure to freeze funds, or that that party automatically be heard after the event in such a context.[1737]

366. The statement of reasons is an essential part of the Council's decision. Neither the Regulation on Terrorism nor the Common Position on Terrorism, unlike the legislative acts already examined, state anything in this regard. However, Article 296 TFEU is applicable; thus, the statement of reasons must disclose in a clear and unequivocal fashion the reasoning followed by the Council so that the persons concerned are able to ascertain the reasons for the measure for the purpose of assessing whether it is well

1731. *Ibid.*, para. 93.
1732. *Ibid.*, para. 127.
1733. *Ibid.*, para. 128, citing *Yusuf 2005* (n. 18) para. 308.
1734. *OMPI* (n. 50) para. 130.
1735. *Ibid.*, para. 133, citing *Yusuf 2005* (n. 18) para. 320; *France v. People's Mojahedin Organization of Iran*, C-27/09 P, Judgment of 21 Dec. 2011, digital ECR para. 67 ('PMOI III').
1736. *OMPI* (n. 50) para. 137.
1737. *Ibid.*

founded and to enable the court having jurisdiction to exercise its power to review.[1738] The statement of reasons must be appropriate to the measure at issue and to the context in which it is adopted. The circumstances of each case dictate the requirements that the statement of reasons needs to satisfy, in particular the content of the measure in question, the nature of the reasons given and the interest which the addresses of the measure, or other parties to whom it is of direct and individual concern, may have in obtaining explanations. In particular, it is not necessary for the reasoning to go into all the relevant facts and points of law or to provide a detailed answer to the considerations set out by the person concerned when consulted prior to the adoption of that same measure. The question of whether the statement of reasons is sufficient must be assessed with regard to its wording, its context and all the legal rules governing the matter in question. Consequently, the reasons provided for a specific measure can be efficient if that measure was adopted in a context, which was known to that person and which enables him or her to understand the scope of the measure concerning him or her.[1739] The degree of precision of the statement of reasons for a decision must be weighed against practical realities and the time and technical facilities available for making the decision.[1740]

367. More specifically, such a decision may not have a statement of reasons that consists merely of a general, stereotypical formulation. Far from that, it is required to state the matters of fact and law, which constitute the legal basis of the decision and the considerations that led to its adoption. Thus, it must indicate the actual and specific reasons why the Council considers that the relevant rules are applicable to the party concerned.[1741] In other words, it must refer to the statutory conditions of application of the Regulation on Terrorism and also to the reasons why the Council considers, in the exercise of its discretion that such a measure must be adopted in respect of the person concerned, unless overriding considerations concerning the security of the Union and its Member States or the conduct of their international relations mitigate against it.[1742] Finally, in the case that the competent authority in question is an authority of a third country, the information to be included in the statement of reasons must include the reasons which led the Council to consider that that decision on which it relies has been adopted in accordance with the principle of the rights of the defence and the right to effective judicial protection.[1743] If necessary, such information may be brief.[1744]

1738. *Al-Aqsa* 2012 (n. 680) para. 138; *LTTE 2017* (n. 390) para. 29; *PKK* 2021 (n. 391) para. 47 ('PKK 2021'); *Stichting Al-Aqsa v. Council*, T-327/03, Judgment of 11 Jul. 2007, digital ECR para. 58 ('Al-Aqsa 2007'); *OMPI* (n. 50) para. 141.
1739. *Al-Aqsa* 2012 (n. 680) paras 139 to 141; *Rosneft* 2017 (n. 32) paras 120-122; *Iran Shipping Lines and Others v. Council*, C-225/17 P, Judgment of 31 Jan. 2019, digital ECR para. 69; *PKK* 2021 (n. 1738) para. 48.
1740. *OMPI* (n. 50) para. 141.
1741. *Ibid*, adopting the approach in *Roman Parra v. Commission*, T-117/01, Judgment of 20 Feb. 2002, digital ECR para. 31, and *Napoli Buzzanca v. Commission*, T-218/02, Judgment of 29 Sep. 2002, digital ECR, para. 74. *See also Al-Aqsa* 2007 (n. 1738) para. 54; *LTTE* 2014 (n. 1667) para. 161.
1742. *OMPI* (n. 50) para. 146; *LTTE* 2014 (n. 1667) para. 162; *Sison* 2009 (n. 1666) para. 60.
1743. *LTTE* 2017 (n. 390) para. 33; *Gamaa Islamya Êgypte* (n. 1704) para. 87.
1744. *Gamaa Islamya Êgypte* (n. 1704) para. 88.

However, the mere indication that the decision in question was published in an official journal of a third country, without providing any further information, is insufficient to establish that the Council carried out the requisite verification as to whether the rights of the defence had been respected in that other country.[1745] The mere reference to sections of legislative provisions and to a periodical revision by an administrative body equally do not suffice for concluding that a thorough examination of the guarantees for the right to defence and the right to effective judicial protection took place.[1746]

368. The issue of publication of the statement of reasons is a separate one. The Courts of the EU, taking into account the regulatory nature of a decision to impose restrictive measures, found that a detailed publication of the complaints put forward against the persons concerned might conflict with overriding considerations of public interest, and cause serious damage to their reputation. Therefore, it adopted the view that, exceptionally, only the operative part of the decision and a general statement of reasons need to be in the version to be published in the Official Journal. The actual, specific statement of reasons for that decision must be formalized and brought to the knowledge of the persons concerned by other appropriate means.[1747] Nonetheless, the aforementioned overriding considerations concerning the security of the Union and its Member States, or the conduct of their international relations discussed above restricting the right to a fair hearing, may preclude disclosure of the specific and complete reasons. Thus, these reservations may equally restrict the obligation to state reasons.[1748]

369. Finally, authentication, especially of the statement of reasons that are sent privately to the person concerned, should be neither overlooked nor treated as a mere formality. The CJEU has reiterated that the authentication procedure provided for by the rules of procedure of the institution issuing the decision could not be assessed as a mere formality for archival purposes. Rather, it is intended to guarantee legal certainty by ensuring that the text adopted became fixed in the languages which were binding,[1749] and thus third parties have a means of verifying that the Council acts which are published or notified correspond to those that have been adopted. Therefore, authentication constitutes an essential procedural requirement[1750] and non-compliance leads to annulment. For instance, in a case, where the statement of reasons sent privately to the person concerned, was neither signed nor dated and the Council acknowledged at the hearing that it had not been signed by its President and Secretary-General, the contested measures were annulled.[1751]

1745. *Ibid.*, paras 100 to 102.
1746. *LTTE* 2014 (n. 1667) paras 146 & 147.
1747. *OMPI* (n. 50) para. 147; *Jose Maria Sison v. Council*, T-47/03, Judgment of 11 Jul. 2007, digital ECR para. 194 ('Sison 2007').
1748. *OMPI* (n. 50) para. 148; *Sison* 2007 (n. 1747) paras 180 & 195.
1749. *Gamaa Islamya Êgypte* (n. 1704) paras 198 & 199; *Commission v. BASF and Others*, C-137/92 P, Judgment of 15 Jun. 1994, digital ECR para. 75; *Hamas v. Council*, T-308/18, Judgment of 4 Sep. 2019, digital ECR, para. 273 ('Hamas 2019 B').
1750. *Gamaa Islamya Êgypte* (n. 1704) paras 200 & 202; *BASF and Others* (n. 1749) para. 76; *Hamas* 2019 B (n. 1749) para. 269 & 274.
1751. *Gamaa Islamya Êgypte* (n. 1704) paras 205, 210 & 230.

370. Turning to review of the lawfulness of the measures, the CJEU initially adopted the approach of the ECtHR and decided that it would examine: (a) whether the rules governing procedure and the statement of reasons have been complied with; (b) whether the facts are materially accurate; and (c) whether there has been a manifest error of assessment of the facts or misuse of power.[1752] However, the ensuing jurisprudence ruled that the Courts of the EU must not only establish whether the evidence relied on is factually accurate, reliable and consistent but must also ascertain whether that evidence contains all the relevant information to be taken into account in order to assess the situation and whether it is capable of substantiating the conclusions drawn from it.[1753]

371. During the proceedings, any objection that the evidence and information used by the Council are secret or confidential shall not deter the Courts of the EU from proceedings reviewing the lawfulness and merits of the measures.[1754] In order to protect and balance all interests involved, such as the government's interest in keeping information secret, the Courts of the EU have conducted confidential inspection, in the sense of inspecting alone documents, following the government's invitation and the applicant's agreement.[1755] Should a party to the trial wish to challenge the evidence adduced by the other party, the latter must satisfy two cumulative requirements.[1756] First, the challenge must be specific and detailed.[1757] Further, challenges to the accuracy of the facts must feature clearly in the first procedural document concerning the contested measures.[1758] Specifically, a person concerned may dispute all material relied on by the Council to demonstrate that the risk of her involvement in terrorist activities is ongoing, irrespective of their source.[1759] Then the burden of proof for establishing that the facts alleged are well-founded shifts to the Council. The Courts of the EU shall determine whether said facts are made out.[1760]

372. Should fund-freezing measures be annulled by the CJEU for any of the aforementioned issues, the Council bears first of all the obligation to ensure that subsequent fund-freezing measures adopted after the annulling judgment and governing periods subsequent to that judgment are not vitiated by the same defects or unlawfulness.[1761] The contested regulation itself that has been annulled does not necessarily cease to

1752. *OMPI* (n. 50) para. 159 citing ECtHR Application No. 9248/81, *Leander v. Sweden*, judgment of 26 Mar. 1987, HUDOC para. 59, and Application No. 50963/99, *Al-Nashify v. Bulgaria*, judgment of 20 Jun. 2002, HUDOC paras 123 & 124; *Sison v. Council*, Joined T-110/03, T-150/03 and T-405/03, Judgment of 26 Apr. 2005, digital ECR, para. 47 ('Sison 2005').

1753. *PMOI I* (n. 48) para. 138 citing *Lenzing* (n. 48) para. 57; *Sison* 2009 (n. 1666) para. 98; *Hamas v. Council*, T-400/10, Judgment of 17 Dec. 2014, digital ECR para. 90 ('Hamas 2014'); *Criminal Proceedings against K.P.*, C-458/15, Judgment of 20 Jun. 2019, digital ECR para. 48 ('K.P.').

1754. *OMPI* (n. 50) para. 155; *PMOI II* (n. 1723) para. 73.

1755. *Al-Aqsa* 2007 (n. 1738) para. 19.

1756. *Hamas* 2018 (n. 1668) para. 333; *Hamas* 2019 A (n. 1729) para. 150.

1757. *Hamas* 2018 (n. 1668) para. 334; *Hamas* 2019 A (n. 1729) para. 151.

1758. *Hamas* 2018 (n. 1668) para. 335; *Hamas* 2019 A (n. 1729) para. 152.

1759. *Hamas* 2018 (n. 1668) paras 104 & 331; *Hamas* 2019 B (n. 1749) para. 147; *LTTE* 2017 (n. 390) para. 71; *PKK* 2018 (n. 1712) para. 104.

1760. *Hamas* 2018 (n. 1668) para. 332; *Hamas* 2019 A (n. 1729) para. 149.

1761. *Al-Aqsa* 2010 (n. 42) para. 39.

produce effects; in truth, the CJEU has the power to provisionally maintain its effects for reasons of avoiding the risk of serious and irreversible harm to the effectiveness of the restrictive measures, and it has done so in a number of cases.[1762] Finally, the CJEU has underlined that annulling contested regulations does not imply any substantive assessment of the question of assessment of the person in question as a terrorist group.[1763]

C *The Procedure at the EU Level: Subsequent Decision(s)*

373. The Council bears the statutory duty to review the list every six months[1764] in order to ensure that grounds for keeping the persons on the list continue to exist. It also ensures that those who no longer meet the necessary criteria for inclusion are removed.[1765] The Council is expected to conclude the existence of an ongoing risk of that person or group being involved in the terrorist activities which justified their initial inclusion in the list,[1766] as maintaining these persons on the list is in essence, an extension of the initial decision to include them on the list.[1767] The Council, in reaching its conclusion, is required to verify whether, since that initial inclusion or, subsequently, the last review the factual situation has changed in such a way that it is no longer possible to draw the same conclusion in relation to the involvement of that person in terrorist activities.[1768] However, it is not obliged to establish that the person concerned is still engaged in terrorist activity.[1769] It further has to verify the consequences of the decision at the national level that initially led to the inclusion of that specific person in the list[1770] and it may not disregard subsequent developments arising out of the investigations or prosecution at hand.[1771] In one instance, the judicial authority competent to review the lawfulness of the acts of the national authority had described the refusal to lift the concerned person's proscription as 'unreasonable' and 'perverse' and, in the other, when the Council adopted the consequent decision, it had been informed on the refusal to grant a leave for appeal. Importantly, the CJEU assessed the gravity of this legal aspect under the institution's duty to state reasons (*see* in this respect paragraphs 378 et seq. below), in the sense that it had failed to provide legal justification for continuing to freeze the applicant's funds.[1772] However, in

1762. *LTTE* 2014 (n. 1667) para. 228; *K.P.* (n. 1753) para. 60; *Hamas* 2014 (n. 1753) para. 145.
1763. *LTTE* 2014 (n. 1667) para. 226; *Hamas* 2014 (n. 1753) para. 142.
1764. Article 2(3) Regulation 2580/2001 and Art. 1(6) Common Position 2001/931/CFSP.
1765. *Hamas* 2018 (n. 1668) para. 189; *Al-Aqsa* 2012 (n. 680) para. 129.
1766. *Council v. Hamas*, C-79/15 P, Judgment of 26 Jul. 2017, digital ECR para. 29 ('Hamas 2017').
1767. *Hamas* 2018 (n. 1668) para. 229; *Hamas* 2019 A (n. 1729) para. 33; *LTTE* 2017 (n.390) para. 61.
1768. *LTTE* 2017 (n. 390) paras 46 & 51; *K.P.* (n. 1753) para. 43; *PKK* 2021 (n. 391) para. 48; *Hamas* 2014 (n. 1753) para. 215.
1769. *PMOI I* (n. 48) para. 107.
1770. *OMPI* (n. 50) para. 117; *Al-Aqsa* 2010 (n. 42) para. 164; *LTTE* 2014 (n. 1667) para. 158; *Hamas* 2014 (n. 1753) para. 85; *Sison* 2009 (n. 1666) para. 116.
1771. *Al-Aqsa* 2010 (n. 42) para. 164; *Sison* 2009 (n. 1666) para. 116.
1772. *PMOI I* (n. 48) paras 184 & 185.

another instance, where the national decision was repealed *ex nunc*, without retroactive effect, for the sole reason of preventing an overlap between the national fund freezing measure imposed by the national authority and the fund freezing measure prescribed at the EU level, the validity of the consequent decision was not affected.[1773]

374. The Council is not obliged to acquire any new material on which it may rely.[1774] Nonetheless, while performing this statutory duty the Council has the power to rely on information that has not derived from decisions of a competent authority, in order to attribute to a person already included in the list, responsibility for incidents and to categorize them as terrorist acts and thus justify her retention on the list.[1775] Thus, the Council can base the decision to retain a person on the list on more recent facts that may come from sources other than national decisions adopted by competent authorities.[1776] Such sources can be the press and the internet[1777] as well as *sensitive documents*[1778] (in regard to the definition *see* the Glossary, Annex I p. 311, at 331). In any event, the Council cannot be required to state with greater precision in what way freezing the specific funds may in concrete terms contribute to the fight against terrorism or to produce evidence to show that the person concerned might use her funds to commit or facilitate acts of terrorism in the future.[1779] The CJEU has accepted the view, according to which cessation of activities by such an organization is not in itself a guarantee that the organization concerned will not resume them at any moment, as well as that a purported renunciation of violence expressed in that context ought not necessarily to be believed. As a matter of fact, the absence of activity might be the result of the effectiveness of the restrictive measures.[1780] On the contrary, in another case, a military defeat was accepted as a significant change in circumstances that called into question the concerned person's involvement in terrorist activities.[1781]

375. Importantly, at this stage, it is no longer necessary to ensure a surprise effect in order to guarantee the effectiveness of the sanctions. Therefore, any such subsequent decision must be preceded by the possibility of a further hearing and, where appropriate, notification of any new evidence.[1782] Thus, the Council must afford the persons concerned the opportunity effectively to make known their views on the matter.[1783] Subsequent to any overriding considerations concerning the security of the Union or its Member States, or the conduct of their international relations, any subsequent decision

1773. *Al-Aqsa* 2010 (n. 42) paras 84, 85 & 110.
1774. *Sison* 2005 (n. 1752) para. 32; *LTTE* 2017 (n. 390) para. 62; *PKK* 2018 (n. 1712) para. 74.
1775. *PKK* 2018 (n. 1712) para. 76.
1776. *Gamaa Islamya Êgypte* (n. 1704) para. 155.
1777. *LTTE*2014 (n. 1667) paras 71 & 72; *LTTE* 2017 (n. 390) paras 47, 63-68 & 72; *Hamas* 2017 (n. 1766) paras 26 & 35; *Hamas* 2018 (n. 1668) para. 94.
1778. *Jose Maria Sison v. Council*, C-266/05 P, Judgment of 1 Feb. 2007, paras 47 & 48.
1779. *Al-Aqsa* 2010 (n. 42) para. 143.
1780. *PMOI I* (n. 48) para. 111.
1781. *LTTE* 2017 (n. 390) para. 79.
1782. *OMPI* (n. 50) para. 131; *PMOI* 2011 (n. 1735) para. 62; *Hamas* 2018 (n. 1668) para. 167; *Sison* 2007 (n. 1747) paras 212 & 213; *Fahas* (n. 796) para. 60.
1783. *OMPI* (n. 50) para. 132.

to freeze funds must, in principle, be preceded by notification of any new evidence adduced and a hearing.[1784]

376. As already discussed in the initial decision, the statement of reasons must refer both to the legal conditions of application of the regulation in question and in particular to the existence of a national decision taken by a competent authority and to the actual and specific reasons why the Council considers, in the exercise of its discretion that the person or entity concerned must be made the subject of a funds freezing measure.[1785] Especially, when the grounds of such a subsequent decision are in essence the same as those already relied on when a previous decision was adopted, a mere statement to that effect may suffice, particularly, when the person concerned is a group or entity.[1786] Moreover, in the absence of any other relevant evidence, a similarity of texts of the reasons stated in the initial decision to include the person on the list and of the reasons stated in the subsequent decision does not establish that the Council failed, when assessing the case, to afford proper consideration to the arguments put forward by the party concerned in arguing its case.[1787] Still, stating that it was 'desirable' or 'decided' to adopt an up-to-date list was not accepted as a valid statement of reasons.[1788] In a specific listing, where the Council was invoking, in general terms, the possession of weapons, without providing a date or location and was implying that the person concerned had an intention which was not substantiated by any given or determinable fact, the CJEU found itself in a situation, where it was impossible for it to carry out the required review. Thus, the aforementioned requirements (*see* in this regard paragraphs 370 et seq. above) were not met.[1789]

377. Turning to judicial review, the first issue that arises relates to the successive decisions issued implementing the Regulation on Terrorism due to the six-month review duty. This results in an applicant filing an application against a decision, which during the proceedings is repealed and replaced by another measure with the same subject matter. The CJEU has taken the view that this constitutes a new factor allowing the applicant to adapt its claims and pleas in law. Requesting a fresh application would be contrary to the principle of due administration of justice and to the requirements of procedural economy.[1790] Furthermore, allowing an institution, in order to counter criticisms of a measure contained in an application to the EU judicature, to amend the contested measure or to substitute another for it and to rely in the proceedings on such an amendment or substitution and in this manner depriving the other party of the opportunity of extending its original pleadings to the latter measure or of submitting supplementary pleadings directed against that decision, would be inequitable.[1791]

1784. *Ibid.*, para. 137; *PMOI III* (n. 1735) para. 75.
1785. *Sison* 2007 (n. 1747) para. 60; *Hamas* 2014 (n. 1753) para. 89.
1786. *PMOI I* (n. 48) para. 81; *Fahas* (n. 796).
1787. *PMOI I* (n. 48) para. 95, citing by analogy *Thyssen Stahl v. Commission*, T-141/94, Judgment of 11 Mar. 1999, digital ECR paras 117 & 118.
1788. *Al-Aqsa* 2007 (n. 1738) para. 55; *Sison* 2007 (n. 1747) para. 216.
1789. *Gamaa Islamya Êgypte* (n. 1704) paras 165 & 166.
1790. *PMOI I* (n. 48) para. 46; *Al-Aqsa* 2010 (n. 42) para. 44.
1791. *OMPI* (n. 50) paras 28 & 29, citing, *Alpha Steel Ltd. v. Commission*, 14/81, Judgment of 3 Mar. 1982, digital ECR para. 8; *Fabrique de fer de Charleroi SA and Dillinger Hüttenwerke AG v.*

However, the CJEU may not perform a speculative review of an act that has not yet been adopted.[1792] In addition, repealing and replacing a measure adversely affecting the applicant with another one with the same subject matter does not deprive the applicant of the interest in obtaining annulment of all contested measures, despite some of them having been repealed and replaced, insofar as such repeal does not constitute recognition of the unlawfulness of the measure and only has prospective effect.[1793]

378. The Courts of the EU are required to determine whether the obligation to state reasons laid down in Article 296 TFEU has been complied with, and therefore, whether the reasons relied on are sufficiently detailed and specific, as well as whether those reasons are substantiated.[1794] Regarding the ability of the person concerned to dispute the material on which the Council relied in order to establish the risk,[1795] the aforementioned apply *mutatis mutandis* (*see* in this regard paragraph 373 above).

V Absences and Absentees

379. Under the statutory provisions elaborated above, both natural and legal persons can become subjects of restrictive measures. The procedure selected has been assessed as appropriate. It is explicitly armed with the advantage of surprise and with restrictions to the right of fair hearing aiming at the efficient implementation of the measures and therefore preserving international security and peace. However, the authors seem to have passed over the reality of the corporate world, where very little can be overlooked and the corporate veil dominates. The EU provisions on company data[1796] are of average velocity and impact, in view of the meagre information on companies' registries and the habitual use of nominees. That cannot be said for the provisions on piercing the corporate veil, which are almost non-existent. Ordinary businesses use elaborate corporate structures for tax purposes. The logic dictates that shadowy and flagrant persons shall opt for serpentine ones making their detection a Herculean task.

Commission, Joined 351/85 and 360/85, Judgment of 29 Sep. 1987, digital ECR, para. 11; *Stahlwerke Peine-Salzgitter AG v. Commission*, 103/85, Judgment of 14 Jul. 1988, digital ECR, paras 11 & 12; and *Council of European Municipalities and Regions (CEMR) v. Commission*, T-46/98 and 151/98, Judgment of 3 Feb. 2000, digital ECR, para. 33.

1792. *Al-Aqsa* 2007 (n. 1738) para. 36.

1793. *Al-Aqsa* 2010 (n. 42) para. 45; *OMPI* (n. 50) para. 35; *PMOI I* (n. 48) paras 45-48; *Sison* 2009 (n. 1666) paras 47 & 48; *Hamas* 2014 (n. 1753) para. 59.

1794. *LTTE 2017* (n. 390) para. 70.

1795. *Ibid.*, para. 71.

1796. Initially introduced by the First Directive on Company Data, First Council Directive 68/151/EEC of 9 Mar. 1968 on co-ordination of safeguards which, for the protection of the interests of members and others, are required by Member States of companies within the meaning of the second paragraph of Article 58 of the Treaty, with a view to making such safeguards equivalent throughout the Community, OJ L 65, 14 Mar. 1968, p. 8. In the meantime this has been repealed and replaced twice. The instrument now in force is Directive (EU) 2017/1132 of the European Parliament and of the Council of 14 Jun. 2017 relating to certain aspects of company law, OJ L 169, 30 Jun. 2017, p. 46.

The Whistleblowing Directive[1797] could shed some hope, although possibly only a grim one, in view of its implementation date, which came twenty years after the Regulation on Terrorism, and of its scope of application that requires fifty or more workers. A small company's incorporation office staffed with four persons can do the trick. And that is just an example.

380. To be fair, the Regulation on Terrorism does include a provision on professional secrecy and mandates to go beyond that. It imposes the duty to provide immediately any information which would facilitate compliance with this regulation to the Member States that shall then convey it to the Commission. Also, it imposes the duty to cooperate in any verification of this information.[1798] It further ensures that any information received in this manner shall be solely used for the purposes for which it was provided or received.[1799] Perhaps the simplicity of this provision disguises its might, or perhaps there is more that can be done.

381. Finally, a brief note on the absentees. The persons against whom the aforementioned measures are imposed are associated with various terrorist groups such as the PKK. Still, some groups indigenous on the European continent, enjoying widespread publicity and having inflicted terror, thus qualifying as terrorist groups, are absent. Indicative of such groups are Camorra of Italy and Conspiracy of Cells of Fire (a.k.a. Synomosia Pyrinon tis Fotias) of Greece, which nonetheless have been enlisted in the US list of terrorist groups.[1800] Equally absent are groups such as Nordkreuz that do inflict terror in the sense of attacking synagogues and opening fire against migrants, and none the less tend to be indicted by the national judiciary for illegal possession of weapons, if at all.[1801] The absence of such groups from the Brussels' list is surprising, if not bewildering, and a solid reasoning for deciding to omit those seems hard to imagine, especially since the aim of the Regulation on Terrorism is to fight terrorism whatever form it may take[1802] and the reference to *international* terrorism[1803] was abandoned for the sake of terrorism in a broad sense that does not differentiate between internal and external terror. Thus, it is here suggested that national authorities and the Council exercise the authority and power given to them to designate further terrorist groups and their members and prevent them from having access to funds and economic resources.

1797. Directive (EU) 2019/1937 of the European Parliament and of the Council of 23 Oct. 2019 on the protection of persons who report breaches of Union law, OJ L 305, 26 Nov. 2019, p. 17.
1798. Article 4(1) Regulation 2580/2001.
1799. Article 4(2) Regulation 2580/200.
1800. *See* in this regard, U.S. Department of Treasury, Office of Foreign Assets Control, *Specially Designated Nationals and Blocked Persons List* (last updated: 10 Jan. 2022), available: https://home.treasury.gov/policy-issues/financial-sanctions/specially-designated-nationals-and-blocked-persons-list-sdn-human-readable-lists (last visited:31 Dec. 2023).
1801. Katrin Bennhold, *Body Bags and Enemy Lists: How Far-Right Police Officers and Ex-Soldiers Planned for* 'Day X', The New York Times, 1 Aug. 2020 (updated 26 May 2021), available: https://www.nytimes.com.
1802. *LTTE* 2014 (n. 1667) para. 58.
1803. Proposal for a Council Regulation on specific restrictive measures directed against certain persons and entities with a view to combating international terrorism, COM/2001/0569 final - CNS 2001/0228, OJ C 25E, 29 Jan. 2002, p. 474.

VI Exchange of Information

382. The fundamental obligation to come forward with information necessary for the implementation of this regulation, despite the professional obligation for confidentiality, has already been explained above (*see* in this respect paragraph 122 above). In addition to this, it is provided that any information on circumventing this regulation – presently or in the past – shall be notified to the competent authorities of the Member States and to the Commission.[1804]

383. This regulation also imposes obligations related to the exchange of information to the Member States, the Council and the Commission. More specifically, it provides that they shall inform each other of the measures taken under this regulation and shall supply each other with information at their disposal in connection with this regulation as well as related to violation and enforcement problems or judgments of the national courts.[1805]

VII Breach of This Regulation

384. The Member States have the power to determine the sanctions to be imposed for infringement of the provisions of this regulation. The only guidance given at the EU level is that these sanctions must be effective, proportionate and dissuasive.[1806] This reflects a general principle that derived from Article 5 of the EEC Treaty (thereafter Article 5 of the EC Treaty, currently Article 5 of the TEU) and has been established via jurisprudence, which found that 'while the choice of penalties remains within their discretion, Member States must ensure in particular that infringements of [Union] law are penalised under conditions, both procedural and substantive, which are analogous to those applicable to infringements of national law of a similar nature and importance and which, in any event, make the penalty effective, proportionate and dissuasive'.[1807] Since then, said guidance has been provided in a number of instruments, such as the General Data Protection Regulation,[1808] the Directive on Internal Market for Electricity[1809] and the

1804. Article 3(2) Regulation 2580/2001.
1805. Article 8 Regulation 2580/2001.
1806. Article 9 Regulation 2580/2001.
1807. *See Commission v. Hellenic Republic*, 68/88, Judgment of 21 Sep. 1989, digital ECR, paras 23 & 24; *Criminal Proceedings against Silvio Berlusconi and Others*, Joined C-387/02, C-391/02 and C-403/02, Judgment of 3 May 2005, digital ECR, para. 35.
1808. Article 84 of Regulation (EU) 2016/679 of the European Parliament and of the Council of 27 Apr. 2016 on the protection of natural persons with regard to the processing of personal data and on the free movement of such data, and repealing Directive 95/46/EC, OJ L 119, 4 May 2016, p. 1.
1809. Article 59(3)(d) of Directive (EU) 2019/944 of the European Parliament and of the Council of 5 Jun. 2019 on common rules for the internal market for electricity and amending Directive 2012/27/EU, OJ L 158, 14 Jun. 2019, p. 125.

Directive on Payment Services.[1810] Thus, it is not indigenous to the fight against terrorism, but a general hallmark of EU law.

§2 RESTRICTIVE MEASURES WITH REGARD TO SPECIFIC TERRORIST ACTS

385. This part analyses restrictive measures which are directed against specific groups associated with terrorist acts, those being Usama bin Laden, the Al-Qaida network, ISIL (Da'esh), the suspected assassins of Rafiq Hariri and the Taliban, who in the meantime have become the government of Afghanistan. The imposed sanctions, which in their majority are UN-mandated, are financial (*see* in this regard paragraphs 393 et seq. below), related to energy (*see* in this regard paragraph 417 below), arms embargo (*see* in this regard paragraphs 418 et seq. below), internet hosting (*see* in this regard paragraphs 422 et seq. below) and travel bans (*see* in this regard paragraph 424 below).

I Overview of Legislative Acts

386. The restrictive measures against Usama bin Laden, the Al-Qaida network and ISIL (Da'esh) are both UN-mandated and autonomous. At the outset, it is noted that frequent mention of 'ISIL (Da'esh) and Al-Qaida or any cell, affiliate, splinter group or derivative thereof' is made. For purposes of brevity and in view of the fact that Al-Qaida was the predecessor of ISIL in Iraq,[1811] mention of *Al-Qaida* shall be deemed to be mention to the aforementioned cluster of persons and groups within the frame of the present analysis. The Union responding to a resolution of the UN Security Council on Afghanistan[1812] adopted a common position[1813] (the 'Decision on Al-Qaida') and a regulation[1814] (the 'Regulation on Al-Qaida'). The Union reiterated its determination to

---

1810. Article 103(1) Directive (EU) 2015/2366 of the European Parliament and of the Council of 25 Nov. 2015 on payment services in the internal market, amending Directives 2002/65/EC, 2009/110/EC and 2013/36/EU and Regulation (EU) No. 1093/2010, and repealing Directive 2007/64/EC, OJ L 337, 23 Dec. 2015, p. 35.

1811. TEABEAMET Estonian Information Board, *International Security and Estonia* (2016) 30; R/RES/2253 of 17 Dec. 2015.

1812. R/RES/1390 of 28 Jan. 2002.

1813. Council Common Position of 27 May 2002 concerning restrictive measures against Usama bin Laden, members of the Al-Qaida organization and the Taliban and other individuals, groups, undertakings and entities associated with them and repealing Common Positions 96/746/CFSP, 1999/727/CFSP, 2001/154/CFSP and 2001/771/CFSP (2002/402/CFSP), OJ L 139, 29 May 2002, p. 4 ('Common Position on Al-Qaida'). In 2016 it was repealed by Council Decision (CFSP) 2016/1693 of 20 Sep. 2016 concerning restrictive measures against ISIL (Da'esh) and Al-Qaeda and persons, groups, undertakings and entities associated with them and repealing Common Position 2002/402/CFSP, OJ L 255, 21 Sep. 2016, p. 25 ('Decision on Al-Qaida'). This was last amended by Council Decision (CFSP) 2023/2231 of 23 Oct. 2023 amending Decision (CFSP) 2016/1693 concerning restrictive measures against ISIL (Da'esh) and Al-Qaeda and persons, groups, undertakings and entities associated with them, digital OJ L of 24 Oct. 2023.

1814. Council Regulation (EC) No. 881/2002 of 27 May 2002 imposing certain specific restrictive measures directed against certain persons and entities associated with Usama bin Laden, the

combat terrorism in every form throughout the world and its pledge to the coalition of the international community to combat terrorism in every shape and form.[1815] To this end and in view of the continued threat posed by these persons, it continued to adopt resolutions of the UN Security Council,[1816] albeit not in full.[1817] The nature of the Regulation on Al-Qaida is not an exclusively legislative one, as despite its application to the generality of economic operators concerned, it is of direct and individual concern to individuals and groups, who are mentioned by name and against whom sanctions are imposed,[1818] the EU Courts ruled. Finally, it is here noted that in 2009 the Regulation on Al-Qaida was amended[1819] following a groundbreaking judgment of the CJEU,[1820] the *Kadi 2008*[1821] as will be discussed below (*see* in this regard paragraph 407 below).

387. The Union proceeded with adopting additional autonomous restrictive measures[1822] (the 'EU Regulation on Al-Qaida') parallel to the UN-mandated sanctions

Al-Qaida network and the Taliban, and repealing Council Regulation (EC) No. 467/2001 prohibiting the export of certain goods and services to Afghanistan, strengthening the flight ban and extending the freeze of funds and other financial resources in respect of the Taliban of Afghanistan, OJ L 139, 29 May 2002, p. 9, as last amended by Commission Implementing Regulation (EU) 2023/2670 of 22 Nov. 2023 amending for the 339th time Council Regulation (EC) No. 881/2002 imposing certain specific restrictive measures directed against certain persons and entities associated with the ISIL (Da'esh) and Al-Qaida organizations, digital OJ L, 24 Nov. 2023.

1815. Recital No. 1 to the preamble of Decision on Al-Qaida.
1816. R/RES/2253 of 17 Dec. 2015 via Decision on Al-Qaida.
1817. The following resolutions of the UN Security Council that are relevant to Al-Qaida condemn various acts and reaffirm the already imposed sanctions have not been transposed into EU law: S/RES/2331 of 20 Dec. 2016; S/RES/2347 of 24 Mar 2017; S/RES/2368 of 20 Jul. 2017; S/RES/2388 of 21 Nov. 2017; S/RES/2462 of 28 Mar. 2019; S/RES/2560 of 29 Dec. 2020. The specific risk of civil aviation being used for terrorist purposes, underlined in S/RES/2396 of 21 Dec. 2017, has been addressed via Directive (EU) 2016/681 of the European Parliament and of the Council of 27 Apr. 2016 on the use of passenger name record (PNR) data for the prevention, detection, investigation and prosecution of terrorist offences and serious crime, OJ L 119, 4 May 2016, p. 132. *See Ligue des droits humains ASBL v. Conseil des ministres*, C-817/19, Opinion of Advocate General of 27 Jan. 2022, digital ECR.
1818. *Yusuf 2005* (n. 18) para. 324; *Kadi* 2008 (n. 15) para. 241; *Omar Mohammed Othman v. Council of the European Union*, T-318/01, Judgment of 11 Jun. 2009, digital ECR para. 54 ('Othman').
1819. Council Regulation (EU) No. 1286/2009 of 22 Dec. 2009 amending Regulation (EC) No. 881/2002 imposing certain specific restrictive measures directed against certain persons and entities associated with Usama bin Laden, the Al-Qaida network and the Taliban, OJ L 346, 23 Dec. 2009, p. 42.
1820. Commission of the European Communities, Proposal for a Council Regulation amending Regulation (EC) No. 881/2002 imposing certain specific restrictive measures directed against certain persons and entities associated with Usama bin Laden, the Al-Qaida network and the Taliban, COM(2009) 0187 final, Explanatory Memorandum, paras 3 and 4, available: https://eur-lex.europa.eu (last visited 24 Jan. 2022). *See also European Parliament* (n. 194) para. 5.
1821. *Kadi* 2008 (n. 15).
1822. Council Regulation (EU) 2016/1686 of 20 Sep. 2016 imposing additional restrictive measures directed against ISIL (Da'esh) and Al-Qaeda and natural and legal persons, entities or bodies associated with them, OJ L 255, 21 Sep. 2016, p. 1, as last amended by Council Implementing Regulation (EU) 2023/1126 of 8 Jun. 2023 implementing Regulation (EU) 2016/1686 imposing additional restrictive measures directed against ISIL (Da'esh) and Al-Qaeda and natural and legal persons, entities or bodies associated with them, OJ L 149, 9 Jun. 2023, p. 13.

already imposed. It decided to do so in view of the threat to international security that Al-Qaida constitutes. It was able to do so, as restrictive measures in the context of the fight against Al-Qaida fall within the objectives of the CFSP of the Union as set out in Article 21(2)(c) of the TEU.[1823] The aim of such targeted measures is to prevent actions in support of Al-Qaida or on behalf thereof.[1824]

388. With regard to Afghanistan, the UN Security Council recognized that the security situation had evolved and reconciliation had progressed; nonetheless it noted that the situation in Afghanistan remained a threat to international peace and security and went on to impose financial sanctions, prohibition of entry and transit, as well as embargo of military equipment to persons designated as the Taliban and persons associated with them.[1825] In response, the Union adopted a decision[1826] ('Decision on Afghanistan') and a regulation[1827] ('Regulation on Afghanistan'). The Union has stated that the Regulation on Afghanistan respects both the fundamental rights and the principles recognized by the Charter of Fundamental Rights of the Union. It further respects the obligations of the Member States under the Charter of the UN as well as the legally binding nature of the resolutions of the UN Security Council.[1828]

389. On 14 February 2005 a terrorist bombing took place in Beirut, Lebanon, that killed former Lebanese Prime Minister Rafiq Hariri and twenty-two other persons and injured dozens of others. The Lebanese authorities were assisted in their investigation by the UN International Independent Investigation Commission that was established by the UN Security Council.[1829] This event was a terrorist act. The UN reaffirmed its commitment to the national unity and stability of Lebanon and underlined that it is unacceptable in principle for anyone to escape accountability for an act of terrorism for any reason. It further determined that this terrorist act and its implications constitute a threat to international peace and security.[1830] In view of these, it decided to assist the investigation of this crime by imposing financial sanctions and by preventing entry and

---

The Union chose not to adopt a specific and separate decision for the aforementioned regulation to implement. Rather, it decided to blend the necessary provisions into the Decision on Al-Qaida (*see*, for example, Arts 1(1), 2(2) and 3(3) Decision on Al-Qaida).

1823. Recital No. 8 to the preamble of Decision on Al-Qaida.
1824. Recital No. 10 to the preamble of Decision on Al-Qaida.
1825. R/RES/1988 of 11 Jun. 2011, paras 1(a), (b) and (c) Decision on Al-Qaida.
1826. Council Decision 2011/486/CFSP of 1 Aug. 2011 concerning restrictive measures directed against certain individuals, groups, undertakings and entities in view of the situation in Afghanistan, OJ L 199, 2 Aug. 2011, p. 57, as last amended by Council Decision (CFSP) 2022/153 of 3 Feb. 2022 amending Decision 2011/486/CFSP concerning restrictive measures directed against certain individuals, groups, undertakings and entities in view of the situation in Afghanistan, OJ L 25, 4 Feb. 2022, p. 17.
1827. Council Regulation (EU) No. 753/2011 of 1 Aug. 2011 concerning restrictive measures directed against certain individuals, groups, undertakings and entities in view of the situation in Afghanistan, OJ L 199, 2 Aug. 2011, p. 1, as last amended by Commission Implementing Regulation (EU) 2022/595 of 11 Apr. 2022 amending certain Regulations concerning restrictive measures and setting out a single list for the Annexes to those Regulations containing the contact details of Member States' competent authorities and the address for notifications to the European Commission, OJ L 114, 12 Apr. 2022, p. 60.
1828. Recital Nos 4 & 5 to the preamble of EU Regulation on Al-Qaida.
1829. R/RES/1595 of 7 Apr. 2005.
1830. R/RES/1636 of 31 Oct. 2005 preamble.

transit to persons designated as suspected of involvement to that act.[1831] The EU responded by adopting a common position[1832] (the 'Common Position with regard to Rafiq Hariri') and a regulation[1833] (the 'Regulation with regard to Rafiq Hariri').

II The Scope of Application

390. The scope of application of the legislative acts at hand is identical to the one already explained.[1834] Thus the aforementioned apply *mutatis mutandis* (*see* in this regard paragraphs 64 et seq. above). On a brief note, the Regulation on Al-Qaida entails an unusual provision that reads:

> This Regulation shall apply notwithstanding any rights conferred or obligations imposed by any international agreement signed or any contract entered into or any licence or permit granted before the entry into force of this Regulation.[1835]

391. It could be purported that this provision reflects the principle of supremacy of EU law or the principle of lex posterior derogat legi priori, or both. It consists of three parts: the one referring to international agreements, the one referring to contracts and the one referring to licences and permits. Thus, it addresses States, private persons and state authorities that have entered into or granted these instruments. The supremacy of Regulation 881/2002 in relation to the latter two parts seems almost self-evident. Even if this provision was absent, a contract, either in whole or in part, would be void due to violating statutory law. Similarly, any licence or permit cannot overhaul statutory provisions. Nevertheless, the first part raises concerns. International agreements are made between two or more sovereign states in exercise of their sovereign powers. They are governed by the Vienna Convention on the Law of the Treaties,[1836] which reflects customary international law. A peripheral international organization can neither interfere nor dictate any rules, regardless of the nobility of the pursued aim. In truth, Member States are under an obligation to comply according to the EU Treaties. However, this obligation does not and cannot extend to their respective counterparties

1831. Paragraph 3(a) R/RES/1636 of 31 Oct. 2005.
1832. Council Common Position 2005/888/CFSP of 12 Dec. 2005 concerning specific restrictive measures against certain persons suspected of involvement in the assassination of former Lebanese Prime Minister Rafiq Hariri, OJ L 327, 14 Dec. 2005, p. 26, as last amended by Council Decision (CFSP) 2022/153 of 3 Feb. 2022 amending Decision 2011/486/CFSP concerning restrictive measures directed against certain individuals, groups, undertakings and entities in view of the situation in Afghanistan, OJ L 25, 4 Feb. 2022, p. 17.
1833. Council Regulation (EC) No. 305/2006 of 21 Feb. 2006 imposing specific restrictive measures against certain persons suspected of involvement in the assassination of former Lebanese Prime Minister Rafiq Hariri, OJ L 51, 22 Feb. 2006, p. 1, as last amended by Council Regulation (EU) 2023/331 of 14 Feb. 2023 amending certain Council regulations concerning restrictive measures in order to insert provisions on a humanitarian exemption, OJ L 47, 15 Feb. 2023, p. 1.
1834. Articles 11 & 13 Regulation on Al-Qaida, Arts 18 & 19 EU Regulation on Al-Qaida, Arts 10 & 11 Regulation with regard to Rafiq Hariri and Arts 14 & 15 Regulation on Afghanistan.
1835. Article 9 Regulation on Al-Qaida.
1836. Vienna Convention on the Law of Treaties (Vienna, 23 May 1969) 1155 UNTS 331.

that have signed the international agreements in question. Hence, Member States have to walk the line of complying with their EU obligations, while respecting their duties under international law. This cannot be achieved by merely invoking a statutory provision, as it would infringe the general principle of international law that a State may not rely on its internal law as a justification for its failure to comply with its international obligations.[1837]

III The Restrictive Measures

392. The restrictive measures imposed by the legislative acts analysed here are financial, related to energy, arms and weapons, internet hosting and travel bans.

A Financial Sanctions

393. Unsurprisingly, the financial restrictive measures have a preventive nature.[1838] They are a precautionary measure, which unlike confiscation does not affect the very substance of the right of persons concerned to property in their financial assets but only the use thereof.[1839] It lacks criminal character and does not have a punitive nature.[1840] Jurisprudence also stressed that this measure constitutes a particularly drastic measure capable of preventing from leading a normal social life and of making a person wholly dependent on the public assistance granted by the authorities.[1841] Aside from seriously disrupting family and working life, and impeding the conclusion of numerous legal acts, public designation of a person further creates opprobrium and suspicion.[1842] These grave negative consequences can nonetheless be justified by the importance of the aims pursued.[1843]

1 The Objective Element

394. The terms *funds* and *economic resources* form the objective element of the financial sanctions, in the pattern discussed above. Their statutory definition is identical to the ones already described (*see* in this regard paragraphs 75 & 76 above and

1837. UN Legislative Treaties, Book 25: Materials on the Responsibility of States for Internationally Wrongful Acts, ST/LEG/SER.B/25 (New York 2012) p. 19.
1838. *Faraj Hassan v. Council of the European Union*, Joined C-399/06 P and C-403/06 P, Judgment of 3 Dec. 2009, digital ECR, para. 55 ('Hassan 2009').
1839. *Yusuf 2005* (n. 18) para. 299; *Ayadi* 2006 (n. 21) para. 135; *Yusef (n. 333)* para. 62.
1840. *Al-Ghabra* (n. 761) para. 119.
1841. *Ayadi* 2006 (n. 21) para. 121.
1842. *Chariq Ayadi v. European Commission*, C-183/12 P, Judgment of 6 Jun. 2013, digital ECR para. 68; *Abdulbasit Abdulrahim v. Council*, C-239/12 P, Judgment of 28 May 2013, digital ECR para. 70 ('Abdulrahim 2013'); *Kadi* 2013 (n. 9) para. 132.
1843. *Ibid.*, para. 123, citing *Bosphorus* (n. 347) para. 23.

Annex I p. 311 at 325 & 318 respectively).[1844] With regard to economic resources, jurisprudence has ruled that the benefit derived by a designated person in the form of assistance in kind, from funds made available to his spouse under a scheme of social allowance, cannot be treated as economic resources in the sense that is here significant.[1845] Only assets that can be turned into funds, goods or services capable of being used to support terrorist activities qualify as economic resources.[1846]

2 The Subjective Element

395. The subjective element differs in each legislative act, as it is affected and influenced by the objectives and purposes that each aims to reach.

a Persons Associated with Usama bin Laden, the Al-Qaida Network and ISIL (Da'esh)

396. According to the Regulation on Al-Qaida, the persons associated with the ISIL (Da'esh) or Al-Qaida organizations are eligible for listing.[1847] These are designated by the UN Security Council or by the sanctions committee[1848] (the '1267 Sanctions Committee'). The Security Council specified that acts and activities indicating that a person is associated with said groups include participating in the financing, planning, facilitating, preparing, or perpetrating of acts or activities by, in conjunction with, under the name of, on behalf of, or in support of same groups.[1849] Supplying, selling or transferring arms and related material to the same groups or recruiting for them equally denote association[1850] and so do otherwise supporting acts or activities of such groups.[1851] Means of financing or support include but are not limited to the use of proceeds derived from crime, such as illicit cultivation, production and trafficking of narcotic drugs and their precursors.[1852] Furthermore, any legal person either owned or

1844. *See* Art. 1(1) Regulation on Al-Qaida, Art. 1(a) EU Regulation on Al-Qaida, Art. 1(2) Regulation with regard to Rafiq Hariri, Art. 1(a) Regulation on Afghanistan and Art. 1(2) Regulation on Al-Qaida, Art. 1(b) EU Regulation on Al-Qaida, Art. 1(4) Regulation with regard to Rafiq Harriri, Art. 1(c) Regulation on Afghanistan respectively. The definitions of *funds* under the Regulation on Afghanistan and the Regulation with regard to Rafiq Hariri slightly differ, as the last component of 'any other instrument of export financing' is absent.
1845. *M and Others* (n. 43) para. 74.
1846. *Ibid.*, para. 56.
1847. Article 2(3) & Annex I Regulation on Al-Qaida.
1848. According to Art. 1(5) Regulation on Al-Qaida *sanctions committee* denotes 'the Committee of the UN Security Council established pursuant to UN Security Council Resolution 1267 (1999) concerning ISIL (Da'esh) and Al-Qaida'. Relevant material, its works and mandate can be retrieved here: https://www.un.org/securitycouncil/sanctions/1267 (last visited 31 Dec. 2023).
1849. R/RES/2610 of 17 Dec. 2021 para. 2(a).
1850. *Ibid.*, para. 2(b).
1851. *Ibid.*, para. 2(c).
1852. *Ibid.*, para. 3.

controlled by any such group or otherwise supporting it is equally eligible for listing.[1853]

397. In parallel, under the EU Regulation on Al-Qaida, six categories of persons are eligible for designation. The first category consists of persons who are associated with Al-Qaida. Within this framework actions indicative of association are: '(i) participating in the financing of ISIL (Da'esh) and Al-Qaeda or any cell, affiliate, splinter group or derivative thereof, or in the financing of acts or activities by, in conjunction with, under the name of, on behalf of, or in support of them; (ii) participating in the planning, facilitating, preparing, or perpetrating of acts or activities or providing or receiving of terrorist training such as instruction related to arms, explosive devices or other methods or technologies with the purpose of committing terrorist acts by, in conjunction with, under the name of, on behalf of, or in support of ISIL (Da'esh) and Al-Qaeda or any cell, affiliate, splinter group or derivative thereof; (iii) engaging in trade with ISIL (Da'esh), Al-Qaeda or any cell, affiliate, splinter group or derivative thereof, in particular of oil, oil products, modular refineries and related material, as well as trade in other natural resources and trade in cultural property; (iv) supplying, selling or transferring arms and related materiel to ISIL (Da'esh), Al-Qaeda or any cell, affiliate, splinter group or derivative thereof'.[1854] Furthermore, eligible for designation are persons travelling or seeking to travel outside of the Union for the following purposes: '(i) the perpetration, planning, or preparation of, or participation in, terrorist acts on behalf of or in support of ISIL (Da'esh), Al-Qaeda, or any cell, affiliate, splinter group or derivative thereof; (ii) the providing or receiving of terrorist training, on behalf of or in support of, ISIL (Da'esh), Al-Qaeda or any cell, affiliate, splinter group or derivative thereof; or (iii) otherwise supporting ISIL (Da'esh), Al-Qaeda or any cell, affiliate, splinter group or derivative thereof'.[1855] At the same time, persons seeking to travel to the Union for these purposes or to participate in acts and activities of Al-Qaida may be listed.[1856] Persons recruiting for and supporting Al-Qaida in other ways can be also listed. Such recruitment and support can be indicated by '(i) providing or collecting, by any means, directly or indirectly, funds in order to finance the travelling of individuals, for the [*aforementioned*] purpose [...]; organising the travel of individuals for the [*aforementioned*] purpose [...], or otherwise facilitating it for that purpose; (ii) soliciting another person to participate in acts or activities by, in conjunction with, under the name of, on behalf of, or in support of ISIL (Da'esh), Al-Qaeda, or any cell, affiliate, splinter group or derivative thereof'.[1857] The next category of actions consists of inciting or publicly provoking acts and activities of Al-Qaida, such as encouraging or glorifying them and thereby causing a danger that terrorist acts may be committed.[1858] Finally, persons being involved or complicit in ordering or committing serious abuses of human rights for Al-Qaida, such as abduction, rape, sexual violence, forced marriage

1853. *Ibid.*, para. 4.
1854. Article 3(1)(a)(i) to (iv) & Annex I EU Regulation on Al-Qaida.
1855. Article 3(1)(b)(i) to (iii) & Annex I EU Regulation on Al-Qaida.
1856. Article 3(1)(c) & Annex I EU Regulation on Al-Qaida.
1857. Article 3(1)(d)(i) & (ii) & Annex I EU Regulation on Al-Qaida.
1858. Article 3(1)(e) & Annex I EU Regulation on Al-Qaida.

and enslavement of persons that are perpetrated outside the territory of the Union may become designated persons.[1859] Under this legal instrument, the Council performs both the assessment and the designation.[1860]

b The Suspected Assassins of Rafiq Hariri

398. The Regulation with regard to Rafiq Hariri is fairly quiet on the designation criteria. It merely mentions that the Commission has been given the power to amend the list on the basis of determinations made by the sanctions committee[1861] (the '1636 Sanctions Committee').[1862] It is here noted that the mandate of the 1636 Sanctions Committee ended in 2009.[1863] Jurisdiction was transferred to the 'Special Tribunal on Lebanon' that commenced functioning that same year with the mandate to investigate and prosecute the perpetrators of the Hariri assassination.[1864]

c Persons Associated with the Taliban

399. Pursuant to the Regulation on Afghanistan, persons eligible for listing are the ones that have been designated by the sanctions committee[1865] (the '1988 Afghanistan Sanctions Committee') as being associated with the Taliban in constituting a threat to the peace, stability and security of Afghanistan.[1866] Equally eligible for designation are persons who had been listed as the Taliban and other persons associated with them prior to the adoption of the resolution that established the 1988 Afghanistan Sanctions Committee.[1867]

3 The Duty to Act and the Obligation to Refuse

400. The imposed obligations consist of freezing funds and economic resources and preventing such from being made available,[1868] including the prohibition of

1859. Article 3(1)(f) & Annex I EU Regulation on Al-Qaida.
1860. Article 4(1) EU Regulation on Al-Qaida.
1861. According to Art. 1(1) Regulation with regard to Rafiq Hariri *sanctions committee* means 'the Committee of the Security Council of the United Nations which was established pursuant to paragraph 3(b) of UNSCR 1636 (2005)'. Relevant material, its works and mandate can be retrieved here: https://www.un.org/securitycouncil/sanctions/1636 (last visited: 31 Dec. 2023).
1862. Article 8(1)(a) EU Regulation on Al-Qaida.
1863. *See* S/2007/424 of 12 Jul. 2007.
1864. *See* R/RES/1757 of 30 May 2007 as well as S/2008/752 of 2 Dec. 2008.
1865. According to Art. 1(g) Regulation on Afghanistan sanctions committee means 'the Committee of the UNSC which was established pursuant to paragraph 30 of UNSC Resolution 1988 (2011)'. Relevant material, its works and mandate can be retrieved here: https://www.un.org/securitycouncil/sanctions/1988 (last visited: 21 Dec. 2023).
1866. Article 4(1)(b) & Annex I Regulation on Afghanistan.
1867. Article 4(1)(a) & Annex I Regulation on Afghanistan.
1868. Article 2(1) & (2) Regulation on Al-Qaida, Art. 2(1) & (2) EU Regulation on Al-Qaida, Art. 2(1) & (2) Regulation with regard to Rafiq Hariri, Art. 3(1) & (2) Regulation on Afghanistan. On the meaning of 'freezing of funds' and 'freezing economic resources' *see* Art. 1(3) & (4) Regulation

circumvention.[1869] Thus the aforementioned apply *mutatis mutandis* (*see* in this respect paragraph 122 above). The Courts of the EU were afforded the opportunity to rule on the notion of *making available* in a case involving the sale of immovable property and transfer of ownership. They affirmed that this phrase has a wide meaning encompassing all the acts necessary under the applicable national law if a person is effectively to obtain full power of disposal in relation to the property concerned.[1870] They further deduced from its wording that the restrictive measure applies to any mode of making available an economic resource. Thus, it also applied to any act flowing from the execution of a contract imposing mutual obligations and agreed in exchange for payment of pecuniary consideration, as the case at hand was.[1871]

401. In addition to the explained obligations and within the same framework, the Regulation on Al-Qaida prohibits the payment of ransom, regardless of how or by whom the ransom is paid.[1872] It is here noted that the UN Security Council has strongly condemned kidnapping and hostage-taking by terrorist groups for any purpose. It also called upon all states' members of the UN to encourage private sector partners to adopt and follow relevant guidelines and good practices for preventing and responding to terrorist kidnappings without paying ransom.[1873] The UN Security Council has further called upon UN Member States to prevent terrorists from benefiting from ransom payments or from political concessions. It also welcomed the endorsement of an addendum to the 'Algiers Memorandum on Good Practices on Preventing and Denying the Benefits of Kidnapping for Ransom by Terrorists'[1874] by the Global Antiterrorism Forum, while urging all states to remain vigilant about kidnapping and hostage-taking by ISIL, Al-Qaida and their affiliates.[1875]

4 The Exceptions

402. The explained restrictive measures are subject to exceptions that can be granted by the competent authorities of the Member States under any conditions that they deem proper. These statutory exceptions, in addition to the already explained humanitarian exception[1876] (*see* in this regard paragraph 145 above), consist of exceptions for

on Al-Qaida, Art. 1(c) & (d) EU Regulation on Al-Qaida, Art. 1(3) & (5) Regulation with regard to Rafiq Hariri, Art. 1(b) & (d) Regulation on Afghanistan respectively.

1869. Article 4 Regulation on Al-Qaida, Art. 11(1) EU Regulation on Al-Qaida, Art. 2(3) Regulation with regard to Rafiq Hariri, Art. 3(3) Regulation on Afghanistan.
1870. *Möllendorf* (n. 45) para. 51.
1871. *Ibid.*, para. 56.
1872. Article 2(2a) Regulation on Al-Qaida, which corresponds to R/RES/2610 of 21 Dec. 2021 para. 8.
1873. *See* S/RES/2199 of 12 Feb. 2015 para. 18, S/RES/2133 of 27 Jan. 2014 paras 3 & 6.
1874. Addendum to the Algiers Memorandum on the Effective Implementation of Certain Good Practices Aimed at Preventing Kidnappings by Terrorists (2015) available: https://www.thegctf.org/About-us/GCTF-framework-documents (last visited: 31 Dec. 2023).
1875. R/RES/2610 of 17 Dec. 2021 preamble.
1876. Article 2(5) Regulation on Al-Qaida, Art. 2(3) EU Regulation on Al-Qaida and Art. 2(4) Regulation on Hariri. The Regulation on Afghanistan does not set out such an exception.

basic needs[1877] (*see* in this regard paragraph 132 above), extraordinary expenses[1878] (*see* in this regard paragraph 132 above), charges for maintenance of the accounts[1879] (*see* in this regard paragraph 133 above) and, but for the EU Regulation on Al-Qaida, addition of interest[1880] (*see* in this regard paragraph 133 above). With the exception of the EU Regulation on Al-Qaida and the Regulation with regard to Rafiq Hariri, payments to a designated person may be performed, as long as they are due under contracts made before the relevant designation was decided and they are made into a frozen account within the Union[1881] (*see* in this regard paragraph 134 above). Payments by a designated person due to a contract may only be undertaken under the EU Regulation on Al-Qaida[1882] (*see* in this regard paragraph 135 above) Professional fees and expenses can be reimbursed[1883] (*see* in this regard paragraph 138 above) and accounts can be credited[1884] (*see* in this regard paragraph 139 above) but awards and decisions can be enforced solely under the EU Regulation on Al-Qaida[1885] (*see* in this regard paragraph 137 above).

403. Furthermore, a single specific exception has been prescribed. It relates to the delivery of humanitarian assistance[1886] (*see* in this regard paragraph 143 above) and unlike in the previously described occasions, delivering such assistance falls outside the scope of the regulations at hand and does not require a previous authorization.

5 *The Decisions Imposing Financial Sanctions*

404. Depending on whether the financial sanctions are UN-mandated or autonomous, the Council, or the Commission as the case may be, amends the lists on the basis of determinations made by the competent sanctions committee[1887] or on the basis of its own assessments.[1888] The lists have statutory specified contents, with the exception of the Regulation with regard to Rafiq Hariri that is silent on this issue. Lists have to include information necessary to identify the persons concerned (*see* in this regard

1877. Article 2a(1)(a)(i) Regulation on Al-Qaida, Art. 5(a) EU Regulation on Al-Qaida, Art. 3(1)(a) Regulation with regard to Rafiq Hariri and Art. 5(1)(a) Regulation on Afghanistan.
1878. Article 2a(1)(a)(iv) Regulation on Al-Qaida, Art. 5(d) EU Regulation on Al-Qaida, Art. 3(1)(d) Regulation with regard to Rafiq Hariri and Art. 5(2) Regulation on Afghanistan.
1879. Article 2a(1)(a)(iii) Regulation on Al-Qaida, Art. 5(c) EU Regulation on Al-Qaida, Art. 3(1)(c) Regulation with regard to Rafiq Hariri and Art. 5(1)(c) Regulation on Afghanistan.
1880. Article 2a(4)(a) Regulation on Al-Qaida, Art. 3(3) Regulation with regard to Rafiq Hariri and Art. 6(1)(a) Regulation on Afghanistan.
1881. Article 2a(4)(b) Regulation on Al-Qaida, Art. 6(1)(b) Regulation on Afghanistan.
1882. Article 7 EU Regulation on Al-Qaida.
1883. Article 2a(1)(a)(ii) Regulation on Al-Qaida, Art. 5(b) EU Regulation on Al-Qaida, Art. 3(1)(b) Regulation with regard to Rafiq Hariri and Art. 5(1)(b) Regulation on Afghanistan.
1884. Article 2b Regulation on Al-Qaida, Art. 8 EU Regulation on Al-Qaida, Art. 4 Regulation with regard to Rafiq Hariri and Art. 6(2) Regulation on Afghanistan.
1885. Article 6 EU Regulation on Al-Qaida.
1886. Article 2(5) Regulation on Al-Qaida, Art. 2(3) EU Regulation on Al-Qaida, Art. 2(4) Regulation with regard to Rafiq Hariri and Art. 3(4) Regulation on Afghanistan.
1887. Articles 7(1)(a) & 7a(1) and Annex I Regulation on Al-Qaida, Art. 8(1)(a) and Annex I Regulation with regard to Rafiq Hariri and Art. 11(1) and Annex I Regulation on Afghanistan.
1888. Article 4(1) EU Regulation on Al-Qaida.

paragraphs 151 & 363 above) that, in UN-mandated sanctions are provided by the competent sanctions committee or the UN Security Council.[1889] Only in a single legislative act it is set out that lists have to include the grounds for listing the person concerned.[1890] In truth, this does not affect the obligations and duties deriving from Article 296 TFEU[1891] (*see* in this regard paragraphs 152, 153 & 365 above).

405. The decision once made, has to be communicated to the person(s) concerned along with the statement of reasons.[1892] Regardless of the actual wording of the legislative acts at hand, Article 296 TFEU mandates that such a decision, just as any decision of an EU institution, must be accompanied by a statement of reasons identifying the individual, specific and concrete reasons, why the competent authorities consider that the individual concerned must be subject to restrictive measures.[1893] Furthermore, the person(s) concerned must equally be given the opportunity to express views on it.[1894] The Regulation with regard to Rafiq Hariri does not set out such obligations for institutions of the Union or equivalent rights of the persons concerned.

406. The procedure under the Regulation on Al-Qaida was much different in the initial legal act and was completely overhauled following the *Kadi 2008* case. Initially it allowed for the Commission to designate a person as associated with Al-Qaida following determinations made by the UN Security Council or the Sanctions Committee.[1895] The Court ruled that the EU institutions had had only circumscribed powers within the frame of this regulation and had lacked any autonomous discretion.[1896] It further held that it had had no authority to review the lawfulness under the (then) community law[1897] and the internal lawfulness of the regulation could only be disputed before the Security Council in the form of diplomatic protection[1898] or before national courts.[1899] Nonetheless, it had accepted its jurisdiction with regard to the right to property noting that only an *arbitrary* deprivation thereof might be regarded as contrary to jus cogens manifested on the face of the resolutions of the Security Council.[1900] Subsequently, this regime was characterized by absence of safeguards of the rights of defence.[1901]

1889. Article 7e Regulation on Al-Qaida, Art. 3(2) EU Regulation on Al-Qaida and Art. 4(3) Regulation on Afghanistan.
1890. Article 4(2) Regulation on Afghanistan.
1891. *Kadi* 2013 (n. 9) para. 116, citing *Al-Aqsa* 2010 (n. 42) paras 140 and 142; *Bamba* (n. 746) paras 49 to 53. *See also Yusef* (n. 333) para. 92.
1892. Article 7c(2) Regulation on Al-Qaida, Art. 4(2) EU Regulation on Al-Qaida and Art. 11(2) Regulation on Afghanistan.
1893. *Kadi* 2013 (n. 9) para. 116, citing *Al-Aqsa* 2010 (n. 42) paras 140 & 142; *Bamba* (n. 746) paras 49 to 53. *See also Yusef* (n. 333) para. 92.
1894. Article 7c(2) Regulation on Al-Qaida, Art. 4(2) EU Regulation on Al-Qaida and Art. 11(2) Regulation on Afghanistan.
1895. Old version Art. 7(1) Regulation on Al-Qaida.
1896. *Yusuf 2005* (n. 18) para. 328; *Ayadi* 2006 (n. 21) para. 116.
1897. *Yusuf 2005* (n. 18) para. 276; *Ayadi* 2006 (n. 21) para. 116.
1898. *Yusuf 2005* (n. 18) paras 265, 266 & 294; *Ayadi* 2006 (n. 21) paras 133 & 141.
1899. *Ayadi* 2006 (n. 21) paras 145 & 147.
1900. *Yusuf 2005* (n. 18) para. 293; *Ayadi* 2006 (n. 21) para. 116.
1901. *Kadi* 2010 (n. 761) para. 187.

407. The *Kadi 2008* case thwarted said regime. At the outset the Court discussed the issue of resolutions of the UN Security Council enjoying immunity from jurisdiction. While reiterating the fundamental obligation to respect international law,[1902] including the undertakings given within the UN,[1903] the Court stated that review of the lawfulness of an EU act giving effect to an international agreement, neither examines nor challenges that international agreement, which enjoys the privilege of primacy.[1904] It then found that the approach of immunity from jurisdiction for an EU measure could be established neither on international law nor on EU law.[1905] Thereafter the Court analysed the relationship between the Charter of the UN and the general principles of the EU law. It reiterated the primacy of international law over secondary EU law,[1906] but specified that that primacy cannot extend to primary law and especially to the general principles of which fundamental rights form part.[1907] Thus, it found that the EU judicature must ensure that the review, in principle the full review, of the lawfulness of all Union acts in the light of the fundamental rights forming an integral part of the general principles of EU law.[1908] Following these findings, the Court proceeded with analysing the breach of the rights of defence, those being the right to be heard and the right to effective judicial review, which were patently not respected.[1909] The effectiveness of judicial protection[1910] mandates that the EU authority in question is bound to communicate the grounds to the person concerned.[1911] The observance of this obligation is necessary in order to enable the person concerned to defend their rights in the best possible conditions and to decide whether there is any point in applying to the Court. It is further necessary in order to put the Court fully in a position in which it may carry out the review of the lawfulness of the EU measure in question.[1912] Turning to the right to be heard, the Court mentioned that the contested regulation provided neither for a procedure for communicating the evidence justifying the inclusion of the names in the list nor for hearing those persons.[1913] Therefore, these persons were not in a

1902. *Kadi* 2008 (n. 15) para. 291, citing *Poulsen* (n. 45) para. 9; *Racke (n. 45)* para. 45.
1903. *Kadi* 2008 (n. 15) para. 292, citing *Commission v. Council*, C-91/05, Judgment of 20 May 2008, digital ECR, para. 65.
1904. *Kadi* 2008 (n. 15) paras 286 & 288.
1905. *Ibid.*, paras 299 & 300.
1906. *Ibid.*, para. 307 citing *The Queen, on the application of International Association of Independent Tanker Owners (Intertanko) and Others v. Secretary of State for Transport*, C-308/06, Judgment of 3 Jun. 2008, digital ECR, para. 42.
1907. *Kadi* 2008 (n. 15) para. 308.
1908. *Ibid.*, para. 326.
1909. *Ibid.*, para. 334.
1910. *See* in this regard *Unibet (London) Ltd and Unibet (International) Ltd v. Justitiekanslern*, C-432/05, Judgment of 13 Mar. 2007, digital ECR para. 37; *Union nationale des entraîneurs et cadres techniques professionnels du football (Unectef) v. Georges Heylens and others*, 222/86, Judgment of 15 Oct. 1987, digital ECR para. 15; *Dansk Rørindustri A/S (C-189/02 P), Isoplus Fernwärmetechnik Vertriebsgesellschaft mbH and Others (C-202/02 P), KE KELIT Kunststoffwerk GmbH (C-205/02 P), LR af 1998 A/S (C-206/02 P), Brugg Rohrsysteme GmbH (C-207/02 P), LR af 1998 (Deutschland) GmbH (C-208/02 P) and ABB Asea Brown Boveri Ltd (C-213/02 P) v. Commission*, Joined C-189/02 P, C-202/02 P, C-205/02 P to C-208/02 P and C-213/02 P, Judgment of 28 Jun. 2005, digital ECR, paras 462 & 463.
1911. *Kadi* 2008 (n. 15) para. 336.
1912. *Ibid.*, para. 337.
1913. *Ibid.*, para. 345.

position to make their point of view in that respect known to advance. Consequently, the right to be heard was not respected.[1914] Moreover, in view of the lack of information of the evidence adduced against them and having regard to the relationship between the rights of defence and the right to effective legal remedy, the persons concerned were also unable to defend their rights with regard to that evidence in satisfactory conditions before the Court. Therefore, their right to an effective legal remedy had also been infringed.[1915] Finally, the infringement had not been remedied during the proceedings and therefore the Court was unable to undertake the review of lawfulness resulting into one more reason for not observing the right to effective legal remedy.[1916]

408. In the aftermath of *Kadi 2008*, the procedure performed by and before the Commission underwent a radical change and resulted in the one already explained (*see* in this regard paragraph 404 & 405 above). Furthermore, the Courts of the EU added the following specifics. The Commission in including a person in the list, as soon as the 1267 Sanctions Committee provides a statement of reasons,[1917] carries out a careful, independent and critical review of the listing decided upon by the 1267 Sanction Committee and it subjects that committee's conclusions to thorough personal scrutiny.[1918] Moreover, the Court has found, and the Commission has conceded, that it has broad discretion[1919] and it is prepared to dissociate itself from the findings of the Sanctions Committee.[1920] Further, the Commission bears a dual procedural obligation towards the person concerned. It must first disclose to the individual concerned the evidence against that person, which is available to the Commission and on which it relied as a basis for its decision, that being at the very least the statement of reasons. Such disclosure takes place directly, when the address is known, or indirectly, through the publication of a notice. This should ensure that that individual is in a position to defend his or her rights in the best possible conditions and to decide, in full knowledge of the relevant facts, whether there is any point in bringing an action before the EU judicature.[1921] The other obligation is to ensure that that individual is placed in a position in which he or she may effectively make known her views on the grounds advanced against him or her.[1922]

1914. *Ibid.*, para. 348.
1915. *Ibid.*, para. 349.
1916. *Ibid.*, paras 350 & 351.
1917. Article 7a(1) Regulation on Al-Qaida. *Statement of reasons* has been defined as 'the publicly releasable portion of the statement of case as provided by the Sanctions Committee and/or, where applicable, the narrative summary of reasons for listing as provided by the Sanctions Committee' Art. 1(6) Regulation on Al-Qaida.
1918. *Al-Bashir Mohammed Al-Faqih and Others v. European Commission*, C-19/16 P, Judgment of 15 Jun. 2017, digital ECR, para. 80.
1919. *Kadi* 2010 (n. 761) para. 141.
1920. *Al-Ghabra* (n. 761) para. 81; *Yusef* (n. 333) para. 91.
1921. *Kadi* 2013 (n. 9) para. 111; *Al-Ghabra* (n. 761) para. 103; *Yusef* (n. 333) para. 93.
1922. *Kadi* 2013 (n. 9) para. 112, citing *Commission v. Lisrestal – Organização Gestão de Restaurantes Colectivos Ld*[a], *Gabinete Técnico de Informática Ld*[a] *(GTI), Lisnico – Serviço Marítimo Internacional Ld*[a], *Rebocalis – Rebocagem e Assistência Marítima Ld*[a] *and Gaslimpo – Sociedade de Desgasificação de Navios SA.*, C-32/95 P, Judgment of 24 Oct. 1996, digital ECR para. 21; *Mediocurso – Estabelecimento de Ensino Particular Ld.*[a] *v. Commission of the European Communities*, C-462/98 P, Judgment of 21 Sep. 2000, digital ECR para. 36; and *M.*

409. The Courts of the EU have the competence to review such decisions, even when the act challenged has ceased to have effect in the course of proceedings, as in such cases the applicant's interest does not necessarily disappear.[1923] This competence also does not cease when the decision is replaced by another during the court proceedings.[1924] The competence to review can be regarded as effective, only if it concerns the substantive assessments of the respective sanctions committee and the evidence underlying them.[1925] Effective judicial protection also enables the person concerned to obtain a declaration from the Court that the listing of his or her name was vitiated by illegality, the recognition of which may re-establish the reputation of that person or constitute for her a form of reparation for the non-material harm that she has suffered.[1926]

410. The Courts of the EU examine the lawfulness of the decision,[1927] in the sense of whether the reasons were sufficiently detailed and specific[1928] as well as whether the factual basis was sufficiently solid. Specifically, regarding the extent and intensity of the review, it has been established that it shall be 'in principle the full review'.[1929] The Courts shall estimate if further evidence and information is necessary. In the affirmative, and under the assumption that the EU institutions provide it, the Courts of the EU shall then assess its value via a balancing technique accommodating, in the one hand legitimate security considerations about the nature and sources of information, which tend to be confidential and classified, and on the other, the need sufficiently to guarantee to an individual respect for her procedural rights.[1930] Should the EU institutions not provide the requested information and evidence, then the EU judicature undertakes an examination of the lawfulness of the contested measure solely on the basis of the material which has been disclosed.[1931] Should this material be insufficient to allow a finding that a reason is well founded, the EU judicature is to disregard this reason as a possible basis for the contested decision to list or to maintain a listing.[1932]

M. v. Minister for Justice, Equality and Law Reform and Others, C-277/11, Judgment of 22 Nov. 2012, digital ECR para. 87. In the meantime, this obligation has been incorporated in the regulation. *See* Art. 7a(2) Regulation on Al-Qaida.

1923. *Abdulrahim* 2013 (n. 1842) paras 61 & 62, citing *Thomas Flaherty (C-373/06 P), Larry Murphy (C-379/06 P) and Ocean Trawlers Ltd (C-382/06 P) v. Commission*, Joined C-373/06 P, C-379/06 P and C-382/06 P, Judgment of 17 Apr. 2008, digital ECR para. 25; *SpA Simmenthal v. Commission*, 92/78, Judgment of 6 Mar. 1979, digital ECR para. 32; *AKZO Chemie BV and AKZO Chemie UK Ltd v. Commission*, 53/85, Judgment of 24 Jun. 1986, digital ECR, para. 21; *Jacques Wunenburger v. Commission*, C-362/05 P, Judgment of 7 Jun. 2007, digital ECR paras 42 & 50.
1924. *Othman* (n. 1818) para. 53.
1925. *Kadi* 2010 (n. 761) para. 129.
1926. *Kadi* 2013 (n. 9) para. 134; *Abdulrahim* 2013 (n. 1842) paras 67 to 84.
1927. *Kadi* 2010 (n. 761) para. 116.
1928. *Kadi* 2013 (n. 9) para. 136; *Abdulrahim* 2013 (n. 1842) para. 70.
1929. *Kadi 2008* (n. 15) para. 326; *Kadi* 2010 (n. 761) paras 132 & 139, citing *OMPI* (n. 50) paras 154, 155 & 159.
1930. *Abdulrahim* 2013 (n. 1842) para. 67.
1931. *Al-Ghabra* (n. 761) para. 142.
1932. *Kadi* 2013 (n. 9) para. 123; *Abdulrahim* 2013 (n. 1842) para. 66.

411. When the Courts of the Union decide the annulment of a contested regulation, they then may consider that annulment with immediate effect could seriously and irreversibly prejudice the effectiveness of the restrictive measures. They thus may make use of its power to maintain the effects of the contested regulation, that it has annulled, for a brief period allowing for the EU institutes to remedy the infringements found.[1933]

6 *The De-Listing*

412. Under the legislative acts at hand, the opportunity is given to submit observations and present substantial new evidence. Then the Council – the Commission under the Regulation on Al-Qaida –is obliged to review its decision and inform the affected persons accordingly.[1934] The Regulation with regard to Rafiq Hariri though is devout of such an opportunity. With regard to multilateral financial sanctions, where the UN decides to de-list a person, the Council, or the Commission as the case may be, proceed with amending the relevant list.[1935] Under the EU Regulation on Al-Qaida only, the Council has the duty to review the lists at regular intervals and at least every twelve months.[1936]

413. Under the Regulation on Al-Qaida, persons previously designated may face specific conditions upon unfreezing their funds or economic resources, as per the decision of the UN Security Council.[1937]

414. It is here noted that in the aftermath of *Kadi 2008* the 'Office of the Ombudsperson' was created at the level of the UN[1938] for the purpose of considering delisting requests within the frame of the 1267 Sanctions Committee.'[1939] Upon receipt of a delisting request by a designated individual, group, undertaking or entity, the Office of the Ombudsperson proceeds with information gathering, a two-month period that results in presenting a written update to the 1267 Sanctions Committee.[1940] Thereafter it facilitates a two-month period of engagement, which *may* include dialogue with the petitioner. The product of this period is a report summarizing the principal arguments for the delisting request.[1941] Finally, a two-month period of Committee discussion and decision takes place, when the 1267 Sanctions Committee may decide to grant or reject the delisting request.[1942] The Courts of the EU assessed this remedy. They took note of

1933. *Kadi* 2008 (n. 15) paras 373 & 375.
1934. Articles 7a(3) & (4) and 7b Regulation on Al-Qaida, Art. 4(3) EU Regulation on Al-Qaida and Art. 11(3) & (4) Regulation on Afghanistan.
1935. Article 7a(5) Regulation on Al-Qaida and Art. 11(3) Regulation on Afghanistan.
1936. Article 4(4) EU Regulation on Al-Qaida.
1937. Article 2(3a) and Annex Ia Regulation on Al-Qaida.
1938. R/RES/1904 of 17 Dec. 2009. The mandate was initially given for a period of eighteen months and it has been subsequently extended by R/RES/1989 of 17 Jun. 2011, R/RES/2083 of 17 Dec. 2012, R/RES/2161 of 17 Jun. 2014, R/RES/2253 of 17 Dec. 2015, R/RES/2368 of 20 Jul. 2017 and R/RES/2610 of 17 Dec. 2021. The current mandate expires on 17 Jun. 2024.
1939. R/RES/1904 (2009) para. 20 & Annex II and R/RES/2610 of 17 Dec. 2021 para. 63 & Annex II.
1940. *Ibid.*, paras 1 to 5 to Annex II.
1941. *Ibid.*, paras 6 to 8 to Annex II.
1942. *Ibid.*, paras 9 to 20 to Annex II.

the consensus within the 1267 Sanctions Committee that is required for delisting, the discretion of the states regarding disclosing evidence to the person concerned and the lack of a mechanism for ensuring that sufficient information is provided to the person concerned. In view thereof, they found that it does not constitute an effective judicial procedure for review of decisions of the 1267 Sanctions Committee.[1943]

7 *Limitation of Liability*

415. The legislative acts at hand provide for limitation of liability when the persons implementing the financial sanctions act in good faith as well as when they did not know that their actions infringe the restrictive measures[1944] (*see* in this regard paragraph 166 above).

416. Furthermore, the EU Regulation on Al-Qaida excludes *claims* of designated persons[1945] (*see* in this regard paragraphs 168 et seq. above).

B Energy Sanctions

417. The Regulation on Al-Qaida sets out indirect energy sanctions. It prohibits trade in oil and refined oil products, modular refineries and related material including chemicals and lubricants, as well as other natural resources.[1946] To this end, it has not set up a separate mechanism. Rather, it has incorporated this prohibition in the financial sanctions by including funds and economic resources used for trade in oil and refined oil products, modular refineries and related material including chemicals and lubricants, as well as other natural resources in the general restrictive measure of funds freezing (*see* in this regard paragraph 394 above). Thus, the aforementioned (*see* in this regard paragraphs 399 et seq. above) apply *mutatis mutandis*. The origins of this prohibition can be traced back to the UN Security Council.[1947]

C Sanctions on Arms and Weapons

418. The Regulation on Al-Qaida, the EU Regulation on Al-Qaida and the Regulation on Afghanistan prescribe sanctions on military activities and items of the EU Common Military List.

1943. *Kadi* 2010 (n. 761) para. 128.
1944. Articles 6 & 2(4) Regulation on Al-Qaida, Art. 12(1) & (2) EU Regulation on Al-Qaida, Art. 6 Regulation with regard to Rafiq Hariri and Art. 7(1) & (2) Regulation on Afghanistan. However, the Regulation with regard to Rafiq Hariri does not provide for exclusion of liability when the person did not know that his or her actions infringe the imposed sanctions.
1945. Article 13 EU Regulation on Al-Qaida. On the definition of 'claim' *see* Art. 1(f) EU Regulation on Al-Qaida.
1946. Article 2(2a) Regulation on Al-Qaida.
1947. R/RES/2255 of 22 Dec. 2015 para. 4.

419. At the outset is noted that, in parallel to the restrictions described below, supplying, selling and transferring arms and related materiel qualifies as a designation criterium for financial sanctions under the Regulation on Al-Qaida.[1948] Thus, the aforementioned applies to persons performing such activities (*see* in this regard paragraphs 399 et seq. above).

420. According to the same regulation, providing technical advice, assistance and training to designated persons with regard to military activities is prohibited. This prohibition entails in particular training and assistance related to the manufacture, maintenance and use of arms and related material of all types.[1949] It is a UN-mandated sanction[1950] that does not have any exceptions; however, the European provision provides a reservation with regard to 'the powers of Member States in the exercise of their public authority'. Furthermore, this is merely a part of the UN-mandated sanction. The UN Security Council also decided to prohibit the 'supply, sale, or transfer [...] of arms and related materiel of all types including weapons and ammunition, military vehicles and equipment, paramilitary equipment, and spare parts for the aforementioned'.[1951] This was not transposed at the EU level.[1952] In parallel, the EU Regulation on Al-Qaida prohibits technical assistance, brokering services and other services related to military activities, as well as providing financing and financial assistance for the same activities to persons designated under this specific regulation.[1953] No exceptions are set out.

421. Sanctions on items of the EU Common Military List (*see* in this respect paragraphs 273 et seq. above) are set out in the EU Regulation on Al-Qaida and the Regulation on Afghanistan. They prohibit the provision of technical assistance[1954] (in regard to the definition *see* Annex I p. 311 at 331) with regard to items of this list and with regard to the provision, manufacture, maintenance and use of goods included in that same list as long as the recipients are designated persons. The first regulation has adopted a wider approach, as it further prohibits the provision of brokering services and other services.[1955] *E contrario* it could be argued that such services are not prohibited under the latter. No exceptions are set out.

1948. R/RES/2610 of 17 Dec. 2021 para. 2(a).
1949. Article 3 Regulation on Al-Qaida. It was introduced via Art. 1(5) Council Regulation (EU) No. 1286/2009 of 22 Dec. 2009 amending Regulation (EC) No. 881/2002 imposing certain specific restrictive measures directed against certain persons and entities associated with Usama bin Laden, the Al-Qaida network and the Taliban, OJ L 346, 23 Dec. 2009, p. 42.
1950. R/RES/2610 of 2021 para. 1(c). It was first decided under R/RES/1333 of 19 Dec. 2000 para. 5(a) and then reaffirmed in S/RES/1390 of 28 Jan. 2002 para. 2(a), S/RES/1989 of 17 Jun. 2011 para. 1(c), S/RES/2368 of 20 Jul. 2017 para. 1(c).
1951. R/RES/2610 of 2021 para. 1(c).
1952. The relevant provision as enacted in the year 2002 read: '[...] it shall be prohibited to grant, sell, supply or transfer, directly or indirectly, technical advice, assistance or training related to military activities, including in particular training and assistance related to the manufacture, maintenance and use of arms and related materiel of all types [...]'. Article 3 Regulation on Al-Qaida (*initial legal act*).
1953. Article 9(b) EU Regulation on Al-Qaida.
1954. Article 1(e) Regulation on Afghanistan. The EU Regulation on Al-Qaida does not define the term *technical assistance*.
1955. Article 9(a) EU Regulation on Al-Qaida and Art. 2(a) Regulation on Afghanistan.

D Restrictive Measures and Internet Hosting

422. Under the Regulation on Al-Qaida, Internet hosting and related services for the support of Al-Qaida and designated persons are prohibited.[1956] Once again, no separate mechanism has been set up; funds and economic resources for such hosting and services are deemed to be included in the notion of funds and resources under that legislative instrument and therefore fall under the general restrictive measure of funds freezing (*see* in this regard paragraph 394 above). Thus, the aforementioned (*see* in this regard paragraph 399 above) apply *mutatis mutandis*. The origins of this prohibition can be traced back to the UN Security Council.[1957]

423. This prohibition pairs with the regulation on the dissemination of terrorist content online[1958] that has created a duty of care to hosting service providers and addresses the misuse of hosting services for the dissemination to the public of terrorist content online.[1959]

E Restrictive Measures and Movement of Persons

424. The legislative acts at hand set out travel bans for the persons that each one has designated and on which it imposed financial sanctions.[1960] Thus the aforementioned (*see* in this regard paragraph 399 above) apply *mutatis mutandis*.

1956. Article 2(2a) Regulation on Al-Qaida.
1957. R/RES/2255 of 22 Dec. 2015 para. 6.
1958. Regulation (EU) 2021/784 of the European Parliament and of the Council of 29 Apr. 2021 on addressing the dissemination of terrorist content online, OJ L 172, 17 May 2021, p. 79.
1959. Article 1(1) Regulation 2021/784.
1960. Article 4 Common Position on Al-Qaida (repealed) and Art. 2(1) Decision on Al-Qaida (now in force); Art. 2(2) and Annex Decision on Al-Qaida; Art. 1 Decision with regard to Rafiq Hariri; and Art. 3 Decision on Afghanistan.

CHAPTER 5
Restrictive Measures and Russia's Aggression

425. This chapter discusses the sanctions that the Union imposed as a reaction to the aggression of Russia against Ukraine and Moldova, as well as the sanctions targeting Belarus. Following an overview of the EU legislation imposing sanctions, these are portrayed according to the sector they impact, those being finance, gold and luxury items, energy, dual-use items, movement of persons, transfer of goods, mining and quarrying, import of certain goods, broadcasting and tourism.

§1 OVERVIEW OF THE EUROPEAN LEGISLATION IMPOSING SANCTIONS DUE TO RUSSIA'S AGGRESSION

426. Russia's aggression towards Ukraine that took place in 2014 and the ensuing war of aggression against Ukraine, initiated on 20 February 2022, have prompted the EU to adopt a series of legislative acts imposing restrictive measures, among other things. The sequence of this series of acts demonstrating the escalation of the imposed measures is also demonstrated in Annexes II, III and IV to the present monograph (*see* in this regard pp. 337, 345 & 353 et seq. below). In chronological order, these legislative acts are portrayed in the following paragraphs; so are the circumstances, in which they were adopted.

427. Russia had been expressing concerns over opposition forces in Ukraine aspiring to change the situation in the country,[1961] an attempt at a coup d'état.[1962] It estimated

1961. *See* Ministry of Foreign Affairs of the Russian Federation, *Comment by the Information and Press Department of the Russian Ministry of Foreign Affairs regarding the situation in Ukraine*, 186-03-02-2014, of 3 Feb. 2014, available: https://www.mid.ru/en/maps/ua/1631708/ (last visited: 31 Dec. 2023).

1962. *See* Ministry of Foreign Affairs of the Russian Federation, *Answer by the Russian Foreign Minister, Sergey Lavrov, to the question about the situation in Ukraine, during the joint press*

that the opposition was out of control and that Ukraine was *en route* to a big crisis.[1963] It was further outraged by the lack of reaction to the criminal activities of radical forces and the opposition, while noting that Ukraine was a friendly and fraternal state for Russia, who would use its influence to assist it in living calmly and in peace.[1964] On 21 February 2014, an agreement was reached between the President of Ukraine and the opposition leaders setting out a process for the settlement of the crisis.[1965] On 12 March 2014, the G-7 leaders called on Russia to cease all efforts to change the status of Crimea and to de-escalate the conflict in Crimea.[1966] A few days later, on 15 March 2014, the UN Security Council was scheduled to vote on a draft resolution on the situation in Ukraine. In this, it reaffirmed its commitment to the sovereignty, independence, unity and territorial integrity of Ukraine, urged all parties to pursue a peaceful resolution of that dispute through political dialogue, called Ukraine to continue to protect the rights of all persons within its territory, including minorities, noted that Ukraine had not authorized the referendum on Crimea, and declared that that referendum would neither be valid nor form a basis for altering the status of Crimea.[1967] As expected, it was not adopted due to Russia's veto.[1968] The referendum was held on Sunday 16 March 2014, as scheduled. On the next day, the legislative acts on restrictive measures due to undermining and threatening Ukraine[1969] ('Decision on Threatening

---

conference summarizing the results of the third session of the Russia-CCASG strategic dialogue at ministerial level, Kuwait City, 19 February 2014, 319-19-02-2014, available: https://www.mid.ru/en/maps/ua/1668301/ (last visited: 31 Dec. 2023).

1963. *See* Ministry of Foreign Affairs of the Russian Federation, *Comment by the Information and Press Department of the Russian Ministry of Foreign Affairs regarding the situation in Ukraine*, 307-18-02-2014, of 18 Feb. 2014, available: https://www.mid.ru/en/maps/ua/1667508/ (last visited: 31 Dec. 2023).
1964. *See* Ministry of Foreign Affairs of the Russian Federation, *Statement by the Russian Ministry of Foreign Affairs regarding the situation in Ukraine*, 313-19-02-2014, of 19 Feb. 2014, available: https://www.mid.ru/en/maps/ua/1667987/ (last visited: 31 Dec. 2023).
1965. *See* UN Secretary-General, *Statement Attributable to the Spokesperson for the Secretary-General on Ukraine*, New York, 21 Feb. 2014, available: https://news.un.org/en/sites/news.un.org.en/files/atoms/files/statement_attributable_to_spokesperson_for_secretary-general_on_ukraine.pdf (last visited: 31 Dec. 2023 2023); Organization for Security and Co-operation in Europe, *OSCE Chair-in-Office welcomes Ukraine agreement*, Bern, 21 Feb. 2014, available: https://www.osce.org/cio/115559 (last visited: 31 Dec. 2023).
1966. The White House, Office of the Press Secretary, *Statement of G-7 Leaders on Ukraine*, 12 Mar. 2014, available: https://obamawhitehouse.archives.gov/the-press-office/2014/03/12/statement-g-7-leaders-ukraine (last visited: 31 Dec. 2023).
1967. S/2014/189 of 15 Mar. 2014.
1968. Security Council Report, *Vote on a Draft Resolution on Ukraine*, 14 Mar. 2014, available: https://www.securitycouncilreport.org/whatsinblue/2014/03/vote-on-a-draft-resolution-ukraine.php (last visited: 31 Dec. 2023).
1969. Council Decision 2014/145/CFSP of 17 Mar. 2014 concerning restrictive measures in respect of actions undermining or threatening the territorial integrity, sovereignty and independence of Ukraine, OJ L 78, 17 Mar. 2014, p. 16, as last amended by Council Decision (CFSP) 2023/2871 of 18 Dec. 2023 amending Decision 2014/145/CFSP concerning restrictive measures in respect of actions undermining or threatening the territorial integrity, sovereignty and independence of Ukraine, digital OJ L, 18 Dec. 2023.

    Council Regulation (EU) No. 269/2014 of 17 Mar. 2014 concerning restrictive measures in respect of actions undermining or threatening the territorial integrity, sovereignty and independence of Ukraine, OJ L 078, 17 Mar. 2014, p. 6, as last amended by Council Regulation (EU) 2023/2873 of 18 Dec. 2023 amending Regulation (EU) No. 269/2014 concerning

Ukraine' & 'Regulation on Threatening Ukraine') were adopted by the EU; and so did the US.[1970]

428. In June 2014, legislative acts restricting the import of goods originating from Crimea and Sevastopol[1971] ('Decision on Goods from Crimea' & 'Regulation on Goods from Crimea') were issued. One month later, the regulation imposing sanctions on Russia due to destabilizing the situation in Ukraine[1972] ('Decision on Russia' & 'Regulation on Russia') was released.

429. The EU responded to Russia's war of aggression against Ukraine not always via enacting new legislation, but also via amending and modifying the aforementioned regulations, including the legislative act on Belarus (*see* in this regard paragraph 433 below).

430. However, the recognition of the 'independence and sovereignty' of Donetsk and Luhansk oblasts of Ukraine by Russia prompted the EU to adopt a new legislative act, the regulation on the recognition of non-government controlled areas of Donetsk and Luhansk of Ukraine[1973] ('Decision with regard to Donetsk and Lahansk' & 'Regulation with regard to Donetsk and Luhansk').

---

restrictive measures in respect of actions undermining or threatening the territorial integrity, sovereignty and independence of Ukraine, digital OJ L, 13 Dec. 2023.

1970. *See* Megan Slack, *President Obama Announces New Ukraine-Related Sanctions*, 17 Mar. 2014, available: https://obamawhitehouse.archives.gov/blog/2014/03/17/president-obama-announces-new-ukraine-related-sanctions (last visited: 21 Dec. 2023).

1971. Council Decision 2014/386/CFSP of 23 Jun. 2014 concerning restrictions on goods originating in Crimea or Sevastopol, in response to the illegal annexation of Crimea and Sevastopol, OJ L 183, 24 Jun. 2014, p. 70, as last amended by Council Decision (CFSP) 2023/1188 of 19 Jun. 2023 amending Decision 2014/386/CFSP concerning restrictive measures in response to the illegal annexation of Crimea and Sevastopol, OJ L 157, 20 Jun. 2023, p. 46.

Council Regulation (EU) No. 692/2014 of 23 Jun. 2014 concerning restrictions on the import into the Union of goods originating in Crimea or Sevastopol, in response to the illegal annexation of Crimea and Sevastopol, OJ L 183, 24 Jun. 2014, p. 9, as last amended by Council Regulation (EU) 2022/1848 of 4 Oct. 2022 amending Regulation (EU) No. 692/2014 concerning restrictive measures in response to the illegal annexation of Crimea and Sevastopol, OJ L 257, 5 Oct. 2022, p. 1.

1972. Council Decision 2014/512/CFSP of 31 Jul. 2014 concerning restrictive measures in view of Russia's actions destabilising the situation in Ukraine, OJ L 229, 31 Jul. 2014, p. 13, as last amended by Council Decision (CFSP) 2023/2874 of 18 Dec. 2023 amending Decision 2014/512/CFSP concerning restrictive measures in view of Russia's actions destabilising the situation in Ukraine, digital OJ L, 18 Dec. 2023.

Council Regulation (EU) No. 833/2014 of 31 Jul. 2014 concerning restrictive measures in view of Russia's actions destabilizing the situation in Ukraine, OJ L 229, 31 Jul. 2014, p. 1, as last amended by Council Regulation (EU) 2023/2878 of 18 Dec. 2023 amending Regulation (EU) No. 833/2014 concerning restrictive measures in view of Russia's actions destabilising the situation in Ukraine, digital OJ L, 18 Dec. 2023.

1973. Council Decision (CFSP) 2022/266 of 23 Feb. 2022 concerning restrictive measures in response to the recognition of the non-government controlled areas of the Donetsk and Luhansk oblasts of Ukraine and the ordering of Russian armed forces into those areas, OJ L 42I, 23 Feb. 2022, p. 109, as last amended by Council Decision (CFSP) 2023/388 of 20 Feb. 2023 amending Decision (CFSP) 2022/266 concerning restrictive measures in response to the illegal recognition, occupation or annexation by the Russian Federation of certain non-government controlled areas of Ukraine, OJ L 53, 21 Feb. 2023, p. 37.

431. Later in that same year, the European Council condemned the military support that Iran provided to Russia, specifically the development and delivery of UAVs, and took action by amending the Regulation on Threatening Ukraine.[1974] On the same day, the Council after strongly cautioning Iran against any new deliveries of weapons to Russia and expressing its great concern, concluded two items. First, the weapons provided by Iran are used by Russia indiscriminately against civil population and infrastructure. Further, it underlined that any transfer of combat drones and missiles to and from Iran lacking permission of the UN Security Council violates the JCPOA.[1975] The European Council reiterated these conclusions on 15 December 2022,[1976] whereas two months later it designated four more individuals of Iran under the Regulation on Threatening Ukraine.[1977] It further condemned the continued military support for Russia's war by Iran in March[1978] and June 2023.[1979] Nonetheless, taking into account the gravity of the situation, which summarizes into the developing and manufacturing of UAVs through a state-sponsored programme run by the Ministry of Defence and Armed Forces Logistics of Iran and the Islamic Revolutionary Guard Corps, the European Council decided to adopt a framework of measures specifically in view of

Council Regulation (EU) 2022/263 of 23 Feb. 2022 concerning restrictive measures in response to the recognition of the non-government controlled areas of the Donetsk and Luhansk oblasts of Ukraine and the ordering of Russian armed forces into those areas, OJ L 42I, 23 Feb. 2022, p. 77, as last amended by Council Regulation (EU) 2022/1903 of 6 Oct. 2022 amending Regulation (EU) 2022/263 concerning restrictive measures in response to the recognition of the non-government controlled areas of the Donetsk and Luhansk oblasts of Ukraine and the ordering of Russian armed forces into those areas, OJ L 259I, 6 Oct. 2022, p. 1.

1974. *See* Council Decision (CFSP) 2022/2432 of 12 Dec. 2022 amending Decision 2014/145/CFSP concerning restrictive measures in respect of actions undermining or threatening the territorial integrity, sovereignty and independence of Ukraine, OJ L 318I, 12 Dec. 2022, p. 32 and Council Implementing Regulation (EU) 2022/2430 of 12 Dec. 2022 implementing Regulation (EU) No. 269/2014 concerning restrictive measures in respect of actions undermining or threatening the territorial integrity, sovereignty and independence of Ukraine, OJ L 318I, 12 Dec. 2022, p. 20.
1975. As adopted in S/RES/2231 of 20 Jul. 2015. *See* Council of the EU, Press Release – Iran: Council approves conclusions of 12 Dec. 2022, available: https://www.consilium.europa.eu/en/press/press-releases/2022/12/12/iran-council-approves-conclusions/ (last visited: 31 Dec. 2023).
1976. European Council, European Council Meeting (15 Dec. 2022) – Conclusions, EUCO 34/22, CO EUR 29, CONCL 7, available: https://www.consilium.europa.eu/media/60872/2022-12-15-euco-conclusions-en.pdf (last visited: 31 Dec. 2023).
1977. *See* Council Decision (CFSP) 2023/432 of 25 Feb. 2023 amending Decision 2014/145/CFSP concerning restrictive measures in respect of actions undermining or threatening the territorial integrity, sovereignty and independence of Ukraine, OJ L 59I, 25 Feb. 2023, p. 437 and Council Regulation (EU) 2023/426 of 25 Feb. 2023 amending Regulation (EU) No. 269/2014 concerning restrictive measures in respect of actions undermining or threatening the territorial integrity, sovereignty and independence of Ukraine, OJ L 59I, 25 Feb. 2023, p. 1.
1978. European Council, European Council Meeting (23 Mar. 2023) – Conclusions, EUCO 4/23, CO EUR 3, CONCL 2, available: https://data.consilium.europa.eu/doc/document/ST-4-2023-INIT/en/pdf (last visited: 31 Dec. 2023).
1979. European Council, European Council Meeting (29 and 30 Jun. 2023) – Conclusions, EUCO 7/23, CO EUR 5, CONCL 3, available: https://data.consilium.europa.eu/doc/document/ST-7-2023-INIT/en/pdf (last visited: 31 Dec. 2023).

Iran's military support to Russia's was of aggression against Ukraine[1980] ('Decision on Iran Assisting Russia' & 'Regulation on Iran Assisting Russia').

432. Moldova has been faced with direct threats to its stability from internal groups with vested interests and from the Russian Federation.[1981] The Union estimates that this crisis poses a threat to democracy and the rule of law in Moldova as well as to its stability and security. It also sees persons who engage in serious financial misconduct concerning public funds and the unauthorized export of capital as a threat to stability, democracy and the rule of law. The Union further stated that destabilization efforts against Moldova threaten the stability and security of its external borders. Moldova did request support from the EU against destabilizing threats.[1982] In view of all these, the Council has set up the legal framework of restrictive measures[1983] ('Decision on Moldova' & 'Regulation on Moldova').

433. Lastly, officials of Belarus have been on the receiving end of restrictive measures at least since 2006, when the here significant regulation was issued[1984] ('Regulation on Belarus'). Still, already before that year, the EU concerned at the lack of investigation on the disappearances of four well-known persons in 1999/2000 and the alleged crimes identified by the Pourgourides report, had imposed restrictions on entering into and

1980. Council Decision (CFSP) 2023/1532 of 20 Jul. 2023 concerning restrictive measures in view of Iran's military support to Russia's war of aggression against Ukraine, OJ L 186, 25 Jul. 2023, p. 20.

Council Regulation (EU) 2023/1529 of 20 Jul. 2023 concerning restrictive measures in view of Iran's military support of Russia's war of aggression against Ukraine, OJ L 186, 25 Jul. 2023, p. 1.

1981. Recital No. 4 to the preamble of Council Decision (CFSP) 2023/891 of 28 Apr. 2023 concerning restrictive measures in view of actions destabilising the Republic of Moldova, OJ L 114, 2 May 2023, p. 15, as last amended by Council Decision (CFSP) 2023/1047 of 30 May 2023 amending Decision (CFSP) 2023/891 concerning restrictive measures in view of actions destabilising the Republic of Moldova, OJ L 140I, 30 May 2023, p. 9 ('Decision 2023/891').

1982. Recital Nos 5, 8-10 Decision (CFSP) 2023/891.

1983. Council Decision (CFSP) 2023/891 of 28 Apr. 2023 concerning restrictive measures in view of actions destabilising the Republic of Moldova, OJ L 114, 2 May 2023, p. 15, as last amended by Council Decision (CFSP) 2023/1047 of 30 May 2023 amending Decision (CFSP) 2023/891 concerning restrictive measures in view of actions destabilising the Republic of Moldova, OJ L 140I, 30 May 2023, p. 9.

Council Regulation (EU) 2023/888 of 28 Apr. 2023 concerning restrictive measures in view of actions destabilising the Republic of Moldova, OJ L 114, 2 May 2023, p. 1, as last amended by Council Implementing Regulation (EU) 2023/1045 of 30 May 2023 implementing Regulation (EU) 2023/888 concerning restrictive measures in view of actions destabilising the Republic of Moldova, OJ L 140I, 30 May 2023, p. 1.

1984. Council Common Position 2006/362/CFSP of 18 May 2006 amending Common Position 2006/276/CFSP concerning restrictive measures against certain officials of Belarus, OJ L 134, 20 May 2006, p. 45.

Council Regulation (EC) No. 765/2006 of 18 May 2006 concerning restrictive measures against President Lukashenko and certain officials of Belarus, OJ L 134, 20 May 2006, p. 1, as last amended by Council Implementing Regulation (EU) 2023/419 of 24 Feb. 2023 implementing Article 8a of Regulation (EC) No. 765/2006 concerning restrictive measures in view of the situation in Belarus and the involvement of Belarus in the Russian aggression against Ukraine, OJ L 61, 27 Feb. 2023, p. 20.

transiting through the Union to certain persons in September 2004.[1985] Further measures had been enacted due to the fraudulent elections and referendum of 17 October 2004.[1986] The grounds for the Regulation on Belarus were the Presidential elections of 19 March 2006 that had been fundamentally flawed and violated international electoral standards as well as the arrest of peaceful demonstrators on that same day.[1987] The title of the regulation was altered from 'restrictive measures against President Lukashenko and certain officials of Belarus' into 'restrictive measures in respect of Belarus' in October 2011[1988] without stating any reason or ground. In March 2022[1989] in response to Belarus' involvement in Russia's aggression against Ukraine,[1990] the title was changed to 'restrictive measures in view of the situation in Belarus *and the involvement of Belarus in the Russian aggression against Ukraine*'. Thus, as the relevant restrictive measures that are explained below demonstrate, this act is analysed here, as it forms a part of the EU legislative framework created due to Russia's invasion of 2014 and the full-scale war that was initiated in 2021.

434. In the following subchapters the restrictive measures on funds and economic resources (*see* in this regard paragraphs 436 et seq. below), financial services (*see* in this regard paragraphs 458 et seq. below), gold and luxury items (*see* in this regard paragraphs 490 et seq. below), energy, that being coal, oil and gas, energy infrastructure, electricity production and nuclear activities (*see* in this regard paragraphs 497 et seq. below), dual-use items (*see* in this regard paragraphs 525 et seq. below), arms and weapons (*see* in this regard paragraphs 535 et seq. below), transfer of persons and movement of goods (*see* in this regard paragraphs 551 et seq. below), mining and quarrying (*see* in this regard paragraphs 576 below), importing and exporting certain goods (*see* in this regard paragraphs 577 et seq. below), broadcasting (*see* in this regard paragraphs 591 et seq. below) and tourism (*see* in this regard paragraphs 593 et seq. below) are set out.

435. The restrictive measures explained below, like the aforementioned ones, are prospective precautionary measures and not penalties. Thus, the mere existence of a risk that an entity may act reprehensibly may be sufficient to impose restrictive

1985. Council Common Position 2004/661/CFSP of 24 Sep. 2004 concerning restrictive measures against certain officials of Belarus, OJ L 301, 28 Sep. 2004, p. 67.
1986. Council Common Position 2004/848/CFSP of 13 Dec. 2004 amending Common Position 2004/661/CFSP concerning restrictive measures against certain officials of Belarus, OJ L 367, 14 Dec. 2004, p. 35.
1987. Recital No. 1 to the preamble of Regulation on Belarus.
1988. *See* Council Decision 2011/666/CFSP of 10 Oct. 2011 amending Decision 2010/639/CFSP concerning restrictive measures against Belarus, OJ L 265, 11 Oct. 2011, p. 17 and Council Regulation (EU) No. 999/2011 of 10 Oct. 2011 amending Regulation (EC) No. 765/2006 concerning restrictive measures in respect of Belarus, OJ L 265, 11 Oct. 2011, p. 6.
1989. *See* Council Decision (CFSP) 2022/356 of 2 Mar. 2022 amending Decision 2012/642/CFSP concerning restrictive measures in view of the situation in Belarus, OJ L 67, 2 Mar. 2022, p. 103.
1990. Recital No. 4 to the preamble of Decision (CFSP) 2022/356.

measures on that entity.[1991] At the same time, the Courts of the EU ruled, that the Council, when deciding the restrictive measures, was entitled to consider that the actions of the Russian Federation undermined or threatened Ukraine's territorial integrity, sovereignty and independence; in view of this the measures could amount to an *emergency in international relations* and the restrictive measures were necessary for the protection of the essential security interests of the Member States of the European Union, within the meaning of Article XXI of GATT.[1992]

§2 FINANCIAL SANCTIONS

436. The Regulation on Threatening Ukraine, the Regulation on Iran Assisting Russia, the Regulation on Moldova and the Regulation on Belarus provide for imposing financial sanctions on certain individuals and persons, similar to the ones already explained (*see* in this respect paragraphs 72 to 170 above). Due to this similarity, they are analysed following the same pattern in the following paragraphs.

437. Before proceeding with the analysis, it must be noted that the Regulation on Russia and the Regulation on Belarus prescribe a peculiar provision in a repeatedly and consistent manner. For a legal person to be owned by another person, either an individual or an entity, in a manner significant for these regulations, the latter must hold a stake of more than 50% either directly or indirectly.[1993] This is how the notion 'owned' stands in the Regulation on Russia and the Regulation on Belarus unless otherwise stated. However, no such threshold is required, when ownership of an entity in a third state by another entity incorporated in a Member State of the EU must be demonstrated.

438. Beginning with the objective element, the term *funds* has been defined in a similar manner[1994] (in regard to the definition *see* Annex I p. 311 at 325) and not in an identical one, as the final component, that being 'any other instrument of export-financing', is absent. In contrast, the term 'economic resources' is identical[1995] (in regard to the definition *see* Annex I p. 311 at 318).

439. With regard to the subjective element, the designation process differs in these four legislative instruments. In the Regulation on Threatening Ukraine, the authority

1991. *Joint-Stock Company 'Almaz-Antey' Air and Space Defence Corp., formerly OAO Concern PVO Almaz-Antey v. Council*, T-255/15, Judgment of 25 Jan. 2017, digital ECR para. 110 ('Almaz-Antey'), citing *Anbouba v. Council*, T–592/11, Judgment of 13 Sep. 2013, digital ECR para. 40 and *Kala Naft* (n. 33) para. 85.
1992. *PAO Rosneft Oil Company and Others v. Council*, C-732/18 P, Judgment of 17 Sep. 2020, digital ECR para. 131 ('Rosneft Oil 2020').
1993. *See*, for example, Arts 5(1)(b), (2)(b), 3(c), 4(b) & (6)(b), 5aa(1), 5b(1), 5h and 5m(1)(c) Regulation on Russia and Arts 1e(4)(e), 1j, 1k(1)(c) and 1zb Regulation on Belarus.
1994. Article 1(g) Regulation on Threatening Ukraine, Art. 1(h) Regulation on Iran Assisting Russia, Art. 1(g) Regulation on Moldova and Art. 1(1) Regulation on Belarus.
1995. Article 1(d) Regulation on Threatening Ukraine, Art. 1(e) Regulation on Iran Assisting Russia, Art. 1(d) Regulation on Moldova and Art. 1(3) Regulation on Belarus.

entrusted with the designation is the Council.[1996] Persons eligible for designation are natural persons who are responsible for undermining or threatening the territorial integrity, sovereignty and independence of Ukraine, including stability and security in this state, and who obstruct the work of international organizations in the same state.[1997] This criterion concerns forms of support which, by their quantitative or qualitative significance, contribute to the continuance of Russia's actions and policies destabilizing Ukraine.[1998] Material support has taken the form of a Russian state-owned company manufacturing heavy weaponry which it supplied to the Russian Federation, which in turn supplied weapons to the separatists in Eastern Ukraine.[1999] However, support is not limited to material support.[2000] Being appointed Head of the State news agency of the Russian Federation Rossiya Segodnya is considered being a central figure of the Russian government propaganda supporting the deployment of Russian forces in Ukraine, satisfying said criterion.[2001] The right to freedom of expression does not change this approach, the Courts of the EU ruled, as long as the conditions for its limitation are fulfilled.[2002] Equally eligible for designation are leading businesspersons operating in Russia, their immediate family members and persons benefitting from them.[2003] Other persons that may be designated are natural or legal persons supporting in a material or financial manner Russian decision-makers, including persons benefitting therefrom.[2004] One more category of natural and legal persons who may face financial sanctions are those who conduct transactions with the separatist groups in the Donbas region of Ukraine,[2005] as well as natural and legal persons who support and benefit from the government of the Russian Federation.[2006] Furthermore, businesspersons and legal persons may become designated when they are involved in economic sectors providing a substantial source of revenue to the government of the Russian Federation.[2007] At the same time, persons eligible for designation are natural and legal persons who circumvent the prohibitions set out in this regulation, in the Regulation on Goods from Crimea, in the Regulation on Russia, in the Regulation with regard to Donetsk and Luhansk as well as the corresponding decisions.[2008] Similarly, persons otherwise significantly frustrating the provisions prohibiting circumvention in said

1996. Article 14(1) Regulation on Threatening Ukraine.
1997. Article 3(1)(a) Regulation on Threatening Ukraine. The designated persons are listed in Annex I Regulation on Threatening Ukraine.
1998. *Kiselev* (n. 581) paras 74 & 114, citing *National Iranian* 2014 (n. 459) para. 119.
1999. *Almaz-Antey'*(n. 1991) para. 141.
2000. *Kiselev* (n. 581) para. 115.
2001. *Ibid.*, paras 43, 44 & 76.
2002. The criteria are: (a) existence of a legal basis for the adoption of the relevant measures; (b) aiming to achieve an objective of general interest; (c) not excessive limitation (*see also* para. 114 above). Regulation on Threatening Ukraine, para. 69, citing *Sarafraz v. Council*, T-273/13, Judgment of 4 Dec. 2015, digital ECR, paras 177-182 & 184.
2003. Article 3(1)(g) Regulation on Threatening Ukraine.
2004. Article 3(1)(d) Regulation on Threatening Ukraine.
2005. Article 3(1)(e) Regulation on Threatening Ukraine.
2006. Article 3(1)(f) Regulation on Threatening Ukraine.
2007. Article 3(1)(g) Regulation on Threatening Ukraine.
2008. The provisions prohibiting circumvention are: Art. 9(1) Regulation on Threatening Ukraine, Art. 2c(3) Regulation on Goods from Crimea, Arts 3m(7)(b) & (8)(b) and 12 Regulation on Russia, Arts 5(3) and 8 Regulation with regard to Donetsk and Luhansk, Arts 4, 4a(3), 4b(5),

legislative acts may face restrictive measures.[2009] Lastly, the following legal persons are eligible for designation: (a) persons supporting, materially or financially, activity that undermines and threatens the territorial integrity, sovereignty and independence of Ukraine; (b) persons in Crimea and Sevastopol whose ownership had been illegally transferred under the law of Ukraine, including persons benefiting from such a transfer; and (c) persons operating in the Russian IT-sector licensed by the Centre for Licensing, Certification, and Protection of State Secrets of the Federal Security Service of the Russian Federation ('FSB') or having a 'weapons and military equipment' licence by the Russian Ministry of Industry.[2010] The twelfth package (*see* in this regard Annex II p. 337 at 343 below) introduced one further group of persons that are eligible for designation: Russian entities that were owned by persons established in the Union but had subsequently their ownership or control transferred by acts of Russia, including entities that benefitted from such transfer and persons appointed to their governing bodies.[2011] In short, the Union reacts to expropriation of foreign investments via sanctions. The objective pursued through freezing the funds of the persons described here is preventing the escalation of the conflict in Ukraine and actions undermining or threatening the territorial integrity, sovereignty and independence of Ukraine. Thus this criterion is not manifestly disproportionate.[2012] Finally, any person associated with all aforementioned categories of persons is eligible for designation.[2013] Should a designated person die while the measures are still in effect, the Council is given the authority to maintain these names on the list, if delisting them would pose a risk of undermining the objectives of the sanctions because of the likelihood that the assets concerned would be used to finance Russia's war of aggression or other actions threatening Ukraine.[2014] It is here noted that the above references to the *government of the Russian Federation* and *Russian decision-maker* are accompanied in the legislative text by the phrase 'responsible for the annexation of Crimea and the destabilization of Ukraine'.[2015] Extraordinarily and exceptionally, the Union did not use the surprise effect upon designating persons under the Regulation on Threatening Ukraine; quite to the contrary, it published a notice for the attention of the persons subject to restrictive measures.[2016]

4c(3) & 4e(5) Decision on Goods from Crimea, Arts 4o(7)(b) & (8)(b) and 8 Decision on Russia and Art. 8 Decision with regard to Donetsk and Luhansk.

2009. Article 3(1)(h)(i) & (ii) Regulation on Threatening Ukraine.
2010. Article 3(1)(b), (c) and (i) respectively Regulation on Threatening Ukraine.
2011. Article 3(1)(j) Regulation on Threatening Ukraine. *See* Art. 2(1)(a) Decision (CFSP) 2023/2871 and Art. 1(1)(a) Regulation (EU) 2023/2873.
2012. *Almaz-Antey* (n. 1991) para. 111.
2013. Article 3(1) Regulation on Threatening Ukraine.
2014. Article 3(1a) Regulation on Threatening Ukraine. *See* Art. 2(1)(a) Decision (CFSP) 2023/2871 and Art. 1(1)(a) Regulation (EU) 2023/2873.
2015. Articles 3(1)(f), (g) & (d) Regulation on Threatening Ukraine.
2016. *See*, for example, *Notice for the attention of the persons and entities subject to the restrictive measures provided for in Council Decision 2014/145/CFSP, as amended by Council Decision 2014/508/CFSP, and in Council Regulation (EU) No 269/2014 as implemented by Council Implementing Regulation (EU) No 826/2014 concerning restrictive measures in respect of actions undermining or threatening the territorial integrity, sovereignty and independence of Ukraine* (2014/C 249/02) OJ C 249, 31 Jul. 2014, p. 29; *Arkady Romanovich Rotenberg v. Council*, T-720/14, Judgment of 30 Nov. 2016, digital ECR para. 10 ('Rotenberg').

440. Under the Regulation on Iran Assisting Russia, the persons that can be designated are natural and legal persons, who are responsible for supporting Iran's UAV programme.[2017] Neither further criteria nor additional information are offered in the regulation allowing for broad discretionary powers of the designating authority, that being the Council, the Commission and the High Representative of the Union for Foreign Affairs and Security Policy.[2018]

441. The Regulation on Moldova prescribes the following designation criteria. They include responsibility for, as well as support and activity with regard to, undermining or threatening the sovereignty and independence of Moldova, or democracy, the rule of law, stability or security in the same state. The actions, through which such responsibility, support and activity can be demonstrated are obstructing or undermining the democratic political process, facilitating in any way violent demonstrations or other acts of violence and serious financial misconduct concerning public funds and the unauthorized export of capital.[2019] Persons associated with them are also eligible for designation.[2020]

442. According to the Regulation on Belarus, the persons eligible for designation are the ones identified by the designating authority, that being the Council, as responsible for serious violations of human rights within that state, for the repression of civil society and democratic opposition, and persons whose activities otherwise seriously undermine democracy or the rule of law in the same state. Persons associated with those are also eligible for designation.[2021] As such qualify the persons responsible for the violations of international electoral standards and the crackdown on civil society and democratic opposition in that country.[2022] The criterion of 'active support' within this framework is less broad than the one in other Union acts.[2023] Further, persons benefiting from and supporting the Lukashenka regime are eligible for designation.[2024] Moreover, persons can face financial sanctions that organize and contribute to activities of the same regime, which facilitate the illegal crossing of the external borders of the Union and the transfer of prohibited goods or restricted goods into the territory of the Union.[2025] Finally, any legal person deemed to be owned or controlled by the aforementioned persons is eligible for designation by the Council.[2026]

443. The obligation imposed, when both the objective element and the subjective element are satisfied, is freezing all funds and economic resources and making no such

2017. Article 3(1) Regulation on Iran Assisting Russia. The designated persons are listed in Annex III Regulation on Iran Assisting Russia.
2018. Article 13(1)(a) & (b) Regulation on Iran Assisting Russia.
2019. Article 2(3)(a)(i)-(iii) Regulation on Moldova.
2020. Article 2(3)(b) Regulation on Moldova.
2021. Article 2(4) Regulation on Belarus and Art. 4(1)(a) Decision 2012/642. The designated persons are listed in Annex I Regulation on Belarus.
2022. *Kiselev* (n. 581) para. 77, citing *Mikhalchanka v. Council*, T-196/11 and T-542/12, Judgment of 23 Sep. 2014, digital ECR, paras 7, 8, 15 & 134-135 ('Mikhalchanka').
2023. *Kiselev* (n. 581) para. 78, citing *Mikhalchanka* (n. 2022) digital ECR.
2024. Article 2(5) Regulation on Belarus and Art. 4(1)(b) Decision 2012/642.
2025. Article 2(6)(a)(i) & (ii) Regulation on Belarus.
2026. Article 2(4),(5) & (6)(b) Regulation on Belarus and Art. 4(1)(a), (b) & (d) Decision 2012/642.

available. Both the obligation per se[2027] and the definitions of *freezing of funds*[2028] and *freezing of economic resources*[2029] are identical to the ones already analysed (*see* in this regard paragraphs 122 et seq. above & with reference to the definitions Annex I p. 311 at 325 & 318). The prohibition of circumvention is quite similar, albeit bearing a significant variation with regard to intent. The Regulation on Threatening Ukraine and the Regulation on Belarus require participation knowingly *and* intentionally,[2030] following the established pattern (*see* in this regard paragraph 122 above) whereas the Regulation on Iran Assisting Russia broadens the scope of application by conditioning participation knowingly *or* intentionally.[2031]

444. Turning to exceptions, it is noted that all widely applied exceptions are also applied in the regulations at hand. These consist of the exception with regard to basic needs,[2032] although the Regulation on Iran Assisting Russia provides that solely natural persons may benefit therefrom, as the Regulation on Mali does (*see* in this regard paragraph 132 above). Further exception is provided for extraordinary expenses (*see* in this regard paragraph 132 above), but the notification obligations towards other Member States and the Commission are not uniform. The Regulation on Threatening Ukraine sets out the condition of notification two weeks *after* a decision has been taken, the Regulation on Iran Assisting Russia provides no time frame and the Regulation on Belarus requires notification two weeks *prior* to reaching a decision.[2033] Similarly, fees and service charges for routine holding and maintenance of frozen funds[2034] (*see* in this regard paragraph 133 above) as well as adding interest and other earnings[2035] (*see* in this regard paragraph 133 above) are also among the widely applied exceptions. Further, payments due under contracts and agreements or obligations predating the designation of the relevant person[2036] (*see* in this regard paragraphs 134 & 135 above), along with reasonable professional fees for legal services[2037] (*see* in this

2027. Article 2(1) & (2) Regulation on Threatening Ukraine, Art. 3(1) & (2) Regulation on Iran Assisting Russia, Art. 2(1) & (2) Regulation on Moldova and Art. 2(1) & (2) Regulation on Belarus.
2028. Article 1(f) Regulation on Threatening Ukraine, Art. 1(i) Regulation on Iran Assisting Russia, Art. 1(f) Regulation on Moldova and Art. 1(2) Regulation on Belarus.
2029. Article 1(e) Regulation on Threatening Ukraine, Art. 1(g) Regulation on Iran Assisting Russia, Art. 1(e) Regulation on Moldova and Art. 1(4) Regulation on Belarus.
2030. Article 9(1) Regulation on Threatening Ukraine, Art. 9 Regulation on Moldova and Art. 2(3) Regulation on Belarus.
2031. Article 12(1) Regulation on Iran Assisting Russia.
2032. Article 4(1)(a) Regulation on Threatening Ukraine, Art. 3a(a) Regulation on Iran Assisting Russia, Art. 3(1)(a) Regulation on Moldova and Art. 3(1)(a) Regulation on Belarus.
2033. Article 4(1)(d) Regulation on Threatening Ukraine, Arts 3a(d) & 6(1)(a) Regulation on Iran Assisting Russia, Art. 3(1)(d) Regulation on Moldova and Art. 3(2) Regulation on Belarus.
2034. Article 4(1)(c) Regulation on Threatening Ukraine, Art. 3a(c) Regulation on Iran Assisting Russia, Art. 3(1)(c) Regulation on Moldova and Art. 3(1)(c) Regulation on Belarus.
2035. Article 7(2)(a) Regulation on Threatening Ukraine, Art. 3d(2) Regulation on Iran Assisting Russia, Art. 7(2)(a) Regulation on Moldova and Art. 4(1)(a) Regulation on Belarus.
2036. Article 7(2)(b) Regulation on Threatening Ukraine, Art. 3d(2) Regulation on Iran Assisting Russia, Art. 7(2)(b) Regulation on Moldova and Art. 4(1)(b) Regulation on Belarus.
2037. Article 4(1)(b) Regulation on Threatening Ukraine, Art. 3a(b) Regulation on Iran Assisting Russia, Art. 4(1)(b) Regulation on Moldova and Art. 3(1)(b) Regulation on Belarus.

regard paragraph 138 above) and crediting of accounts[2038] (*see* in this regard paragraph 139 above). Moreover, designated persons may under conditions and following authorization perform payments under contracts and agreements (*see* in this regard paragraphs 134 & 135 above).[2039] The Commission and other Member States need to be notified within an unspecified period of time after the authorization has been granted; specifically with regard to Moldova, this notification needs to be done within two weeks.[2040] Specifically with regard to persons listed under the Regulation on Belarus, payments can be done, when these persons shall not be benefitted therefrom and the authority intending to grant the authorization has informed accordingly the Commission and the other Member States two weeks prior to doing so.[2041] Further, awards and judgments can be enforced both against a designated person[2042] (*see* in this regard paragraph 137 above) and in favour of such a person[2043] (*see* in this regard paragraph 137 above) with the exception of the Regulation on Belarus that lacks such provision. The Commission and other Member States must be informed of enforcement proceedings against a designated person, albeit within different time-frames.[2044]

445. The specific exceptions common to the regulations at hand are two. First, derogations may take place for diplomatic missions[2045] in the same manner as already explained (*see* in this regard paragraph 142 above). The second exception relates to humanitarian assistance and differs from the aforementioned. It provides that funds and economic resources can be made available by organizations and agencies that are pillar-assessed by the Union when such funds and economic resources are necessary for exclusively humanitarian purposes within the respective states. Furthermore, it is essential that the Union has signed with such organizations and agencies a financial framework partnership agreement that serves as a basis for them to act as humanitarian partners of the Union.[2046] Should these conditions not be fulfilled, funds and economic resources may still serve humanitarian purposes, when the competent authorities grant specific or general authorizations. The authorities shall have to inform other Member States and the Commission of any such authorization within two weeks

2038. Article 7(1) Regulation on Threatening Ukraine, Art. 3d(1) Regulation on Iran Assisting Russia, Art. 7(1) Regulation on Moldova and Art. 4(2) Regulation on Belarus.
2039. Article 6(1) Regulation on Threatening Ukraine, Art. 3c Regulation on Iran Assisting Russia, Art. 6(1) Regulation on Moldova and Art. 4(2) Regulation on Belarus.
2040. Article 6(1) Regulation on Threatening Ukraine, Art. 6(1)(a) Regulation on Iran Assisting Russia and Art. 6(2) Regulation on Moldova.
2041. Article 4a(i) & (ii) Regulation on Belarus.
2042. Article 5(1) Regulation on Threatening Ukraine, Art. 3b Regulation on Iran Assisting Russia, Art. 5(1) Regulation on Moldova and Art. 3a(1) Regulation on Belarus.
2043. Article 7(2)(c) Regulation on Threatening Ukraine, Art. 3d(2) Regulation on Iran Assisting Russia and Art. 7(2)(c) Regulation on Moldova.
2044. Article 5(2) Regulation on Threatening Ukraine, Art. 6(1)(a) Regulation on Iran Assisting Russia, Art. 5(2) Regulation on Moldova and Art. 3a(2) Regulation on Belarus.
2045. Article 4(1)(e) Regulation on Threatening Ukraine, Art. 3a(e) Regulation on Iran Assisting Russia, Art. 4(1)(e) Regulation on Moldova and Art. 3(1)(d) Regulation on Belarus.
2046. Article 2a(1) Regulation on Threatening Ukraine, Art. 3e(1) Regulation on Iran Assisting Russia and Art. 4(1) Regulation on Moldova.

of granting it.[2047] The Regulation on Belarus also provides an exception on the basis of humanitarian action but under different conditions. More specifically, competent authorities may authorize the release of funds and economic resources or make them available under conditions, if they deem this appropriate when these are intended exclusively for humanitarian purposes, such as the operation of flights for the evacuation or repatriation of persons, or for initiatives supporting victims of natural, nuclear or chemical disasters.[2048] The same authorities shall have to inform other Member States and the Commission of any such authorization within an unspecified time period.[2049]

446. The Regulation on Threatening Ukraine entails further derogations, mostly in the form of authorizing activities otherwise prohibited. They are related to human health and environment, maritime safety and Crimean ports, agricultural and food products, termination of agreements and electronic communication services. Issuing authorizations under the conditions explained below requires that the authorities doing so inform accordingly the other Member States and the Commission within two weeks.[2050] In more detail, competent authorities have the power to issue an authorization under the condition that any resulting proceeds are frozen when the release of funds and economic resources is necessary for urgent prevention or mitigation of an event that could have a serious and significant impact on human health and safety or the environment.[2051]

447. Further, for the purpose of maritime safety funds and economic resources are released, when these are needed for the provision of pilot services.[2052] No notification of other Member States and the Commission is needed.

448. With regard to Crimean Sea Ports, competent authorities may issue an authorization for payments to these ports for services provided at Kerch Fishery Port, Yalta Commercial Port and Evpatoria Commercial Port. They may also authorize payments for services provided by Gosgidrografiya and by Port-Terminal branches of the Crimean Sea Ports.[2053]

449. In addition, funds and economic resources belonging to certain entities necessary for the purchase, import and transport of agricultural and food products, including wheat and fertilizers, may be exempt from freezing as a result of the competent authorities issuing an authorization.[2054] At the same time, on the basis of a specific and

2047. Article 2a(2) & (4) Regulation on Threatening Ukraine and Art. 3e(2) & (4) Regulation on Iran Assisting Russia and Art. 4(2) & (4) Regulation on Moldova.
2048. Article 3(1)(d)(i) Regulation on Belarus.
2049. Article 3(3) Regulation on Belarus.
2050. *See* Arts 6d(2), 6a(2), 6e(2) & 6b(6) Regulation on Threatening Ukraine.
2051. Article 6d(1)(a) & (b) Regulation on Threatening Ukraine.
2052. Article 6f Regulation on Threatening Ukraine.
2053. Article 6a(1) Regulation on Threatening Ukraine.
2054. Article 6e(1) Regulation on Threatening Ukraine. These entities are: Bank Rossiya, Promsvyazbank, VEB.RF, Otkritie FC Bank, Novikombank, Sovcombank, VTB Bank, Sberbank, Credit Bank of Moscow, JSC 'Far Eastern Bank', JSC Ural Civil Aviation Factory, Alfa-Bank JSC, Public joint-stock company Rosbank, MRB Bank, CMRBank & AlfaStrakhovanie Group

case-by-case assessment, competent authorities may authorize the release of funds and economic resources of designated persons, who prior to the listing held a significant role in international trade in agricultural and food products, including wheat and fertilizers. It is pertinent that these funds and economic resources are necessary for the sale, supply, transfer or export of such products to third countries for the purpose of addressing food security.[2055]

450. The following set of exceptions relates to releasing funds and economic resources for the performance of certain agreements by specific designated persons, usually. More specifically, when competent authorities deem that funds and economic resources are necessary for the termination by a specific point in time, the latest being 30 June 2024, of operations, contracts and other agreements, including correspondent banking relations, concluded with designated persons before a different point in time, the latest being 19 December 2023.[2056] In a similar manner, the competent authorities are given the power to release funds and economic resources deemed necessary for completing, within a specific time frame, the sale and transfer of proprietary rights in a legal person established in the Union, when these rights are owned by designated persons.[2057] In the same way, they may unfreeze funds and economic resources of specific designated persons, that are estimated as necessary for the completion of transactions strictly necessary for the wind-down of a joint venture or similar legal arrangement,[2058] as well as for disposing or transferring securities, as long as these were controlled by bank, the disposal or action is completed within a specific time frame and it is based on agreements of VTB Bank or National Settlement Depository of Russia concluded before a certain point in time.[2059] Furthermore, they have the power to authorize EU nationals, including legal persons, and residents of a Member State to convert repository receipts with Russian underlying security held by the National

a.k.a. Alfa Insurance (Nos 53, 54, 55, 79, 80, 81, 82, 108, 126, 127, 198, 199, 200, 214, 215 & 270, Entities, Annex I Regulation on Threatening Ukraine).

2055. Article 6e(1a) Regulation on Threatening Ukraine.

2056. These designated persons are the ones already mentioned with regard to agricultural and foods products, but for MRB Bank, CMRBank, JSC 'Alabuga' Special Economic Zone of Industrial and Production Type a.k.a. Alabuga special economic zone (SEZ) a.k.a. Yelabuga special economic zone (SEZ) a.k.a. JSC Alabuga and additionally National Settlement Depository and Joint Stock Company 'Scientific and Production Association "Impuls"'. Article 6b(1) and Nos 53, 54 & 55, Entities, Annex I; Art. 6b(2) and Nos 79, 80, 81 & 82, Entities, Annex I; Art. 6b(2a) and No. 108, Entities, Annex I; Art. 6b(2c) and Nos 126 & 127, Entities, Annex I; Art. 6b(2d) and Nos 198, 199 & 200; Art. 6b(5) and No. 101, Entities, Annex I; Art. 6b(5b) and No. 190, Entities, Annex I; (without time limit) Art. 6b(5e) and No. 270, Entities, Annex I; and Art. 6b(5g) and No. 333, Entities, Annex I, *ibid*. The exception also applies with regard to certain natural persons. *See* Art. 6b(5f) and Nos 92, 674, 675, 694, 880, 882, 909 & 920, Individuals, Annex I *ibid*.

2057. This exception is provided solely to Sberbank for completing a sale by 17 Jun. 2023 (Art. 6b(2b) and No. 108, Entities, Annex I *ibid.*) and to all designated persons for a sale by 31 May 2023 or within six months since the designation (Art. 6b(3) and Annex I *ibid.*).

2058. With regard to PJSC KAMAZ the wind-down of the joint venture that was concluded before 12 Mar. 2022 must take place before 31 Dec. 2022 (Art. 6b(4) and No. 91, Entities, Annex I *ibid.*), whereas with regard to Alexey Alexandrovits MORDASHOV, Chairman of Severstal and Severgroup, the wind-down of the joint venture that was concluded before 28 Feb. 2022 must take place before 31 Aug. 2023 (Art. 6b(5c) and No. 695, Persons, Annex I *ibid.*).

2059. Article 6b(5a) and Nos 82 & 101, Entities, Annex I *ibid*.

Settlement Depository of Russia for the purpose of selling that security upon fulfilment of certain conditions, including compliance with the Regulation on Russia and not making funds available to any designated legal person.[2060] Lastly, competent authorities have the authority to release funds and economic resources belonging to any designated natural and legal person in order to set-up, certify or evaluate a firewall for the purpose of removing control of a designated person over the assets of a non-listed legal person, which is established in the EU and owned by a designated person, as long as no funds benefit the designated person. To the same end, they may also allow for the provision of such services.[2061]

451. Finally, funds and economic resources are not frozen, when they are strictly necessary for the following services: (a) electronic communications services provided by communication operators operating in the Union; (b) associated facilities and services necessary for the operation, maintenance and security of such electronic communication services, in Russia, in Ukraine, in the Union, between Russia and the Union, and between Ukraine and the Union; and (c) data centre services in the Union.[2062] No notification is required.

452. The Regulation on Belarus allows for some further derogations associated with aviation. More specifically, competent authorities may unfreeze or make available funds and economic resources intended exclusively for the operation of flights in the framework of international adoption procedures, flights required for attending meetings for solving the crisis in Belarus or promoting the policy objectives of the sanctions, or an emergency landing, take-off or overflight by an EU air carrier.[2063] Moreover, they may authorize so, following consultation with the European Union Aviation Safety Agency, when such funds and economic resources are necessary for critical and clearly identified air safety matters.[2064]

453. The twelfth package (*see* in this regard Annex II p. 337 at 343 below) introduced, subtly, the alienation of funds and economic resources frozen under the Regulation on Threatening Ukraine. Such may be made available or released following an authorization of the competent authorities, which have to establish that an administrative or judicial authority decided their *deprivation* in the public interest under the condition that compensation is paid, which however shall remain frozen.[2065] It also established the authority of competent authorities to release frozen funds and economic resources belonging to expropriated foreign investments (*see* in this regard paragraph 439 above) or permit to make funds and economic resources available to them, when this is necessary for enabling payment of consideration, as this is agreed by parties, established by a juridical or administrative authority or set out in law. Outside the scope of

2060. Article 6b(5aa) and No. 101, Entities, Annex I *ibid*.
2061. Article 6b(5d) and Annex I *ibid*.
2062. Article 6c *ibid*.
2063. Article 3(1)(d)(ii), (iii) & (iv) Regulation on Belarus.
2064. Article 3(1)(e) Regulation on Belarus.
2065. Article 5a(1) Regulation on Threatening Ukraine. *See* Art. 1(2)(c) Decision (CFSP) 2023/2871 and Art. 1(2) Regulation (EU) 2023/2873.

this exception fall frozen funds and economic resources held by central securities depositories.[2066] Releasing frozen funds and economic resources in such a manner, notwithstanding the nobility of public interest, equals to alienation of property of foreign legal persons that, provided that such legal persons are evaluated as investors having performed investments under international investment law, has been wrongfully expropriated under the applicable international investment agreement as the Hull formula of prompt, adequate and effective compensation has not been met. With the enactment of such legal provisions, the future of international investment arbitration shall be glorious and captivating.

454. Designation decisions that take the form of inclusion in a list of persons subject to restrictive measures are similar to an individual decision.[2067] Such lists include the grounds for deciding so[2068] and where available, information necessary to identify the persons concerned. With regard to natural persons, such information may include names including aliases, date and place of birth, nationality, passport and ID card numbers, gender, address, if known, and function or profession. With regard to legal persons, such information may include names, place and date of registration, registration number and place of business.[2069] The aforementioned statement of reasons, notification and evidence (*see* in this regard paragraphs 152 et seq. above) apply *mutatis mutandis*.[2070]

455. In deviation from the already described designations, the persons listed under the here-described criteria have the statutory obligation to report their funds and economic resources located within the jurisdiction of a Member State of the EU to the authority of that Member State within six weeks. Funds and economic resources are deemed to be theirs when they are owned, held or controlled by them, or when they belong to them. They also have to cooperate with the authorities to verify any such information.[2071] Not doing so is deemed as participation in activities the object or effect of

2066. Article 5a(2) Regulation on Threatening Ukraine. *See* Art. 1(2)(c) Decision (CFSP) 2023/2871 and Art. 1(2) Regulation (EU) 2023/2873. On 'central securities depositories' *see* Regulation (EU) No. 909/2014 of the European Parliament and of the Council of 23 Jul. 2014 on improving securities settlement in the European Union and on central securities depositories and amending Directives 98/26/EC and 2014/65/EU and Regulation (EU) No. 236/2012, OJ L 257 28 Aug. 2014, p. 1, as last amended by Regulation (EU) 2022/858 of the European Parliament and of the Council of 30 May 2022 on a pilot regime for market infrastructures based on distributed ledger technology, and amending Regulations (EU) No. 600/2014 and (EU) No. 909/2014 and Directive 2014/65/EU, OJ L 151, 2 Jun. 2022, p. 1.

2067. *DenizBank A.Ş. v. Council*, T-798/14, Judgment of 13 Sep. 2018, digital ECR para. 57, citing *Kala Naft* (n. 33) para. 50, *National Iranian* 2016 (n. 33) para. 44, *Rosneft*2017 (n. 347) para. 103.

2068. Article 3(2) Regulation on Threatening Ukraine, Art. 8(1) Regulation on Iran Assisting Russia, Art. 14(1) Regulation on Moldova and Art. 2b(1) Regulation on Belarus.

2069. Article 3(3) Regulation on Threatening Ukraine, Art. 8(2) Regulation on Iran Assisting Russia, Art. 14(2) Regulation on Moldova and Art. 2b(2) Regulation on Belarus.

2070. *See Rotenberg* (n. 2016) paras 47-49, 58 & 146; *Almaz-Antey'* (n. 1991) paras 54-56, 61 & 68.

2071. Article 9(2)(a) & (b) Regulation on Threatening Ukraine, Art. 12(2)(a) & (b) Regulation on Iran Assisting Russia.

which is to circumvent the measures.[2072] Such obligations are set out neither in the Regulation on Belarus nor in the Regulation on Moldova.

456. With regard to de-listing, the lists need to be reviewed at regular intervals and at least every twelve months, whereas the Council has the duty to communicate its decisions to affected persons, who have the right to submit or present observations,[2073] as already explained (*see* in this regard paragraphs 149 et seq. above).

457. The regulations at hand further limit the liability of third parties that in truth give effect to the restrictive measures[2074] in the already explained manner (*see* in this regard paragraph 161 above), also with regard to claims[2075] that have the aforementioned meaning[2076] and the relevant onus of proof[2077] (*see* in this regard paragraphs 167 et seq. above). Still, the Regulation on Iran Assisting Russia and the Regulation on Belarus differentiate, as they prohibit claims not only by designated persons but also by any Iranian or Belarussian person respectively.[2078]

§3 FURTHER RESTRICTIONS ON FUNDS AND FINANCIAL SERVICES

458. The Regulation on Russia and the Regulation on Belarus prescribe further financial restrictions that range from *any transaction* and *public financing and financial assistance for trade and investment* to certain *services*.

I Any Transaction

459. At the outset, under the Regulation on Russia, it is prohibited to perform *any transaction*, an undefined term, both directly and indirectly, with legal persons established in Russia that are either controlled or owned by the state or in whose profits the state has the right to participate, or that has been designated by the EU as having other substantial economic relationship with Russia.[2079] It also applies to legal persons established outside the EU, when they are controlled or owned by a legal person, which

2072. Article 9(3) & (1) Regulation on Threatening Ukraine, Art. 12(3) & (1) Regulation on Iran Assisting Russia.

2073. Article 14(4), (2) & (3) Regulation on Threatening Ukraine, Art. 7(4), (2) & (3) Regulation on Iran Assisting Russia, Art. 14(4), (2) & (3) Regulation on Moldova and Art. 8a(4), (2) & (3) Regulation on Belarus.

2074. Article 10(1) & (2) Regulation on Threatening Ukraine, Art. 10(1) & (2) Regulation on Iran Assisting Russia, Art. 10(1) & (2) Regulation on Moldova and Arts 6 & 2a Regulation on Belarus.

2075. Article 11(1) Regulation on Threatening Ukraine, Art. 11(1) Regulation on Iran Assisting Russia, Art. 11(1) Regulation on Moldova and Art. 8d(1) Regulation on Belarus.

2076. Article 1(a) Regulation on Threatening Ukraine, Art. 1(b) Regulation on Iran Assisting Russia, Art. 1(a) Regulation on Moldova and Art. 1(15) Regulation on Belarus.

2077. Article 11(2) Regulation on Threatening Ukraine, Art. 11(2) Regulation on Iran Assisting Russia, Art. 11(2) Regulation on Moldova and Art. 8d(2)(b) Regulation on Belarus.

2078. Article 11(1)(b) Regulation on Iran Assisting Russia and Art. 8d(1)(c) Regulation on Belarus.

2079. At the time of writing these were: OPK Oboronprom, United Aircraft Corporation, Uralvagonzavod, Rosneft, Transneft, Gazprom Neft, Almaz-Antey, Kamaz, Rostec (Russian

has other substantial economic relationship with Russia, as per the EU's designation.[2080] Similarly, it is prohibited to engage in a transaction with a person acting on behalf of or at the direction of such a Russian person or a designated person.[2081] Three exceptions are attached to this general prohibition of transactions in the form of transactions either falling outside the scope of this provision or being authorized by competent authorities under conditions deemed appropriate. First, such an authorization may be granted when the relevant transactions are strictly necessary for all aforementioned entities and their subsidiaries in the Union to divest and withdraw by the end of 2023 from a person established in the EU.[2082] Payments on the basis of such contracts are equally exempt from the prohibition.[2083] Lastly, unless otherwise prohibited, the following items fall outside the scope of application of the general prohibition of transactions:

- those strictly necessary for the purchase, import and transport of natural gas, titanium, aluminium, copper, nickel, palladium and iron ore from or though Russia into the Union, the European Economic Area, Switzerland or the Western Balkans;[2084]
- those strictly necessary for the purchase, import and transport of oil, including refined petroleum products, from or through Russia, unless otherwise prohibited (*see* in this regard paragraphs 505 et seq. below);[2085]
- those related to energy projects outside Russia in which a designated person is a minority shareholder;[2086]
- such for purchase import and transport of coal and other solid fossil fuel until 10 August 2022;[2087]
- those strictly necessary for the wind-down within a specific time frame of a joint-venture made before a point in time involving a designated person;[2088]
- those strictly necessary for providing electronic communication services, data centre services, as well as services and equipment necessary for their operation, maintenance, and security, including the provision of firewalls, and call centre services, to a designated person;[2089]

Technologies State Corporation), JSC PO Sevmash, Sovcomflot, United Shipbuilding Corporation, Russian Maritime Register of Shipping (RMRS) and Russian Regional Development Bank. Article 5aa(1)(a) and Annex XIX Regulation on Russia.

2080. At the time of writing these were the aforementioned persons. Article 5aa(1)(b) and Annex XIX Regulation on Russia.
2081. Article 5aa(1)(c) Regulation on Russia.
2082. Article 5aa(3e) Regulation on Russia.
2083. Article 5aa(2a), (2c) & (2e) Regulation on Russia.
2084. Article 5aa(3)(a) Regulation on Russia.
2085. Articles 5aa(3)(aa), 3m & 3n Regulation on Russia.
2086. Article 5aa(3)(b) Regulation on Russia.
2087. Article 5aa(3)(c) Regulation on Russia.
2088. The joint venture, or similar legal arrangement must have been concluded before 16 Mar. 2022 and the wind-down has to take place by 31 Dec. 2024. Article 5aa(3)(d) Regulation on Russia.
2089. Article 5aa(3)(e) Regulation on Russia.

- those necessary for the purchase, import or transport of pharmaceutical, medical, agricultural and food products, including wheat and fertilizers as long as such import, purchase and transport is not prohibited thereunder;[2090] and
- those strictly necessary for access to judicial, arbitral and administrative proceedings in the Union, including recognition and enforcement of an award or judgment rendered in a Member State, under the condition that such transactions are consistent with the objectives of the Regulation on Russia.[2091]

460. In relation to the aforementioned general prohibition on transactions and the provided exceptions, two notes must be made. At the outset, a process facilitating remedy or making a complaint against the designation of persons as having a substantial economic relationship with Russia is absent, thus giving to the EU institution that performs the designations under Annex XIX, supreme, absolute and unchecked power. Furthermore, the Regulation on Russia aspires to bend the New York Convention[2092] by introducing additional conditions for the execution of arbitral awards, in an act that defies the 1969 Vienna Convention.[2093]

461. The twelfth package introduced a duty to report transfer of funds of more than EUR 100,000. First, this duty is imposed on legal persons established in the Union that are owned by Russian natural and legal persons or persons residing in Russia as of 1 May 2024. Within this frame, ownership requires holding at least 40% of the shares of a legal person. The bearers of this duty have to fulfil this reporting requirement quarterly and within two weeks of the end of each quarter to the competent authority of the Member State of their incorporation.[2094] Second, this duty is imposed on credit and financial institutions as of 1 July 2024 with regard to transfers of funds that cumulatively exceed EUR 100,000 and are initiated by legal persons owned by Russian natural and legal persons or persons residing in Russia. Credit and financial institutions have to perform this duty every semester and within two weeks of the end of each semester, notwithstanding the applicable rules concerning reporting, confidentiality and professional secrecy.[2095] The Member States shall then assess the information received and identify transactions, legal persons and business sectors that indicate a serious risk of breaches or circumvention of the Regulation on Russia, the Regulation on Threatening Russia, the Regulation on Goods from Crimea and the Regulation with regard to Donetsk and Luhansk.[2096]

2090. Article 5aa(3)(f) Regulation on Russia.
2091. Article 5aa(3)(g) Regulation on Russia.
2092. Convention on the Recognition and Enforcement of Foreign Arbitral Awards (New York 1958) 330 UNTS 3.
2093. Vienna Convention on the Law of Treaties (Vienna 1969) 1155 UNTS 331.
2094. Article 5r(1)(a), (b) & (c) Regulation on Russia.
2095. Article 5r(2) Regulation on Russia.
2096. Article 5r(3) Regulation on Russia.

II Public Financing and Financial Assistance for Trade and Investment

462. The Regulation on Russia as well as the Regulation on Belarus, prohibit public financing or financial assistance for trade with, or investment in, these states.[2097] *Financing or financial assistance* has been defined as any action, whereby the person, entity or body concerned disburses or commits to disburse its own funds or economic resources, excluding those made in line with normal business practice[2098] (in regard to the definition *see* Annex I p. 311 at 323). Specifically with regard to Belarus, it is prohibited to provide insurance and re-insurance to the state, including its government, public bodies, corporations and agencies, and anyone acting on their behalf or at their direction, with the exception of compulsory or third-party liability insurance to legal persons established in Belarus, where the risk is situated in the Union, as well as for diplomatic missions of Belarus.[2099] The prohibition on public financing and financial assistance does not apply to binding relevant commitments made before a specific point in time,[2100] as well as to the provision of such assistance for trade in food and for agricultural, medical and humanitarian purposes.[2101] It equally does not apply to providing such assistance for the benefit of small and medium-sized enterprises established in the Union, as long as it does not exceed the value of EUR 10 million per project.[2102]

463. Making new credit and loans to certain persons after a specific date are also prohibited per se under said two regulations[2103] as well as under the Regulation on Goods from Crimea and the Regulation with regard to Donetsk and Luhansk. The Regulation on Russia has designated persons ineligible for such loans from major credit institutions *or* other major institutions having an explicit mandate to promote the competitiveness of the Russian economy, its diversification and encouragement of investment, established in Russia and publicly owned or controlled.[2104] The same applies to legal persons established outside the Union that are owned by the designated persons and any other legal person acting on behalf of or at the direction of such a person.[2105] These prohibitions put in place measures necessary to give effect to the

2097. Article 2e(1) Regulation on Russia. and Art. 1t(1) Regulation on Belarus.
2098. Article 1(o) Regulation on Russia and Art. 1(17) Regulation on Belarus.
2099. Article 1l Regulation on Belarus.
2100. For Russia this is 26 Feb. 2022 and for Belarus 10 Mar. 2022. *See* Art. 2e(2)(a) Regulation on Russia and Art. 1t(2)(a) Regulation on Belarus, respectively.
2101. Article 2e(2)(c) Regulation on Russia and Art. 1t(2)(c) Regulation on Belarus.
2102. Article 2e(2)(b) Regulation on Russia and Art. 1t(2)(b) Regulation on Belarus.
2103. With regard to Russia this date is 26 Feb. 2022 and in relation to Belarus 29 Jun. 2021. In the latter case, new loans or credits need to have a maturity exceeding ninety days in order to fall within the scope of the prohibition. *See* Art. 5(6)(i) & (ii) Regulation on Russia and Art. 1k(1) Regulation on Belarus.
2104. The designated persons are Sberbank, VTB Bank, Gazprombank, Vnesheconombank (VEB) and Rosselkhozbank. Articles 5(6) & 5(1)(a) and Annex III Regulation on Russia. *See* in regard to the latter provision *Sberbank of Russia OAO v. Council*, T-732/14, Judgment of 13 Sep. 2018, digital ECR paras 83-85 and *VTB Bank PAO, formerly VTB Bank OAO v. Council*, C-729/18 P, Judgment of 25 Jun. 2020, digital ECR paras 30 & 31 ('VTB Bank').
2105. Articles 5(6) & 5(1)(b) & (c) and Annex III Regulation on Russia.

general prohibition of investment services and financial services explained immediately above.[2106] The objective of designations made under such criteria is to increase the costs of the actions of the Russian Federation designed to undermine Ukraine's territorial integrity, sovereignty and independence.[2107] In a similar manner, the EU has designated legal persons for being major credit institutions established in Belarus and owned or controlled by the state.[2108] The prohibition also applies to legal persons established in a third state that are owned by the designated persons and any other legal person acting on their behalf or at their direction.[2109] The Regulation on Belarus differs as it additionally prohibits the provision of credit and loans to the Republic of Belarus, its Government, its public bodies and corporations or agencies.[2110] Outside the scope of said prohibition fall loans and credits having a specific and documented objective to provide financing for non-prohibited imports or exports of goods and non-financial services between the Union and any third state. These include the expenditure for goods and services from another third state that is necessary for executing the export or import contracts. Specifically with regard to Russia, the competent authority must be notified within three months.[2111] Furthermore, outside the scope of said prohibition also fall loans aiming to provide emergency funding to meet solvency and liquidity criteria for legal persons established in the EU, whose proprietary rights are owned by a designated legal person, as long as the competent authorities are notified within the same time frame.[2112] The Regulation on Goods from Crimea and the Regulation with regard to Donetsk and Luhansk prohibit the making of loans, credit or other financing, including equity capital, to an *entity in Crimea or Sevastopol*[2113] (in regard to the definition *see* Annex I p. 311 at 319), to an *entity in the specified territories*[2114] (in regard to the definition *see* Annex I p. 311 at 319) or for the documented purpose of financing such an entity.[2115] These prohibitions do not apply to the conduct of legitimate business with legal persons outside Crimea, Sevastopol and the specified territories as long as the related investments are not destined for said entities.[2116] Obligations arising from contracts concluded before a specific point in time, as well as from ancillary contracts necessary for their execution are also excluded from these prohibitions, under the condition that the competent authorities are

2106. *VTB Bank* (n. 2104) para. 33 citing *Rosneft* 2017 (n. 347) para. 141.
2107. *DenizBank* (n. 2067) para. 77, citing *Rosneft* 2017 (n. 347) para. 123.
2108. The designated persons are Belarusbank, Belivestbank (Belarusian Bank for Development and Reconstruction), Belagroprombank, Bank Dabrabyt and Development Bank of the Republic of Belarus. Article 1k(1)(b) and Annex IX Regulation on Belarus.
2109. Article 1k(1)(c) & (d) and Annex IX Regulation on Belarus.
2110. Article 1k(1)(a) Regulation on Belarus.
2111. Article 5(6)(a) Regulation on Russia and Art. 1k(2) Regulation on Belarus.
2112. The designated persons are Sberbank, VTB Bank, Gazprombank, Vnesheconombank (VEB) and Rosselkhozbank. Article 5(6)(b) and Annex III Regulation on Russia.
2113. Article 1(h) Regulation on Goods from Crimea.
2114. Article 1(e) Regulation with Regard to Donetsk and Luhansk.
2115. Article 2a(1)(c) Regulation on Goods from Crimea and Art. 3(1)(c) Regulation with regard to Donetsk and Luhansk.
2116. Article 2a(2) Regulation on Goods from Crimea and Art. 3(2) Regulation with regard to Donetsk and Luhansk.

informed at least five days in advance.[2117] With regard to the above-explained prohibition, it must be reiterated that no legal remedy against the designation of legal persons by, once again, an undisclosed institution of the EU is available.

464. Lastly, it is prohibited to invest, participate or otherwise contribute to projects co-financed by the Russian Direct Investment Fund, unless this is due under contracts made before 2 March 2022, including ancillary contracts necessary for their execution. In such a case, the competent authorities must provide authorization under any conditions deemed appropriate.[2118]

III Transferable Securities and Other Money Market Instruments

465. Transferable securities and money market instruments are at the front-stage of the ensuing prohibition in the Regulation on Russia and in the Regulation on Belarus. Within this frame, *transferable securities* have been defined as classes of securities, such as shares, bonds or other forms of scrutinized debt, negotiable on the capital market, but for instruments of payment[2119] (in regard to the definition *see* Annex I p. 311 at 335). *Money-market instruments* however are those classes of instruments which are normally dealt in on the money market, excluding instruments of payment[2120] (in regard to the definition *see* Annex I p. 311 at 329). Transferable securities and money-market instruments may neither be purchased, sold, provided or otherwise dealt with irrespective of their date of maturity, by certain persons, when said instruments have been issued after a specific point in time.[2121] With regard to Russia, this point in time is 12 April 2022 and the persons have been designated in five groups, whereas with regard to Belarus, the point in time is 29 June 2021 and the persons consist of the state itself, including the government and public bodies, corporations and agencies, as well as of a group of designated persons.

466. Russian designated persons are the following: (a) major credit institutions and other major institutions having an explicit mandate to promote the competitiveness of the Russian economy, its diversification and encouragement of investment that have been established in Russia and are owned or controlled by the state;[2122] (b) major credit institutions, other institutions owned or controlled publicly, or other credit institution that have a significant role in supporting the activities of Russia, the Russian government or the Central Bank of Russia and are established in Russia;[2123] (c) legal persons that are predominantly engaged in concepting, producing, selling and exporting

2117. Article 2a(3) Regulation on Goods from Crimea and Art. 3(3) Regulation with regard to Donetsk and Luhansk.
2118. Article 2e(3) & (4) Regulation on Russia.
2119. Article 1(f) Regulation on Russia and Art. 1(10) Regulation on Belarus.
2120. Article 1(g) Regulation on Russia and Art. 1(11) Regulation on Belarus.
2121. Article 5(1), (2), (3) & (4) Regulation on Russia and Art. 1j Regulation on Belarus.
2122. These are: Sberbank, VTB Bank, Gazprombank, Vnesheconombank (VEB) and Rosselkhozbank. Article 5(1)(a) and Annex III Regulation on Russia.
2123. These are, at the time of writing: Alfa Bank, Bank Otkritie, Bank Rossiya and Promvyazbank. Article 5(2)(a) and Annex XII Regulation on Russia.

military equipment or services and are established in Russia, with the exception of legal persons active in the space or the nuclear energy sectors;[2124] (d) legal persons generating at least half of their revenues from the sale or the transportation of crude oil or petroleum products that are owned or controlled by the state, have estimated assets of more than RUB 1 trillion and are established in Russia;[2125] and (e) publicly owned or controlled legal persons, in whose profits Russia, its government or the Central Bank participate or with which Russia, its government or the Central Bank have other substantial economic relationships.[2126] This prohibition also applies to legal persons resident in a third country, that are owned or controlled both directly and indirectly by said designated persons and legal persons acting on behalf of or at the direction of said designated persons.[2127] The latter designation criterion is fulfilled by plain ownership of a foreign person by a designated legal person.[2128]

467. With regard to Belarus, the persons designated, apart from the state of Belarus, are major credit institutions that are under state ownership or public control.[2129] As already seen in Russia, said prohibition equally applies to legal persons resident in a third country, that are owned or controlled both directly and indirectly by these designated persons, and legal persons acting on their behalf or at their direction.[2130]

468. Furthermore, it is prohibited, after 29 January 2023, to list and provide services for transferable securities of any legal person that is registered in Russia and is state-owned. Specifically with regard to trading venues,[2131] that being a regulated market,[2132] a multilateral trading facility[2133] or an organized trading facility,[2134] that are registered or recognized in the Union, no such securities may be admitted to trading, after 29 January 2023.[2135]

2124. These are, at the time of writing: ORK Oboronprom, United Aircraft Corp, Uralvagonzavod. Article 5(3)(a) and Annex V Regulation on Russia.
2125. These are: Rosneft, Transneft and Gasprom Neft. Article 5(3)(b) and Annex VI Regulation on Russia.
2126. These are: Almaz-Antey, Kamaz, Novorossiysk Commercial Sea Port, Rostec, Russia Railways, JSC Po Sevmash, Sovcomflot, United Shipbuilding Corporation and Russian Maritime Registration of Shipping. Article 5(4)(a) and Annex XIII Regulation on Russia.
2127. Article 5(1)(b) & (c) and Annex III, (2)(b) & (c) and Annex XII, (3)(c) & (d) and Annexes V & VI and (4)(b) & (c) and Annex XIII Regulation on Russia.
2128. *DenizBank A.Ş. v. Council*, T-798/14, Judgment of 13 Sep. 2018, digital ECR para. 82.
2129. These are: Belarusbank, Belinvestbank (Belarusian Bank for Development and Reconstruction), Belagroprombank, Bank Dabrabyt and Development Bank of the Republic of Belarus. Article 1j(b) and Annex IX Regulation on Belarus.
2130. Article 1j(c) & (d) Regulation on Belarus.
2131. With regard to the definition *see* Art. 1(n) Regulation on Belarus. and Art. 4(24) Directive 2014/65/EU of the European Parliament and of the Council of 15 May 2014 on markets in financial instruments and amending Directive 2002/92/EC and Directive 2011/61/EU, OJ L 173, 12 Jun. 2014, p. 349.
2132. In regard to the definition of *regulated market* set out in Art. 4(21) Directive 2014/65/EU *see* Annex I p. 311 at 330.
2133. In regard to the definition of *multilateral trading facility* set out in Art. 4(22) Directive 2014/65/EU *see* Annex I p. 311 at 329.
2134. In regard to the definition of *organized trading facility* set out in Art. 4(23) Directive 2014/65/EU *see* Annex I p. 311 at 329.
2135. Article 5(5) Regulation on Russia.

469. Similarly, Union central securities depositories[2136] after 12 April 2022 must refrain from providing any of the following services for transferable securities to any Russian or Belarusian national or legal person established in Russia or Belarus:[2137] (a) core services of central securities depositories; (b) non-banking-type ancillary services of central securities depositories that do not entail credit or liquid risk; and (c) banking-type ancillary services.[2138] Exempt from this prohibition are nationals of a Member State and natural persons having a residence permit, temporary or permanent in those states.[2139] The Regulation on Russia extends the derogation to include nationals and residents of the European Economic Area and Switzerland.[2140]

470. Furthermore, transferable securities denominated in any official currency of a Member State and issued after 12 April 2022 may not be sold to any Russian or Belarusian national, natural and legal person, as well as to any natural person residing in Russia or in Belarus. Units in collective investment undertakings providing exposure to such securities may also not be sold to any such person.[2141] Exempt from this prohibition are nationals of a Member State and natural persons having a residence permit, temporary or permanent in those states.[2142] The Regulation on Russia extends the derogation to include nationals and residents of the European Economic Area and Switzerland.[2143]

471. Moreover, purchasing, selling and providing *investment services*[2144] for transferable securities and money-market instruments issued after 9 March 2022 by Russia, its government, its Central Bank and anyone acting on their behalf or at their direction is prohibited. Assisting in the issuance of transferable securities and money-market instruments is also prohibited.[2145] Similar is the prohibition with regard to Belarus, whereby the transferable securities and money-market instruments need to have maturity exceeding ninety days and be issued after 29 June 2021. Further same instruments need to have been issued by Belarus, its government, its public bodies, corporations and agencies, or a major credit institution established in Belarus and

2136. In regard to the statutory definition of *central securities depository* (Art. 2(1) and Annex Regulation (EU) No. 909/2014 of the European Parliament and of the Council of 23 Jul. 2014 on improving securities settlement in the European Union and on central securities depositories and amending Directives 98/26/EC and 2014/65/EU and Regulation (EU) No. 236/2012, OJ L 257 28 Aug. 2014, p. 1, as last amended by Regulation (EU) 2022/858 of the European Parliament and of the Council of 30 May 2022 on a pilot regime for market infrastructures based on distributed ledger technology, and amending Regulations (EU) No. 600/2014 and (EU) No. 909/2014 and Directive 2014/65/EU, OJ L 151, 2 Jun. 2022, p. 1) *see* Annex I p. 311 at 312.
2137. Article 5e(1) Regulation on Russia and Art. 1x(1) Regulation on Belarus.
2138. Sections A, B & C Annex Regulation (EU) 909/2014.
2139. Article 5e(2) Regulation on Russia and Art. 1x(2) Regulation on Belarus.
2140. Article 5e(2) Regulation on Russia.
2141. Article 5f(1) Regulation on Russia and Art. 1y(1) Regulation on Belarus.
2142. Article 5f(2) Regulation on Russia and Art. 1y(2) Regulation on Belarus.
2143. Article 5f(2) Regulation on Russia.
2144. In regard to the definition of *investment services* set out in Art. 1(e) Regulation on Russia and Art. 1(9) Regulation on Belarus *see* Annex I p. 311 at 327.
2145. Article 5a(1)(a), (b) & (c) Regulation on Russia.

owned or controlled by the state.[2146] The same applies to instruments issued by a legal person established in a third state that is owned by an aforementioned entity as well as by anyone acting on their behalf or at their direction.[2147]

IV Specialized Financial Messaging Services

472. Specialized financial messaging services, which are used to exchange financial data, may not be provided to designated persons in Russia[2148] and Belarus[2149] as well as to any legal person controlled or owned by such persons directly or indirectly.[2150] No exceptions are set out.

V Central Bank and Banknotes

473. Restrictions are imposed on the Central Bank of Russia and the Central Bank of Belarus, as well as on banknotes of Russia and Belarus. Generally, transactions related to the management of reserves and assets of said central banks, including with any legal person acting on their behalf or at their direction, are prohibited.[2151] Such prohibition could be infringing the law of state immunity.[2152] Nonetheless, it is argued that in view of the nature and scale of Russia's violation of international law, the portrayed prohibition could well qualify as lawful countermeasures in the sense of Articles 49 and 51 Articles on Responsibility of States for Internationally Wrongful Acts ('ARSIWA')[2153] although the fact that the measures are taken by states not directly injured could raise controversial questions.[2154] In any event, the Courts of the EU did

2146. At the time of writing, these are: Belarusbank, Belinvestbank (Belarusian Bank for Development and Reconstruction), Belagroprombank, Bank Dabrabyt and Development Bank of the Republic of Belarus. Article 1j(a) & (b) and Annex IX Regulation on Belarus.

2147. Article 1j(c) & (d) Regulation on Belarus.

2148. From 12 Mar. 2022 onwards to: Bank Otkritie, Novikombank, Promsvyazbank, Bank Rossiya, Sovcombank and Vnesheconombank (VEB), whereas from 14 Jun. 2022 onwards to: Sberbank, Credit Bank of Moscow and Joint Stock Company Russian Agricultural Bank, JSC Rosselkhozbank. Article 5h and Annex XIV Regulation on Russia.

2149. From 20 Mar. 2022 onwards to: Belagroprombank, Bank Dabrabyt and Development Bank of the Republic of Belarus, whereas from 14 Jun. 2022 onwards to: Belinvestbank (Belarusian Bank for Development and Reconstruction). Article 1zb and Annex XV Regulation on Belarus.

2150. Article 5h(1) Regulation on Russia and Art. 1zb(1) Regulation on Belarus.

2151. Article 5a(4) Regulation on Russia and Art. 1ja(1) Regulation on Belarus.

2152. Anton Moiseienko, *Legal: The Freezing of the Russian Central Bank's Assets* (chad050) EJIL 1 at 2 (2023) https://doi.org/10.1093/ejil/chad050; Ron van der Horst, *Illegal, Unless: Freezing the Assets of Russia's Central Bank* (chad053) EJIL 1 at 3 (2023) https://doi.org/10.1093/ejil/chad053.

2153. Anton Moiseienko, *Legal: The Freezing of the Russian Central Bank's Assets* (chad050) EJIL 1 at 9 & 10 (2023) https://doi.org/10.1093/ejil/chad050.

2154. Ron van der Horst, *Illegal, Unless: Freezing the Assets of Russia's Central Bank* (chad053) EJIL 1 at 10 (2023) https://doi.org/10.1093/ejil/chad053. On questioning the legality of restrictive measures as countermeasures against Central Bank of Iran (in the meantime the provision has been repealed) *see* Pierre-Emmanuel Dupont, *Countermeasures and Collective Security: The Case of the EU Sanctions Against Iran*, 17(3) J.C.&S.L. 301 at 323 et seq. (2012) https://doi.org/10.1093/jcsl/krs020.

not view restrictive measures as countermeasures[2155] (*see* in this regard paragraphs 68 & 191 above). Exceptionally, such transactions may be authorized by the competent authorities, when this is strictly necessary for the financial stability of the Union as a whole or of a specific Member State.[2156] Should a Member State wish to proceed with authorizing such a transaction, it must immediately inform accordingly the other Member States and the Commission.[2157]

474. The Regulation on Russia additionally prohibits transactions related to reserves and assets of the Russian National Wealth Fund that may be exempt under the same conditions as the ones already explained for funds and assets of the Central Bank of Russia.[2158]

475. With regard to the explained prohibitions on reserves and assets of the Central Bank of Russia and the Russia National Wealth Fund, a special reporting obligation has been imposed generally on *natural and legal persons*, including but not limited to the European Central Bank, Central Banks of the Member States, financial sector entities,[2159] insurance and reinsurance undertakings,[2160] central securities depositories[2161] and central counterparties[2162,2163] These persons, notwithstanding their statutory duties on reporting, confidentiality and professional secrecy, have to provide to the

2155. *Venezuela* 2023 (n. 12) para. 92.
2156. Article 5a(5) Regulation on Russia and Art. 1ja(2) Regulation on Belarus.
2157. Article 5a(6) Regulation on Russia and Art. 1ja(3) Regulation on Belarus.
2158. Article 5a(4) & (5) Regulation on Russia.
2159. In regard to the definition of *financial sector entity* (Art. 4a Regulation on Russia and Art. 4(27) Regulation (EU) No. 575/2013 of the European Parliament and of the Council of 26 Jun. 2013 on prudential requirements for credit institutions and amending Regulation (EU) No. 648/2012, OJ L 176, 27 Jun. 2013, p. 1, as last amended by Regulation (EU) 2022/2036 of the European Parliament and of the Council of 19 Oct. 2022 amending Regulation (EU) No. 575/2013 and Directive 2014/59/EU as regards the prudential treatment of global systemically important institutions with a multiple-point-of-entry resolution strategy and methods for the indirect subscription of instruments eligible for meeting the minimum requirement for own funds and eligible liabilities, OJ L 275, 25 Oct. 2022, p. 1) *see* Annex I p. 311 at 322.....
2160. In regard to the definition of *insurance undertaking* (Art. 5a(4a) Regulation on Russia and Art. 13(1) & (4) Directive 2009/138/EC of the European Parliament and of the Council of 25 Nov. 2009 on the taking-up and pursuit of the business of Insurance and Reinsurance (Solvency II), OJ L 335 17 Dec. 2009, p. 1, as last amended by Directive (EU) 2019/2177 of the European Parliament and of the Council of 18 Dec. 2019 amending Directive 2009/138/EC on the taking-up and pursuit of the business of Insurance and Reinsurance (Solvency II), Directive 2014/65/EU on markets in financial instruments and Directive (EU) 2015/849 on the prevention of the use of the financial system for the purposes of money-laundering or terrorist financing, OJ L 334, 27 Dec. 2019, p. 155) *see* Annex I p. 311 at 326.
2161. In regard to the definition of *central securities depository see* Annex I p. 311 at 312. Article 5a(4a) Regulation on Russia and Art. 2(1) and Annex Regulation (EU) 909/2014.
2162. In regard to the definition of *central counterparty* also abbreviated as CCP (Art. 5a(4a) Regulation on Russia and Art. 2(1) Regulation (EU) No. 648/2012 of the European Parliament and of the Council of 4 Jul. 2012 on OTC derivatives, central counterparties and trade repositories, OJ L 201 27 Jul. 2012, p. 1, as last amended by Regulation (EU) 2021/168 of the European Parliament and of the Council of 10 Feb. 2021 amending Regulation (EU) 2016/1011 as regards the exemption of certain third-country spot foreign exchange benchmarks and the designation of replacements for certain benchmarks in cessation, and amending Regulation (EU) No. 648/2012, OJ L 49, 12 Feb. 2021, p. 6) *see* Annex I p. 311 at 312.
2163. Article 5a(4a) Regulation on Russia.

competent national authority and the Commission information on the assets and reserves which they hold or control or they are counterparty to. Such information, which must be updated every three months, entails: (a) information identifying the natural or legal persons holding or controlling such assets and reserves; (b) the amount or market value of such assets and reserves at the date of reporting and at the date of immobilization;[2164] and (c) types of the assets and reserves,[2165] including crypto-assets and economic resources within the meaning of 'assets of every kind, whether tangible or intangible, movable or immovable, which are not funds but may be used to obtain funds, goods or services'.[2166]

476. Further, said natural and legal persons along with Member States have the obligation to cooperate with the Commission in any effort to verify information provided received under the above-explained process. The Commission also has the power to request any additional information for the purposes of verification from such persons, whereas this request shall be simultaneously transmitted to the competent authority of the relevant Member State.[2167] Any received information under the explained processes is to be used by the Commission and the competent authorities of the Member States solely for the purposes for which it has been given.[2168]

477. Turning to banknotes, it is prohibited to sell, supply, transfer and export banknotes denominated in any official currency of a Member State to Russia and Belarus, to any natural or legal person in Russia and in Belarus, including their Central Banks, or for use in said states.[2169] Sale, supply, transfer and export for personal use of natural persons travelling to Russia are exempt. So is sale, supply, transfer and export for official purposes of diplomatic missions, consular posts or international organizations in Russia enjoying immunities under International Law.[2170]

VI Deposits

478. Within the present framework *deposit* (in regard to the definition *see* Annex I p. 311 at 318) is understood as a credit balance which results from funds left in an account or from temporary situations deriving from normal banking transactions and which a credit institution is required to repay, including a fixed-term deposit and a savings deposit, but for such balance that can only be proven by a *financial instrument*[2171] (in

2164. Article 5a(4a)(a) & (b) Regulation on Russia.
2165. These are to be broken down according to the categories included in the definition of *funds* (*see* in this regard para. 428 above). Article 5a(4a)(c) Regulation on Russia and Art. 1(g) Regulation on Threatening Ukraine.
2166. Article 5a(4a)(c) Regulation on Russia and Art. 1(d) Regulation on Threatening Ukraine.
2167. Article 5a(4c) Regulation on Russia.
2168. Article 5a(4d) Regulation on Russia.
2169. Article 5i(1) Regulation on Russia and Art. 1za(1) Regulation on Belarus.
2170. Article 5i(2)(a) & (b) Regulation on Russia and Art. 1za(2)(a) & (b) Regulation on Belarus.
2171. *Financial instrument* stands for the following instruments, including such instruments issued by means of distributed ledger technology: Transferable securities; Money-market instruments; Units in collective investment undertakings; Options, futures, swaps, forward rate agreements and any other derivative contracts relating to securities, currencies, interest rates

regard to the definition *see* Annex I p. 311 at 321) or when its principal is not repayable at par, or when its principal is repayable at par but only under a particular guarantee or agreement.[2172] Deposits in this sense of more than EUR 100,000 per credit institution are not accepted in the Union when the person wishing to make a deposit is a Russian or Belarusian national, natural persons residing in Russia or Belarus, as well as legal persons established in Russia or Belarus.[2173] In particular, with regard to deposits originating from Russia, legal persons established in a third state that are owned by Russian nationals or other nationals residing in Russia, are also precluded from performing deposits to credit institutions in the Union.[2174] No mention of legal persons or otherwise exercising control over such legal persons is made. The Regulation on Russia further prohibits providing crypto-asset wallet, account and custody services to Russian nationals, other nationals residing in Russia and legal persons established in Russia;[2175] it equally prohibits nationals of and residents in Russia from owning, controlling or holding posts in any legal person providing such services.[2176] The Regulation on Belarus is silent on this matter. Exempt from all these prohibitions are nationals of a Member State, a member of the European Economic Area and Switzerland as well as other nationals residing in said states both temporarily and permanently.[2177]

479. Competent authorities of Member States, in a manner quite similar to the derogations allowing for releasing frozen funds (*see* in this regard paragraphs 444 et seq. above), may allow for such a deposit to be accepted by a credit institution in the Union, under conditions that it may deem appropriate, should the purpose of the

---

or yields, emission allowances or other derivatives instruments, financial indices or financial measures which may be settled physically or in cash; Options, futures, swaps, forwards and any other derivative contracts relating to commodities that must be settled in cash or may be settled in cash at the option of one of the parties other than by reason of default or other termination event; Options, futures, swaps, and any other derivative contract relating to commodities that can be physically settled provided that they are traded on a regulated market, a MTF, or an OTF, except for wholesale energy products traded on an OTF that must be physically settled; Options, futures, swaps, forwards and any other derivative contracts relating to commodities, that can be physically settled not otherwise mentioned in point 6 of this Section and not being for commercial purposes, which have the characteristics of other derivative financial instruments; Derivative instruments for the transfer of credit risk; Financial contracts for differences; Options, futures, swaps, forward rate agreements and any other derivative contracts relating to climatic variables, freight rates or inflation rates or other official economic statistics that must be settled in cash or may be settled in cash at the option of one of the parties other than by reason of default or other termination event, as well as any other derivative contracts relating to assets, rights, obligations, indices and measures not otherwise mentioned in this section, which have the characteristics of other derivative financial instruments, having regard to whether, *inter alia*, they are traded on a regulated market, OTF, or an MTF; Emission allowances consisting of any units recognized for compliance with the requirements of Directive 2003/87/EC (Emissions Trading Scheme). Article 4(1)(15) and Annex I section C Nos 1-11 Directive 2014/65.

2172. Article 1(k) Regulation on Russia and Art. 1(21) Regulation on Belarus.
2173. Article 5b(1) Regulation on Russia and Art. 1u(1) Regulation on Belarus.
2174. Article 5b(1) Regulation on Russia.
2175. Article 5b(2) Regulation on Russia.
2176. Article 5b(2a) Regulation on Russia.
2177. Article 5b(3) Regulation on Russia and Art. 1u(2) Regulation on Belarus.

intended deposit be: (a) satisfying the basic needs of persons intending to proceed with it, their dependent family members, including payments for food, rent, mortgage, medicines and medical treatment, taxes, insurance payments and public utility charges, as long as they are necessary;[2178] (b) payment of professional fees, including reimbursement of incurred expenses associated with the provision of legal services, to the extent that they are reasonable;[2179] (c) extraordinary expenses only to the extent that they are necessary and under the condition that other Member States and the Commission are informed two weeks in advance;[2180] (d) the official ones of a diplomatic mission, consular posts or international organizations, when these are necessary;[2181] and (e) non-prohibited cross-border trade in goods and services between the Union and Russia or Belarus and as long as they are deemed necessary.[2182] With regard to Russia, deposits may also be authorized, when they are intended for the payment of fees and service charges for routine holding and maintenance of frozen funds and economic resources.[2183] Competent authorities may also authorize the acceptance of deposits when these are deemed necessary for humanitarian purposes, such as the delivery of assistance, that could include medical supplies, food and transfer of humanitarian workers, related assistance and evacuations,[2184] as well as for civil society activities that directly promote democracy, human rights and the rule of law in Russia or Belarus.[2185] Any such authorization, with the exception of any related to extraordinary expenses and cross-border trade on the part of Belarus, shall be notified to other Member States and the Commission within two weeks of it having been granted.[2186]

VII Certain Contracts

480. Russian nationals, other nationals residing in Russia, legal persons established in Russia,[2187] as well as legal persons established in third states but owned by such persons,[2188] including persons acting on their behalf or at their directions may neither be awarded nor continue the execution of certain contracts.[2189] These are any public contracts or concession contracts covered by the EU public procurement framework.[2190]

2178. Article 5c(1)(a) Regulation on Russia and Art. 1v(1)(a) Regulation on Belarus.
2179. Article 5c(1)(b) Regulation on Russia and Art. 1v(1)(b) Regulation on Belarus.
2180. Article 5c(1)(d) Regulation on Russia and Art. 1v(1)(c) Regulation on Belarus.
2181. Article 5c(1)(e) Regulation on Russia and Art. 1v(1)(d) Regulation on Belarus.
2182. Article 5c(1)(f) Regulation on Russia and Art. 1u(3) Regulation on Belarus.
2183. Article 5c(1)(c) Regulation on Russia.
2184. Article 5d(1)(a) Regulation on Russia and Art. 1w(1)(a) Regulation on Belarus.
2185. Article 5d(1)(b) Regulation on Russia and Art. 1w(1)(b) Regulation on Belarus.
2186. Articles 5c(2) and 5d(2) Regulation on Russia and Arts 1v(2) and 1w(2) Regulation on Belarus.
2187. Article 5k(1)(a) Regulation on Russia.
2188. Article 5k(1)(b) Regulation on Russia.
2189. Article 5k(1)(c) Regulation on Russia.
2190. Article 5k(1) Regulation on Russia. This framework entails: Directive 2014/23/EU of the European Parliament and of the Council of 26 Feb. 2014 on the award of concession contracts, OJ L 094, 28 Mar. 2014, p. 1, as last amended by Commission Delegated Regulation (EU) 2021/1951 of 10 Nov. 2021 amending Directive 2014/23/EU of the European Parliament and

Contracts concluded before 9 April 2022 do not fall within the scope of this prohibition.[2191]

481. Competent authorities of the Member States are given the power to authorize the award and continued execution of contracts related to energy, metals, space and diplomatic missions. The exception with regard to energy covers civil nuclear facilities, such as the Paks II project, including decommissioning, nuclear waste management and fuel supply, nuclear energy for medical applications, environmental radiation monitoring and civil nuclear cooperation.[2192] It also covers the purchase, import and transport of natural gas and oil, unless otherwise prohibited[2193] (*see* in this regard paragraphs 497 et seq. below) and coal and other fossil fuels until 10 August 2022.[2194] The metals exception includes titanium, aluminium copper, nickel, palladium and iron ore.[2195] Lastly, said prohibition is not intended to impede intergovernmental cooperation in space programmes and the functioning of diplomatic and consular representations of the Union and its Member States in Russia or of international organizations in Russia that under international law enjoy immunities.[2196] When an authorization is

of the Council in respect of the thresholds for concessions, OJ L 398, 11 Nov. 2021, p. 21; Directive 2014/24/EU of the European Parliament and of the Council of 26 Feb. 2014 on public procurement and repealing Directive 2004/18/EC, OJ L 94, 28.3.2014, p. 65, as last amended by Commission Delegated Regulation (EU) 2021/1952 of 10 Nov. 2021 amending Directive 2014/24/EU of the European Parliament and of the Council in respect of the thresholds for public supply, service and works contracts, and design contests, OJ L 398, 11 Nov. 2021, p. 23; Directive 2014/25/EU of the European Parliament and of the Council of 26 Feb. 2014 on procurement by entities operating in the water, energy, transport and postal services sectors and repealing Directive 2004/17/EC, OJ L 94, 28 Mar. 2014, p. 243, as last amended by Commission Delegated Regulation (EU) 2021/1953 of 10 Nov. 2021 amending Directive 2014/25/EU of the European Parliament and of the Council in respect of the thresholds for supply, service and works contracts, and design contests, OJ L 398, 11 Nov. 2021, p. 25; Directive 2009/81/EC of the European Parliament and of the Council of 13 Jul. 2009 on the coordination of procedures for the award of certain works contracts, supply contracts and service contracts by contracting authorities or entities in the fields of defence and security, and amending Directives 2004/17/EC and 2004/18/EC, OJ L 216, 20 Aug. 2009, p. 76, as last amended by Commission Delegated Regulation (EU) 2021/1950 of 10 Nov. 2021 amending Directive 2009/81/EC of the European Parliament and of the Council in respect of the thresholds for supply, service and works contracts, OJ L 398, 11 Nov. 2021, p. 19; and Regulation (EU, Euratom) 2018/1046 of the European Parliament and of the Council of 18 Jul. 2018 on the financial rules applicable to the general budget of the Union, amending Regulations (EU) No. 1296/2013, (EU) No. 1301/2013, (EU) No. 1303/2013, (EU) No. 1304/2013, (EU) No. 1309/2013, (EU) No. 1316/2013, (EU) No. 223/2014, (EU) No. 283/2014, and Decision No. 541/2014/EU and repealing Regulation (EU, Euratom) No. 966/2012, OJ L 193, 30 Jul. 2018, p. 1, as last amended by Regulation (EU, Euratom) 2022/2434 of the European Parliament and of the Council of 6 Dec. 2022 amending Regulation (EU, Euratom) 2018/1046 as regards the establishment of a diversified funding strategy as a general borrowing method, OJ L 319, 13 Dec. 2022, p. 1.

2191. Article 5k(4) Regulation on Russia.
2192. Article 5k(2)(a) Regulation on Russia.
2193. Articles 5k(2)(e) and 3m or 3n Regulation on Russia.
2194. Article 5k(2)(f) and Annex XXII Regulation on Russia. These *other solid fossil fuels* are goods with the CN Code: 2701, 2702, 2703 00 00, 2704 00, 2705 00 00, 2706 00 00, 2707 and 2708.
2195. Article 5k(2)(e) Regulation on Russia.
2196. Article 5k(b) & (d) Regulation on Russia.

granted, other Member States and the Commission shall be informed thereof within two weeks thereof.[2197]

482. Furthermore, legal persons owned or controlled by Russia may receive no support, both direct and indirect, including financing, financial assistance and any other benefit under a programme or contract of the Union, Euratom or a Member State.[2198] Outside the scope of this prohibition falls support for humanitarian purposes, public health emergencies, prevention and mitigation of events with potentially serious and significant impact on human health and safety or on the environment, response to natural disasters,[2199] phytosanitary and veterinary programmes,[2200] intergovernmental cooperation in space programmes and under the International Thermonuclear Experimental Reactor Agreement,[2201] civil nuclear facilities, such as the Paks II project, nuclear energy for medical applications, environmental radiation monitoring, civil nuclear cooperation,[2202] mobility exchanges for individuals and people-to-people contacts,[2203] climate and environmental programmes[2204] and diplomatic and consular representations in Russia.[2205] Nonetheless, support of climate and environmental programmes in the context of research and innovation is prohibited.[2206]

483. Finally, in relation to Belarus, payments arising out of existing agreements between the state, including its public authorities, and the European Investment Bank may not be performed. Existing Technical Assistance Service Contracts related to such agreements and intended for the benefit of the state are suspended.[2207]

VIII Certain Services

484. The provision of a number of services is prohibited as part of the maze of restrictive measures against Russia, with regard to Crimea as well as in relation to Donetsk and Luhansk. Following the chronological order of their imposition, these are the following.

485. With the fourth package of sanctions in response to Russia's invasion of Ukraine[2208] (*see* in this regard Annex II p. 337 at 339 below), the EU prohibited the provision of credit rating services. *Credit rating* has been defined as 'an opinion

2197. Article 5k(3) Regulation on Russia.
2198. Article 5l(1) Regulation on Russia. On the meaning of 'support' *see* Regulation (EU, Euratom) 2018/1046 (n. 2190).
2199. Article 5l(2)(a) Regulation on Russia.
2200. Article 5l(2)(b) Regulation on Russia.
2201. Article 5l(2)(c) Regulation on Russia.
2202. Article 5l(2)(d) Regulation on Russia.
2203. Article 5l(2)(e) Regulation on Russia.
2204. Article 5l(2)(f) Regulation on Russia.
2205. Article 5l(2)(g) Regulation on Russia.
2206. Article 5l(2)(f) Regulation on Russia.
2207. Article 1n(a) & (b) Regulation on Belarus.
2208. *See* Art. 1(2) Council Decision (CFSP) 2022/430 of 15 Mar. 2022 amending Decision 2014/512/CFSP concerning restrictive measures in view of Russia's actions destabilising the situation in Ukraine, OJ L 87I, 15 Mar. 2022, p. 56 and Art. 1(10) Council Regulation (EU)

regarding the creditworthiness of an entity, a debt or financial obligation, debt security, preferred share or other financial instrument, or of an issuer of such a debt or financial obligation, debt security, preferred share or other financial instrument, issued using an established and defined ranking system of rating categories'.[2209] Credit rating services may not be provided to Russian nationals, other nationals residing in Russia and any legal person established in Russia.[2210] The same persons may neither be provided with access to any subscription services with regard to credit rating activities from 15 April 2022 onwards.[2211] However, such services may be provided to natural persons having the nationality of a Member State or residing, both temporarily and permanently, in the Union.[2212]

486. The sixth package of sanctions[2213] (*see* in this regard Annex II p. 337 at 340) introduced a ban on services to trusts and similar legal arrangements. More specifically, it is prohibited to register, provide a registered office, business or administrative address and management services with regard to trusts and similar legal arrangements, when the trustor or beneficiary is a Russian national, another national residing in Russia, a legal person established in Russia, other legal persons owned or controlled by said persons or anyone acting on their behalf or at their direction.[2214] It is also prohibited to act as a trustee, nominee shareholder, director, secretary or to hold a similar position for said legal arrangements from 5 July 2022 onwards.[2215] Outside the scope of these prohibitions fall arrangements having as a trustor or beneficiary a national of a Member State, a member of the European Economic Area or Switzerland or a national of a third state residing in said states. Equally outside the scope of these prohibitions fall operations strictly necessary for terminating contracts in violation of the explained provisions made before 9 April 2022 and terminated by 5 July 2022, including necessary ancillary contracts.[2216] Furthermore, competent authorities may authorize, under conditions deemed appropriate, the provision of services of a trustee, a nominee shareholder, a director and a secretary beyond 5 July 2022 for the purpose of terminating contracts until 5 September 2022, when relevant activity had commenced before 11 May 2022.[2217] The same services may also be authorized for other reasons, under the condition that funds and economic resources or other benefit is not

2022/428 of 15 Mar. 2022 amending Regulation (EU) No. 833/2014 concerning restrictive measures in view of Russia's actions destabilising the situation in Ukraine, OJ L 87I, 15 Mar. 2022, p. 13.

2209. Article 1(s) Regulation on Russia.
2210. Article 5j(1) Regulation on Russia.
2211. Article 5j(2) Regulation on Russia.
2212. Article 5j(3) Regulation on Russia.
2213. *See* Art. 1(6) Council Decision (CFSP) 2022/884 of 3 Jun. 2022 amending Decision 2014/512/CFSP concerning restrictive measures in view of Russia's actions destabilising the situation in Ukraine, OJ L 153, 3 Jun. 2022, p. 128 and Art. 1(13) Council Regulation (EU) 2022/879 of 3 Jun. 2022 amending Regulation (EU) No. 833/2014 concerning restrictive measures in view of Russia's actions destabilising the situation in Ukraine, OJ L 153, 3 Jun. 2022, p. 53.
2214. Article 5m(1)(a) to (e) Regulation on Russia.
2215. Article 5m(2) Regulation on Russia.
2216. Article 5m(4) & (3) Regulation on Russia.
2217. Article 5m(5)(a) Regulation on Russia.

provided to Russian nationals, other nationals residing in Russia or legal persons established in the same state.[2218] Moreover, competent authorities have the power to authorize the provision of all aforementioned services related to trusts, under appropriate conditions, for humanitarian purposes,[2219] for civil society activities[2220] and for the operation of trusts, whose purpose is the administration of occupational pension schemes, insurance policies or employee share scheme, charities, amateur sports clubs and funds for minor or vulnerable adults.[2221] Other Member States and the Commission shall be informed of any such authorizations granted within two weeks.[2222]

487. The ninth package of economic and individual sanctions[2223] (*see* in this regard Annex II p. 337 at 341 below) introduced restrictions to the provision of accounting, auditing, bookkeeping and tax consulting services, business and management consulting or public relations services ('cluster (a) services'),[2224] architectural and engineering services, legal advisory services, IT consulting services ('cluster (b) services'),[2225] market research and public opinion polling services, technical testing and analysis services, as well as advertising services ('cluster (c) services').[2226] The twelfth package (*see* in this regard Annex II p. 337 at 343 below) added restrictions to supplying software for the management of enterprises, such as enterprise resource planning, customer relationship management, business intelligence, supply chain management, project management software and product lifecycle management, and design and manufacturing software used in architecture, engineering, construction, manufacturing, media, education and entertainment ('cluster (d) services').[2227] These services may not be provided to the Government of Russia and to legal persons established in Russia.[2228] Moreover, it is prohibited to provide technical assistance, brokering services, financing, financial services and other services related to the aforementioned goods and services to the same persons and bodies.[2229]

2218. Article 5m(5)(b) Regulation on Russia.
2219. Such purposes include delivering and facilitating the delivery of assistance, including medical supplies, food, transfer of humanitarian workers and related assistance, as well as for evacuations. Article 5m(6)(a) Regulation on Russia.
2220. These activities need to directly promote democracy, human rights or the rule of law in Russia. Article 5m(6)(b) Regulation on Russia.
2221. Article 5m(6)(c) Regulation on Russia.
2222. Article 5m(7) Regulation on Russia.
2223. *See* Art. 1(3) Council Decision (CFSP) 2022/2478 of 16 Dec. 2022 amending Decision 2014/512/CFSP concerning restrictive measures in view of Russia's actions destabilising the situation in Ukraine, OJ L 322I, 16 Dec. 2022, p. 614 and Art. 1(13) Council Regulation (EU) 2022/2474 of 16 Dec. 2022 amending Regulation (EU) No. 833/2014 concerning restrictive measures in view of Russia's actions destabilising the situation in Ukraine, OJ L 322I, 16 Dec. 2022, p. 1.
2224. Article 5n(1) Regulation on Russia.
2225. Article 5n(2) Regulation on Russia.
2226. Article 5n(2a) Regulation on Russia.
2227. Article 5n(2b) and Annex XXXIX Regulation on Russia.
2228. Article 5n(1)(a) & (b), (2)(a) & (b), (2a)(a) & (b) and (2b)(a) & (b) & Annex XXXIX Regulation on Russia.
2229. Article 5n(3a)(a) & (b) Regulation on Russia.

488. Cluster (a), (b) and (c) services were given grace periods of a few weeks that have since lapsed.[2230] Cluster (d) services were given a three months grace period including for ancillary contracts necessary for the execution of such contracts.[2231] In addition, providing cluster (d) services may be provided upon authorization of the competent authorities, when those are necessary for the contribution of Russian nationals to international open-source projects.[2232] At the same time, cluster (a) services and cluster (b) services shall be provided for exercising the right to defence and the right to an effective legal remedy, though only when this is strictly necessary. Similarly, they are provided for ensuring access to judicial, administrative and arbitral proceedings as well as for recognizing and enforcing judgments and awards, under the further condition that providing the same services is consistent with the objective of the Regulation on Threatening Ukraine.[2233] Cluster (b), (c) and (d) services shall further be provided for public health emergencies, the urgent prevention or mitigation of an event with possible serious and significant impact on human health and safety or the environment, or as a response to natural disasters.[2234] Lastly, all aforementioned services are available to the exclusive use of legal persons established in Russia but are owned or controlled by a legal person established in a Member State of the Union, a state of the European Economic Area, Switzerland or a *partner country*[2235] for a grace period of six months that expires on 20 June 2024.[2236]

489. The above-explained cluster (a), (b), (c) and (d) services, as well as relevant technical assistance, brokering services, financing, financial services and other services, may be provided, when the competent authority authorizes so for the following purposes, under conditions it deems appropriate and when it deems this to be necessary. At the outset, such services may be provided for humanitarian purposes, that being delivering assistance and offering evacuations, for civil society activities (*see* in this respect paragraph 482 above) and for the functioning of diplomatic and consular representations of the Member States, the partner countries and international organizations.[2237] Authorizations may also be granted for energy purposes, those being ensuring critical energy supply within the Union and purchasing, importing or transporting titanium, aluminium, copper, nickel, palladium and iron ore, as well as for civil nuclear capabilities, civil nuclear facilities, such as the Paks II project, nuclear energy for medical applications, environmental radiation monitoring and civil nuclear cooperation.[2238] Authorizations may further be given for the continuing operation of *critical*

2230. Article 5n(3), (4) & (4a) Regulation on Russia repealed by the 12th package (*see* Art. 1(22)(c) Council Regulation (EU) 2023/2878 of 18 Dec. 2023 amending Regulation (EU) No. 833/2014 concerning restrictive measures in view of Russia's actions destabilising the situation in Ukraine, digital OJ L, 18 Dec. 2023).
2231. Article 5n(4b) Regulation on Russia.
2232. Article 5n(9b) Regulation on Russia.
2233. Article 5n(5) & (6) Regulation on Russia.
2234. Article 5n(8) Regulation on Russia.
2235. In regard to the definition of *partner country* set out in Art. 1(p) and Annex VIII Regulation on Russia. *see* Annex I p. 311 at 329.
2236. Article 5n(7) Regulation on Russia.
2237. Article 5n(10)(a),(b) & (c) Regulation on Russia.
2238. Article 5n(10)(d) & (f) Regulation on Russia.

infrastructures,[2239] as well as for hardware and software that is critical for human health and safety and for the safety of the environment.[2240] Furthermore, authorizations may be issued for the purpose of providing electronic communication services by Union telecommunication operators, as long as this is necessary for the operation, maintenance, security, also cybersecurity, of electronic communication services in Russia, Ukraine, the Union, between Russia and the Union, between Ukraine and the Union, as well as for data centre services in the Union.[2241] Lastly, this may be done for the exclusive use of legal persons established in Russia that are owned or controlled by a legal person established within the Union, the European Economic Area, Switzerland or a *partner country*.[2242] Other Member States and the Commission shall be informed of any such authorization within two weeks.[2243]

§4 SANCTIONS ON GOLD AND LUXURY ITEMS

490. Gold and luxury items are prohibited under the Regulation on Russia and the Regulation on Goods from Crimea. Restrictions on diamonds are also in place.

491. Gold unwrought, in semi-manufactured or powder form and waste and scrap of gold,[2244] that originate in Russia and have been exported from Russia into the Union or any third state after 22 July 2022, may be neither purchased, imported, nor transferred. This also applies to such gold, when it is processed in a third country.[2245] Gold in the sense of articles of jewellery, goldsmiths' or silversmiths' wares, as well as parts thereof,[2246] that also originate in Russia and have been exported from Russia into the Union in the same time period, may also not be purchased, imported or transferred.[2247] These prohibitions do not apply to gold necessary for the official purposes of diplomatic missions and consular posts or international organizations in Russia, as well as to gold in the latter sense for personal use of natural persons travelling to the Union that is owned by them and is not intended for sale.[2248] Furthermore, competent authorities of Member States may, in deviation from the aforementioned prohibitions, authorize the

2239. *In regard to the definition of critical infrastructure* (Art. 1z Regulation on Russia, Art. 2(a) Council Directive 2008/114/EC of 8 Dec. 2008 on the identification and designation of European critical infrastructures and the assessment of the need to improve their protection, OJ L 345, 23 Dec. 2008, p. 75 & Art. 2(4) Directive (EU) 2022/2557 of the European Parliament and of the Council of 14 Dec. 2022 on the resilience of critical entities and repealing Council Directive 2008/114/EC, OJ L 333, 27 Dec. 2022, p. 164) *see* Annex I p. 311 at 316.
2240. Articles 1(z) and 5n(10)(e) Regulation on Russia.
2241. Article 5n(10)(g) Regulation on Russia.
2242. Article 5n(10)(h) Regulation on Russia. On the notion of a 'partner country' *see* para. 479 above (Art. 1(p) and Annex VIII Regulation on Russia).
2243. Article 5n(11) Regulation on Russia.
2244. Goods with the following CN codes qualify as such: 7108, 71112 91 and ex 7118 90. Annex XXVI Regulation on Russia.
2245. Article 3o(1) & (2) and Annex XXVI Regulation on Russia.
2246. Goods with the following CN codes qualify as such: ex 7113 and ex 7114. Annex XXVII Regulation on Russia.
2247. Article 3o(3) and Annex XXVII Regulation on Russia.
2248. Article 3o(5) & (6) Regulation on Russia.

transfer or import of *cultural goods* that are on loan in the context of formal cultural cooperation with Russia.[2249]

492. Furthermore, in relation to gold in the aforementioned sense no technical assistance,[2250] brokering services,[2251] other services and financing or financial assistance may be offered.[2252] Neither deviations nor exceptions are set out in relation to this prohibition. On a final note, gold is estimated to be an item suited for use in the energy sector and the sector of prospection, exploration and production of oil, gas and mineral resources. Thus, it undergoes the relevant restrictive measures (*see* in this regard paragraphs 497 et seq. below).

493. The twelfth package (*see* in this regard Annex II p. 337 at 342 below) introduced prohibitions on diamonds and products incorporating diamonds that are divided into three groups. The first one consists of unsorted diamonds and non-industrial diamonds,[2253] the second of synthetic or reconstructed diamonds[2254] and the third of articles of jewellery, articles of goldsmiths' or silversmiths' wares, and other articles of precious metal or pearls incorporating diamonds, including wristwatches.[2255] All these goods and items, when they have been exported from Russia, may not be purchased, imported or transferred into the Union or to any third country. The same applies when the same goods and items are transited via the territory of Russia.[2256] Specifically for such goods and products that are processed in a third country and weigh equal to or more than 0.5 carats or 0.1 grams, a grace period of nine months has been given. Diamonds falling under the first group processed in a third country with a weight equal to or above 1.0 carats have been granted a briefer grace period of three months.[2257] For the purpose of implementing these provisions, a specific procedure has been set up that shall apply in parallel to the Kimberley Process.[2258,2259] At the same time, importers are called to provide evidence of the country of origin, which as of 1 September 2024 shall include a corresponding certificate establishing that the diamonds are not mined,

2249. Article 3o(7) Regulation on Russia.
2250. In regard to the meaning of *technical assistance* set out in Art. 1(c) Regulation on Russia. *see* Annex I p. 311 at 331.
2251. In regard to the meaning of *brokering services* set out in Art. 1(d) Regulation on Russia. *see* Annex I p. 311 at 312.
2252. Articles 3o(4)(a) & (b) and 1(o) Regulation on Russia. On the definition of *financing and financial assistance see* para. 452 above & Annex I p. 311 at 323.
2253. These are goods and products falling under CN codes 7102 10, 7102 31 and 7102 39. Article 3p and Part A Annex XXXVIIIA Regulation on Russia.
2254. These are goods and products falling under CN codes 7104 21 & 7104 91. Article 3p and Part B Annex XXXVIIIA Regulation on Russia.
2255. These are goods and products falling under CN codes ex 7113, ex 7114, ex 7115 90, ex 7116 20 & ex 9101. Article 3p and Part C Annex XXXVIIIA Regulation on Russia.
2256. Article 3p(1) & (2) Regulation on Russia.
2257. Article 3p(3) & (4) Regulation on Russia.
2258. Council Regulation (EC) No. 2368/2002 of 20 Dec. 2002 implementing the Kimberley Process certification scheme for the international trade in rough diamonds, OJ L 358, 31 Dec. 2002, p. 28, as last amended by Commission Implementing Regulation (EU) 2022/1359 of 27 Jul. 2022 amending Council Regulation (EC) No. 2368/2002 implementing the Kimberley Process certification scheme for the international trade in rough diamonds, OJ L 205, 5 Aug. 2022, p. 99.
2259. Article 3p(8) & (9) Regulation on Russia.

processed or produced in Russia.[2260] The prohibition of technical assistance, brokering services, other services and financing or financial assistance had an immediate effect.[2261]

494. The exceptions with regard to personal use of persons travelling into the Union and transfer of goods in the context of cultural cooperation with Russia (*see* in this regard paragraph 491 above) also apply here.[2262]

495. The meaning of *luxury items* that form the core of the ensuing restrictive measures is related to the one encountered under the Regulation on DPRK (*see* in this regard paragraph 192 above) and at the same time, it is dissimilar. At first, the items are specified in lists with nomenclature codes and accompanying descriptions[2263] similar to the approach of the Regulation on DPRK. However, for any of these listed items to qualify as a luxury item under the Regulation on Russia, it must have a value exceeding EUR 300.[2264] Further, most of the listed items, those being some items under horses,[2265] truffles,[2266] coats,[2267] coins,[2268] cutlery,[2269] lead crystal,[2270] electronic items for domestic use[2271] and articles and equipment for sports[2272] as well as all items under caviar,[2273] wines,[2274] cigars,[2275] perfumes,[2276] carpets,[2277] pearls, precious and semi-precious stones,[2278] tableware,[2279] clocks,[2280] musical instruments,[2281] works of art[2282] and articles and equipment for billiard, automatic bowling, casino games and games operated by coins or banknotes,[2283] have the notation 'ex' in front of the respective codes. This denotes that it covers more products, thus widening its scope of application. At the same time, certain value thresholds have been added that are either different from the ones in the Regulation on DPRK or even absent therefrom. The value

2260. Article 3p(10) Regulation on Russia.
2261. Article 3p(5)(a) & (b) Regulation on Russia.
2262. Article 3p(6) & (7) Regulation on Russia.
2263. Annex XVIII Regulation on Russia.
2264. Article 3h(2) Regulation on Russia.
2265. CN code ex 0101 21 00 Annex XVII (1) Regulation on Russia.
2266. CN code ex 0709 5950, ex 2003 9010 Annex XVIII (3) Regulation on Russia.
2267. CN code ex 6112 20 00, ex 6112 31 00, ex 6112 39 00, ex 6112 41 00, ex 6112 49 00, ex 6211 11 00, ex 6211 12 00, ex 6211 20 00 Annex XVIII (8) Regulation on Russia.
2268. CN code ex 7118 10 00 Annex XVIII (11) Regulation on Russia.
2269. CN code ex 7114 00 00, ex 7115 0000 Annex XVIII (12) Regulation on Russia.
2270. CN code ex 7013 22 00, ex 7013 33 00, ex 7013 41 00, ex 7013 41 00, ex 7013 91 00 Annex XVIII (14) Regulation on Russia.
2271. CN code ex 9504 50 00, 9504 90 80 Annex XVIII (15) Regulation on Russia.
2272. CN code ex 6211 11 00 to ex 6211 20 00, ex 6402 12 00 to ex 9507 00 00 Annex XVIII (21) Regulation on Russia.
2273. *See* Annex XVIII (2) Regulation on Russia.
2274. *See* Annex XVIII (4) Regulation on Russia.
2275. *See* Annex XVIII (5) Regulation on Russia.
2276. *See* Annex XVIII (6) Regulation on Russia.
2277. *See* Annex XVIII (9) Regulation on Russia.
2278. *See* Annex XVIII (10) Regulation on Russia.
2279. *See* Annex XVIII (13) Regulation on Russia.
2280. *See* Annex XVIII (18) Regulation on Russia.
2281. *See* Annex XVIII (19) Regulation on Russia.
2282. *See* Annex XVIII (20) Regulation on Russia.
2283. *See* Annex XVIII (22) Regulation on Russia.

of vehicles and motorcycles has to exceed EUR 50,000 and EUR 5,000 respectively[2284] and the value of a musical instrument has to be more than EUR 1,500.[2285] Only then do they qualify as *luxury items*. Furthermore, certain items listed as luxury items under the Regulation on DPRK are not deemed luxury items under the Regulation on Russia,[2286] and vice versa.[2287] Importantly, the Regulation on Russia has introduced a new category of luxury items, the 'optical articles and equipment'.[2288] As the preparatory documents are unavailable to the public, the reasons that promoted these deviations, are not explained and thus remain in the dark.

496. Luxury items in the aforementioned sense may neither be sold, supplied, transferred nor exported to any natural or legal person in Russia or for use in Russia.[2289] The latter component, that being the phrase 'for use in Russia', denotes a prohibition harsher than the one imposed on DPRK (*see* in this respect paragraph 192 above). *Luxury items* necessary for diplomatic and consular missions of Member States and of international organizations fall outside the scope of this prohibition, along with articles of jewellery and goldsmiths' or silversmiths' wares, including parts thereof, that are for the personal use of persons travelling from the Union, owned by them and not intended for sale.[2290] The exception for personal use is meagre when compared with the similar one set out under the Regulation on DPRK that allows travellers, both from and into the Union, to carry items as personal effects or goods of non-commercial nature in their luggage (*see* in this respect paragraph 194 above). Additionally, the competent authorities may authorize the transfer or transport to Russia luxury items that double as cultural goods that are on loan in the context of formal cultural cooperation with Russia. Other Member States and the Commission shall be informed thereof within two weeks.[2291] Authorization on such ground may not be provided under the Regulation on DPRK that nonetheless allows for authorization for humanitarian purposes (*see* in this respect paragraph 194 above).

§5 ENERGY RELATED SANCTIONS

497. The sanctions imposed on Russia, initially as a response to the annexation of Crimea and the military support given to Ukrainian separatists, are meant to exert a

2284. *See* Annex XVIII (17) Regulation on Russia.
2285. *See* Annex XVIII (19) Regulation on Russia.
2286. *See* 7104 20 00 & 7104 90 00 Annex VIII (10), ex 9405 10 50 & ex 9405 20 50 Annex VIII (14), ex 8472 90 40, ex 8472 90 90, ex 8517 12 00, ex 8529 10 31 & ex 8529 10 39 Annex VIII (15), ex 8525 80 30, ex 8525 80 91 & ex 8525 80 99 Annex VIII (16), ex 8801 00 00, ex 8802 11 00, ex 8802 12 00, ex 8802 20 00, ex 8802 30 00, ex 8802 30 00, ex 8802 40 00, ex 8803 10 00, ex 8803 20 00, ex 8803 30 00, ex 8803 90 10, ex 8803 90 90 & ex 8805 10 00 Annex VIII (17) Regulation on DPRK.
2287. *See* ex 7104 91 00 Annex XVIII (10), ex 8472 90 80 & ex 8517 13 00 Annex XVIII (15) Regulation on Russia.
2288. *See* Annex XVIII (23) Regulation on Russia.
2289. Article 3h(1) Regulation on Russia.
2290. Article 3h(3a) and CN 7113 00 00 & CN 7114 00 00 Regulation on Russia.
2291. Article 3h(4) & (5) Regulation on Russia.

greater impact on energy companies, including Rosneft and Gazprom, that seem to represent the specific target of the Union's reaction.[2292] Nonetheless, the introduced restrictions, targeting the oil sector have not been deemed to target identified or identifiable persons, thus depriving anyone of challenging them before the Courts of the EU,[2293] granting once again absolute and unchecked power to the Commission. In addition to the aforementioned measures on services and gold (*see* in this regard paragraphs 489 & 492 above), the measures relate to the energy sector of Russia, coal, gas and oil, including pipeline-borne oil, energy infrastructure, electricity production and, in a very limited way, nuclear activities.

I Sanctions with Regard to Coal

498. Berlaymont has taken on the *energy sector* of Russia via the ninth package of sanctions of December 2022 (*see* in this regard paragraph 487 above and Annex II p. 337 at 343 below), in which this has been specified as a sector covering certain activities with the exception of civil nuclear-related activities, such as the Paks II project. The covered activities are exploration, production and distribution of crude oil, natural gas or solid fossil fuels, including the refining of fuels and the liquefaction of natural gas or regasification, as well as the manufacture or distribution of solid fossil fuel products, refined petroleum products or gas, and the construction of facilities or installation of equipment for power generation or electricity production, including relevant services, equipment or technology.[2294] Thus the measures target both coal, that is analysed in the present subchapter, as well as oil and gas and electricity that are set out in the ensuing ones.

499. The restrictions consist of prohibiting creating any new or expanding any existing participation in any legal person, regardless of its state of incorporation, when this operates in the energy sector in Russia.[2295] They also prohibit granting any new loan, credit or otherwise financing to such legal persons and creating any new joint venture with the same persons.[2296] In parallel, they proscribe providing investment services to such legal persons.[2297]

500. Still, the energy sector is not placed under the restrictions explained above, when the competent authorities authorize so, under conditions deemed appropriate and for the purpose of ensuring critical energy supply within the Union, including transport of natural gas, oil and refined petroleum products from or through Russia into the Union,

2292. Rafael Leal-Arcas, Juan Alemany Ríos & Costantino Grasso, *The European Union and its Energy Security Challenges* 8(4) J.W.E.L. & B. 291 at 325 & 326 (2015).
2293. *Rosneft Oil* 2020 (n. 1992) para. 63.
2294. In regard to the definition of *energy sector* that has been set out in Art. 1(u) Regulation on Russia *see* Annex I p. 311 at 319.
2295. Article 3a(1)(a) Regulation on Russia.
2296. Article 3a(1)(b) & (c) *ibid.*
2297. Article 3a(1)(d) *ibid.* On the meaning of *investment services see* (n. 2099) above.

as long as this is not otherwise prohibited[2298] (*see* in this respect paragraphs 538 et seq. below). Similarly, restrictions may be lifted following authorization of competent authorities for legal persons operating in the energy sector in Russia that are nonetheless owned by a legal person incorporated in the Union.[2299] Finally, a photographic exception was introduced with the twelfth package. According to this, new loans, credit or other funding is permitted when this is necessary for ensuring the operation of a deep-water offshore gas project in the Mediterranean Sea in which certain designated persons were minority shareholders before 31 October 2017 and remain so. It is equally required that this project is solely or jointly controlled by a legal person incorporated in the Union. The competent authority shall assess whether these conditions have been met and shall issue the necessary authorization under any conditions it deems proper.[2300]

501. The fifth package of sanctions of April 2022[2301] (*see* in this regard Annex II p. 337 at 339 below) introduced a ban on purchasing, importing and transferring coal and other products[2302] that originated in Russia or were exported from Russia, including providing technical assistance, brokering services, other services and financing or financial assistance.[2303] The eleventh package of June 2023 (*see* in this regard Annex II p. 337 at 342 below) repealed this separate provision and incorporated the ban on coal into a pre-existing prohibition of importing certain goods (*see* in this respect paragraph 624 below) via amending the respective list of goods and technology.[2304]

II Sanctions with Regard to Oil and Gas

502. The sanctions on oil and gas are fourfold. At the outset, it is noted that oil and gas are sanctioned within the frame of the 'energy sector' as already explained (*see* in this respect paragraphs 498 et seq. above). Furthermore, it is prohibited to import, purchase and transfer certain oil, including to provide certain related services (*see* in this respect paragraphs 503 et seq. below), while sanctions have been imposed on goods and technology suited for use in oil refining and liquefaction of natural gas (*see* in this respect paragraphs 511 et seq. below) as well as on storage capacity in storage facilities (*see* in this respect paragraphs 513 et seq. below).

503. The sixth package of sanctions of June 2022 (*see* in this regard Annex II p. 337 at 340 below), imposed restrictive measures on importing, purchasing and transferring

2298. Articles 3a(3)(a) and 3m or 3n *ibid.*
2299. Article 3a(3)(b) *ibid.*
2300. Article 3a(3a) and Annex XIX *ibid. See* Art. 1(13) Decision 2014/512/CFSP and Art. 1(5) Regulation (EU) 2023/2878.
2301. *See* Art. 1(20) Decision 2022/578 and Art. 1(13) Regulation (EU) 2022/576.
2302. These were the goods with the CN codes 2701, 2702, 2703 00 00, 2704 00, 2705 00 00, 2706 00 00, 2707 and 2708 (repealed) Annex XXII *ibid.*
2303. Article 3j(1) & (2) *ibid.* (repealed).
2304. *See* recital No. 47 to the preamble of & Art. 1(17) Decision 2023/1217 and Art. 1(15) Regulation (EU) 2023/1214; Art. 3i and Annex XXI Regulation on Russia.

crude oil or petroleum products[2305] that originate in Russia or are exported from Russia.[2306] Providing technical assistance, brokering services, financing and financial assistance as well as any other services with regard to said oil ('group (a) oil services') is also prohibited.[2307] At the same time trading, brokering and transporting such oil to third countries, including through ship-to-ship transfers ('group (b) oil services') is prohibited,[2308] and so is providing technical assistance, brokering services, financing or financial assistance with regard to such activities ('group (c) oil services'), as Berlaymont decided later that year.[2309] Importantly, the prohibition on group (b) oil services enters into force at the same time that a council decision depicting the prices agreed by the Price Cap Coalition does after 3 December 2022.[2310] The term Price Cap Coalition is a term used in the legislative text, albeit a definition is absent. The U.S. Department of the Treasury equally uses the term coalition, but differs, as it offers a description of the participants. These are Australia and the Group of Seven ('G7'),[2311] the informal bloc of industrialized democracies that has its roots as a response to the establishment of OPEC, and in which the EU has participated fully since 1981.[2312] The Federal Foreign Office of Germany also clarifies that the countries participating in the Price Cap Coalition are the G7 and Australia.[2313] To date, two such council decisions have been issued.[2314]

504. Said prohibitions are not absolute, as they may be overlooked under conditions. At the outset, it is permitted to purchase in Russia oil falling under CN codes 2709 00 and 2710 that is required for essential needs of the purchaser in Russia or for essential

2305. Within this frame crude oil and petroleum products have been specified with the CN codes: ex 2709 00 & 2701. Annex XXV Regulation on Russia.
2306. Article 3m(1) Regulation on Russia. *See* Art. 1(13) Decision 2022/884 and Art. 1(1) Regulation 2022/879.
2307. Article 3m(2) Regulation on Russia.
2308. The prohibition with regard to crude oil in the sense of CN code 2709 00 commences on 5 Dec. 2022 and with regard to petroleum products in the sense of CN code 2710 on 5 Feb. 2023. Article 3n(4) *ibid.*
2309. Article 3n(1) *ibid. See* Art. (1) Decision 2022/2369 and Art. 1(1) Regulation (EU) 2022/2367.
2310. Article 3n(5) 1st subparagraph Regulation on Russia. *See also* Art. 4p(9) and Annex XI Decision 2014/512.
2311. Elizabeth Rosenberg & Eric Van Nostrand, *The Price Cap on Russian Oil: A Progress Report*, U.S. Department of the Treasury, 18 May 2023, available: https://home.treasury.gov/news/featured-stories/the-price-cap-on-russian-oil-a-progress-report (last visited: 21 Dec. 2023).
2312. Editors, *What Does the G7 Do?* Council on Foreign Relations, 28 Jun. 2023, available: https://www.cfr.org/backgrounder/what-does-g7-do (last visited: 21 Dec. 2023).
2313. Editors, *Statement of the G7 and Australia on a price cap for seaborne Russian-origin crude oil*, Press release, Federal Foreign Office of Germany, 2 Dec. 2022, available: https://www.auswaertiges-amt.de/en/newsroom/news/g7-australia-price-cap-seaborne-russian-origin-crude-oil/2567026 (last visited: 21 Dec. 2023).
2314. These are: Council Decision (CFSP) 2022/2369 of 3 Dec. 2022 amending Decision 2014/512/CFSP concerning restrictive measures in view of Russia's actions destabilising the situation in Ukraine, OJ L 311I, 3. Dec. 2022, p. 8; and Council Decision (CFSP) 2023/252 of 4 Feb. 2023 amending Decision 2014/512/CFSP concerning restrictive measures in view of Russia's actions destabilizing the situation in Ukraine, OJ L 32I, 4 Feb. 2023, p. 11.

needs of humanitarian projects in Russia,[2315] as it was decided by the sixth package[2316] that did not provide any further clarifications.

505. The prohibitions on oil import and group (a) oil services are paired with the derogations described below. Such oil can be imported and such services can be provided to seaborne oil in transit through Russia or departing from Russia, when the goods in question and their owner are not Russian.[2317] Further, oil from Russia falling under CN code 2709 00 may be imported, purchased and transferred into the Union until 5 December 2022 on the basis of one-off transactions for near-term delivery, when they have been made before that date and they are notified to the Commission within ten days after the transaction. This may also take place on the basis of contracts made before 4 June 2022, including ancillary contracts, under the condition that they have been notified to the Commission by 24 June 2022.[2318] Oil from Russia falling under CN code 2710 may also be imported, purchased and transferred into the Union until 5 February 2023 on the basis of identical instruments and conditions.[2319]

506. Specifically, the competent authorities of Bulgaria and Croatia are given the power to allow for derogations from the prohibitions on oil import and group (a) oil services. Starting with the authorities of Bulgaria, these may decide that contracts made before 4 June 2022 for the purchase, import and transfer of seaborne oil from Russia falling under CN codes 2709 00 and 2710, including ancillary contracts, can be performed until 31 December 2024.[2320] The authorities of Croatia are being given the power to allow the purchase, import and transfer of vacuum gas oil with CN code 2710 19 71 from Russia until 31 December 2024, as long as no alternative supply of said good is available. The Commission must be informed two weeks prior to the intended decision of the relevant grounds and during this time, it may express its objection.[2321] Any oil purchases under said authorizations of authorities of Bulgaria and Croatia may be sold to buyers located neither in another Member State nor in a third state.[2322] Specifically, oil with CN code 2710 imported to Bulgaria may neither be transferred nor transported abroad,[2323] unless certain conditions take place. The first set of conditions consists of certain petroleum products[2324] obtained from crude oil imported by

2315. Article 3m(9) Regulation on Russia.
2316. Article 1(7) Regulation (EU) 2022/879.
2317. Article 3m(3)(c) Regulation on Russia.
2318. Article 3m(3)(a) Regulation on Russia.
2319. Article 3m(3)(b) Regulation on Russia.
2320. Article 3m(5) and Annex XXV Regulation on Russia.
2321. Article 3m(6)(a) & (b) Regulation on Russia.
2322. Article 3m(7) first subparagraph Regulation on Russia.
2323. Article 3m(7) second subparagraph Regulation on Russia.
2324. These are gas oils (CN codes: 2710 19 31, 2710 19 35, 2710 19 43, 2710 19 46, 2710 19 47, 2710 19 48, 2710 20 11, 2710 20 16 & 2710 20 19), light oils and preparations (CN codes: 2710 12 11, 2710 12 15, 2710 12 21, 2710 12 25, 2710 12 31, 2710 12 41, 2710 12 45, 2710 12 49, 2710 12 50, 2710 12 70 & 2710 12 90), medium oils (CN codes: 2710 19 21 & 2710 19 25), heavy oils (CN codes: 2710 19 51, 2710 19 55, 2710 19 62, 2710 19 66, 2710 19 66, 2710 19 67) and petroleum oils and oils obtained from bituminous minerals and preparations not elsewhere specified or included, other than waste oils (CN codes: 2710 20 32, 2710 20 38 & 2710 20 90). Annex XXXI Regulation on Russia.

Bulgaria, the receiving state being Ukraine and exclusive use of the relevant products in Ukraine, as long as the intended transaction is not intended to circumvent the prohibition here in question.[2325] The second set of conditions consists of other petroleum products obtained from crude oil imported by Bulgaria under export volume quotes,[2326] the receiving state being any third state and impossibility of storage in Bulgaria due to environmental and safety risks, as long as no circumvention is intended.[2327]

507. The group (c) oil services prohibition does not apply to contracts concluded before 4 June 2022 and their ancillary contracts as long as they are executed by 5 December 2022, when they relate to crude oil falling under CN code 2709 00, or 5 February 2023, when they relate to petroleum products falling under CN code 2710.[2328] This is also true for insurance claims after 5 December 2022, when they relate to crude oil falling under CN code 2709 00, and 5 February 2023, when they relate to petroleum products falling under CN code 2710, as long as the relevant insurance contracts were made before 4 June 2022 and the insurance coverage is ceased by said date.[2329]

508. Furthermore, both prohibitions on group (b) and group (c) oil services are not applicable to oil in transit through Russia or departing from Russia, under the condition that both the goods and their owner are not Russian.[2330] Similarly, services necessary for urgent prevention or mitigation of an event likely to have a serious and significant impact on human health and safety or the environment, including response to natural disasters,[2331] are immune from said prohibitions, as is at least until 31 March 2024, crude oil originating in the Sakhalin-2 **(Сахалин-2)** project, located in Russia's Far East, in order to ensure Japan's energy security needs.[2332] Some context could be offered with regard to this latter exception that was introduced with the set of legislative acts issued upon the agreement on the price cap in December 2022[2333] (on the price cap *see* paragraph 499 below). In the summer of that same year, Moscow enacted legislation expropriating foreign stakes in the Sakhalin-2 project by creating a new company that took over all rights and obligations. The Russian government would then decide whether the foreign partners, those being Shell, Mitsui and Mitsubishi, that at the time owned 27.5% minus one share, 12.5% and 10% stakes respectively, could

2325. Article 3m(7) third subparagraph Regulation on Russia.
2326. These are light oils and preparations (CN codes 2710 12 25, 2710 12 41, 2710 12 45 & 2710 12 49) and heavy oils for other purposes (CN codes 2710 19 66 & 2710 19 67). Annex XXXII Regulation on Russia.
2327. Article 3m(7) forth subparagraph Regulation on Russia.
2328. Article 3n(2)(a) & (b) Regulation on Russia.
2329. Article 3n(3) Regulation on Russia.
2330. Such oil must fall under the CN codes ex 2709 00 and 2701. Article 3n(6)(b) and Annex XXV Regulation on Russia.
2331. Article 3m(9) Regulation on Russia.
2332. Such oil must fall under CN code 2709 00. Article 3n(6)(c) and Annex XXIX Regulation on Russia. *See also* recital No. 39 to the preamble of Regulation (EU) 2023/1214.
2333. *See* Art. 1(d) Decision 2022/2369 and Art. 1(4) Regulation (EU) 2022/2367.

continue to take part in the project or not.[2334] In April 2023, following the above-described derogation's enactment by Brussels, the Russian government ordered Shell's share to be sold and, in a surprise move, allowed the proceeds to be paid directly to Shell.[2335] Mitsui and Mitsubishi retained their stakes.[2336] There might be no causal connection between the moves of Moscow and Brussels, but they certainly are a very happy coincidence, perhaps indicating intensive lobbying or even Europe's apparent disregard for the manifest unlawfulness of Russia's aggression and its consequences.

509. Finally, the last set of exceptions explained below is related to and dependent on the price cap set by the Price Cap Coalition. The prohibitions on group (b) and group (c) oil services may be lifted when the purchase price does not exceed the set price cap. This may take place, only for a period of ninety days, for contracts already made at the date that a price cap has been set, as long as they relate to crude oil falling under CN codes 2709 00 and 2710 that is transported or exported from Russia.[2337] It may also take place for new contracts from 5 December 2022 onwards with regard to crude oil falling under CN code 2709 00 originating in or exported from Russia and from 5 February 2023 onwards for such oil falling under CN code 2710.[2338] Said prohibitions are also lifted when the purchase price does exceed the set price cap on the ensuing two occasions. The first one is applicable from 5 December 2022 onwards and relates to crude oil falling under CN 2709 00 that has been already loaded onto a vessel before this date, as long as it is unloaded at the final port before 19 January 2023.[2339] The second one is applicable from 5 February 2023 onwards and relates to crude oil falling under CN 2710 under the same conditions, whereby the date of unloading is 1 April 2023.[2340] If however, the purchase price of a contract that has been made, exceeds the

2334. Yuka Obayashi, Emily Chow & Ron Bousso, *Russia Seizes Control of Sakhalin Gas Project, Raises Stakes with West*, 1 Jul. 2022, Reuters, available: https://www.reuters.com/business/energy/russia-decree-sakhalin-2-project-knocks-mitsui-mitsubishi-shares-2022-07-01/ (last visited: 21 Dec. 2023); Stanley Reed, *Putin Moves to Seize a Large Gas Venture in Russia's Far East*, 1 Jul. 2022, The New York Times, available: https://www.nytimes.com/2022/07/01/business/putin-sakhalin-natural-gas.html (last visited: 21 Dec. 2023); Editors, *Russia to Take Full Control of Sakhalin-2 Oil and Gas Project*, 4 Jul. 2022, NS Energy, available: https://www.nsenergybusiness.com/news/russian-president-vladimir-putin-decree-sakhalin-2/ (last visited: 21 Dec. 2023).

2335. Alexander Marrow et al., *Russia Allows USD1.2 bln Sakhalin-2 Payment to Shell: Kommersant*, 4 Apr. 2023, Reuters, available: https://www.reuters.com/markets/deals/russia-allows-12-bln-sakhalin-2-payment-shell-kommersant-2023-04-04/ (last visited: 21 Dec. 2023); Jillian Ambrose, *Shell May Get Nearly UKP1bn from Sale of Stake in Russian Gas Project*, 12 Apr. 2023, The Guardian, available: https://www.theguardian.com/business/2023/apr/12/shell-sakhalin-2-gas-project-stake (last visited: 21 Dec. 2023).

2336. Editors, Japan's Mitsui says no plans to exit Russia's Sakhalin-2 LNG project, Reuters 21 Jun. 2023, available: https://www.reuters.com/business/energy/japans-mitsui-says-no-plans-exit-russias-sakhalin-2-lng-project-2023-06-21/ (last visited: 21 Dec. 2023). *See* also Mitsubishi Corporation, *Our business > Energy Business Department*, *undated*, available: https://www.mitsubishicorp.com/ru/en/bg/energy-business-department/ (last visited: 21 Dec. 2023).

2337. Article 3n(5) second sub-paragraph Regulation on Russia.

2338. Article 3n(6)(a) Regulation on Russia.

2339. Article 3n(6)(d) Regulation on Russia.

2340. Article 3n(6)(e) Regulation on Russia.

price cap that is later specified and the transport has been already concluded, the prohibition on group (c) oil services shall apply for ninety days following unloading, when the operator knew or had reasonable cause to suspect that said price discrepancy was taking place.[2341] Specifically with regard to group (b) oil services and Russian crude oil or petroleum products loaded as of 20 February 2024, service providers have the opportunity to collect itemized price information for ancillary costs by operators further up the supply chain, when these providers lack access to the set price cap.[2342]

510. To the end of facilitating the implementation and enforcement of the aforementioned prohibitions on Russian crude oil and petroleum products, the Commission and the Member States have the right to share information for identifying vessels and persons of concern carrying out deceptive practices while transporting such goods and products.[2343]

511. With the fifth[2344] and the 'maintenance and alignment' package of sanctions[2345] (*see* in this regard Annex II p. 337 at 339 below), restrictive measures were imposed on goods and technology suited for use in oil refining and liquefaction of natural gas. These may neither be sold, supplied, transferred nor exported to any person in Russia or for use therein.[2346] In the already familiar pattern technical assistance, brokering services, financing and financial assistance as well as any other services related to such goods and technology, transferring intellectual property rights and trade secrets are also prohibited.[2347] Contracts concluded before 26 February 2022, including ancillary contracts, fall outside the scope of said prohibitions, when they have been executed before 27 May 2022. Competent authorities may authorize derogations when such goods and technology are necessary for the urgent prevention or mitigation of an event likely to have a serious and significant impact on human health and safety or the environment. In fact, in cases of emergency, a sale, supply, transfer or export may take place without an authorization, under the condition that the authorities are informed within five working days and are given detailed reasoning about the unauthorized action.[2348]

512. In a similar manner, selling goods and technologies suited for use in the energy sector and the sector of prospection, exploration and production of oil, gas and mineral

2341. Article 3n(7) Regulation on Russia.
2342. Article 3n(6a), (4) & (6)(a) and Annex XXV Regulation on Russia.
2343. Article 3na Regulation on Russia. It was introduced with the twelfth package. *See* recital No. 16 to the preamble of Decision 2014/512/CFSP Art. & Art. 1(15) Regulation (EU) 2023/2878.
2344. *See* Art. 1(8) Regulation (EU) 2022/576.
2345. *See* Art. 1(22) and Annex IV Regulation (EU) 2022/1269.
2346. The specific goods and technologies prohibited are the ones falling under the following ex CN codes: 8414 10 81, 8418 69 00, 8419 40 00, 8419 50 20, 8419 50 80, 8419 60 00, 8419 60 00, 8419 89 98, 8421 39 15, 8421 39 25, 8421 39 35, 8421 39 85, 8419 89 10, 8419 89 98 & 8479 89 97. Article 3b(1) and Annex X Regulation on Russia.
2347. Article 3b(2)(a), (b) & (c) Regulation on Russia.
2348. Article 3b(3) & (4) Regulation on Russia.

resources[2349] is prohibited to anyone in Crimea, Sevastopol[2350] and the non-government-controlled areas of Ukraine.[2351] Providing technical assistance, brokering services, financing and financial assistance as well as any other services related to such goods and technology are also prohibited.[2352] Still, contracts concluded prior to the relevant legislation coming into force shall be executed within three months in Crimea and Sevastopol and six months with regard to the non-government-controlled areas of Ukraine, including any ancillary contracts.[2353] Specifically with regard to Crimea and Sevastopol, the prohibitions at hand do not apply, when there are no reasonable grounds to determine that the relevant goods and technology are to be used in these areas.[2354]

513. Finally, Brussels took measures to avoid Russia's weaponization of gas supply and risks of market manipulation.[2355] To this end, it is prohibited to provide *storage capacity*[2356] (in regard to the definition *see* Annex I p. 311 at 331) in *storage facilities*[2357] to Russian nationals and legal persons and individuals residing in Russia as well as to legal persons owned by them, including persons acting on their behalf or at their direction.[2358] The part of liquified natural gas facilities used for storage does not fall within the realm of the prohibition at hand.[2359] At the same time, the competent authorities of EU Member States may authorize deviation from the aforementioned prohibition, when this is necessary for ensuring critical energy supply within the Union.[2360]

2349. These products are described in detail and include among others salt, sulphur, earths and stone, cement, ores, slag and ash, mineral fuels, mineral oils, inorganic chemicals, organic chemicals, iron and steel, copper, nickel, aluminium, lead, zinc, tin, rock-drilling or earth-boring tools, nuclear reactors, steam boilers, central heating boilers, steam turbines, turbo-jets, railway or tramway locomotives, aircraft, spacecraft, ships, gold, silver and platinum. Annex II Regulation on Goods from Crimea and Annex II Regulation with regard to Donetsk and Luhansk.

2350. Article 2b(1)(a) & (b), (iii) & (iv) Regulation on Goods from Crimea.

2351. More specifically, the areas under non-governmental control are the oblasts of Donetsk, Kherson, Luhansk and Zaporizhzhia. Article 4(1)(a) & (b), (iii) & (iv) and Art. 1(d) Regulation with regard to Donetsk & Luhansk.

2352. Article 2b(2)(a) & (b) Regulation on Goods from Crimea and Art. 4(2)(a) & (b) Regulation with regard to Donetsk & Luhansk.

2353. Article 2b(4) Regulation on Goods from Crimea and Art. 4(4) Regulation with regard to Donetsk & Luhansk.

2354. Article 2b(3) Regulation on Goods from Crimea.

2355. Recital No. 7 to the preamble of Decision (CFSP) 2023/434 and recital No. 19 to the preamble of Regulation (EU) 2023/427.

2356. In regard to the definition of *storage capacity* (Art. 2(1)(28) Regulation (EC) No. 715/2009 of the European Parliament and of the Council of 13 Jul. 2009 on conditions for access to the natural gas transmission networks and repealing Regulation (EC) No. 1775/2005, OJ L 211, 14 Aug. 2009, p. 36) *see* Annex I p. 311 at 331.

2357. In regard to the definition of *storage facility* (Art. 2(9) Directive 2009/73/EC of the European Parliament and of the Council of 13 Jul. 2009 concerning common rules for the internal market in natural gas and repealing Directive 2003/55/EC, OJ L 211, 14 Aug. 2009, p. 94) *see* Annex I p. 311 at 331.

2358. Article 5p(1)(a), (b) & (c) Regulation on Russia.

2359. Article 5p(1) Regulation on Russia.

2360. Article 5p(3) Regulation on Russia.

514. Other Member States and the Commission are to be informed of authorized derogations that competent authorities have issued under the circumstances and according to the procedures explained above within two weeks.[2361]

III Specifically Pipeline-Borne Oil

515. Oil qualifying as CN code 2709 00 delivered by pipeline from Russia into the Union, is not affected by the aforementioned prohibitions (*see* in this regard paragraphs 503 et seq. above), at least not until the Council decides otherwise.[2362] Brussels justifies this course of action due to the 'geographical situation of several Member States that generated specific dependence on importing crude oil from Russia by pipeline',[2363] a dubious argument. Brussels seems to have forgotten that it has been repeatedly warned against the danger of dependence on Russian gas[2364] and decided to ignore them, including the threat assessments of security services of EU Member States. The Council did decide to extend the aforementioned prohibitions with regard to Germany and Poland on 23 June 2023,[2365] while allowing the operation of the Caspian Pipeline Consortium (*see* in this regard paragraph 516 below), but not Slovakia and Hungary, which continues to habitually import oil by pipeline.[2366] Such pipeline-borne crude oil, once imported, may neither be transferred nor transported to other Member States or third states.[2367] Similarly, petroleum products falling under CN code 2710 obtained from pipeline-borne crude oil may neither be transferred, transported nor sold to other Member States or third states from 5 February 2023 onwards,[2368] specifically for Czechia from 5 December 2023 onwards, unless alternative supplies for such products are available before that date.[2369] At the same time, competent authorities of Hungary and Slovakia may authorize the sale, supply and export of certain petroleum products to Ukraine, as long as these shall be used exclusively in Ukraine and shall not

2361. Article 3m(7) fifth sub-paragraph, 3m(8) sixth sub-paragraph, 5q(3), 3b(4), 5p(4) Regulation on Russia.
2362. Article 3m(3)(d) Regulation on Russia.
2363. Recital No. 16 to the preamble of Regulation (EU) 2022/879.
2364. Editors, *The Nord Stream 2 Gas Pipeline is a Russian Trap: And Germany Has Fallen Into It*, The Economist, 16 Feb. 2019, available: https://www.economist.com/leaders/2019/02/16/the-nord-stream-2-gas-pipeline-is-a-russian-trap (last visited: 21 Dec. 2023); Paul Belkin, Michael Ratner & Cory Wel, *Russia's Nord Stream 2 Natural Gas Pipeline to Germany Halted*, 10 Mar. 2022, Congressional Research Service, available: https://crsreports.congress.gov/product/pdf/IF/IF11138 (last visited: 21 Dec. 2023); TEABEAMET Estonian Information Board, *International Security and Estonia*, 2016, pp. 27 et seq., available: https://raport.valisluureamet.ee/2023/en/previous-reports/ (last visited: 21 Dec. 2023); Drošības Policija, Latvijas Republika, *Annual Report About the Activities of the Security Police in 2013* (Riga, May 2014) pp. 17 & 18.
2365. Article 3m(3a) Regulation on Russia.
2366. *See* Jakob Hanke Vela, *Brussels Playbook from Politico: Road to 2024*, 4 Sep. 2023, available: https://www.politico.eu/newsletter/brussels-playbook/ (last visited: 21 Dec. 2023).
2367. Article 3m(8) first subparagraph Regulation on Russia.
2368. Article 3m(8) third subparagraph Regulation on Russia.
2369. Article 3m(8) forth subparagraph Regulation on Russia.

circumvent the explained prohibitions.[2370] Lastly, it would be fair to suggest that the supply of crude oil delivered by pipeline from Russia is in fact protected. Should its supply be interrupted for reasons beyond a state's control, seaborne oil from Russia with the same classification may be imported into that specific state until supply is resumed or until the Council decides to activate the prohibitions on oil import and group (a) oil services.[2371] Neither authorization nor notification of other Member States and the Commission is necessary.

516. According to another statutory derogation, authorities may facilitate the operation and maintenance of the Caspian Pipeline Consortium, through which the majority of the oil produced in Kazakhstan en route to Europe passes[2372] and whose major shareholder holding 24 % of the shares is Russia.[2373] Brussels has not considered the Baku – Tbilisi – Ceyhan pipeline as an alternative and instead insists on delivering oil via Russia to Germany.[2374] For the operation and maintenance of the pipelines and infrastructure of the Caspian Pipeline Consortium, competent authorities of EU Member States have been given the power to authorize the sale, supply, transfer, export and transit through Russia of the following goods and technology: double use items;[2375] goods and technology which might contribute to Russia's military and technological enhancement or the development of the defence and security sector;[2376] maritime navigation goods and technology;[2377] and goods which could contribute in particular to the enhancement of Russian industrial capacities.[2378] Supplying these items must be necessary for oil classified as CN 2709 00 that originates in Kazakhstan and is transiting through, departing from or loaded in Russia.[2379] In reaching their decision, the authorities must determine that such sales and supplies, including export and transit through Russia, are necessary for the operation and maintenance of the Caspian Pipeline Consortium, whereas specifically for such goods exported to Russia they must not go beyond the ones previously exported from the Union, the European Economic Area, Switzerland, the US, Japan, the UK, South Korea, Australia, Canada, New

2370. Article 3m(8) fifth subparagraph Regulation on Russia.
2371. Article 3m(4) Regulation on Russia.
2372. *See* Vladimyr Afanasiev, *EU Offers Kazakhstan 'Targeted' Exemptions for Oil Exports Through Russia*, 23 Jun. 2023, Upstream, available: https://www.upstreamonline.com/production/eu-offers-kazakhstan-targeted-exemptions-for-oil-exports-through-russia/2-1-1473915 (last visited: 21 Dec. 2023).
2373. *See* Caspian Pipeline Consortium, *About, Shareholders*, available: https://www.cpc.ru/en/about/pages/shareholders.aspx (last visited: 21 Dec. 2023); Vladimyr Afanasiev, *EU offers Kazakhstan 'Targeted' Exemptions for Oil Exports Through Russia*, 23 Jun. 2023, Upstream, available: https://www.upstreamonline.com/production/eu-offers-kazakhstan-targeted-exemptions-for-oil-exports-through-russia/2-1-1473915 (last visited: 21 Dec. 2023).
2374. Vladimir Afanasiev, *Kazakhstan Upgrades Legacy Pipeline to Russia to Grow Oil Supplies to Germany*, 6 Sep. 2023, Upstream, available: https://www.upstreamonline.com/production/kazakhstan-upgrades-legacy-pipeline-to-russia-to-grow-oil-supplies-to-germany/2-1-1511298(last visited: 21 Dec. 2023).
2375. Articles 5q(1), 2(1) and 1(a) Regulation on Russia.
2376. Articles 5q(1), 2a(1) and Annex VII Regulation on Russia.
2377. Articles 5q(1), 3f(1) and Annex XVI Regulation on Russia.
2378. Articles 5q(1), 3k(1) and Annex XXIII Regulation on Russia.
2379. Article 5q(1) Regulation on Russia.

Zealand and Norway.[2380] Furthermore, the requested volumes must not be commensurate with the ones already used and at the same time, such goods and technology must be provided exclusively for end use in the operation and maintenance of the Caspian Pipeline Consortium.[2381] Upon granting the authorization, the holder shall have to present an end-user certificate to the authorities, as well as detailed regular reports stating that the items in question have not been diverted from their intended purpose.[2382] In the same manner, technical assistance related to the operation and maintenance of said consortium, brokering or other services and financing or financial assistance can be provided.[2383] However, auditing services, engineering services, legal advisory services, technical testing and analysis services to the same end may be provided, when this is necessary.[2384]

IV Sanctions on Energy Infrastructure

517. Energy infrastructure faces twofold restrictive measures. At the outset, certain goods and technology are prohibited in Crimea, Sevastopol and the non-government-controlled areas of Ukraine. At the same time, new investments in the energy sector in Russia are restricted, with the exception of the nuclear industry and the downstream sector of energy transport.

518. The infrastructure of the energy sector and of the sector of prospection, exploration and production of oil, gas and mineral resources in Crimea, Sevastopol and the non-government-controlled areas of Ukraine is under sanctions. The imposed restrictions consist of the prohibition to sell, supply, transfer and export goods suited for use in these industries, regardless of their origin.[2385] They further sanction technical assistance, brokering services, financing and financial assistance,[2386] as well as the provision of technical assistance, brokering, construction and engineering services, when they are directly related to such infrastructure.[2387] Obligations related to contracts concluded before the respective legislative acts came into force[2388] are not affected by the explained prohibitions, as long as they are satisfied within nine months or six months respectively.[2389]

2380. Article 5q(1)(a) & (b) and Annex VIII Regulation on Russia.
2381. Article 5q(1)(c) & (d) Regulation on Russia.
2382. Article 5q(4) Regulation on Russia.
2383. Article 5q(1)(a) to (d) Regulation on Russia.
2384. Article 5q(2)(a) & (b) Regulation on Russia.
2385. Article 2b(1)(a) & (b) (iii) & (iv) & Annex II Regulation on Goods from Crimea and Art. 4(1)(a) & (b) (iii)(iv) & Annex II Regulation with regard to Donetsk & Luhansk.
2386. Article 2b(2)(a) & (b) & Annex II Regulation on Goods from Crimea and Art. 4(2)(a) & (b) & Annex II Regulation with regard to Donetsk.
2387. Article 2c(1) & Annex II Regulation on Goods from Crimea and Art. 5(1) & Annex II Regulation with regard to Donetsk & Luhansk.
2388. *See* Art. 1(1) Decision (CFSP) 2014/933 & Art. 1(2) Regulation (EU) 1351/2014 and Art. 7 Decision (CFSP) 2022/266 & Art. 5(2) Regulation (EU) 2022/263.
2389. Article 2c(2) Regulation on Goods from Crimea and Art. 5(2) & Annex II Regulation with regard to Donetsk & Luhansk.

519. Deviations may be authorized by competent authorities when this is necessary for official purposes of consular missions or international organizations enjoying immunities. Authorizations may also be issued for goods, technology and services that relate to projects in support of hospitals, other public health institutions or civilian education establishments, or for appliances and equipment having medical use.[2390] Deviations may equally be permitted when this is necessary for urgently preventing or mitigating events likely to have a serious and significant impact on human health and safety or the environment. In fact, this is the sole ground for deviation from the prohibition to provide technical assistance, brokering, construction and engineering services.[2391]

520. Brussels has deemed it appropriate to prohibit new investments in the energy sector in Russia.[2392] To this end, it prohibited the sale, supply, transfer and export of certain line pipes, casting and tubing, rock-drilling and earth-boring tools and pumps, to anyone in Russia or for use in Russia.[2393] The relevant legislative act mentions the Exclusive Economic Zone and the Continental Self of Russia explicitly, albeit unnecessarily as they are an undeniable part of a state's territory. In the familiar pattern, providing technical assistance, brokering services or other services as well as financing and financial assistance is not permitted, as is selling, licensing or transferring in any other way intellectual property rights and trade secrets.[2394]

521. Outside the scope of these prohibitions fall the transport of natural gas and oil, unless otherwise prohibited (*see* in this regard paragraph 503 above) and preventing and mitigating events likely to have a serious and significant impact on human health and safety or the environment.[2395] Also unaffected remains providing insurance and re-insurance to any legal person incorporated in a Member State with regard to its activities outside the energy sector in Russia, however after 20 June 2024 providing such insurance or reinsurance shall have to be authorized by the competent authorities.[2396] Furthermore, the competent authorities have been given authorization to allow for the sale, supply, transfer and export of these goods and technology and the provision of technical and financial assistance when doing so is necessary for ensuring critical energy supply within the Union.[2397] They may further allow for such transactions when this is intended for the exclusive use of legal persons owned or controlled by an entity incorporated in a Member State.[2398]

2390. Article 2e(1)(a), (b) & (c) Regulation on Goods from Crimea and Art. 7(1)(a), (b) & (c) Regulation with regard to Donetsk & Luhansk.
2391. Article 2e(3) Regulation on Goods from Crimea and Art. 7(3) Regulation with regard to Donetsk & Luhansk.
2392. *See* recital No. 5 to the preamble of Decision (CFSP) 2022/430 and recital No. 5 to the preamble of Regulation (EU) 2022/428.
2393. Article 3(1) Regulation on Russia. *See* the detailed description in Annex II Regulation on Russia.
2394. Article 3(2)(a), (b) & (c) Regulation on Russia.
2395. Articles 3(3)(a) & (b) and 3m & 3n Regulation on Russia.
2396. Article 3(4) & (5) Regulation on Russia. *See* Art. 1(12) Decision (CFSP) 2023/2874 & Art. 1(4) Regulation (EU) 2023/2878.
2397. Article 3(6)(a) Regulation on Russia.
2398. Article 3(6)(b) Regulation on Russia.

522. Other Member States and the Commission are informed of granted authorizations within two weeks.[2399]

V Sanctions with Regard to Electricity Production

523. Electricity production is sanctioned by the EU within the frame of the 'energy sector' as already explained (*see* in this respect paragraph 498 above). No other restrictive measures are set out.

VI Sanctions with Regard to Nuclear Activities

524. No restrictive measures with regard to nuclear activity have been prescribed. Certain provisions on nuclear energy and activities falling under different categories are explained in the respective categories (*see* in this regard paragraphs 498 above & 529 et seq. below).

§6 SANCTIONS ON DUAL-USE ITEMS

525. With the second package of sanctions on Russia[2400] (*see* in this regard Annex II p. 337 at 338 below) and the third package with regard to Belarus[2401] (*see* in this regard Annex III p. 345 at 346 below) restrictions have been imposed on *dual-use goods and technology*. Furthermore, with the eleventh package on Russia[2402] (*see* in this regard Annex II p. 337 at 342 below) restrictions on specific dual-use goods and technology intended for persons in third states were introduced.

526. Dual-use items have been defined as 'the items listed in Annex I to Regulation (EU) 2021/821 of the European Parliament and the Council'.[2403] Thus they are identical to the notion of *dual-use items* already explained (*see* in this respect paragraphs 241 et seq. above). For the purpose of consistency, the term *dual-use items*, instead of *dual-use goods and technology*, shall be used in the ensuing paragraphs.

527. Dual-use items may be neither sold, supplied, transferred nor exported to anyone in Russia or Belarus, or for use in Russia or Belarus.[2404] Providing technical assistance, brokering services or other services as well as financing and financial assistance is also prohibited,[2405] as is selling, licensing or transferring in any other way intellectual

2399. Article 3(7) Regulation on Russia.
2400. *See* Art. 1(3) Decision (CFSP) 2022/327 and Art. 1(2) Regulation (EU) 2022/328.
2401. *See* Art. 1(2) Decision (CFSP) 2012/642 and Art. 1(4) Regulation (EU) 2022/355.
2402. *See* Art. 1(23) Decision (CFSP) 2023/1217 and Art. 1(29) Regulation (EU) 2023/1214.
2403. Article 1(a) Regulation on Russia and Art. 1(8) Regulation on Belarus.
2404. Article 2(1) Regulation on Russia and Art. 1e(1) Regulation on Belarus.
2405. Article 2(2)(a) & (b) Regulation on Russia and Art. 1e(2)(a) & (b) Regulation on Belarus.

property rights or trade secrets in relation to dual-use items, however only with regard to Russia.[2406] Furthermore, dual-use items exported from the Union may not transit through the territory of Russia.[2407]

528. These restrictions are not applicable when they are for non-military use and non-military end users and serve one of the following purposes or have one of the ensuing uses. The purposes include humanitarian, medical or pharmaceutical, health emergencies, or urgent prevention or mitigation of an event likely to have a serious and significant impact on human health and safety or the environment or as a response to natural disasters.[2408] The uses include use by news media, use as consumer communication devices, software updates and personal use of individuals travelling to Russia or members of their immediate families travelling with them and limited to personal effects, household effects, vehicles or tools of trade owned by them and not intended for sale.[2409] Specifically in relation to Belarus, these restrictions are not applicable to dual-use items that ensure cyber-security and information security of persons in Belarus with the exception of the government and undertakings controlled by it.[2410] Finally, dual-use items in transit via the territory of Russia are exempt from said prohibitions, when they are intended for all said purposes as well as for use by news media, use as consumer communication devices and for software updates.[2411]

529. At the same time, competent authorities may authorize, under the rules and procedures of the Dual Use Regulation, deviations from the prohibitions at hand, when the dual-use items are for non-military use and for a non-military end user, as long as they are intended for one of the following purposes.[2412] These include cooperation in civilian matters between the Union, the Member States and Russia, intergovernmental cooperation in space programmes, operation of civil nuclear capabilities, such as the Paks II project, including safety, or civil nuclear cooperation.[2413] They further include maritime safety, civilian non-publicly available electronic communications networks which are not owned or controlled by the state, diplomatic representations of the Union or its Member States and partner countries, or are for the exclusive use of entities owned or controlled by entities registered in a Member State or a partner country.[2414] Furthermore, competent authorities may authorize the sale, supply, transfer and export of dual-use items, when this is due under contracts made before the legislative

2406. Article 2(2)(c) Regulation on Russia.
2407. Article 2(1a) Regulation on Russia.
2408. Article 2(3)(a) & (b) Regulation on Russia and Art. 1e(3)(a) & (b) Regulation on Belarus.
2409. Article 2(3)(c), (d), (e) & (g) Regulation on Russia and Art. 1e(3)(c), (d), (e) & (g) Regulation on Belarus.
2410. Article 1e(3)(f) Regulation on Belarus.
2411. Article 2(3a) and (3)(a) to (e) Regulation on Russia.
2412. Article 2(4) & (6) Regulation on Russia and Art. 1e(4) & (6) Regulation on Belarus. *See also* Art. 2b(2) Regulation on Russia and Art. 1fa(2) Regulation on Belarus.
2413. Article 2(4)(a), (b) & (c) Regulation on Russia and Art. 1e(4)(a), (b) & (c) Regulation on Belarus.
2414. Article 2(4)(d), (e), (f) & (g) Regulation on Russia and Art. 1e(4)(d), (e), (f) & (g) Regulation on Belarus.

at came into force as long as fulfilment is completed within two months.[2415] Lastly, competent authorities may authorize deviation from said prohibitions for Russia, when they are intended to ensure cyber-security and information security for anyone except the government and entities controlled or owned by them, regardless of the stake that the state has in those.[2416] Competent authorities shall not issue an authorization when the end user may be a military end user or a designated person. They shall equally refrain from doing so, when the items might have a military end use or might be intended for aviation or the space industry[2417] or, with regard to Russia, the energy sector.[2418] In these last cases but solely with regard to Russia, competent authorities have the discretion to apply certain statutory exemptions for events impacting human health and safety or the environment,[2419] intergovernmental cooperation in space programmes,[2420] transport of natural gas and oil, (once again) events impacting human health and safety or the environment and insurance for persons established in the Union active in the energy sector in Russia[2421] (*see* in this regard paragraphs 530, 529 and 521 below and above respectively).

530. Moreover, competent authorities may issue an authorization for the sale of dual-use items to designated persons, when these are necessary for the urgent prevention or mitigation of an event likely to have a serious and significant impact on human health and safety or the environment. They may also do so for items due under contracts made before the relevant legislative acts entered into force, under the condition that these are fulfilled within two months.[2422]

531. Competent authorities are given the authority to annul, suspend, modify or revoke such an authorization, should they deem that doing so is necessary for the effective implementation of the EU legislative instruments.[2423]

532. The newest prohibition refers to a specific cluster of dual-use items, those being 'sensitive' or 'goods and technology that might contribute to the enhancement of Russia's military, technological or industrial capacities' or 'goods and technology that might contribute to the development of Russia's defence and security sector, in a way that strengthens its ability to wage war'. These goods and technology are to be listed and specified in a separate annex.[2424] Still, this has not yet taken place, thus attributing a stand-by quality to the prohibition here at hand. In truth, it has been stated that this

2415. Article 2(5) Regulation on Russia and Art. 1e(5) Regulation on Belarus. *See also* Art. 1(3) Decision (CFSP) 2022/327, Art. 1(2) Regulation (EU) 2022/328 and Art. 1(2) Decision (CFSP) 2022/356, Art. 1(4) Regulation (EU) 2022/355.
2416. Article 2(4)(h) Regulation on Russia.
2417. Article 2(7)(i) & (ii) Regulation on Russiaand Art. 1e(7)(i) & (ii) Regulation on Belarus.
2418. Article 2(7)(iii) Regulation on Russia.
2419. Articles 2(7)(i) and 2b(1)(a) Regulation on Russia.
2420. Article 2(7)(ii) & (4)(b) Regulation on Russia.
2421. Articles 2(7)(iii) and 3(3) to (6) Regulation on Russia.
2422. *See* Art. 2b(1)(a) & (b) and Annex IV Regulation on Russia. and Art. 1fa(1)(a) & (b) & Annex V Regulation on Belarus.
2423. Articles 2(8) & 2b(3) Regulation on Russia and Art. 1e(8) Regulation on Belarus. *See also* Art. 2b(3) Regulation on Russia and Art. 1fa(3) Regulation on Belarus.
2424. *See* Annex XXXIII Regulation on Russia.

provision introduced to Brussels the possibility to take exceptional and last-resort measures.[2425] For such measures to be taken, the items have to meet the following two criteria. The export of such, yet to be specified, items to Russia must be prohibited under different provisions of the same legislative act while presenting a high and continuous risk of being forwarded from third states to Russia after being sold, supplied, transferred or exported from the Union. These third states shall have to be identified by the Council as having systematically and persistently failed to prevent the sale, supply, transfer and export of such specific items to Russia.[2426] It was noted that such third states shall have to demonstrate a continuing and particularly high risk of being used for circumvention.[2427] Nonetheless, before any measure is adopted, the Commission shall take into account a thorough technical analysis of the circumvention issues in question. The analysis shall have to include available trade data, alternative issues that were ineffective, and information on efforts that the Union made in order to address the matter with the third state along with a clear indication that these efforts failed. The decision to include a third state in the list shall be taken by the Council.[2428]

533. Such dual-use items, as they shall be determined, may not be sold, supplied, transferred and exported to anyone in third states, as they shall be determined. No technical assistance, brokering services or other services, financing and financial assistance may be offered. No intellectual property rights and trade secrets may be sold, licensed or transferred in any other way.[2429]

534. Existing provisions delineating the scope of application of certain prohibitions and authorizing deviations apply *mutatis mutandis*.[2430]

§7 SANCTIONS ON ARMS AND WEAPONS

535. The restrictive measures with regard to arms and weapons include bans and restrictions on military items, equipment for internal repression, missiles and other means of delivery. They are similar, but not identical to the ones already described in Chapter 3.

I Sanctions with Regard to Military Items

536. Military items sanctioned under the regulations at hand are the items listed in the EU Common Military List, items contributing to military and technological enhancement and finally firearms, components and ammunition.

2425. *See* recital No. 13 to the preamble of Regulation (EU) 2023/1214.
2426. Article 12f(3) Regulation on Russia.
2427. *See* recital No. 13 to the preamble of Decision (CFSP) 2023/1217.
2428. *See* recital Nos 16 & 17 to the preamble of Decision (CFSP) 2023/1217.
2429. Article 12f(1) & (2)(a), (b) & (c) Regulation on Russia.
2430. Article 12f(4) & (5) Regulation on Russia.

A The EU Common Military List

537. The restrictive measures set out on goods and technology listed in the EU Common Military List (*see* in this regard paragraphs 273 et seq. above) with regard to Russia and Belarus[2431] are identical to the ones set out in the Regulation on the DPRK (*see* in this regard paragraphs 281 et seq. above), although the prohibition of brokering services with regard to Russia was introduced in June 2023 through the eleventh package of sanctions[2432] (*see* in this regard Annex II p. 337 at 342 below) and with regard to Belarus brokering is still not prohibited.

538. These prohibitions are not absolute, as derogations have been put in place. The ones set in relation to Belarus follow those already set and explained above with regard to humanitarian purposes, for protective use, including non-combat vehicles, and for institution-building programmes, and authorization is required, as the case may be[2433] (*see* in this regard paragraphs 289 et seq. above).

539. The derogations set with regard to Russia are different. Contracts made before the Regulation on Russia came into force do not fall within the scope of said prohibitions, making therefore their execution possible, and so does maintenance, repair and safety of existing civil nuclear capabilities within the Union, enabling import, export, purchase, sale, supply and transfer of relevant space parts and services.[2434] This latter derogation relates to utilities with VVER reactors in the Union that are dependent on Russian-produced nuclear fuel.[2435] Currently, within the Union twenty VVER reactors operate; two in Bulgaria, six in Czechia, two in Finland, four in Hungary, and six in Slovakia.[2436] Equally exempt from said prohibitions regarding prohibition of technical assistance and financing or financial assistance are specific pyrotechnics in the Common Military List[2437] destined for launchers operated by European launch service providers, for launches of European space programmes and for fuelling satellites by European satellite manufacturers, those being hydrazine (CAS 302-01-2), unsymmetrical dimethyl

---

2431. Article 4(1)(a) & (b) Regulation on Russiaand Art. 1b(1)(a) & (c) Regulation on Belarus. The prohibition of activities aiming to circumvent the set prohibitions is set, in a general manner, in Art. 12 Regulation on Russia, and in a specific manner, in Art. 1b(1)(d) Regulation on Belarus.

2432. *See* Art. 1(19) Regulation 2023/1214.

2433. Article 1b(2)(a) & (b) & (3) Regulation on Belarus.

2434. Article 4(2)(a) & (b) Regulation on Russia.

2435. *See* Martina Etzmuss et al, *Analysis of Nuclear Fuel Availability at EU Level from a Security of Supply Perspective, Report*, Euratom Supply Agency Advisory Committee: Working Group on Prices and Security of Supply, (European Union, 2020) p. 9.

2436. European Commission, Cordis EU research results, *Safety of Alternative Nuclear Fuel for VVER Reactors*, October 2022, available: https://cordis.europa.eu/programme/id/HORIZON_HORIZON-EURATOM-2022-NRT-01-01(last visited: 31 Dec. 2023). *See also* Editors, *Early Soviet Reactors and EU Accession*, World Nuclear Association, June 2019, available: https://www.world-nuclear.org/information-library/safety-and-security/safety-of-plants/appendices/early-soviet-reactors-and-eu-accession.aspx (last visited: 31 Dec. 2023).

2437. *See* recital No. 3 to the preamble of Regulation (EU) 2015/1797.

hydrazine (CAS 57-14-7) and monomethyl hydrazine (CAS 60-34-4).[2438] Hydrazine (CAS 302-01-2) is also outside the scope of said prohibitions when it is destined for tests and flights of the ExoMars 2020 mission.[2439] These hydrazine-related exemptions are subject to prior authorization of the competent authorities that are obliged to inform the Commission of any granted authorizations.[2440]

B Items for Military and Technological Enhancement

540. Goods and technology that might contribute to the military and technological enhancement of Russia and Belarus or the development of their defence and security sector are the object of restrictive measures. These are listed in much detail in the Regulation on Russia and the Regulation on Belarus, and entail the categories of electronic, computers, telecommunications, information security, sensors and lasers, navigation and avionics, marine, aerospace and propulsion, miscellaneous items, special materials and related equipment and materials processing and contain mainly items other than those specified in the EU Common Military List and in the Dual Use Regulation.[2441]

541. The relevant prohibitions are very close to the ones on items on the EU Common Military List but for three exceptions. At first, they are wider, as they prohibit 'any other services' along with technical assistance and brokering services.[2442] Further, they also prohibit selling, licensing and transferring intellectual property rights or trade secrets, however solely with regard to Russia.[2443] Finally, transit of such goods and technology through Russia while being exported from the EU is prohibited.[2444]

542. The prescribed exemptions are identical to the ones provided with regard to dual-use items, including already concluded contracts that must be executed within two months[2445] (*see* in this regard paragraphs 528 et seq. above). The specifics of issuing an authorization as well as annulling, suspending, modifying and revoking it[2446] are also identical to the ones already described under the dual-use items (*see* in this regard paragraph 531 above).

2438. Article 4(2a)(a), (b) & (c) Regulation on Russia.
2439. Article 4(2aa)(a) & (b) Regulation on Russia.
2440. Article 4(2b) Regulation on Russia.
2441. Annex VII Regulation on Russiaand Annex Va Regulation on Belarus.
2442. Article 2a(1) & (2)(a) & (b) Regulation on Russia and Art. 1f(1) & (2)(a) & (b) Regulation on Belarus.
2443. Article 2a(2)(c) Regulation on Russia.
2444. Article 2a(1a) Regulation on Russia.
2445. Article 2a(3)(a) to (g), (4)(a) to (h) & (5) Regulation on Russia and Art. 1f(3)(a) to (g), (4)(a) to (h) & (5) Regulation on Belarus.
2446. Article 2a(6), (7) & (8) Regulation on Russia and Art. 1f(6), (7) & (8) Regulation on Belarus. *See also* Art. 2b(1), (2) & (3) Regulation on Russia and Art. 1fa(1), (2) & (3) Regulation on Belarus.

C Firearms, Components and Ammunition

543. The following set of restrictive measures applicable with regard to Russia relates to firearms, their parts and essential components and ammunition. They are described in much detail[2447] and include short and long firearms,[2448] parts that were specifically designed for a firearm and are essential to its operation,[2449] ammunition[2450] as well as collections and collectors' pieces.[2451] The eleventh package of measures[2452] (*see* in this regard Annex II p. 337 at 342 below) enlarged the scope by adding further items because this was 'appropriate'.[2453] The added items are other firearms and similar devices which operate by firing an explosive charge and other arms, excluding those heading CN 9307.[2454]

544. The restrictive measures put in place for these items[2455] are identical to the ones regarding items for military and technological enhancement, including the prohibition on transit (*see* in this regard paragraphs 540 et seq. above). These measures are absolute.

II Sanctions with Regard to Equipment for Internal Repression

545. Equipment for internal repression is under restrictions solely with regard to Belarus. This equipment[2456] is very similar to the one described in the Regulation on Libya (*see* in this regard paragraph 296 above). The only variation has been adding riot control agents[2457] with the fourth package of sanctions[2458] (*see* in this regard Annex II p. 337 at 339 below).

546. The restrictive measures[2459] are equally very similar to the ones set out in the Regulation on Libya (*see* in this regard paragraph 298 above), with the exception of the

2447. Article 2aa(1) Regulation on Russia and Annex I Regulation (EU) I Regulation No. 258/2012 of the European Parliament and of the Council of 14 Mar. 2012 implementing Article 10 of the United Nations' Protocol against the illicit manufacturing of and trafficking in firearms, their parts and components and ammunition, supplementing the United Nations Convention against Transnational Organized Crime (UN Firearms Protocol), and establishing export authorization, and import and transit measures for firearms, their parts and components and ammunition, OJ L 94, 30 Mar. 2012, p. 1.
2448. CN codes: ex 9302 00 00, ex 9303 20 10, ex 9303 20 95, ex 9303 30 00, ex 9303 90 00, & 9303 10 00. Annex I Nos 1-12 Regulation (EU) 258/2012.
2449. CN codes: ex 9305 10 00, ex 9305 21 00, ex 9305 29 00 & ex 9305 99 00. Annex I No. 13 Regulation (EU) 258/2012.
2450. CN codes ex 3601 00 00, ex 3603 00 90, ex 9306 21 00, ex 9306 29 00, ex 9306 30 10, ex 9306 30 90 & ex 9306 90 90. Annex I No. 14 Regulation (EU) 258/2012.
2451. CN codes: ex 9705 00 00 & 9706 00 00. Annex I No. 15 Regulation (EU) 258/2012.
2452. Article 1(7) Decision (CFSP) 2023/1217 and Art. 1(3) Regulation (EU) 2023/1214.
2453. Recital No. 20 to the preamble of Decision (CFPS) 2023/1217.
2454. CN codes 9303 & ex 9304. Annex XXXV Regulation on Russia.
2455. Article 2aa(1), (1a) & (2)(a), (b) & (c) Regulation on Russia.
2456. Annex III Nos 1 to 11 Regulation on Belarus.
2457. Annex III No. 9a Regulation on Belarus.
2458. *See* Annex I Regulation (EU) 2021/1030.
2459. Article 1a(1)(a) & (b) Regulation on Belarus.

prohibition of exporting and transporting such items that is absent in the Regulation on Belarus. Finally, the exceptions with regard to protective clothing and items used for protective or humanitarian use, following authorization of the competent authorities, as the case may be,[2460] are identical to the ones in force regarding Libya (*see* in this regard paragraph 301 above). Derogations with regard to certain rifles and ammunition complying with the specifications for biathlon equipment and related to sporting rifles, sporting pistols and their ammunition that were introduced in February 2017[2461] and in February 2018[2462] respectively, were repealed by the fourth package[2463] (*see* in this regard Annex II p. 337 at 339 below).

III Sanctions with Regard to Missiles and Other Systems of Delivery

547. Sanctions with regard to missiles and other systems of delivery are encountered solely in the Regulation on Iran Assisting Russia. This legislation sets out restrictive measures on goods and technology that might contribute to Iran's capability to manufacture UAVs, regardless of their country of origin.[2464] The items that have been identified as such include UAVs other than those designed for carrying passengers,[2465] propulsion and navigation items,[2466] electronic components and devices[2467] and other items,[2468] such as satellite navigation systems. Said items may double as items qualifying as *dual-use items* under the Dual Use Regulation[2469] (*see* in this regard paragraphs 241 et seq. above).

548. This legislative act restricts the sale, supply, transfer and export of said items to anyone in Iran or for use in Iran. It equally restricts their transit through Iran, along with technical assistance, brokering services, other services, financing or financial assistance, as well as sale, license and transfer in any other way of intellectual property rights and trade secrets.[2470]

549. Contracts made before this legislative act came into force, including necessary ancillary contracts, that are executed within three months, do not fall within its scope

2460. Article 1a(2) & (3) Regulation on Belarus.
2461. *See* Art. 1(1) Regulation (EU) 2017/331.
2462. *See* Art. 1(1) Regulation (EU) 2018/275.
2463. *See* Art. 1(2) Regulation (EU) 2021/1030.
2464. Article 2(1) Regulation (EU) 2023/1529.
2465. CN codes 8806.91, 8806.92, 8806.93, 8806.94 & 8806.99, category 1 to Annex II Regulation on Iran Assisting Russia.
2466. CN codes ex 8411.11, ex 8411.12, ex 8411.21, ex 8411.22, ex 8411.91, 8407.10, ex 8408.90, 9014.20, ex 8526.10, ex 8529.90, ex 8526.91, ex 8529.90, ex 8807.30 & ex 8807.30 category 2 to Annex II Regulation on Iran Assisting Russia.
2467. CN codes ex 8542.31, ex 8542.39, ex 8542.33, ex 8548.00, 8525.83, ex 8525.89, ex 9006.30, ex 8529.90, ex 9013.80, ex 9025.80, ex 9026.90 & ex 9027.50 category 3 to Annex II Regulation on Iran Assisting Russia.
2468. These include airborne laser rangefinder, LIDAR systems and technology, designed or specifically adapted for the test, development or production of equipment listed above. Category 4 to Annex II Regulation on Iran Assisting Russia.
2469. *See* Art. 2(3) & (5) Regulation on Iran Assisting Russia.
2470. Article 2(1) & (2)(a), (b) & (c) *ibid.*

of application.[2471] Derogation is possible via authorizations issued by competent authorities, as long as the transaction is for non-military use and for non-military end user and under the condition that the items at hand are necessary for medical, pharmaceutical or humanitarian purposes. Preventing or mitigating an event likely to have a serious and significant impact on human health and safety or on the environment may equally serve as a purpose and so does a response to natural disasters.[2472] Any such authorization may be annulled, suspended, modified or revoked, when the competent authorities deem that this is necessary for the effective implementation of the regulation at hand.[2473]

550. The above described are without prejudice to authorization requirements under the Dual Use Regulation; any such other authorization is granted separately and is valid throughout the Union.[2474]

§8 SANCTIONS ON MOVEMENT OF PERSONS AND TRANSFER OF GOODS

551. The restrictive measures discussed here disrupt persons' movement and transfer of goods, in the sense of road transport and transport via vessels and aircraft. Furthermore, a few remarks on the interplay of sanctions and transfer of goods are offered.

I Sanctions on Movement of Persons

552. Sanctions on movement of natural persons, that are widely known as *travel bans*, are prescribed in the Decision accompanying the Regulation on Threatening Ukraine, the Decision accompanying the Regulation on Iran Assisting Russia and the Decision accompanying the Regulation on Belarus. The other legislative instruments do not set out such restrictive measures.

A The Restrictive Measures

553. Both the objective and the subjective elements that constitute the prohibition of entering into and transiting through the territories of the Member States[2475] follow the pattern already explained above (*see* in this regard paragraphs 308 et seq.). Thus, the aforementioned apply *mutatis mutandis*. Exceptionally, although the Regulation on Threatening Ukraine does freeze the funds of persons operating in the Russian IT sector

2471. Article 2(7) *ibid.*
2472. Article 2(3)(a) & (b) *ibid.*
2473. Article 2(4) *ibid.*
2474. Article 2(3) & (5) *ibid.*
2475. Article 1 Decision 2014/145/CFSP, Art. 2 Decision (CFSP) 2023/1532 (*see also* Art. 4 Regulation on Iran Assisting Russia) & Art. 3 Decision 2012/642/CFSP.

with a licence administered by the Federal Security Service of Russia Centre for Licensing, Certification, and Protection of State Secrets or a 'weapons and military equipment' license administered by the Russian Ministry of Industry and Trade, the corresponding decision does not impose any travel restrictions.

B *The Exceptions*

554. Unlike the restrictive measures, the exceptions and derogations therefrom rather resemble and do not follow the (uneven) pattern explained above. Obligations under international law[2476] (*see* in this respect paragraph 316 above) do remain unaffected from said restrictive measures creating to the Member States granting an exception on such a base, the duty to duly inform the Council.[2477] Member States may further grant an exception for urgent humanitarian needs as well as for attending intergovernmental meetings hosted by the Union or a Member State that directly promote the policy objectives of the restrictive measures, may that be support for the territorial integrity, sovereignty and independence of Ukraine or democracy, human rights and the rule of law in Belarus.[2478] Member States intending to grant an exemption on these grounds have the duty to inform the Council in writing. Council members are then given the right to raise an objection within two working days, which lacks the power to block the intended decision, as the Council may reach a decision by a qualified majority.[2479]

II Sanctions on Movement of Goods

A *Sanctions with Regard to Road Transport*

555. Transporting goods by road has been sanctioned with regard to Russia and Belarus with the fifth package of sanctions[2480] (*see* in this regard Annex II p. 337 at 339 below). It is prohibited for *any road transport undertaking*[2481] established in Russia and Belarus to transport goods by road within the Union, including transit.[2482] As it has been specified with the eleventh package of sanctions[2483] (*see* in this regard Annex II p. 337 at 342 below), this prohibition applies to road transportation carried out by means

2476. Article 1(3) & (4) Decision 2014/145/CFSP, Art. 2(3) & (4) Decision (CFSP) 2023/1532 & Art. 3(3) & (4) Decision 2012/642/CFSP.
2477. Article 1(5) Decision 2014/145/CFSP, Art. 2(5) Decision (CFSP) 2023/1532 & Art. 3(5) Decision 2012/642/CFSP.
2478. Article 1(6) Decision 2014/145/CFSP, Art. 2(6) Decision (CFSP) 2023/1532 & Art. 3(6) Decision 2012/642/CFSP.
2479. Article 1(7) Decision 2014/145/CFSP, Art. 2(7) Decision (CFSP) 2023/1532 & Art. 3(7) Decision 2012/642/CFSP.
2480. *See* Art. 1(20) Decision (CFSP) 2022/578 & Art. 1(13) Regulation (EU) 2022/576 and Art. 1(3) Decision (CFSP) Decision 2022/579 & Art. 1(4) Regulation (EU) 2022/577.
2481. In regard to the definition of *road transport undertaking* that has been set out in Art. 1(w) Regulation on Russia and Art. 1(25) Regulation on Belarus *see* Annex I p. 311 at 330.
2482. Article 3l(1) Regulation on Russia and Art. 1zc(1) Regulation on Belarus.
2483. *See* recital No. 30 to the preamble of and Art. 1(17) Regulation (EU) 2023/1214.

of trailers or semi-trailers registered in Russia, including such trailers or semi-trailers having been hauled by trucks registered in other countries.[2484]

556. Outside the scope of this prohibition falls road transport undertakings transporting mail as a universal service.[2485] Specifically with regard to Belarus, transport of goods already in the territory of the Union, when the regulations came in force were not affected, as long as the transport was completed within a week or the transit through the Union was necessary in order to return to Belarus.[2486] Specifically with regard to Russia, goods in transit to through the Union between the Kaliningrad Oblast and Russia also fall outside the scope, under the condition that transporting such goods is not otherwise prohibited under the Regulation on Russia.[2487]

557. Road transportation of goods may be authorized by competent authorities for oil and natural gas, titanium, aluminium, copper, nickel, palladium and iron ore,[2488] unless otherwise prohibited (*see* in this regard paragraphs 509 & 515 above). Road transportation of pharmaceutical, medical, agricultural and food products may also be authorized.[2489] Authorization of road transport of goods may further serve humanitarian purposes as well as facilitate the functioning of diplomatic and consular representations in Russia, including international organizations.[2490] Finally, road transport may be authorized within the context of formal cultural cooperation with Russia and relate to the transfer to Russia of cultural goods on loan.[2491]

558. Other Member States and the Commission shall be informed of granting any such authorization within two weeks.[2492]

B Sanctions with Regard to Vessels

559. The restrictive measures that relate to vessels include refusal of port and lock, which have been extended in response to increased deceptive practices, and prohibition to provide maritime navigation goods and technology.

560. In a manner similar to the restrictions imposed on the DPRK, any vessel registered under the flag of Russia as well as any vessel certified by the Russian Maritime Register of Shipping, regardless of them changing flag or registration after 24 February 2022, does not have access to ports in the Union.[2493] Furthermore, such vessels do not have access to locks, unless their use serves the purpose of leaving the

2484. Article 3l(1a) Regulation on Russia.
2485. Article 3l(2)(a) Regulation on Russia and Art. 1zc(2) Regulation on Belarus.
2486. Article 1zc(3) Regulation on Belarus.
2487. Article 3l(2)(b) Regulation on Russia.
2488. Article 3l(4)(a) Regulation on Russia and Art. 1zc(4)(a) Regulation on Belarus.
2489. Article 3l(4)(b) Regulation on Russia and Art. 1zc(4)(b) Regulation on Belarus.
2490. Article 3l(4)(c) & (d) Regulation on Russia and Art. 1zc(4)(c) & (d) Regulation on Belarus.
2491. Article 3l(4)(e) Regulation on Russia.
2492. Article 3l(5) Regulation on Russia and Art. 1zc(5) Regulation on Belarus.
2493. Article 3ea(1), (1a) & (2) Regulation on Russia.

territory of the Union.[2494] Within this frame *vessel* has been defined as 'a ship falling within the scope of the relevant international conventions; a yacht, of 15 metres in length or more, which does not carry cargo and carrying no more than 12 passengers; or recreational craft[2495] or personal watercraft[2496]'.[2497]

561. These prohibitions do not apply in cases of a vessel in need of assistance seeking a place of refuge, of an emergency port call for reasons of maritime safety, or for saving life at sea.[2498] At the same time, authorizations may be granted for derogating from same prohibitions, when the competent authorities deem this necessary for reasons and items[2499] fairly similar to the ones mentioned under road transport (*see* in this respect paragraph 557 above). In addition, authorizations may be granted for the transport of certain iron and chemical products[2500] and nuclear fuels and other goods necessary for civil nuclear capabilities, such as the Paks II project.[2501] Coal and other solid fossil fuels may no longer be authorized for seaborne transport.[2502] Lastly, two specifically targeted exceptions are foreseen in the Regulation on Russia. According to the first, accessing a port or a lock may be authorized for vessels that have changed their Russian flag or registration to such of another state before 16 April 2022, when acquiring a Russian flag or registration was required under a contract. Cumulatively, access to ports and locks of the Union must be necessary for unloading goods necessary for completing renewable energy projects in the Union, as long as importing such is not otherwise prohibited.[2503] The second exception permits vessels to access a port or a lock, then they have flown the Russian flag under a bareboat charter registration initially affected prior to 24 February 2022. Parallel thereto the vessels at hand must have resumed their right to fly the flag of the underlying Member State registry before 31 January 2023, while not being owned, chartered, operated or otherwise controlled by a Russian national or legal person established in Russia.[2504]

562. Other Member States and the Commission shall be informed of granting any such authorization within two weeks.[2505]

563. The eleventh package of sanctions (*see* in this regard Annex II p. 337 at 342 below) has widened the prohibition on access to ports and locks of the Union, as a

2494. Article 3ea(1) Regulation on Russia.
2495. In regard to the definition of *recreational craft* (Art. 3ea(3)(c) Regulation on Russia & Art. 3(2) Directive 2013/53/EU of the European Parliament and of the Council of 20 Nov. 2013 on recreational craft and personal watercraft and repealing Directive 94/25/EC, OJ L 354 28 Dec. 2013, p. 90) *see* Annex I p. 311 at 330.
2496. In regard to the definition of *personal watercraft* set out in Art. 3ea(3)(c) Regulation on Belarus & Art. 3(3) Directive (EU) 2013/35 *see* Annex I p. 311 at 329.
2497. Article 3ea(3)(a), (b) & (c) Regulation on Russia.
2498. Article 3ea(4) Regulation on Russia.
2499. *See* Art. 3ea(5)(a), (b) & (c) Regulation on Russia.
2500. Article 3ea(5)(a) Regulation on Russia. The items are specified in Annex XXIV Regulation on Russia.
2501. Article 3ea(5)(d) Regulation on Russia.
2502. *See* Art. 3ea(5)(e) Regulation on Russia [repealed] and Art. 1(9) Regulation 2023/1214.
2503. Article 3ea(5a) Regulation on Russia.
2504. Article 3ea(5b) Regulation on Russia.
2505. Article 3ea(6) Regulation on Russia.

response to increased deceptive practices,[2506] without widening its scope of application.[2507] It allows the competent authorities to refuse access, when they have reasonable cause to suspect illegal interference with or disabling the shipborne automatic identification system at any point of the voyage, only in cases where the transported goods are crude oil and petroleum products.[2508] They also have the power to refuse access upon reasonable cause to suspect that a vessel performed ship-to-ship transfer in breach of the Regulation on Russia.[2509] Any ship-to-ship transfer taking place within the Exclusive Economic Zone of a Member State or within 12 nautical miles from the baseline of that Member State's coast must be notified to the competent authority at least forty-eight hours in advance.[2510] As a derogation access to ports and locks of the Union may be authorized, when this is necessary for humanitarian purposes.[2511]

564. Refusal of port access must be notified immediately to the competent authorities of other Member States, whereas the other Member States and the Commission must be notified without delay.[2512] Authorizations need not be notified.

565. Maritime goods and technology that have been specified in detail in the Regulation on Russia,[2513] may not be sold, supplied, transferred or exported to anyone in Russia, for use in Russia or for placing on board of a Russian-flagged vessel.[2514] Technical assistance, brokering services, other services, financing or financial assistance, as well as sale, license and transfer in any other way of intellectual property rights and trade secrets may also not be provided.[2515] This restriction does not apply on items and services for non-military use and for non-military end-user, when they are intended to satisfy humanitarian purposes, to respond to health emergencies or natural disasters, or to prevent or mitigate events likely having a serious and significant impact on human health and safety or on the environment.[2516] Competent authorities may issue derogations for items and services not having military use or military end-user, when they are intended for maritime safety.[2517]

566. Other Member States and the Commission shall be informed of granting any such authorization within two weeks.[2518]

2506. *See* recital Nos 29-33 to the preamble of & 1(13) Article Decision 2023/1217 and recital Nos 31-34 to the preamble of & Art. 1(10) Regulation (EU) 2023/1214.
2507. Vessels in need of assistance seeking a place of refuge, of an emergency port call for reasons of maritime safety, including pilot services in innocent passages, or for saving life at sea equally do not fall within the scope of application. Articles 3eb(3), 3ee(2) & 5aa(3)(h) Regulation on Russia.
2508. Article 3ec(1) Regulation on Russia.
2509. Articles 3eb(1) and 3m(1) & (2), 3n(1) & (4) Regulation on Russia.
2510. Article 3eb(2) Regulation on Russia.
2511. Articles 3eb(4) & 3ec(3) Regulation on Russia.
2512. Articles 3eb(5) & 3ec(4) Regulation on Russia.
2513. *See* Annex XVI Regulation on Russia.
2514. Article 3f(1) Regulation on Russia.
2515. Article 3f(2)(a), (b) & (c) Regulation on Russia.
2516. Article 3f(3) Regulation on Russia.
2517. Article 3f(4) Regulation on Russia.
2518. Article 3f(5) Regulation on Russia.

C Sanctions with Regard to Aircraft

567. In a manner similar to the restrictions imposed on the DPRK (*see* in this regard paragraphs 327 et seq. above), aircraft operated by Russian and Belarusian air carriers may not land in, take off and overfly over the Union. Marketing carriers in code-sharing or blocked-space arrangements may also not do so.[2519] Specifically with regard to Russia, the prohibition extends to any Russian-registered aircraft and any non-Russian-registered aircraft that is owned, chartered or otherwise controlled by any Russian person.[2520]

568. Said prohibitions do not apply in emergency landings or emergency overflights.[2521] Competent authorities may authorize derogations from the prohibitions discussed here when doing so is required for humanitarian purposes or for any other purpose consistent with the objectives of the legislative acts in question.[2522]

569. Specifically with regard to Russia, a specific notification obligation was introduced with the tenth package of sanctions (*see* in this regard Annex II p. 337 at 342 below), for the purpose of avoiding circumvention of and ensuring compliance with the aforementioned prohibition on non-Russian-registered aircrafts.[2523] This prescribes that aircraft operators of non-scheduled flights between Russia and a Member State, regardless of being operated directly or through a third country, are to notify at least forty-eight hours in advance the competent authorities of the Member State of departure or destination and communicate all relevant information concerning the flight.[2524] Any refusal to such a flight notification is communicated immediately to other Member States, the Commission and the Network Manager.[2525] The Network Manager is the body entrusted with the tasks necessary for the execution of the network management and design of the single European sky.[2526]

570. Goods and technology for the aviation and space industry,[2527] including jet fuel and fuel additives,[2528] are under restrictions with regard to Russia. They may be neither

2519. Article 3d(1) Regulation on Russia and Art. 8b(1) Regulation on Belarus.
2520. Article 3d(1) Regulation on Russia.
2521. Article 3d(2) Regulation on Russiaand Art. 8b(2) Regulation on Belarus.
2522. Article 3d(3) Regulation on Russia and Art. 8c(1) Regulation on Belarus.
2523. Recital No. 8 to the preamble of Decision (CFSP) 2023/434 and recital No. 20 to the preamble of Regulation (EU) 2023/427.
2524. Article 3d(5) Regulation on Russia.
2525. Article 3d(6) Regulation on Russia.
2526. Article 2(6) Commission Implementing Regulation (EU) 2019/123 of 24 Jan. 2019 laying down detailed rules for the implementation of air traffic management (ATM) network functions and repealing Commission Regulation (EU) No. 677/2011, OJ L 28, 31 Jan. 2019, p. 1 and Art. 6 Regulation (EC) No. 551/2004 of the European Parliament and of the Council of 10 Mar. 2004 on the organization and use of the airspace in the single European sky, OJ L096, 31 Mar. 2004, p. 20.
2527. These goods bear the following CN codes: 88, ex 2710 19 83, ex 2710 19 99, 4011 30 00, ex 6813 20 00, 6813 81 00, 8517 71 00, ex 8517 79 00, 9024 10 00, 9026 00 00, 8407 10, 8409 10, 8411, 8411 12, 8411 21, 8411 22 & 8411 91. *See* Parts A to D Annex XI Regulation on Russia.
2528. These goods bear the following CN codes: 2710 12 70, 2710 19 29, 2710 19 21, 2710 20 90, 3811 21 00, 3811 29 00, 3811 90 00. *See* Annex XX Regulation on Russia.

sold, supplied, transferred nor exported to anyone in Russia or for use in Russia.[2529] No technical assistance, brokering services, other services, financing or financial assistance, insurance and re-insurance, as well as sale, license and transfer in any other way of intellectual property rights and trade secrets with regard to said goods may be provided.[2530] They may also not transit via Russia when exported from the Union.[2531] Importantly, any one of the following activities, as well as any combination thereof, may not be provided to any one in Russia or for use in Russia: overhaul, repair, inspection, replacement, modification or defect rectification of an aircraft or component. Pre-flight inspection with regard to goods and technology for the aviation and space industry is exempt.[2532]

571. In the following cases, competent authorities may authorize deviation from certain prohibitions, those being the ones of selling, supplying, transferring, exporting and providing technical assistance, brokering services, other services, financial and financial assistance. They have not been given the authority to authorize deviation from the other prohibitions. The first case concerns the execution of existing aircraft financial leases when this is necessary to ensure repayments to a person established in a Member State that does not fall under any of the restrictions set in the Regulation on Russia. In addition, authorities must have determined that no economic resources shall be made available to the Russian contracting party, but for full reimbursement of the financial lease upon the transfer of ownership of the aircraft.[2533] Competent authorities may further issue an authorization for certain goods when this is necessary for producing titanium goods required in the aeronautic industry and no alternative supply is available.[2534] They also have the competence to authorize the sale, supply, transfer and export of aerials and aerial reflectors and instruments and apparatus for measuring the flow, level, pressure or other variables of liquids or gases, when this is necessary for medical or pharmaceutical purposes or for humanitarian purposes. For these purposes and for these goods, technical assistance, brokering services, financing and financial assistance may also be afforded.[2535] However, no such authorization shall be given, when authorities have reasonable grounds to believe that the goods might have a military end-use.[2536]

572. To the end of avoiding collision between satellites or their unintended re-entry into the atmosphere, competent authorities may allow the provision of technical

2529. Article 3c(1) Regulation on Russia.
2530. Article 3c(4)(a), (b) & (c) & (2) Regulation on Russia.
2531. Article 3c(1a) & (2) Regulation on Russia.
2532. Article 3c(3) Regulation on Russia.
2533. Article 3c(6)(a) & (b) Regulation on Russia.
2534. These specific goods are the ones listed in Part B of Annex XI. Article 3c(6a) Regulation on Russia.
2535. These specific goods are the ones falling under the CN codes 8517 71 00, 8517 79 00 & 9026 00 00 of Part B of Annex XI. Article 3c(6c) first sub-paragraph Regulation on Russia.
2536. Article 3c(6c) second sub-paragraph Regulation on Russia.

assistance, brokering services, financing and financial assistance.[2537] They may further authorize the sale, supply, transfer and export of certain goods, when the specific goods in question shall be used to fulfil maintenance obligations in areas under long-term lease agreement between a Member State and Russia, as long as these goods shall be under the full control of the authorizing Member State.[2538] Finally, competent authorities have the discretion to permit transit via Russia of the goods and technology for aviation and space industry, including jet fuel and fuel additives, when this is necessary for producing titanium goods, for avoiding collision between satellites, for avoiding unintended re-entry of satellites into the atmosphere, for medical purposes, for pharmaceutical purposes and for humanitarian purposes.[2539]

573. Other Member States and the Commission shall be informed of any granted authorizations within two weeks.[2540]

III Sanctions and Movement of Goods

574. With regard to items exempt from export prohibitions, those being dual-use items,[2541] items that might contribute to the military and technological enhancement of Russia and Belarus[2542] and certain machinery,[2543] the exporter bears the obligation to state in the customs declaration that the items in question are being exported under the relevant exception. The exporter also bears the obligation to notify the competent authority of the first use of the exception in question within thirty days of the first export taking place.[2544] These obligations do not apply for exceptions related to items for personal use of persons travelling to Russia or Belarus[2545] and cybersecurity.[2546]

575. Other items exempt from export prohibitions[2547] do not create such declaration and notification obligations to exporters.

2537. Article 3c(6b) Regulation on Russia.
2538. Article 3c(6e) Regulation on Russia.
2539. Article 3c(6d) Regulation on Russia.
2540. Article 3c(7) Regulation on Russia.
2541. Article 2(3) first sub-paragraph Regulation on Russia and Art. 1e(3) first sub-paragraph Regulation on Belarus.
2542. Article 2a(3) first sub-paragraph Regulation on Russia and Art. 1f(3) first sub-paragraph Regulation on Belarus.
2543. Article 1s(3) first sub-paragraph Regulation on Belarus.
2544. Articles 2(3) second sub-paragraph & 2s(3) second sub-paragraph Regulation on Russia and Arts 1e(3) second sub-paragraph, 1f(3) second sub-paragraph & 1s(3) second sub-paragraph Regulation on Belarus.
2545. Articles 2(3) first sub-paragraph (g) & 2a(3) first sub-paragraph (g) Regulation on Russia and Arts 1e(3) first sub-paragraph (f), 1f(3) first sub-paragraph (f) & 1s(3) first sub-paragraph (f) Regulation on Belarus.
2546. Article 1s(3) first sub-paragraph (g) Regulation on Belarus.
2547. *See* Arts 3(3), 3b(3) & (4), 3f(3), 3h(3) & (3a), 3k(4), 4(2), (2a) & (2aa) and 12f(4) Regulation on Russia, Art. 2b(3) & (4) Regulation on Goods from Crimea, Arts 1a(2) & 1h(2) Regulation on Belarus and Arts 4(3) & 4a(1) Regulation with regard to Donetsk & Luhansk.

§9 MINING AND QUARRYING

576. Within the frame of restrictive measures against Russia, the *mining and quarrying sector* has been defined as 'a sector covering the location, extraction, management and processing activities relating to non-energy producing materials'.[2548] Legal persons operating in this sector are subject to restrictions identical to the ones in the energy sector.[2549] Therefore, the aforementioned (*see* in this regard paragraphs 498 et seq. above) apply *mutatis mutandis*. Mining and quarrying activities that yield their highest value from the production of aluminium, chromium, cobalt, copper, iron ore, mineral fertilizers, molybdenum, nickel, palladium, rhodium, scandium, titanium, vanadium, heavy rare earths or light rare earths fall outside the scope of this restriction. So do mining and quarrying activities that have as their primary objective the production of any of said minerals.[2550]

§10 RESTRICTIONS ON IMPORTING AND EXPORTING CERTAIN GOODS

577. Goods that could contribute to the enhancement of the industrial capacities of Russia, as described and detailed in the Regulation on Russia,[2551] may not be sold, supplied, transferred or exported, regardless of whether they originate in the Union or not. At the same time, in the familiar pattern, no technical assistance, brokering or other services, financing and financial assistance may be provided. Similarly, no sale, license and transfer in any other way of intellectual property rights and trade secrets with regard to said goods may take place.[2552]

578. Grace periods of one, two or three months for contracts already made before the initial legislative act came into force have long expired.[2553] Still, the twelfth package (*see* in this regard Annex II p. 337 at 343 below) took note of contracts related to certain

2548. Article 1(x) Regulation on Russia.
2549. Article 3a(2)(a) to (d) Regulation on Russia.
2550. Article 3a(5) and Annex XXX Regulation on Russia.
2551. *See* Annex XXIII Regulation on Regulation on Russia.
2552. Article 3k(1) & (2)(a), (b) & (c) Regulation on Russia.
2553. Contracts made before 24 Jun. 2023 had to be executed within one month according to Art. 3k(3), (3a) & (eb) Regulation on Russia. Under the repealed provisions contracts made before 9 Apr. 2022 had to be executed by 10 Jul. 2022 (*see* Art. 1(20) Decision (CFSP) 2022/578 & Art. 1(13) Regulation (EU) 2022/576). Contracts made before 7 Oct. 2022 had to be executed by 8 Jan. 2023 (*see* Art. 1(13) Decision (CFSP) 2022/1909 and Art. 1(7) Regulation (EU) 2022/1904). Contracts made before 17 Dec. 2022 had to be executed by 16 Jan. 2023 (*see* Art. 1(9)(c) Decision (CFSP) 2022/2478 and Art. 1(7)(c) Regulation (EU) 2022/2474). Contracts made before 26 Feb. 2023 have to be executed until 27 Mar. 2023 (*see* Art. 1(8)(a) Decision (CFSP) 2023/434 and Art. 1(7)(a) Regulation (EU) 2023/427). These grace periods were repealed by Art. 1(19)(c) Decision (CFSP) 2023/2874 & Art. 1(11)(c) Regulation (EU) 2023/2878.

goods and granted renewed grace periods of three[2554] or six months,[2555] depending on the specific goods.[2556] Outside the scope of this prohibition fall goods necessary for the official purposes of diplomatic or consular missions of Member States and partner countries in Russia or of international organizations enjoying immunities.[2557]

579. Competent authorities may authorize deviations from said prohibition for medical purposes, pharmaceutical purposes or humanitarian purposes, including transfer of humanitarian workers and evacuations. Authorizations may further be based on the need to maintain obligations in areas under long-term lease agreements between a Member State and Russia[2558] as well as on establishing, operating and maintaining civil nuclear capabilities, completing civil nuclear facilities, such as the Paks II project, and supplying material for medical radioisotopes and similar medical applications or environmental radiation monitoring.[2559] Specifically, the sale, supply, transfer or export of goods falling under CN Chapters 72, 84, 85 and 90 may be authorized, when the competent authorities deem this necessary for the production of titanium goods required in the aeronautic industry, under the condition that no alternative supply is available.[2560] Lastly, 'bakery ovens, incl. biscuit ovens, non-electric' may be sold, supplied, transferred or exported following authorization when it is established that they are necessary for personal household use of natural persons.[2561] However, no authorization shall be granted, when the competent authorities have reasonable grounds to believe that the goods in question might have a military end use.[2562]

2554. These are goods falling under the CN codes: 2825, 2905 31, 3812 10, 3812 31, 3812 39, 3816 00 90, 3910, 3911 90, 3912 12, 3912 20, 3912 31, 3912 39, 3917 22, 3917 29, 4011 80, 7201, 7202 11, 7202 19, 7202 19, 7202 21, 7202 29, 7202 30, 7202 41, 7202 49, 7202 50, 7202 60, 7202 70, 7202 80, 7202 91, 7202 93, 7202 99, 7203, 7204, 7205, 7206, 7214, 7215 10, 7215 90, 7217, 7221, 7222 11, 7222 19, 7222 20, 7222 40, 7223, 7227, 7229 20, 7301 10, 7302, 7303, 7304 11, 7304 19, 7304 22, 7304 23, 7304 29, 7304 31, 7304 39, 7304 41, 7304 49, 7304 51, 7304 59, 7304 90, 7305 12, 7305 19, 7305 20, 7305 31, 730590, 7306 11, 7306 19, 7306 21, 7306 29, 7306 30, 7306 40, 7306 40, 7306 61, 7306 69, 7306 90, 7411 10, 7411 21, 7411 22, 7413, 7606 11, 7606 12, 7606 91, 7608, 7609, 8207 13, 8207 19, 8207 20, 8207 30, 8207 40, 8207 50, 8207 70, 8207 80, 8207 90, 8412 31, 8412 80, 8413 20, 8413 40, 8413 82, 8413 92, 8417 10, 8430 20, 8430 31, 8430 61, 8456 11, 8456 12, 8456 30, 8456 50, 8456 90, 8461 50, 8757, 8474 20, 8474 32, 8480 10, 8480 41, 8480 49, 8480 50, 8480 79, 8501 10, 8501 32, 8501 40, 8501 51, 8501 52, 8501 71, 8501 72, 8501 80, 8506 10, 8506 30, 8506 40, 8506 50, 8506 80, 8507 50, 8507 60, 8507 80, 8705 90, 8515 31, 8515 39, 8515 80, 8515 90, 8904, 8905, 9013 20, 9013 90, 9027 20, 9027 30, 9027 50, 9027 90, 9030 10, 9030 20, 9030 31, 9030 33, 9030 84 and 9030 90. Article 3k(3aa) and Annex XXIIIA Regulation on Russia. It is here noted that some of these items, such as lasers and spectrometers double as dual use items.

2555. These are goods falling under CN codes 3917 21, 3917 39, 3917 40, 7305 11, 7307 11, 7307 19, 7307 21, 7307 23, 7307 29, 7307 91, 7307 92, 7307 93, 7307 99, 7412, 8412 90, 8413 70, 8413 91, 8417 80, 8417 90, 8430 41, 8430 49, 8465 10, 8465 91, 8465 92, 8465 95, 8465 99, 8474 90 and 8480 71. Article 3k(3ab) and Annex XXIIIB Regulation on Russia.

2556. *See* Art. 1(19)(d) Decision (CFSP) 2023/2874 & Art. 1(11)(d) Regulation (EU) 2023/2878.

2557. Article 3k(4) Regulation on Russia.

2558. Article 3k(5)(a) & (b) Regulation on Russia.

2559. Article 3k(5)(c) Regulation on Russia.

2560. Article 3k(5b) Regulation on Russia.

2561. Goods falling under CN code 8417 20. Article 3k(5a) Regulation on Russia.

2562. Article 3k(6) Regulation on Russia.

580. Other Member States and the Commission shall be informed of any granted authorizations within two weeks.[2563]

581. The 12th package (*see* in this regard Annex II p. 337 at 343 below) introduced a prohibition of transit through the territory of Russia of certain goods and technology[2564] that could contribute to the enhancement of Russian industrial capacities exported from the Union.[2565] Nonetheless, competent authorities may authorize such action, when they determine that such goods and technology are intended for medical or pharmaceutical purposes, for purposes of fulfilling maintenance obligations, for civil nuclear facilities and for the production of titanium goods required in the aeronautic industry (*see* in this regard paragraph 579 above).[2566]

582. The export, as well as selling, supplying and transferring of certain goods to anyone in Belarus or for use in Belarus is prohibited.[2567] Providing technical assistance, brokering services, financing and financial assistance as well as insurance and re-insurance is equally not permitted.[2568] These restricted goods are the ones used for the production or manufacturing of tobacco products[2569] and machinery, such as nuclear reactors, furnaces, bookbinding machinery and knitting machines.[2570] The scope of application of the latter prohibition on machinery[2571] is identical to the one of dual-use items (*see* in this regard paragraph 528 above). Lastly, contracts related to such machinery made before the relevant legislative act came into force are unaffected, as long as they are executed within three months.[2572]

583. At the same time, since June 2021,[2573] exporting equipment, technology and software intended primarily for use in the monitoring or interception of internet or

2563. Article 3k(7) Regulation on Russia.
2564. These are principally engines, filters for engines, valves and crane lorries. More specifically they fall under the CN codes 840999, 841221, 841350, 842123, 842131, 842839, 842959, 843139, 847130, 847170, 848120, 850220, 850710 and 870510. Annex XXXVII Regulation on Russia.
2565. Article 3k(1a) Regulation on Russia. *See* Art. 1(19)(b) Decision (CFSP) 2023/2874 & Art. 1(11)(a) Regulation (EU) 2023/2878.
2566. Article 3k(5c) Regulation on Russia. *See* Art. 1(19)(d) Decision (CFSP) 2023/2874 & Art. 1(11)(f) Regulation (EU) (EU) 2023/2878.
2567. Articles 1g(1) & (2) and Regulation on Belarus.
2568. Articles 1g(1) & (1a) and 1s(1)(a) & (b) Regulation on Belarus.
2569. These are the goods falling under CN codes ex 4823 90, 4813, ex 3302 90, 8478 & ex 8208 90 00. Article 1g(2) and Annex VI Regulation on Belarus.
2570. These are the goods and technology falling under CN codes 8401, 8402, 8404, 8405, 8406, 8407, 8408, 8409, 8410, 8412, 8413, 8415, 8416, ex 8418, 8420, 8421, ex 8422, 8423, 8424, 8425, 8426, 8427, 8428, 8429, 8430, 8431, 8439, 8440, 8441, 8442, 8443, 8444 00, 8445, 8447, 8448, 8449 00 00, 8453, 8454, 8455, 8457, 8458, 8466, 8467, 8468, 8471, 8474, 8475, 8477, 8479, 8480, 8481, 8482, 8483, 8484, 8501, 8502, 8503, 8504, 8405, 8507, 8511, 8514, 8529, 8537, 8538, 8539, 8544, 8545, 8547, 8548 and confidential products under Chapter 85 and goods under Chapter 85 transported by post or by parcel post (extra)/reconstituted code for statistical distribution. Article 1s(1) and Annex XIV Regulation on Belarus.
2571. Article 1s(2)(a) to (g) Regulation on Belarus.
2572. *See* Art. 1(10) Decision (CFSP) 2022/356 & Art. 1(13) Regulation (EU) 2022/355. Article 1s(3) Regulation on Belarus.
2573. Article 1(2) Decision (CFSP) 2021/1031 and Art. 1(4) Regulation (EU) 2021/1030.

telephone communications has been restricted.[2574] Within this frame, the notion 'telecommunication or internet monitoring or interception services' denotes *services that provide access to and delivery of a subject's incoming and outgoing telecommunications and call-associated data for the purpose of its extraction, decoding, recording, processing, analysis or storing, or any other related activity.*[2575] For any such export to take place, the competent authorities must issue a prior authorization. They may not do so, when they have reasonable grounds to determine that the goods in question would be used for repression by the government of Belarus, public bodies, corporations and agencies, including anyone acting on their behalf or at their direction.[2576] The same applies to providing technical assistance, brokering services, financing or financial assistance as well as providing any telecommunication or internet monitoring or interception services of any kind to Belarus, that being the government, public bodies, corporations and agencies or anyone acting on their behalf or at their direction.[2577]

584. Other Member States and the Commission shall be informed of any granted authorizations within two weeks.[2578]

585. Goods and technology suited for use in telecommunications and transport may neither be exported to Crimea, Sevastopol and the non-government-controlled areas of Ukraine, nor sold, supplied or transferred to anyone in those areas or for use therein.[2579] Infrastructure in the same areas in the same sectors is equally under restrictive measures.[2580] These prohibitions, including the exceptions and authorizations,[2581] are identical to the restrictions in the energy sector and the prospecting, exploration and production of oil, gas and mineral resources. Thus, the aforementioned (*see* in this regard paragraph 498 above) apply *mutatis mutandis*.

586. With the fourth package of sanctions[2582] (*see* in this regard Annex II p. 334 below) trade restrictions on iron and steel products[2583] were introduced. Importing iron and steel products originating in Russia or being exported from Russia is prohibited, and so is purchasing such when they originated or are located in Russia and transporting them

2574. Article 1c(1) & (3) Regulation on Belarus.
2575. In regard to the definition of *telecommunication or internet monitoring or interception services* that has been set out in Art. 1d(2) and Annex IV Regulation on Belarus. *see* Annex I p. 311 at 332.
2576. Article 1c(1) & (2) Regulation on Belarus.
2577. Article 1d(a), (b) & (c) Regulation on Belarus.
2578. Article 1c(4) Regulation on Belarus.
2579. Article 2b(1) & (2) Regulation on Goods from Crimea and Art. 4(1) & (2) Regulation with regard to Donetsk & Luhansk.
2580. Article 2c(1) Regulation on Goods from Crimea and Art. 5(1) Regulation with regard to Donetsk & Luhansk.
2581. Articles 2b(3) & (4), 2c(2) & 2e(1) Regulation on Goods from Crimea and Arts 4(3), 4a, 5(2) & 7(1) Regulation with regard to Donetsk & Luhansk.
2582. *See* recital No. 5 to the preamble of & Article 1(9) Decision (CFSP) and recital No. 3 to the preamble of & Art. 1(8) Regulation (EU) 2022/428.
2583. These are the iron and steel products falling under CN codes 7206, 7207, 7208, 7209, 7210, 7211, 7212, 7213, 7214, 7215, 7216, 7217, 7218, 7219, 7220, 7221, 7222, 7223, 7223, 7224, 7225, 7226, 7227, 7228, 7229, 7301, 7302, 7303, 7304, 7305, 7306, 7307, 7307, 7308, 7309, 7310, 7311, 7312, 7313, 7314, 7315, 7316, 7317, 7318, 7319, 7320, 7321, 7322, 7323, 7324, 7325 & 7326. *See* Annex XVII Regulation in Russia.

if they originated in Russia or were exported from Russia to any other state.[2584] Providing technical assistance, brokering services, financing or financial assistance as well as insurance and re-insurance is also prohibited.[2585] The same restrictions apply to the trade of a wider range of iron and steel products from Belarus.[2586] These latter measures were in fact introduced earlier in time with the third package of sanctions[2587] (*see* in this regard Annex II p. 337 at 338 below).

587. The Regulation on Russia contains an additional peculiar prohibition with regard to iron and steel products and more specifically with regard to such products that have been processed in a third state incorporating iron and steel products originating in Russia. Such processed products in a third state may not be purchased or imported into the Union as from 30 September 2023, whereby in particular for semi-finished products of iron or non-alloy steel (CN code 7207 11) this shall apply as from 1 April 2024 and for semi-finished products of iron or non-alloy steel and semi-finished products of alloy steel other than stainless (CN codes 7207 12 10 & 7224 90) as from 1 October 2028.[2588] In other words, the grace period granted ranges from twelve to seventy-two months and is independent of any previously concluded contracts and agreements. The twelfth package (*see* in this regard Annex II p. 337 at 343-- below) introduced the requirement of providing evidence of the country of origin with the exception of imports from a 'partner country for importation of iron and steel', those being Switzerland and Norway.[2589]

588. Contracts made before the legislative acts came into force fall outside the scope of this prohibition as long as they were executed within three months and so did any necessary ancillary contracts.[2590] The same applies to specific quantities of semi-finished products of iron or non-alloy steel (CN codes 7207 12 10 and 7207 11) and semi-finished products of alloy steel other than stainless (CN code 7224 90) from Russia calculated within specific time frames,[2591] whereby the set import volume quotas are managed by the Commission and the Member States under the management system for tariff-rate quotas.[2592] Goods necessary for civil nuclear capabilities, civil

2584. Article 3g(1)(a), (b) & (c) Regulation in Russia.
2585. Article 3g(1)(e) Regulation in Russia.
2586. These are the iron and steel products falling under CN codes 72 & 73. Article 1q(1)(a), (b), (c) & (d) and Annex XII Regulation on Belarus.
2587. Article 1(10) Decision (CFSP) 2022/356 & Art. 1(13) Regulation (EU) 2022/355.
2588. Article 3g(1 (d) Regulation on Russia. *See* Art. 1(10) Decision (CFSP) 2022/1909 & Art. 1(4)(a) Regulation (EU) 2022/1904.
2589. Article 3g(1)(d) second subparagraph and Annex XXXVI Regulation on Russia. *See* Art. 1(16)(a) and Annex (3) Decision (CFSP) 2023/2874 Art. 1(8)(a) and Annex VII Regulation (EU) 2023/2878.
2590. [Repealed] Art. 3g(2) & (3) Regulation on Russia and Art. 1q(2) Regulation on Belarus.
2591. The time frames are: 7 Oct. 2002 to 30 Sep. 2023; 1 Oct. 2023 to 30 Sep. 2024; 1 Oct. 2024 to 30 Sep. 2025; 1 Oct. 2025 to 30 Sep. 2026; 1 Oct. 2026 to 30 Sep. 2027; 1 Oct. 2027 to 30 Sep. 2028; 7 Oct. 2022 to 30 Sep. 2023; 1 Oct. 2023 to 31 Dec. 2023; 1 Jan. 2024 to 31 Mar. 2024; 17 Dec. 2022 to 31 Dec. 2023; 1 Jan. 2024 to 30 Sep. 2024; 1 Oct. 2024 to 30 Sep. 2025; 1 Oct. 2025 to 30 Sep. 2026; 1 Oct. 2026 to 30 Sep. 2027; and 1 Oct. 2027 to 30 Sep. 2028. Article 3g(4), (5) & (5a) Regulation on Russia.
2592. Article 3g(6) Regulation on Russia. and Arts 49 to 54 Commission Implementing Regulation (EU) 2015/2447 of 24 Nov. 2015 laying down detailed rules for implementing certain

nuclear facilities, such as the Paks II project, medical radioisotopes or similar medical applications and civil nuclear cooperation may be purchased, transferred and imported from Russia following authorization granted by competent authorities. Other Member States and the Commission shall be informed of any granted authorizations within two weeks.[2593]

589. Import, including purchase and transfer, of certain items is prohibited and so is providing technical assistance, brokering services or other services, financing or financial assistance.[2594] In some instances, providing insurance and re-insurance is also prohibited.[2595] The prohibited goods and technology are those that generate significant revenues, including coal[2596] and potassium chloride products.[2597] Specifically with regard to Russia purchases for the functioning of diplomatic and consular representations of the Union and of the Member States are permitted; and so are purchases for the personal use of Union nationals.[2598] Import of goods for the personal use of persons travelling to the Union may also be authorized, whereas specifically vehicles (CN code 8703) The import of mineral products,[2599] wood,[2600] cement[2601] and

provisions of Regulation (EU) No. 952/2013 of the European Parliament and of the Council laying down the Union Customs Code, OJ L 343, 29 Dec. 2015, p. 558, as last amended by Commission Implementing Regulation (EU) 2023/403 of 8 Feb. 2023, OJ L 56, 23 Feb. 2023, p. 18.

2593. Article 3g(7) & (8) Regulation on Russia.
2594. Article 3i(1) & (2)(a) & (b) and Annex XXI Regulation on Russia, Art. 1i(1) & (1a) and Annex VIII Regulation on Belarus.
2595. Article 1i(1a) Regulation on Belarus.
2596. These are the goods and technology that fall under CN codes: 0306, 1604 31 00, 1604 32 00, 2208, 2303, 2402, 2523, 2701, 2702, 2703, 2704, 2705, 2706, 2707, 2708, 2712, 2713, 2714, 2715, 2803, 2811, 2818, ex 2825, 2834, ex 2835, 2836, ex 2901, 2902, 2903, 2905, 2907, 2909, 2914, 2915, 2917, 2922, 2923, 2931, 2933, 3104 20, 3105 20, 3105 60, ex 3105 90 20, ex 3105 90 80, 3301, 3304, 3305, 3306, 3307, 3401, 3402, 3801, 3811, 3812, 3817, 3819, 3823, 3824, 3901, 3902, 3903, 3904, 3907, 3908, 3916, 3917, 3919, 3920, 3921, 3923, 3925, 3926, 4002, 4011, 4107, 4202, 4301, 44, 4703, 4705, 4801, 4802, 4803, 4804, 4805, 4810, 4811, 4818, 4819, 4823, 5402, 5601, 5603, 6204, 6305, 6403, 6806, 6807, 6808, 6810, 6814, 6815, 6902, 6907, 7005, 7007, 7010, 7019, 7104, 7106, 7112, 7115, 7606, 7801, 8207, 8212, 8302, 8309, 8407, 8408, 8409, ex 8411, 8412, 8413, 8414, 8418, 8419, 8421, 8422, 8424, 8426, 8431, 8450, 8455, 8466, 8467, 8471, 8474, 8477, 8479, 8480, 8481, 8482, 8483, 8487, 8501, 8502, 8503, 8504, 8511, 8516, 8517, 8523, 8525, 8526, 8531, 8535, 8536, 8537, 8538, 8539, 8541, 8542, 8543, 8544, 8545, 8603, 8606, 8701, 8703, 8704, 8716, 8802, 8901, 8903, 8904, 8905, 9001, 9006, 9014, 9026, 9027, 9030, 9031, 9032, 9401, 9403, 9404, 9405 & 9406. Article 3i(1) & (2)(a) & (b) and Annex XXI Regulation on Russia.
2597. These are the goods that fall under CN codes: 3104 20, 3105 20 10, 3105 20 90, 3105 60 00, ex 3105 90 20 & ex 3105 90 80. Article 1i(1) & (1a) and Annex VIII Regulation on Belarus.
2598. Article 3i(3a) Regulation on Russia. This exception was introduced with the eighth package (*see* in this regard Annex II p. 337 at 341).
2599. These are the goods that fall under CN codes: 2707, 2710, 2711, 2712, 2713 & 2715. Article 1h(1)(a), (b), (c) & (d) and Annex VII Regulation on Belarus.
2600. These are wood and articles of wood, including wood charcoal that fall under the CN code 44. Article 1o(1)(a), (b), (c) & (d) and Annex X Regulation on Belarus.
2601. These are cement, whether or not coloured, (CN code 2523) and articles of cement, concrete or artificial stone, whether or not reinforced (CN code 6810). Article 1p(1)(a), (b), (c) & (d) and Annex XI Regulation on Belarus.

rubber[2602] from Belarus is also prohibited in a manner similar to iron and steel products from Russia (*see* in this regard paragraph 587 above), but for the grace periods.

590. Outside the scope of these prohibitions fall purchases of mineral products required to meet essential needs of the purchaser in Belarus or of humanitarian projects in Belarus.[2603] Transit of mineral products through Belarus is also not affected[2604] and so are already concluded contracts regarding wood, cement and rubber, as long as they are concluded within three months.[2605]

§11 SANCTIONS ON BROADCASTING

591. The third package of sanctions (*see* in this regard Annex II p. 337 at 338 below) introduced a set of unusual restrictive measures, that of broadcasting.[2606] The EU resorted to this measure as a response to disinformation, a hybrid threat. It has been estimated that Russia has engaged in a systematic, international campaign of media manipulation and distortion of facts targeting political parties, civil society, asylum seekers, Russian ethnic minorities, gender minorities and the functioning of democratic institutions.[2607] The propaganda actions were channelled through a number of media outlets under the control of the leadership of Russia, thus posing a significant and direct threat to the public order and security of the EU.[2608] In view of these, the EU introduced the suspension of broadcasting activities of the relevant media outlets in the Union, a temporary measure that shall cease as soon as the aggression against Ukraine is put to an end and as soon as the propaganda actions are discontinued.[2609]

592. The set of restrictive measures prohibits for operators to broadcast as well as any enabling, facilitating or otherwise contribution to broadcast, any content by certain designated persons.[2610] Broadcasting includes through transmission or distribution of any means such as cable, satellite, IP-TV, internet service providers, internet video-sharing platforms or applications, both new and pre-installed.[2611] Broadcasting licenses and authorizations as well as transmission and distribution arrangements with

2602. These are new pneumatic tyres, of rubber (CN code 4011). Article 1r(1)(a), (b), (c) & (d) and Annex XIII Regulation on Belarus.
2603. Article 1h(2) Regulation on Belarus.
2604. Article 1h(4) Regulation on Belarus.
2605. Articles 1o(2), 1p(2) & 1r(2) Regulation on Belarus.
2606. *See* Art. 1(1) Decision (CFSP) 2022/351 and Art. 1(1) Regulation (EU) 2022/350.
2607. *See* recital Nos 5 & 6 to the preamble of Decision (CFSP) 2022/351 and recital Nos 5 & 6 to the preamble of Regulation (EU) 2022/350.
2608. *See* recital No. 8 to the preamble of Decision (CFSP) 2022/351 and recital No. 8 to the preamble of Regulation (EU) 2022/350.
2609. *See* recital No. 10 to the preamble of Decision (CFSP) 2022/351 and recital No. 10 to the preamble of Regulation (EU) 2022/350.
2610. The designated persons are: RT- Russia Today English, RT – Russia Today UK, RT – Russia Today Germany, RT – Russia Today France, RT – Russia Today Spanish, Sputnik (designated via Art. 1(21) & Annex VI Regulation (EU) 2022/879), Rossiya RTR/RTR Planeta, Rossiya 24/Russia 24, TV Centre International (Art. 1(19) & Annex V Regulation (EU) 2022/2474), RT Arabic, Sputnik Arabic (Art. 1(20) & Annex V Regulation (EU) 2023/427).
2611. Article 2f(1) and Annex XV Regulation on Russia.

designated persons are suspended.[2612] Furthermore, advertising products and services in any content produced or broadcasted by the designated persons is prohibited.[2613] This set of prohibitions is absolute, acknowledges neither exceptions nor derogations and accepts no legal remedies.

§12 SANCTIONS ON TOURISM

593. Services directly related to tourism activities in Crimea, Sevastopol and the non-government-controlled areas of Ukraine may not be provided.[2614] Specifically, ships providing cruising services and flying the flag of a Member State may not enter into or call at any port situated in the Crimea Peninsula.[2615] This also applies to ships providing cruising services and are owned, while being under the operational control of a shipowner of a Member State, or any ship over which an operator of a Member State assumes overall responsibility for its operation.[2616] Reasons for maritime safety in cases of emergency allow for entering into or calling at these ports, as long as the competent authorities are informed within five working days.[2617]

594. The legislator gave a grace period of three months with regard to Crimea and Sevastopol and six months for non-government controlled areas of Ukraine, under the condition that competent authorities were informed at least five working days in advance.[2618]

2612. Article 2f(2) Regulation on Russia.
2613. Article 2f(3) Regulation on Russia.
2614. Articles 2d(1) Regulation on Goods from Crimea and Art. 6(1) Regulation with regard to Donetsk & Luhansk.
2615. These are the ports of Sevastopol, Kerch, Yalta, Theodosia, Evpatoria, Chernomorsk and Kamysh-Burun. Annex III Regulation on Goods from Crimea.
2616. Article 2d(2) Regulation on Goods from Crimea.
2617. Article 2d(3) Regulation on Goods from Crimea.
2618. Article 2d(4) Regulation on Goods from Crimea. and Art. 6(2) Regulation with regard to Donetsk & Luhansk.

CHAPTER 6

'New Generation' Restrictive Measures

595. The restrictive measures examined in this chapter differentiate from the ones already examined with regard to their scope of application, in the sense that the legislative acts portrayed below relate to specific activities regardless of the territory where they unfold. The previously examined legislative acts were being consistently enacted 'in view of a situation' in a specific state and therefore, the condemned activity was always being framed within a specific territory. Here this territorial element is missing. This absence is the unconventional and novel element that differentiates the legislative acts described here from the ones already portrayed above.

§1 OVERVIEW OF THE EUROPEAN LEGISLATION IMPOSING 'NEW GENERATION' SANCTIONS

596. Brussels decided to impose sanctions in view of serious human rights violations and abuses, in view of cyber-attacks threatening the Union or its Member States and in view of the proliferation and use of chemical weapons.

597. Serious human rights violations can trigger the imposition of sanctions under the relevant EU regulation[2619] ('Regulation on Human Rights Violation') and the accompanying decision.[2620] While issuing the Regulation on Human Rights Violation, the EU underlined the states' primary responsibility to 'respect, protect and fulfil human

2619. Council Regulation (EU) 2020/1998 of 7 Dec. 2020 concerning restrictive measures against serious human rights violations and abuses, OJ L 410I, 7 Dec. 2020, p. 1, as last amended by Council Implementing Regulation (EU) 2023/1715 of 8 Sep. 2023 implementing Regulation (EU) 2020/1998 concerning restrictive measures against serious human rights violations and abuses, OJ L 221I, 8 Sep. 2023, p. 1.

2620. Council Decision (CFSP) 2020/1999 of 7 Dec. 2020 concerning restrictive measures against serious human rights violations and abuses, OJ L 410I, 7 Dec. 2020, p. 13, as last amended by Council Decision (CFSP) 2023/1716 of 8 Sep. 2023 amending Decision (CFSP) 2020/1999 concerning restrictive measures against serious human rights violations and abuses, OJ L 221I, 8 Sep. 2023, p. 6.

rights' and marked the worldwide concern about human rights violations and abuses and their severity, perpetrated also by non-state actors.[2621] It further took the view that such acts violate the principles of the Union's external action and threaten its objectives.[2622] It thus established a framework for targeted restrictive measures to address the worldwide serious violation and abuse of human rights and emphasized that the interaction between international human rights law and international humanitarian law was to be considered upon the implementation of sanctions.[2623] The EU neither acts in solitude nor is pioneering in deploying restrictive measures against grave violation of human rights and abuse. Already before this legislation, the US had issued the Global Magnitsky Act,[2624] imposing economic sanctions and denying entry to any foreign person abusing human rights or perpetrating corruption,[2625] that was implemented and built upon by further legislation.[2626] The US works closely with other states in pursuing coordinated actions against persons violating or abusing human rights and seeks additional allies and partners to jointly leverage all tools at their disposal to deny access to their territory and international financial systems,[2627] including the EU.[2628]

598. The regulation concerning restrictive measures against cyber-attacks[2629] ('Regulation Against Cyber-Attacks') and the accompanying decision,[2630] both issued in May

2621. Recital No. 2 to the preamble of Decision 2020/1999.
2622. Article 21(1) & (2) TEU and recital No. 2 to the preamble of Decision 2020/1999.
2623. Recital No. 4 to the preamble of Decision 2020/1999 and recital No. 1 to the preamble of Regulation on Human Rights Violation.
2624. The Global Magnitsky Human Rights Accountability Act, National Defence Authorization Act for Fiscal Year 2017, Title XII, Subtitle F of Public Law 114-328, 130 Stat. of 23 Dec. 2016, p. 2000.
2625. Michael A. Weber & Edward J. Collins-Chase, *The Global Magnitsky Human Rights Accountability Act*, Congressional Research Service, 28 Oct. 2020, p. 1, available: https://crsreports.congress.gov/product/pdf/IF/IF10576 (last visited: 31 Dec. 2023).
2626. Executive Order Blocking the Property of Persons Involved in Serious Human Rights Abuse or Corruption, of December 20, 2017, Federal Register Vol. 82 No. 246 of 26 Dec. 2017, p. 60839, available: https://www.federalregister.gov/d/2017-27925 (last visited: 31 Dec. 2023).
2627. David Hale, *Global Magnitsky Human Rights Accountability Act Annual Report*, 23 Dec. 2020, Federal Register Vol. 86 No. 1 of 4 Jan. 2021, p. 175.
2628. Alexandra King-Pile, *2021 Global Magnitsky Human Rights Accountability Act Annual Report*, Federal Register Vol. 88 No. 60 of 29 Mar. 2023, p. 18624; Andrew Self, *2022 Global Magnitsky Human Rights Accountability Act Annual Report*, Federal Register Vol. 88 No. 62 of 31 Mar. 2023, p. 19344.
2629. Council Regulation (EU) 2019/796 of 17 May 2019 concerning restrictive measures against cyber-attacks threatening the Union or its Member States, OJ L 129I, 17 May 2019, p. 1, as last amended by Commission Implementing Regulation (EU) 2022/595 of 11 Apr. 2022 amending certain Regulations concerning restrictive measures and setting out a single list for the Annexes to those Regulations containing the contact details of Member States' competent authorities and the address for notifications to the European Commission, OJ L 114, 12 Apr. 2022, p. 60.
2630. Council Decision (CFSP) 2019/797 of 17 May 2019 concerning restrictive measures against cyber-attacks threatening the Union or its Member States, OJ L 129I 17 May 2019, p. 13, as last amended by Council Decision (CFSP) 2023/964 of 15 May 2023 amending Decision (CFSP) 2019/797 concerning restrictive measures against cyber-attacks threatening the Union or its Member States, OJ L 129, 16 May 2023, p. 16.

2019, were preceded by the Cyber Diplomacy Toolbox of the EU[2631] that was adopted as a diplomatic response to malicious cyber activities. The EU reiterated the need to prevent conflict and mitigate cybersecurity threats while expressing concerns in view of states' and non-state actors' willingness to achieve their objectives through malicious cyber activities of various scope, scale, duration, intensity, complexity, sophistication and impact.[2632] It also took note of the ongoing work of the United Nations Groups of Governmental Experts on Developments ('UN GEE') in the Field of Information and Telecommunications in the context of international security, urging to uphold the consensus that existing international law is applicable to cyberspace.[2633] The EU took the view that measures, including restrictive measures, were a necessary response to such threats, encouraging cooperation, facilitating mitigation of immediate and long-term threats in cyberspace and influencing the behaviour of potential aggressors in the long term.[2634] To this end, the aforementioned legal instruments were issued, establishing a framework for targeted restrictive measures to deter and respond to cyber-attacks with significant effect which constitute an external threat to the Union or its Member States. Moreover, if deemed necessary for the purpose of achieving the objectives set in Article 21 TEU, restrictive measures can be applied in response to cyber-attacks with significant effect against third states or international organizations.[2635] Once again, the EU neither acts in solitude nor is pioneering when imposing sanctions against cyber-attacks. The US has been doing so since 2015,[2636] when the Lazarus Group hacked Sony Pictures Entertainment unleashing chaos and havoc.[2637]

2631. Council of the European Union, *Council Conclusions on a Framework for a Joint EU Diplomatic Response to Malicious Cyber Activities* ('Cyber Diplomacy Toolbox'), 19 Jun. 2017, 10474/17, available: https://www.consilium.europa.eu/.

2632. *Ibid.*, paras 1 & 2.

2633. *Ibid.*, para. 3. Reiterated in recital No. 4 to the preamble of Decision (CFSP) 2019/797.

2634. Council of the European Union, *Cyber Diplomacy Toolbox* (n. 2631) para. 5. Reiterated in recital No. 2 to the preamble of Decision (CFSP) 2019/797.

2635. Recital No. 7 to the preamble.

2636. The President, *Blocking the Property of Certain Persons Engaging in Significant Malicious Cyber-Enabled Activities*, Executive Order 13694 of 1 Apr. 2015, Federal Register Vol. 80 No. 63 of 2 Apr. 2015, p. 18077, as amended by the President, *Taking Additional Steps to Address the National Emergency With Respect to Significant Malicious Cyber-Enabled Activities*, Executive Order 13757 of 28 Dec. 2016, Federal Register Vol. 82 No. 1 of 3 Jan. 2017, p. 1. *See also* Office of Foreign Assets Control, 31 CFR Part 578 *Cyber-Related Sanctions Regulations*, Federal Register Vol. 80 No. 251 of 31 Dec. 2015, p. 81752, and Office of Foreign Assets Control, 31 CFR Part 578 Cyber-Related Sanctions Regulations, Federal Register Vol. 87 No. 171 of 6 Sep. 2022, p. 54373.

2637. Jason Bartlett & Megan Ophel, *Sanctions by the Numbers: Spotlight on Cyber Sanctions*, Center for a New American Security, 4 May 2021, available: https://www.cnas.org/publications/reports/sanctions-by-the-numbers-cyber (last visited: 31 Dec. 2023). *Hear* also the podcast: Jean Lee & Geoff White (hosts/reporters), Estelle Doyle (producer), *The Lazarus Heist, S1.1 Hacking Hollywood*, 19 Apr. 2021 & *S1.2 The Disaster Movie*, 26 Apr. 2021, BBC World Service, wherever you get your podcasts.

599. The regulation with regard to the proliferation and use of chemical weapons[2638] ('the Regulation on Chemical Weapons') and the accompanying decision[2639] were adopted in October 2018 and thus followed by a decision of the Conference of the States Parties to the Chemical Weapons Convention[2640] of 27 June 2018.[2641] Therein the States Parties condemned the use of chemical weapons by anyone under any circumstances as well as that such weapons had been used in Iraq, Malaysia, Syria and the UK, where the nerve agent Novichok was used in Salisbury, while also condemning their use by state and non-state actors.[2642] The EU expressed its support to this decision, to other international initiatives addressing the threat of chemical weapons, such as the AG, as well as to relevant resolutions of the UN Security Council.[2643] It concluded that the use of chemical weapons is completely unacceptable, must be condemned and constitutes a security threat.[2644] It thus adopted a new regime of restrictive measures to address this threat adopting the scope and definition set in the Chemical Weapons Convention.[2645] The US has been imposing sanctions for the use of chemical weapons in the explained occasions under the Chemical and Biological Weapons Control and Warfare Elimination Act.[2646,2647]

§2 THE SCOPE OF APPLICATION

600. The scope of application of the Regulation on Human Rights Violation, as explicitly defined as such therein, extends to:

2638. Council Regulation (EU) 2018/1542 of 15 Oct. 2018 concerning restrictive measures against the proliferation and use of chemical weapons, OJ L 259, 16 Oct. 2018, p. 12, as last amended by Council Implementing Regulation (EU) 2022/2228 of 14 Nov. 2022 implementing Regulation (EU) 2018/1542 concerning restrictive measures against the proliferation and use of chemical weapons, OJ L 293I, 14 Nov. 2022, p. 1.
2639. Council Decision (CFSP) 2018/1544 of 15 Oct. 2018 concerning restrictive measures against the proliferation and use of chemical weapons, OJ L 259, 16 Oct. 2018, p. 25, as last amended by Council Decision (CFSP) 2022/2232 of 14 Nov. 2022 amending Decision (CFSP) 2018/1544 concerning restrictive measures against the proliferation and use of chemical weapons, OJ L 293I, 14 Nov. 2022, p. 32.
2640. Convention on the Prohibition of the Development, Production, Stockpiling and Use of Chemical Weapons and on their Destruction (Geneva 1992) 1975 UNTS 45.
2641. Conference of the States Parties, Decision 'Addressing the Threat from Chemical Weapons Use' C-SS-4/DEC.3 of 27 Jun. 2018, available: https://www.opcw.org/sites/default/files/documents/CSP/C-SS-4/en/css4dec3_e_.doc.pdf (last visited: 31 Dec. 2023).
2642. *Ibid.*, paras 1, 2, 3, 13 & 17. *See also* Executive Council, Decision 'Addressing the Threat Posed by the Use of Chemical Weapons by Non-State Actors' EC-86/DEC.9 of 13 Oct. 2017, available: https://www.opcw.org/sites/default/files/documents/EC/86/en/ec86dec09_e_.pdf (last visited: 31 Dec. 2023).
2643. Recital Nos 1-4 to the preamble of Decision (CFSP) 2018/1544.
2644. Recital No. 5 to the preamble of Decision (CFSP) 2018/1544.
2645. Recital No. 6 to the preamble of Decision (CFSP) 2018/1544.
2646. Chemical and Biological Weapons Control and Warfare Elimination Act of 1991, An Act to Provide for the Termination of the Application of Title IV of the Trade Act of 1974 to Czechoslovakia and Hungary, Title III of Public Law 102-182, 105 Stat. of 4 Dec. 1991, p. 1245.
2647. Dianne E. Rennack & Cory Welt, *Russia, the Skripal Poisoning, and U.S. Sanctions*, Congressional Research Service, 28 Oct. 2020, pp. 1 et seq., available: https://crsreports.congress.gov/product/pdf/IF/IF10962 (last visited: 31 Dec. 2023).

- genocide;
- crimes against humanity;
- the following serious human rights violations or abuses: (i) torture and other cruel, inhuman or degrading treatment or punishment; (ii) slavery; (iii) extrajudicial, summary or arbitrary executions and killings; (iv) enforced disappearance of persons; (v) arbitrary arrests or detentions; and
- other human rights violations or abuses, including but not limited to the following, in so far as those violations or abuses are widespread, systematic or are otherwise of serious concern as regards the objectives of the common foreign and security policy set out in Article 21 TEU: (i) trafficking in human beings, as well as abuses of human rights by migrant smugglers as referred to in this Article; (ii) sexual and gender-based violence; (iii) violations or abuses of freedom of peaceful assembly and of association; (iv) violations or abuses of freedom of opinion and expression; (v) violations or abuses of freedom of religion or belief.[2648]

601. While applying the aforementioned scope of application, the EU considers 'customary international law and widely accepted instruments of international law'.[2649] Indicatively, and not exclusively the following are named as such: the International Covenant on Civil and Political Rights of 1966,[2650] the International Covenant on Economic, Social and Cultural Rights of 1966,[2651] the Convention on the Prevention and Punishment of the Crime of Genocide of 1948,[2652] the Convention against Torture and other Cruel, Inhuman or Degrading Treatment or Punishment of 1984,[2653] the International Convention on the Elimination of All Forms of Racial Discrimination of 1966,[2654] the Convention on the Elimination of All Forms of Discrimination against Women of 1979,[2655] the Convention on the Rights of the Child of 1989,[2656] the International Convention for the Protection of All Persons from Enforced Disappearance of 2006,[2657] the Convention on the Rights of Persons with Disabilities of 2006,[2658] the Protocol to Prevent, Suppress and Punish Trafficking in Persons, Especially Women and Children, supplementing the United Nations Convention against

2648. Article 2(1)(a) to (d) Regulation on Human Rights Violation.
2649. Article 2(2)(a) to (l) Regulation on Human Rights Violation.
2650. International Covenant on Civil and Political Rights (New York 1966) 999 UNTS 171.
2651. International Covenant on Economic, Social and Cultural Rights (New York 1966) 993 UNTS 3.
2652. Convention on the Prevention and Punishment of the Crime of Genocide (Paris 1948) 78 UNTS 277.
2653. Convention against Torture and other Cruel, Inhuman or Degrading Treatment or Punishment (New York 1984) 1465 UNTS 85.
2654. International Convention on the Elimination of All Forms of Racial Discrimination (New York 1966) 660 UNTS 195.
2655. Convention on the Elimination of All Forms of Discrimination against Women (New York 1979) 1249 UNTS 13.
2656. Convention on the Rights of the Child (New York 1989) 1577 UNTS 3.
2657. International Convention for the Protection of All Persons from Enforced Disappearance (New York 2006) 2716 UNTS 3.
2658. Convention on the Rights of Persons with Disabilities (New York 2006) 2515 UNTS 3.

Transnational Organized Crime of 2000,[2659] the Rome Statute of the International Criminal Court[2660] and the European Convention for the Protection of Human Rights and Fundamental Freedoms.[2661]

602. The scope of application of the Regulation Against Cyber-Attacks is defined by the meaning of 'cyber-attacks with a significant effect, including attempted cyber-attacks with a potentially significant effect, which constitute an external threat to the Union or its Member States'.[2662] This notion consists of the following four components: *cyber-attacks*; *cyber-attacks constituting an external threat*; *cyber-attacks constituting a threat to Member States*; and *cyber-attacks constituting a threat to the Union*. Within this framework *cyber-attacks* are actions that are unauthorized or illegal and involve access to information systems,[2663] information system interference,[2664] data interference[2665] or data interception.[2666,2667] The notion *cyber-attacks constituting an external threat* is built on the term *cyber-attack*, whereby the relevant activities take place outside the Union either literally or due to them being under the control of persons located outside the Union.[2668] *Cyber-attacks* are perceived as constituting *a threat to Member States* when they affect information systems, such as critical infrastructure, services necessary for the maintenance of essential social and economic activities, that include energy, transport, banking, health and drinking water, critical State functions, storage or processing of classified information and government emergency response teams.[2669] Finally, *cyber-attacks constituting a threat to the Union* are those carried out against the institutions, bodies and offices of the Union.[2670] Importantly, the Regulation Against Cyber-Attacks allows response to cyber-attacks with significant effect against third states or international organizations.[2671]

603. Furthermore the factors to be considered upon determining that a cyber-attack had a *significant* effect are any of the following: the scope, scale, impact or severity of

2659. The Protocol to Prevent, Suppress and Punish Trafficking in Persons, Especially Women and Children, supplementing the United Nations Convention against Transnational Organized Crime (New York 2000) 2237 UNTS 319.
2660. Rome Statute of the International Criminal Court (Rome 1998) 2187 UNTS 3.
2661. European Convention for the Protection of Human Rights and Fundamental Freedoms (Rome 1950) 213 UNTS 221.
2662. Article 1(1) Regulation Against Cyber-Attacks.
2663. In regard to the definition of *Information system* set out in Art. 1(7)(a) Regulation Against Cyber-Attacks. *see* Annex I p. 311 at 325.
2664. In regard to the definition of *information system interference* set out in Art. 1(7)(b) Regulation Against Cyber-Attacks. *see* Annex I p. 311 at 325.
2665. In regard to the definition of *data interference* set out in Art. 1(7)(c) Regulation Against Cyber-Attacks. *see* Annex I p. 311 at 318.
2666. In regard to the definition of *data interception* set out in Art. 1(7)(d) Regulation Against Cyber-Attacks. *see* Annex I p. 311 at 318.
2667. Article 1(3) Regulation Against Cyber-Attacks. In regard to the definition *see* Annex I p. 311 at 317.
2668. Article 1(2) Regulation Against Cyber-Attacks. In regard to the definition *see* Annex I p. 311 at 317.
2669. Article 1(4) Regulation Against Cyber-Attacks. In regard to the definition *see* Annex I p. 311 at 317.
2670. Article 1(5) Regulation Against Cyber-Attacks.
2671. Article 1(6) Regulation Against Cyber-Attacks.

disruption caused, including to economic and societal activities, essential services, critical State functions, public order or public safety; the number of natural or legal persons, entities or bodies affected; the number of Member States concerned; the amount of economic loss caused, such as through large-scale theft of funds, economic resources or intellectual property; the economic benefit gained by the perpetrator, for himself or for others; the amount or nature of data stolen or the scale of data breaches; or the nature of commercially sensitive data accessed.[2672]

604. The scope of the Regulation Against Chemical Weapons aligns with the one set in the Chemical Weapons Convention, as already explained above. Thus, it outlaws chemical weapons and mandates the destruction of all chemical weapons within ten years.[2673] This is allied to the general purpose criterion that lies in the notion of *chemical weapons.*[2674] It encompasses *toxic chemicals*[2675] as long as their intended use, including types and quantities of the chemicals, is for purposes prohibited under the Chemical Weapons Convention, as well as munitions and devices, specifically designed to cause death or other harm through the toxic properties of those chemicals and any equipment specifically designed for use directly in connection with the employment of such munitions and devices.[2676]

§3 THE RANGE OF RESTRICTIVE MEASURES

605. The restrictive measures that the regulations here at hand provide are twofold: financial and restricting the movement of persons.

I The Financial Sanctions

606. The financial sanctions that can be imposed under the Regulation on Human Rights Violation, the Regulation Against Cyber-Attacks and the Regulation Against Chemical Weapons follow the familiar pattern (*see* in this regard paragraph 74 above) and thus consist of an objective and a subjective element. Starting with the objective element, the notion of *funds*[2677] is very similar to the one already explained (*see* in this regard paragraph 75 above & Annex I p. 311 at 325), as it lacks the last indicative item of 'any other instrument of export-financing'. At the same time, the meaning of

2672. Article 2(a) to (g) Regulation Against Cyber-Attacks.
2673. Article I Chemical Weapons Convention. *See also* Editors, *The Chemical Weapons Convention* 30(3) Arms Control Today 37 at 37 (2000).
2674. Terence Taylor, *The Chemical Weapons Convention and Prospects for Implementation* 42(4) ICLQ 912 at 913 (1993) https://doi.org/10.1093/iclqaj/42.4.912.
2675. In regard to the definition of *toxic chemicals* set out in Art. II(2) Chemical Weapons Convention *see* Annex I p. 311 at 334.
2676. Article 1(a) Regulation Against Chemical Weapons and Art. II(1) Chemical Weapons Convention. In regard to the definition *see* Annex I p. 311 at 313.
2677. Article 1(g) Regulation on Human Rights Violation; Art. 1(8)(g) Regulation Against Cyber-Attacks; and Art. 1(h) Regulation Against Chemical Weapons.

economic resources[2678] is identical to the one previously described (*see* in this regard paragraph 76 above & Annex I p. 311 at 318.).

607. Before discussing the subjective element, it is noted that the regulations at hand refer to 'natural or legal persons, entities of bodies'. Once again, the term 'person' is used in the paragraphs below in order to lend clarity, and denotes all aforementioned terms. Specifically in the Regulation on Human Rights Violation, it is set out that this phrase also includes state actors, other actors exercising effective control or authority over a territory and other non-state actors.[2679]

608. Turning to the subjective element, this differs in each legislative act and depends on its scope of application. According to the Regulation on Human Rights Violation, the persons that are eligible for designation are persons responsible for actions and omissions falling under its scope, including those that provide financial, technical and material support and those that are otherwise involved, along with persons associated with them.[2680] Under the Regulation Against Cyber-Attacks persons responsible for cyber-attacks and attempted cyber-attacks may become designated persons, including persons providing financial, technical and material support for such activities, or persons otherwise involved therein. Persons associated with said persons may equally become designated.[2681] Finally, the Regulation Against Chemical Weapons provides for the designation of persons using chemical weapons or otherwise being involved with such weapons, that being manufacturing, acquiring, possessing, developing, transporting, stockpiling and transferring, as well as persons engaging in any preparations for the use of same.[2682] It further prescribes that persons assisting, encouraging or inducing anyone to engage in such activities and thereby contributing to a danger that these might be carried out, may become designated, along with anyone associated with them.[2683]

609. When the subjective and objective elements discussed above are fulfilled, funds and economic resources are frozen and none is made available.[2684] Circumvention, when it is done knowingly and intentionally, is equally prohibited.[2685]

610. The exceptions that the regulations at hand provide, allow for derogation on the basis of basic needs,[2686] extraordinary expenses,[2687] fees for routine holding of bank

2678. Article 1(d) Regulation on Human Rights Violation; Art. 1(8)(d) Regulation Against Cyber-Attacks; and Art. 1(e) Regulation Against Chemical Weapons.
2679. Article 2(3) Regulation on Human Rights Violation and Art. 1(4) Decision (CFSP) 2020/1999.
2680. Articles 3(3) & 2(1) and Annex I Regulation on Human Rights Violation.
2681. Articles 3(3)(a) to (c) Regulation Against Cyber-Attacks and Art. 5(1) of Decision (CFSP) 2019/797.
2682. Article 2(3)(a)(i) to (iii) Regulation Against Chemical Weapons.
2683. Article 2(3)(b) & (c) Regulation Against Chemical Weapons.
2684. Article 3(1) & (2) Regulation on Human Rights Violation; Art. 3(1) & (2) Regulation Against Cyber-Attacks; and Art. 2(1) & (2) Regulation Against Chemical Weapons.
2685. Article 10 Regulation on Human Rights Violation; Art. 9 Regulation Against Cyber-Attacks; and Art. 8 Regulation Against Chemical Weapons.
2686. Article 4(1)(a) Regulation on Human Rights Violation; Art. 4(1)(a) Regulation Against Cyber-Attacks; and Art. 3(1)(a) Regulation Against Chemical Weapons.
2687. Article 4(1)(d) Regulation on Human Rights Violation; Art. 4(1)(d) Regulation Against Cyber-Attacks; and Art. 3(1)(d) Regulation Against Chemical Weapons.

accounts,[2688] crediting of interest and other earnings,[2689] payments under contracts, agreements and obligations,[2690] payments under judgments and decisions,[2691] payment of legal costs[2692] and crediting the frozen accounts.[2693] Thus, they also set out the specific exceptions already described (*see* in this regard paragraphs 123 et seq. above). They further allow for payments into or from accounts of a diplomatic or consular mission[2694] and, solely under the Regulation on Human Rights Violation, for extraordinary expenses[2695] (*see* in this respect paragraphs 142 and 132 above respectively).

611. The designation of a person under the criteria explained above takes the form of inclusion in a list. Such lists have to state the grounds for deciding so[2696] and where available, information necessary to identify the persons concerned. With regard to natural persons, such information may include names including aliases, date and place of birth, nationality, passport and ID card numbers, gender, address, if known, and function or profession. With regard to legal persons, such information may include names, place and date of registration, registration number and place of business.[2697] The aforementioned statement of reasons and notification (*see* in this respect paragraphs 142 et seq. above) apply *mutatis mutandis*.

II The Sanctions on Movement of Persons

612. The travel ban imposed by the decisions accompanying the regulations at hand follows the pattern already explained, that of the objective element and the subjective element[2698] (*see* in this respect paragraphs 307 et seq. above). Thus, the aforementioned apply here *mutatis mutandis*.

613. The explained exceptions on the grounds of urgent humanitarian need, fulfilling a judicial process and in compliance with international law (*see* in this respect

2688. Article 4(1)(c) Regulation on Human Rights Violation; Art. 4(1)(c) Regulation Against Cyber-Attacks; and Art. 3(1)(c) Regulation Against Chemical Weapons.
2689. Article 8(2)(a) Regulation on Human Rights Violation; Art. 7(2)(a) Regulation Against Cyber-Attacks; and Art. 6(2)(a) Regulation Against Chemical Weapons.
2690. Articles 7(1) & 8(2)(b) Regulation on Human Rights Violation; Arts 6(1) & 7(2)(b) Regulation Against Cyber-Attacks; and Arts 5(1) & 6(2)(b) Regulation Against Chemical Weapons.
2691. Articles 6(1) & 8(2)(c) Regulation on Human Rights Violation; Arts 5(1) & 7(2)(c) Regulation Against Cyber-Attacks; and Arts 4(1) & 6(2)(c) Regulation Against Chemical Weapons.
2692. Article 4(1)(b) Regulation on Human Rights Violation; Art. 4(1)(b) Regulation Against Cyber-Attacks; and Art. 3(1)(b) Regulation Against Chemical Weapons.
2693. Article 8(1) Regulation on Human Rights Violation; Art. 7(1) Regulation Against Cyber-Attacks; and Art. 6(1) Regulation Against Chemical Weapons.
2694. Article 4(1)(e) Regulation on Human Rights Violation; Art. 4(1)(e) Regulation Against Cyber-Attacks; and Art. 3(1)(e) Regulation Against Chemical Weapons.
2695. Article 5(1) Regulation on Human Rights Violation.
2696. Article 15(1) Regulation on Human Rights Violation, Art. 14(1) Regulation Against Cyber-Attacks; Art. 13(1) Regulation Against Chemical Weapons.
2697. Article 15(2) Regulation on Human Rights Violation, Art. 14(2) Regulation Against Cyber-Attacks; Art. 13(2) Regulation Against Chemical Weapons.
2698. Article 2(1) & (2) Decision (CFSP) 2020/1999; Art. 4(1) & (2) Decision (CFSP) 2019/797; and Art. 2(1) & (2) Decision (CFSP) 2018/1544.

paragraphs 312 et seq. above) equally find application.[2699] Therefore, the aforementioned apply here *mutatis mutandis*.

§4 THE ABSENTEES

614. The Lazarus Group is absent from the list of derogated persons, unlike in the US.[2700] This is a group of IT hackers allegedly earning money and operating for the regime of DPRK. It has performed a number of bold, highly sophisticated and flagrant cyber-attacks and bank heists. In 2016 after hacking the SWIFT software, they smashed and grabbed, digitally, USD 951 million from the Bangladesh Bank, although they managed to get their hands *only* on USD 81 million.[2701] They manipulated the software of the Cosmos Bank in India into dispensing cash from ATMs; with the help of an army of money mules, they grabbed nearly USD 14 million that was spat out from ATMs across twenty-eight countries in just two hours and thirty minutes.[2702] Posing as the French stock exchange regulator, they interfered with the SWIFT system through the Bank of Valletta in Malta leading to the shutdown of its system, meaning that its credit cards and ATM machines ceased working, while USD 13 million disappeared into drop-accounts.[2703] Cryptocurrency that lacks the logistical challenge posed by actually stealing cash, did not escape their attention. They raided KuCoin, a Singapore-based crypto exchange, and stole USD 300 million.[2704] All this stolen money is used to bankroll the nuclear and ballistic missile programs of the DPRK, especially following the harsh sanctions imposed in 2017 by the UN Security Council that disrupted the

2699. Article 2(3) & (4), (6) to (9) Decision (CFSP) 2020/1999; Art. 4(3) & (4), (6) to (9) Decision (CFSP) 2019/797; and Art. 2(3) & (4), (6) to (8) Decision (CFSP) 2018/1544.
2700. *See* Office of Foreign Assets Control, Notice of OFAC Actions, Federal Register Vol. 87 No. 75 of 19 Apr. 2022, p. 23320.
2701. *Hear* the podcast: Jean Lee & Geoff White (hosts/reporters), Estelle Doyle (producer), *The Lazarus Heist, S1.4 Billion Dollar Hack*, 9 May 2021, BBC World Service, *Wherever You Get Your Podcasts*; *Still on the Trail: The Investigation Into the Bangladesh Bank Heist Continues*, The Economist, 23 Mar. 2017, available: https://www.economist.com/finance-and-economics/2017/03/23/the-investigation-into-the-bangladesh-bank-heist-continues? (last visited: 21 Dec. 2023).
2702. *Hear* the podcast: Jean Lee & Geoff White (hosts/reporters), Estelle Doyle (producer), *The Lazarus Heist, S2.1 Jackpotting*, 27 Mar. 2023, BBC World Service, *Wherever You Get Your Podcasts*.
2703. Ivan Martin, *North Korean Hackers Charged in US with €13 Million Bank of Valletta Heist*, 20 Feb. 2021, available: https://timesofmalta.com/articles/view/north-korean-hackers-charged-in-us-with-13million-bank-of-valletta.852902 (last visited: 21 Dec. 2023); Ivan Martin, *How BOV Hackers Got Away with €13 million: Phishing E-mails Did the Job … and Bank Still Doesn't Know How Long Hackers Had Access*, 25 Mar. 2019, The Times of Malta, available: https://timesofmalta.com/articles/view/how-bov-hackers-got-away-with-13-million.702800 (last visited: 21 Dec. 2023). *Hear* the podcast: Jean Lee & Geoff White (hosts/reporters), Estelle Doyle (producer), *The Lazarus Heist, S2.3 Hushpuppi*, 27 Mar. 2023, BBC World Service, *Wherever You Get Your Podcasts*.
2704. Ada Hui & Wolfie Zhao, *Over $280M Drained in KuCoin Crypto Exchange Hack*, 26 Sep. 2020, CoinDesk, available: https://www.coindesk.com/markets/2020/09/26/over-280m-drained-in-kucoin-crypto-exchange-hack/ (last visited: 21 Dec. 2023). *Hear* the podcast: Jean Lee & Geoff White (hosts/reporters), Estelle Doyle (producer), *The Lazarus Heist, S2.8 Bitcoin bandits*, 1 May 2023, BBC World Service, *Wherever You Get Your Podcasts*.

main exports and income of the DPRK and blocked the flow of income and fuel. The Lazarus Group has also simply caused chaos by unleashing WannaCry and attacking essential infrastructure in 150 countries, such as the National Health System in the UK, *die Bahn*, the German railways, the Ministry of Interior of Russia, the Spanish Telefonica, FedEx and Boeing.[2705] Against this grand backdrop, their absence from the list of the Regulation Against Cyber-Attacks is remarkable.

2705. Editors, *The WannaCry Attack Reveals the Risks of a Computerised World*, 20 May 2017, The Economist, available: https://www.economist.com/leaders/2017/05/20/the-wannacry-attack-reveals-the-risks-of-a-computerised-world? (last visited: 21 Dec. 2023). *Hear* the podcast: Jean Lee & Geoff White (hosts/reporters), Estelle Doyle (producer), *The Lazarus Heist, S.10 Kill switch*, 20 Jun. 2021, BBC World Service, *Wherever You Get Your Podcasts*.

Conclusions

615. Sanctions is a political tool that the Union applies in various political contexts for certain policy reasons. The policy reasons double as the values and principles that the Union strives to uphold and promote and entail international peace and security, human rights, democracy, prevention of violent repression and political stalemate, misappropriation of state funds and EU's security and interests; these values and principles have formed the foundation for outlining the EU legislation that sets out sanctions in the present monograph. As already noted, they frequently overlap, mingle and mix prohibiting any stiff distinction or brisk categorization. For example, undermining the electoral process was one of the reasons that triggered the introduction of sanctions targeting Guinea-Bissau; it was also one of the reasons for imposing sanctions against Myanmar/Burma and Burundi. Still, for the purposes of said outlining, the first was portrayed under international peace and security, the second under human rights and the latter under democracy and human rights. It is here apposite to remind that international peace and security has been used as an umbrella principle that denotes not merely the policy reasons for issuing certain EU legislation, but also that that same legislation was preceded by resolutions of the UN Security Council, thus having the relevant sanctions qualifying as UN-mandated or multilateral.

616. What is though unique, is the political context of each and every one state targeted by sanctions of the EU; and although it has been attempted to portray the political context in the present monograph, it did not receive the merit that it deserved. One can hardly dispute the uniqueness of the DPRK, nicknamed the Hermit Kingdom, the Maduro regime in Venezuela or the reality in Haiti, where criminal gangs control vital ports and fuel terminals. At the same time and from a very simplistic viewpoint, certain events that have triggered the imposition of sanctions have a common denominator; these are civil war (*see* the regulations on Sudan, Somalia), activities of foreign armed groups (*see* the regulations on DRC and the CAR), fighting of armed groups (*see* the regulations on Libya, Yemen, South Sudan, Mali, Haiti), terrorist activities (*see* the regulations on Terrorism, Afghanistan and Rafiq Hariri), violent repression (*see* the regulations on Iran, Venezuela, Guinea and Syria) as well as coup d'états and/or undermining electoral process (*see* the regulations on Guinea-Bissau,

Zimbabwe, Myanmar/Burma, Burundi, Venezuela, Nicaragua and Lebanon) or violating or threatening sovereignty and territorial integrity of a state (*see* the regulations on Threatening Ukraine, Russia, Donetsk and Lahansk, Iran Assisting Russia and Moldova). One cannot help but notice that violence is met with sanctions at all times; the source and direction of violence however is indicative of the nature of sanctions that are likely to be imposed. When groups, armed but unassociated with the state apparatus of the territory, where they operate, exercise violence, UN-mandated sanctions are likely to be imposed; when groups, armed and associated with the state apparatus of the territory, where they operate, exercise violence, autonomous sanctions are likely imposed, as attempts within the UN Security Council are met with veto. The latter are also very likely to be imposed in the aftermath of coup d'états and/or when the electoral process is undermined by actions or inactions of the state apparatus. The UN Security Council is reluctant to lecture states on how to exercise their authority within their territory whether this is police force performing its tasks or the national authorities holding elections. The EU is happy to oblige and assess the proportionality of actions and inactions of third states. At this point, it merits to reiterate that the uniqueness of every event in every state cannot be overstated. For example, a coup d'état might be the result of a set of events; however, these events, as well as the power dynamics, the specifics of culture and society differ greatly, not only from state to state but also throughout time. Thus, although the result, a coup d'état, is common the events, reasons and dynamics that lead to such a result differ greatly. Furthermore, it is highly unlikely to truly grasp what lead to a coup d'état, even if all bits and pieces are put together, when they are viewed from a *European* perspective and understood under *European* standards.

617. Withal certain political contexts are idiosyncratic to such an extent that they cannot fit into any group. That would be the case of *unauthorized drilling* and *illegal actions* that the Union assesses as a threat to its interests and security. In 2004, the EU – then the European Community – took the decision to expand and include in the common market a frozen conflict, the Cyprus problem. EU law and membership in the EU are not a panacea for all evils and perils; the frozen conflict was not solved, when all was bright and sunny, and it was – and still is – due to lead to complications sometime in the future. This begs the question, did the threat to the Union's interests and security arise already at the time that the expansion was decided, only to become more intense with the exploration of hydrocarbons? Or even, is there any threat at all, when the Union knowingly, intentionally and wilfully took in a frozen conflict? Or, should the threat to the Union's interests and security as a policy reason vanish, would it lead to the collapse of the EU legislation that it supports? These are lovely and intriguing academic questions that are very much likely to become flesh and blood, as the Union started the accession process to an actual conflict; Ukraine. Is the EU ready to take in a *hot* conflict?

618. The sanctions imposed, as a response to the aforementioned unique political contexts and different sets of policy reasons, are nonetheless the same; financial, in the sense of freezing assets of certain targeted persons and economic resources and not making such available to the same persons. The imposition of these exact restrictions is attended to uniformly with much zeal and religious devotion. Said restrictions, that have been conceived within the Western financial system, entail also the assumption that the Western financial system is the sole financial system. This is not accurate, as the operation of informal funds transfer systems, such as the *hawala*,[2706] demonstrates. Notwithstanding the parallel operation of such systems, even the generic traits of any financial system are not received in the same manner everywhere. For example, from the *European* perspective large corporate taxpayers pay large taxes, employ large number of employees and contribute largely to the gross domestic product. Thus, ensuring the sustainability of large corporate taxpayers sounds reasonable and a sound component of any financial system. It is not. States can be – and have been – *unprincipled hostile* towards them;[2707] states have frozen their assets forcing them into liquidation, whereby the most valuable assets were grabbed on a Sunday under the pretence of a bankruptcy auction.[2708] Thus, the question arises, how can one expect that a measure conceived, designed and tested in a certain environment, shall operate *successfully* in another alien environment? After all, specifically with regard to Russia, the regime has been already using its geographical position, its military power and its control over oil and gas pipelines to make up for economic weakness.[2709]

619. One more feature that stands at odds with the meticulously uniform deployment of financial sanctions, is the non-uniformity of the preambles to the respective legislative instruments. Some state that the respective Union act observes the principles of the Charter of Fundamental Rights of the European Union (i.e., the regulations on Burundi, Nicaragua and Tunisia), other that it respects the obligations of Member States under the Charter of the UN and the legally binding nature of UN Security Council resolutions (i.e., the Regulation on Somalia), other that the respective situation poses a specific threat to international peace and security (i.e., the Regulation on Burundi) and other that designated persons should be provided with the reasons for their designation so as to give them an opportunity to present observations (i.e., the regulations on Somalia and on CAR). Such recitals are absent in other Union acts imposing sanctions. This begs the question, of whether any conclusions can be drawn or any assumptions could be made on the basis of their absence. And if not, why has the Union chosen to differentiate the preambles with respect to such fundamental principles, values and rules. Unless the legislative acts have been hastily assembled.

620. The preambles of the legislative acts present an interesting feature. This is the reference in some acts to competition (*see*, for example, Regulation on Iraq, Regulation on DRC and Regulation on Zimbabwe) and in other acts to uniform application by

2706. On the issue of informal funds transfer systems, including the *hawala*, *see* Mohammed El-Qorchi, *Hawala* 39(4) Finance & Development (December 2002).

2707. *See Quasar de Valores SICAV S.A. et al. v. The Russian Federation*, SCC Case No. 24/2007, Award of 20 Jul. 2012, para. 80, available: https://www.italaw.com/cases/915 (last visited: 31 Dec. 2023).

2708. *See Yukos Universal Limited (Isle of Man) v. the Russian Federation*, PCA Case No. AA 227, Final Award of 18 Jul. 2014, paras 997, 1016 & 1036, available: https://www.italaw.com/cases/1175 (last visited: 31 Dec. 2023).

2709. Dominic Lieven, *Empire, the Russian Empire and Its Rivals* (London: Pimlico 2003) p. 408.

economic operators (*see*, for example, Regulation on Lebanon, Regulation on Somalia, Regulation on Iran, Regulation on Libya and Regulation on Haiti). The Courts of the EU had the opportunity to adjudicate on this issue within the frame of the Regulation on Terrorism. The applicant alleged that this reason has no foundation in fact, perhaps not without merit. The General Court refrained from making a finding on this issue, adopting the approach that even if it constituted a procedural defect, it could not lead to annulment of the measures.[2710] Later, the CJEU noted that implementing restrictive measures of an economic nature could have a particular effect on trade between the Member States as well as on the exercise by economic operators of their right of establishment. It went on to find that any differences between measures taken unilaterally by the Member States benefiting or damaging the competitive position of certain economic operators could lead to distortion of competition. Therefore, the aforementioned reason was indeed relevant.[2711] Interestingly, later amendments of the Regulation on Terrorism adopted the view that action at the level of the Union was necessary 'with a view to ensuring their uniform application by economic operators in all Member States'.[2712] This could serve as a solid basis for the assumption that these two reasons are indeed associated. At this point, the US legislative act on Iran and Libya sanctions[2713] is noteworthy. The sanctions imposed that had to be implemented via US corporations and undertakings, led to these persons having to abandon multi-million contracts that were later taken on by European corporations and undertakings, who went on to win further contracts for the development of massive gas fields.[2714] It is highly probable, that *this* is the distortion of competition that the Union wishes to avoid and thus strives to create a *wide* common playing field. This assumption is supported by the Union's call to encourage third States to adopt measures similar both with regard to unilateral sanctions and with regard to multilateral, with the aim to maximize the impact of the adopted measures.

621. In truth, alongside the financial sanctions, certain legislative instruments provide for additional restrictive measures in the finance sector that have the form of obligations and prohibitions. Credit and financial institutions of Syria and the DPRK may not open a new bank account or a representative office, including a branch and a subsidiary in the Union, or establish a new banking corresponding relationship. Reserves and assets of the Central Bank of Russia, the Russian National Wealth Fund and the Central Bank of Belarus may not be managed in the Union, provoking a debate on whether this prohibition infringes the law of state immunity. This prohibition is paired with the obligation of anyone in the Union, such as banks, central securities

2710. *Ayadi* 2006 (n. 21) para. 165.
2711. *Kadi* 2008 (n. 15) paras 230 & 231.
2712. *See*, for example, recital No. 4 to the preamble of Regulation 2016/363.
2713. An Act to impose sanctions on persons making certain investments directly and significantly contributing to the enhancement of the ability of Iran or Libya to develop its petroleum resources, and on persons exporting certain items that enhance Libya's weapons or aviation capabilities or enhance Libya's ability to develop its petroleum resources, and for other purposes, Public Law 104-172 of 5 Aug. 1996, 110 Stat. 1541.
2714. David Strahan, *The Last Oil Shock, a Survival Guide to the Imminent Extinction of Petroleum Man* (London: John Murray (Publishers) 2007) p. 4.

depositories and central counterparties, to inform the authorities of the assets and reserves that they hold or control. Further measures set out the prohibition to sell banknotes of a Member State to Russia or Belarus, including to Russian and Belarusian persons and for use in these states. Deposits of more than EUR 100,000 are not accepted in the Union from Russian and Belarusian persons, as well as to persons residing in said states. Russia and Russian enterprises may also not receive services related to: crypto-assets; credit rating; trusts; accounting and auditing; tax, business and management consulting; legal advisory; public relations; architecture and engineering; IT consulting; market research and public opinion; technical testing, analysis and advertising; and public relations. They neither may be supplied software for managing enterprises nor software used in architecture, engineering, construction, manufacturing, media, education and entertainment. Public financing and financial assistance for trade and investment with regard to Russia, Belarus and the DPRK are also prohibited. So do loans for Russian and Belarussian persons and participation in projects co-financed by the Russian Direct Investment Fund. Russian persons are furthermore prohibited from making any transaction, whereas certain Russian and Belarusian persons may not acquire transferable securities. Moreover, Russian persons may not be awarded public contracts or concession contracts, whereas if this has already been done, they are prohibited from continuing their performance. Bonds issued by Syria or the DPRK may not be acquired by anyone in the Union, whereas no transfer of funds both to and from the DPRK may take place. At the same time, credit institutions and financial institutions in the Union may not perform transactions with their counterparts in the DPRK. Undertakings in the Union may not provide insurance and re-insurance to the state of Syria and all its public bodies, as well as financing any undertaking active in the oil and gas sector. Finally, certain report obligations have been introduced. The first relates to transfers of EUR 100,000 or more and has been imposed on legal persons established in the Union that are owned by Russians. Credit and financial institutions established in the Union also have to report such transfers, when they are initiated by persons in Russia. Same institutions have to apply customer due diligence measures – not enhanced customer due diligence measures, as one would expect – and ensure that they comply with the anti-money laundering legislation and the counter-terrorist-financing procedures as set out in EU law when they engage in activities with credit and financial institutions in the DPRK. They equally have to report suspicious transactions as well as suspicions of proliferation financing.

622. With the exception of the aforementioned obligations, the prohibitions described above are usually accompanied by a series of exceptions, grace periods or cases being carved out of their scope, as these have been set out throughout the monograph. Yet, said prohibitions are unaccompanied by any form or means of legal remedy, leading to unchecked, absolute and opulent power of the Commission. At the same time, same prohibitions create an environment of clean-cut discrimination against the relevant enterprises and undertakings that is finely justified in view of the specific circumstances, which gave rise to the need to adopt measures. Nonetheless, these measures are unmistakably discriminatory as they are adopted against persons due to their nationality or the nationality of persons controlling the respective legal persons. Should the affected assets or activity qualify as an investment under international investment law, the Union could be facing anytime soon a wave of requests for arbitration under the respective investment treaties, as explained below (*see* in this respect paragraph 624 below).

623. Undertakings and corporations established in the Union are further prohibited from exporting, as well as importing, gold, precious metals, diamonds and luxury goods to and from the DPRK, Syria and Russia. These imposed sanctions targeting said states, are not uniform however, as the statutory definition of the respective items varies. Nonetheless, these measures obstruct both access of 'rogue' regimes to treats, into which they indulge, and the flow of proceeds into the coffers of the targeted regimes, as these goods habitually form a component of money laundering.

624. As the book was going to press, there has been talk about appropriating frozen Russian assets to use them for Ukraine's needs,[2715] something like Switzerland deciding to use the profits of Krups for the reconstruction of Paris, if one was to draw parallels to a previous war. It also entails the – wishful but baseless – assumption that Ukraine will win the war. This move was characterized as *morally justified*.[2716] It might be so. Legally though this could mark the start of a wild ride; a ride that shall not necessarily take place before the Courts of the EU and does not require the war to end. Such a scenario could unfold in the following manner. The corporations that had their assets frozen and subsequently used for a purpose set by the authorities that froze them, could file for protection under the applicable investment treaty, that being the treaty signed between the state, where the investment is located, and the state where the corporation that owns that specific investment is registered. Depending on the standards of protection that the specific investment treaty provides, the corporation, whose investment is used for purposes other than the ones that its owner wishes, could complain for unlawful expropriation, violation of the fair and equitable treatment or discrimination.[2717] Taking as an example, that a frozen asset is located in Belgium and the corporation owning the investment is registered in Russia, the applicable treaty would be the Belgium/Luxembourg – Russian Federation Bilateral Investment Treaty of 1989,[2718] which protects under both the fair and equitable treatment standard (Article 4(1)) and the prohibition of unlawful expropriation (Article 5). Also applicable

2715. Gregorio Sorgi, *EU Capitals Fear Russian Retaliation and Cyberattacks after Asset Freezes: G7 is Drafting a Workaround to Use Frozen Assets to Rebuild Ukraine*, 5 Feb. 2024, Politico, available: https://www.politico.eu/article/russia-cyberattack-retaliation-asset-freezes-eu-war-ukraine/ (last visited: 5 Feb. 2024).

2716. Alexander Kolyandr, *Russia's Frozen Assets Present a Policy Dilemma*, 5 Feb. 2024, Carnegie Endowment for International Peace (https://carnegieendowment.org/politika/91556).

2717. On these standards of treatment *see* Meg Kinnear, Geraldine R. Fischer et al. (eds), *Building International Investment Law: The First 50 Years of ICSID* (Kluwer Law International 2015); UNCTAD, *Expropriation: UNCTAD Series on Issues in International Investment Agreements II* (New York and Geneva 2012); and UNCTAD, *Fair and Equitable Treatment: UNCTAD Series on Issues in International Investment Agreements II* (New York and Geneva 2012).

2718. Accord entre les gouvernements du Royaume de Belgique et du Grand-Duche de Luxembourg, et le gouvernment de l' Union des Républiques Socialistes Soviétiques concernant l' encouragement et la protection réciproques des investissements (Moscow 1989) Belgische Kamer van Volksvertegenwoordigers – 1106/1 – 89/90.

in the set example, is the Energy Charter Treaty,[2719] as long as the investment in question qualifies as an investment in the energy sector. This provides the widest possible protection against violation of the fair and equitable treatment (Article 10(1)), discrimination (Article 10(1)) and unlawful expropriation (Article 13). A note to self: under international investment law, nothing prohibits two – or more – arbitration proceedings between the same parties and under different treaties from taking place in parallel. The Union and the respondent state could object by invoking the principle of autonomy of EU law and the principle of supremacy of EU law, an argument that has been put forward numerous times and has invariably failed to persuade the arbitral tribunals.[2720] In the scenario that Ukraine does not win the war, the wild ride shall take place at unchartered waters, whereby the habit of grabbing assets and land will have been reinforced by the victorious outcome.

625. In parallel to the imposed financial sanctions, the Union has adopted restrictions on admission, also named 'travel bans'. This type of restriction was initiated at UN level and was then duplicated in Brussels, when unilateral sanctions were introduced. With a couple of exceptions related to Iran and Russia, all persons who had their assets and economic resources frozen, get simultaneously a travel ban.

626. The energy sector is also sanctioned. Coal is under restrictive measures with respect to the DPRK and Russia. Oil and gas however are under restrictions in relation not only to the DPRK and Russia but also to Iraq, Libya and Syria. These measures are far from uniform, as both the definitions of the respective items and the measures per se fluctuate from mere granting of loans and credits to actual export and transfer. Furthermore, electricity production in Syria is also under sanctions. Alongside said prohibitions, the legislative instruments provide for exceptions, derogations, grace periods and cases that fall outside their scope. Among those some photographic exceptions are set out, such as coal exports from the Rajin (Rason) port, crude oil from the Sakhalin-2 project, operation of the Caspian Pipeline Consortium and a deep-water offshore gas project in the Mediterranean Sea, suggesting the works of lobbyists. As seen already above with regard to additional financial sanctions and the appropriation of frozen assets, no legal remedies are offered to the persons affected by these measures.

2719. Energy Charter Treaty (Lisbon 1994) 2080 UNTS 95.

2720. *See*, for example, *Eureko B.V. v. The Slovak Republic*, UNCITRAL, PCA Case No. 2008-13, Award on Jurisdiction, Arbitrability and Suspension of 26 Oct. 2010 available: https://www.italaw.com/cases/417 (last visited: 31 Dec. 2023); *Rupert Joseph Binder v. Czech Republic*, UNCITRAL, Award on Jurisdiction of 6 Jun. 2007, available:https://www.italaw.com/cases/151 (last visited: 31 Dec. 2023); *Electrabel S.A. v. Republic of Hungary*, ICSID Case No. ARB/07/19, Decision on Jurisdiction, Applicable Law and Liability of 30 Nov. 2012, available: https://www.italaw.com/cases/380 (last visited: 31 Dec. 2023); *Cube Infrastructure Fund SICAV and others v. Kingdom of Spain*, Decision on Jurisdiction, Liability and Partial Decision on Quantum of 19 Feb. 2019, available: https://www.italaw.com/cases/7477 (last visited: 31 Dec. 2023); *Greentech Energy Systems A/S et al. v. Kingdom of Spain*, SCC Case No. 2015/150, Final Award of 14 Nov. 2018, available:https://www.italaw.com/cases/7001, (last visited: 31 Dec. 2023); and *Landesbank Baden-Württemberg and others v. Kingdom of Spain*, ICSID Case No. ARB/15/45, Decision on the Intra-EU Jurisdictional Objection of 25 Feb. 2019, available: https://www.italaw.com/cases/7586 (last visited: 31 Dec. 2023).

627. Notably oil and gas sanctions on Russia may be bent, as long as this is authorized on the basis of having been appropriate for the critical energy supply of the Union or the relevant oil and gas is the product of a European doing business in Russia. The criterium of ensuring the Union's energy supply as an exceptional reason for allowing for derogation from sanctions imposed due to Russia's violation of the principles on which European security is built[2721] fails to impress. The Union, already in its capacity as European Communities was well aware of its dependency on Soviet, and then Russian, oil and gas. Nonetheless, in 2007, it abandoned the Nabucco pipeline project that would carry oil and gas from the Caspian Sea, promoting instead renewables. Moscow was delighted; the Russian press commented 'the EU is giving up on solving the issue of dependence on energy supplies from Russia, CIS, and North Africa by new pipeline projects and reforms on the market'.[2722] After all, Russia has been supplying the West with oil since at least the time of Khrushchev.[2723] The Union has opted for energy efficiency, in the sense of decreasing the consumed energy and thus increasing its dependency on (Russian) oil and gas. Perhaps led by naïveté, the Union did not address the matter of energy security, resulting in Moscow holding a fairly firm grip on the Union's energy grid. Choosing to further its dependence on Russian oil and gas by allowing for derogations, the EU not only allows Moscow's coffers to fil up at an unforgiving time in history but it also allows for a critical weakness in the Union's security to persist.

628. Special mention deserve the restrictive measures imposed on nuclear energy and nuclear activities in the DPRK and Iran, along with the note that no such measures have been imposed on Russia. Specific goods and technology that have the capability to contribute to nuclear-related programs and at the same time qualify as dual use items, may not be exported to and imported from the DPRK, whereas they may be traded with Iran, as long as the competent authorities have authorized such actions. Another set of items, styled as 'goods and technology listed in Annex I', is also sanctioned with regard to Iran in the sense that a prior authorization is necessary for those to be provided to the DPRN or acquired therefrom. This set of items are items listed both under the 'trigger list' of the NSG as well as under the list of dual use items of the Dual Use Regulation. Items related to the modification of cascades at the Fordow facility and modernization of the Arak reactor fall outside the scope of this prohibition.

629. At this point, it is fair to say that in essence the two pillars of Russia's great power status, that being oil & gas and the nuclear retaliation capability,[2724] have not been sanctioned.

2721. Recital No. 4 to the preamble of Council Decision (CFSP) 2022/264 of 23 Feb. 2022 amending Decision 2014/512/CFSP concerning restrictive measures in view of Russia's actions destabilising the situation in Ukraine, OJ L 42I, 23 Feb. 2022, p. 95.
2722. Martin Walker, *Russia v. Europe: The Energy Wars* 24(1) World Policy Journal 1 at 5 & 6 (2007) https://doi.org/10.1162/wopj.2007.24.1.1.
2723. Veljko Mićunović, *Moscow Diary* (London: Chatto & Windus 1980) pp. 205 & 233.
2724. Norwegian Intelligence Service, *Focus 2019: The Norwegian Intelligence Service's Assessment of Current Security Challenges*, 21 Jan. 2019, p. 25, available: https://www.etterretningstjenesten.no/publikasjoner/fokus (last visited: 31 Dec. 2023). *See also* David Strahan, (n. 2714) p. 193.

630. Dual use in their capacity as dual use items, that encompass in addition to the 'goods and technology listed in Annex I' explained above nine more categories of items, are under sanctions targeting the DPRK, Iran, Myanmar/Burma, Syria, Russia and Belarus. This list of items was not initially drafted by the EU; rather, the EU adopted lists prepared by the AG, the MTCR, the NSG and the Wassenaar Agreement. In parallel to the usual controls imposed on such items by the Dual Use Regulation, the Union prohibits their supply and acquisition when the DPRK, Myanmar/Burma, Syria, Russia and Belarus are involved, a prohibition resembling the prohibition of money laundering in reverse. Should Iran be involved in any intended transaction, a prior authorization is required. Exceptions on the grounds of humanitarian or protective use are set out, but any supply of dual use items to Syria must be done in accordance with the scope of eliminating Syria's chemical weapons program and the objective of the Chemical Weapons Convention. Non-military use of dual use items falls outside the scope of the prohibition in Russia and Belarus.

631. Arms and weapons, in the form of items listed in the EU Common Military List, the abstract notion of *arms and related materiel of all types*, equipment for internal repression as well as missiles and other systems of delivery, face restrictions with regard to Sudan, the DRC, Lebanon, Yemen, South Sudan, Myanmar/Burma, Zimbabwe, the DPRK, Somalia, Iran, Libya, the CAR, Venezuela, Syria, Russia and Belarus. Iran faces restrictions only with regard to missiles and other systems of delivery. Exceptions such as for humanitarian reasons, assistance to governments and state institutions, demining operations or the ExoMars 2020 mission, and grace periods are provided alongside the prohibitions and requirements for prior authorization. The Regulation on DRC even provides an exception for items that are not sanctioned, whereas the Regulation on Somalia does not set out exceptions, despite the implemented UN Security Council resolution doing so.

632. At the outset of the monograph, it has been noted that all sanctions imposed by the Union are smart, in the sense of discriminating and minimizing adverse consequences for the ones not responsible for policies and actions causing the violations. This could be questionable for three reasons. The first reason has been already described above under the additional non-financial sanctions, whereby the flow of categories of goods and services towards and from a state is interrupted. The other two reasons are the *new generation sanctions* and the *effects* of certain imposed sanctions; these are elaborated below.

633. A handful of recently decided sanction regimes, styled as new generation sanctions in the monograph, depart from the established modus of targeting individuals in a state. Instead, they target individuals regardless of their nationality or their position in a state apparatus. They target individuals seriously violating human rights, individuals performing cyber-attacks and proliferate or use chemical weapons. In view of this particularity, it is here suggested that these prohibitions stimulate the approach of piercing the *state* veil, paraphrasing the established institution of corporate law.

634. The effects of the sanctions imposed against Russia are felt across the country, both by the population and by the elite.[2725] Furthermore, Iran's environmental problems are enhanced by imposed sanctions resulting into prolonged use of older vehicles, impossibility to obtain equipment and technology to reduce vehicle emissions and foreign investors abandoning large projects of solar power plants. This leads to higher levels of respiratory and other diseases and thousands of premature deaths.[2726] These facts call into question the view that all imposed restrictive measures are smart, in the sense of targeting the regime of a state and not its population. It would be more accurate to suggest that solely the financial sanctions and the travel bans qualify as smart; all other sanctions, whereby the flow of goods and technology to and from a state is disrupted, do not seem to be smart.

635. Having explored the vast political context under which sanctions are imposed, the policy reasons that sanctions aspire to accomplice, the issues that could arise from the repetitious, tepid and inflexible financial sanctions, the question bears mention, is the Union ready to take the credit and bear the consequences? This question is significant, as in the past the introduction of Western principles of law and democracy did lead to the collapse of the Soviet system and the disintegration of the Soviet Union.[2727] At the time, Europe decided to 'fix' the issue of its energy security and deal with the neglected energy infrastructure of the former Soviet Union by adopting the Energy Charter Treaty,[2728] and dismissed the option of providing long-term loans.[2729] Short-sightedness and lack of imagination lead to a persisting energy security issue for the old continent and 'intra-EU' claims of investors against Member States of the EU under the Energy Charter Treaty[2730] that the Union now strives to annihilate.[2731] Still, the unlikely scenario of the Moscow regime collapsing has been assessed to lead to democratization attempts that are just short-lived.[2732]

2725. Norwegian Intelligence Service, *Focus 2023: The Norwegian Intelligence Service's Assessment of Current Security Challenges*, 27 Jan. 2023, p. 11, available:https://www.etterretningstjenesten.no/publikasjoner/fokus (last visited: 31 Dec. 2023) ('Focus 2023').

2726. UN News, *Iran: US Sanctions Violating Human Rights of All Living There, Say UN Experts*, 20 Dec. 2022, available: https://news.un.org/en/story/2022/12/1131887 (last visited: 31 Dec. 2023).

2727. Dominic Lieven (n. 2709) pp. 302 & 336.

2728. Energy Charter Treaty (Lisbon 1994) 2080 UNTS 95.

2729. Natalia Charalampidou, *Range of Disputes under the Energy Charter Treaty* 16(5) OGEL 2 (2018) (joint OGEL & TDM Special Issue with ArbitralWomen on 'Strategic Considerations in Energy Disputes').

2730. On the *intra-EU* issue *see* Florian Stefan, *Intra-EU Disputes under the Energy Charter Treaty: Quo Vadis?* Kluwer Arbitration Blog, 18 Aug. 2019, available: https://arbitrationblog.kluwerarbitration.com/2019/08/18/intra-eu-disputes-under-the-energy-charter-treaty-quo-vadis/ (last visited: 31 Dec. 2023).

2731. *See* Laura Halonen, *Termination of Intra-EU BITs: Commission and Most Member States Testing the Principle of Good Faith under International Law*, Kluwer Arbitration Blog, 13 May 2020, available: https://arbitrationblog.kluwerarbitration.com/2020/05/13/termination-of-intra-eu-bits-commission-and-most-member-states-testing-the-principle-of-good-faith-under-international-law/ (last visited: 31 Dec. 2023); Proposal for a COUNCIL DECISION on the position to be taken on behalf of the European Union in the Energy Charter Conference, COM/2024/104 final, 1 Mar. 2024 (https://eur-lex.europa.eu).

2732. Estonian Foreign Intelligence Service, *International Security and Estonia 2023*, 31 Jan. 2023, p. 37 (https://raport.valisluureamet.ee/2023/en/).

636. An equally tectonic question, is whether the Union is ready to take the credit and bear the *unplanned, unintended* and *undesired* consequences of the imposed sanctions. As already seen, the EU has taken the decision to impose autonomous (or unilateral) sanctions, not infrequently as a result of proposals for sanctions being vetoed within the UN Security Council. Targeting states for not respecting human rights, the rule of law and democracy and imposing restrictive measures, could have the effect of pushing the targets to a *get-together* leading to *talks* and possibly *cross-pollination*. Moscow does anyhow intend to create a geopolitical coalition of authoritarian regimes whose common ground is to oppose the West, democracy and the rule of law.[2733] It would be a good idea for the EU not to give a helping hand. Iran has already provided Russia with drones and missiles that were splashed all over Ukraine. P'yŏngyang's arsenal of missiles and bombs having access to Moscow's petrol and kerosene is the stuff of nightmares. And the Union does not do well with unpremeditated consequences, as the history of the Energy Charter Treaty shows.

637. Conclusively, the Union imposes restrictive measures, financial or non-financial, smart or not, multilateral or unilateral, following the rupture of violence in the form of shattering international peace and security, violating human rights or democracy, including political stalemate and misappropriation of state funds, or the interests and security of the Union. In order to maximize the effectiveness of these measures and to protect its own interests and security, the Union has to seriously reconsider its energy security policy. The already adopted policies have been proven to be woefully insufficient, as demonstrated by the exceptions to the energy-related sanctions. Energy policy can spare diplomatic niceties.

638. Reviewing the energy policy is furthermore prudent as the possibility of a local war that escalates into a wider military conflict involving Russia and NATO cannot be discounted.[2734] Specifically with regard to Russia's military power, the overwhelming economic challenges that Russia is facing in rebuilding its conventional military power elevate the role of non-strategic nuclear weapons. This also means that the threshold for nuclear escalation becomes lower.[2735] Another war, whether it be with conventional weapons or nuclear ones, shall be a form of violence, where sanctions, as contemplated, designed and put into effect until now, have proven to be ineffective, at least partially. The loudest example is the fact that the sanctions imposed upon the annexation of Crimea, did not deter Russia from launching its attack against Kiev eight years later. Should another war erupt in the old continent, the Union shall have to react and respond. In view of the outcome and effects of the already imposed sanctions, perhaps it is time to re-think, re-invent and re-design measures that aim to align their targets with the desired political preferences. At least then, the Union shall have learned from its mistakes.

2733. *Ibid.* p. 25. *See* also *Focus 2023* (n. 2725) p. 17.
2734. *Focus 2023* (n. 2725) p. 27.
2735. *Ibid.*, p. 34.

Annexes

ANNEX I
Glossary of Statutory Definitions

Affecting the performance of a contract or transaction

[t]he performance of a contract or transaction shall be regarded as having been affected by the measures imposed by this Regulation where the existence or content of the claim results directly or indirectly from those measures.[2736]

Armoured combat vehicles

tracked, semi-tracked or wheeled self-propelled vehicles, with armoured protection and cross-country capability, either: (a) designed and equipped to transport a squad of four or more infantrymen, or (b) armed with an integral or organic weapon of at least 12.5 millimetres calibre or a missile launcher.[2737]

Attack helicopters

rotary-wing aircraft designed, equipped or modified to engage targets by employing guided or unguided anti-armour, air-to-surface, air-to-subsurface, or air-to-air weapons and equipped with an integrated fire control and aiming system for these weapons, including versions of these aircraft which perform specialized reconnaissance or electronic warfare missions.[2738]

Basic scientific research

experimental or theoretical work undertaken principally to acquire new knowledge of the fundamental principles of phenomena or observable facts, not primarily directed towards a specific practical aim or objective.[2739]

2736. Article 53(2) Regulation on DPRK & Art. 38(2) Regulation on Iran.
2737. *See* A/71/259 Annex I, Category II.
2738. *See* A/71/259 Annex I, Category V.
2739. Definitions of Terms Used in This Annex, Annex I Dual Use Regulation.

Battle tanks

tracked or wheeled self-propelled armoured fighting vehicles with high cross-country mobility and a high-level of self-protection, weighing 16.5 metric tons unladen weight, with a high muzzle velocity direct fire main gun of at least 75 millimetres calibre.[2740]

Branch

a place of business which forms a legally dependent part of an institution and which carries out directly all or some of the transactions inherent in the business of institutions.[2741]

Brokering services

(i) the negotiation or arrangement of transactions for the purchase, sale or supply of goods and technology or of financial and technical services, including from a third country to any other third country, or (ii) the selling or buying of goods and technology or of financial and technical services, including where they are located in third countries for their transfer to another third country.[2742]

Central counterparty, ('CCP')

a legal person that interposes itself between the counterparties to the contracts traded on one or more financial markets, becoming the buyer to every seller and the seller to every buyer.[2743]

Central securities depository

a legal person that operates a securities settlement system and provides at least one other core service from the following: (a) providing cash accounts to, and accepting deposits from, participants in a securities settlement system and holders of securities accounts, within the meaning of point 1 of Annex I to Directive 2013/36/EU; (b) providing cash credit for reimbursement no later than the following business day, cash lending to pre-finance corporate actions and lending

2740. A/RES/46/36 p. 75.
2741. Article 1(a) Regulation on DPRK and Art. 4(1)(17) Regulation 575/2013.
2742. Article 1(f) Regulation on Goods from Crimea, Art. 1(d) Regulation on Russia, Art. 1(a) Regulation with regard to Donetsk, Art. 1(a) Regulation on Iran Assisting Russia, Art. 1(13) Regulation on Belarus.
The Regulation on Threatening Ukraine, the Regulation on Moldova, the Regulation on Human Rights Violation, the Regulation Against Cyber-Attacks & the Regulation Against Chemical Weapons do not provide a definition of brokering services.
2743. Article 5a(4a) Regulation on Russia and Art. 2(1) Regulation (EU) No. 648/2012 of the European Parliament and of the Council of 4 Jul. 2012 on OTC derivatives, central counterparties and trade repositories, OJ L 201 27 Jul. 2012, p. 1, as last amended by Regulation (EU) 2021/168 of the European Parliament and of the Council of 10 Feb. 2021 amending Regulation (EU) 2016/1011 as regards the exemption of certain third-country spot foreign exchange benchmarks and the designation of replacements for certain benchmarks in cessation, and amending Regulation (EU) No. 648/2012, OJ L 49, 12 Feb. 2021, p. 6.

securities to holders of securities accounts, within the meaning of point 2 of Annex I to Directive 2013/36/EU; (c) payment services involving processing of cash and foreign exchange transactions, within the meaning of point 4 of Annex I to Directive 2013/36/EU; (d) guarantees and commitments related to securities lending and borrowing, within the meaning of point 6 of Annex I to Directive 2013/36/EU; and (e) treasury activities involving foreign exchange and transferable securities related to managing participants' long balances, within the meaning of points 7(b) and (e) of Annex I to Directive 2013/36/EU.[2744]

Chemical weapons

(a) Toxic chemicals[2745] and their precursors, except where intended for purposes not prohibited under this Convention, as long as the types and quantities are consistent with such purposes;
(b) Munitions and devices, specifically designed to cause death or other harm through the toxic properties of those toxic chemicals specified in subparagraph (a), which would be released as a result of the employment of such munitions and devices;
(c) Any equipment specifically designed for use directly in connection with the employment of munitions and devices specified in subparagraph (b).[2746]

Combat aircraft and unmanned combat aerial vehicles

fixed-wing or variable-geometry wing aerial vehicles as defined below:

(a) Manned fixed-wing or variable-geometry wing aircraft, designed, equipped or modified to engage targets by employing guided missiles, unguided rockets, bombs, guns, cannons or other weapons of destruction, including versions of these aircraft which perform specialized electronic warfare, suppression of air defence or reconnaissance missions.
(b) Unmanned fixed-wing or variable-geometry wing aircraft, designed, equipped or modified to engage targets by employing guided missiles, unguided rockets, bombs, guns, cannons or other weapons of destruction.

The terms combat aircraft and unmanned combat aerial vehicles do not include primary trainer aircraft, unless designed, equipped or modified as described above.[2747]

2744. Article 2(1) and Annex Regulation (EU) No. 909/2014 of the European Parliament and of the Council of 23 Jul. 2014 on improving securities settlement in the European Union and on central securities depositories and amending Directives 98/26/EC and 2014/65/EU and Regulation (EU) No. 236/2012, OJ L 257 28 Aug. 2014, p. 1, as last amended by Regulation (EU) 2022/858 of the European Parliament and of the Council of 30 May 2022 on a pilot regime for market infrastructures based on distributed ledger technology, and amending Regulations (EU) No. 600/2014 and (EU) No. 909/2014 and Directive 2014/65/EU, OJ L 151, 2 Jun.2022, p. 1.
2745. In regard to the definition of *toxic chemicals* set out in Art. II(2) Chemical Weapons Convention *see* this Annex p. 331.
2746. Article 1(a) Regulation Against Chemical Weapons and Art. II(1) Chemical Weapons Convention.
2747. *See* A/71/259 para. 81.

Claim

any claim, whether asserted by legal proceedings or not, made before or after the date of entry into force of this Regulation, under or in connection with a contract or transaction, including in particular: (i) a claim for performance of any obligation arising under or in connection with a contract or transaction; (ii) a claim for extension or payment of a bond, financial guarantee or indemnity of whatever form; (iii) a claim for compensation in respect of a contract or transaction; (iv) a counterclaim; or (v) a claim for the recognition or enforcement, including by the procedure of *exequatur*, of a judgment, an arbitration award or an equivalent decision, wherever made or given.[2748]

Contracts and transactions

any transaction of whatever form and whatever the applicable law, whether comprising one or more contracts or similar obligations made between the same or different parties; for that purpose 'contract' includes a bond, guarantee or indemnity, particularly a financial guarantee or financial indemnity, and credit, whether legally independent or not, as well as any related provision arising under, or in connection with, the transaction.[2749]

Controlling a legal person, group or entity

(a) having the right to appoint or remove a majority of the members of the administrative, management or supervisory body of such legal person, group or entity; (b) having appointed solely as a result of the exercise of one's voting rights a majority of the members of the administrative, management or supervisory bodies of a legal person, group or entity who have held office during the present and previous financial year; (c) controlling alone, pursuant to an agreement with other shareholders in or members of a legal person, group or entity, a majority of shareholders' or members' voting rights in that legal person, group or entity; (d) having the right to exercise a dominant influence over a legal person, group or entity, pursuant to an agreement entered into with that legal person, group or entity, or to a provision in its Memorandum or Articles of Association, where the law governing that legal person, group or entity permits its being subject to such agreement or provision; (e) having the power to exercise the right to exercise a dominant influence referred to in the aforementioned point, without being the holder of that right; (f) having the right to use all or part of the assets of a legal

2748. Article 1(b) Regulation on Sudan, Art. 1(a) Regulation on DRC, Art. 2(3) Regulation on DPRK, Art. 1(c) Regulation on Iran, Art. 1(b) Regulation on CAR, Art. 1(a) Regulation on Yemen, Art. 1(b) Regulation on South Sudan, Art. 1(a) Regulation on Mali, Art. 1(a) Regulation on Haiti, Art. 1(a) Regulation on Myanmar/Burma, Art. 1(a) Regulation on Burundi, Art. 1(a) Regulation on Venezuela, Art. 1(a) Regulation on Nicaragua, Art. 1(a) EU Regulation on Lebanon, Art. 1(a) Funds Regulation Ukraine & Art. 1(a) Regulation on Drilling. The Regulation on Libya and the Regulation on Syria do not set out a definition of *claims*.

2749. Article 1(c) Regulation on Sudan, Art. 1(b) Regulation on DRC, Art. 2(5) Regulation on DPRK, Art. 1(d) Regulation on Iran, Art. 1(c) Regulation on CAR, Art. 1(d) Regulation on Yemen, Art. 1(c) Regulation on South Sudan, Art. 1(d) Regulation on Mali, Art. 1(b) Regulation on Haiti, Art. 1(b) Regulation on Myanmar/Burma, Art. 1(b) Regulation on Burundi, Art. 1(b) Regulation on Venezuela, Art. 1(b) Regulation on Nicaragua, Art. 1(b) EU Regulation on Lebanon, Art. 1(c) Regulation on Syria, Art. 1(b) Funds Regulation Ukraine & Art. 1(b) Regulation on Drilling. The Regulation on Libya does not set out a definition of *contract or transaction*.

person, group or entity; (g) managing the business of a legal person, group or entity on a unified basis, while publishing consolidated accounts; and (h) sharing jointly and severally the financial liabilities of a legal person, group or entity, or guaranteeing them.[2750]

Credit institution

an undertaking the business of which consists of any of the following:

(a) to take deposits or other repayable funds from the public and to grant credits for its own account;

(b) to carry out [any of the following investment services and activities: dealing on own account; or underwriting of financial instruments and/or placing of financial instruments on a firm commitment basis773], where one of the following applies, but the undertaking is not a commodity and emission allowance dealer, a collective investment undertaking or an insurance undertaking:

 (i) the total value of the consolidated assets of the undertaking is equal to or exceeds EUR 30 billion;

 (ii) the total value of the assets of the undertaking is less than EUR 30 billion, and the undertaking is part of a group in which the total value of the consolidated assets of all undertakings in that group that individually have total assets of less than EUR 30 billion and that carry out any of [the following investment services and activities: dealing on own account; or underwriting of financial instruments and/or placing of financial instruments on a firm commitment basis] is equal to or exceeds EUR 30 billion; or

 (iii) the total value of the assets of the undertaking is less than EUR 30 billion, and the undertaking is part of a group in which the total value of the consolidated assets of all undertakings in the group that carry out any of the activities referred [any of the following investment services and activities: dealing on own account; or underwriting of financial instruments and/or placing of financial instruments on a firm commitment basis] is equal to or exceeds EUR 30 billion, where the consolidating supervisor, in consultation with the supervisory college, so decides in order to address potential risks of circumvention and potential risks for the financial stability of the Union;

for the purposes of points (b)(ii) and (b)(iii), where the undertaking is part of a third-country group, the total assets of each branch of the third-country group authorised in the Union shall be included in the combined total value of the assets of all undertakings in the group.[2751]

Credit transfer

a national or cross-border payment service for crediting a payee's payment account with a payment transaction or a series of payment transactions from a

2750. Article 1(6) Regulation on Terrorism.

2751. Article 1(d) Regulation on Syria and Art. 4(1)(1) Regulation (EU) No. 575/2013 of the European Parliament and of the Council of 26 Jun. 2013 on prudential requirements for credit institutions and amending Regulation (EU) No. 648/2012, OJ L 176 27 Jun. 2013, p. 1.

payer's payment account by the PSP which holds the payer's payment account, based on an instruction given by the payer.[2752]

Critical infrastructure

'an asset, system or part thereof located in Member States which is essential for the maintenance of vital societal functions, health, safety, security, economic or social well-being of people, and the disruption or destruction of which would have a significant impact in a Member State as a result of the failure to maintain those functions' *and* 'an asset, a facility, equipment, a network or a system, or a part of an asset, a facility, equipment, a network or a system, which is necessary for the provision of an essential service'.[2753]

Cryptoanalysis

analysis of a cryptographbhv ccic system or its inputs and outputs to derive confidential variables or sensitive data, including clear text.[2754]

Cryptographic activation

any technique that specifically activates or enables cryptographic capability of an item, by means of a mechanism implemented by the manufacturer of the item, where this mechanism is uniquely bound to any of the following: (1) A single instance of the item; or (2) One customer, for multiple instances of the item.[2755]

Cryptography

the discipline which embodies principles, means and methods for the transformation of data in order to hide its information content, prevent its undetected modification or prevent its unauthorized use. [It] is limited to the transformation of information using one or more secret parameters (e.g., crypto variables) or associated key management.[2756]

2752. Article 2(23)(a)(i) and Art. 2(1) Regulation (EU) No. 260/2012 of the European Parliament and of the Council of 14 Mar. 2012 establishing technical and business requirements for credit transfers and direct debits in euro and amending Regulation (EC) No. 924/2009, OJ L 94, 30 Mar. 2012, p. 1.
2753. Article 1z Regulation on Russia, Art. 2(a) Council Directive 2008/114/EC of 8 Dec. 2008 on the identification and designation of European critical infrastructures and the assessment of the need to improve their protection, OJ L 345, 23 Dec. 2008, p. 75, & Art. 2(4) Directive (EU) 2022/2557 of the European Parliament and of the Council of 14 Dec. 2022 on the resilience of critical entities and repealing Council Directive 2008/114/EC, OJ L 333, 27 Dec. 2022, p. 164.
2754. Definitions of Terms Used in This Annex, Annex I Dual Use Regulation.
2755. Definitions of Terms Used in This Annex, Annex I Dual Use Regulation, that corresponds to Definitions of Terms Used in These Lists of the WA-List p. 220.
2756. Definitions of Terms Used in This Annex, Annex I Dual Use Regulation, that corresponds to Definitions of Terms Used in These Lists of the WA-List p. 221.

Customs declaration

the act whereby a person indicates, in the prescribed form and manner, a wish to place goods under a given customs procedure, with an indication, where appropriate, of any specific arrangements to be applied.[2757]

Cyber-attacks

(a) access to information systems;[2758] (b) information system interference;[2759] (c) data interference;[2760] or (d) data interception,[2761] where such actions are not duly authorised by the owner or by another right holder of the system or data or part of it, or are not permitted under the law of the Union or of the Member State concerned.[2762]

Cyber-attacks constituting a threat to Member States

those affecting information systems relating to, inter alia: (a) critical infrastructure, including submarine cables and objects launched into outer space, which is essential for the maintenance of vital functions of society, or the health, safety, security, and economic or social well-being of people; (b) services necessary for the maintenance of essential social and/or economic activities, in particular in the sectors of: energy (electricity, oil and gas); transport (air, rail, water and road); banking; financial market infrastructures; health (healthcare providers, hospitals and private clinics); drinking water supply and distribution; digital infrastructure; and any other sector which is essential to the Member State concerned; (c) critical State functions, in particular in the areas of defence, governance and the functioning of institutions, including for public elections or the voting process, the functioning of economic and civil infrastructure, internal security, and external relations, including through diplomatic missions; (d) the storage or processing of classified information; or (e) government emergency response teams.[2763]

Cyber-attacks constituting a threat to the Union

those carried out against its institutions, bodies, offices and agencies, its delegations to third countries or to international organisations, its common security and defence policy (CSDP) operations and missions and its special representatives.[2764]

2757. Article 5(12) Regulation (EU) 952/2013.
2758. In regard to the definition of *information system* set out in Art. 1(7)(a) Regulation (EU) 952/2013. *see* this Annex p. 321.
2759. In regard to the definition of *information system interference* set out in Art. 1(7)(b) Regulation (EU) 952/2013. *see* this Annex p 321.
2760. In regard to the definition of *data interference* set out in Art. 1(7)(c) Regulation (EU) 952/2013. *see* this Annex p. 314.
2761. In regard to the definition of *data interception* set out in Art. 1(7)(d) Regulation (EU) 952/2013. *see* this Annex p. 314.
2762. Article 1(3) Regulation Against Cyber-Attacks.
2763. Article 1(4) Regulation Against Cyber-Attacks.
2764. Article 1(5) Regulation Against Cyber-Attacks.

Cyber-attacks constituting an external threat

(a) originate, or are carried out, from outside the Union; (b) use infrastructure outside the Union; (c) are carried out by any natural or legal person, entity or body established or operating outside the Union; or (d) are carried out with the support, at the direction or under the control of any natural or legal person, entity or body operating outside the Union.[2765]

Data interference

deleting, damaging, deteriorating, altering or suppressing digital data on an information system, or rendering such data inaccessible; it also includes theft of data, funds, economic resources or intellectual property.[2766]

Data interception

'intercepting, by technical means, non-public transmissions of digital data to, from or within an information system, including electromagnetic emissions from an information system carrying such digital data'.[2767] Article 1(7)(d) *ibid.*

Deposit

a credit balance which results from funds left in an account or from temporary situations deriving from normal banking transactions and which a credit institution is required to repay under the legal and contractual conditions applicable, including a fixed-term deposit and a savings deposit, but excluding a credit balance where: (i) its existence can only be proven by a *financial instrument* [...],[2768] unless it is a savings product which is evidenced by a certificate of deposit made out to a named person and which exists in a Member State on 2 July 2014; (ii) its principal is not repayable at par; (iii) its principal is only repayable at par under a particular guarantee or agreement provided by the credit institution or a third party.[2769]

Development

all phases prior to serial production, such as: design, design research, design analyses, design concepts, assembly and testing of prototypes, pilot production schemes, design data, process of transforming design data into a product, configuration design, integration design, layouts.[2770]

Direct debit

a national or cross-border payment service for debiting a payer's payment account, where a payment transaction is initiated by the payee on the basis of the payer's consent.[2771]

2765. Article 1(2) Regulation Against Cyber-Attacks.
2766. Article 1(7)(c) Regulation Against Cyber-Attacks.
2767. Article 1(7)(d) Regulation Against Cyber-Attacks.
2768. In regard to the definition of the term 'financial instrument' *see* this Annex p. 317.
2769. Article 1(k) Regulation on Russia and Art. 1(21) Regulation on Belarus.
2770. Definitions of Terms Used in This Annex, Annex I Dual Use Regulation.
2771. Article 2(23)(a)(ii) and Art. 2(2) Regulation (EU) No. 260/2012.

Economic resources

assets of every kind, whether tangible or intangible, movable or immovable, which are not funds but can be used to obtain funds, goods or services.[2772]

Energy sector (with regard to Russia)

a sector covering the following activities with the exception of civil nuclear related activities, such as the Paks II project: (i) the exploration, production, distribution within Russia or mining of crude oil, natural gas or solid fossil fuels, the refining of fuels, the liquefaction of natural gas or regasification; (ii) the manufacture or distribution within Russia of solid fossil fuel products, refined petroleum products or gas; or (iii) the construction of facilities or installation of equipment for, or the provision of services, equipment or technology for, activities related to power generation or electricity production.[2773]

Entity in Crimea or Sevastopol

any entity having its registered office, central administration or principal place of business in Crimea or Sevastopol, its subsidiaries or affiliates under its control in Crimea or Sevastopol, as well as branches and other entities operating in Crimea or Sevastopol.[2774]

Entity in the specified territories

any entity having its registered office, central administration or principal place of business in the specified territories, its subsidiaries or affiliates under its control in the specified territories, as well as branches and other entities operating in the specified territories.[2775]

Entry summary declaration

the act whereby a person informs the customs authorities, in the prescribed form and manner and within a specific time-limit, that goods are to be brought into the customs territory of the Union.[2776]

2772. Article 1(3) Regulation on Iraq, Art. 1(e) Regulation on Sudan, Art. 1(d) Regulation on DRC, Art. 2(8) Regulation on DPRK, Art. 1(c) Regulation on Somalia, Art. 1(h) Regulation on Iran, Art. 1(c) Regulation on Guinea-Bissau, Art. 1(c) Regulation on Libya, Art. 1(e) Regulation on CAR, Art. 1(d) Regulation on Yemen, Art. 1(e) Regulation on South Sudan, Art. 1(d) Regulation on Mali, Art. 1(d) Regulation on Haiti, Art. 1(d) Regulation on Zimbabwe, Art. 1(c) EU Regulation on Iran, Art. 1(d) Regulation on Myanmar/Burma, Art. 1(g) Regulation on Burundi, Art. 1(d) Regulation on Venezuela, Art. 1(d) Regulation on Nicaragua, Art. 1(f) Regulation on Guinea, Art. 1(f) Regulation on Syria, Art. 1(c) Regulation on Tunisia, Art. 1(d) Funds Regulation on Ukraine & Art. 1(d) Regulation on Drilling; Art. 1(d) Regulation on Threatening Ukraine, Art. 1(e) Regulation on Iran Assisting Russia, Art. 1(d) Regulation on Moldova and Art. 1(3) Regulation on Belarus; Art. 1(d) Regulation on Human Rights Violation; Art. 1(8)(d) Regulation Against Cyber-Attacks; and Art. 1(e) Regulation Against Chemical Weapons.
2773. Article 1(u) Regulation on Russia.
2774. Article 1(h) Regulation on Goods from Crimea.
2775. Article 1(e) Regulation with Regard to Donetsk and Luhansk.
2776. Article 5(9) Regulation (EU) 952/2013.

Exit summary declaration

the act whereby a person informs the customs authorities, in the prescribed form and manner and within a specific time-limit, that goods are to be taken out of the customs territory of the Union.[2777]

Financial institution

(i) an undertaking, other than a credit institution, which carries out one or more of the [following] operations [...], including the activities of currency exchange offices (bureau de change) [lending including, inter alia: consumer credit, credit agreements relating to immovable property, factoring, with or without recourse, financing of commercial transactions (including forfeiting); financial leasing;[2778] payment services;[2779] issuing and administering other means of payment such as travelers' cheques and bankers' drafts; guarantees and commitments; trading for own account or for account of customers in any of the following: (a) money market instruments, such as cheques, bills, certificates of deposit, (b) foreign exchange, (c) financial futures and options, (d) exchange and interest-rate instruments, and (e) transferable securities; participation in securities issues and the provision of services relating to such issues; advice to undertakings on capital structure, industrial strategy and related questions and advice as well as services relating to mergers and the purchase of undertakings; money broking; portfolio management and advice; safekeeping and administration of securities; safe custody services; and issuing electronic money[2780]][2781]

(ii) an insurance undertaking in the sense of a direct life or non-life insurance undertaking which has received authorization under the EU provisions, insofar as it carries out life assurance activities covered by the Solvency II Directive;[2782]

2777. Article 5(10) Regulation (EU) 952/2013.
2778. Points 2 & 3 Annex I Directive 2013/36/EU of the European Parliament and of the Council of 26 Jun. 2013 on access to the activity of credit institutions and the prudential supervision of credit institutions, amending Directive 2002/87/EC and repealing Directives 2006/48/EC and 2006/49/EC, OJ L 176 27.6.2013, p. 338, as last amended by Directive (EU) 2021/338 of the European Parliament and of the Council of 16 Feb. 2021 amending Directive 2014/65/EU as regards information requirements, product governance and position limits, and Directives 2013/36/EU and (EU) 2019/878 as regards their application to investment firms, to help the recovery from the COVID-19 crisis, OJ L 68, 26 Feb. 2021, p. 14.
2779. Point 4 Annex I Directive 2013/36. With regard to the definition of *payment service see* this Annex p. 326.
2780. Points 5 to 15 Annex I Directive 2013/36.
2781. Article 1(g)(i) Regulation on Syria and Annex I points (2) to (12), (14) and (15) Directive 2013/36.
2782. Article 1(g)(ii) Regulation on Syria and Arts 13(1) and 14 Directive 2009/138/EC of the European Parliament and of the Council of 25 Nov. 2009 on the taking-up and pursuit of the business of Insurance and Reinsurance, OJ L 335, 17 Dec. 2009, p. 1, as last amended by Directive (EU) 2019/2177 of the European Parliament and of the Council of 18 Dec. 2019 amending Directive 2009/138/EC on the taking-up and pursuit of the business of Insurance and Reinsurance (Solvency II), Directive 2014/65/EU on markets in financial instruments and Directive (EU) 2015/849 on the prevention of the use of the financial system for the purposes of money-laundering or terrorist financing, OJ L 334, 27 Dec. 2019, p. 155. The Regulation on Syria makes explicit reference to Directive 2004/39, albeit this has been repealed by Directive 2009/138.

(iii) an investment firm;[2783,2784]
(iv) a collective investment undertaking marketing its units or shares;[2785]
(v) an insurance intermediary;[2786,2787]

including its branches, whether inside or outside the Union.[2788]

Financial instrument

[the] instruments specified [below], including such instruments issued by means of distributed ledger technology:

(1) Transferable securities;
(2) Money-market instruments;
(3) Units in collective investment undertakings;
(4) Options, futures, swaps, forward rate agreements and any other derivative contracts relating to securities, currencies, interest rates or yields, emission allowances or other derivatives instruments, financial indices or financial measures which may be settled physically or in cash;
(5) Options, futures, swaps, forwards and any other derivative contracts relating to commodities that must be settled in cash or may be settled in cash at the option of one of the parties other than by reason of default or other termination event;
(6) Options, futures, swaps, and any other derivative contract relating to commodities that can be physically settled provided that they are traded on a regulated market, a MTF, or an OTF, except for wholesale energy products traded on an OTF that must be physically settled;
(7) Options, futures, swaps, forwards and any other derivative contracts relating to commodities, that can be physically settled not otherwise mentioned in point 6 of this Section and not being for commercial purposes, which have the characteristics of other derivative financial instruments;
(8) Derivative instruments for the transfer of credit risk;
(9) Financial contracts for differences;
(10) Options, futures, swaps, forward rate agreements and any other derivative contracts relating to climatic variables, freight rates or inflation rates or other official economic statistics that must be settled in cash or may be settled in cash at the option of one of the parties other than by reason of default or other termination event, as well as any other derivative contracts relating to assets, rights, obligations, indices and measures not otherwise mentioned in this Section, which have the characteristics of other derivative financial instruments, having regard to whether, inter alia, they are traded on a regulated market, OTF, or an MTF;

2783. With regard to the definition of *investment firm see* this Annex p. 323.
2784. Article 1(g)(iii) Regulation on Syria. This provision refers to Directive 2002/83; albeit this has been repealed by Directive 2014/65.
2785. Article 1(g)(iv) Regulation on Syria.
2786. With regard to the definition of *insurance intermediary see* this Annex p. 321.
2787. Article 1(g)(v) Regulation on Syria. This provision further sets out 'with the exception of intermediaries referred to in Article 2(7) of [Directive 2002/92/EC], when they act in respect of life insurance and other investment related services'. However, Directive 2002/92 has been repealed by Directive 2016/97 and the repealed Art. 2(7) has not been replaced by any provision of the directive now in force. Therefore, it may be suggested that the exception set out in Art. 1(g)(v) Regulation on Syria has been repealed.
2788. Article 1(g) last sentence Regulation on Syria.

(11) Emission allowances consisting of any units recognised for compliance with the requirements of Directive 2003/87/EC (Emissions Trading Scheme).[2789]

Financial sector entity

any of the following: (a) an institution; (b) a financial institution; (c) an ancillary services undertaking included in the consolidated financial situation of an institution; (d) an insurance undertaking; (e) a third-country insurance undertaking; (f) a reinsurance undertaking; (g) a third-country reinsurance undertaking; (h) an insurance holding company as defined in point (f) of Article 212(1) of Directive 2009/138/EC;(k) an undertaking excluded from the scope of Directive 2009/138/EC in accordance with Article 4 of that Directive; (l) a third-country undertaking with a main business comparable to any of the entities referred to in points (a) to (k).[2790]

Financial services

any service of a financial nature, including all insurance and insurance-related services, and all banking and other financial services (excluding insurance) as follows:

Insurance and insurance-related services

(i) Direct insurance (including co-insurance): (A) life assurance; (B) non-life;
(ii) Reinsurance and retrocession;
(iii) Insurance intermediation, such as brokerage and agency;
(iv) Services auxiliary to insurance, such as consultancy, actuarial, risk assessment and claim settlement services.

Banking and other financial services (excluding insurance)

(v) Acceptance of deposits and other repayable funds;
(vi) Lending of all types, including consumer credit, mortgage credit, factoring and financing of commercial transaction;
(vii) Financial leasing;
(viii) All payment and money transmission services, including credit, charge and debit cards, travellers' cheques and bankers' drafts;
(ix) Guarantees and commitments;
(x) Trading for own account or for account of customers, whether on an exchange, in an over-the-counter market or otherwise, the following: (A) money market instruments (including cheques, bills, certificates of deposits); (B) foreign exchange; (C) derivative products including, but not limited to,

2789. Article 4(1)(15) and Annex I Section C Nos 1-11 Directive 2014/65.

2790. Article 4a Regulation on Russia and Art. 4(27) Regulation (EU) No. 575/2013 of the European Parliament and of the Council of 26 Jun. 2013 on prudential requirements for credit institutions and amending Regulation (EU) No. 648/2012, OJ L 176, 27 Jun. 2013, p. 1, as last amended by Regulation (EU) 2022/2036 of the European Parliament and of the Council of 19 Oct. 2022 amending Regulation (EU) No. 575/2013 and Directive 2014/59/EU as regards the prudential treatment of global systemically important institutions with a multiple-point-of-entry resolution strategy and methods for the indirect subscription of instruments eligible for meeting the minimum requirement for own funds and eligible liabilities, OJ L 275, 25 Oct. 2022, p. 1.

futures and options; (D) exchange rate and interest rate instruments, including products such as swaps and forward rate agreements; (E) transferable securities; (F) other negotiable instruments and financial assets, including bullion;

(xi) Participation in issues of all kinds of securities, including underwriting and placement as agent (whether publicly or privately) and provision of services related to such issues;

(xii) Money brokering;

(xiii) Asset management, such as cash or portfolio management, all forms of collective investment management, pension fund management, custodial, depository and trust services;

(xiv) Settlement and clearing services for financial assets, including securities, derivative products, and other negotiable instruments;

(xv) Provision and transfer of financial information, and financial data processing and related software by suppliers of other financial services;

(xvi) Advisory, intermediation and other auxiliary financial services on all the activities listed in subparagraphs (v) to (xv), including credit reference and analysis, investment and portfolio research and advice, advice on acquisitions and on corporate restructuring and strategy [2791]

Financing or financial assistance

any action, irrespective of the particular means chosen, whereby the person, entity or body concerned, conditionally or unconditionally, disburses or commits to disburse its own funds or economic resources, including but not limited to grants, loans, guarantees, suretyships, bonds, letters of credit, supplier credits, buyer credits, import or export advances and all types of insurance and reinsurance, including export credit insurance; payment as well as terms and conditions of payment of the agreed price for a good or a service, made in line with normal business practice, do not constitute financing or financial assistance.[2792]

Freezing of economic resources

preventing their use to obtain funds, goods or services in any way, including, but not limited to, by selling, hiring or mortgaging them.[2793]

2791. Article 1(3) Regulation on Terrorism.

2792. Article 1(o) Regulation on Russia and Art. 1(17) Regulation on Belarus.

2793. Article 1(5) Regulation on Iraq, Art. 1(f) Regulation on Sudan, Art. 1(e) Regulation on DRC, Art. 2(10) Regulation on DPRK, Art. 1(d) Regulation on Somalia, Art. 1(j) Regulation on Iran, Art. 1(d) Regulation on Guinea-Bissau, Art. 1(d) Regulation on Libya, Art. 1(f) Regulation on CAR, Art. 1(e) Regulation on Yemen, Art. 1(f) Regulation on South Sudan, Art. 1(e) Regulation on Mali, Art. 1(e) Regulation on Zimbabwe, Art. 1(d) EU Regulation on Iran, Art. 1(e) Regulation on Myanmar/Burma, Art. 1(e) EU Regulation on Lebanon, Art. 1(e) Regulation on Burundi, Art. 1(e) Regulation on Venezuela, Art. 1(e) Regulation on Nicaragua, Art. 1(g) Regulation on Guinea, Art. 1(h) Regulation on Syria, Art. 1(d) Regulation on Tunisia, Art. 1(e) Funds Regulation Ukraine & Art. 1(e) Regulation on Drilling; Art. 1(e) Regulation on Threatening Ukraine, Art. 1(g) Regulation on Iran Assisting Russia, Art. 1(e) Regulation on Moldova and Art. 1(4) Regulation on Belarus.

Freezing of funds

preventing any move, transfer, alteration, use of, access to, or dealing with funds in any way that would result in any change in their volume, amount, location, ownership, possession, character, destination or other change that would enable the funds to be used, including portfolio management.[2794]

Full Authority Digital Electronic Engine Controls

'an electronic control system for gas turbine or combined cycle engines utilising a digital computer to control the variables required to regulate engine thrust or shaft power output throughout the engine operating range from the beginning of fuel metering to fuel shutoff'.[2795]

Full Authority Digital Engine Control Systems

digital electronic control system for a gas turbine engine that is able to autonomously control the engine throughout its whole operating range from demanded engine start until demanded engine shut-down, in both normal and fault conditions.[2796]

Funds

financial assets and economic benefits of every kind, including but not limited to: (a) cash, cheques, claims on money, drafts, money orders and other payment instruments; (b) deposits with financial institutions or other entities, balances on accounts, debts and debt obligations; (c) publicly- and privately-traded securities and debt instruments, including stocks and shares, certificates representing securities, bonds, notes, warrants, debentures and derivatives contracts; (d) interest, dividends or other income on or value accruing from or generated by assets; (e) credit, right of set-off, guarantees, performance bonds or other financial commitments; (f) letters of credit, bills of lading, bills of sale; and (g) documents evidencing an interest in funds or financial resources.[2797]

2794. Article 1(4) Regulation on Iraq, Art. 1(g) Regulation on Sudan, Art. 1(f) Regulation on DRC, Art. 2(11) Regulation on DPRK, Art. 1(b) Regulation on Somalia, Art. 1(k) Regulation on Iran, Art. 1(b) Regulation on Guinea-Bissau, Art. 1(b) Regulation on Libya, Art. 1(g) Regulation on CAR, Art. 1(f) Regulation on Yemen, Art. 1(g) Regulation on South Sudan, Art. 1(f) Regulation on Mali, Art. 1(c) Regulation on Zimbabwe, Art. 1(b) EU Regulation on Iran, Art. 1(f) Regulation on Myanmar/Burma, Art. 1(f) EU Regulation on Lebanon, Art. 1(f) Regulation on Burundi, Art. 1(f) Regulation on Venezuela, Art. 1(f) Regulation on Nicaragua, Art. 1(e) Regulation on Guinea, Art. 1(i) Regulation on Syria, Art. 1(b) Regulation on Tunisia, Art. 1(f) Funds Regulation on Ukraine & Art. 1(f) Regulation on Drilling; Art. 1(f) Regulation on Threatening Ukraine, Art. 1(i) Regulation on Iran Assisting Russia, Art. 1(f) Regulation on Moldova and Art. 1(2) Regulation on Belarus.

2795. Definitions of Terms Used in this Annex, Annex I Dual Use Regulation.

2796. Definitions of Terms Used in These Lists of the WA-List p. 223.

2797. Article 1(h) Regulation on Sudan; Art. 1(g) Regulation on DRC; Art. 2(12) Regulation on DPRK; Art. 1(a) Regulation on Somalia; Art. 1(l) Regulation on Iran; Art. 1(a) Regulation on Guinea-Bissau; Art. 1(a) Regulation on Libya; Art. 1(a) Regulation on Libya; Art. 1(h) Regulation on CAR; Art. 1(g) Regulation on Yemen; Art. 1(h) Regulation on South Sudan; Art. 1(g) Regulation on Mali; Art. 1(g) Regulation on Haiti; Art. 1(g) Regulation on Threatening

In the public domain

technology or software which has been made available without restrictions upon its further dissemination; copyright restrictions do not remove technology or software from being in the public domain.[2798]

Information system

a device or group of interconnected or related devices, one or more of which, pursuant to a programme, automatically processes digital data, as well as digital data stored, processed, retrieved or transmitted by that device or group of devices for the purposes of its or their operation, use, protection and maintenance.[2799]

Information system interference

hindering or interrupting the functioning of an information system by inputting digital data, by transmitting, damaging, deleting, deteriorating, altering or suppressing such data, or by rendering such data inaccessible.[2800]

Insulation

is applied to the components of a rocket motor and includes cured or semi-cured compounded rubber sheet stock containing an insulating or refractory material. It may also be incorporated as stress relief boots or flaps.[2801]

Insurance intermediary

any natural or legal person, other than an insurance or reinsurance undertaking or their employees and other than an ancillary insurance intermediary, who, for remuneration, takes up or pursues the activity of insurance distribution.[2802]

Insurance undertaking

'a direct life or non-life insurance undertaking which has received authorisation in accordance with Article 14' and *reinsurance undertaking* means 'an undertaking

Ukraine, Art. 1(h) Regulation on Iran Assisting Russia, Art. 1(g) Regulation on Moldova and Art. 1(1) Regulation on Belarus; Art. 1(g) Regulation on Human Rights Violation; Art. 1(8)(g) Regulation Against Cyber-Attacks; and Art. 1(h) Regulation Against Chemical Weapons.

2798. Definitions of Terms Used in This Annex, Annex I Dual Use Regulation.
2799. Article 1(7)(a) Regulation Against Cyber-Attacks.
2800. Article 1(7)(b) Regulation Against Cyber-Attacks.
2801. Definitions of Terms Used in this Annex, Annex I Dual Use Regulation, which corresponds to the technical note of No. 3.A.3 of the MTCR Annex.
2802. Article 2(1)(3) Directive (EU) 2016/97 of the European Parliament and of the Council of 20 Jan. 2016 on insurance distribution, OJ L 026, 2 Feb. 2016, p. 19, as last amended by Commission Delegated Regulation (EU) 2019/1935 of 13 May 2019 amending Directive (EU) 2016/97 of the European Parliament and of the Council with regard to regulatory technical standards adapting the base euro amounts for professional indemnity insurance and for financial capacity of insurance and reinsurance intermediaries, OJ L 301, 22 Nov. 2019, p. 3.

which has received authorisation in accordance with Article 14 to pursue reinsurance activities'.[2803]

Interior lining

suited for the bond interface between the solid propellant and the case or insulating liner is usually a liquid polymer based dispersion of refractory or insulating materials, e.g. carbon filled hydroxyl terminated polybutadiene (HTPB) or other polymer with added curing agents sprayed or screeded over a case interior.[2804]

Intrusion software

software specially designed or modified to avoid detection by *monitoring tools*, or to defeat *protective countermeasures*, of a computer or network-capable device, and performing any of the following:

a. The extraction of data or information, from a computer or network-capable device, or the modification of system or user data; or
b. The modification of the standard execution path of a program or process in order to allow the execution of externally provided instructions.

Notes:

1. *Intrusion software* does not include any of the following:
   a. Hypervisors, debuggers or Software Reverse Engineering (SRE) tools;
   b. Digital Rights Management (DRM) *software*; or
   c. *Software* designed to be installed by manufacturers, administrators or users, for the purposes of asset tracking or recovery.
2. Network-capable devices include mobile devices and smart meters.

Technical Notes:

1. *Monitoring tools*: *software* or hardware devices, that monitor system behaviours or processes running on a device. This includes antivirus (AV) products, end point security products, Personal Security Products (PSP), Intrusion Detection Systems (IDS), Intrusion Prevention Systems (IPS) or firewalls.
2. *Protective countermeasures*: techniques designed to ensure the safe execution of code, such as Data Execution Prevention (DEP), Address Space Layout Randomisation (ASLR) or sandboxing.[2805]

2803. Article 5a(4a) Regulation on Russia and Art. 13(1) & (4) Directive 2009/138/EC of the European Parliament and of the Council of 25 Nov. 2009 on the taking-up and pursuit of the business of Insurance and Reinsurance (Solvency II), OJ L 335 17 Dec. 2009, p. 1, as last amended by Directive (EU) 2019/2177 of the European Parliament and of the Council of 18 Dec. 2019 amending Directive 2009/138/EC on the taking-up and pursuit of the business of Insurance and Reinsurance (Solvency II), Directive 2014/65/EU on markets in financial instruments and Directive (EU) 2015/849 on the prevention of the use of the financial system for the purposes of money-laundering or terrorist financing, OJ L 334, 27 Dec. 2019, p. 155.
2804. Definitions of Terms Used in this Annex, Annex I Dual Use Regulation, which corresponds to the technical note of No. 3.C.1 of the MTCR Annex.
2805. Definitions of Terms Used in this Annex, Annex I Dual Use Regulation.

Investment firm

means any legal person whose regular occupation or business is the provision of one or more investment services to third parties and/or the performance of one or more investment activities on a professional basis.

Member States may include in the definition of investment firms undertakings which are not legal persons, provided that:

(a) their legal status ensures a level of protection for third parties' interests equivalent to that afforded by legal persons; and
(b) they are subject to equivalent prudential supervision appropriate to their legal form.

However, where a natural person provides services involving the holding of third party funds or transferable securities, that person may be considered to be an investment firm for the purposes of this Directive and of Regulation (EU) No. 600/2014 only if, without prejudice to the other requirements imposed in this Directive, in Regulation (EU) No. 600/2014, and in Directive 2013/36/EU, that person complies with the following conditions:

(a) the ownership rights of third parties in instruments and funds must be safeguarded, especially in the event of the insolvency of the firm or of its proprietors, seizure, set-off or any other action by creditors of the firm or of its proprietors;
(b) the firm must be subject to rules designed to monitor the firm's solvency and that of its proprietors;
(c) the firm's annual accounts must be audited by one or more persons empowered, under national law, to audit accounts;
(d) where the firm has only one proprietor, that person must make provision for the protection of investors in the event of the firm's cessation of business following the proprietor's death or incapacity or any other such event.[2806]

Investment services (with regard to Somalia)

'(i) reception and transmission of orders in relation to one or more financial instruments;
(ii) execution of orders on behalf of clients;
(iii) dealing on own account;
(iv) portfolio management;
(v) investment advice;
(vi) underwriting of financial instruments and/or placing of financial instruments on a firm commitment basis;
(vii) placing of financial instruments without a firm commitment basis; or
(viii) operating of multilateral trading facilities,

provided that the activity relates to any of the [following] financial instruments'[2807] [: transferable securities; money-market instruments: units in collective investment undertakings; options, futures, swaps, forward rate agreements and other derivative contracts related to securities, commodities or climatic variables freight rates, inflation rates or other official economic statistics; derivative instruments for the transfer of credit risk; financial contracts for instruments; and

2806. Article 4(1)(1) Directive 2014/65.
2807. Article 1(g) Regulation on Somalia.

emission allowances consisting of any units under the Emissions Trading Scheme[2808]].

Investment services (with regard to Russia and Belarus)

the following services and activities: (i) reception and transmission of orders in relation to one or more financial instruments; (ii) execution of orders on behalf of clients; (iii) dealing on own account; (iv) portfolio management; (v) investment advice; (vi) underwriting of financial instruments and/or placing of financial instruments on a firm commitment basis; (vii) placing of financial instruments without a firm commitment basis; and (viii) any service in relation to the admission to trading on a regulated market or trading on a multilateral trading facility.[2809]

Iranian person, entity of body

(i) the State of Iran or any public authority thereof; (ii) any natural person in, or resident in, Iran; (iii) any legal person, entity or body having its registered office in Iran; (iv) any legal person, entity or body, inside or outside Iran, owned or controlled directly or indirectly by one or more of the above-mentioned persons or bodies.[2810]

Missile

complete rocket systems and unmanned aerial vehicle systems, capable of delivering at least 500 kg payload to a range of at least 300 km.[2811]

Missiles and missile launchers

(a) Guided or unguided rockets, ballistic or cruise missiles capable of delivering a warhead or weapon of destruction to a range of at least 25 kilometres, and means designed or modified specifically for launching such missiles or rockets, if not covered by categories I through VI. For the purpose of the Register, this sub-category includes remotely piloted vehicles with the characteristics for missiles as defined above but does not include ground-to-air missiles.
(b) Man-Portable Air-Defense Systems (MANPADS).[2812]

2808. Points 1 to 11 Annex I section C Directive 2014/65/EU. It is noted that the Regulation on Somalia refers to Directive 2004/39; nonetheless this has been repealed and replaced by Directive 2014/65/EU. On the *Emissions Trading Scheme see* Directive 2003/87/EC of the European Parliament and of the Council of 13 Oct. 2003 establishing a scheme for greenhouse gas emission allowance trading within the Community and amending Council Directive 96/61/EC, OJ L 275, 25 Oct. 2003, p. 32, as last amended by Directive (EU) 2023/959 of the European Parliament and of the Council of 10 May 2023 amending Directive 2003/87/EC establishing a system for greenhouse gas emission allowance trading within the Union and Decision (EU) 2015/1814 concerning the establishment and operation of a market stability reserve for the Union greenhouse gas emission trading system, OJ L 130, 16 May 2023, p. 134.
2809. Article 1(e) Regulation on Russia and Art. 1(9) Regulation on Belarus.
2810. Article 1(o) Regulation on Iran.
2811. Definitions of Terms Used in This Annex, Annex I, Dual Use Regulation.
2812. *See* A/58/274 para. 112.

Money remittance

a payment service where funds are received from a payer, without any payment accounts being created in the name of the payer or the payee, for the sole purpose of transferring a corresponding amount to a payee or to another payment service provider acting on behalf of the payee, and/or where such funds are received on behalf of and made available to the payee.[2813]

Multilateral trading facility

a multilateral system, operated by an investment firm or a market operator, which brings together multiple third-party buying and selling interests in financial instruments – in the system and in accordance with non-discretionary rules – in a way that results in a contract in accordance with Title II of this Directive.[2814]

Large-calibre artillery systems

guns, howitzers, artillery pieces, combining the characteristics of a gun or a howitzer, mortars or multiple-launch rocket systems, capable of engaging surface targets by delivering primarily indirect fire, with a calibre of 75 millimetres and above.[2815]

Lighter-than-air vehicles

balloons and airships that rely on hot air or other lighter-than-air gases such as helium or hydrogen for their lift.[2816]

Money-market instruments

those classes of instruments which are normally dealt in on the money market, such as treasury bills, certificates of deposit and commercial papers and excluding instruments of payment.[2817]

Multilateral trading facility

a multilateral system, operated by an investment firm or a market operator, which brings together multiple third-party buying and selling interests in financial instruments – in the system and in accordance with non-discretionary rules – in a way that results in a contract in accordance with Title II of this Directive.[2818]

2813. Article 2(23)(a)(iii) and Art. 4(22) Directive (EU) 2015/2366 of the European Parliament and of the Council of 25 Nov. 2015 on payment services in the internal market, amending Directives 2002/65/EC, 2009/110/EC and 2013/36/EU and Regulation (EU) No. 1093/2010, and repealing Directive 2007/64/EC, OJ L 337, 23 Dec. 2015, p. 35.
2814. Article 4(22) Directive 2014/65/EU.
2815. *See* A/58/274 para. 112.
2816. Definitions of Terms Used in This Annex, Annex I Dual Use Regulation that corresponds to Definitions of Terms Used in These Lists of the WA-List p. 226, Definition of Terms of the Control List of Dual-Use Biological Equipment and Related Technology and Software of the AG as of 16 Aug. 2020.
2817. Article 1(g) Regulation on Russia and Art. 1(11) Regulation on Belarus.
2818. Article 4(22) Directive 2014/65/EU.

Organized trading facility

a multilateral system which is not a regulated market or an MTF and in which multiple third-party buying and selling interests in bonds, structured finance products, emission allowances or derivatives are able to interact in the system in a way that results in a contract in accordance with Title II of this Directive.[2819]

Owning a legal person, group or entity

being in possession of 50 % or more of the proprietary rights of a legal person, group or entity, or having a majority interest therein.[2820]

Partner country

a country applying a set of export control measures substantially close to those set out in Regulation on Russia and as such the following have been identified as partner countries: US, Canada, UK, Norway, Japan, South Korea, Australia, New Zealand.[2821]

Payment service

any of the following business activities: (i) services enabling cash to be placed on a payment account as well as all the operations required for operating a payment account; (ii) services enabling cash withdrawals from a payment account as well as all the operations required for operating a payment account; (iii) Execution of payment transactions, including transfers of funds on a payment account with the user's payment service provider or with another payment service provider: execution of direct debits, including one-off direct debits; execution of payment transactions through a payment card or a similar device; and execution of credit transfers, including standing orders; (iv) Execution of payment transactions where the funds are covered by a credit line for a payment service user: execution of direct debits, including one-off direct debits; execution of payment transactions through a payment card or a similar device; and execution of credit transfers, including standing orders; (v) issuing of payment instruments and/ or acquiring of payment transactions; (vi) money remittance; (vii) payment initiation services; and (viii) account information services.[2822]

Personal watercraft

a watercraft intended for sports and leisure purposes of less than 4 m in hull length which uses a propulsion engine having a water jet pump as its primary source of propulsion and designed to be operated by a person or persons sitting, standing or kneeling on, rather than within the confines of, a hull.[2823]

2819. Article 4(23) Directive 2014/65/EU.
2820. Article 1(5) Regulation on Terrorism.
2821. Article 1(p) and Annex VIII Regulation on Russia.
2822. Article 4(3) and Annex I Directive (EU) 2015/2366 of the European Parliament and of the Council of 25 Nov. 2015 on payment services in the internal market, amending Directives 2002/65/EC, 2009/110/EC and 2013/36/EU and Regulation (EU) No. 1093/2010, and repealing Directive 2007/64/EC, OJ L 337, 23 Dec. 2015, p. 35.
2823. Article 3ea(3)(c) Regulation on Belarus & Art. 3(3) Directive (EU) 2013/35.

Persons, groups and entities involved in terrorist acts

- persons who commit, or attempt to commit, terrorist acts or who participate in, or facilitate, the commission of terrorist acts,
- groups and entities owned or controlled directly or indirectly by such persons; and persons, groups and entities acting on behalf of, or under the direction of, such persons, groups and entities, including funds derived or generated from property owned or controlled directly or indirectly by such persons and associated persons, groups and entities.[2824]

Production

all production phases, such as: construction, production engineering, manufacture, integration, assembly (mounting), inspection, testing, quality assurance.[2825]

Re-export declaration

the act whereby a person indicates, in the prescribed form and manner, a wish to take non-Union goods, with the exception of those under the free zone procedure or in temporary storage, out of the customs territory of the Union.[2826]

Recreational craft

any watercraft of any type, excluding personal watercraft, intended for sports and leisure purposes of hull length from 2,5 m to 24 m, regardless of the means of propulsion.[2827]

Regulated market

a multilateral system operated and/or managed by a market operator, which brings together or facilitates the bringing together of multiple third-party buying and selling interests in financial instruments – in the system and in accordance with its non-discretionary rules – in a way that results in a contract, in respect of the financial instruments admitted to trading under its rules and/or systems, and which is authorised and functions regularly and in accordance with Title III of this Directive.[2828]

Road transport undertaking

any natural or legal person, entity or body engaged with a commercial purpose in the transport of freight by means of motor vehicles or combinations of vehicles.[2829]

2824. Article 1(2) Common Position on Terrorism.
2825. Definitions of Terms Used in This Annex, Annex I Dual Use Regulation.
2826. Article 5(13) Regulation (EU) 952/2013.
2827. Article 3ea(3)(c) Regulation on Russia & Art. 3(2) Directive 2013/53/EU of the European Parliament and of the Council of 20 Nov. 2013 on recreational craft and personal watercraft and repealing Directive 94/25/EC, OJ L 354 28 Dec. 2013, p. 90.
2828. Article 4(21) Directive 2014/65/EU.
2829. Article 1(w) Regulation on Russia and Art. 1(25) Regulation on Belarus.

Sensitive documents

Sensitive documents are documents originating from the institutions or the agencies established by them, from Member States, third countries or International Organisations, classified as 'TRÈS SECRET/TOP SECRET', 'SECRET' or 'CONFIDENTIEL' in accordance with the rules of the institution concerned, which protect essential interests of the European Union or of one or more of its Member States in the areas covered by Article 4(1)(a) [*the public interest as regards public security, defence and military matters, international relations, the financial, monetary or economic policy of the Community or a Member State*], notably public security, defence and military matters.[2830]

Storage capacity

any combination of space, injectability and deliverability.[2831]

Storage facility

a facility used for the stocking of natural gas and owned and/or operated by a natural gas undertaking, including the part of LNG facilities used for storage but excluding the portion used for production operations, and excluding facilities reserved exclusively for transmission system operators in carrying out their functions.[2832]

Syrian credit or financial institution

(i) any credit or financial institution domiciled in Syria, including the Central Bank of Syria;
(ii) any branch or subsidiary, where it falls within the scope of Article 35, of a credit or financial institution domiciled in Syria;
(iii) any branch or subsidiary, where it does not fall within the scope of Article 35, of a credit or financial institution domiciled in Syria;
(iv) any credit or financial institution that is not domiciled in Syria but is controlled by one or more persons or entities domiciled in Syria.[2833]

Technical assistance

any technical support related to repairs, development, manufacture, assembly, testing, maintenance, or any other technical service, and may take forms such as

2830. Article 9(1) Regulation (EC) No. 1049/2001 of the European Parliament and of the Council of 30 May 2001 regarding public access to European Parliament, Council and Commission documents, OJ L 145, 31.5.2001, p. 43.
2831. Article 2(1)(28) Regulation (EC) No. 715/2009 of the European Parliament and of the Council of 13 Jul. 2009 on conditions for access to the natural gas transmission networks and repealing Regulation (EC) No. 1775/2005, OJ L 211, 14 Aug. 2009, p. 36.
2832. Article 2(9) Directive 2009/73/EC of the European Parliament and of the Council of 13 Jul. 2009 concerning common rules for the internal market in natural gas and repealing Directive 2003/55/EC, OJ L 211, 14 Aug. 2009, p. 94.
2833. Article 1(n) Regulation on Syria.

instruction, advice, training, transmission of working knowledge or skills or consulting services; including verbal forms of assistance.[2834]

Telecommunication or internet monitoring or interception services

services that provide, in particular using [the following] *equipment, technology* or *software*:

[- *equipment:*
  - Deep Packet Inspection equipment,
  - Network Interception equipment including Interception Management Equipment (IMS) and Data Retention Link Intelligence equipment,
  - Radio Frequency monitoring equipment,
  - Network and Satellite jamming equipment,
  - Remote Infection equipment,
  - Speaker recognition/processing equipment,
  - International Mobile Subscriber Identity, Mobile Subscriber Integrated Services Digital Network Number, International Mobile Equipment Identity, Temporary Mobile Subscriber Identity interception and monitoring equipment,
  - Systems, equipment, and components therefor, specially designed or modified for the generation, command and control, or delivery of *intrusion software,*[2835]
  - Equipment designed or modified to perform cryptanalysis,
  - Tactical Short Message System/Global System for Mobile Communications / Global Positioning System /General Package Radio Service /Universal Mobile Telecommunication System /Code Division Multiple Access /Public Switch Telephone Networks interception and monitoring equipment,
  - Dynamic Host Configuration Protocol /Simple Mail Transfer Protocol, GPRS Tunneling Protocol information interception and monitoring equipment,
  - Pattern Recognition and Pattern Profiling equipment,
  - Remote Forensics equipment,
  - Semantic Processing Engine equipment,
  - WEP and WPA code breaking equipment,
  - Interception equipment for VoIP proprietary and standard protocol [...];

2834. Article 1(j) Regulation on Sudan, Art. 1(h) Regulation on DRC, Art. 1(1) Regulation on Lebanon, Art. 1(21) Regulation on DPRK, Art. 1(f) Regulation on Somalia, Art. 1(r) Regulation on Iran, Art. 1(e) Regulation on Libya, Art. 1(j) Regulation on CAR, Art. 1(j) Regulation on Yemen, Art. 1(j) Regulation on South Sudan, Art. 1(i) Regulation on Haiti, Art. 1(a) Regulation on Zimbabwe, Art. 1(h) Regulation on Myanmar/Burma, Art. 1(h) Regulation on Venezuela, Art. 3(1)(a) Regulation on Nicaragua, Art. 1(p) Regulation on Syria & Art. 4(1)(a) Regulation on Tunisia. Article 1(e) Regulation on Afghanistan, Art. 1(r) Regulation on Iran, Art. 1(g) Regulation on Goods from Crimea, Art. 1(c) Regulation on Russia, Art. 1(h) Regulation with regard to Donetsk, Art. 1(j) Regulation on Iran Assisting Russia & Art. 1(6) Regulation on Belarus. The EU Regulation on Iran, the Regulation on Burundi, the Regulation on Nicaragua, the EU Regulation on Lebanon, the Regulation on Guinea, the Regulation on Tunisia, the Funds Regulation on Ukraine, the Regulation on Drilling, the EU Regulation on Al-Qaida, the Regulation Threatening Ukraine, the Regulation on Moldova the Regulation on Human Rights Violation, the Regulation Against Cyber-Attacks & the Regulation Against Chemical Weapons do not define the term *technical assistance.*

2835. With regard to the definition of *intrusion software see* this Annex p. 322.

- *software* for the development, production or use of the aforementioned equipment and software having the characteristics of, or performing or simulating, the functions of the [aforementioned] equipment;
- *technology* for the development, production or use of the aforementioned equipment]

[as well as services that provide] access to and delivery of a subject's incoming and outgoing telecommunications and call-associated data for the purpose of its extraction, decoding, recording, processing, analysis or storing, or any other related activity', as long as it does not qualify as a dual-use item, an item listed in the EU Common Military List or software available to the public without restriction.[2836]

Territory of the Union

the territories of the Member States to which the Treaty is applicable, under the conditions laid down in the Treaty, including their airspace.[2837]

Terrorist act

one of the following intentional acts, which, given its nature or its context, may seriously damage a country or an international organisation, as defined as an offence under national law, where committed with the aim of:

(i) seriously intimidating a population, or
(ii) unduly compelling a Government or an international organisation to perform or abstain from performing any act, or
(iii) seriously destabilising or destroying the fundamental political, constitutional, economic or social structures of a country or an international organisation:
  (a) attacks upon a person's life which may cause death;
  (b) attacks upon the physical integrity of a person;
  (c) kidnapping or hostage taking;
  (d) causing extensive destruction to a Government or public facility, a transport system, an infrastructure facility, including an information system, a fixed platform located on the continental shelf, a public place or private property, likely to endanger human life or result in major economic loss;
  (e) seizure of aircraft, ships or other means of public or goods transport;
  (f) manufacture, possession, acquisition, transport, supply or use of weapons, explosives or of nuclear, biological or chemical weapons, as well as research into, and development of, biological and chemical weapons;

2836. Article 1d(2) and Annex IV Regulation on Belarus.

2837. Article 1(k) Regulation on Sudan, Art. 11(j) Regulation on DRC, Art. 2(22) Regulation on DPRK, Art. 1(s) Regulation on Iran, Art. 1(g) Regulation on Libya, Art. 1(k) Regulation on the CAR, Art. 1(i) Regulation on Yemen, Art. 1(j) Regulation on South Sudan, Art. 1(i) Regulation on Mali, Art. 1(e) EU Regulation on Iran, Art. 1(m) Regulation on Myanmar/Burma, Art. 1(h) Regulation on Burundi, Art. 1(j) Regulation on Venezuela, Art. 1(h) Regulation on Nicaragua, Art. 1(q) Regulation on Syria, Art. 1(e) Regulation on Tunisia and Art. 1(h) Funds Regulation on Ukraine. The definition in the Regulations on Lebanon (Art. 1(2)), on Somalia (Art. 1(h)), on Guinea-Bissau (Art. 1(e)), on Guinea (Art. 1(h)) make no mention of airspace. The Regulations on Iraq and on Zimbabwe do not contain a definition.

(g) release of dangerous substances, or causing fires, explosions or floods the effect of which is to endanger human life;
(h) interfering with or disrupting the supply of water, power or any other fundamental natural resource, the effect of which is to endanger human life;
(i) threatening to commit any of the acts listed under (a) to (h);
(j) directing a terrorist group;
(k) participating in the activities of a terrorist group, including by supplying information or material resources, or by funding its activities in any way, with knowledge of the fact that such participation will contribute to the criminal activities of the group.[2838]

Toxic chemicals

Any chemical which through its chemical action on life processes can cause death, temporary incapacitation or permanent harm to humans or animals. This includes all such chemicals, regardless of their origin or of their method of production, and regardless of whether they are produced in facilities, in munitions or elsewhere. (For the purpose of implementing this Convention, toxic chemicals which have been identified for the application of verification measures are listed in Schedules contained in the Annex on Chemicals.).[2839]

Transfer of funds

'any transaction at least partially carried out by electronic means on behalf of a payer through a payment service provider, with a view to making funds available to a payee through a payment service provider, irrespective of whether the payer and the payee are the same person and irrespective of whether the payment service provider of the payer and that of the payee are one and the same, including a credit transfer,[2840] a credit debit,[2841] a money remittance[2842] whether national or cross border and a transfer carried out using a payment card, an electronic money instrument, or a mobile phone, or any other digital or IT prepaid or postpaid device with similar characteristics' including 'any transaction by non-electronic means, such as in cash, cheques or accountancy orders, with a view to making funds available to a payee irrespective of whether the payer and the payee are the same person'.[2843]

Transferable securities

the following classes of securities, including in the form of crypto-assets, which are negotiable on the capital market, with the exception of instruments of payment: (i)

2838. Council Common Position of 27 Dec. 2001 on the application of specific measures to combat terrorism (2001/931/CFSP) OJ L 344, 28 Dec. 2001, p. 93, as last amended by Council Decision (CFSP) 2023/1514 of 20 Jul. 2023 updating the list of persons, groups and entities subject to Arts 2, 3 and 4 of Common Position 2001/931/CFSP on the application of specific measures to combat terrorism, and repealing Decision (CFSP) 2023/422, OJ L 184, 21 Jul. 2023, p. 33.
2839. Article II(2) Chemical Weapons Convention.
2840. With regard to the definition of *credit transfer* see this Annex p. 311.
2841. With regard to the definition of *direct debit see* this Annex p. 314.
2842. With regard to the definition of *money remittance see* this Annex p. 325.
2843. Article 2(23)(a) & (b) Regulation on DPRK.

shares in companies and other securities equivalent to shares in companies, partnerships or other entities, and depositary receipts in respect of shares; (ii) bonds or other forms of securitized debt, including depositary receipts in respect of such securities; (iii) any other securities giving the right to acquire or sell any such transferable securities or giving rise to a cash settlement determined by reference to transferable securities.[2844]

Unmanned Aerial Vehicle (UAV)

any aircraft capable of initiating flight and sustaining controlled flight and navigation without any human presence on board.[2845]

Use

operation, installation (including on-site installation), maintenance (checking), repair, overhaul and refurbishing.[2846]

vessel crewed by the DPRK

(a) a vessel whose manning is controlled by: (i) a natural person of DPRK nationality; or (ii) a legal person, entity of body incorporated or constituted under the law of the DPRK; (b) a vessel entirely manned by DPRK nationals.[2847]

Warship

vessels or submarines armed and equipped for military use with a standard displacement of 500 metric tons or above, and those with a standard displacement of less than 500 metric tons, equipped for launching missiles with a range of at least 25 kilometres or torpedoes with similar rang.[2848]

2844. Article 1(f) Regulation on DPRK and Art. 1(10) Regulation on Belarus.
2845. Definitions of Terms Used in This Annex, Annex I Dual Use Regulation.
2846. *Ibid.*
2847. Article 2(24) Regulation on DPRK.
2848. *See* A/61/261 para. 124.

Annex II

Moscow's Aggression & Brussels' Packages

(Part I of III)

- Amendments on the Decision on Russia (Decision 2014/512/CFSP) & the Regulation on Russia (Regulation (EU) 833/2014) -

<table>
<tr><td rowspan="2">First package (23 Feb. 2022)</td><td>Council Decision (CFSP) 2022/264 of 23 February 2022 amending Decision 2014/512/CFSP concerning restrictive measures in view of Russia's actions destabilising the situation in Ukraine, OJ L 421, 23 Feb. 2022, p. 95.</td><td rowspan="2">Press release: https://www.consilium.europa.eu/en/press/press-releases/2022/02/23/russian-recognition-of-the-non-government-controlled-areas-of-the-donetsk-and-luhansk-oblasts-of-ukraine-as-independent-entities-eu-adopts-package-of-sanctions/</td></tr>
<tr><td>Council Regulation (EU) 2022/262 of 23 Feb. 2022 amending Regulation (EU) No 833/2014 concerning restrictive measures in view of Russia's actions destabilising the situation in Ukraine, OJ L 421, 23 Feb. 2022, p. 74.</td></tr>
<tr><td rowspan="2">Second package (25 Feb. 2022)</td><td>Council Decision (CFSP) 2022/327 of 25 Feb. 2022 amending Decision 2014/512/CFSP concerning restrictive measures in view of Russia's actions destabilising the situation in Ukraine, OJ L 48, 25 Feb. 2022, p. 1</td><td rowspan="2">Press release: https://www.consilium.europa.eu/en/press/press-releases/2022/02/25/russia-s-military-aggression-against-ukraine-eu-imposes-sanctions-against-president-putin-and-foreign-minister-lavrov-and-adopts-wide-ranging-individual-and-economic-sanctions/</td></tr>
<tr><td>Council Regulation (EU) 2022/328 of 25 Feb. 2022 amending Regulation (EU) No 833/2014 concerning restrictive measures in view of Russia's actions destabilising the situation in Ukraine, OJ L 49, 25 Feb. 2022, p. 1</td></tr>
</table>

<table>
<tr><td rowspan="2">Third package (28 Feb. 2022 & 2 Mar. 2022)</td><td>Council Decision (CFSP) 2022/356 of 2 Mar. 2022 amending Decision 2012/642/CFSP concerning restrictive measures in view of the situation in Belarus, OJ L 67, 2 Mar. 2022, p. 103</td><td rowspan="2">Press releases: https://www.consilium.europa.eu/en/press/press-releases/2022/03/02/eu-imposes-sanctions-on-state-owned-outlets-rt-russia-today-and-sputnik-s-broadcasting-in-the-eu/ https://www.consilium.europa.eu/en/press/press-releases/2022/03/02/russia-s-military-aggression-against-ukraine-eu-bans-certain-russian-banks-from-swift-system-and-introduces-further-restrictions/ https://www.consilium.europa.eu/en/press/press-releases/2022/02/28/eu-adopts-new-set-of-measures-to-respond-to-russia-s-military-aggression-against-ukraine/</td></tr>
<tr><td>Council Regulation (EU) 2022/355 of 2 Mar. 2022 amending Regulation (EC) No 765/2006 concerning restrictive measures in view of the situation in Belarus, OJ L 67, 2 Mar. 2022, p. 1.</td></tr>
<tr><td rowspan="2">Fourth package (15 Mar. 2022)</td><td>Council Decision (CFSP) 2022/430 of 15 Mar. 2022 amending Decision 2014/512/CFSP concerning restrictive measures in view of Russia's actions destabilising the situation in Ukraine, OJ L 87I, 15 Mar. 2022, p. 56</td><td rowspan="2">Press release: https://www.consilium.europa.eu/en/press/press-releases/2022/03/15/russia-s-military-aggression-against-ukraine-fourth-eu-package-of-sectoral-and-individual-measures/</td></tr>
<tr><td>Council Regulation (EU) 2022/428 of 15 Mar. 2022 amending Regulation (EU) No 833/2014 concerning restrictive measures in view of Russia's actions destabilising the situation in Ukraine, OJ L 87I, 15 Mar. 2022, p. 13</td></tr>
<tr><td rowspan="2">Fifth package (8 Apr. 2022)</td><td>Council Decision (CFSP) 2022/578 of 8 Apr. 2022 amending Decision 2014/512/CFSP concerning restrictive measures in view of Russia's actions destabilising the situation in Ukraine, OJ L 111, 8 Apr. 2022, p. 70.</td><td rowspan="2">Press release: https://www.consilium.europa.eu/en/press/press-releases/2022/04/08/eu-adopts-fifth-round-of-sanctions-against-russia-over-its-military-aggression-against-ukraine/</td></tr>
<tr><td>Council Regulation (EU) 2022/576 of 8 Apr. 2022 amending Regulation (EU) No 833/2014 concerning restrictive measures in view of Russia's actions destabilising the situation in Ukraine, OJ L 111, 8 Apr. 2022, p. 1.</td></tr>
</table>

Sixth package (3 Jun. 2022)	Council Decision (CFSP) 2022/884 of 3 Jun. 2022 amending Decision 2014/512/CFSP concerning restrictive measures in view of Russia's actions destabilising the situation in Ukraine, OJ L 153, 3Jun. 2022, p. 128.	Press release: https://www.consilium.europa.eu/en/press/press-releases/2022/06/03/russia-s-aggression-against-ukraine-eu-adopts-sixth-package-of-sanctions/
	Council Regulation (EU) 2022/879 of 3 Jun. 2022 amending Regulation (EU) No 833/2014 concerning restrictive measures in view of Russia's actions destabilising the situation in Ukraine, OJ L 153, 3 Jun. 2022, p. 53.	
Seventh package (21 Jul. 2022)	Council Decision (CFSP) 2022/1271 of 21 Jul. 2022 amending Regulation (EU) No 833/2014 concerning restrictive measures in view of Russia's actions destabilising the situation in Ukraine, OJ L 65, 21 Jul. 2022, p. 196.	Press release: https://www.consilium.europa.eu/en/press/press-releases/2022/07/21/russia-s-aggression-against-ukraine-eu-adopts-maintenance-and-alignment-package/
	Council Regulation (EU) 2022/1269 of 21 Jul. 2022 amending Regulation (EU) No 833/2014 concerning restrictive measures in view of Russia's actions destabilising the situation in Ukraine, OJ L 65, 21 Jul. 2022, p. 1.	
Eighth package (6 Oct. 2022)	Council Decision (CFSP) 2022/1909 of 6 Oct. 2022 amending Decision 2014/512/CFSP concerning restrictive measures in view of Russia's actions destabilising the situation in Ukraine, OJ L 259I, 6 Oct. 2022, p. 122.	Press release: https://www.consilium.europa.eu/en/press/press-releases/2022/10/06/eu-adopts-its-latest-package-of-sanctions-against-russia-over-the-illegal-annexation-of-ukraine-s-donetsk-luhansk-zaporizhzhia-and-kherson-regions/
	Council Regulation (EU) 2022/1904 of 6 Oct. 2022 amending Regulation (EU) No 833/2014 concerning restrictive measures in view of Russia's actions destabilising the situation in Ukraine, OJ L 259I, 6 Oct. 2022, p. 3.	
Ninth package (16 Dec. 2022)	Council Decision (CFSP) 2022/2478 of 16 Dec. 2022 amending Decision 2014/512/CFSP concerning restrictive measures in view of Russia's actions destabilising the situation in Ukraine, OJ L 322I, 16.12.2022, p. 614.	Press release: https://www.consilium.europa.eu/en/press/press-releases/2022/12/16/russia-s-war-of-aggression-against-ukraine-eu-adopts-9th-package-of-economic-and-individual-sanctions/
	Council Regulation (EU) 2022/2474 of 16 Dec. 2022 amending Regulation (EU) No 833/2014 concerning restrictive measures in view of Russia's actions destabilising the situation in Ukraine, OJ L 322I, 16 Dec. 2022, p. 1.	

<table>
<tr><td rowspan="2">Tenth package (25 Feb. 2023)</td><td>Council Decision (CFSP) 2023/434 of 25 Feb. 2023 amending Decision 2014/512/CFSP concerning restrictive measures in view of Russia's actions destabilising the situation in Ukraine, OJ L 59I, 25 Feb. 2023, p. 593.</td><td rowspan="2">Press release: https://www.consilium.europa.eu/en/press/press-releases/2023/02/25/one-year-of-russia-s-full-scale-invasion-and-war-of-aggression-against-ukraine-eu-adopts-its-10th-package-of-economic-and-individual-sanctions/</td></tr>
<tr><td>Council Regulation (EU) 2023/427 of 25 Feb. 2023 amending Regulation (EU) No 833/2014 concerning restrictive measures in view of Russia's actions destabilising the situation in Ukraine, OJ L 59I, 25 Feb. 2023, p. 6.</td></tr>
<tr><td rowspan="2">Eleventh package (23 Jun. 2023)</td><td>Council Decision (CFSP) 2023/1217 of 23 Jun. 2023 amending Decision 2014/512/CFSP concerning restrictive measures in view of Russia's actions destabilising the situation in Ukraine, OJ L 159I, 23 Jun. 2023, p. 451.</td><td rowspan="2">Press release: https://www.consilium.europa.eu/en/press/press-releases/2023/06/23/russia-s-war-of-aggression-against-ukraine-eu-adopts-11th-package-of-economic-and-individual-sanctions/</td></tr>
<tr><td>Council Regulation (EU) 2023/1214 of 23 Jun. 2023 amending Regulation (EU) No 833/2014 concerning restrictive measures in view of Russia's actions destabilising the situation in Ukraine, OJ L 159I, 23 Jun. 2023, p. 1.</td></tr>
<tr><td rowspan="2">Twelfth package (18 Dec. 2023)</td><td>Council Decision (CFSP) 2023/2871 of 18 Dec. 2023 amending Decision 2014/145/CFSP concerning restrictive measures in respect of actions undermining or threatening the territorial integrity, sovereignty and independence of Ukraine, digital OJ L, 18 Dec. 2023.</td><td rowspan="2">Press release: Council, 12th package of sanctions on Russia's war of aggression against Ukraine, available: https://www.consilium.europa.eu/en/press/press-releases/2023/12/18/12th-package-of-sanctions-on-russia-s-war-of-aggression-against-ukraine-additional-61-individuals-and-86-entities-included-in-the-eu-s-sanctions-list/</td></tr>
<tr><td>Council Regulation (EU) 2023/2878 of 18 Dec. 2023 amending Regulation (EU) No 833/2014 concerning restrictive measures in view of Russia's actions destabilising the situation in Ukraine,
digital OJ L, 18 Dec. 2023.</td></tr>
</table>

ANNEX III

Moscow's Aggression & Brussels' Packages

(Part II of III)

- Amendments on the Decision Threatening Ukraine (Decision 2014/145/CFSP) and the Regulation Threatening Ukraine (Regulation (EU) 269/2014) -

<table>
<tr><td rowspan="2">First package (23 Feb. 2022)</td><td>Council Decision (CFSP) 2022/264 of 23 February 2022 amending Decision 2014/512/CFSP concerning restrictive measures in view of Russia's actions destabilising the situation in Ukraine, OJ L 421, 23 Feb. 2022, p. 95.</td><td rowspan="2">Press release: https://www.consilium.europa.eu/en/press/press-releases/2022/02/23/russian-recognition-of-the-non-government-controlled-areas-of-the-donetsk-and-luhansk-oblasts-of-ukraine-as-independent-entities-eu-adopts-package-of-sanctions/</td></tr>
<tr><td>Council Regulation (EU) 2022/262 of 23 Feb. 2022 amending Regulation (EU) No 833/2014 concerning restrictive measures in view of Russia's actions destabilising the situation in Ukraine, OJ L 421, 23 Feb. 2022, p. 74.</td></tr>
</table>

Second package (25 Feb. 2022)	Council Decision (CFSP) 2022/327 of 25 Feb. 2022 amending Decision 2014/512/CFSP concerning restrictive measures in view of Russia's actions destabilising the situation in Ukraine, OJ L 48, 25 Feb. 2022, p. 1	Press release: https://www.consilium.europa.eu/en/press/press-releases/2022/02/25/russia-s-military-aggression-against-ukraine-eu-imposes-sanctions-against-president-putin-and-foreign-minister-lavrov-and-adopts-wide-ranging-individual-and-economic-sanctions/
	Council Regulation (EU) 2022/328 of 25 Feb. 2022 amending Regulation (EU) No 833/2014 concerning restrictive measures in view of Russia's actions destabilising the situation in Ukraine, OJ L 49, 25 Feb. 2022, p. 1	
Third package (28 Feb. 2022 & 2 Mar. 2022)	Council Decision (CFSP) 2022/356 of 2 Mar. 2022 amending Decision 2012/642/CFSP concerning restrictive measures in view of the situation in Belarus, OJ L 67, 2 Mar. 2022, p. 103	Press releases: https://www.consilium.europa.eu/en/press/press-releases/2022/03/02/eu-imposes-sanctions-on-state-owned-outlets-rt-russia-today-and-sputnik-s-broadcasting-in-the-eu/ https://www.consilium.europa.eu/en/press/press-releases/2022/03/02/russia-s-military-aggression-against-ukraine-eu-bans-certain-russian-banks-from-swift-system-and-introduces-further-restrictions/ https://www.consilium.europa.eu/en/press/press-releases/2022/02/28/eu-adopts-new-set-of-measures-to-respond-to-russia-s-military-aggression-against-ukraine/
	Council Regulation (EU) 2022/355 of 2 Mar. 2022 amending Regulation (EC) No 765/2006 concerning restrictive measures in view of the situation in Belarus, OJ L 67, 2 Mar. 2022, p. 1.	

<table>
<tr><td rowspan="2">Fourth package (15 Mar. 2022)</td><td>Council Decision (CFSP) 2022/430 of 15 Mar. 2022 amending Decision 2014/512/CFSP concerning restrictive measures in view of Russia's actions destabilising the situation in Ukraine, OJ L 87I, 15 Mar. 2022, p. 56</td><td rowspan="2">Press release: https://www.consilium.europa.eu/en/press/press-releases/2022/03/15/russia-s-military-aggression-against-ukraine-fourth-eu-package-of-sectoral-and-individual-measures/</td></tr>
<tr><td>Council Regulation (EU) 2022/428 of 15 Mar. 2022 amending Regulation (EU) No 833/2014 concerning restrictive measures in view of Russia's actions destabilising the situation in Ukraine, OJ L 87I, 15 Mar. 2022, p. 13</td></tr>
<tr><td rowspan="2">Fifth package (8 Apr. 2022)</td><td>Council Decision (CFSP) 2022/578 of 8 Apr. 2022 amending Decision 2014/512/CFSP concerning restrictive measures in view of Russia's actions destabilising the situation in Ukraine, OJ L 111, 8 Apr. 2022, p. 70.</td><td rowspan="2">Press release: https://www.consilium.europa.eu/en/press/press-releases/2022/04/08/eu-adopts-fifth-round-of-sanctions-against-russia-over-its-military-aggression-against-ukraine/</td></tr>
<tr><td>Council Regulation (EU) 2022/576 of 8 Apr. 2022 amending Regulation (EU) No 833/2014 concerning restrictive measures in view of Russia's actions destabilising the situation in Ukraine, OJ L 111, 8 Apr. 2022, p. 1.</td></tr>
</table>

<table>
<tr><td rowspan="2">Sixth package (3 Jun. 2022)</td><td>Council Decision (CFSP) 2022/884 of 3 Jun. 2022 amending Decision 2014/512/CFSP concerning restrictive measures in view of Russia's actions destabilising the situation in Ukraine, OJ L 153, 3Jun. 2022, p. 128.</td><td rowspan="2">Press release: https://www.consilium.europa.eu/en/press/press-releases/2022/06/03/russia-s-aggression-against-ukraine-eu-adopts-sixth-package-of-sanctions/</td></tr>
<tr><td>Council Regulation (EU) 2022/879 of 3 Jun. 2022 amending Regulation (EU) No 833/2014 concerning restrictive measures in view of Russia's actions destabilising the situation in Ukraine, OJ L 153, 3 Jun. 2022, p. 53.</td></tr>
<tr><td rowspan="2">Seventh package (21 Jul. 2022)</td><td>Council Decision (CFSP) 2022/1271 of 21 Jul. 2022 amending Regulation (EU) No 833/2014 concerning restrictive measures in view of Russia's actions destabilising the situation in Ukraine, OJ L 65, 21 Jul. 2022, p. 196.</td><td rowspan="2">Press release: https://www.consilium.europa.eu/en/press/press-releases/2022/07/21/russia-s-aggression-against-ukraine-eu-adopts-maintenance-and-alignment-package/</td></tr>
<tr><td>Council Regulation (EU) 2022/1269 of 21 July 2022 amending Regulation (EU) No 833/2014 concerning restrictive measures in view of Russia's actions destabilising the situation in Ukraine, OJ L 65, 21 Jul. 2022, p. 1.</td></tr>
</table>

Eighth package (6 Oct. 2022)	Council Decision (CFSP) 2022/1909 of 6 Oct. 2022 amending Decision 2014/512/CFSP concerning restrictive measures in view of Russia's actions destabilising the situation in Ukraine, OJ L 259I, 6 Oct. 2022, p. 122.	Press release: https://www.consilium.europa.eu/en/press/press-releases/2022/10/06/eu-adopts-its-latest-package-of-sanctions-against-russia-over-the-illegal-annexation-of-ukraine-s-donetsk-luhansk-zaporizhzhia-and-kherson-regions/
	Council Regulation (EU) 2022/1904 of 6 Oct. 2022 amending Regulation (EU) No 833/2014 concerning restrictive measures in view of Russia's actions destabilising the situation in Ukraine, OJ L 259I, 6 Oct. 2022, p. 3.	
Ninth package (16 Dec. 2022)	Council Decision (CFSP) 2022/2478 of 16 Dec. 2022 amending Decision 2014/512/CFSP concerning restrictive measures in view of Russia's actions destabilising the situation in Ukraine, OJ L 322I, 16.12.2022, p. 614.	Press release: https://www.consilium.europa.eu/en/press/press-releases/2022/12/16/russia-s-war-of-aggression-against-ukraine-eu-adopts-9th-package-of-economic-and-individual-sanctions/
	Council Regulation (EU) 2022/2474 of 16 Dec. 2022 amending Regulation (EU) No 833/2014 concerning restrictive measures in view of Russia's actions destabilising the situation in Ukraine, OJ L 322I, 16 Dec. 2022, p. 1.	

<table>
<tr><td rowspan="2">Tenth package (25 Feb. 2023)</td><td>Council Decision (CFSP) 2023/434 of 25 Feb. 2023 amending Decision 2014/512/CFSP concerning restrictive measures in view of Russia's actions destabilising the situation in Ukraine, OJ L 59I, 25 Feb. 2023, p. 593.</td><td rowspan="2">Press release: https://www.consilium.europa.eu/en/press/press-releases/2023/02/25/one-year-of-russia-s-full-scale-invasion-and-war-of-aggression-against-ukraine-eu-adopts-its-10th-package-of-economic-and-individual-sanctions/</td></tr>
<tr><td>Council Regulation (EU) 2023/427 of 25 Feb. 2023 amending Regulation (EU) No 833/2014 concerning restrictive measures in view of Russia's actions destabilising the situation in Ukraine, OJ L 59I, 25 Feb. 2023, p. 6.</td></tr>
<tr><td rowspan="2">Eleventh package (23 Jun. 2023)</td><td>Council Decision (CFSP) 2023/1217 of 23 Jun. 2023 amending Decision 2014/512/CFSP concerning restrictive measures in view of Russia's actions destabilising the situation in Ukraine, OJ L 159I, 23 Jun. 2023, p. 451.</td><td rowspan="2">Press release: https://www.consilium.europa.eu/en/press/press-releases/2023/06/23/russia-s-war-of-aggression-against-ukraine-eu-adopts-11th-package-of-economic-and-individual-sanctions/</td></tr>
<tr><td>Council Regulation (EU) 2023/1214 of 23 Jun. 2023 amending Regulation (EU) No 833/2014 concerning restrictive measures in view of Russia's actions destabilising the situation in Ukraine, OJ L 159I, 23 Jun. 2023, p. 1.</td></tr>
</table>

<table>
<tr>
<td rowspan="2">Twelfth package (18 Dec. 2023)</td>
<td>Council Decision (CFSP) 2023/2871 of 18 Dec. 2023 amending Decision 2014/145/CFSP concerning restrictive measures in respect of actions undermining or threatening the territorial integrity, sovereignty and independence of Ukraine, digital OJ L, 18 Dec. 2023.</td>
<td rowspan="2">Press release:
Council, 12th package of sanctions on Russia's war of aggression against Ukraine, available: https://www.consilium.europa.eu/en/press/press-releases/2023/12/18/12th-package-of-sanctions-on-russia-s-war-of-aggression-against-ukraine-additional-61-individuals-and-86-entities-included-in-the-eu-s-sanctions-list/</td>
</tr>
<tr>
<td>Council Regulation (EU) 2023/2878 of 18 Dec. 2023 amending Regulation (EU) No 833/2014 concerning restrictive measures in view of Russia's actions destabilising the situation in Ukraine, digital OJ L, 18 Dec. 2023.</td>
</tr>
</table>

Annex IV

Moscow's Aggression & Brussels' Packages

(Part III of III)

- Amendments on the Decision with regard to Donetsk & Luhansk (Decision (CFSP) 2022/266) and the Regulation with regard to Donetsk & Luhansk (Regulation (EU) 2022/263) in the time frame from 23 February 2022 until 23 December 2023 -

<table>
<tr><td rowspan="2">First package (23 Feb. 2022)</td><td>Council Decision (CFSP) 2022/266 of 23 of 23 Feb. 2022 concerning restrictive measures in response to the recognition of the non-government controlled areas of the Donetsk and Luhansk oblasts of Ukraine and the ordering of Russian armed forces into those areas, OJ L 42 I, 23 Feb. 2022, p. 109.</td><td rowspan="2">Press release: https://www.consilium.europa.eu/en/press/press-releases/2022/02/23/russian-recognition-of-the-non-government-controlled-areas-of-the-donetsk-and-luhansk-oblasts-of-ukraine-as-independent-entities-eu-adopts-package-of-sanctions/</td></tr>
<tr><td>Council Regulation (EU) 2022/263 of 23 Feb. 2022 amending Regulation (EU) No 269/2014 concerning restrictive measures in response to the recognition of the non-government controlled areas of the Donetsk and Luhansk oblasts of Ukraine and the ordering of Russian armed forces into those areas, OJ L 42 I, 23 Feb. 2022, p. 77.</td></tr>
</table>

Second package (25 Feb. 2022)	Council Decision (CFSP) 2022/327 of 25 Feb. 2022 amending Decision 2014/512/CFSP concerning restrictive measures in view of Russia's actions destabilising the situation in Ukraine, OJ L 48, 25 Feb. 2022, p. 1	Press release: https://www.consilium.europa.eu/en/press/press-releases/2022/02/25/russia-s-military-aggression-against-ukraine-eu-imposes-sanctions-against-president-putin-and-foreign-minister-lavrov-and-adopts-wide-ranging-individual-and-economic-sanctions/
	Council Regulation (EU) 2022/328 of 25 Feb. 2022 amending Regulation (EU) No 833/2014 concerning restrictive measures in view of Russia's actions destabilising the situation in Ukraine, OJ L 49, 25 Feb. 2022, p. 1	
Third package (28 Feb. 2022 & 2 Mar. 2022)	Council Decision (CFSP) 2022/356 of 2 Mar. 2022 amending Decision 2012/642/CFSP concerning restrictive measures in view of the situation in Belarus, OJ L 67, 2 Mar. 2022, p. 103	Press releases: https://www.consilium.europa.eu/en/press/press-releases/2022/03/02/eu-imposes-sanctions-on-state-owned-outlets-rt-russia-today-and-sputnik-s-broadcasting-in-the-eu/ https://www.consilium.europa.eu/en/press/press-releases/2022/03/02/russia-s-military-aggression-against-ukraine-eu-bans-certain-russian-banks-from-swift-system-and-introduces-further-restrictions/ https://www.consilium.europa.eu/en/press/press-releases/2022/02/28/eu-adopts-new-set-of-measures-to-respond-to-russia-s-military-aggression-against-ukraine/
	Council Regulation (EU) 2022/355 of 2 Mar. 2022 amending Regulation (EC) No 765/2006 concerning restrictive measures in view of the situation in Belarus, OJ L 67, 2 Mar. 2022, p. 1.	
Fourth package (15 Mar. 2022)	Council Decision (CFSP) 2022/430 of 15 Mar. 2022 amending Decision 2014/512/CFSP concerning restrictive measures in view of Russia's actions destabilising the situation in Ukraine, OJ L 87I, 15 Mar. 2022, p. 56	Press release: https://www.consilium.europa.eu/en/press/press-releases/2022/03/15/russia-s-military-aggression-against-ukraine-fourth-eu-package-of-sectoral-and-individual-measures/
	Council Regulation (EU) 2022/428 of 15 Mar. 2022 amending Regulation (EU) No 833/2014 concerning restrictive measures in view of Russia's actions destabilising the situation in Ukraine, OJ L 87I, 15 Mar. 2022, p. 13	

<table>
<tr><td rowspan="2">Fifth package (8 Apr. 2022)</td><td>Council Decision (CFSP) 2022/578 of 8 Apr. 2022 amending Decision 2014/512/CFSP concerning restrictive measures in view of Russia's actions destabilising the situation in Ukraine, OJ L 111, 8 Apr. 2022, p. 70.</td><td rowspan="2">Press release: https://www.consilium.europa.eu/en/press/press-releases/2022/04/08/eu-adopts-fifth-round-of-sanctions-against-russia-over-its-military-aggression-against-ukraine/</td></tr>
<tr><td>Council Regulation (EU) 2022/576 of 8 Apr. 2022 amending Regulation (EU) No 833/2014 concerning restrictive measures in view of Russia's actions destabilising the situation in Ukraine, OJ L 111, 8 Apr. 2022, p. 1.</td></tr>
<tr><td rowspan="2">Sixth package (3 Jun. 2022)</td><td>Council Decision (CFSP) 2022/884 of 3 Jun. 2022 amending Decision 2014/512/CFSP concerning restrictive measures in view of Russia's actions destabilising the situation in Ukraine, OJ L 153, 3Jun. 2022, p. 128.</td><td rowspan="2">Press release: https://www.consilium.europa.eu/en/press/press-releases/2022/06/03/russia-s-aggression-against-ukraine-eu-adopts-sixth-package-of-sanctions/</td></tr>
<tr><td>Council Regulation (EU) 2022/879 of 3 Jun. 2022 amending Regulation (EU) No 833/2014 concerning restrictive measures in view of Russia's actions destabilising the situation in Ukraine, OJ L 153, 3 Jun. 2022, p. 53.</td></tr>
<tr><td rowspan="2">Seventh package (21 Jul. 2022)</td><td>Council Decision (CFSP) 2022/1271 of 21 Jul. 2022 amending Regulation (EU) No 833/2014 concerning restrictive measures in view of Russia's actions destabilising the situation in Ukraine, OJ L 65, 21 Jul. 2022, p. 196.</td><td rowspan="2">Press release: https://www.consilium.europa.eu/en/press/press-releases/2022/07/21/russia-s-aggression-against-ukraine-eu-adopts-maintenance-and-alignment-package/</td></tr>
<tr><td>Council Regulation (EU) 2022/1269 of 21 Jul. 2022 amending Regulation (EU) No 833/2014 concerning restrictive measures in view of Russia's actions destabilising the situation in Ukraine, OJ L 65, 21 Jul. 2022, p. 1.</td></tr>
</table>

Eighth package (6 Oct. 2022)	Council Decision (CFSP) 2022/1909 of 6 Oct. 2022 amending Decision 2014/512/CFSP concerning restrictive measures in view of Russia's actions destabilising the situation in Ukraine, OJ L 259I, 6 Oct. 2022, p. 122.	Press release: https://www.consilium.europa.eu/en/press/press-releases/2022/10/06/eu-adopts-its-latest-package-of-sanctions-against-russia-over-the-illegal-annexation-of-ukraine-s-donetsk-luhansk-zaporizhzhia-and-kherson-regions/
	Council Regulation (EU) 2022/1904 of 6 Oct. 2022 amending Regulation (EU) No 833/2014 concerning restrictive measures in view of Russia's actions destabilising the situation in Ukraine, OJ L 259I, 6 Oct. 2022, p. 3.	
Ninth package (16 Dec. 2022)	Council Decision (CFSP) 2022/2478 of 16 Dec. 2022 amending Decision 2014/512/CFSP concerning restrictive measures in view of Russia's actions destabilising the situation in Ukraine, OJ L 322I, 16.12.2022, p. 614.	Press release: https://www.consilium.europa.eu/en/press/press-releases/2022/12/16/russia-s-war-of-aggression-against-ukraine-eu-adopts-9th-package-of-economic-and-individual-sanctions/
	Council Regulation (EU) 2022/2474 of 16 Dec. 2022 amending Regulation (EU) No 833/2014 concerning restrictive measures in view of Russia's actions destabilising the situation in Ukraine, OJ L 322I, 16 Dec. 2022, p. 1.	
Tenth package (25 Feb. 2023)	Council Decision (CFSP) 2023/434 of 25 Feb. 2023 amending Decision 2014/512/CFSP concerning restrictive measures in view of Russia's actions destabilising the situation in Ukraine, OJ L 59I, 25 Feb. 2023, p. 593.	Press release: https://www.consilium.europa.eu/en/press/press-releases/2023/02/25/one-year-of-russia-s-full-scale-invasion-and-war-of-aggression-against-ukraine-eu-adopts-its-10th-package-of-economic-and-individual-sanctions/
	Council Regulation (EU) 2023/427 of 25 Feb. 2023 amending Regulation (EU) No 833/2014 concerning restrictive measures in view of Russia's actions destabilising the situation in Ukraine, OJ L 59I, 25 Feb. 2023, p. 6.	

Eleventh package (23 Jun. 2023)	Council Decision (CFSP) 2023/1217 of 23 Jun. 2023 amending Decision 2014/512/CFSP concerning restrictive measures in view of Russia's actions destabilising the situation in Ukraine, OJ L 159I, 23 Jun. 2023, p. 451. Council Regulation (EU) 2023/1214 of 23 Jun. 2023 amending Regulation (EU) No 833/2014 concerning restrictive measures in view of Russia's actions destabilising the situation in Ukraine, OJ L 159I, 23 Jun. 2023, p. 1.	Press release: https://www.consilium.europa.eu/en/press/press-releases/2023/06/23/russia-s-war-of-aggression-against-ukraine-eu-adopts-11th-package-of-economic-and-individual-sanctions/
Twelfth package (18 Dec. 2023)	Council Decision (CFSP) 2023/2871 of 18 December 2023 amending Decision 2014/145/CFSP concerning restrictive measures in respect of actions undermining or threatening the territorial integrity, sovereignty and independence of Ukraine, digital OJ L, 18 Dec. 2023. Council Implementing Regulation (EU) 2023/2875 of 18 December 2023 implementing Regulation (EU) No 269/2014 concerning restrictive measures in respect of actions undermining or threatening the territorial integrity, sovereignty and independence of Ukraine, digital OJ L, 18 Dec. 2023.	Press release: https://ec.europa.eu/commission/presscorner/detail/en/ip_23_6566

Bibliography

Vladimyr Afanasiev, *EU Offers Kazakhstan 'Targeted' Exemptions for Oil Exports Through Russia*, 23 June 2023, Upstream, available: https://www.upstreamonline.com/production/eu-offers-kazakhstan-targeted-exemptions-for-oil-exports-through-russia/2-1-1473915 (last visited: 31 December 2023).

Vladimir Afanasiev, *Kazakhstan Upgrades Legacy Pipeline to Russia to Grow Oil Supplies to Germany*, 6 September 2023, Upstream, available: https://www.upstreamonline.com/production/kazakhstan-upgrades-legacy-pipeline-to-russia-to-grow-oil-supplies-to-germany/2-1-1511298 (last visited: 31 December 2023).

Yamiche Alcindor & Ali Rogin, *Who Assassinated the Haitian President, and Why? Here's What We Know So Far*, 7 July 2021, PBS, available: https://www.pbs.org/newshour/show/who-assassinated-the-haitian-president-and-why-heres-what-we-know-so-far (last visited: 31 December 2023).

Jillian Ambrose, *Shell May Get Nearly UKP1bn from Sale of Stake in Russian Gas Project*, 12 April 2023, The Guardian, available: https://www.theguardian.com/business/2023/apr/12/shell-sakhalin-2-gas-project-stake (last visited: 31 December 2023).

N. Bărbulescu, *20 Years of the Australia Group Coordination*, Romania, National Agency for Export Controls 2005, available: https://www.dfat.gov.au/publications/minisite/theaustraliagroupnet/site/en/20years.pdf(last visited: 31 December 2023).

Mehmet Bardakçı, *Turkey and the Major Powers in the Eastern Mediterranean Crisis from the 2010s to the 2020s* 70(3) Comparative Southeast European Studies 516 (2022).

Jason Bartlett & Megan Ophel, *Sanctions by the Numbers: Spotlight on Cyber Sanctions*, Center for a New American Security, 4 May 2021, available: https://www.cnas.org/publications/reports/sanctions-by-the-numbers-cyber (last visited: 31 December 2023).

Sibylle Bauer, Kolja Brockmann, Mark Bromley & Giovanna Maletta, *Internal Compliance and Export Control Guidance Documents for the Nuclear Sector*, Stockholm International Peace Research Institute, 2017.

Paul Belkin, Michael Ratner & Cory Wel, *Russia's Nord Stream 2 Natural Gas Pipeline to Germany Halted*, Congressional Research Service, 10 March 2022, available: https://crsreports.congress.gov/product/pdf/IF/IF11138 (last visited: 31 December 2023).

Katrin Bennhold, *Body Bags and Enemy Lists: How Far-Right Police Officers and Ex-Soldiers Planned for 'Day X'*, 1 August 2020, The New York Times (updated 26 May 2021), available: https://www.nytimes.com.

Tibor Besedeš, Stefan Goldbach & Volker Nitsch, *Financial Sanctions* Econ. Policy 263 (2017).

Thomas J. Biersteker, Marcos Tourinho & Sue E. Eckert (eds), Targeted Sanctions (Cambridge University Press 2016).

Andreas Boogaerts, *Beyond Norms: A Configurational Analysis of the EU's Arab Spring Sanctions* 14 Foreign Policy Analysis 408 (2018).

M. Bothe, Convention on the Prohibition of the Development, Production, Stockpiling and Use of Chemical Weapons and on their Destruction, in: *United Nations Audiovisual Library of International Law*, Geneva: United Nations 2011, available: https://legal.un.org/avl/ha/disarmament.html (last visited: 31 December 2023).

Kolta Brockmann, Mark Bromley & Lauriane Hau, *The Missile Technology Control Regime at a Crossroads*, Stockholm International Peace Research Institute, 2022.

Mark Bromley & Giovanna Maletta, *The Challenge of Software and Technology Transfers to Non-Proliferation Efforts*, Stockholm International Peace Research Institute, 2018.

Michael Brzoska, *International Sanctions Before and Beyond UN Sanctions* 91(6) Int'l Aff.(UK) 1339 (2015).

Paul D. Burns et al., *Trade Sanctions and Export Controls: A Multijurisdictional Analysis for the Energy Sector* 3(2) J.W.E.L. & B. 214 (2010).

Andrea Charron & Clara Portela, *The UN, Regional Sanctions and Africa* 91 (6) Int'l Aff. (UK) 1369 (2015).

Council of the European Union, *Association with Turkey: Establishment of the Position of the European Union for the 54th Meeting of the Association Council*, Brussels, 1 March 2019, p. 7, available: https://data.consilium.europa.eu/doc/document/ST-6965-2019-INIT/en/pdf (last visited: 31 December 2023).

Council of the European Union, *Council Conclusions on Turkey's Illegal Drilling Activities in the Eastern Mediterranean*, 13092/19, Brussels, 14 October 2019, available: https://data.consilium.europa.eu/doc/document/ST-13092-2019-INIT/en/pdf (last visited: 31 December 2023).

Council of the European Union, *Guidelines on Implementation and Evaluation of Restrictive Measures (Sanctions) in the Framework of the EU Common Foreign and Security Policy*, 15579/03, Brussels, 3 December 2003.

Council of the European Union, *Sanctions Guidelines*, 5664/18, Brussels, 4 May 2018.

Council of the European Union, *Turkish Drilling Activities in the Eastern Mediterranean – Council Conclusions*, 11257/19, Brussels, 15 July 2019, p. 2, available: https://data.consilium.europa.eu/doc/document/ST-11257-2019-INIT/en/pdf (last visited: 31 December 2023).

Daniel W. Drezner, *Sanctions Sometimes Smart: Targeted Sanctions in Theory and Practice* 13(1) Int. St. Rev. 96 (2011).

Thomas Dörfler, *Why Rules Matter: Shaping Security Council Sanctions Policy in Counterterrorism and Beyond* 8(1) J.Glob.Secur.Stud. 1 (2023).

Pierre-Emmanuel Dupont, *Countermeasures and Collective Security: The Case of the EU Sanctions Against Iran*,17(3) J.C.&S.L. 301 (2012).

Jonathan Eaton & Maxim Engers, *Sanctions* 100(5) J.Pol.Econ. 899 (1992).

Editors, *Still on the Trail: The Investigation into the Bangladesh Bank Heist Continues*, 23 March 2017, The Economist, available: https://www.economist.com/finance-and-economics/2017/03/23/the-investigation-into-the-bangladesh-bank-heist-continues? (last visited: 21 December 2023).

Editors, *Chronology of Events: DPRK (North Korea)*, Security Council Report, 2 September 2020, available: https://www.securitycouncilreport.org/chronology/dprk-north-korea.php (last visited: 31 December 2023).

Editors, *'Cup of Blood': Haiti Official Decries Impunity in Moise Killing*, Aljazeera, 6 July 2023, available: https://www.aljazeera.com/news/2023/7/6/cup-of-blood-haiti-official-decries-impunity-in-moise-killing (last visited: 31 December 2023).

Editors, *Early Soviet Reactors and EU Accession*, World Nuclear Association, June 2019, available: https://www.world-nuclear.org/information-library/safety-and-security/safety-of-plants/appendices/early-soviet-reactors-and-eu-accession.aspx (last visited: 31 December 2023).

Editors, *Fact Sheet: North Korea Missile Test Activity*, 14 November 2023 (updated 5 February 2024), Center for Arms Control and Non-Proliferation, available: https://armscontrolcenter.org/fact-sheet-north-korea-missile-test-activity/ (last visited: 31 December 2023).

Editors, *Japan's Mitsui says no plans to exit Russia's Sakhalin-2 LNG project*, Reuters 21 Jun. 2023, available: https://www.reuters.com/business/energy/japans-mitsui-says-no-plans-exit-russias-sakhalin-2-lng-project-2023-06-21/ (last visited: 31 December 2023).

Editors, *Missile Launches by North Korea, Ministry of Foreign Affairs of Japan*, available: https://www.mofa.go.jp/files/100469370.pdf (last visited: 31 December 2023).

Editors, *North Korea's Missile Activity in 2022*, IISS, December 2022, available: https://www.iiss.org/sv/publications/strategic-comments/2022/north-koreas-missile-activity-in-2022/ (last visited: 31 December 2023).

Editors, *November 2019 Monthly Forecast, Europe, Cyprus*, Security Council Report, 31 October 2019, available: https://www.securitycouncilreport.org/monthly-forecast/2019-11/cyprus-4.php (last visited: 31 December 2023).

Editors, *Russia to Take Full Control of Sakhalin-2 Oil and Gas Project*, 4 July2022, NS Energy, available: https://www.nsenergybusiness.com/news/russian-president-vladimir-putin-decree-sakhalin-2/ (last visited: 31 December 2023).

Editors, *Statement of the G7 and Australia on a Price Cap for Seaborne Russian-Origin Crude Oil*, Press release, Federal Foreign Office of Germany, 2 December 2022, available: https://www.auswaertiges-amt.de/en/newsroom/news/g7-australia-price-cap-seaborne-russian-origin-crude-oil/2567026 (last visited: 31 December 2023).

Editors, *The Chemical Weapons Convention* 30(3) Arms Control Today 37 (2000).
Editors, *The Nord Stream 2 Gas Pipeline is a Russian Trap – and Germany has Fallen Into It*, 16 February 2019, The Economist, available: https://www.economist.com/leaders/2019/02/16/the-nord-stream-2-gas-pipeline-is-a-russian-trap (last visited: 31 December 2023).
Editors, *The WannaCry Attack Reveals the Risks of a Computerised World*, 20 May 2017, The Economist, available: https://www.economist.com/leaders/2017/05/20/the-wannacry-attack-reveals-the-risks-of-a-computerised-world? (last visited: 21 December 2023).
Editors, *What Does the G7 Do?*, Council on Foreign Relations, 28 June 2023, available: https://www.cfr.org/backgrounder/what-does-g7-do (last visited: 31 December 2023).
Matthias Efing, Stefan Goldbach & Volker Nitsch, *Freeze! Financial Sanctions and Bank Responses* 36(11) The Review of Financial Studies 4417 (2023).
Brigit Embaló, *Civil-Military Relations and Political Order in Guinea-Bissau* 50(2) J. Mod. Afr. Stud. 253 (2012).
Joris van Esch et al. (eds), *Strategic Monitor 2014: Four Strategic Challenges* (Hague Centre for Strategic Studies 2014).
European Commission, *Commission Staff Working Document Accompanying the Document Report from the Commission to the European Parliament and the Council on the Assessment of the Risk of Money Laundering and Terrorist Financing Affecting the Internal Market and Relating to Cross-Border Activities*, SWD/2022/344 final, Brussels, 27 October 2022, available: https://eur-lex.europa.eu (last visited: 21 December 2023).
European Commission, *Commission Staff Working Document, Turkey 2018 Report*, SWD(2018) 153 final, Strasbourg, 17 April 2018, p. 60, available: https://data.consilium.europa.eu/doc/document/ST-8080-2018-INIT/en/pdf (last visited: 31 December 2023).
European Commission, *Commission Staff Working Document, Turkey 2019 Report*, SWD(2019) 220 final, Brussels, 29 May 2019, p. 7, available: https://data.consilium.europa.eu/doc/document/ST-9816-2019-INIT/en/pdf (last visited: 31 December 2023).
European Commission, *Cordis EU Research Results, Safety of Alternative Nuclear Fuel for VVER Reactors*, October 2022, available: https://cordis.europa.eu/programme/id/HORIZON_HORIZON-EURATOM-2022-NRT-01-01 (last visited: 31 December 2023).
European Council, *European Council Meeting (20 June 2019): Conclusions*, EUCO 9/19, Brussels, 20 June 2019, available: https://data.consilium.europa.eu/doc/document/ST-9-2019-INIT/en/pdf (last visited: 31 December 2023).
European Parliament, Situation in Nicaragua P8_TA(2019)0219 of 14 March 2019.
European Parliament, Situation in Nicaragua P9_TA(2022)0238 of 9 June 2022.
Martina Etzmuss et al., *Analysis of Nuclear Fuel Availability at EU Level from a Security of Supply Perspective, Report*, Euratom Supply Agency Advisory Committee – Working Group on Prices and Security of Supply (European Union, 2020).

Financial Times, *North Korea and the Triads: Gangsters, Ghost Ships and Spies*, FT Film, 31 March 2023, available: https://www.youtube.com/watch?v=o-6J5X9E-lE (last visited: 21 December 2023).

Dieter Fleck, *Developments of the Law of Arms Control as a Result of the Iraq-Kuwait Conflict* 13 EJIL 105 at 107-108 (2002).

Andreas de Guttry, Michaela Frulli, Federico Casolari & Ludovica Poli (eds), *International Law and Chemical, Biological, Radio-Nuclear (CBRN) Events* (Brill 2022).

David Hale, Global Magnitsky Human Rights Accountability Act Annual Report, 23 December 2020, Federal Register Vol. 86 No. 1 of 4 January 2021, p. 175.

P. Holtom, *Transparency in Transfers of Small Arms and Light Weapons*, Stockholm International Peace Research Institute, 2008.

Ron van der Horst, *Illegal, Unless: Freezing the Assets of Russia's Central Bank* (chad053) EJIL 1 (2023).

Ada Hui & Wolfie Zhao, *Over $280M Drained in KuCoin Crypto Exchange Hack*, 26 September 2020, CoinDesk, available: https://www.coindesk.com/markets/2020/09/26/over-280m-drained-in-kucoin-crypto-exchange-hack/ (last visited: 21 December 2023).

Kristine Karsten & Andrew Berkley (eds), Arbitration: Money Laundering, Corruption and Fraud (Paris: International Chamber of Commerce 2003)

Alexandra King-Pile, *2021 Global Magnitsky Human Rights Accountability Act Annual Report*, Federal Register Vol. 88 No. 60 of 29 March 2023, p. 18624.

Vladyslav Lanovoy, *The Use of Force by Non-State Actors and the Limits of Attribution of Conduct* 28 (2) EJIL 563 (2017).

Rafael Leal-Arcas, Juan Alemany Ríos & Costantino Grasso, *The European Union and its Energy Security Challenges* 8(4) J.W.E.L. & B. 291 (2015).

Jean Lee & Geoff White (hosts/reporters), Estelle Doyle (producer), *The Lazarus Heist, S1.1 Hacking Hollywood*, 19 April 2021 & *S1.2 The Disaster Movie*, 26 April 2021, BBC World Service, *Wherever You Get Your Podcasts.*

Jean Lee & Geoff White (hosts/reporters), Estelle Doyle (producer), *The Lazarus Heist, S1.4 Billion Dollar Hack*, 9 May 2021, BBC World Service, *Wherever You Get Your Podcasts.*

Jean Lee & Geoff White (hosts/reporters), Estelle Doyle (producer), *The Lazarus Heist, S1.5 Cyber Warriors,* 17 May 2021, BBC World Service, *Wherever You Get Your Podcasts.*

Jean Lee & Geoff White (hosts/reporters), Estelle Doyle (producer), *The Lazarus Heist, S1.9 The Macau Connection,* 14 June 2021, BBC World Service, *Wherever You Get Your Podcasts.*

Jean Lee & Geoff White (hosts/reporters), Estelle Doyle (producer), *The Lazarus Heist, S1.10 Kill Switch*, 20 June 2021, BBC World Service, *Wherever You Get Your Podcasts.*

Jean Lee & Geoff White (hosts/reporters), Estelle Doyle (producer), *The Lazarus Heist, S2.1 Jackpotting*, 27 March 2023, BBC World Service, *Wherever You Get Your Podcasts.*

Jean Lee & Geoff White (hosts/reporters), Estelle Doyle (producer), *The Lazarus Heist, S2.3 Hushpuppi*, 27 March 2023, BBC World Service, *Wherever You Get Your Podcasts*.

Jean Lee & Geoff White (hosts/reporters), Estelle Doyle (producer), *The Lazarus Heist, S2.8 Bitcoin Bandits*, 1 May 2023, BBC World Service, *Wherever You Get Your Podcasts*.

Jean Lee & Geoff White (hosts/reporters), Estelle Doyle (producer), *The Lazarus Heist, S2.9 Big Spenders*, 22 May 2023, BBC World Service, *Wherever You Get Your Podcasts*.

Magdalena Ličková, *European Exceptionalism in International Law* 19(3) EJIL 463 at 482 (2008).

Siegfried Magiera, *Governments* MPEPIL 2007.

Alexander Marrow et al., *Russia Allows USD1.2 Bln Sakhalin-2 Payment to Shell: Kommersant*, 4 April 2023, Reuters, available: https://www.reuters.com/markets/deals/russia-allows-12-bln-sakhalin-2-payment-shell-kommersant-2023-04-04/ (last visited: 31 Dec. 2023).

Ivan Martin, *How BOV Hackers Got Away with €13 Million: Phishing E-mails Did the Job ... and Bank Still Doesn't Know How Long Hackers Had Access*, 25 March 2019, The Times of Malta, available: https://timesofmalta.com/articles/view/how-bov-hackers-got-away-with-13-million.702800 (last visited: 21 December 2023).

Ivan Martin, *North Korean Hackers Charged in US with €13 Million Bank of Valletta Heist*, 20 February 2021, available: https://timesofmalta.com/articles/view/north-korean-hackers-charged-in-us-with-13million-bank-of-valletta.852902 (last visited: 21 December 2023).

Timothy V. McCarthy, McCarthy, The Missile Technology Control Regime, in: Michael Barletta & Amy Sands (eds), *Nonproliferation Regimes at Risk* (James Martin Center for Nonproliferation Studies (CNS), 1999).

Ministry of Foreign Affairs, Japan, *Gaiko-Seisho (Diplomatic Bluebook) 1991*, in English, available: https://www.mofa.go.jp/policy/other/bluebook/1991/1991-2-1.htm#Section%201.%20How%20the%20Gulf%20Crisis%20Began%20and%20Ended (last visited: 31 December 2023).

Ministry of Foreign Affairs of the Russian Federation, *Answer by the Russian Foreign Minister, Sergey Lavrov, to the Question about the Situation in Ukraine, During the Joint Press Conference Summarizing the Results of the Third Session of the Russia-CCASG Strategic Dialogue at Ministerial Level, Kuwait City, 19 February 2014*, 319-19-02-2014, available: https://www.mid.ru/en/maps/ua/1668301/ (last visited: 31 December 2023).

Ministry of Foreign Affairs of the Russian Federation, *Comment by the Information and Press Department of the Russian Ministry of Foreign Affairs Regarding the Situation in Ukraine*, 186-03-02-2014, of 3 February 2014, available: https://www.mid.ru/en/maps/ua/1631708/ (last visited: 31 December 2023).

Ministry of Foreign Affairs of the Russian Federation, *Comment by the Information and Press Department of the Russian Ministry of Foreign Affairs Regarding the Situation in Ukraine*, 307-18-02-2014, of 18 February 2014, available: https://www.mid.ru/en/maps/ua/1667508/ (last visited: 31 December 2023).

Ministry of Foreign Affairs of the Russian Federation, *Statement by the Russian Ministry of Foreign Affairs Regarding the Situation in Ukraine*, 313-19-02-2014, of 19 February 2014, available: https://www.mid.ru/en/maps/ua/1667987/ (last visited: 31 December 2023).

Mitsubishi Corporation, *Our Business > Natural Gas Group > Project cases > Sakhalin 2 Project*, 8 September 2023, available: https://www.mitsubishicorp.com/jp/en/bg/natural-gas-group/project/sakhalin-2/ (last visited: 31 December 2023).

Anton Moiseienko, *Legal: The Freezing of the Russian Central Bank's Assets* (chad050) EJIL 1 (2023).

Daragh Murray, *How International Humanitarian Law Treaties Bind Non-State Armed Groups* 20 (1) J.C. & S. L. 101 at 120 & 121 (2015).

Sean D. Murphy, *Democratic Legitimacy and the Recognition of States and Governments* 48(3) ICLQ 545 (1999).

Michelle Nichols, *UN Sanctions in Mali to End after Russia Blocks Renewal*, 30 August 2023, Reuters, available: https://www.reuters.com/world/russia-seeks-end-un s-mali-sanctions-monitoring-2023-08-30/ (last visited: 31 December 2023).

John O'Loughlin, Gearóid Ó Tuathail & Vladimir Kollov, *A 'Risky Westward Turn'? Putin's 9-11 Script and Ordinary Russians* 56(1) Eur.-Asia Stud. 3 (2004).

Joseph O'Mahoney, Denying the Spoils of War (Edinburgh University Press 2018).

Yuka Obayashi, Emily Chow & Ron Bousso, *Russia Seizes Control of Sakhalin Gas Project, Raises Stakes with West*, 1 July 2022, Reuters, available: https://www.reuters.com/business/energy/russia-decree-sakhalin-2-project-knocks-mitsui-mitsubishi-shares-2022-07-01/ (last visited: 31 December 2023).

Office of Foreign Assets Control, 31 CFR Part 578 *Cyber-Related Sanctions Regulations*, Federal Register Vol. 80 No. 251 of 31 December 2015, p. 81752.

Office of Foreign Assets Control, 31 CFR Part 578 Cyber-Related Sanctions Regulations, Federal Register Vol. 87 No. 171 of 6 September 2022, p. 54373.

Office of Foreign Assets Control, Notice of OFAC Actions, Federal Register Vol. 87 No. 75 of 19 April 2022, p. 23320.

Organization for Security and Co-operation in Europe, *OSCE Chair-in-Office Welcomes Ukraine Agreement*, 21 February 2014, Bern, available: https://www.osce.org/cio/115559 (last visited: 31 December 2023).

Drošības Policija & Latvijas Republika, *Annual Report about the Activities of the Security Police in 2013* (Riga, May 2014).

Clara Portela, *Where and Why does the EU Impose Sanctions?* 17(3) Politique Eur. 83 at 84 (2005).

Stanley Reed, *Putin Moves to Seize a Large Gas Venture in Russia's Far East*, 1 July 2022, The New York Times, available: https://www.nytimes.com/2022/07/01/business/putin-sakhalin-natural-gas.html (last visited: 31 December 2023).

Dianne E. Rennack & Cory Welt, *Russia, the Skripal Poisoning, and U.S. Sanctions*, Congressional Research Service, 28 October 2020, pp. 1 et seq., available: https://crsreports.congress.gov/product/pdf/IF/IF10962 (last visited: 21 December 2023).

Republic of Türkiye, Ministry of Foreign Affairs, No: 199, *Press Release Regarding the Activities of Our Drilling Ship Yavuz*, 10 July 2019, available: https://www.mfa.

gov.tr/no_199_-yavuz-sondaj-gemimizin-faaliyetleri-hk.en.mfa (last visited: 31 December 2023).

Republic of Türkiye, Ministry of Foreign Affairs, No: 321, *Press Release Regarding the Escalatory Activities of Greece and the Greek Cypriot Administration in the Eastern Mediterranean*, 2 October 2021, available: https://www.mfa.gov.tr/no_-321_-yunanistan-ve-gkry-nin-dogu-akdeniz-de-gerginligi-arttiran-faaliyetleri-hk.en.mfa (last visited: 31 December 2023).

Elizabeth Rosenberg & Eric Van Nostrand, *The Price Cap on Russian Oil: A Progress Report*, U.S. Department of the Treasury, 18 May 2023, available: https://home.treasury.gov/news/featured-stories/the-price-cap-on-russian-oil-a-progress-report (last visited: 31 December 2023).

Tom Ruys & Cedric Ryngaert, *Secondary Sanctions: A Weapon Out of Control? The International Legality of, and European Responses to, US Secondary Sanctions* (braa007) BYIL 1 (2020).

Julia Schmidt, *The Legality of Unilateral Extra-territorial Sanctions under International Law* 27(1) J.C.&S.L. 53 (2022).

Joanne Scott, *Extraterritoriality and Territorial Extension in EU Law* 62(1) Am.J. Comp.L. 87 at 94 (2014).

Andrew Self, *2022 Global Magnitsky Human Rights Accountability Act Annual Report*, Federal Register Vol. 88 No. 62 of 31 March 2023, p. 19344.

Issaka K. Souaré, *The African Union as a Norm Entrepreneur on Military Coups D'état in Africa (1952-2012): An Empirical Assessment* 52 (1) J. Mod. Afr. Stud. 69 (2014).

Leonard S. Spector, *The Missile Technology Control Regime and Shifting Proliferation Challenges* 48(3) Arms Controls Today 14 (2018).

Terence Taylor, *The Chemical Weapons Convention and Prospects for Implementation* 42(4) ICLQ 912 (1993).

Teabeamet Estonian Information Board, *International Security and Estonia*, 2016, available: https://raport.valisluureamet.ee/2023/en/previous-reports/.

Andrea Teftedaria et al., *Non-State Actors and Individuals*, in: Jan Rood & Rosa Dinnissen (eds), An Uncertain World: Clingendael Strategic Monitor (2013).

The New York Times, *How a Mysterious Ship Helps North Korea Evade Oil Sanctions*, Visual Investigations, 22 March 2021, available: https://www.youtube.com/watch?v=hDTCHdcPYTQ (last visited: 21 December 2023).

UN, *UN Condemns 'Abhorrent' Assassination of Haiti President Jovenel Moïse*, 7 July 2021, UN News, available: https://news.un.org/en/story/2021/07/1095422 (last visited: 31 December 2023).

UN Secretary-General, *Statement Attributable to the Spokesperson for the Secretary-General on Ukraine*, New York, 21 February 2014, available: https://www.un.org/sg/en/content/sg/statement/2014-02-21/statement-attributable-spokesperson-secretary-general-ukraine (last visited: 31 December 2023).

Jakob Hanke Vela, *Brussels Playbook from Politico: Road to 2024*, 4 September 2023, available: https://www.politico.eu/newsletter/brussels-playbook/ (last visited: 31 December 2023).

Markus Wagner, *Non-State Actors* MPEIL (2013).

Michael A. Weber & Edward J. Collins-Chase, *The Global Magnitsky Human Rights Accountability Act*, Congressional Research Service, 28 October 2020, p. 1, available: https://crsreports.congress.gov/product/pdf/IF/IF10576 (last visited: 31 December 2023).

Rüdiger Wolfrum & Anne Peters (eds), Max Planck Encyclopedias of International Law (OUP 2013).

Table of Cases

Table of Treaties, Legislation and Texts

International Treaties and Texts

Legislation of the European Union

restrictive measures in order to insert provisions on humanitarian exceptions, digital OJ, 28 November 2023, 34.

Council Decision 2011/101/CFSP of 15 February 2011 concerning restrictive measures against Zimbabwe, OJ L 42, 16 February 2011, p. 6, as last amended by Council Decision (CFSP) 2023/2686 of 27 November 2023 amending certain Council Decisions concerning restrictive measures in order to insert provisions on humanitarian exceptions, digital OJ, 28 November 2023, 27.

Council Decision 2011/235/CFSP of 12 April 2011 concerning restrictive measures directed against certain persons and entities in view of the situation in Iran, OJ L 100, 14 April 2011, p. 51, as last amended by Council Implementing Decision (CFSP) 2023/1780 of 15 September 2023 implementing Decision 2011/235/CFSP concerning restrictive measures directed against certain persons and entities in view of the situation in Iran, OJ L 228I, 15 September 2023, p. 6, 28

Council Decision 2011/486/CFSP of 1 August 2011 concerning restrictive measures directed against certain individuals, groups, undertakings and entities in view of the situation in Afghanistan, OJ L 199, 2 August 2011, p. 57, as last amended by Council Decision (CFSP) 2022/153 of 3 February 2022 amending Decision 2011/486/CFSP concerning restrictive measures directed against certain individuals, groups, undertakings and entities in view of the situation in Afghanistan, OJ L 25, 4 February 2022, p. 17, 190

Council Decision 2012/35/CFSP of 23 January 2012 amending Decision 2010/413/CFSP concerning restrictive measures against Iran, OJ L 19, 24 January 2012, p. 22, 20

Council Decision 2012/285/CFSP of 31 May 2012 concerning restrictive measures directed against certain persons, entities and bodies threatening the peace, security or stability of the Republic of Guinea-Bissau and repealing Decision 2012/237/CFSP, OJ L 142, 1 June 2012, p. 36, as last amended by Council Decision (CFSP) 2023/1598 of 3 August 2023 amending Decision 2012/285/CFSP concerning restrictive measures in view of the situation in Guinea-Bissau, OJ L 196, 4 August 2023, p. 23, 21, 81

Council Decision 2013/184/CFSP of 22 April 2013 concerning restrictive measures against Myanmar/Burma and repealing Decision 2010/232/CFSP, OJ L 111, 23 April 2013, p. 75, as last amended by Council Decision (CFSP) 2023/2788 of 11 December 2023 amending Decision 2013/184/CFSP concerning restrictive measures in view of the situation in Myanmar/Burma, digital OJ L, 11 December 2023, 29.

Council Decision 2013/255/CFSP of 31 May 2013 concerning restrictive measures against Syria, OJ L 147, 1 June 2013, p. 14, as last amended by Council Decision (CFSP) 2023/2876 of 18 December 2023 amending Decision 2013/255/CFSP concerning restrictive measures in view of the situation in Syria, digital OJ L, 18 Dec. 2023, 33.

Council Decision 2013/798/CFSP of 23 December 2013 concerning restrictive measures against the Central African Republic, OJ L 352, 24 December 2013, p. 51, as last amended by Council Decision (CFSP) 2023/2487 of 9 November 2023 amending certain Council decisions and common positions concerning restrictive

2023 amending Decision (CFSP) 2019/797 concerning restrictive measures against cyber-attacks threatening the Union or its Member States, OJ L 129, 16 May 2023, p. 16, 282

Council Decision (CFSP) 2019/1720 of 14 October 2019 concerning restrictive measures in view of the situation in Nicaragua, OJ L 262, 15 October 2019, p. 58, as last amended by Council Decision (CFSP) 2023/2686 of 27 November 2023 amending certain Council Decisions concerning restrictive measures in order to insert provisions on humanitarian exceptions, digital OJ L, 28 November 2023, 31..

Council Decision (CFSP) 2019/1894 of 11 November 2019 concerning restrictive measures in view of Turkey's unauthorised drilling activities in the Eastern Mediterranean, OJ L 291, 12 November 2019, p. 47, as last amended by Council Decision (CFSP) 2023/2488 of 9 Nov. 2023 amending Decision (CFSP) 2019/1894 concerning restrictive measures in view of Turkey's unauthorised drilling activities in the Eastern Mediterranean, digital OJ L, 10 November 2023, 35.

Council Decision (CFSP) 2020/1999 of 7 December 2020 concerning restrictive measures against serious human rights violations and abuses, OJ L 410I, 7 December 2020, p. 13, as last amended by Council Decision (CFSP) 2023/1716 of 8 September 2023 amending Decision (CFSP) 2020/1999 concerning restrictive measures against serious human rights violations and abuses, OJ L 221I, 8 September 2023, p. 6, 281

Council Decision (CFSP) 2021/1277 of 30 July 2021 concerning restrictive measures in view of the situation in Lebanon, OJ L 277I, 2 August 2021, p. 16, as last amended by Council Decision (CFSP) 2023/2686 of 27 Nov. 2023 amending certain Council Decisions concerning restrictive measures in order to insert provisions on humanitarian exceptions, digital OJ L, 28 Nov. 2023, 32.

Council Decision (CFSP) 2022/266 of 23 February 2022 concerning restrictive measures in response to the recognition of the non-government controlled areas of the Donetsk and Luhansk oblasts of Ukraine and the ordering of Russian armed forces into those areas, OJ L 42I, 23 February 2022, p. 109, as last amended by Council Decision (CFSP) 2023/388 of 20 February 2023 amending Decision (CFSP) 2022/266 concerning restrictive measures in response to the illegal recognition, occupation or annexation by the Russian Federation of certain non-government controlled areas of Ukraine, OJ L 53, 21 February 2023, p. 37, 209

Council Decision (CFSP) 2022/2319 of 25 November 2022 concerning restrictive measures in view of the situation in Haiti, OJ L 307, 28 November 2022, p. 135, as last amended by Council Decision (CFSP) 2023/2575 of 13 Nov. 2023 amending Decision (CFSP) 2022/2319 concerning restrictive measures in view of the situation in Haiti, digital OJ L, 14 November, 26 2023.

Council Decision (CFSP) 2022/2432 of 12 December 2022 amending Decision 2014/145/CFSP concerning restrictive measures in respect of actions undermining or threatening the territorial integrity, sovereignty and independence of Ukraine, OJ L 318I, 12 December 2022, p. 32 and Council Implementing Regulation (EU) 2022/2430 of 12 December 2022 implementing Regulation (EU) No.

April 2021 establishing the Union Anti-Fraud Programme and repealing Regulation (EU) No. 250/2014, OJ L 172, 17 May 2021, p. 110, 115

Council Regulation (EC) No. 2580/2001 of 27 December 2001 on specific restrictive measures directed against certain persons and entities with a view to combating terrorism, OJ L 344, 28 December 2001, p. 70, as last amended by Commission Implementing Regulation (EU) 2022/595 of 11 April 2022 amending certain Regulations concerning restrictive measures and setting out a single list for the Annexes to those Regulations containing the contact details of Member States' competent authorities and the address for notifications to the European Commission, OJ L 114, 12 April 2022, p. 60, 169

Council Regulation (EC) No. 2368/2002 of 20 December 2002 implementing the Kimberley Process certification scheme for the international trade in rough diamonds, OJ L 358, 31 December 2002, p. 28, as last amended by Commission Implementing Regulation (EU) 2022/1359 of 27 July 2022 amending Council Regulation (EC) No. 2368/2002 implementing the Kimberley Process certification scheme for the international trade in rough diamonds, OJ L 205, 5 August 2022, p. 99, 242

Council Regulation (EC) No. 2368/2002 of 20 December 2002 implementing the Kimberley Process certification scheme for the international trade in rough diamonds, OJ L 358, 31 December 2002, p. 28, as last amended by Commission Implementing Regulation (EU) 2022/1359 of 27 July 2022 amending Council Regulation (EC) No. 2368/2002 implementing the Kimberley Process certification scheme for the international trade in rough diamonds, OJ L 205, 5 August 2022, p. 99, 242

Council Regulation (EC) No. 1210/2003 of 7 July 2003 concerning certain specific restrictions on economic and financial relations with Iraq and repealing Regulation (EC) No. 2465/96, OJ L 169, 8 July 2003, p. 6, as last amended by Commission Implementing Regulation (EU) 2023/2185 of 11 October 2023 amending Council Regulation (EC) No. 1210/2003 concerning certain specific restrictions on economic and financial relations with Iraq, digital OJ L, 12 October 2023, 13.

Council Regulation (EC) No. 314/2004 of 19 February 2004 concerning certain restrictive measures in respect of Zimbabwe, OJ L 55, 24 February 2004, p. 1, as last amended by Council Regulation (EU) 2023/2694 of 27 November 2023 amending certain Council Regulations concerning restrictive measures in order to insert provisions on humanitarian exceptions, digital OJ L, 28 November 2023, 27-28.

Council Regulation (EC) No. 1183/2005 of 18 July 2005 imposing certain specific restrictive measures directed against persons acting in violation of the arms embargo with regard to the Democratic Republic of the Congo, OJ L 193, 23 July 2005, p. 1, as last amended by Council Regulation (EU) 2023/1565 of 28 July 2023 amending Regulation (EC) No. 1183/2005 concerning restrictive measures in view of the situation in the Democratic Republic of the Congo, OJ L 190I, 28 July 2023, 14

Council Regulation (EC) No. 305/2006 of 21 February 2006 imposing specific restrictive measures against certain persons suspected of involvement in the assassination of former Lebanese Prime Minister Rafiq Hariri, OJ L 51, 22 February 2006, p. 1, as last amended by Council Regulation (EU) 2023/331 of 14 February 2023 amending certain Council regulations concerning restrictive measures in order to insert provisions on a humanitarian exemption, OJ L 47, 15 February 2023, p. 1, 191

Council Regulation (EC) No. 765/2006 of 18 May 2006 concerning restrictive measures against President Lukashenko and certain officials of Belarus, OJ L 134, 20 May 2006, p. 1, as last amended by Council Implementing Regulation (EU) 2023/419 of 24 February 2023 implementing Article 8a of Regulation (EC) No. 765/2006 concerning restrictive measures in view of the situation in Belarus and the involvement of Belarus in the Russian aggression against Ukraine, OJ L 61, 27 February 2023, p. 20, 211

Council Regulation (EC) No. 1412/2006 of 25 September 2006 concerning certain restrictive measures in respect of Lebanon, OJ L 267, 27 September 2006, p. 2, as last amended by Commission Implementing Regulation (EU) 2022/595 of 11 April 2022 amending certain Regulations concerning restrictive measures and setting out a single list for the Annexes to those Regulations containing the contact details of Member States' competent authorities and the address for notifications to the European Commission, OJ L 114, 12 April 2022, p. 60, 16

Council Regulation (EC) No. 423/2007 of 19 April 2007 concerning restrictive measures against Iran, OJ L 103, 20 April 2007, p. 1, later repealed by Council Regulation (EU) No. 267/2012 of 23 March 2012 concerning restrictive measures against Iran and repealing Regulation (EU) No. 961/2010, OJ L 88, 24 March 2012, p. 1, 19

Council Regulation (EU) No. 1284/2009 of 22 December 2009 imposing certain specific restrictive measures in respect of the Republic of Guinea, OJ L 346, 23 December 2009, p. 26, as last amended by Council Regulation (EU) 2023/2694 of 27 November 2023 amending certain Council Regulations concerning restrictive measures in order to insert provisions on humanitarian exceptions, digital OJ L, 28 November 2023, 33.

Council Regulation (EU) No. 356/2010 of 26 April 2010 imposing certain specific restrictive measures directed against certain natural or legal persons, entities or bodies, in view of the situation in Somalia, OJ L 105, 27 April 2010, p. 1, as last amended by Council Implementing Regulation (EU) 2023/1147 of 12 June 2023 implementing Article 12 of Regulation (EU) No. 356/2010 imposing certain specific restrictive measures directed against certain natural or legal persons, entities or bodies, in view of the situation in Somalia, OJ L 151I, 12 June 2023, p. 1, 18

Council Regulation (EU) No. 961/2010 of 25 October 2010 on restrictive measures against Iran and repealing Regulation (EC) No. 423/2007, OJ L 281, 27 October 2010, p. 1, 19

Council Regulation (EU) No. 101/2011 of 4 February 2011 concerning restrictive measures directed against certain persons, entities and bodies in view of the situation in Tunisia, OJ L 31, 5 February 2011, p. 1, as last amended by Council

Implementing Regulation (EU) 2023/156 of 23 January 2023 implementing Regulation (EU) No. 101/2011 concerning restrictive measures directed against certain persons, entities and bodies in view of the situation in Tunisia, OJ L 22, 24 January 2023, p. 8, 34

Council Regulation (EU) No. 359/2011 of 12 April 2011 concerning restrictive measures directed against certain persons, entities and bodies in view of the situation in Iran, OJ L 100, 14 April 2011, p. 1, as last amended by Council Implementing Regulation (EU) 2023/1298 of 26 June 2023 implementing Regulation (EU) No. 359/2011 concerning restrictive measures directed against certain persons, entities and bodies in view of the situation in Iran, OJ L 160I, 26 June 2023, p. 1, 28

Council Regulation (EU) No. 753/2011 of 1 August 2011 concerning restrictive measures directed against certain individuals, groups, undertakings and entities in view of the situation in Afghanistan, OJ L 199, 2 August 2011, p. 1, as last amended by Commission Implementing Regulation (EU) 2022/595 of 11 April 2022 amending certain Regulations concerning restrictive measures and setting out a single list for the Annexes to those Regulations containing the contact details of Member States' competent authorities and the address for notifications to the European Commission, OJ L 114, 12 April 2022, p. 60, 190

Council Regulation (EU) No. 36/2012 of 18 January 2012 concerning restrictive measures in view of the situation in Syria and repealing Regulation (EU) No. 442/2011, OJ L 16, 19 January 2012, p. 1, as last amended by Council Regulation (EU) 2023/2877 of 18 December 2023 amending Regulation (EU) No. 36/2012 concerning restrictive measures in view of the situation in Syria, digital OJ L, 19 December 2023, 33.

Council Regulation (EU) No. 267/2012 of 23 March 2012 concerning restrictive measures against Iran and repealing Regulation (EU) No. 961/2010, OJ L 88, 24 March 2012, p. 1, as last amended by Council Implementing Regulation (EU) 2023/2196 of 16 October 2023 implementing Regulation (EU) No. 267/2012 concerning restrictive measures against Iran, digital OJ L, 17 October 2023, 19.

Council Regulation (EU) No. 377/2012 of 3 May 2012 concerning restrictive measures directed against certain persons, entities and bodies threatening the peace, security or stability of the Republic of Guinea-Bissau, OJ L 119, 4 May 2012, p. 1, as last amended by Council Regulation (EU) 2023/1593 of 3 August 2023 amending Regulation (EU) No. 377/2012 concerning restrictive measures in view of the situation in Guinea-Bissau, OJ L 196, 4 August 2023, p. 1, 21

Council Regulation (EU) No. 401/2013 of 2 May 2013 concerning restrictive measures in respect of Myanmar/Burma and repealing Regulation (EC) No. 194/2008, OJ L 121, 3 May 2013, p. 1, as last amended by Council Implementing Regulation (EU) 2023/2789 of 11 December 2023 implementing Regulation (EU) No. 401/2013 concerning restrictive measures in view of the situation in Myanmar/Burma, digital OJ L, 11 December, 292023.

Council Regulation (EU) No. 208/2014 of 5 March 2014 concerning restrictive measures directed against certain persons, entities and bodies in view of the situation in Ukraine, OJ L 66, 6 March 2014, p. 1, as last amended by Council Implementing Regulation (EU) 2023/449 of 2 March 2023 implementing Regulation (EU) No.

208/2014 concerning restrictive measures directed against certain persons, entities and bodies in view of the situation in Ukraine, OJ L 67, 3 March 2023, p. 1.

Council Regulation (EU) No. 224/2014 of 10 March 2014 concerning restrictive measures in view of the situation in the Central African Republic, OJ L 70, 11 March 2014, p. 1, as last amended by Council Regulation (EU) 2023/2506 of 9 November 2023 amending certain Council regulations concerning restrictive measures in order to insert provisions on a humanitarian exemption, digital OJ L, 10 November 2023, 23.

Council Regulation (EU) No. 269/2014 of 17 March 2014 concerning restrictive measures in respect of actions undermining or threatening the territorial integrity, sovereignty and independence of Ukraine, OJ L 078, 17 March 2014, p. 6, as last amended by Council Regulation (EU) 2023/2873 of 18 December 2023 amending Regulation (EU) No. 269/2014 concerning restrictive measures in respect of actions undermining or threatening the territorial integrity, sovereignty and independence of Ukraine, digital OJ L, 18 December 2023, 208-209.

Council Regulation (EU) No. 692/2014 of 23 June 2014 concerning restrictions on the import into the Union of goods originating in Crimea or Sevastopol, in response to the illegal annexation of Crimea and Sevastopol, OJ L 183, 24 June 2014, p. 9, as last amended by Council Regulation (EU) 2022/1848 of 4 October 2022 amending Regulation (EU) No. 692/2014 concerning restrictive measures in response to the illegal annexation of Crimea and Sevastopol, OJ L 257, 5 October 2022, p. 1, 209

Council Regulation (EU) No. 747/2014 of 10 July 2014 concerning restrictive measures in view of the situation in Sudan and repealing Regulations (EC) No. 131/2004 and (EC) No. 1184/2005, OJ L 203, 11 July 2014, p. 1, as last amended by Council Regulation (EU) 2023/720 of 31 March 2023 amending certain Council Regulations concerning restrictive measures in order to insert provisions on a humanitarian exemption, OJ L 94, 3 April 2023, p. 1, 14

Council Regulation (EU) No. 833/2014 of 31 July 2014 concerning restrictive measures in view of Russia's actions destabilizing the situation in Ukraine, OJ L 229, 31 July 2014, p. 1, as last amended by Council Regulation (EU) 2023/2878 of 18 December 2023 amending Regulation (EU) No. 833/2014 concerning restrictive measures in view of Russia's actions destabilizing the situation in Ukraine, digital OJ L, 18 Dec. 2023, 209.

Council Regulation (EU) No. 1352/2014 of 18 December 2014 concerning restrictive measures in view of the situation in Yemen, OJ L 365, 19 December 2014, p. 60, as last amended by Council Regulation (EU) 2023/331 of 14 February 2023 amending certain Council regulations concerning restrictive measures in order to insert provisions on a humanitarian exemption, OJ L 47, 15 February 2023, p. 1, 24

Council Regulation (EU) 2015/735 of 7 May 2015 concerning restrictive measures in respect of the situation in South Sudan, and repealing Regulation (EU) No. 748/2014, OJ L 117, 8 May 2015, p. 13, as last amended by Council Regulation

(EU) 2023/720 of 31 March 2023 amending certain Council Regulations concerning restrictive measures in order to insert provisions on a humanitarian exemption, OJ L 94, 3 April 2023, p. 1, 25

Council Regulation (EU) 2015/1755 of 1 October 2015 concerning restrictive measures in view of the situation in Burundi, OJ L 257, 2 October 2015, p. 1, as last amended by Council Regulation (EU) 2023/2694 of 27 November 2023 amending certain Council Regulations concerning restrictive measures in order to insert provisions on humanitarian exceptions, digital OJ L, 28 November 2023, 30.

Council Regulation (EU) 2016/44 of 18 January 2016 concerning restrictive measures in view of the situation in Libya and repealing Regulation (EU) No. 204/2011, OJ L 12, 19 January 2016, p. 1, as last amended by Council Regulation (EU) 2023/1433 of 10 July 2023 amending Regulation (EU) 2016/44 concerning restrictive measures in view of the situation in Libya, OJ L 176, 11 July 2023, p. 1, 22

Council Regulation (EU) 2016/1686 of 20 September 2016 imposing additional restrictive measures directed against ISIL (Da'esh) and Al-Qaeda and natural and legal persons, entities or bodies associated with them, OJ L 255, 21 September 2016, p. 1, as last amended by Council Implementing Regulation (EU) 2023/1126 of 8 June 2023 implementing Regulation (EU) 2016/1686 imposing additional restrictive measures directed against ISIL (Da'esh) and Al-Qaeda and natural and legal persons, entities or bodies associated with them, OJ L 149, 9 June 2023, p. 13, 189

Council Regulation (EU) 2017/1509 of 30 August 2017 concerning restrictive measures against the Democratic People's Republic of Korea and repealing Regulation (EC) No. 329/2007, OJ L 224, 31.8.2017, p. 1, as last amended by Council Regulation (EU) 2023/720 of 31 March 2023 amending certain Council Regulations concerning restrictive measures in order to insert provisions on a humanitarian exemption, OJ L 94, 3 April 2023, p. 1, 16

Council Regulation (EU) 2017/1770 of 28 September 2017 concerning restrictive measures in view of the situation in Mali, OJ L 251, 29 September 2017, p. 1, as last amended by Council Regulation (EU) 2023/720 of 31 March 2023 amending certain Council Regulations concerning restrictive measures in order to insert provisions on a humanitarian exemption, OJ L 94, 3 April 2023, p. 1, 26

Council Regulation (EU) 2017/2063 of 13 November 2017 concerning restrictive measures in view of the situation in Venezuela, OJ L 295, 14 November 2017, p. 21, as last amended by Council Regulation (EU) 2023/2694 of 27 November 2023 amending certain Council Regulations concerning restrictive measures in order to insert provisions on humanitarian exceptions, digital OJ L, 28 November 2023, 30.

Council Regulation (EU) 2018/1542 of 15 October 2018 concerning restrictive measures against the proliferation and use of chemical weapons, OJ L 259, 16 October 2018, p. 12, as last amended by Council Implementing Regulation (EU) 2022/2228 of 14 November 2022 implementing Regulation (EU) 2018/1542 concerning restrictive measures against the proliferation and use of chemical weapons, OJ L 293I, 14 November 2022, p. 1, 284

Council Regulation (EU) 2019/796 of 17 May 2019 concerning restrictive measures against cyber-attacks threatening the Union or its Member States, OJ L 129I, 17 May 2019, p. 1, as last amended by Commission Implementing Regulation (EU) 2022/595 of 11 April 2022 amending certain Regulations concerning restrictive measures and setting out a single list for the Annexes to those Regulations containing the contact details of Member States' competent authorities and the address for notifications to the European Commission, OJ L 114, 12 April 2022, p. 60, 282

Council Regulation (EU) 2019/1716 of 14 October 2019 concerning restrictive measures in view of the situation in Nicaragua, OJ L 262, 15 October 2019, p. 1, as last amended by Council Regulation (EU) 2023/2694 of 27 November 2023 amending certain Council Regulations concerning restrictive measures in order to insert provisions on humanitarian exceptions, digital OJ L, 28 November 2023, 31.

Council Regulation (EU) 2019/1890 of 11 November 2019 concerning restrictive measures in view of Turkey's unauthorised drilling activities in the Eastern Mediterranean, OJ L 291, 12 November 2019, p. 3, as last amended by Commission Regulation (EU) 2023/2507 of 9 November 2023 amending Regulation (EU) 2019/1890 concerning restrictive measures in view of Turkey's unauthorised drilling activities in the Eastern Mediterranean, digital OJ L, 10 November 2023, 35.

Council Regulation (EU) 2020/1998 of 7 December 2020 concerning restrictive measures against serious human rights violations and abuses, OJ L 410I, 7 December 2020, p. 1, as last amended by Council Implementing Regulation (EU) 2023/1715 of 8 September 2023 implementing Regulation (EU) 2020/1998 concerning restrictive measures against serious human rights violations and abuses, OJ L 221I, 8 September 2023, p. 1, 281

Council Regulation (EU) 2021/1275 of 30 July 2021 concerning restrictive measures in view of the situation in Lebanon, OJ L 277I, 2 August 2021, p. 1, as last amended by Commission Regulation (EU) 2023/2694 of 27 November 2023 amending certain Council Regulations concerning restrictive measures in order to insert provisions on humanitarian exceptions, digital OJ L, 28 November 2023, 32.

Council Regulation (EU) 2022/263 of 23 February 2022 concerning restrictive measures in response to the recognition of the non-government controlled areas of the Donetsk and Luhansk oblasts of Ukraine and the ordering of Russian armed forces into those areas, OJ L 42I, 23 February 2022, p. 77, as last amended by Council Regulation (EU) 2022/1903 of 6 October 2022 amending Regulation (EU) 2022/263 concerning restrictive measures in response to the recognition of the non-government controlled areas of the Donetsk and Luhansk oblasts of Ukraine and the ordering of Russian armed forces into those areas, OJ L 259I, 6 October 2022, p. 1, 210

Council Regulation (EU) 2022/2309 of 25 November 2022 concerning restrictive measures in view of the situation in Haiti, OJ L 307, 28 November 2022, p. 17, as last amended by Council Regulation (EU) 2023/1569 of 28 July 2023 amending Regulation (EU) 2022/2309 concerning restrictive measures in view of the situation in Haiti, digital OJ L, 31 July 2023, 27.

as regards the prudential treatment of global systemically important institutions with a multiple-point-of-entry resolution strategy and methods for the indirect subscription of instruments eligible for meeting the minimum requirement for own funds and eligible liabilities, OJ L 275, 25 October 2022, p. 1, 232, 318

Regulation (EU) No. 952/2013 of the European Parliament and of the Council of 9 October 2013 laying down the Union Customs Code, OJ L 269 10 October 2013, p. 1, as last amended by Regulation (EU) 2022/2399 of the European Parliament and of the Council of 23 November 2022 establishing the European Union Single Window Environment for Customs and amending Regulation (EU) No. 952/2013, OJ L 317 9 December 2022, p. 1, 165

Regulation (EU) No. 909/2014 of the European Parliament and of the Council of 23 July 2014 on improving securities settlement in the European Union and on central securities depositories and amending Directives 98/26/EC and 2014/65/EU and Regulation (EU) No. 236/2012, OJ L 257 28 August 2014, p. 1, as last amended by Regulation (EU) 2022/858 of the European Parliament and of the Council of 30 May 2022 on a pilot regime for market infrastructures based on distributed ledger technology, and amending Regulations (EU) No. 600/2014 and (EU) No. 909/2014 and Directive 2014/65/EU, OJ L 151, 2 June 2022, p. 1, 222, 230, 309

Regulation (EU) 2015/847 of the European Parliament and of the Council of 20 May 2015 on information accompanying transfers of funds and repealing Regulation (EC) No. 1781/2006, OJ L 141, 5 June 2015, p. 1, 98

Regulation (EU) 2016/679 of the European Parliament and of the Council of 27 April 2016 on the protection of natural persons with regard to the processing of personal data and on the free movement of such data, and repealing Directive 95/46/EC, OJ L 119, 4 May 2016, p. 1, 187

Regulation (EU, Euratom) 2018/1046 of the European Parliament and of the Council of 18 July 2018 on the financial rules applicable to the general budget of the Union, amending Regulations (EU) No. 1296/2013, (EU) No. 1301/2013, (EU) No. 1303/2013, (EU) No. 1304/2013, (EU) No. 1309/2013, (EU) No. 1316/2013, (EU) No. 223/2014, (EU) No. 283/2014, and Decision No. 541/2014/EU and repealing Regulation (EU, Euratom) No. 966/2012, OJ L 193, 30 July 2018, p. 1, as last amended by Regulation (EU, Euratom) 2022/2434 of the European Parliament and of the Council of 6 December 2022 amending Regulation (EU, Euratom) 2018/1046 as regards the establishment of a diversified funding strategy as a general borrowing method, OJ L 319, 13 December 2022, p. 1, 236

Regulation (EU) 2021/821 of the European Parliament and of the Council of 20 May 2021 setting up a Union regime for the control of exports, brokering, technical assistance, transit and transfer of dual-use items, OJ L 206, 11 June 2021, p. 1, as last amended by Commission Delegated Regulation (EU) 2023/996 of 23 February 2023 amending Regulation (EU) 2021/821 of the European Parliament and of the Council as regards the list of dual-use items, OJ L 138, 25 May 2023, p. 1, 114, 125

Legislation of the United States of America

Index

Q

R

S

EUROPEAN MONOGRAPH SERIES

1. Lammy Betten (ed.), *The Future of European Social Policy,* 1991 (ISBN 90-654-4585-4).
2. Annemarie Loman, Kamiel Mortelmans, Harry H.G. Post & Stewart Watson, *Culture and Common Law: Before and After Maastricht,* 1992 (ISBN 90-654-4638-9).
3. John A.E. Vervaele, *Fraud against the Community: The Need for European Fraud Legislation,* 1994 (ISBN 90-654-4634-6).
4. Philip Raworth, *The Legislative Process in the European Community,* 1993 (ISBN 90-654-4690-7).
5. Jules Stuyck, *Financial and Monetary Integration in the European Economic Community,* 1993 (ISBN 90-654-4718-0).
6. Jules Stuyck & A.J. Vossestein (eds), *State Entrepreneurship, National Monopolies and European Community Law,* 1993 (ISBN 90-654-4773-3).
7. Jules Stuyck & A. Looijestijn-Clearie (eds), *The European Economic Area EC-EFTA,* 1994 (ISBN 90-654-4815-2).
8. Rosita B. Bouterse, *Competition and Integration: What Goals Count?,* 1995 (ISBN 90-654-4816-0).
9. René Barents, *The Agricultural Law of the EU, 2nd Edition,* 2022 (ISBN 978-94-035-4411-3).
10. Nicholas Emiliou, *Principles of Proportionality in European Law: A Comparative Study,* 1996 (ISBN 90-411-0866-1).
11. Eivind Smith, *National Parliaments as Cornerstones of European Integration,* 1996 (ISBN 90-411-0898-X).
12. Jan H. Jans, *European Environmental Law,* 1996 (ISBN 90-411-0877-7).
13. Síofra O'Leary, *The Evolving Concept of Community Citizenship: From the Free Movement of Persons to Union Citizenship,* 1997 (ISBN 90-411-0878-5).
14. Laurence W. Gormley (ed.), *Current and Future Perspectives on EC Competition Law,* 1983 (ISBN 90-411-0691-X).
15. Simone White, *Protection of the Financial Interests of the European Communities: The Fight against Fraud and Corruption,* 1998 (ISBN 90-411-9647-1).
16. Morten P. Broberg, *Broberg on the European Commission's Jurisdiction to Scrutinise Mergers,* 4th Edition, 2013 (ISBN 978-90-411-3339-7).
17. Doris Hildebrand, *The Role of Economic Analysis in the EC Competition Rules: The European School,* 2nd Edition, 2002 (ISBN 90-411-1706-7).
18. Christof R.A. Swaak, *European Community Law and the Automobile Industry,* 1999 (ISBN 90-411-1140-9).

19. Dorthe Dahlgaard Dingel, *Public Procurement: A Harmonization of the National Judicial Review of the Application of European Community Law*, 1999 (ISBN 90-411-1161-1).
20. John A.E. Vervaele (ed.), *Compliance and Enforcement of European Community Law*, 1999 (ISBN 90-411-1151-4).
21. Martin Trybus, *European Defence Procurement Law: International and National Procurement Systems as Models for a Liberalized Defence Procurement Market in Europe*, 1999 (ISBN 90-411-1167-0).
22. Helen Staples, *The Legal Status of Third Country Nationals Resident in the European Union*, 1999 (ISBN 90-411-1277-4).
23. Damien Geradin (ed.), *The Liberalization of State Monopolies in the European Union and Beyond*, 1999 (ISBN 90-411-1264-2).
24. Katja Heede, *European Ombudsman: Redress and Control at Union Level*, 2000 (ISBN 90-411-1413-0).
25. Ulf Bernitz & Joakim Nergelius (eds), *General Principles of European Community Law*, 2000 (ISBN 90-411-1402-5).
26. Michaela Drahos, *Convergence of Competition Laws and Policies in the European Community*, 2002 (ISBN 90-411-1562-5).
27. Damien Geradin (ed.), *The Liberalization of Electricity and Natural Gas in the European Union*, 2001 (ISBN 90-411-1560-9).
28. Gisella Gori, *Towards an EU Right to Education*, 2001 (ISBN 90-411-1670-2).
29. Brendan P.G. Smith, *Constitution Building in the European Union*, 2001 (ISBN 90-411-1695-8).
30. Friedl Weiss & Frank Wooldridge, *Free Movement of Persons within the European Community*, 2nd Edition, 2007 (ISBN 978-90-411-2545-3).
31. Ingrid Boccardi, *Europe and Refugees: Towards an EU Asylum Policy*, 2002 (ISBN 90-411-1709-1).
32. John A.E. Vervaele & André Klip (eds), *European Cooperation Between Tax, Customs and Judicial Authorities*, 2001 (ISBN 90-411-1747-4).
33. Wouter P.J. Wils, *The Optimal Enforcement of EC Antitrust Law: Essays in Law and Economics*, 2002 (ISBN 90-411-1757-1).
34. Damien Geradin (ed.), *The Liberalization of Postal Services in the European Union*, 2002 (ISBN 90-411-1780-6).
35. Nick Bernard, *Multilevel Governance in the European Union*, 2002 (ISBN 90-411-1812-8).
36. Jill Wakefield, *Judicial Protection through the Use of Article 288(2) EC*, 2002 (ISBN 90-411-1823-3).
37. Sebastiaan Princen, *EU Regulation and Transatlantic Trade*, 2002 (ISBN 90-411-1871-3).
38. Amaryllis Verhoeven, *The European Union in Search of a Democratic and Constitutional Theory*, 2002 (ISBN 90-411-1872-1).
39. Paul L.C. Torremans, *Cross Border Insolvencies in EU, English and Belgian Law*, 2002 (ISBN 90-411-1888-8).

40. Malcolm Anderson & Joanna Apap (eds), *Police and Justice Cooperation and the New European Borders,* 2002 (ISBN 90-411-1893-4).
41. Christin M. Forstinger, *Takeover Law in EU and USA: A Comparative Analysis,* 2002 (ISBN 90-411-1919-1).
42. Antonio Bavasso, *Communications in EU Antitrust Law: Market Power and Public Interest,* 2003 (ISBN 90-411-1974-4).
43. Fiona G. Wishlade, *Regional State Aid and Competition Policy in the European Union,* 2003 (ISBN 90-411-1975-2).
44. Gareth Davies, *Nationality Discrimination in the European Internal Market,* 2003 (ISBN 90-411-1998-1).
45. René Barents, *The Autonomy of Community Law,* 2003 (ISBN 90-411-2251-6).
46. Gerhard Dannecker & Oswald Jansen (eds), *Competition Law Sanctioning in the European Union,* 2004 (ISBN 90-411-2100-5).
47. Nauta Dutilh (ed.), *Dealing with Dominance: The Experience of National Competition Authorities,* 2004 (ISBN 90-411-2211-7).
48. Stefaan van den Bogaert, *Practical Regulation of the Mobility of Sportsmen in the EU Post Bosman,* 2005 (ISBN 90-411-2327-X).
49. Katalin Judit Cseres, *Competition Law and Consumer Protection,* 2005 (ISBN 90-411-2380-6).
50. Philipp Kiiver, *The National Parliaments in the European Union: A Critical View on EU Constitution Building,* 2006 (ISBN 978-90-411-2452-4).
51. Alexander Turk, *The Concept of Legislation in European Community Law,* 2006 (ISBN 978-90-411-2472-2).
52. Dimitrios Sinaniotis, *The Interim Protection of Individuals before the European and National Courts,* 2006 (ISBN 978-90-411-2498-2).
53. M. Holoubek & D. Damjanovic, M. Traimer (eds), *Regulating Content: The European Regulatory Framework for the Media and Related Creative Sectors,* 2006 (ISBN 978-90-411-2597-2).
54. Anneli Albi & Jacques Ziller (eds), *The European Constitution and National Constitutions: Ratification and Beyond,* 2006 (ISBN 978-90-411-2524-8).
55. Gustavo E. Luengo, *Regulation of Subsidies and State Aids in WTO and EC Law: Conflicts in International Trade Law,* 2007 (ISBN 978-90-411-2547-7).
56. Eniko Horvath, *Mandating Identity: Citizenship, Kinship Laws and Plural Nationality in the European Union,* 2007 (ISBN 978-90-411-2662-7).
57. Rass Holdgaard, *External Relations Law of the European Community: Legal Reasoning and Legal Discourses,* 2007 (ISBN 978-90-411-2604-7).
58. Jill Wakefield, *The Right to Good Administration,* 2007 (ISBN 978-90-411-2697-9).
59. Dimitry Kochenov, *EU Enlargement and the Failure of Conditionality: Pre- accession Conditionality in the Fields of Democracy and the Rule of Law,* 2008 (ISBN 978-90-411-2696-2).
60. Despina Mavromati, *The Law of Payment Services in the EU: The EC Directive on Payment Services in the Internal Market,* 2008 (ISBN 978-90-411-2700-6).

61. Anne Meuwese, *Impact Assessment in EU Lawmaking*, 2008 (ISBN 978-90-411-2720-4).
62. Ulf Bernitz, Joakim Nergelius & Cecilia Cardner (eds), *General Principles of EC Law in a Process of Development*, 2008 (ISBN 978-90-411-2705-1).
63. Johan van de Gronden (ed.), *The EU and WTO Law on Services: Limits to the Realisation of General Interest Policies within the Services Markets?*, 2008 (ISBN 978-90-411-2809-6).
64. Alina Tryfonidou, *Reverse Discrimination in EC Law*, 2009 (ISBN 978-90-411-2751-8).
65. Mikael Berglund, *Cross-Border Enforcement of Claims in the EU: History Present Time and Future*, 2014 (ISBN 978-90-411-4564-2).
66. Theodore Konstadinides, *Division of Powers in European Union Law: The Delimitation of Internal Competence between the EU and the Member States*, 2009 (ISBN 978-90-411-2615-3).
67. Mattias Derlén, *Multilingual Interpretation of European Union Law*, 2009 (ISBN 978-90-411-2853-9).
68. René Barents, *Directory of EU Case Law on the Preliminary Ruling Procedure*, 2009 (ISBN 978-90-411-3150-8).
69. Yan Luo, *Anti-dumping in the WTO, the EU and China: The Rise of Legalization in the Trade Regime and Its Consequences*, 2010 (ISBN 978-90-411-3207-9).
70. Patrick Birkinshaw & Mike Varney (eds), *The European Union Legal Order after Lisbon*, 2010 (ISBN 978-90-411-3152-2).
71. Thomas Gr. Papadopoulos, *EU Law and Harmonization of Takeovers in the Internal Market*, 2010 (ISBN 978-90-411-3340-3).
72. Bas van Bockel, *The* Ne Bis In Idem *Principle in EU Law*, 2010 (ISBN 978-90-411-3156-0).
73. Veljko Milutinović, *The 'Right to Damages' under EU Competition Law: From* Courage v. Crehan *to the White Paper and Beyond*, 2010 (ISBN 978-90-411-3235-2).
74. Amandine Garde, *EU Law and Obesity Prevention*, 2010 (ISBN 978-90-411-2706-8).
75. Leonard Besselink, Frans Pennings & Sacha Prechal (eds), *The Eclipse of the Legality Principle in the European Union*, 2011 (ISBN 978-90-411-3262-8).
76. Sacha Garben, *EU Higher Education Law: The Bologna Process and Harmonization by Stealth*, 2011 (ISBN 978-90-411-3365-6).
77. Dimitry Kochenov (ed.), *EU Law of the Overseas: Outermost Regions, Associated Overseas Countries and Territories, Territories Sui Generis*, 2011 (ISBN 978-90-411-3445-5).
78. Pablo Ibáñez Colomo, *European Communications Law and Technological Convergence: Deregulation, Re-regulation and Regulatory Convergence in Television and Telecommunications*, 2012 (ISBN 978-90-411-3829-3).
79. Elise Muir, *EU Regulation of Access to Labour Markets: A Case Study of EU Constraints on Member State Competences*, 2012 (ISBN 978-90-411-3823-1).
80. Tim Corthaut, *EU Ordre Public*, 2012 (ISBN 978-90-411-3232-1).

81. Oana Ştefan, *Soft Law in Court: Competition Law, State Aid and the Court of Justice of the European Union*, 2013 (ISBN 978-90-411-3997-9).
82. Francesco Rossi dal Pozzo, *Citizenship Rights and Freedom of Movement in the European Union*, 2013 (ISBN 978-90-411-4660-1).
83. Jens Hartig Danielsen, *EU Agricultural Law*, 2013 (ISBN 978-90-411-3280-2).
84. Ulf Bernitz, Xavier Groussot & Felix Schulyok (eds), *General Principles of EU Law and European Private Law*, 2013 (ISBN 978-90-411-4683-0).
85. Michelle Everson, Cosimo Monda & Ellen Vos (eds), *European Agencies in between Institutions and Member States*, 2014 (ISBN 978-90-411-2843-0).
86. Stefan Leible & Matthias Lehmann (eds), *European Contract Law and German Law*, 2014 (ISBN 978-90-411-2588-0).
87. Piero Leanza & Ondrej Pridal, *The Right to a Fair Trial: Article 6 of the European Convention on Human Rights*, 2014 (ISBN 978-90-411-4855-1).
88. Patrick J. Birkinshaw, *European Public Law: The Achievement and the Brexit Challenge*, 3rd Edition, 2020 (ISBN 978-90-411-9751-1).
89. George Cumming, *Expert Evidence Deficiencies in the Judgments of the Courts of the European Union and the European Court of Human Rights*, 2014 (ISBN 978-90-411-4123-1).
90. Vesna Rijavec, Tomaž Keresteš & Tjaša Ivanc (eds), *Simplification of Debt Collection in the EU*, 2014 (ISBN 978-90-411-4854-4).
91. Nina Półtorak, *European Union Rights in National Courts*, 2015 (ISBN 978-90-411-5863-5).
92. Kyriaki-Korina Raptopoulou, *EU Law and Healthcare Services: Normative Approaches to Public Health Systems*, 2015 (ISBN 978-90-411-5013-4).
93. Torsten Frank Koschinka & Piero Leanza, *Preliminary Injunctions: Germany, England/Wales, Italy and France*, 2015 (ISBN 978-90-411-5833-8).
94. Vesna Rijavec, Tomaž Keresteš & Tjaša Ivanc (eds), *Dimensions of Evidence in European Civil Procedure*, 2016 (ISBN 978-90-411-6662-3).
95. Stefan Leible (ed.), *General Principles of European Private International Law*, 2016 (ISBN 978-90-411-5955-7).
96. Patrick J. Birkinshaw & Andrea Biondi (eds), *Britain Alone!: The Implications and Consequences of United Kingdom Exit from the EU*, 2016 (ISBN 978-90-411-5832-1).
97. René Barents, *Remedies and Procedures before the EU Courts*, 2nd Edition, 2020 (ISBN 978-94-035-1140-5).
98. Luca Prete, *Infringement Proceedings in EU Law*, 2017 (ISBN 978-90-411-6900-6).
99. Robert van den Hoven van Genderen, *Privacy Limitation Clauses: Trojan Horses under the Disguise of Democracy*, 2017 (ISBN 978-90-411-8599-0).
100. Mariusz Krzysztofek, *Post-Reform Personal Data Protection in the European Union: General Data Protection Regulation (EU) 2016/679*, 2017 (ISBN 978-90-411-6237-3).
101. Gianni Lo Schiavo, *The Role of Financial Stability in EU Law and Policy*, 2017 (ISBN 978-90-411-8230-2).

102. Emmanuel Guinchard & Marie-Pierre Granger (eds), *The New EU Judiciary: An Analysis of Current Judicial Reforms*, 2017 (ISBN 978-90-411-6834-4).
103. Kirsten Henckel, *Cross-Border Transfers of Undertakings: A European Perspective*, 2017 (ISBN 978-90-411-9227-1).
104. Vesna Rijavec, Wendy Kennett, Tomaž Keresteš & Tjaša Ivanc, *Remedies Concerning Enforcement of Foreign Judgements: Brussels I Recast*, 2018 (ISBN 978-90-411-9416-9).
105. Albert Sanchez-Graells & Constant De Koninck, *Shaping EU Public Procurement Law: A Critical Analysis of the CJEU Case Law 2015–2017*, 2018 (ISBN 978-94-035-0160-4).
106. Andrea Biondi, Patrick J. Birkinshaw & Maria Kendrick, *Brexit: The Legal Implications*, 2019 (ISBN 978-90-411-9540-1).
107. Mariusz Krzysztofek, *GDPR: General Data Protection Regulation (EU) 2016/679: Post-Reform Personal Data Protection in the European Union*, 2019 (ISBN 978-94-035-0594-7).
108. Giovanni Bassani, *The Legal Framework Applicable to the Single Supervisory Mechanism: Tapestry or Patchwork?*, 2019 (ISBN 978-94-035-0872-6).
109. Piotr Staszczyk, *A Legal Analysis of NGOs and European Civil Society*, 2019 (ISBN 978-94-035-1251-8).
110. Patrizio Messina, *Finance for SMEs: European Regulation and Capital Markets Union – Focus on Securitization and Alternative Finance Tools*, 2019 (ISBN 978-94-035-0161-1).
111. Jacques H.J. Bourgeois (ed.), *EU Framework for Foreign Direct Investment Control*, 2020 (ISBN 978-94-035-1883-1).
112. Ulf Bernitz, Xavier Groussot, Jaan Paju & Sybe de Vries (eds), *General Principles of EU Law and the EU Digital Order*, 2020 (ISBN 978-94-035-1165-8).
113. Aleksandra Drożdż, *Protection of Natural Persons with Regard to Automated Individual Decision-Making in the GDPR*, 2020 (ISBN 978-94-035-2045-2).
114. Mariusz Krzysztofek, *GDPR: Personal Data Protection in the European Union*, 2021 (ISBN 978-94-035-3270-7).
115. Katarzyna Gromek-Broc (ed.), *Public Law in a Troubled Era: A Tribute to Professor Patrick Birkinshaw*, 2023 (ISBN 978-94-035-3576-0).
116. Guido Alpa, *Solidarity: A Normative Principle*, 2023 (ISBN 978-94-035-3596-8).
117. Frederik Behre, *Fixing the Euro Within the National Constitutional Guardrails: A Comparative Assessment of the National Constitutional Space for EU (Fiscal) Integration*, 2023 (ISBN 978-94-035-3586-9).
118. Berdien B.E. van der Donk, *Digital Bouncers: A European Roadmap to Navigate Access Rights and Moderation Issues on Social Media Platforms*, 2024 (ISBN 978-94-035-2858-8).
119. Natalia Charalampidou, *The Financial and Other Sanctions of the European Union*, 2025 (ISBN 978-94-035-4357-4).